Orchestrating Value

Population Health in the Digital Age

Orchestrating Value

Population Health in the Digital Age

Pam W. Arlotto, MBA, FHIMSS
Susan P. Irby, MSHS

CRC Press
Taylor & Francis Group
Boca Raton London New York

CRC Press is an imprint of the
Taylor & Francis Group, an **informa** business
A PRODUCTIVITY PRESS BOOK

CRC Press
Taylor & Francis Group
6000 Broken Sound Parkway NW, Suite 300
Boca Raton, FL 33487-2742

International Standard Book Number-13: 978-1-138-36791-3 (Hardback)
International Standard Book Number-13: 978-1-138-36734-0 (Paperback)

Library of Congress Cataloging-in-Publication Data

Names: Arlotto, Pam, author. | Irby, Susan P., author.
Title: Orchestrating value : population health in the digital age / Pam W. Arlotto, Susan P. Irby.
Other titles: Rethinking return on investment.
Description: 2 edition. | Boca Raton, FL : CRC Press, Taylor & Francis Group, 2020. | Preceded by Rethinking return on investment / Pam Arlotto, editor ; with Susan Irby, associate editor. c2012. | Includes bibliographical references and index.
Identifiers: LCCN 2019046127 (print) | LCCN 2019046128 (ebook) | ISBN 9781138367340 (paperback) | ISBN 9781138367913 (hardback) | ISBN 9780429429507 (ebook)
Subjects: MESH: Medical Informatics--economics | Investments--economics | Health Information Management--economics | Population Health Management
Classification: LCC R858 (print) | LCC R858 (ebook) | NLM W 26.5 | DDC 610.285--dc23
LC record available at https://lccn.loc.gov/2019046127
LC ebook record available at https://lccn.loc.gov/2019046128

Visit the Taylor & Francis Web site at
http://www.taylorandfrancis.com

and the CRC Press Web site at
http://www.crcpress.com

Contents

List of Figures

List of Tables

Foreword

Many of today's healthcare leaders came up through the ranks during a time when their career goal was to become a hospital chief executive officer. Our mentors taught us that the physician was the primary customer, and success would be gauged by the number of patients in our hospital beds. Cost was all but impossible to measure, but certainly controlled by the physician and his/her pen. Today these views have the potential to make us quickly irrelevant.

Healthcare leaders must create a sense of urgency and examine the following questions:

- How can we transform our healthcare system in an increasingly digital world?
- Are we able to give ourselves permission to experiment with new business and operating models?
- What is the role of population health within our organizations?
- Do we fully understand what it takes to reinvent the consumer experience?
- Are we willing to partner with others who bring something different to the table?

In *Orchestrating Value: Population Health in the Digital Age*, Pam W. Arlotto and Susan P. Irby introduce the challenge of transitioning from volume to value in a siloed, fragmented, facility and provider centric health system. They pervasively describe the pivot leaders must make to embrace the consumer and to design disruptive business models and operating platforms. They share cultural lessons learned from healthcare leaders who have embraced the intersection of the digital age and population health management.

At Froedtert Health and the Medical College of Wisconsin, we created Inception Health as our innovation arm to solve key health care problems, develop new ideas, and scale those solutions across the health network. We collaborate with innovators locally and across the country to combine a commitment to "meet people where they are" with digital technologies to transform healthcare. Our efforts are resulting in improvements that

- Empower people to stay healthy at home.
- Increase the reliability of care for the most complex cases.
- Engage consumers in understanding and using their personal health data.
- Expand access to mental health services and management of chronic disease 24/7.
- Enhance the health care experience by helping people get the right care at the right place at the right time.
- Reduce the cost and improve the efficiency of care.

Simultaneously, at Froedtert Health we are working to reinvent traditional healthcare delivery. Through initiatives such as our micro-hospital strategy, we are partnering with others to change traditional cultural views and deploy new care delivery models. Our efforts at Inception Health and to reposition our core business have generated important lessons about taking risks, encouraging entrepreneurial and collaborative mindsets, and challenging the status quo.

Orchestrating Value questions "business as usual" mindsets including reliance on traditional revenue models, command and control organization structures, and legacy information technology infrastructures. Leaders are encouraged to reimagine health and healthcare through the new combinations of talent, digital technology, and information. Through multiple frameworks and examples, *Orchestrating Value* describes an evolving healthcare innovation ecosystem that focuses on solving old problems and creating new value. The book suggests that the coming digital revolution will touch all that we do, from the most simple patient encounter to the most complex clinical intervention.

Last year, as Chairman of the American College of Healthcare Executives, I had the opportunity to meet with healthcare leaders across the country and around the world. Through these conversations, it is clear, our greatest obstacle is our past success. We must roll up our sleeves, change the rules of engagement, and adapt innovative approaches. Digital disruption will occur, either through our own leadership or from outside the industry. Artificial intelligence, the Internet of Things, genomics, and other digital platforms have the potential to change the very nature of work. Leaders across the healthcare industry should consider their role in orchestrating value.

David A. Olson, FACHE
Senior Vice President and Chief Strategy Officer
Froedtert Health and the Medical College of Wisconsin
Past Chairman, American College of Healthcare Executives

Preface

This book is about value, not about value realization and return on investment (ROI) as in our previous books. A casual conversation at a Healthcare Information and Management Systems Society conference in 2002 led to a seventeen-year journey exploring the increasingly complex effort required to drive ROI from healthcare information technology (HIT). In those books we focused on the operational change and incremental performance required to manage the value from electronic health records, enterprise resource planning, revenue management, and other information systems into reality. Over the years, we have heard from many information technology, informatics, operational, financial, and clinical leaders about the insights gained from applying business principles to the adoption and deployment of HIT. Yet, something was missing. The promise of data and technology was not being realized and many healthcare leaders struggle with the dollars spent, the difficulty of use, and other challenges such as burn-out, poor data quality, and lack of interoperability.

In our previous books, change management and culture were always mentioned, but often as an afterthought. Across the healthcare industry, information technology implementations were accompanied by change strategies and road maps. After interviewing healthcare executives, completing research on digital transformation across multiple industries, and advising health systems and solution companies on their journey to value-based care, our focus has shifted. Much like the leadership pivot we describe in this book, our message became less about the value of information technology and change management, and more about building new capabilities and operating models. We recognize that the fragmented, siloed delivery system requires reinvention, transformation, and innovation. While data and technology are core to future digital health and connected care platforms, we must design new competencies and cultures. Collaboration and partnership are essential to our future success.

Orchestrating Value: Population Health in the Digital Age starts a conversation. Based on an orchestra analogy, we discuss transitioning the industry from brick-and-mortar–based care to consumer-centric, virtual care. While never intended to replace all episodic visits or healthcare facilities, we hope to challenge traditional leadership thinking. Our basic premise is that progress to population health and value-based care stalls when tacked on to the traditional healthcare delivery system as a program or project. To scale, digital strategies and consumer centered design are needed. Rather than viewing value as a payer contract for select populations, health system incumbents, digital health start-ups, Big Tech, and other innovators are partnering to create new value and new consumer experiences for unique populations. Data and technology, when combined with collaborative platform-based operating models, will provide continuous intelligence, predictive and prescriptive insights, and allow personalized medicine.

We look forward to advancing these conversations further and receiving your feedback and insights.

Pam Arlotto
Atlanta, Georgia
November 2019

Acknowledgments

This book is dedicated to the many change agents driving digital health innovation. For most of us, this is personal— our own interactions with the healthcare system, or those of a family member or a close friend, make change essential. Thank you for sharing the vision of a healthcare system transformed through the power of data, technology, and consumer-centric value. Your hard work is inspirational. Appreciation is extended to Heidi Davies and Jamie Lovett for their diligence during the editing process. We are grateful to our family and friends who have supported us during our careers and the countless hours we have given to making this book possible.

About the Authors

Pam Arlotto, MBA, FHIMSS, is chief executive officer and president of Maestro Strategies, LLC, a management consulting firm focused on transformation, innovation, and the orchestration of change in the healthcare industry. She advises chief executive officers and other executives on digital strategy and consumer-centric design of new health and healthcare business and operating models. Ms. Arlotto created the award-winning series *Return on Investment: Maximizing the Value of Healthcare Information Technology* and has authored four previous books on planning for and realizing the value of data and technology. She has held a number of important healthcare and industry leadership positions that include

- Board of trustees member, Georgia Tech Foundation
- Advisory board member, Wallace H. Coulter School of Biomedical Engineering at Georgia Tech and Emory University, Scheller College of Business at Georgia Tech
- National president and fellow of the Healthcare Information and Management Systems Society
- Adjunct faculty member in the Healthcare Informatics program at University of Alabama at Birmingham
- Board member of numerous privately held companies and not-for-profit organizations

Ms. Arlotto is a popular and frequent speaker at healthcare industry and corporate meetings and has authored a number of journal and magazine articles.

Susan P. Irby, MSHS, is the managing director of Business Intelligence and Analytics for Maestro Strategies, LLC, and has over 30 years of healthcare experience with providers and as a consultant. Ms. Irby built the firm's *ROI Toolkit* and specializes in financial planning, decision support, and information technology benefits realization. Her experience includes:

- Transformation strategy advisory consulting work, including planning for care management platforms, enterprise analytics management systems, clinical integration, and population health management, for a variety of health systems
- Return on investment and value management strategies for health systems, solution companies, and associations
- Director of strategic planning and decision support at Alta Bates Health System, where she pioneered early decision support system and benefits realizations applications in healthcare
- Arthur Young consultant with experience in strategic planning, operating and capital budgeting, cost accounting, financial planning, and forecasting

SETTING THE STAGE

*The greatest danger in times of turbulence is not the
turbulence—it is to act with yesterday's logic.*

Peter Drucker

A New Cadence of Change

There is a new cadence in healthcare. Value-based care is
making an indelible imprint on the U.S. healthcare industry.
Providers are investing in care management platforms (CMP)
to support alternative payment models, clinical integration,
and improved clinical outcomes. Payers, both commercial
and governmental, are rolling out new value-based contracts
and joining forces with providers to launch new "payvider"
partnerships. Employers are developing work-site clinics and
exploring creative alternatives to traditional health plans.
Venture-backed digital health companies and Big Tech (i.e.,
Amazon, Google, Apple, etc.) are launching dramatic population health and consumer-centric digital innovations.

Yet, the phrase "a foot in two canoes" is frequently used
to describe the fact that the fee-for-service and value-based

reimbursement models appear to be diametrically opposed. "Today, many health systems appear to be in a holding pattern," according to research from the Deloitte Center for Health Solutions, delaying investment in the analytics and technology infrastructure, care delivery models, and the expertise needed to support population health until the risk–reward tide shifts. "Waiting to invest could put organizations at risk of falling behind on the adoption curve," the researchers concluded. "Once the industry reaches a tipping point, revenue based on outcomes and risk could exponentially increase, leaving fewer resources for new investments."[1]

The chapters within Section I examine a framework for the Journey to High-Value Healthcare—1.0: Brick and Mortar Healthcare, 2.0: The Transition, and 3.0: Digital Health and Connected Care. Additionally, the impact of the previous three industrial revolutions on industry and healthcare are explored while considering the most dramatic change yet—the Fourth Industrial Revolution and its simultaneous tidal wave of physical, digital, and biological disruptive innovation. In these chapters, we set the stage for this book's primary message—value-based care and population health management cannot scale using traditional brick and mortar healthcare business and operating models. Digital health and connected care provide the promise for the future, where disease is prevented, chronic conditions managed, and equitable, transparent services are personalized for each and every person.

Bonus Materials

Digital health and population health management topics are changing daily. There were so many additional concepts and examples we could have explored within the pages of this book. The solution was to provide several extras as bonus materials available online at www.maestrostrategies.com/ orchestratingvalue. All the bonus materials are easy to access.

Note

1. Kent, Jessica. "Value-Based Hospitals More Likely to Adopt Population Health Tools." HealthITAnalytics, January 17, 2019. https://healthitanalytics.com/news/value-based-hospitals-more-likely-to-adopt-population-health-tools.

Chapter 1

Orchestrating Value in the Digital Age

Transformation is a difficult thing to do; it doesn't happen overnight. I like to say we're twenty-five years into a forty-year transformation.

Mike Leavitt, Secretary of Health and Human Services, George W. Bush Administration, HIMSS Global Conference & Exhibition, 2019

Purpose

To introduce the concept of value orchestration and the convergence of digital transformation, population health, and consumerism.

In this chapter, the reader will consider

- The opportunity for new value creation and the orchestra analogy

- What digital transformation is, and more importantly, what it is not
- The varying stakeholder definitions of value and increase in consumer expectations
- The Value Management Maturity Model as it relates to Next-Generation Value Management Strategy
- The purpose, organization, and content of the remaining chapters of this book

Introduction

Just as an orchestra comes together to deliver a performance, a new wave of connectors and collaborators are rethinking and reinventing healthcare. Digital native companies and startups, as well as progressive healthcare industry incumbents, are working in concert to orchestrate innovative ecosystems for health and connected care. The tempo (speed and agility) and harmony (ability to work together) are creating the music (value) of digital health and connected care. Organizations are collaborating around shared ideas, leveraging synergies and complementary strategies, engineering new business and operating models, and developing new customer experiences. While they will continue to play their individual instruments (core businesses and capabilities), the convergence of value-based care, rising consumerism, and interconnected digital technologies will accelerate a new value creation to

- Design breakthrough solutions to persistent and well-recognized industry problems.
- Identify and solve new problems and seize new opportunities.
- Redefine existing industry problems and resolve the redefined problem.[1]

ORCHESTRATING VALUE

Great orchestras are more than their individual musicians. String, woodwind, brass, and percussion instruments work in concert, in the right balance, so that the musical score can be heard clearly, with the same rhythm, and often to convey the orchestra's own unique sound, message, and feeling. Rehearsals ensure that musicians hone their craft and the collective performance of the team improves. If one instrument is missing or not played well, the performance at best would be flat. A great orchestra provides listeners with experiences they can't get elsewhere and takes them on a journey of different musical scores that combine to create a satisfying whole. Evoking images, inspiring emotion, it reveals the depths of the composers' musical thinking without telling the audience what to think, what to feel, or how to interpret what they heard.

Healthcare's digital transformation *is not* about

- Digitizing the existing silos
- Electronic health records (EHRs), apps, fast healthcare interoperability resources (FHIR), artificial intelligence, or any of the other emerging technologies we see in the headlines
- Infusing information into the hospital, ambulatory practice, or accountable care organization
- A new executive role or organization structure

Healthcare's digital transformation *is* about

- Reimagining relationships, customer journeys, and economic incentive

- Orchestrating new value from the interconnection of physical, digital, and biologic assets through data and the creation of new ways of working in the digital age
- A fundamental change in business and organizational activities, processes, competencies, business and operating models, and data and technology
- Leadership that owns the transformation, guides the development of new mindsets and cultures, and articulates a forward-looking vision for the future

Defining Value

Modern medicine provides value every day. Genomic and personalized medicine are saving lives. Heart disease deaths have dropped by 40% in the last 25 years, and cancer and HIV/AIDS have transitioned from fatal diagnoses to chronic diseases.[2] Progress, however, has come at a significant cost. U.S. national health expenditures are projected to grow at an average annual rate of 5.5% for 2018–27 and to represent 19.4% of gross domestic product in 2027.[3] Recent research by the Institute for Health Improvement indicates that 41% of adults in the United States have either experienced a medical error in their own care or been personally involved in a situation where a medical error was made in the care of someone close to them.[4] The current model of providing healthcare is increasingly unsustainable and the status quo no longer feasible.

Over a decade ago, Harvard economist Michael Porter put forward the concept of value-based care as an approach to improving health outcomes at a lower cost. He encouraged health systems to focus on what patients value and to allocate resources according to health outcomes.[5] In Chapter 2, we examine the journey to high-value healthcare and explore a framework for understanding the required changes along the way. We acknowledge that even though value-based care has made progress in the past few years, forward momentum has stalled in many healthcare organizations and markets. We recognize that change is difficult for our legacy health system, and barriers and roadblocks abound. Rigid silos, bureaucracy, and decision-making styles become obstacles. Leaders frequently become cautious and talk themselves out of transformation.

One of the major challenges to change is the fact that healthcare's various stakeholders have different goals and multiple definitions of value, including:

- Health systems emphasize quality, safety, and efficiency.
- Clinicians often define value as clinical efficacy.
- Payers emphasize alignment of economic incentives and interventions with high benefit to cost ratios.
- Employers seek to influence factors that impact work performance, including reduced absenteeism and increased workplace productivity.
- The Centers for Medicare and Medicaid Services (CMS), the Food and Drug Administration (FDA), and other governmental agencies focus on a variety of compliance, risk management, public health and welfare regulations, and value improvement opportunities.
- Device manufacturers, pharmaceutical companies, software providers, and suppliers concentrate on product attributes and features in their value conversations.

Paul Keckley, a healthcare policy analyst and strategic advisor to the healthcare industry, comments: "In healthcare, we are more comfortable using an assembly line model to capture attributes and measures of value; i.e. value is the sum of component parts plus labor plus overhead divided by price."[6] In Chapter 3, we trace healthcare's adoption of technology enabled by three previous industrial revolutions. We consider how this assembly line mindset came into existence. We explore the accelerated pace of the coming Fourth Industrial Revolution and healthcare's unique opportunity to orchestrate new value through the fusion of the physical, digital, and biological worlds. According to Keckley, "What's missing in this (traditional) view is an understanding of value as defined by end users: patients, members, users (or more appropriately consumers). Arguably, the industry's most important constituent."[7] The Fourth Industrial Revolution will provide an unprecedented opportunity to focus on and exceed the expectations of the healthcare consumer. Through the development of new networks and collaborative platforms, stakeholders will come together to create new value. Success will require new digital leadership thinking and development of next-generation strategies for managing value into reality.

The Next-Generation Value Management Strategy

In 2003, in the award-winning book *Return on Investment: Maximizing the Value of Healthcare Information Technology*, we discussed the potential of healthcare information technology (HIT). We emphasized that while financial return on investment (ROI) was important, strategic value realization was increasingly critical. In other words, investment in HIT while managing value into reality through organizational change could result in enterprise performance improvement.[8] We continued to make these points in three additional books on the topic, including the most recent (2019) book, *Beyond Return on Investment: Expanding the Value of Healthcare Information Technology, Second Edition.*[9] The primary premise was simple. Rather than viewing HIT as a cost of doing business, organizations should apply the following definition:

$$\text{Value of Healthcare IT} = \frac{\text{Degree of Change in the Business}}{\text{Total IT and Business Investment}}$$

The Health Information Technology for Economic and Clinical Health (HITECH) Act of 2009 sought to accelerate the adoption of EHRs through a mix of front-loaded incentives and back-loaded penalties. While meaningful use was often criticized, it did distribute first-generation clinical systems capability to hospitals, clinics, and physician offices across the country. As implemented, however, EHRs "paved the cow paths" or automated existing clinical processes without considering the efficiency or effectiveness of those processes. Legacy reimbursement systems, care delivery models, organization structures, and operating processes and practices remained the same. The inherent inefficiencies, waste, and lack of consumer focus within the traditional fee-for-service health system prevented much return on investment or value from being realized from investment in these systems.

As we consider meaningful use in our rearview mirror, it is important to recognize that in almost every industry, the first generation of any technology was not perfect. Today's personal computers and smartphones are almost inconceivably more usable, powerful, and prolific in their value delivery than their predecessors were in the 1990s. As new payment models are introduced to reward providers for improving health outcomes, and next-generation technologies become usable and customer friendly, the potential now lies in the reinvention of the delivery system. We are on the threshold of delivering greater value to patients, their clinicians, and other industry stakeholders. Innovations fast-tracked through actionable clinical information and intelligence will drive population health programs and enable the transition to precision medicine.[10] "Whether you are a provider, a payer, or a patient, your experience with value-based health care will be shaped by digital health in inevitable and myriad ways," indicates Joanna Bergmann, an attorney at Ropes and Gray, LLP. "If digital health is the engine of value-based health care, then data is its fuel."[11]

The Value Management Maturity Model, illustrated in Figure 1.1, depicts the healthcare industry's historical view of the HIT return on investment and value realization. Enterprise-centric methods have traditionally focused on support of the legacy enterprise, including its organization structures, people, and processes. In recent years, the focus has moved away from single IT projects or IT-centric measures toward integrated strategic programs. The *Next-Generation Value Management Strategy* will focus on the extended enterprise, or ecosystems of stakeholders working together to orchestrate value through new mindsets, operating models, and digital platforms.

The levels of the Value Management Maturity Model are defined as follows:

- *Level 1—Initial:* Application/Functionality Orientation. Consists of informal, general benefit statements from the requesting department or software vendor. Typically ad hoc and unstructured.
- *Level 2—Basic:* Budget Justification. One-time business case and ROI analysis (i.e., benefits/cost ratio, payback period, net present value, and internal rate of return) used to justify capital or operating expenditure during annual budget process. Hurdle rates established by finance, or the board allows project-by-project comparison for new capital and operating expense requests.
- *Level 3—IT Centric:* IT Performance Focus. Internal IT service-level measures focused on efficiency, effectiveness, and user satisfaction. Developed from an IT perspective, these metrics are generally IT project or operations centric (i.e., on time, on budget, customer satisfaction, help desk resolution percentage and response time, etc.).
- *Level 4—Project/Program:* Value of Strategic Programs. As business, clinical, and financial executives play a more active role in redesigning processes, organization structures, and data assets in conjunction with technology

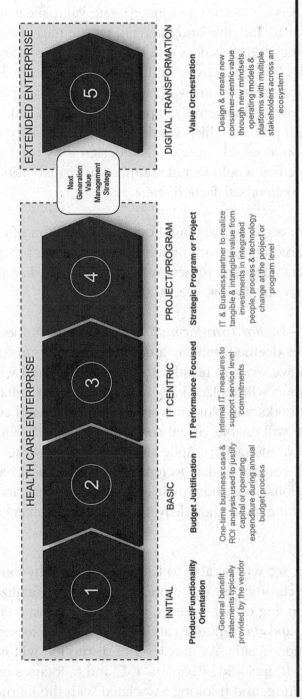

Figure 1.1 The Value Management Maturity Model.

deployments, leadership should move beyond financial and IT service metrics and incorporate value-measure dashboards. Tangible and intangible value measures for each integrated (business and IT) project or program are needed. Plans, incentives, and road maps help drive value into reality over the life of the initiative. For example, a patient engagement strategic program might include a telehealth project, which would include technology implementation alongside operations redesign for virtual care. Value metrics would include number of virtual visits, cost of visit, patient satisfaction, etc.

As healthcare organizations build out the continuum of care, they create accountable care organizations, develop provider–payer partnerships, explore new relationships with disruptors, and create new platforms, specifically

■ *Level 5—Digital Transformation:* Value Orchestration. Advances deemed unlikely a decade ago will transform the way we work in healthcare in unprecedented ways. Automation will replace jobs; new partnerships, alliances, and networks will blur enterprise boundaries; and connectivity will enable virtual communication and reduce the cost of interaction. Agile value generation strategies will compel leaders to rethink even the most basic assumptions about how their organizations work and the resulting value they deliver to health consumers and patients.

In the future, we will be able to keep people healthy longer, manage chronic diseases more effectively, personalize our understanding of our patients, improve the consumer's experiences, and reinvent our care delivery models to support population health. Yet, this level of disruption will not be easy. Section II, including Chapters 4, 5, and 6, focuses on the mindsets, culture, and thinking associated with the journey to high-value healthcare. Chapter 4 will introduce the chief executive officer (CEO) as the conductor of the value orchestra. The CEO must ensure that the core business continues to operate, answering specific questions, including:

- Why change?
- What are we changing?
- How are we changing?
- At what cost?
- For what results?
- How will we measure the value of the change?

Figure 1.2 illustrates the conductor's role and the key components of the *Next-Generation Value Management Strategy*.

Chapter 5 introduces the concept of the leadership pivot and the changes in mindset and culture the leadership team must make in this new environment. Specifically, the impact of silos and the silo mentality, which must be overcome by leadership pivots in decision making from hierarchy, command and control, and functional organization structures to collaboration, multidisciplinary teams, and networks will be explored. Chapter 6 will introduce platform thinking as the new operating model for digital health and connected care.

Section III provides an example of a platform strategy for health systems, provider groups, health plans, and others seeking to drive value-based care: the care management platform (CMP). The CMP is the ecosystem of tools, technologies, information, people, and care processes needed to support population health in the digital age. Chapters 7–12 will review the five layers of the CMP:

- Foundational systems or EHRs
- Interoperability and high-performing networks
- Knowledge management and analytics
- Advanced care management
- Consumer and patient engagement

MINDSETS & CULTURE
New ways of thinking & leadership pivots to orchestrate value

OPERATING MODELS
Capabilities & competencies needed to create hypotheses, experiment & scale

CARE MANAGEMENT PLATFORM
Foundational systems, network connectivity, knowledge management & analytics, care management & consumer activation

CEO AS CONDUCTOR
Value orchestration through convergence of shift from volume to value, emerging digital technology & focus on consumer

Figure 1.2 Next-Generation Management Strategy.

Finally, Section IV will introduce the population health services organization (PHSO) in Chapter 13 and provide final thoughts of value measurement in the digital age in Chapter 14.

Conclusion

Digital health and connected care will require change at every level of the healthcare system.

The future will move from patient-centric thinking to consumer-led health and participatory care. Value orchestration will occur through the interconnection of cultures and mindsets, operating models, and care management platforms. This book sets the stage and identifies the needed leadership pivots, capabilities, and systems needed to build the high-performing healthcare networks of the future.

Notes

1. Kim, W Chan, and Rene Mauborgne. "Nondisruptive Creation Rethinking Innovation and Growth." *MIT Sloan Management Review*, 60 (3): 52, 2019.
2. Cox, Lauren. "The Top 10 Medical Advances of the Decade." MedPage Today: Medical News and Free CME. MedpageToday, December 17, 2009. www.medpagetoday.com/infectiousdisease/publichealth/17594.
3. Sisko, Andrea, Sean Keehan, John Poisal, Gigi Cuckler, Sheila Smith, Andrew Madison, Kathryn Rennie, and James Hardesty. "National Health Expenditure Projections, 2018–27: Economic and Demographic Trends Drive Spending and Enrollment Growth." *Health Affairs*, 38 (3): 491, February 20, 2019.
4. NORC at the University of Chicago and IHI/NPSF Lucian Leape Institute. *Americans' Experiences with Medical Errors and Views on Patient Safety*. Cambridge, MA: Institute for Healthcare Improvement and NORC at the University of Chicago, 2017.

5. Michael Porter, "Institute for Strategy & Competitiveness." Value-Based Health Care Delivery—Institute For Strategy and Competitiveness—Harvard Business School. Accessed June 8, 2019. www.isc.hbs.edu/health-care/vbhcd/Pages/default.aspx.
6. Keckley, Paul. "The Meaning of 'Value' in Health Care." The Health Care Blog, December 4, 2015. https://thehealthcareblog. com/blog/2015/12/03/the-meaning-of-value-in-health-care/.
7. Keckley, Paul. "The Meaning of 'Value' in Health Care." The Health Care Blog, December 4, 2015. https://thehealthcareblog. com/blog/2015/12/03/the-meaning-of-value-in-health-care/.
8. Arlotto, Pam, and Jim Oaks. *Return on Investment: Maximizing the Value of Healthcare Information Technology.* Chicago, IL: Healthcare Information and Management Systems Society, 2003.
9. Arlotto, Pam W., and Susan P. Irby. *Beyond Return on Investment: Expanding the Value of Healthcare Information Technology.* Boca Raton, FL: CRC Press, Taylor & Francis Group, 2019.
10. Gellert, George A., et al. "In Defense of Meaningful Use: The Potential of Electronic Health Records Systems to Support Value-Based Care." Journalofclinicalpathways.com, Christus Health, August 2016, www.journalofclinicalpathways.com/arti-cle/defense-meaningful-use-potential-electronic-health-records-systems-support-value-based-care.
11. Bergmann, Joanna, Ira Parghi, and Christine Moundas. "The Role of Digital Health in the Shift to Value-Based Health Care." Lexology, May 10, 2017. www.lexology.com/library/detail. aspx?g=24b1056a-7f07-41ff-a5da-72c869b5caf7.

Chapter 2

The Journey to High-Value Healthcare: A Framework

As we look to 2030, everyone engaged in healthcare is focused on creating a system that consistently delivers quality care, improves health outcomes and delivers better value.

David Orbuch, Optum UK

Purpose

To explore the journey to high-value healthcare, a framework for the transition, and the capabilities needed along the journey.

In this chapter, the reader will review

- A framework for the transition to value-based care, and its three distinct phases: 1.0: Brick and Mortar Healthcare; 2.0: Transitional, and 3.0: Digital Health and Connected Health

- The business goals of each phase and the shift to a risk-based population health business model
- The changing role of information technology throughout the journey
- Capabilities and competencies needed for the transition and the challenges
- The concepts of value in healthcare and in relation to the role of data, technology, and change in phases 2.0 and beyond

The Transition from Volume to Value

Value-based care is simply the concept of improving quality and care outcomes. The focus is on a holistic, proactive approach to healthcare delivery that stresses wellness, stronger integration of preventative screenings and practices, a program on social determinants, best practice standards, and the elimination of unwarranted clinical variation. Population health management (PHM) has been discussed by many as an effective approach to helping healthcare organizations and providers meet their value-based care goals and objectives. Three major tenets of PHM involve

- Integration of hospitals, physicians, care managers, post-acute providers, community services, payers, and other stakeholders
- Improvement of health and management of chronic disease among defined populations
- Alignment of desired outcomes with incentives initially for participation and ultimately through assumption of risk

For executives at forward-looking organizations, the future is already here. "We are working to provide our patients with the best quality care at the lowest cost," says Tal Heppenstall, executive vice president of UPMC Health System, based in

Pittsburgh, and chief executive officer (CEO) of its development arm, UPMC Enterprises. "We don't really see volume and value as contradictory," Heppenstall continues. "From our standpoint, it's always about giving patients the best care, which often isn't the most care. Half of our revenue is volume-based, and half is value-based. And our clinicians don't even want to know what kind of insurance a patient has."[1]

Don Lovasz leads CommonSpirit's population health strategy development and is president/CEO CHI Saint Joseph Health Partners. With over 2 million covered lives and $6 billion in total medical spend, managed by 25 different organizations and supported by 15 different software systems, CommonSpirit is addressing population health at scale. But, according to Lovasz, it's simple: "Everyone talks about the transition from volume to value. I prefer to say volume and value. Under DRGs we have essentially been operating under a fixed payment system—if you spend more than you are paid, you lose; if you spend less, you do well. We have to focus on working efficiently, effectively and delivering value for the long term."[2]

The Journey to High-Value Healthcare—A Framework

In interviews with CEOs, chief marketing officers, chief information officers, chief medical information officers, and leaders of innovation and transformation at over 80 leading health systems, 20 academic medical centers, and dozens of accountable care organizations (ACOs), alliances, and provider organizations, we found that the most successful organizations viewed the transition from volume to value as a journey. The journey was not an event but a series of changes to strategy and development of new capabilities for value-based care and population health management. Investment and commitment levels depended on the degree of change and resulting value desired along with consideration of unique factors impacting the organization such as market positioning, payer contractual obligations, enterprise strengths, leadership priorities, etc. Based on these interviews, we developed a framework or simple model to explain three distinct phases of the journey—1.0: Fee-for-Service, Brick and Mortar Healthcare to 3.0: Value-Based, Digital Health and Connected Care, as illustrated in Figure 2.1.

The framework is easily understood and should help organizations and individuals step outside the day-to-day to identify current positioning within the journey, plan for and build capabilities to support value-based care and digital health, and improve readiness for movement to the next phase of the journey. The framework can also serve as a tool for change agents to use as they educate key stakeholders, ensure clear alignment across the enterprise or team, slow down actions that may be premature or accelerate actions that may have been ignored, and provide a comparison to competitors or the industry at large. Ultimately, the framework should serve as a guide toward value orchestration along the journey to high-value healthcare.

Figure 2.1   The journey to high-value healthcare.

For individuals to apply this framework within their own organization or to their own situation, it is important to consider:

- The framework provides conceptual understanding, not hard and fast rules for the transition.
- No two organizations move through each phase in the same way and on the same timeline.
- Each phase builds upon the previous phase, and activities in one phase may continue through the next.
- Success depends on the integration of strategy, new leadership roles, organization and operating model design, new competencies and capabilities, and new tools and measures.
- Investment level depends on the goals for value, and while return on investment is still important, it is viewed from a longer-term perspective.
- As organizations mature in their journey, the focus becomes less about the individual entity and more about the connected ecosystem.
- Cultural change is the most difficult aspect of the journey.

The remaining sections of this chapter will provide a high-level overview of the framework, the goals, the characteristics, and the challenges of each phase. The remaining sections of the book will provide more detail on the specifics of the journey.

1.0: Brick and Mortar Healthcare

In 1.0: Brick and Mortar Healthcare, fee-for-service reimbursement drives revenues, and health systems are facility or hospital centric. Ambulatory practices are primarily independent, composed of small group or independent practices. Three primary goals of this phase are to

- Introduce value-based care and digital PHM platform concepts to key stakeholders.

■ Implement "systems of record" (i.e., electronic health records [EHR]) and quality measures.
■ Conduct high-level planning regarding positioning and strategy.

Phase 1.0 organizations frequently exhibit the following characteristics:

■ Care is delivered through localized acute care, primary care, specialty care, and services with limited post-acute interaction.
■ Care is provided at the micro level or during an encounter between a physician and a patient. Typically, the patient presents with symptoms, the provider completes a diagnostic and treatment process, and depending on needed interventions, the clinician hands the patient off to other professionals.
■ The clinical decision-making process protects the autonomy of the health professional and is separated from the business decision-making process.
■ Administrative or business decisions are siloed according to entity, specialty, function, or reporting relationship and are often made through consensus or "command-and-control" hierarchies.
■ Exposure to value-based care during 1.0 comes through programs that link economic rewards and penalties to quantification and reporting of quality, such as
  – The Centers for Medicare and Medicaid Services (CMS) Hospital Value-Based Purchasing Program—rewards acute care hospitals with incentive payments for the quality of care for Medicare beneficiaries
  – The Physician Quality Reporting System (PQRS)—incents and promotes awareness among providers of the opportunities for quality improvement present in daily care and processes

Challenges for 1.0 organizations include:

- Most stakeholders view value-based care from their own perspective (i.e., specialty role, functional responsibilities, entity, geographic location, facility, etc.). While 1.0 presents an opportunity to educate all stakeholders from a holistic or systemic view so that they understand both the short-term and the long-term implications, only the most advanced organizations do so.
- Quality measures (i.e., structural, process, and outcome measures) are collected manually through chart abstraction and reporting through registries or niche quality systems. Many organizations find that the number of tools, dashboards, metrics, and reporting requirements has expanded exponentially. Harmonization and automation of the metrics is needed.
- The Health Information Technology for Economic and Clinical Health (HITECH) Act of 2009 accelerated the implementation of EHRs or "systems of record" by physicians and hospitals. Meaningful use (MU) and the accompanying incentives, however, may have "overshadowed" the importance of these foundation systems in paving the path for the development of highly configurable, connected care digital platforms to support PHM in later phases.

In 2019, progressive organizations have moved beyond 1.0: Brick and Mortar Healthcare. Those that remain in 1.0 are in markets with limited to no payer activity, have small Medicare populations, have delegated population health platform development to a partner, and/or are cash strapped and cannot make the investment needed to progress.

2.0: Transition

The transition period between 1.0: Brick and Mortar Healthcare and 3.0: Digital Health and Connected Care is a time of building new capabilities to support risk assumption, care management, and patient-centered care processes. Specific goals include:

- Participate in one or two value-based contracts with CMS or a commercial payer.
- Launch initial PHM strategies and develop new care coordination competencies.
- Shift from implementing "systems of record" to building "systems of insight."

Through legal structures such as patient-centered medical homes (PCMH), clinical integration networks (CINs), and ACOs, providers come together to support a variety of value-based care programs. While the structures are often complementary, each model does have its own objectives and capabilities to develop. The structures include:

- PCMHs focus on improvement for primary care services. Care teams work with the physician to provide preventative and chronic disease management. Disease registries are used to track patients. New processes for cross-continuum care coordination and patient engagement are developed.[3] In 2019, the National Committee for Quality Assurance (NCQA) has recognized approximately 13,000 practices (with 67,000 clinicians) as PCMHs, and more than 100 payers support the NCQA recognition through financial incentives and other programs.[4]
- CINs include a collection of health providers, such as physicians, hospitals, and post-acute specialists, joined together to improve care and reduce costs. CINs can incorporate under a "safe harbor" from antitrust laws and are able to negotiate collectively for commercial payer contracts. Compliance requirements include physician-led governance and commitment, development and implementation of clinical practice guidelines to improve

performance, development of infrastructure and technology, and financial incentives for achieving goals.[5]

▪ ACOs focus on care improvement for a patient population across the continuum. Often launched through a Medicare Shared Savings Program (MSSP), the organization works to generate savings and develop the necessary care management, data, and technology infrastructure. As of January 2019, there are 538 Medicare ACOs serving more than 12.3 million beneficiaries with hundreds more commercial and Medicaid ACOs serving millions of additional patients.[6]

In some markets, management service organizations (MSOs), independent practice associations (IPAs), and provider-led health plans are the driving force for value-based care. Typical characteristics of 2.0 organizations include:

▪ Initially, the contracts focus on "upside risk" only, and participation is incentivized through shared savings. Minimum quality performance standards are established, and no penalties are incurred if the benchmarks are not met.

▪ Patient care shifts to a macro view that considers managing patients with multiple chronic conditions and, treatment provided by numerous clinicians from different care delivery organizations. While not replacing the micro-level care of the 1.0 health system, processes such as referral management and management of transitions become progressively impactful.

▪ Advanced analytics tools and expertise combine claims, clinical, cost accounting, social determinants of health, and other data to support insight-driven decision making.

▪ Team-based care models and care management process design initiatives focus on quality and outcome improvement, efficient service, cost reduction, etc. Stratified high-risk and rising-risks patients are the initial focus as communication and collaboration tools are developed

for patient assessment, care planning and intervention,
performance measurement, etc. Ultimately, the entire
population has specific protocols and standards of care
developed in order to transcend time, location, and traditional clinical practice across prevention, diagnosis, treatment, and prognosis processes.

■ As the number of active contracts and covered lives
increases, this often signals an ACO's desire and readiness to assume responsibility or risk for an attributed
patient population. As the number of "covered lives" and
increased "downside risk" are assumed, the ACO typically commits to scaling their care management, data, and
technology infrastructure.

■ Traditional hierarchical structures give way to matrixed,
service line and process–oriented organization structures
and reporting relationships.

There are a number of challenges to 2.0 organizations, and
the majority of these challenges relate to the inability to scale.
They include

■ Single enterprise leadership of clinical integration and
care management capability development, with limited
work to improve overall market readiness
■ Limited investment beyond EHRs and analytic tools,
such as enhanced revenue management and enterprise
resource planning systems, care management, or consumer engagement platforms
■ Long-established provider centricity versus consumer and
patient focus
■ Reliance on traditional care models and limited redesign
of key processes
■ Lack of governance and decision-making structures to
support care management across an ecosystem of partners and affiliates
■ The financial implications and cost of scale

While the goal is to improve value as soon as possible, it takes time to build sufficient infrastructure and redesign care processes. In fact, in 2018, 74 ACOs dropped out of the CMS MSSP[7] (Figure 2.2).

A Numerof & Associates Survey, conducted in conjunction with Dr. David Nash, dean of the School of Population Health at Jefferson Health every year since 2014, indicates that 82% of surveyed executives view population health as very or critically important to their healthcare organization's future success.[8] Yet, for health systems, providers, and payers, their progress toward value-based care and PHM has stalled. Investment and actual engagement in value-based arrangements remain symbolic and experience in this new way of operating nominal, along with comfort levels.[9] A 2018 study by Quest Diagnostics indicates that more than two-thirds (67%) of physicians and health plan executives said that the United States still has a fee-for-service system and that little progress has been made.[10] For many, the 2.0 transition feels overwhelming and chaotic. Even though most executives understand the level of change needed, they are uncertain how to lead their organizations through the transformation and are often unwilling to forgo payments associated with fee-for-service care delivery. [11]

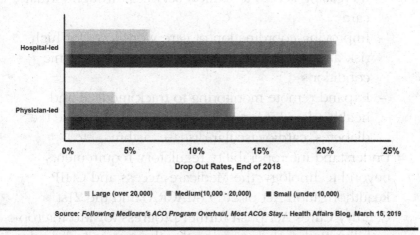

Source: *Following Medicare's ACO Program Overhaul, Most ACOs Stay...* Health Affairs Blog, March 15, 2019

Figure 2.2   Percentage of ACOs dropping out of MSSP (end of 2018).

3.0: Digital Health and Connected Health

There are two primary goals for 3.0: Digital Health and Connected Care, and they are:

- Scale value-based care and PHM strategies to impact larger population groups and communities.
- Design "systems of engagement" to activate consumers and patients in their own health and healthcare.

In 3.0, game-changing digital technologies such as genomics and sequencing, analytics and artificial intelligence, biosensors, telemedicine, mobile applications, and digital therapeutics will combine with new business and operating models to create new value. Consumers and patients will participate in design of digital innovation with health systems, payers, clinical researchers, and suppliers across the health and healthcare ecosystem. If stalled, a "jump-start" or bridge strategy may be needed to move from 2.0 to 3.0, such as:

- Make the complex simple: Focus on a targeted digital initiative such as
  - Increasing access to clinical services through virtual care
  - Improving coordination of care workflows for high-risk and rising-risk patients with multiple chronic conditions
  - Expand remote monitoring to track medical and health-related information for a specific disease (i.e., diabetes, cardiovascular disease, asthma, etc.)
- Understand interoperability regulatory requirements beyond technology: the Medicare Access and CHIP Reauthorization Act of 2015 (MACRA) and the 21st Century Cures Act push further progress toward interoperability. Rather than viewing the changes as technical

requirements alone, think about care practice changes across the continuum enabled through connectivity and data exchange requirements.

■ Engage clinicians in the digital conversation: in a survey conducted by the American Medical Association (AMA), 85% of physicians surveyed see the potential for digital tools to improve patient care, and 82% believe they will improve practice efficiency,[12] indicating the opportunity for shared exploration throughout the journey. The AMA has launched a number of digital health innovation programs in recent years to engage physicians and others in transforming health and healthcare.

■ Create collaborative innovation partnerships: According to the IBM Institute for Business Value, more than half of chief officers (CXOs) expect to open up their enterprises—bringing down barriers to extend collaboration both inside and outside their organizations, resulting in a shift from organization centricity to ecosystem centricity.[13]

■ Spend time understanding the consumer and patient perspective: when surveyed, healthcare consumers indicate that they want.
  – A personalized experience—to be known by and understood by their provider
  – Economically manageable care choices
  – Convenient, accessible care—when, where, and how it best suits their unique situation
  – Easy-to-use digital capabilities to assist in management of their care[14]

Conclusion

Transformation of the healthcare industry and the transition to value-based care and population health will take time. While the specifics of how each market and organization moves

forward are unique, there are a number of common characteristics, including:

- Iteration and experimentation precede scale.
- EHRs are just the beginning; digital care management
  platforms designed in conjunction with new operating
  models are essential.
- Enterprise-centric initiatives will shift to collaboration of
  partners across ecosystems.
- While value-based contracts often launch efforts, consumer expectations and demand will ultimately drive the
  need for value orchestration.
- Cultural change is the most difficult aspect of the journey.

Table 2.1 summarizes each phase of the journey.

Yet, there is a coming tsunami of change. With much to
offer healthcare, the Fourth Industrial Revolution will challenge traditional roles and structures. If purposeful technology and clinical operating models can be combined to deliver
better outcomes, experiences, and economics, the under-
pinnings of fee-for-service healthcare become less secure.
Next-generation EHRs and data enablement tools provide
the opportunity to change the way we prevent and manage
chronic disease. Consumers expect and demand seamless customer experiences, and a new group of disrupters, including
Big Tech, employers, and payers, are targeting the failings of
traditional models.

Table 2.1 Phases of the Journey to High-Value Healthcare

	Brick and Mortar Healthcare 1.0	Transition 2.0	Digital Health and Connected Care 3.0
Enterprise strategic direction	• Fee-for-service reimbursement • Horizontal and vertical consolidation	• Clinical integration • Coordination of care • Quality measurement and reporting • Patient experience	• Risk management • Population health management • Consumerism • New business and care models
Customer	Provider	Patient	Consumer
Leadership domain	Acute care and physician practices	Continuum of care	Anytime, anywhere
Decision-making culture	Siloed—command and control, consensus	Dyads and matrixed—dotted lines, insight-driven decision making	Collaboration, networked, predictive, and prescriptive
New capabilities and competencies	Meaningful use and EHR adoption	Interoperability, analytics, care management, and patient engagement	Digital health, design thinking, innovation
Return on investment (ROI) and value potential	Enterprise centric—tactical benefits and ROI	Network centric—incremental value realization	Consumer centric—disruptive and transformational, value orchestration

Notes

1. Hagland, Mark. "That 'One Foot in the Boat' Problem Is Going to Last for a While." *Healthcare Innovation*, July 2019, www.hcin-novationgroup.com/policy-value-based-care/article/21089669/that-one-foot-in-the-boat-problem-is-going-to-last-for-a-while.
2. Arlotto, Pam, and Don Lovasz. "Orchestrating Value: Population Health in the Digital Age." Telephone Interview, August 28, 2019.
3. "The Care Transformation Alphabet: What's the Difference between CI, ACO, and PCMH?" The Advisory Board Company. The Advisory Board, September 24, 2014. www.advisory.com/research/care-transformation-center-blog/2014/09/deciphering-the-reform-alphabet.
4. "Patient-Centered Medical Home (PCMH)." NCQA. Accessed July 2, 2019. www.ncqa.org/programs/health-care-providers-practices/patient-centered-medical-home-pcmh/.
5. Gallegos, Alicia, Neil Osterweil, and Christine Kilgore. "Clinically Integrated Networks: 5 Roadblocks and How to Overcome Them." MDedge ObGyn, January 18, 2019. www.mdedge.com/obgyn/article/142735/business-medicine/clinically-integrated-networks-5-roadblocks-and-how-overcome.
6. LaFayette, Anna. "NACCOS." National Association of ACOs. Accessed July 1, 2019. www.naacos.com/.
7. Bleser, William, Robert Saunders, David Muhlestein, Andrew Olson, Donald Taylor, and Mark McClellan. "Following Medicare's ACO Program Overhaul, Most ACOs Stay—But Physician-Led ACOs Leave at a Higher Rate." *Health Affairs*, March 15, 2019. www.healthaffairs.org/do/10.1377/hblog20190311.776139/full/.
8. "State of Population Health Survey, Conducted by Numerof & Associates in Collaboration with David Nash, Dean of the Jefferson College of Population Health." *Numerof*, March 25, 2019. nai-consulting.com/numerof-state-of-population-health-survey/.
9. "State of Population Health Survey, Conducted by Numerof & Associates in Collaboration with David Nash, Dean of the Jefferson College of Population Health." *Numerof*, March 25, 2019, nai-consulting.com/numerof-state-of-population-health-survey/.

10. "New Study Reveals Stalled Progress toward Value-Based Care." Quest Diagnostics Newsroom. Accessed July 3, 2019. http://newsroom.questdiagnostics.com/2018-07-17-New-Study-Reveals-Stalled-Progress-Toward-Value-Based-Care.
11. "State of Population Health Survey, Conducted by Numerof & Associates in Collaboration with David Nash, Dean of the Jefferson College of Population Health." *Numerof*, March 25, 2019. nai-consulting.com/numerof-state-of-population-health-survey/.
12. "Digital Health Study Physicians' Motivations and Requirements for Adopting Digital Clinical Tools." American Medical Association, 2016. www.ama.org.
13. Davidson, Steven, Martin Harmer, and Anthony Marshall. "The New Age of Ecosystems—Redefining Partnering in an Ecosystem Environment." IBM, 2014. www.ibm.com/downloads/cas/BXE7OEP5.
14. Read, Leslie, David Betts, Matt Kaye, and Aaron Patton. "Consumer Priorities in Health Care Survey: Deloitte US." Deloitte, June 15, 2017. www2.deloitte.com/us/en/pages/life-sciences-and-health-care/articles/us-lshc-consumer-priorities-promo.html.

Chapter 3

Digital Health and the Fourth Industrial Revolution

AMARA's Law:

We tend to overestimate the effect of a technology in the short run and underestimate the effect in the long run.

**Roy Charles Amara, past president
Institute of the Future**

Purpose

To examine the Fourth Industrial Revolution and its potential to disrupt the healthcare industry while exploring healthcare's resistance to change in previous times of transformation.

In this chapter, the reader will review

- The potential disruption associated with the Fourth Industrial Revolution
- The healthcare industries' historic resistance to adapting during times of significant change for other industries

- The history of the First, Second, and Third Industrial Revolutions and healthcare's tendency to lag in adoption of new technology
- Big Tech and the potential impact on healthcare and population health management

The Coming Tsunami of Change

Change is not new to the healthcare industry. Wave after wave of new reimbursement programs, government regulations, clinical technologies and devices, organizational models, and information systems continue to pummel the healthcare system and the people in it. During times of major change, some healthcare organizations and their leaders paddle directly into the coming tidal surge, others batten down the hatches in preparation, and the least prepared are caught unaware. Yet, the coming tsunami of technologically driven change will converge with new business models, and according to Klaus Schwab, founder and executive chairman of the World Economic Forum, these models will result in a "revolution unlike any previous one in history, and it will affect us all in ways we cannot even begin to image."[1]

Stephanie Woerner and Peter Weill, in their book *What's Your Digital Business Model*, share that "Digital transformation is not about technology—it's about change. And it is not a matter of if, but a question of when and how ... the digital revolution is disrupting virtually every industry."[2] Defined as the integration of digital technology into all areas of a business, digital transformation will fundamentally change the way an organization operates and delivers value to its customers. The required cultural change will result in organizations that continually challenge the status quo, experiment, and get comfortable with failure.[3]

In healthcare, confluent disruptions in biology, business models, computer science, and culture have the potential to transform the healthcare system like never before—impacting the speed and location of care, the role of patients in managing their own care, and the relationships across the clinical care community. Smart connected services focused on preventing chronic disease, accessing clinical care, providing diagnosis and treatment, managing the health of populations, and designing personalized care and experiences will be powered by artificial intelligence, biosensors, speech recognition, robotics, and other cognitive technologies that mimic human behavior and decision-making styles. To survive the tsunami and ultimately thrive, healthcare systems, providers, payers, and their partners will have to challenge their organizational structures, information systems, and operating models to digitally transform the value they provide to their customers.

Yet, transforming an industry as complex as healthcare will be difficult. No other industry or sector has the equivalent range and breadth—the intricate funding models, multiple moving parts, complicated clients with diverse needs, and so many options and interventions for any one person's needs. Healthcare has numerous stakeholders, with different roles and interests, and uneven regulations that tightly control some matters and barely touch others. The various combinations of care, activities, events, interactions, and outcomes are infinite.[4] Factors such as the following only exacerbate this problem:

- Six in ten adults in the United States have a chronic disease (i.e., diabetes, heart disease, cancer, stroke, lung disease, Alzheimer's, kidney disease, etc.), and four in ten adults have multiple chronic diseases.[5]
- In 2017, U.S. healthcare spending topped US$3.5 trillion (17.9% of the gross domestic product [GDP]),[6] and by 2025, the healthcare sector is projected to account for one-third of all new employment and will represent 20% of the GDP.[7]
- According to industry data, retiring baby boomers will more than double Medicare and Medicaid costs by 2020.

As healthcare costs increase faster than economic growth, Medicare taxes and the Trust Fund will cover less and less. By 2033, some pundits say, the Trust Fund will be bankrupt, and taxes will pay only for 48% of the costs.[8]

Looking Back to Look Forward

According to Schwab, "The changes associated with the Fourth Industrial Revolution are so profound that, from the perspective of human history, there has never been a time of greater promise or potential peril." Schwab defines an industrial revolution as the appearance of "new technologies and novel ways of perceiving the world [that] trigger a profound change in economic and social structures."[9] A significant majority of executives surveyed in a poll conducted by the Economist Intelligence Unit (45%) believe that healthcare is the sector that will benefit most from the merging of physical, digital, and biological systems offered in this next industrial revolution.[10] Before exploring this possible future of the Fourth Industrial Revolution, it may be helpful to revisit the previous three industrial revolutions, the technologies that sparked them, and healthcare's response to each (Figure 3.1).

The First Industrial Revolution and the Growth of the Hospital

Prior to the mid-1700s, society was primarily agrarian. People worked and lived on farms. During the First Industrial Revolution, with innovations such as the transcontinental railroad, the cotton gin, and electricity, society became more industrialized and urban, causing villages and towns to swell in size, sometimes into vast cities. Despite the technological advancements of the day, disease spread quickly. In response, Dr. Thomas Bond and Benjamin Franklin founded Pennsylvania Hospital, America's first hospital, "to care for the sick-poor and insane who were

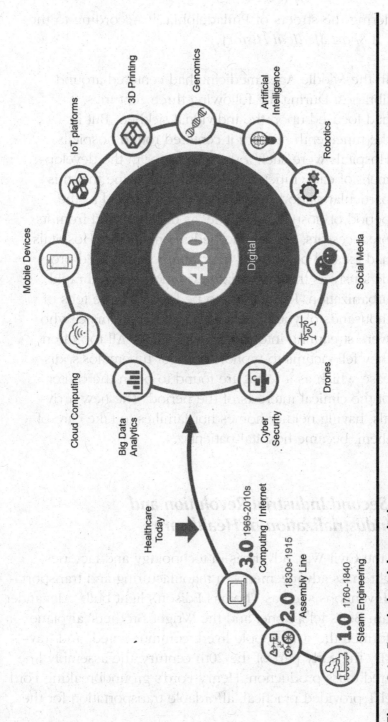

Figure 3.1 Four industrial revolutions.

wandering the streets of Philadelphia."[11] According to the book *A Short Medical History,*

> In the Middle Ages medicine had centered around libraries. During the following three centuries, it had focused upon the individual sickbed. But in the nineteenth century it centered round hospitals. Hospitals were such a decisive factor in the development of early nineteenth-century medicine that this particular period might well be categorized as the period of hospital medicine, as distinguished from its predecessors, library and bedside medicine. Hospitals had existed before, but their number increased prodigiously as the Industrial Revolution fostered rapid urbanization. Refuge had to be found for the tens of thousands of young peasants, male and female, who were streaming into the growing cities. All too often they fell victims to typhoid fever or tuberculosis, disease which as a result are found to be in the center of the clinical interests of the period. The new arrivals, having neither homes nor families to take care of them, became hospital patients.[12]

The Second Industrial Revolution and the Industrialization of Healthcare

After the Civil War, advances in technology and factories brought mass advancements in manufacturing and transportation. Inventions such as Thomas Edison's light bulb, Alexander Graham Bell's telephone, and the Wright Brothers' airplane transformed the way people lived, communicated, and traveled. By the early part of the 20th century, the assembly line powered mass production. Henry Ford's groundbreaking Ford Model T provided practical, affordable transportation for the

common man. Fredrick W. Taylor pioneered scientific management techniques to improve productivity on the factory floor
through the deployment of time-and-motion studies, best practices, and routinization of work.

Healthcare, however, was slow to adopt the efficiencies
of the factory. It was considered by most a cottage industry, and physicians were viewed as skilled craftsmen, so
that adoption of the attributes or characteristics of industri-
alizations were viewed with skepticism. While healthcare
accepted some practices of the industrial setting, such as
colocation, specialization, and shared core facilities, many of
the innovations of the Second Industrial Revolution, including standardization of activities, comprehensive quality
assurance programs, and hierarchical management structure,
were not deployed within the industry until many years
later. Most often, the reasons for the reluctance to change
were based on the differences between the delivery of
healthcare and the assembly of automobiles. Clear and deep-
seated impediments, such as the fierce culture of independence developed by medical practitioners and the resistance
to top-down management techniques, were also associated
with the factory.[13]

Healthcare, previously spared from the assembly line
organization of work associated with the Second Industrial
Revolution, began a process of "industrialization" in the second half of the 20th century. Darius A. Rastegar, MD noted in
a 2004 journal article, "Health Care Becomes an Industry":

> The delivery of health care is in the process of
> "industrialization" in that it is undergoing changes
> in the organization of work which mirror those that
> began in other industries a century ago. This pro-
> cess is characterized by an increasing division of
> labor, standardization of roles and tasks, the rise of
> a managerial superstructure, and the degradation (or

de-skilling) of work. The consolidation of the health care industry, the fragmentation of physician roles, and the increasing numbers of nonphysician clinicians will likely accelerate this process. Although these changes hold the promise of more efficient and effective health care, physicians should be concerned about the resultant loss of autonomy, disruption of continuity of care, and the potential erosion of professional values.[14]

Examples include

- Increasing specialization and development of sub- and superspecialties focused on increasingly narrow disciplines such as particular organs, illnesses, processes, or stage of care, with over 120 recognized specialty designations.[15]
- Use of hierarchical, functionally driven management structures and decision-making processes resulting in a rise in healthcare administrative roles of 3200% over a 35 year period, while numbers of physicians only increased by 150% in the same time period.[16]
- Vertical and horizontal consolidation of hospitals, ambulatory practices, and post-acute services is the norm. Software companies, pharmaceuticals, insurance companies, and adjacent companies also were part of this trend. In 2018, Definitive Healthcare tracked an astounding 803 mergers and acquisitions (M&As) and 858 affiliation and partnership announcements.[17]
- Adoption of improvement techniques from big manufacturers, such as process reengineering and lean methodology or the Toyota Production System, Six Sigma, and Quality Improvement approaches with the goal of eliminating waste, adding value to processes, redesigning work, and maximizing operational efficiency, quality, and speed while reducing costs.

The Third Industrial Revolution and the Electronic Health Record

In the middle of the 20th century, the Third Industrial Revolution brought semiconductors, mainframe computing, personal computing, and the Internet. The shift from analog electronic and mechanic devices to digital technologies—that is, an old television with an antenna and a fixed broadcast schedule versus an Internet-connected device that lets you stream movies—set the stage for disruption. Newspapers, banking, retail, communications, movies, music, and a variety of other industries faced reinvention. The HITECH Act's Meaningful Use program paid more than 5000 hospitals and 500,000 physicians financial incentives to adopt certified electronic health record (EHR) technology.[18] Most agree today that the EHRs mirrored paper records, were implemented for the purpose of billing versus patient care, were focused on technology-centric features, functions, and requirements, and virtually ignored the people, data, process, organization design, change management, and decision-making structures. The additional workload placed on clinicians and the lack of return on investment resulting from these systems have generated a great deal of dissatisfaction across the healthcare industry. Specific examples include:

- On March 18, 2019, the cover story of *Fortune* magazine, "Botched Operation: Death By 1,000 Clicks: Where Electronic Health Records Went Wrong" describes in detail that 10 years and $36 billion after the U.S. government claimed that turning American medical charts into electronic records would make healthcare better, safer, and cheaper, the healthcare industry has yet to reap the benefits and is dealing with unintended consequences of a digital revolution that took a bad turn.[19]
- A recent Harris poll conducted on behalf of Stanford Medicine indicates that even though roughly two-thirds of

primary care physicians think EHRs have led to improved care and are somewhat satisfied with their EHRs, they continue to report problems. The majority believe that EHRs contribute to physician burnout and need a complete overhaul (71% and 59%, respectively).[20]

■ 64% of healthcare leaders surveyed say EHRs don't do enough to support new care and reimbursement models. In a *Harvard Business Review* article entitled "We Interviewed Healthcare Leaders about Their Industry and They're Worried," Poku and Schulman report: "the technology needs of the emerging population-health strategy differ significantly from those of the current fee-for-service model ... there is a growing realization that the transformation of the health care system will require existing organizations to develop new business models and new organizational structures."[21]

The Next Great Revolution—Healthcare Is Primed for Disruption

The three previous industrial revolutions liberated human-kind from animal power, made mass production possible, and brought digital capabilities to billions of people. The emerging Fourth Industrial Revolution is, however, fundamentally different. It is characterized by a range of new technologies that are fusing the physical, digital, and biological worlds, impacting all disciplines, economies, and industries, and even challenging ideas about what it means to be human. Unlike anything we have experienced before, in its velocity, scope, and systematic impact, it will progress at an exponential rather than a linear pace.[22]

Healthcare has been slow to respond to innovations brought by the three previous revolutions. According to Clayton Christenson in his book *The Innovator's Prescription*, "high costs and uneven levels of access are typical hallmarks for an industry that is ripe for disruption."[23] According to a PWC Money Tree Report on venture capital money flow, the healthcare industry will benefit more than other industries from the merging of physical, digital, and biological systems. In 2017, the top sectors for investment flows were the Internet ($6.5 billion) followed by healthcare ($4 billion). These two sectors were ahead of mobile and telecommunications and software (non-Internet and mobile).[24] Artificial intelligence (AI), a specific example of Fourth Industrial Revolution technology, has seen a significant rise in investment dollars. According to CB Insights in 2018, healthcare AI startups have raised $4.3 billion across 576 deals since 2013, topping all other industries in AI deal activity[25] (Figure 3.2).

In fact, early signs of digital disruption are already having an impact on care quality, clinical efficiency, consumer experience, and reduction of the cost of care. Examples include:

- Telehealth is promoted by physicians to patients and used to care for cancer, behavioral health, post-surgical recovery, substance abuse, at-home dialysis, and more. Telemedicine parity reimbursement laws are being adopted, payers are adding telehealth to their benefits, and Congress has passed the CHRONIC Care Act, which opens the door for elderly Americans to benefit from telehealth in their home.[26]
- Continuous, remote monitoring: for chronic conditions such as heart failure, atrial fibrillation, and diabetes, the ability to monitor the patient's condition remotely through wearables, mobile devices, and wireless technologies integrated seamlessly into people's daily lives allows care teams to make real-time decisions and reduces the need for hospital admissions and bedside evaluations.
- Intelligent treatment plans: the inclusion of clinical and genomic data on specific patients to update clinical protocols using AI algorithms to continuously learn and personalize and develop real-time conclusions for

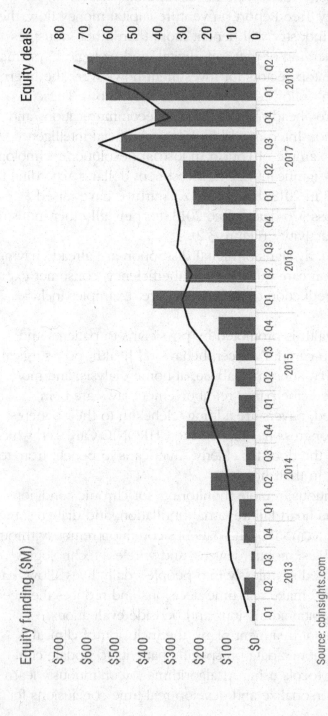

Figure 3.2 AI in healthcare.

early diagnosis, treatment, and management of chronic conditions.

■ Connected ecosystems: clinical, social determinants, claims, and other data are coordinated across networks that include retail clinics, hospitals, post-acute, home, and other venues while interacting with the health consumer, their immediate care providers, and seamless provision of payment for services.

Enter Big Tech

Big Tech or Alphabet (parent company of Google), Apple, Amazon, Microsoft, and a crowded field including Facebook, Oracle, Uber, IBM, and Salesforce have entered the health and healthcare market in a big way. With Fourth Revolution success across a broad array of industries, each company is leaning on its specific field of expertise to support health-care providers, payers, systems, and their patients through tools, solutions, and expertise. From 2013 to 2017, Alphabet, Apple, and Microsoft filed 313 healthcare patents between them. Recently, Google, Microsoft, Amazon, IBM, Oracle, and Salesforce have pledged to work toward greater interoperability in healthcare, especially related to cloud and AI-based technologies. Stey, Kanzaria, and Brook, in an American Medical Association Article entitled "How Disruptive Innovation by Business and Technology Firms Could Improve Population Health," challenged the Big Tech companies to benefit patients with complex needs who rely on the extensive resources and infrastructure of modern-day hospitals and health systems.[27] Leveraging accessible platforms, analytics, and marketing expertise, these companies have the ability to increase connectivity, collect data, predict preferences, and forecast market choices. These companies have the ability to simultaneously improve population health by helping to promote healthy lifestyle choices and reduce barriers to access.[28]

Conclusion

The healthcare industry has resisted disruptive forces in three previous industrial revolutions and is on the precipice of the fourth. Confluent changes in demographics, regulatory emphasis, computer science, clinical discovery, and consumer expectations have the potential to prevent or delay the onset of chronic conditions, to improve the speed of care, to reduce the fragmentation of clinical decision making, and to improve the relationships among the various stakeholders. While each industrial revolution changed the trajectory of mankind, the healthcare industry must address the dual challenges of high cost and variable quality. For most healthcare systems and providers, the transformation and innovation required are overwhelming. This book launches a conversation, building on the capabilities of previous industrial revolutions and the potential of the fourth to leapfrog healthcare's ability to orchestrate value through population health in the digital age.

Notes

1. Schwab, Klaus. *The Fourth Industrial Revolution.* World Economic Forum, 2016.
2. "What Is Digital Transformation?" The Enterprisers Project. Accessed July 16, 2019. https://enterprisersproject.com/what-is-digital-transformation.
3. Weill, Peter. *What's Your Digital Business Model?* Brighton: Harvard Business Review Press, Kindle Edition, 2018.
4. Golden, Brian. "Transforming Healthcare Organizations." *Healthcare Quarterly*, November 15, 2006. www.longwoods.com/content/18490/healthcare-quarterly/transforming-healthcare-organizations.
5. "About Chronic Diseases | CDC." Centers for Disease Control and Prevention. Accessed July 15, 2019. www.cdc.gov/chronicdisease/about/index.htm.
6. "NHE-Fact-Sheet." CMS.gov Centers for Medicare & Medicaid Services, April 26, 2019. www.cms.gov/research-statistics-data-and-systems/statistics-trends-and-reports/nationalhealthexpenddata/nhe-fact-sheet.html.

7. "U.S. Health Expenditure as GDP Share 1960–2019 | Statistic." Statista. Accessed June 4, 2019. www.statista.com/ statistics/184968/ us-health-expenditure-as-percent-of-gdp-since-1960/.
8. Landau, Joel. "Health-Care Dilemma: 10,000 Baby Boomers Are Now Retiring Each Day." CNBC, October 3, 2017. www.cnbc. com/2017/10/03/health-care-dilemma-10000-boomers-retiring-each-day.html.
9. Schwab, Klaus. *The Fourth Industrial Revolution*. World Economic Forum, 2016.
10. The Economist Intelligence Unit Flash poll. Healthcare to Benefit Most from the Fourth Industrial Revolution Executives Predict. The Economist Intelligent Unit Limited. January 2016.
11. "Pennsylvania Hospital History: Stories - Nation's First Hospital." Accessed July 27, 2019. www.uphs.upenn.edu/paharc/features/ creation.html.
12. "Massachusetts in the Industrial Revolution." History of Massachusetts Blog, July 30, 2018. https://historyofmassachu-setts.org/massachusetts-industrial-revolution/.
13. Panko, Walter B. "Clinical Care and the Factory Floor." *Journal of the American Medical Informatics Association: JAMIA* (American Medical Informatics Association, 1999). www.ncbi. nlm.nih.gov/pmc/articles/PMC61377/.
14. Rastegar, Darius A. "Health Care Becomes an Industry." *Annals of Family Medicine* (Copyright 2004 Annals of Family Medicine, Inc., January 2004). www.ncbi.nlm.nih.gov/pmc/articles/PMC1466626/.
15. "Medical Specialties—Explore Options—Choose Your Specialty—Careers in Medicine." Accessed June 5, 2019. www. aamc.org/cim/specialty/exploreoptions/list/.
16. "The Rise (and Rise) of the Healthcare Administrator." athe-naInsight, March 26, 2019. www.athenahealth.com/insight/ expert-forum-rise-and-rise-healthcare-administrator.
17. Waldron, Tory. "Top 8 Healthcare Trends in 2019." Definitive Healthcare, May 9, 2019. https://blog.definitivehc.com/ top-8-healthcare-trends-2019.
18. Halamka, John D., and Micky Tripathi. "The HITECH Era in Retrospect | NEJM." *New England Journal of Medicine*, Oxford University Press, September 7, 2017. www.nejm.org/doi/ full/10.1056/NEJMp1709851.
19. Fry, Erika, and Fred Schulte. "Death by a Thousand Clicks: Where Electronic Health Records Went Wrong." *Fortune*, March 18, 2019. http://fortune.com/longform/medical-records/.

20. "How Doctors Feel about Electronic Health Records." Stanford Medicine & The Harris Poll. med.stanford.edu/content/dam/sm/ehr/documents/EHR-Poll-Presentation.pdf.

21. Poku, Michael, and Kevin A Schulman. "We Interviewed Health Care Leaders about Their Industry, and They're Worried." *Harvard Business Review*, April 5, 2017. https://hbr.org/2016/12/we-interviewed-health-care-leaders-about-their-industry-and-theyre-worried.

22. Schwab, Klaus. *The Fourth Industrial Revolution*. World Economic Forum, 2016.

23. Christensen, Clayton M., Jerome H. Grossman, and Jason Hwang. *The Innovator's Prescription: a Disruptive Solution for Health Care*. New York: McGraw-Hill Education, 2017.

24. Hassan, Fred. "The Big Bang Is Coming in Health Care, and It Will Spark the Next Industrial Revolution." CNBC (CNBC, January 23, 2018). www.cnbc.com/2018/01/19/a-health-care-revolution-is-emerging-in-biopharma.html.

25. "The AI Industry Series: Top Healthcare AI Trends To Watch." cbinsights.com. CB Insights Research, September 2018. https://www.cbinsights.com/research/report/ai-trends-healthcare/.

26. American Well. "2019 Telehealth Predictions: The Emergence of a Game-Changer for Healthcare." American Well, February 13, 2019. www.americanwell.com/2019-telehealth-predictions/.

27. Stey, Anne, Hemal Kanzaria, and Robert Brook. "How Disruptive Innovation by Business and Technology Firms Could Improve Population Health," *JAMA* (U.S. National Library of Medicine, September 11, 2018). www.ncbi.nlm.nih.gov/pubmed/30128483.

28. Ibid.

The measurement of starlight

The measurement of starlight
Two centuries of
astronomical photometry

J. B. Hearnshaw

Reader in Astronomy

University of Canterbury

Christchurch, New Zealand

CAMBRIDGE UNIVERSITY PRESS
Cambridge, New York, Melbourne, Madrid, Cape Town, Singapore, São Paulo

Cambridge University Press
The Edinburgh Building, Cambridge CB2 2RU, UK

Published in the United States of America by Cambridge University Press, New York

www.cambridge.org
Information on this title: www.cambridge.org/9780521403931

First published 1996
This digitally printed first paperback version 2005

A catalogue record for this publication is available from the British Library

Library of Congress Cataloguing in Publication data

Hearnshaw, J. B.
The measurement of starlight : two centuries of astronomical
photometry / J. B. Hearnshaw.
   p.   cm.
Includes index.
ISBN 0 521 40393 6 (hc)
1. Astronomical photometry – History.   2. Stars – Photographic
measurements – History.   I. Title.
QB815.H43   1996
522′.62′09–dc20   95-34046   CIP

ISBN-13 978-0-521-40393-1 hardback
ISBN-10 0-521-40393-6 hardback

ISBN-13 978-0-521-01828-9 paperback
ISBN-10 0-521-01828-5 paperback

To Vickie, Alice and Edward

Contents

Preface

This book tells the story of the historical development of stellar photometry, the science of the measurement of the magnitudes and colours of the stars. I wrote it as a sequel to my earlier work *The Analysis of Starlight*, which described the development of stellar spectroscopy. As for *The Analysis of Starlight*, the present book has been written for the practising astronomer interested in the background and development of the subject. To this end I have endeavoured to provide an extensive and accurate bibliography of the principal references that cover the development of stellar photometry, with the view that this will make this book a useful reference work as well as one that is read for interest and for enjoyment. Neither science historians nor amateur astronomers were my primary readership targets, but hopefully there will be material here of interest to both these groups.

Over half of *The Measurement of Starlight* was written in the excellent library of the Royal Observatory, Edinburgh (including the famous Crawford Collection) during my sabbatical leave there in 1989, and again briefly in 1991. Chapter 6 was largely written in the library of Harvard College Observatory, also in 1989. The remainder of the book was written in the library of the University of Canterbury from 1990 to 1994. In addition I have made visits to the libraries of the Royal Astronomical Society, London, the Observatories, Cambridge, the Carter Observatory, Wellington, the South African Astronomical Observatory, Cape Town, Dunsink Observatory, Dublin, Konkoly Observatory, Budapest, to the Widener Library of Harvard University and to the Auckland University Library in New Zealand in order to research additional items, and I have borrowed materials from the Neils Bohr Library of the American Institute of Physics, College Park, Maryland. I am grateful to all these institutions for their assistance. In these libraries I filled eight large notebooks with hundreds of pages of detailed notes. The present book is much shorter and less detailed than my notebooks, and represents no more than a summary of what I have learnt. Researching and writing this book has been stimulating and rewarding, although at times it was also arduous; I trust both the stimulation and rewards can be shared with my readers.

Stellar photometry has at all stages been closely linked to developments in detector technology and instrumentation. The subject has experienced four major revolutions in the past two centuries – those of visual photometry, photographic photometry, photomultiplier photometry and photometry with the charge-coupled device (CCD). The first three of these are recorded in these pages, which take the story to about 1970. Since this is also the year that marks the invention of the CCD, I have decided to terminate my account at about that time. Astronomy from space was already being undertaken by 1970, but only the early beginnings of space-age photometry are discussed here. The subtitle of the book is *Two centuries of astronomical photometry*. The two centuries in question start in the early 1780s with the work of William Herschel, whom many would regard as the founder of stellar astronomy. However, a few earlier references to observations of stellar magnitudes are discussed in chapter 1, including those of Hipparchus and Ptolemy in classical times.

It is instructive to compare the respective developments of observational stellar spectroscopy and photometry. The former relied heavily on atomic and stellar-atmosphere theory for its progress, and at each stage it built on the knowledge and understanding that had been accumulated in the past. Photometry on the other hand, was tied almost slavishly to detector technology and instrumentation, to such an extent that the subject was practically started from scratch after each major revolution in detectors. Curiously, though, photometrists were always reluctant after each upheaval to abandon the cumbersome magnitude scale of stellar photometry (a legacy of ancient Greek science), fearing that to do so would render many decades of dedicated photometric effort obsolete. In practice, however, the poorer precision and accuracy of the older photometric data have in any case led to their being rarely cited in the modern literature.

Some major disasters have beset stellar photometry at different times, which sent shock-waves through the astronomical community. The failure of the *Carte du Ciel* project and the collapse of the International System of photometry based on the so-called North Polar Sequence were the two most notable misfortunes. The reasons for each event and the bitter lessons which astronomers have had to learn from them form an important part of this story.

Finally, I found that stellar photometry, being such an instrumental technique, itself provides a quintessential picture of the development of technology as a whole. In particular the general progress in photography, electronics, optical instrumentation and computing has in all cases had profound influences on astronomical photometry. The story told here portrays a fascinating microcosm of the wider developments in these diverse fields of technological endeavour. This in itself provides an important reason for writing this book, as an illustration of the relationships between different branches of science and technology.

A note on various matters of style: Dates have been included for those people who figure prominently in the text, provided these could be readily ascertained. I have used either imperial or metric units for indicating telescope apertures, whichever was the more common usage for that particular instrument. Frequently I have followed the practice in the older literature of specifying the precision of observations by quoting a probable error (p.e.), which is defined so that half the observations would lie at more than one p.e. from the mean. The standard error used in the more modern literature is close to 1.5 times the probable error, provided the random errors are normally distributed.

Acknowledgements

I am grateful to Prof. Malcolm Longair, the former director of the Royal Observatory, Edinburgh, for welcoming me as a guest in that institution where I wrote much of this book in 1989. Also I thank Prof. Owen Gingerich for his hospitality and interest in my project during my three-month stay at the Harvard-Smithsonian Center for Astrophysics, also in 1989. Prof. Brian Warner (Cape Town), Dr Chris Sterken (Brussels), Dr Alan Batten (Victoria) and Dr Michael Bessell (Canberra) all read large parts of this book and commented critically on the manuscript, which resulted in numerous improvements. Mrs Gill Evans (University of Canterbury) efficiently entered most of the text into a computer. Mrs Barbara Cottrell and Ms Merilyn Hooper (photographic section, University of Canterbury) and Mr Brian Hadley and his staff (ROE) undertook most of the photographic work for the illustrations. Dr Kaylene Murdoch received a grant from the Frank Bradshaw and Elizabeth Pepper Wood Fund at the University of Canterbury and she compiled part of the index and checked the references in chapters 1 to 7. Prof. A. G. McLellan undertook much of the index compilation. Mark Seymour's careful copy-editing at Cambridge University Press has resulted in numerous stylistic improvements.

While in Scotland in 1989 I received grants from the British Council which allowed me to visit libraries at the Royal Astronomical Society, London, and the Observatories, Cambridge, as well as to visit the Science Museum, London, where the late Dr Jon Darius showed me the Lindemann photoelectric photometer belonging to that institution.

Numerous people have offered me assistance, advice and material relating to stellar photometry, either verbally or by correspondence. Mr Angus Macdonald, the ROE librarian, was exceptionally helpful in this respect, but I also wish to thank Drs R. A. Arnold (Leiden), R. C. Bless (Wisconsin), Prof. H. A. and Dr M. T. Brück (Edinburgh), Drs V. I. Burnashev (Crimea), A. W. J. Cousins (Cape Town), D. W. Dewhirst (Cambridge), R. J. Dodd (Wellington), I. Elliott (Dublin), M. D. Guarnieri (Edinburgh), Prof. M. Golay (Geneva), Mr P. D. Hingley (RAS, London), the late Dr J. S. Hall (Sedona, Arizona), Mrs R. Hiltner (Ann Arbor), Dr G. E. Kron

(Honolulu), Mrs E. E. Lastovica (Cape Town), Dr D. E. Osterbrock and Mrs I. H. Osterbrock (Santa Cruz), Dr E. E. Salpeter (Ithaca), Mr J. Sharpe (Hythe, Kent, formerly of EMI), the late Dr R. H. Stoy (Edinburgh), Drs J. Tenn (Sonoma State Univ.), W. Tobin (Christchurch), Mrs M. Vargha (Budapest), Drs P. Wayman (Dublin), A. E. Whitford (Santa Cruz), G. Wlérick (Paris-Meudon), R. V. Willstrop (Cambridge), Prof. F. B. Wood (Gainesville), Drs A. G. Wright (Thorn-EMI, Middlesex) and A. T. Young (San Diego). This book would certainly have been less informative without the generous assistance of those cited above.

Finally I wish to thank the University of Canterbury for granting me sabbatical leave in 1989, for a Frank Bradshaw and Elizabeth Pepper Wood grant in 1991 and for an Erskine Fellowship in 1992, which enabled me to visit the institutions mentioned in the Preface, where I did the library research for this book.

1 The first stellar magnitudes

1.1 Classical stellar magnitudes

The earliest record to give quantitative information on the brightness of the stars is in Books VII and VIII of the *Almagest* by Claudius Ptolemaeus (Ptolemy) (c. AD 100 – c. AD 170). The star catalogue of the *Almagest*, or Μεγαλη Συνταξις, lists 1028 stars (some sources give as few as 1022 stars owing to possibly duplicate or misidentified objects) in 48 constellations, which had been recognized in ancient times (early third century BC) by Aratus and Eudoxus. The catalogue epoch is about AD 137. Each star in the catalogue has a description of its location in the constellation, its ecliptic coordinates of longitude and latitude (generally specified to a sixth of a degree but occasionally in quarters) as well as the magnitude on a scale from 1 to 6, based on a visual estimate of the star's brightness. Some of the stars have additional brightness descriptions of μειζων or ελασων for respectively brighter than or fainter than the integral values to which these labels are appended. According to the recent compilation of Grasshoff [1], 156 stars were assigned to such intermediate classes, which have frequently been interpreted as representing stars one third of a magnitude (or sometimes $0^{\mathrm{m}}3$) from the integral values. In addition, 12 stars were listed in the *Almagest* as 'faint' and 5 as 'nebulous', but these terms are not precisely defined.

Ptolemy says almost nothing in the *Almagest* about how he defines a magnitude. In Book VII he wrote: '... we observed as many stars as we could sight down to the sixth magnitude' (see for example Toomer's recent English translation of the *Almagest* (Book VII, Section 4) [2, see p. 339]) implying that magnitude 6 is indeed the limit of naked-eye visibility. Compared with the detailed discussion on his positional observations and reductions, this lack of comment on the scale of magnitudes is perplexing.

The original work of Ptolemy's *Almagest* is no longer available, but numerous manuscript copies from the ninth to sixteenth centuries have survived. Peters and Knobel, whose English translation and discussion

Fig. 1.1 Sample from Ptolemy's *Almagest*, from the Paris Codex 2389, ninth century Greek transcription.

of the *Almagest* has been a standard reference since 1915 [3], list 33 such manuscripts, 21 being in the original Greek, 8 in Latin and 4 in Arabic. Some of these are incomplete and most contain transcription errors (especially errors in assignments to the intermediate magnitude classes). Two in Greek dating from the ninth century (known as the Paris Codex 2389 and the Vatican Codex 1594) are usually deemed to be the most accurate.

There is a vigorous and continuing debate concerning the extent to which Ptolemy relied on the observations of Hipparchus (c. 129 BC) to compile his catalogue. This debate is largely based on evidence relating to the stars' coordinates, including the average 1° systematic error in Ptolemy's longitudes, the occasional use of quarters of a degree instead of sixths for the coordinate angle (suggesting the use of two different instruments) and the fact that all the *Almagest* stars rise above the horizon from Rhodes (latitude 36°), even though Ptolemy claimed to observe all of them from Alexandria, some 5 degrees further south. The arguments for and against have been presented by Delambre [4], Baily [5], Dreyer [6, 7], Vogt [8], Newton [9], Grasshoff [1], Rawlins [10], and Evans [11, 12] among others.

The magnitudes themselves play a relatively minor role in this debate. However, Rawlins [10] has derived the probability for the inclusion of a star in the *Almagest* as a function of its magnitude. This is 99 per cent for magnitude 4.05 or brighter, 75 per cent for $m = 5$, but only 2.5 per cent for $m = 6$. He then points out that eleven bright stars visible from Alexandria (magnitudes 3.4 to 4.9 after extinction by the terrestrial atmosphere) were omitted from the *Almagest*. They appear low on the southern horizon in Alexandria, but would be invisible or very low and faint from Rhodes. Their omission from the *Almagest* strengthens the case against Ptolemy as the observer. However, Evans [11, 12] considered the six southernmost stars in the catalogue (these included Canopus, Acrux and α Cen) and finds that atmospheric extinction would have rendered them much fainter than given in the *Almagest* (by nearly 2 magnitudes), had they been observed from Rhodes. The magnitudes of these stars therefore favour the original observations having been made by Ptolemy.

Even if Ptolemy was the observer for the *Almagest* star catalogue, was he also the originator of the system of magnitudes? Toomer [2, see p. 16] claims he was not, but concedes it is conjecture to ascribe the origin of the magnitude scale to Hipparchus. Hipparchus indeed had a star catalogue. His work is frequently referred to by Ptolemy in the *Almagest*, as well as by Pliny [13], who mentioned that Hipparchus had recorded the positions and brightnesses of stars. Although this catalogue is unfortunately long since lost, Hipparchus' commentary on the early third-century BC poem called *Phaenomena* by Aratus (in turn based on an earlier work by Eudoxus) has survived. Here Hipparchus refers to stars of 'brilliant light' ($\lambda\alpha\mu\pi\rho\sigma\tau\alpha\tau\sigma\varsigma$), 'of second degree' ($\epsilon\chi\phi\alpha\nu\eta\varsigma$) and 'faint' ($\epsilon\chi\phi\alpha\nu\epsilon\varsigma\tau\alpha\tau\sigma\varsigma$), corresponding roughly to the *Almagest*'s magnitudes 1–3, 4–5 and 6 respectively. Such qualitative descriptions therefore represent some of the earliest known references to the brightness of individual stars, and date from about 130 BC.

For the purposes of the present discussion, the identity of the observer of the *Almagest* star catalogue is of minor importance. Not only was the system of assigning a numerical scale of magnitudes to represent the brightness of stars the first known quantitative record of the apparent brightness of celestial objects, but the magnitude system of the *Almagest* has been amazingly resilient and therefore influential – a classical legacy which astronomy has retained to this day. Taking the *Almagest* as a whole, its application of mathematics to interpret celestial phenomena showed an elegance and rigour unequalled in classical times, and unsurpassed for the next fourteen centuries. Whatever its faults, the *Almagest* is without doubt a great work of the first rank in the history of science.

1.1.1   Note on the Almagest's magnitude scale

The magnitudes of the *Almagest* represent the earliest data on the visual estimation of stellar brightness. The technique is quite distinct from that of visual photometry, in which an instrument is used to measure the intensity of starlight, even though the eye is still the detector. Visual photometry flourished mainly in the second half of the nineteenth century (see chapter 3) and data from it allowed comparisons between the estimated and photometrically measured magnitudes, the latter being usually derived from the intensities using the adopted logarithmic law of Fechner (discussed in detail in section 3.5).

The early photometrists used their results to make comparisons with the estimated magnitudes, to investigate the random errors of the estimates and to explore systematic deviations between the photometric (ostensibly logarithmic) and estimated magnitudes. C. S. Peirce [14] and E. C. Pickering [15] at Harvard and E. Zinner at Bamberg [16] made some of the most exhaustive comparisons between the data of different observers available to them. Zinner, for example, derived mean photometric magnitudes for 2373 stars from the best data from Harvard and Potsdam, and used these results to obtain error bars for all the observers of estimated and photometric magnitudes that were to be found in the then existing literature. His value for the mean probable error of an *Almagest* magnitude was $\pm0^{m}.47$ (corresponding to a standard error of about $\pm0^{m}.7$ – see note in the Preface). This figure includes the rounding error, taken to be to the nearest third of a magnitude, as well as systematic deviations between the photometric and *Almagest* scales, which were substantial for the brightest stars. Numerous other systematic effects may intervene and were discussed by Zinner, notably those of extinction in the earth's atmosphere (Zinner applied approximate extinction corrections to the southernmost *Almagest* stars to bring their magnitudes to zenith values), whether the star is in or well away from the Milky Way and the colour equation (systematic effect of star colour on estimated magnitude).

Other authors have also obtained values for the errors in the *Almagest* magnitudes. For example Lundmark found the probable error of one observation by Ptolemy to be $\pm 0^m37$, a value which reflects the random error of a typical *Almagest* magnitude [17].

Peirce [14], Pickering [15], Lundmark [17] and Zinner [16] also considered the deviations of the *Almagest* scale from the photometric magnitudes, a topic discussed further in chapter 3. A summary of their findings is given by Weaver [18] in the first of his six articles on the development of photometry. The results of all investigators showed that Ptolemy's scale was far from the logarithmic or photometric one. The photometric magnitude difference between stars of first and second magnitude in the *Almagest* was in fact found to be 1^m4, but between $m = 5$ and $m = 6$ in the *Almagest*, the photometric difference was only 0^m3. Thus the bright end of the scale was much expanded relative to a logarithmic scale, while the faint end was compressed.†

The reader should beware of any suggestion that Ptolemy's scale was in error. This cannot be, for the *Almagest* magnitudes themselves define the scale. The error was the belief, prevalent in the nineteenth century, that a logarithmic relationship would indeed fit the scale of estimated stellar magnitudes.

1.2   Al-Sûfi's star catalogue

The one major catalogue of stellar magnitudes from the Middle Ages is that of the tenth-century Persian astronomer al-Sûfi (903–986). His work, the *Book on the Constellations of the Fixed Stars*, was especially valuable since it was based on his own observations of stellar brightness,

† A recent analysis by the author shows, however, that previous analyses of the Ptolemaic magnitudes were all erroneous in their treatment, and are strongly affected by a selection effect for the fainter stars. The correct statistical treatment finds the relation between mean Ptolemaic magnitude and a photometric (or Pogson) magnitude. This is, indeed, found to be linear [19], which implies that the Ptolemaic magnitude scale is accurately logarithmic in intensity, with a constant intensity ratio of $R = 3.26$ for two stars differing by one *Almagest* magnitude. The standard error of one *Almagest* magnitude was found to be $\pm 0^m62$.

whereas other works of this period had simply transcribed the values from Ptolemy. However, the stellar coordinates were not original but precessed from the *Almagest* to the epoch AD 964. A translation of manuscript copies of al-Sûfi's catalogue into French was published by the Danish astronomer H. C. F. C. Schjellerup in 1874 [20]. He also published a preliminary account of al-Sûfi's catalogue and magnitudes in 1869 [21].

Al-Sûfi's catalogue retained the 48 constellations of classical times. It added a few additional stars to those given by Ptolemy, bringing the total to 1151. The magnitude system closely resembles Ptolemy's, with intermediate classes to denote slightly more or less than integral values. However, Lundmark [22] listed 374 out of 1014 identified stars in al-Sûfi's catalogue with these intermediate magnitude labels, a proportion about twice that in the *Almagest*.

Lundmark also commented on ' ... the strong impression of the critical mind and extreme carefulness of Al-Sûfi' [22] and remarked on his practice of intercomparing stars of the same magnitude as a check on his estimation procedure. Indeed al-Sûfi's catalogue discussed the relative magnitudes of stars within each constellation in great detail and also made numerous references to Ptolemy whenever discrepancies arose. Al-Sûfi emphasized that he recorded the magnitudes 'as they were seen by his own eyes', implying that his observations rather than Ptolemy's were the ones appearing in his catalogue.

Zinner [16] derived a mean probable error of $\pm 0^m\!.38$ for al-Sûfi's magnitudes, comparable to that of the *Almagest*. The magnitude scale itself closely follows that of the *Almagest*, so even though al-Sûfi independently re-estimated the individual *Almagest* stars, he was clearly guided by Ptolemy's definition of the mean brightness of the stars in each magnitude class. His scale therefore shows the same departures from a logarithmic scale as does that of Ptolemy, as tabulated for example by Weaver [18].

Other medieval star catalogues did not contain new observations of stellar magnitudes. Ulugh Begh's (1394–1449) catalogue of the positions of 1018 stars observed from Samarkand (epoch 1437) simply copied the magnitudes from al-Sûfi [23, 24], while the ninth-century Mesopotamian astronomer al-Battani (c. 858–929) included a catalogue of about 500 stars (epoch AD 899) in his major astronomical work the *Zij*, but borrowed all the magnitudes from the *Almagest*.

Fig. 1.2 Constellation figures as they appeared in the St Petersburg manuscript by H. C. F. C. Schjellerup, 1874, being a translation of al-Sūfi's star catalogue.

1.3   Tycho Brahé's magnitude estimates and Bayer's *Uranometria*

The great Danish astronomer and aristocrat, Tycho Brahé (1546–1601), working nearly 15 centuries after Ptolemy and more than 600 years after al-Sûfi, was only the third major observer of stellar magnitudes. His introduction to stellar astronomy was spurred by the famous supernova of 1572. He recorded both its magnitude and colour, the record of the former being mainly descriptions of the new star's brightness relative to Venus, Jupiter and nearby stars in Cassiopeia [25, 26]. These observations were later interpreted by W. Baade in 1945 to reconstruct the light curve [27].

This extraordinary and very rare event of a galactic supernova probably inspired Tycho to pursue further observations in stellar astronomy. He established his Uraniborg Observatory on the island of Hven in 1576 and here produced his first star catalogue of 777 stars for the epoch 1600, which was published posthumously in the *Progymnasmata* of 1602 [26], the observations having been completed a decade earlier. Although Tycho's positional accuracy was superb, his magnitudes were relatively poor. Like Ptolemy and al-Sûfi, he introduced a scale with two intermediate grades between integral values (for example successively fainter stars were denoted by 3, 3., 3: and 4), but according to Zinner, his probable errors were no better than $\pm 0^{m}.54$.

Tycho had observed magnitudes for a further several hundred stars by 1598 and constructed a new catalogue of 1000 stars, which was eventually published by Kepler in the *Rudolphine Tables* of 1627 [28]. Another version of Tycho's catalogue was edited by Francis Baily in 1843. [29]. The fact that magnitudes were now quoted to only the nearest integer indicates that precision was not a major aim of these estimates, as Tycho himself conceded. Tycho's magnitude scale has been analysed by Peirce [14] and by Zinner [16] and is very similar to those of Ptolemy and al-Sûfi, in spite of the centuries that separated these three observers. Details can also be found in the articles by Lundmark [22] and Weaver [18].

In spite of the modest accuracy of Tycho's magnitude estimates, their use by Johann Bayer (1572–1625) for the construction of his famous star chart, the *Uranometria* of 1603 [30], greatly contributed to Tycho's reputation as an observer. This highly influential work comprised 51 copper engraved maps, 48 of them portraying the original constellations of classical times for which Tycho's second catalogue (at the time unpublished) provided the principal positions and magnitudes. Bayer embellished the constellations with drawings by Albrecht Dürer.

The influence of the *Uranometria* was enhanced by the practice of naming the stars with Greek or Roman letters, approximately in order of descending brightness within each constellation, as given by Tycho's magnitudes (although with many exceptions). This provided an elegant system of stellar nomenclature, far more practical than the Ptolemaic descriptions of location within a constellation.

Bayer's *Uranometria* was greatly superior to Alessandro Piccolomini's (1508–1579) charts *De le Stelle Fisse* of 1540 [31] which represent the first printed star atlas, produced from woodcuts. Piccolomini's atlas showed stars to only fourth magnitude, and was of lower accuracy and less highly embellished than the *Uranometria*. Although Piccolomini also used letters to label the stars, it is Bayer's nomenclature that has survived.

1.4 The southern constellations: Keyzer, de Houtman and Halley

The charting of the far southern skies, which were omitted from the catalogues of Ptolemy, al-Sûfi and Tycho Brahé, represents one of the more fascinating episodes of astronomical history. As early as 1589 a Flemish monk named Petrus Plancius (1552–1622) had drawn a celestial globe with several non-Ptolemaic constellations added in the far south. Some stars down to sixth magnitude were shown. Plancius ascribed the source of observations for the southern globe to early navigators, such as Andrea Corsali, Amerigo Vespucci and Pedro de Medina.

In 1601 the globe of Jodocus Hondius (1563–1612) showed stars in 12 far southern constellations which were not in the *Almagest*. Two years later three further works appeared showing southern stars: a catalogue by Frederick de Houtman (c. 1560 – c. 1605), Bayer's atlas (the *Uranometria*) and another globe by Willem Janszoon Blaeu (1571–1638) with 300 southern stars.

It is likely that all four of these early seventeenth century works relied mainly on the observations of two Dutch seafarers, Pieter Dircksz Keyzer (d. 1596) and Frederick de Houtman. They sailed on the same ship for the Dutch East Indies in 1595. Keyzer, whose Latin name was Petrus Theodorus, was a pupil of Plancius. He observed the positions and estimated magnitudes of southern stars in Madagascar and Sumatra in 1595–96, but died on the return voyage. His observations nevertheless reached Holland and were almost certainly used by Hondius, and very probably by Bayer.

De Houtman observed in Sumatra in 1596 (probably assisting Keyzer) and there again from 1599–1600 while on a second voyage. He published

Fig. 1.3   New south polar constellations in Bayer's *Uranometria* (1661 edition).

a catalogue of 303 stars, of which 196 were new ones not in the *Almagest*. Curiously, it appeared as an appendix to a dictionary on Malayan and Madagascan native dialects [32]. The catalogue was edited by Edward Knobel (1841–1930), who ascribed, however, the observations to Keyzer [33], but de Houtman published them as his own after the death of his colleague. Whatever the true source of the observations, the catalogue was the basis for the southernmost stars on the globe of Willem Janszoon Blaeu. On the other hand, a series of celestial maps drawn by Jacob Bartsch (1600–33), the first dating from 1624, is believed to be based on the unpublished observations of Keyzer – see [34, p. 14].

The various early seventeenth century sources, be they charts, globes or catalogue, recognized 12 new southern constellations, and magnitudes of about 130 stars were given to the nearest integer. Zinner has analysed the magnitudes in de Houtman's catalogue and found a mean probable error of $\pm0^m.52$, while the observations of Keyzer, with magnitudes taken from the maps of Bartsch where they are clearly indicated, gave a probable error of $\pm 0^{m}54$ [16]. In practice, stars assigned to magnitude 6 by Keyzer were about magnitude 4.7 to 5.0 on Zinner's photometric scale.

The early observations of the southern sky by Keyzer and de Houtman still left this region of the heavens far less well charted than the equatorial and northern regions. The main requirement was to improve the positional accuracy of the stars for navigational purposes, and Flamsteed as Astronomer Royal was one of those to undertake new observations from Greenwich using a sextant equipped with telescopic sights. In 1676 Edmond Halley (1656–1742), at that time a student at Oxford, proposed an expedition to the southern hemisphere to extend the work of Tycho and Flamsteed to the southernmost stars. The expedition to Saint Helena (latitude 16° S) was funded by Halley's father, but had the support of the Royal Society, of King Charles II and of the East India Company.

Halley's stellar observations during 1676–78 were made with a large sextant, which, like Flamsteed's, was equipped with telescopic sights. A few stars were observed on the return voyage and by the end of 1678 his *Catalogus Stellarum Australium* [35] was published. It contained 341 southern stars in 23 constellations. Although positional accuracy was the principal goal, naked-eye magnitudes were also estimated, generally in integers, but for 31 stars the values $1\frac{1}{2}$, $3\frac{1}{2}$ or $4\frac{1}{2}$ were used. Halley also gave the first account of the fine southern globular cluster, ω Centauri, in this catalogue. An edited version of the catalogue was prepared by Francis Baily in 1843 [36]. According to Zinner the mean probable error of Halley's estimates was $\pm 0^{m}42$ [16].

The Czech astronomer and Jesuit priest Father Frantisek Noël (1651–1729) was the only other notable observer of stellar magnitudes for southern stars before Lacaille. His observations were made from China and India (including Macao and Goa) between 1684 and 1707. His two catalogues [37, 38] contained respectively 220 and 352 stars with integral magnitudes and a probable error of $\pm 0^{m}45$ [16].

1.5   Early magnitude estimates through the telescope

The invention of the telescope, attributed to Hans Lippershey in Holland in 1608, and its subsequent use in astronomy by Galileo Galilei (1564–1642), represents one of the great moments in the history of astronomy. Yet the telescope had relatively little beneficial effect on the quality of stellar magnitudes in the seventeenth and eighteenth centuries. Although fainter stars became accessible, there were no guidelines concerning what magnitudes should be assigned to them, so that the scales of different observers diverged widely. Moreover the telescope introduces a different colour equation to that of the unaided eye, which is in part caused by the Purkinje effect.† The advent of the telescope was therefore a mixed blessing for observers of stellar magnitudes, and this was the case until William Herschel and especially Argelander made improvements in the technique of magnitude estimation. This section records some of the limited progress before such improvements were devised.

Galileo's amazing discoveries with the telescope were described in his essay *Sidereus Nuncius* (the *Sidereal Messenger*) [39]. He had some interesting and eloquent comments on stars and the Milky Way seen through a telescope:

> But beyond the stars of the sixth magnitude you will behold through the telescope a host of other stars, which escape the unassisted sight, so numerous as to be almost beyond belief, for you may see more than six other differences of magnitude, and the largest of these, which I may call stars of the seventh magnitude, or of the first magnitude of invisible stars, appear with the aid of the telescope larger and brighter than stars of the second magnitude seen with the unassisted sight ...

> The next object I have observed is the Milky Way. By the aid of a telescope any one may behold this in a manner which so distinctly appeals to the senses ... for the Galaxy is nothing else but a mass of innumerable stars planted together in clusters. Upon whatever part of it you direct the telescope straightway a vast crowd of stars presents itself to view; many of them are tolerably large and extremely bright, but the number of small ones is quite beyond determination [39].

Galileo clearly states that stars were over 5 magnitudes brighter in a telescope (this would be expected for a telescope aperture about ten times that of the iris of the unaided eye), and he implies that the faintest stars just visible in his telescope should be assigned to about magnitude 12, which is roughly consistent with the principle that all stellar images on the human retina should be increased in brightness by the same factor when the telescope is employed.

Galileo did not explicitly record magnitudes of stars. The first observer to do so through a telescope was probably John Flamsteed (1646–1719). His sextant and mural arc at Greenwich were fitted with small sighting telescopes to improve the positional accuracy of the stars observed for his *Historia Coelestis Britannica* [40]. This famous catalogue improved the positional

---

† The Purkinje effect (1825), named after the Czech physiologist Jan Purkinje (1787–1869), describes the apparent brightnesses of blue and red objects initially of equal intensity. In low intensity illumination the eye perceives blue objects as the brighter, owing to the shift from photopic (cones as sensors) to scotopic vision (rods as sensors).

accuracy of nearly 3000 stars to about 10 arc seconds, but the magnitudes were not recorded with any great care. Baily [41], in his introduction to his edited version of the catalogue, states that the magnitudes were 'not sufficiently attended to'. Generally Flamsteed used naked-eye observation and for the bright stars he borrowed magnitude data from other sources. However, some stars in the catalogue are given as 7th or 8th magnitude, which represent the first estimates to extend the Ptolemaic scale beyond the naked-eye limit.

1.5.1   Eighteenth century meridian-circle observations

The popularity of telescopic meridian-circle observations in the eighteenth century led to a large number of magnitude estimates being made for fainter stars. This was considered a useful by-product of positional astronomy, mainly as an aid to identification.

The third Astronomer Royal, James Bradley (1693–1762), estimated magnitudes in this way at Greenwich from 1750 [42]. The individual observations were not at that time published, but this was done by Arthur Auwers (1838–1915) over a century later in a catalogue of proper motions for 3222 stars observed by Bradley [43]. Here the mean magnitude estimates of nearly 400 stars by Bradley and his assistants are reproduced from the original notebooks. The original estimates were generally in quarter magnitude intervals, and with few exceptions they pertain to fainter stars between magnitudes 5.5 and 8.

By far the most extensive of the eighteenth century transit-circle catalogues was that published by Jérome de Lalande (1732–1807) in his *Histoire Céleste Française* [44]. The actual observer was probably Lalande's nephew Michel Lalande, using a telescope of $2\frac{2}{3}$-inches aperture at the École Militaire in Paris. Some 50 000 stars were observed, but the full reduction to equatorial coordinates (epoch 1800) was not made until Francis Baily reduced and published a catalogue of 47 390 stars based on Lalande's observations [45]. Magnitudes are given for nearly all these objects, the estimates being in half magnitude intervals to $m = 9\frac{1}{2}$.

One of the greatest pioneers of southern hemisphere astronomy, Nicolas-Louis de Lacaille (1713–62), was another very productive astrometric observer. He was at the Cape of Good Hope for two years from March 1751 and established a small observatory there with the assistance of the Dutch authorities. For his stellar observations he mounted a half-inch aperture telescope on his mural quadrant and was able to observe nearly 10 000 stars on just 126 nights. Only about a fifth of these data were fully reduced by Lacaille in his *Coelum Australe Stelliferum* [46], and it was not until 1847 that

Francis Baily's edition of Lacaille's work gave the equatorial coordinates (epoch 1750) for 9766 stars (based largely on the reductions of Thomas Henderson), as well as their magnitudes. This catalogue was produced with the financial support of the British Association and the British government, and was published after Baily's death in 1844 with a preface by Sir John Herschel, who was himself a noted telescopic observer of stellar magnitudes in the early nineteenth century – see section 2.2. The magnitudes go to 7, with half-magnitude intervals being occasionally used. Herschel gives no information on Lacaille's observing procedure for the magnitude scale.

In his original catalogue [46] Lacaille had added 14 new southern constellations to those of the early Dutch seafarers; they are still in use today and names such as Telescopium, Horologium and Octans are among several based on Lacaille's own astronomical tools. One can rightly marvel at Lacaille's prodigious output, which was nearly thirty times that of Halley over a similar period of time. His catalogue of the far southern sky was only exceeded for accuracy and number of stars when the third volume of the *Cape Photographic Durchmusterung* was published in 1900 for the south polar region [47] – see section 4.4.

1.5.2   *Two notable catalogues compiled by Francis Baily*

Two notable catalogues compiled by Francis Baily (1774–1844) in the early nineteenth century deserve mention because of their widespread use. Both gave valuable compendia of magnitudes, although positions were their main purpose. The first was the *Astronomical Society Catalogue* of 1826, published as an appendix in the second volume of the Society's *Memoirs* [48]. The society was later to become the Royal Astronomical Society, and Baily was one of its founders and the first president. His astronomical reputation was largely made from the editing and compiling of stellar catalogues. The *Astronomical Society Catalogue* gave positions and magnitudes for 2881 stars, including all to magnitude 5 over the whole sky, all to magnitude 6 within 30° of the equator and all to magnitude 7 within 10° of the ecliptic. It was compiled from the catalogues of Flamsteed (2934 stars), Bradley (3222 stars), Lacaille, Mayer (998 stars) [49], Piazzi (7646 stars) [50], and von Zach (1826 stars) [51]. Unfortunately the catalogue gives no information on how the magnitudes were obtained. Many are quoted in half magnitude intervals with the notation such as $6 \cdot 7$ for magnitude $6\frac{1}{2}$.

Baily's second catalogue, the *Catalogue of Stars of the British Association*, was compiled from 32 separate sources and encompassed 8377 stars [52]. It included at least all stars to $m = 6$, and all to $m = 7$ within 10° of the ecliptic; in practice a few stars to magnitude 8 were also included.

Fig. 1.4   Francis Baily.

Magnitudes are given in half magnitude intervals and the positions are to a
precision of about 5 arc seconds for the epoch 1850. Of the catalogues used
by Baily for this compilation, that by Thomas Granville Taylor (1804–48)
from the Madras Observatory was one of the most extensive [53], giving
data for 11 015 stars, some as far south as −62° declination. Two Dollond
telescopes of $3\frac{3}{4}$-inch aperture were employed, one being in the Madras

transit circle, the other belonging to the mural circle. Magnitude estimates were made for stars as faint as magnitude $9\frac{1}{2}$.

This summary of early magnitude estimates by no means refers to all the early sources of magnitudes in stellar catalogues. A particularly useful reference list is to be found in chapter 17 of Houzeau's *Répertoire des Constantes de l'Astronomie* [54].

1.6   Concluding remarks on early magnitude estimates

The scale of stellar magnitudes used by Ptolemy has now survived for nearly two thousand years. For the first 17 centuries, until the mid-nineteenth century, neither the utility nor even the precise definition of a stellar magnitude was seriously questioned. By modern standards it must be regarded as a cumbersome scale, with several defects. First, it is an inverse scale, with the magnitudes of fainter stars being specified by larger numbers. Secondly, a difference of one magnitude on the *Almagest* scale was neither a constant intensity difference nor a constant intensity ratio. By the mid-nineteenth century it was believed to approximate the latter quite closely (see section 3.5.4), in which case it would be a logarithmic scale, but the constant ratio (or base of the logarithms) is far from any convenient integral value (a base of ten would indeed result in a more convenient scale than that in use).

In the event, the Ptolemaic scale was shown by Pickering, Zinner and others to depart significantly from a logarithmic one. A consequence of this is that the magnitude difference perceived between two stars, which is understood to be an ill-defined expression of the difference in visual sensation, will change when the stars are viewed in a telescope, and indeed the value will depend on the light collecting power of the telescope. That the early telescopic observers should encounter such a pitfall but not clearly recognize the dangers was a recipe for numerous problems in extending the scale beyond magnitude 6.

In reading the early literature on visual magnitude estimates, one is struck by the extreme paucity of discussion concerning the basis on which the magnitudes were assigned or of the observational procedures. In contrast, the wealth of detail on stellar positions clearly shows where the priorities of early observers lay. Magnitude estimates were made principally as an aid to identification, or for no better reason than the fact that stars so clearly differed among themselves in their brilliance, that some succinct notation for such perceived differences was required.

In the catalogues referred to in this first phase of stellar magnitude estimation, there is no discussion of physiological effects, of colour equation, of eye fatigue, of the influence of sky brightness or of atmospheric extinction. Some of these ideas, which are so crucial to photometry, began to germinate with Bouguer and Lambert in the mid-eighteenth century, but it was another century after that before they really entered the realm of stellar photometry, or were discussed extensively by observational astronomers.

It is not surprising that the lack of critical appraisal of observational techniques in the long early period of magnitude estimation should also be accompanied by an almost total lack of interpretation or analysis of stellar magnitude data. One of the notable exceptions was a short paper presented by Edmund Halley to the Royal Society in March 1721, the year following his appointnment as Astronomer Royal, and a paper all the more remarkable on account of its uniqueness [55]. Halley considered that the brightest stars, of first magnitude, must also be the nearest, and continued:

> If therefore the number of them be supposed Thirteen, omitting Niceties in a Matter of such Irregularity, at twice the distance from the Sun there may be placed four times as many, or 52; which, with the same allowance, would nearly represent the number of the Stars we find to be of the 2d magnitude: so 9 × 13 or 117, for those at three times the distance: and at ten times the distance 100 × 13 or 1300 Stars; which distance may perhaps diminish the light of any of the Stars of the first magnitude to that of the sixth.

Halley was interested in showing that the stellar universe has infinite extent†, a consequence of his belief that ever fainter and more numerous stars could be found in larger telescopes. His assertion that second magnitude stars are on average at twice the distance of those of first magnitude, as well as being four times as numerous, is flawed. But his calculation for the relative brightness of those of sixth magnitude is, remarkably, on the right tracks, even if the result for the number of sixth magnitude stars in the sky is somewhat low.

References

[1] Grasshoff, G., The History of Ptolemy's Star Catalogue, Springer-Verlag (1990).
[2] Toomer, G.J., Almagest (Book vii, Section 4) (1984).
[3] Peters, C.F.H. and Knobel, E.B., Ptolemy's catalogue of stars, a revision of the Almagest, Carnegie Institution of Washington Publ. No. 86, Washington (1915).

---

† His paper represents an early but flawed attempt to explain the paradox later associated with the name of Wilhelm Olbers, that the sky should be bright at night in an infinite starry universe.

[4]   Delambre, J.B.J., *Histoire de l'Astronomie ancienne*, 2 vols., Paris (1817).
[5]   Baily, F., *Mem. R. Astron. Soc.*, **13**, 1 (1843).
[6]   Dreyer, J.L.E., *Mon. Not. R. Astron. Soc.*, **77**, 528 (1917).
[7]   Dreyer, J.L.E., *Mon. Not. R. Astron. Soc.*, **78**, 343 (1918).
[8]   Vogt, H., *Astron. Nachr.*, **224**, 17 (1925).
[9]   Newton, R.R., *The Crime of Claudius Ptolemy*, Johns Hopkins University Press, Baltimore (1977).
[10] Rawlins, D., *Publ. Astron. Soc. Pacific*, **94**, 359 (1982).
[11] Evans, J., *J. Hist. Astron.*, **18**, 155 (1987).
[12] Evans, J., *J. Hist. Astron.*, **18**, 233 (1987).
[13] Pliny, *Plinius, Naturalis Historia II*, 95, Beaujeau ed. 41–42.
[14] Peirce, C.S., *Ann. Harvard Coll. Observ.*, **9**, 1 (1878).
[15] Pickering, E.C., *Ann. Harvard Coll. Observ.*, **14**, 325 (1885).
[16] Zinner, E., *Veröff. Remeis-Sternw. Bamberg*, **2**, 1 (1926).
[17] Lundmark, K., *Vierteljahrschr. Astron. Ges.*, **61**, 230 (1926).
[18] Weaver, H., *Pop. Astron.*, **54**, 211 (1946).
[19] Hearnshaw, J.B. and Khan, D.A., *Southern Stars*, **36**, 169 (1995).
[20] Schjellerup, H.C.F.C., *Description des Etoiles Fixes composée au milieu du dixième siècle de notre ère par l'Astronome Persan Abd-al-Rahman al-Sûfi*, St Petersburg (1874).
[21] Schjellerup, H.C.F.C., *Astron. Nachr.*, **74**, 97 (1869).
[22] Lundmark, K., *Handbuch der Astrophys.*, **5**, 210 (1932).
[23] Peters, C.H.F., *Astron. Nachr.*, **99**, 235 (1881).
[24] Knobel, E.B., *Mon. Not. R. Astron. Soc.*, **45**, 417 (1885).
[25] Brahé, T., *De Stella Nova* (1573).
[26] Brahé, T., *Progymnasmata*, (1602).
[27] Baade, W., *Astrophys. J.*, **102**, 309 (1945).
[28] Kepler, J., *Rudolphine Tables* (1627).
[29] Baily, F., *Mem. R. Astron. Soc.*, **13**, 29 and 127 (1843).
[30] Bayer, J., *Uranometria* (1603).
[31] Piccolomini, A., *De le Stelle Fisse* (1540).
[32] de Houtman, F., *Spraechende woordboeck Inde Maleysche ende Madagaskarsche Talen*, Amsterdam (1603).
[33] Knobel, E.B., *Mon. Not. R. Astron. Soc.*, **77**, 414 (1917).
[34] Warner, D.J., *The Sky Explored: Celestial Cartography 1500–1800*, Alan R. Liss Inc., New York (1979).
[35] Halley, E., *Catalogus Stellarum Australium*, (1679).
[36] Baily, F., *Mem. R. Astron. Soc.*, **13**, 35 and 167 (1843).
[37] Noël, F., Observationes de l'ascension droite, de la déclinasion et de la grandeur de plusieurs étoiles australes, *Mém. Acad. Paris 1699*, **7** (2), 221 (1729).
[38] Noël, F., *Observations math. et phys. in India et China factae a Patre Francisco Noël S.J. ab anno 1684 usque ad annum 1708*, Prague (1710).
[39] Galilei, G., *Sidereus Nuncius* (1610). See English translation by E. Stafford Carlos, *The Sidereal Messenger of Galileo*, London, Dawson's of Pall Mall (1960).
[40] Flamsteed, J., *Historia Coelestis Britannica*, London (1725).
[41] Baily, F., *An account of the Rev. John Flamsteed ...to which is added his British Catalogue of Stars*, London (1835).
[42] Bradley, J., *Fundamenta atronomine pro anno 1755*, F. Bessel, Königsberg (1818).
[43] Auwers, A., *Neue Reduction der Bradley'schen Beobachtungen aus den Jahren 1750 bis 1762*, **3**, St Petersburg (1888).

[44]   de Lalande, J., *Histoire Céleste Française, contenant les observations de plusieurs Astronomes français*, Paris (1801).

[45]   Baily, F., *A catalogue of those stars in the Histoire Céleste Française of Jérome de Lalande*, London (1847).

[46]   de Lacaille, N-L., *Coelum Australe Stelliferum*, Paris (1763).

[47]   Gill, D. and Kapteyn, J.C., *Ann. Cape Observ.*, **5**, 1 (1900).

[48]   Baily, F., *Mem. R. Astron. Soc.*, **2**, 1 (appendix) (1826).

[49]   Mayer, T., *Opera Inedita*, **1**, Göttingen (1775).

[50]   Piazzi, G., *Praecipuarum stellarum inerrantium positiones mediae*, Palermo (1814).

[51]   von Zach, F.X., *Tabulae speciales aberrationis*, Gotha, 2 vols. (1806).

[52]   Baily, F., *The Cat. of Stars of the British Association for the Advancement of Science*, London (1845).

[53]   Taylor, T.G., *A general catalogue of the principal fixed stars from observations made at the honorable East India Company's Observatory at Madras in the years 1830–43*, Madras (1844).

[54]   Houzeau, J.-C., *Ann. Observ. R. Bruxelles*, **1** (Part 2) (1878).

[55]   Halley, E., *Phil. Trans. R. Soc. Lond.*, **31**, 24 (1720–21).

2 Visual magnitude estimates

2.1 William Herschel and the method of sequences

William Herschel (1738–1822) is frequently acclaimed as the father of stellar astronomy. His accomplishments as a stellar observer far exceeded those of his contemporaries, and his instruments, especially his 20-foot reflector, were superior to those available to any other astronomer at this time in light-gathering power and resolution.

Herschel turned his attention to astronomy in 1773, the year in which he constructed his first telescopes. At this time he was living in Bath with his sister Caroline. In 1782 the Herschels moved to Datchet near Windsor, and by the end of the following year, the famous 20-foot reflector (aperture 18.8 inches) had been completed. These years marked the start of his researches in stellar astronomy. The telescope was re-erected in Slough when the Herschels finally moved there in 1786.

Here the main achievements of William Herschel in stellar astronomy will be summarized. He produced two catalogues of double stars, in 1782 and 1784, comprising respectively 269 and 434 objects. He studied stellar proper motions, and concluded that they gave information on the sun's motion as a star moving through space, with the direction of solar motion, the solar apex, being near the star λ Herculis. By 1786 his 'sweeps' with the 20-foot telescope had produced his first catalogue of a thousand new nebulae and clusters, which was followed by second and third catalogues in the years 1789 and 1802. He considered nebulae were composed of numerous faint stars, though later (1811) he modified this opinion, finding many to be made of nebulous matter from which stars formed. Above all, Herschel published two famous papers 'On the construction of the heavens' (1784, 1785). Here he showed, as Galileo had done before him, that the Milky Way itself was resolvable into many faint stars [1, 2]. From his 'gauges', or star counts, he determined the shape of the boundary of our Milky Way system, based on the premise that a star's apparent brightness is a measure of its distance,

Fig. 2.1   William Herschel, from a painting by I. Russell, R.A., 1794.

even though the shortcomings of this assumption must have become evident to him later on – see section 8.4.

William Herschel was the first astronomer to produce reliable naked-eye estimates of stellar brightness. In this work he greatly surpassed the accuracy achieved by his predecessors by devising the method of sequences. His motivation was to improve upon the many discrepancies found in the magnitudes by Flamsteed and other observers, which frequently amounted to half a magnitude for the bright stars and $1\frac{1}{2}$ magnitudes for fainter ones. Herschel described his new technique as follows:

> I place each star, instead of giving its magnitude, into a short series, constructed upon the order of brightness of the nearest proper stars. For instance to express the lustre of D, I say CDE. By this short notation, instead of referring star D to an imaginary uncertain standard, I refer it to a precise, and determined, existing one. C is a star that has a greater lustre than D; and E is another of less brghtness [sic] than D [3].

When work began in July 1781, stars were simply placed in decreasing order of brightness. By 1783 he assigned approximate magnitudes and subdivided each whole magnitude into 'three degrees of difference'. Thus:

May 12, 1783. Order of the stars in Boötes
α 1′ ε 2″ η 2‴ γ β δ 3′ ρ 3″ ζ 3‴ π 4

By August of that year he had devised special symbols for magnitude differences between closely neighbouring stars. The main symbols he used were as follows:

.   indicates equality

,   separates two stars where 'upon a longer inspection of them we always return to decide it in favour of the same [star]'

-      indicates a small but readily discernible difference

-,

and --   indicate progressively larger magnitude intervals

---   shows any large difference in brightness

With these symbols, Herschel connected together, in a descending sequence, the stars within a constellation, writing down the Flamsteed numbers separated by the appropriate symbol. His object was to devise a system capable of detecting possible changes in the brightness of the stars, without resorting to the unreliable magnitude estimates of Flamsteed and others. In addition, the question of the distribution of the stars in space and the distribution of their luminosities was always to the fore in Herschel's mind from the outset of his stellar researches.

The possibility of finding new variable stars was an important aspect of this work, and Herschel remarks that as many as 1 in 30 of the 3000 or so stars so far examined may prove to be variable. As the sun itself could in principle be variable, he saw his stellar research as being potentially able to give some information on the sun:

> Who, for instance, would not wish to know what degree of permanency we ought to ascribe to the lustre of our sun? Not only the stability of our climates, but the very existence of the whole animal and vegetable creation itself is involved in the question ... If it be allowed to admit the similarity of stars with our sun as a point established, how necessary will it be to take note of the fate of our neighbouring suns, in order to guess at the fate of our own [3]!

Herschel's observations for his sequences were nearly all naked eye, although a telescope was used on numerous occasions for fainter objects. All the stars observed, however, were in Flamsteed's catalogue, and were therefore naked-eye objects. He completed 3010 estimates for 1251 stars, and a total of six catalogues of stellar sequences were produced. Four of these were published in the *Philosophical Transactions* between 1796 and 1799 [3, 4, 5, 6], while two were discovered posthumously in June 1883 by Edward Pickering in a form ready for the printer [7].

2.1.1 Later analysis of Herschel's sequences

William Herschel did not assign numerical magnitudes to the stars he observed. But Charles Peirce (1839–1914) at Harvard College Observatory [8] was able to put Herschel's work on a quantitative magnitude scale. He first calibrated Herschel's symbols in terms of magnitude intervals. In arbitrary units these were:

$$. \; = 0$$
$$, \; = 1$$
$$- \; = 2$$
$$-, \; = 3$$
$$-- \; = 4$$

By comparing the magnitudes for the same stars obtained with his Zöllner photometer, Peirce showed that one unit corresponded to $0^{m}.17$, falling to $0^{m}.27$ for fainter stars ($m > 3.75$).

The calibration was repeated more rigorously by Pickering, who found that $. \; = 0^{m}.06$; $, \; = 0^{m}.23$ and $- \; = 0^{m}.38$ were the average intervals, with negligible dependence on stellar magnitude or on which of Herschel's six catalogues a star appeared in [7]. Pickering later wrote:

> Herschel furnished observations of nearly 3000 stars, from which their magnitudes a hundred years ago can now be determined with an accuracy approaching that of the best modern catalogues. The average difference from the photometric catalogues is only $\pm 0^{m}.16$, which includes the actual variations of the stars during a century, as well as the errors of both catalogues. The error of a single comparison but little exceeds a tenth of a magnitude [9, see p. 231].

Pickering and his coworkers converted the Herschelian scale into photometric magnitudes by tying it to the magnitude scale of the Harvard meridian photometry. In the *Harvard Photometry* of 1884–85 the magnitude scale was that of Pogson with a zero-point set to achieve the best agreement with the estimated magnitudes of Argelander. When the later photometry with the 4-inch meridian photometer began at Harvard, the zero-point of the photometric scale was tied to 722 standard stars observed by Gould and his assistants from Córdoba in the $+5°$ to $+15°$ declination zone for the *Uranometria Argentina*. Pickering gave a full tabulation of the magnitudes deduced for all Herschel's stars on this photometric scale in 1899 [9].

Ernst Zinner (1886–1970) in Bamberg later recalibrated Herschel's sequences, this time carefully taking into account the effects of colour difference and stellar magnitude in assigning numerical values for the magnitude differences that correspond to Herschel's symbols. He also showed that one

Herschel observation resulted in a magnitude with a typical probable error of $\pm 0^{m}\!.17$ [10].

2.2   Photometric observations by J. Herschel

John Herschel (1792–1871) continued his father's northern work on stellar sequences in the southern hemisphere when he visited the Cape of Good Hope from 1834 to 1838. During the voyage home to England he also attempted to link these southern observations to the northern stars. Observations were made on 46 clear nights between July 1835 and April 1838 – the last three of these being at sea, and the remainder from his observing station at Feldhausen.

The method of recording the results differed somewhat from that of his father. Each night's data resulted in a sequence of stars in descending order of brightness, mainly observed by naked eye. These nightly sequences were then merged into one continuous sequence of stars in order of brightness, using the numerous stars in common to different sequences [11]. Further stars were then interpolated into the 'normal' sequence so obtained. This method was used for stars down to the fifth magnitude.

Herschel's next step was to assign magnitudes for 452 stars in his sequence. For this purpose the magnitudes given in Francis Baily's *Astronomical Society Catalogue* were adopted [12] – see section 1.5.2. This major early nineteenth century work was a compilation of 2881 stars with magnitudes taken from the work by Flamsteed, Bradley, Lacaille and others. For the southern stars Baily had used primarily Lacaille's *Caelum Australe Stelliferum* [13], and the magnitudes are quoted in whole magnitudes with an intermediate step (such as $4 \cdot 5$). Herschel used these data to calibrate his sequences. His procedure was to derive a smooth sequence of magnitudes by taking the mean magnitudes of five consecutive stars in Baily's catalogue. Apart from the shortcomings of this system of standards, Herschel applied no corrections for extinction, nor did he take the effects of stellar colour into account. He states:

> Care, however, was taken to avoid low altitudes, and the exceeding purity of the atmosphere at the Cape allowed a range of 60 or even 70 degrees in all directions [11, p. 306].

Pickering (see [7, p. 356]) estimated that this neglect of extinction 'might account for a large part of the residual errors'. Herschel also observed during bright moon, and even though he avoided stars lying close to the moon, this would nevertheless also have impaired his results.

Herschel was clearly aware of the problems of comparing differently coloured stars. In a passage which foresaw the need for spectrophotometry, he wrote with admirable vision:

> Some of these difficulties, indeed, seem altogether insuperable – those namely which arise from the diversity of colour in the light of the stars themselves; since it seems hardly possible to assign any precise meaning to the equality or other proportion of total brightness of two stars differing sensibly in colour ...
>   Nothing short of a separate and independent estimation of the total amount of the red, the yellow, and the blue rays in the spectrum of each star would suffice for the resolution of the problem [11, Chap. 3].

In spite of the problems, Herschel's magnitudes appear to be remarkably precise. C. S. Peirce has estimated a probable error of $\pm 0^{m}.18$ for Herschel's magnitudes [8]. W. Doberck also analysed Herschel's results by comparing them with the photometric scale of Benjamin Gould's *Uranometria Argentina* [14] and also with that of the *Revised Harvard Photometry* [15]. The estimated probable errors vary from about $\pm 0^{m}.08$ for second magnitude stars to $\pm 0^{m}.20$ for those of fifth magnitude. E. Zinner rereduced Herschel's results, taking into account the considerable colour equation of his original catalogues. In doing so he found a probable error of $\pm 0^{m}.12$ for one observation, or only $\pm 0^{m}.07$ for a star observed on several nights, a result which represented higher precision than that achieved by William Herschel [10].

John Herschel was one of the notable pioneers of magnitude estimation through the telescope. In his *Results of astronomical observations made at the Cape of Good Hope*, he gave an account of his star 'gauges' in the southern hemisphere, in which he counted 68 948 stars in 2299 fields. Towards the end of a discussion on the distribution of the stars in the Milky Way, he then surprises the reader with the statement:

> In counting the gauges, however, not only the total numbers were set down, but those of all the magnitudes down to the 11th inclusive, and even of the estimated half magnitudes intermediate, so that we are not left without data for entering with considerable detail into this part of the general inquiry [11, Chap. 4].

He then tabulated the numbers of stars counted in magnitude intervals between eighth and twelfth visual magnitude, but gave no information on his methods of extrapolating the scale to these fainter stars.

After his return to England, John Herschel resolved to continue his magnitude work in the northern hemisphere. Sixty-one northern sequences were observed, and the magnitude results were used for the preparation of sky charts. However, the programme was discontinued, once Herschel learned of Argelander's *Uranometria Nova* [16] with over 3000 stellar magnitudes. Many of the charts for both hemispheres had, however, been completed, and these were presented to the Royal Astronomical Society in London in 1867 in 'their present state, rough and imperfect as it is' [17].

2.3   Struve's double star photometry

Wilhelm Struve (1793–1864) commenced his astronomical work at Dorpat, Estonia, where he was appointed to a professorship in astronomy in 1813. Even before the famous 9-inch (240-mm) Fraunhofer refractor had been installed at the observatory in 1824, Struve's interest was in the measurement of double stars. However, the new telescope was used for two major catalogues, the *Catalogus Novus* of 1827 [18] and the *Mensurae Micrometricae* of 1837 [19]. The latter work contained the micrometer measurements of 2640 pairs to which were added visual estimates of both magnitude and colour. Struve's double star magnitudes thus represent a significant body of data for many fainter telescopic stars, which were estimated on an arbitrary scale to a limiting magnitude assigned to be $m = 12$. The results were quoted to a tenth of a magnitude, and are reproduced in the edited and extended edition of *Mensurae Micrometricae* by Thomas Lewis (1856–1927) in 1906 [20].

The question of whether Struve could preserve the approximate Ptolemaic light ratios for the naked-eye stars in extrapolating the magnitude scale is of some interest. The task may well be easier for double stars, because magnitude differences can be assigned while two stars are under simultaneous observation. This question was considered by Norman Pogson at the time that he made his celebrated proposal that the light ratio of successive magnitudes should be 2.512 [21] – see section 3.5.5. Pogson compared the magnitude estimates of Wilhelm Struve, John Herschel [22], Admiral William Smyth [23] and George Bond at Harvard with his assumed extrapolation of Argelander's scale in the *Uranometria Nova* using the 2.512 ratio. All the scales were considered to coincide at $m = 6.0$, but Pogson's $m = 15$. was given as 11^m9 by Struve and 17^m9 by Herschel, showing Struve's ratio to be greater than and Herschel's less than Pogson's.

A similar comparison was made by George Knott (1835–94) in 1866 [24]. Knott compared the results of Smyth, Struve and Argelander and, in a later paper [25], also those of John Herschel. From Knott's tables, Struve's magnitude 10.9 is the same as Herschel's 15.9, indicating a discrepancy of comparable size to that found by Pogson.

When Pickering published his first meridian photometry in 1884 using the

Pogson scale, a more reliable determination of the departures from a uniform (constant ratio) scale in Struve's magnitudes was possible. Pickering found only small discrepancies between his scale and Struve's from $m = 5.5$ to 9.5. But for fainter stars Struve's magnitudes were progressively estimated too bright, the difference exceeding a magnitude at $m_{Struve} = 12.0$ [7, see p. 357]. On the other hand, Struve's magnitudes were about half a magnitude too faint for third magnitude stars.

2.4 Argelander's *Uranometria Nova* and his step estimation method

Sir John Herschel was one of the few astronomers interested in determining stellar magnitudes in the first half of the nineteenth century. The great German-Prussian astronomer Friedrich Argelander (1799–1875) was one of the few people active in this area towards the middle of the century. Argelander had his early training from Friedrich Bessel (1784–1846) at the Königsberg Observatory, and he then worked at Åbo Observatory near Helsinki (now Turku Observatory), where his interest was in stellar proper motions. In 1837 he was able to repeat and greatly improve upon William Herschel's earlier work on the solar motion from the analysis of the proper motion of nearby stars.

When Argelander moved to Bonn in 1836 to take up the directorship of the observatory there, his interest turned to uranography and uranometry, the production of celestial charts and the measurement of stellar magnitudes. Argelander's first major undertaking in this area was his *Uranometria Nova* of 1843 [16], containing 17 charts and a catalogue of 3256 naked-eye stars north of declination −35°. This work can be regarded as a transitional one between older charts such as Bayer's *Uranometria* (1603) or Flamsteed's *Atlas Coelestis* (1729) and the modern era of cartography, often taken to start with Argelander's charts in his later *Bonner Durchmusterung*, published from 1852 to 1859. Thus the constellation boundaries are indicated in the *Uranometria Nova* by freely drawn curves, and mythical constellation figures were used to adorn the charts. For the magnitude estimates no telescope was used. Intermediate classes of a third of a magnitude were indicated with the notation: 2, 2 · 3, 3 · 2, 3 – in this example for successively fainter stars from second to third magnitude. The fact that the great majority of the stars still were assigned integral values indicated that Argelander had not adopted a smoothly varying scale. Nor does one Argelander division represent a minimum discernible change. Thus the nine brightest stars were all assigned to first magnitude, even though striking differences in their

F. W. ARGELANDER.

Fig. 2.2 Friedrich Argelander.

brilliance are readily observed. Hassenstein has estimated a mean error of $\pm 0^m\!\!.27$ in the *Uranometria Nova* [26]. This value is typical of naked-eye magnitude estimates not based on the method of sequences.

Although William Herschel had developed the method of sequences for naked-eye observations aimed at detecting possible long-term variability in the brightness of stars, Argelander in Bonn independently arrived at and perfected the same method, which he called the 'Stufenschätzungsmethode' or step estimation method. Instead of assigning arbitrary symbols to magnitude differences as Herschel had done, he employed numerical estimates of the number of magnitude steps between two stars. He defined a step as follows:

If two stars at a first glance appear to be equally bright, but I
recognize on more careful observation and repeatedly going from **a** to
b and then **b** to **a**, that **a** is always or with very few exceptions
noticeably the brighter, then I say that **a** is one step brighter than **b**
and my notation for this is **a1b**. If on the other hand **b** is the brighter,
then I write **b1a**, so that the brighter star always precedes the number,
and the fainter one follows [27].

Thus Argelander's step corresponded to Herschel's comma. Greater magnitude differences were represented by 2, 3 or 4 steps, equality by zero.
Sometimes Argelander even used half steps (such as **a2.5b**), although it is
hard to reconcile this practice with the definition of the step.

The step estimation method was described in detail in Argelander's *Aufforderung an Freunde der Astronomie* (Invitation to friends of astronomy)
[27] – (see p. 185 for section on magnitudes and colours of the stars). The
technique was developed by Argelander in Bonn from 1839 to 1842 and
used for studying variable stars. An example of this work is Argelander's
paper on δ Cephei, β Lyrae and η Aquilae, in which he asserts that one of
his steps corresponds to about a tenth of a magnitude [28].

2.5   The *Bonner Durchmusterung*

2.5.1   *Origins of the* Bonner Durchmusterung

By the middle of the nineteenth century the magnitudes and
approximate positions were known for all the stars in both hemispheres
visible to the naked eye, but the magnitudes were not determined to better
than a few tenths or even to half a magnitude in many cases. Francis
Baily had compiled in 1845 the *British Association Catalogue* of 8377 stars
in both hemispheres, based on observations in some 32 other catalogues
[29]. Although this was the principal compendium of stellar data in its day,
replacing Baily's earlier *Astronomical Society Catalogue* of 1826 [12], the
photometric data were nevertheless meagre and inhomogeneous and clearly
subsidiary in importance to the astrometric positions – see section 1.5.2.

Argelander's *Uranometria Nova* encompassed naked-eye stars to declination $-26°$, while the observations of Nicolas-Louis de Lacaille at the Cape,
as published by Baily in 1847 [30], recorded the approximate brightnesses
for nearly ten thousand southern stars to magnitude 7, the values also being
quoted in half magnitude intervals.

Thus no systematic record of the sky for the many thousands of fainter
telescopic stars existed. It was Argelander at Bonn who undertook to rectify
this situation, in a gigantic programme of visual observing through a small

'comet seeker' telescope to determine the magnitudes and positions of all stars to the ninth magnitude north of −2° declination.

The programme of telescopic magnitude estimates had been begun before the main survey was commenced, as part of Argelander's work with his 4-inch meridian circle between 1841 and 1867. As many as 73 500 stars were observed by Argelander and his assistants with this instrument, and the magnitude estimates were included as a by-product of the astrometry, initially to half a magnitude, but, after 1853, in tenths [31]. The meridian circle work was in itself a substantial programme, yet it presaged yet more ambitious goals to come.

Argelander was clearly aware of some of the problems of extrapolating Ptolemy's magnitude scale for naked-eye stars to fainter telescopic objects. He discussed these problems in the first volume of the Bonn Observatory publications:

> The estimation of the magnitudes of stars in the telescope is one of the most difficult tasks in astronomy. The impression that light makes upon the eye is very much dependent on the condition of the atmosphere, on the brightness or faintness of the illumination of the field of view, on how tired the observer's eye might be as well as on other circumstances that might arise, with the result that each determination becomes very uncertain. In addition, the estimation of the next star is unwittingly influenced by the effect of the previous one – thus a brighter star coming after a substantially fainter one, we will estimate as too bright, and vice versa. Thus such magnitude estimates can make no claim to great precision, even if the boundaries of the magnitude classes were better defined as is in fact the case [32].

2.5.2   The Bonner Durchmusterung – the observational programme

The *Bonner Durchmusterung* (or Bonn 'survey', frequently abbreviated BD) was based on observations by Argelander and his assistants Thormann (till May 1853), Eduard Schönfeld and A. Krüger between 1852 and 1859. In all, 324 198 mainly northern stars to magnitude 9.5 were recorded with a small 76-mm aperture refractor used normally for comet searches. This huge undertaking was designed to give approximate stellar positions for all stars to the ninth magnitude, with magnitudes down to 9.5 being assigned to some fainter objects. The *Durchmusterung* comprised a catalogue in three volumes published between 1859 and 1862 [33] as well as 37 charts (published in 1863).

The goal which Argelander set himself for this work is described in the introduction to the first volume of the catalogue:

The charts should encompass the whole of the northern sky. At first it was my intention to go significantly further to the south, as far as the Tropic of Capricorn or even to 25° southern declination, and by no means negligible preliminary work was made in the southern part of the sky. But although we chose for this the darkest of nights and the clearest air, it soon became obvious that the absorption of light rays in these regions was too great to observe the fainter stars with reasonable certainty, and hence to bring this part of the work into even approximate concordance with the other regions ... I therefore decided to limit myself to the northern sky, in the hope that a similar programme for the southern sky would be taken up at one or other of the observatories of the other hemisphere. However, in order to be able to intercompare the two completed programmes, should my hope ever be fulfilled, I included the first two degrees of southerly declination in the present work.

Within this scope, the charts should contain all stars to the ninth magnitude, if possible all those brighter than $9^{m}10$, and as many of the remainder of this class as conditions allowed [33].

Each star was observed two or three times, so nearly a million observations were made in the course of 625 nights spread over seven years. Two observers (these were mainly Schönfeld and Krüger) were required to work together, one at the eyepiece and one to record the data including the times of meridian transit. The magnitudes were purely estimates on a memorized scale made during the brief duration of meridian transit and without direct reference to comparison stars. Extinction was not explicitly corrected for, although there was an attempt to make a mental allowance for its effect during the estimations themselves.

Argelander evidently regarded approximate *Durchmusterung* positions as more critical than magnitudes, so observations were continued on slightly hazy nights or during bright moon.

2.5.3 The magnitude scale and errors in the Bonner Durchmusterung

The magnitude scale that Argelander adopted for the fainter stars in the *Bonner Durchmusterung* was ostensibly based on the magnitudes that Bessel had obtained for telescopic stars from Königsberg with the 4-inch meridian circle at that observatory. Bessel had assigned magnitude 9 to the faintest stars visible at a first glance through the telescope, while those still fainter, requiring some effort to discern, were labelled as magnitude 9.1. For the brighter stars, the same scale as used in the *Uranometria Nova* was adopted.

The whole system of the *Bonner Durchmusterung* is known not to be a uniform one. Thus Schönfeld, in a letter to C. S. Peirce at Harvard (see [8, see p. 27]), identified three periods as follows:

(a) 1852–54   20 per cent of all observations. Magnitudes were estimated in whole magnitudes, or in intermediate steps (such as 7-8).

(b) 1854–57   50 per cent of all observations. The notation for magnitudes from, for example, 7 to 8 was: 7, 7s, 7-8gt, 7-8, 7-8s, 8gt, 8 with therefore six divisions of each whole magnitude. Note that s = *schwach*: weak, faint; gt = *gut*: bright.

(c) 1857–59   30 per cent of all observations. The magnitudes were estimated directly in tenths.

In spite of this evolution in the method of making the individual estimates, the *mean* magnitudes, however, were always expressed in tenths in the final catalogue.

The errors in the visual estimates of Argelander and his assistants when observing through the telescope were comparable to those for brighter stars with the naked eye, about $\pm 0^m\!.24$ near the zenith, but larger for the southern objects [10]. The results thus show that the visual magnitude estimates based on a memorized scale are not as precise as can be obtained by Herschel's method of sequences.

Numerous studies have been made of the magnitude system of the *Bonner Durchmusterung*. One of the earliest by Peirce compared Argelander's magnitudes to those from Harvard visual photometry with a Zöllner photometer. He found a magnitude scale error for the BD results for stars within 10° of the North Pole [8, see p. 27].

Pickering, Searle and Wendell compared the results of Harvard meridian photometry for 16 865 BD stars with the Bonn magnitudes, and found that the BD scale was too narrow compared with the Pogson scale used at Harvard [7]. Thus the faintest BD ninth magnitude stars were nearly a magnitude fainter on the Harvard photometric scale. Further extensive studies were made by Pickering as more photometric data were amassed at Harvard. Thus the large 12-inch meridian photometer was used to observe 11 139 BD stars [34], and Pickering published an exhaustive analysis of the comparison in 1913 [35].

Müller and Kempf at Potsdam compared the results of the Potsdam photometric survey with the BD and found the latter was generally brighter by $0^m\!.2$ for naked-eye stars, rising to half a magnitude for stars brighter than third magnitude. There is also a substantial colour equation in the Bonn magnitudes. The faint red stars were underestimated by $0^m\!.20$ to $0^m\!.37$ relative to those of white colour. Stars in crowded Milky Way fields were also estimated to be systematically too faint, a common error of visual estimates.

Other notable early studies of the BD scale were undertaken by Antonie Pannekoek [36] in Amsterdam and by J. Hopmann in Bonn, the latter using photometric data for 10 663 stars observed photometrically by F. Küstner (1856–1936), Argelander's successor in Bonn [37].

2.5.4 *The* Bonn Southern Durchmusterung

Argelander died in 1875, leaving unfulfilled his hope that his survey of the sky to −2° might be further extended into more southerly declinations. However, Eduard Schönfeld (1828–91) undertook this work to −23°. The observing was commenced in September 1875 using the Schröder telescope of 159 mm aperture, which was about twice the size of the instrument used earlier for the northern stars. In spite of the increased atmospheric extinction at these lower altitudes, it was still possible to reach a limiting magnitude of 10 on the BD scale, thanks to the more powerful telescope.

Schönfeld noted that the early tests

> ... only confirmed for the fainter stars our earlier experiences, namely
> that especially in the divisions of 9.4 and 9.5 of the Bonn star
> catalogue, there exist stars of very different brightnesses, encompassing
> at least half a magnitude ... The old Bonn magnitude division of 9.5
> contains a great many stars, which, if the scale of the brighter stars
> had been uniformly extended, must have been allocated to the
> magnitude 10.0, or often even still fainter, not infrequently to 10.5.

In practice, although 10 was the limiting magnitude quoted in the *Southern Durchmusterung* (frequently abbreviated SD), completeness was achieved only to $9^m\!.2$ or $9^m\!.3$, which was only slightly fainter than for the BD.

The magnitude estimates for 133 569 stars were made by Schönfeld for the southern extension to the BD [38]. The magnitudes were estimated in tenths on the same scale as used for the main Bonn survey.

As with the BD, the results of the SD have been carefully analysed for systematic and random errors, for example by Pannekoek, who compared Schönfeld's results with Harvard photometry [36]. The most striking differences were for the stars fainter than ninth magnitude, which were estimated progressively too bright, by as much as a magnitude for $m_{SD} = 10.0$.

2.6   Four catalogues of visual magnitude estimates in the 1870s

In the decade of the 1870s four catalogues containing the results of mainly naked-eye visual magnitude estimates were published. These all came towards the end of an era when visual estimates, especially those with the naked eye, could make a useful contribution to astronomy. All four catalogues therefore had relatively short useful lifetimes before being overtaken by photometric or photographic observations through telescopes.

2.6.1   The Atlas Coelestis Novus of Eduard Heis

Eduard Heis (1806–77) was professor of mathematics and astronomy at the University of Münster from 1852. He was renowned for his unusually sharp eyesight which enabled him to see stars to visual magnitude 6.7 with the unaided eye.

Heis published his *Atlas Coelestis Novus* [39] in 1872 with the visual magnitude estimates of 5421 stars from the North Pole to −35° declination. He based his magnitude scale on Argelander's *Uranometria Nova*, but presumably was motivated to undertake this work, because he was able to record 2200 more stars than Argelander had done in the same area of the sky. His results were quoted in steps of one third of a magnitude, with a typical mean error of $\pm 0\overset{m}{.}27$ [10]. His faintest quoted magnitude was $6\frac{1}{3}$. Heis attempted to take into account the influence of star colour, of the background sky brightness and atmospheric extinction when making his estimates.

2.6.2   Carl Behrmann's atlas of southern stars

The German astronomer and astronavigator Carl Behrmann (1843–1927) made a survey of the southern sky with the unaided eye during a sea voyage lasting ten months· which he made during 1866–67 to Brazil, Chile and the Cape of Good Hope. Nearly all his observations were undertaken while at sea, and his stated aim was:

> ... the construction of star charts for all stars in the southern sky visible with the naked eye ... In order to have as true a picture as possible, I have produced charts according to the same plan that Argelander followed for his *Uranometria Nova* [40].

Behrmann's photometry encompassed six magnitude classes with intervals of a third of a magnitude being distinguished. The observations covered the region from −20° to the South Pole. The resulting *Atlas des südlichen*

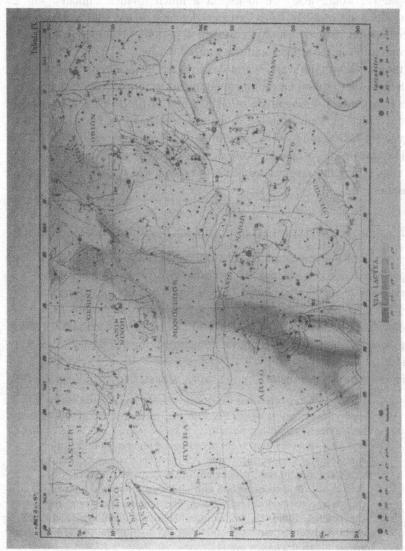

Fig. 2.3   Part of the *Atlas Coelestis* by Eduard Heis.

gestirnten Himmels [41] gave the results for 2344 stars, and he remarked: 'The number of stars surpasses 2000, whereas a glance in Argelander's *Uranometria* would lead one to expect a much smaller number' [40], a result which he ascribes to the greater richness of the southern sky, his better eyesight than Argelander's and the especially favourable conditions of observation in the tropics and the south Atlantic.

Although Behrmann's aim was to extend the *Uranometria Nova* to the South Pole, his results were unfortunately rather imprecise. Zinner gives mean errors at third magnitude of $\pm 0^m.28$ and at fourth of $\pm 0^m.40$, which is lower precision than achieved by either Argelander or Heis [10]. Stars assigned by Behrmann to $m = 5$ could be anywhere from $m = 3.7$ to 6.7 in Gould's *Uranometria Argentina* – see section 2.6.4. Nevertheless, this was the first atlas giving the magnitudes of all the naked-eye stars in the southern hemisphere.

2.6.3   The Uranométrie Générale of J.-C. Houzeau

The Belgian astronomer Jean-Charles Houzeau de Lehaie (1820–88) produced his *Uranométrie Générale* in 1878, which is notable for its observations of all the naked-eye stars in both hemispheres from a single site [42]. The observations were undertaken from Jamaica in the short space of time of 13 months (28 Jan 1875 to 28 Feb 1876), each of 5719 stars being observed two or three times on consecutive nights. No telescope was employed.

His motivation for undertaking this work is described as follows:

> During my stay of several years near the equator, I thought that a general examination of the sky with the naked eye, encompassing both hemispheres, would not be entirely without interest. All I had to do was go a short distance from my home in Jamaica in order to complete this whole programme. All the stars that can be seen with unaided vision in the entire extent of the heavens would then be determined for a recent epoch and under uniform conditions of climate and method of observation. The different sections of this *Uranométrie* would thus be comparable among themselves, and one could study, on a homogeneous basis, the distribution of the stars that are visible to the naked eye [42].

In practice, his goal of uniformity of magnitudes observed from a single site was quite illusory, given that the polar stars were necessarily seen close to the horizon. Houzeau used half magnitude steps for his estimates, with the notation of, for example, 3 · 4 for an intermediate estimate between magnitudes 3 and 4. His faintest value used was 6 · 7. According to Zinner, the mean error was $\pm 0^m.34$ for brighter stars [10].

Houzeau's catalogue was accompanied by five star charts on which con-stellation boundaries were also demarcated. He was able to find several new variable stars, and he analysed the star densities per square degree for the naked-eye stars in his catalogue. In particular, he found an average of 0.139 stars per square degree in his catalogue, compared to 0.114 for Argelander's *Uranometria Nova*, and he studied the distribution of stars with galactic latitude. The concentration towards the galactic equator was found to be more marked for bright stars than for fainter ones, but he surprisingly missed discovering the inclined orientation of the bright ones, since named Gould's Belt.

Houzeau returned to Brussels from the New World in 1876, to take up the directorship of the Royal Observatory there. He is well known for his subsequent compilation with Lancaster, the *Bibliographie Générale de l'Astronomie* of 1882 [43]. His *Répertoire des Constantes de l'Astronomie* [44] is less well known, and is a useful and comprehensive compilation of astronomical data known at that time.

2.6.4   *Benjamin Gould and the* Uranometria Argentina

Benjamin Gould (1824–96) was born in Boston and had his early astronomical training under Gauss at Göttingen, from where he gained his doctorate in 1848. He is renowned as the founder and first editor of the *Astronomical Journal* in 1849, as well as for his major contributions to southern hemisphere astronomy.

In 1865 Gould, who was then at the Dudley Observatory in Albany, New York, had resolved to compile a catalogue of the stars of the southern skies. To this end he travelled to Córdoba in Argentina in 1870, where he set up the Argentine National Observatory at an altitude of 450 m, with the support of the president of the Argentine Republic. He was the observatory's first director from 1870–85.

Observing commenced in 1872 for the *Uranometria Argentina* [45], a work which, as with Behrmann's and Houzeau's catalogues, was designed to extend Argelander's *Uranometria Nova* to the South Pole. Four assistants (M. Rock, W. M. Davies, C. L. Hathaway and J. M. Thome) were employed at the new observatory, and they observed 7756 stars south of $+10°$ on an average of four times for each star during 1872–73. The observations were mainly by naked eye, although occasionally opera glasses or a telescope were used for double stars or other difficult objects. Gould directed the work, but on account of his extreme myopia, he was unable to participate in the observing programme itself.

The magnitude estimates of the *Uranometria Argentina* were given in

Fig. 2.4   Benjamin Gould.

tenths of a magnitude, and the mean error was about $\pm 0^m.15$ [26]. This figure was significantly better than achieved by Argelander or by Heis, a result which can probably be attributed to the careful use of standard comparison stars in the programme. A total of 722 primary standards was observed by all four observers in the northern zone $+5°$ to $+15°$, the so-called 'type belt'. The purpose was to tie the Córdoba magnitudes to those of the *Uranometria Nova*, which had been obtained from Bonn by Argelander at the same mean zenith distance as the type-belt stars seen from Córdoba. Secondary comparison stars were then established in southern fields at $-55°$ and $-78°$, thus allowing all programme stars to be compared with comparison stars at the same altitude, which was always a minimum of $30°$ from the horizon.

The *Uranometria Argentina* includes stars as faint as magnitude 7.0 visible under exceptionally favourable conditions. One problem was to fix standards for this limiting magnitude, as Argelander had not observed such faint objects. Gould therefore did this through the telescope, by comparing the images of stars estimated as being of seventh magnitude with brighter ones for which the telescope was stopped down by a known factor, so as to achieve in both cases the criterion of 'marginal visibility at a first glance'.

The *Uranometria Argentina* thus surpassed that of all its predecessors in the quality of its magnitudes for southern stars. It became the standard reference work until about the turn of the century, by which time the

Harvard meridian photometry had been extended to all the bright stars as far as the South Pole, mainly by S. I. Bailey from Harvard's Boyden Station in Peru – see section 3.7.2.

The *Uranometria Argentina* contains a detailed discussion of the distribution of bright stars in the sky. In particular Gould gave a full description of the belt of bright stars now generally named after him:

> A belt or stream of bright stars appears to girdle the heavens very nearly in a great circle, which intersects the Milky Way at about the points of its highest declination and forms with it an angle not far from 20° ... Its position is clearly recognizable on our map ... it appears as a stream of especially conspicuous stars ... In the northern hemisphere its course is less distinctly marked [45, chap. 8].

The discovery of Gould's Belt had been announced briefly a few years earlier [46], and its presence was also alluded to much earlier by Sir John Herschel [11, p.385] – see also section 2.6.3.

2.7   The *Córdoba Durchmusterung*

After Schönfeld had completed the Bonn *Southern Durchmusterung* in 1886, there was still a need for a comparable catalogue of stars to at least ninth magnitude in the southern hemisphere south of −23°. Indeed, Argelander had expressed the hope that some southern observatory would take up this work. When John Thome (1843–1908) took on the directorship of the Córdoba Observatory in 1885, following Gould's retirement, the continuation of Schönfeld's work to more southerly declinations became his major programme. Although most of the staff had been disbanded and the observatory faced severe financial difficulties, the major work of the *Córdoba Durchmusterung* (frequently abbreviated CoD) was commenced by Thome in 1885, using the observatory's 125-mm equatorial refractor as a transit instrument.

Thome described his work as follows:

> The method employed has been essentially the same as that which guided Argelander in his great work ... All the observations at the telescope were made by me and my first assistant, Richard H. Tucker, jr.
>
> Our telescope was made by Alvan Clark and Sons, and has an objective of 12.5 cm aperture and 168 cm focal length, and an ocular magnifying 15 times, showing stars to the $10\frac{1}{2}$- magnitude in dark field under the best conditions of sky. The magnitudes are estimated in quarters. Our aim has been ... to obtain a position and magnitude for every object down to the 10.0 magnitude inclusive. It is, perhaps, too much to expect that the absolute total has been reached, but I have

> every reason to believe, from the evidence which will follow, and from rigorous tests in many regions, that our approach to completeness is very close [47, vol. 16].

This huge undertaking took many years to complete. By 1900 positions and magnitudes for nearly half a million stars to −52° had been published in the first three volumes of the *Durchmusterung* [47]. Work on the zone from −52° to −62° was 90 per cent complete when Thome died in September 1908. The new observatory director in Córdoba was C. D. Perrine (1868–1951), who completed the observations in the zone to −62° and saw to the publication of the fourth volume of the *Durchmusterung* in 1914, which contained 89 000 stars. In all, 578 802 stars from −22° to −62° were included in these four volumes of the Córdoba catalogue. The fourth volume contained some fainter stars to magnitude $11\frac{3}{4}$.

The magnitude scale of the CoD is not homogeneous. Initially the magnitudes were tied to those obtained by Schönfeld, using stars in the −22° zone observed from both Córdoba and Bonn. In the later part of the work, the Córdoba magnitudes were influenced increasingly by the Harvard photometric magnitudes (for stars from −42° to −62°) on the Pogson scale. Thus Pannekoek has shown how the Córdoba magnitude 9.0 for a star in the zones −22° to −42° would on average be assigned magnitude 9.57 in the Harvard meridian photometry, a divergence of the Córdoba scale from the photometric Pogson scale very similar to that shown in the BD magnitudes.

However, for the more southerly stars in the Córdoba catalogue, the ninth magnitude stars correspond to Harvard magnitude 9.07, showing an evolution of the faint end of the Córdoba scale by half a magnitude after about a decade of observation [36].

The mean error of the Córdoba magnitudes is $\pm0^{m}\!.2$ at $m_{\mathrm{CoD}} = 6.5$, and $\pm0^{m}\!.4$ at $m_{\mathrm{CoD}} = 9.0$, typical of visual estimates, nevertheless less precise than the magnitudes in the *Uranometria Argentina*. Pickering has also made a careful study of the magnitudes of the CoD in comparison with the Harvard values [48].

After the publication of the fourth volume, the observing programme of the *Córdoba Durchmusterung* languished for many years as other programmes took priority under Perrine's directorship. However, the work was recommenced in 1923 by E. Chaudet and later continued by J. Tretter who completed the survey to the South Pole [49]. From the first observation to the final publication had taken nearly half a century, although the labour was not continuous over this whole period.

The last section of the work was now undertaken on the Harvard Pogson scale and 10. was the limiting magnitude, which was therefore considerably brighter than had been adopted for the earlier parts of the catalogue. In the zone −82° to the Pole, Chaudet used a polarizing photometer on loan from Harvard. Apart from this, visual estimates were made elsewhere in the sky for this last volume, but with frequent reference to standard stars observed in the Harvard programme.

The *Córdoba Durchmusterung* was the last great catalogue of stellar magnitudes based on visual estimates. Thome had the misfortune of commencing this laborious programme of observations when other observatories, at Oxford, Harvard and Potsdam, began experimenting with visual photometers for large scale surveys of the sky. These instruments had the potential of delivering a precision with which simple eye estimates could not compete, a typical probable error with a photometer being about one tenth of a magnitude, but two to three tenths for a visually estimated value. However, the usefulness of the Córdoba work was in its recording of many thousands of southern stars for the first time, to a limiting magnitude considerably fainter than the early visual photometers were able to reach. The introduction of photographic photometry, in particular the *Photographic Durchmusterung* at the Cape from 1895, further proscribed the usefulness of the visual estimates at Córdoba. In these circumstances it is rather surprising that the programme was ever completed after Thome had died in 1908.

2.8   Visual estimates of stellar colours

The visual estimation of stellar colours flourished in the nineteenth and very early twentieth centuries. The early pioneers were both Herschels, F. G. W. Struve, W. H. Smyth, Argelander and Sestini (all before 1850). By the end of the century it had become an important branch of observational astronomy. The data could be notoriously unreliable (see [50]) and subject to a range of physiological effects, yet it is from this work that the first results pertaining to the correlation between colour and spectral type were obtained.

The fact that coloured or reddish stars exist at all was noted by Ptolemy, who assigned in the *Almagest* this description to six first magnitude stars, including Sirius (for a recent discussion of the controversy over the red colour of Sirius reported in ancient times see [51]).

Wilhelm Struve, during the time of his professorship at Dorpat, Estonia, was the first systematic observer of star colours, as part of his extensive work from 1814 on double stars, although both William and John Herschel also recorded some observations of the colours of visual binaries. Struve's *Catalogus Novus* of 1827 [18] and the *Mensurae Micrometricae* of a decade later [19] (see section 2.3) contained visual estimates of the magnitudes and colours of several thousand visual binary stars, including 596 pairs in which the colours of both components were noted. For this purpose he adopted a scale of ten colours from blue, through white then to yellow and red with various intermediate steps (see [50] for Struve's colour scale). The observations appear in English in the edited and expanded version of the *Mensurae Micrometricae* by Thomas Lewis [20]

John Herschel, during his time at the Cape from 1835, found a number of unusually red stars, and he published a list of 76 whose colours he described as 'ruby or very intensely red', mainly of magnitude 8 or 9 and occurring in either hemisphere [11, p. 448].

Several pioneers of stellar colour estimation were active from the 1840s. One was Father Benedetto Sestini (1816–90) who began observing stellar colours in Rome in 1843. His catalogue of star colours comprised 2540 objects north of −30° declination and made use of the colours blue, white, yellow, orange and red or of combinations of these, and often with further adjectives such as 'bright', 'dark' etc. [52, 53]. Sestini's catalogue was later re-edited by Father Johann Hagen (1847–1930) at the Vatican Observatory, in which Sestini's descriptions of stellar colours were replaced by the symbols B, W, Y, O or R, or by combinations of two consecutive letters in this sequence [54]. Like Struve, Sestini was also interested in the colours of double stars, and during his exile at Georgetown College Observatory in America he continued his work on the colours of binaries initiated in Rome [55].

We know that Sestini corresponded with Admiral Smyth in England, who recorded numerous references to the colours of double stars in his *Cycle of Celestial Objects* in 1844 [23]. Smyth's later work under the title *Sidereal Chromatics* [56] of 1864 was a landmark in the early development of the subject. It was a book that not only compared observations of the colours of double stars by Smyth and Sestini, but also gave a colour chart (resembling the modern pamphlets from paint manufacturers!) reproducing standard tints and shades. Smyth recognized a sequence of red, orange, yellow, green, blue and purple and each colour was further divided into four shades from bright to pale, giving a two-dimensional array of standard colours. However, simultaneous observation of the chart and a star through the telescope was not practicable. The problems of chart illumination, the need for dark adaption of the eye and the errors arising from the use of charts have been discussed by William Pickering, who himself had attempted to use a 12-point colour scale [57].

Another of the early pioneers was Argelander in Bonn who in 1844, in his well-known essay *Aufforderung an Freunde der Astronomie*, proposed a six-point scale of purple (possibly meaning dark red), red, orange, yellow, white and bluish-white, with up to 2 or 3 subdivisions of each [27, see pp. 206–7]. However, no observations were reported, and Argelander remarked that his own eyesight lacked the sensitivity needed for this type of work.

A clear statement of the problems of accurate stellar colour estimation can be found in a paper by Sidney Kincaid in 1867. He discusses the personal equation of the observer, atmospheric effects, instrumental effects (especially in reflectors with their unreliable, mainly speculum metal, mirrors) and the need for standards of comparison [58]. The use of a painted chart he found to be objectionable, coloured precious stones were 'beyond the reach of most observers' and he advocated chemical solutions as the best colour standards.

The next development was the adoption of an arbitrary numerical scale to represent the different visually observed colours, in the same spirit as the magnitude scale was intended to categorize stars by their brightness. The originator of such a scale was Hermann Klein (1844–1914), the owner of a private observatory in Cologne. His interest was restricted to the coloured or orange-red stars, and for these he devised a scale that ran from 0 (yellow) to 5 (deep fiery red) [59].

At this time the study of stars of unusual reddish colouration was a topic of considerable interest, following the publication of H. C. F. C. Schjellerup's (1827–87) first catalogue, listing 280 objects of this type [60]. The catalogue included an assortment of colour descriptions from diverse observers – often expressed in eloquent terms, such as for Mira: 'Very full ruby, sanguine'. No doubt Klein's scale was intended to bring some order to such observations. However, numerical colours for only a few stars were reported, and his main concern was an attempt to demonstrate periodic colour variability in α UMa.

Klein's colour scale was the start of a substantial tradition of stellar colour estimates from German astronomers over some fifty years. Julius Schmidt (1825–84) in Athens extended the scale to run from 0 to 10 and encompass all stars, including those of white colour [61]. Here 0 represented white, 4 was for bright yellow and 10 pure red. He claimed his interest in star colours dated from 1841, in which case his earliest observations may even have predated Sestini's by several years.

The Schmidt scale was widely used in Germany and became the standard for several catalogues, most notably the work of Krüger, Osthoff and Lau. The colours could be indicated by a superscript 'c' (e.g. $5^{c}.6$), a notation resembling the superscript 'm' for magnitudes. Schmidt himself observed 162 red stars in Schjellerup's catalogue [62] and was also interested in the possibility of detecting colour variability, which he falsely claimed to have found for Arcturus [63].

Apart from the German school, the observations of William Franks (1851–1935) were the other major contribution to this subject in the later nineteenth century. Like Admiral Smyth, Franks chose a two-dimensional colour scale, with the second dimension being the shade from bright to pale. With his 5-inch refractor, he estimated the colours of 3890 naked-eye stars and presented his catalogue to the Royal Astronomical Society (see [64] for a brief description). The colours were published in America as part of Pickering's meridian photometry in 1884 [65], and were based on a system comprising 8 colours (represented by letters) with capital letters for very bright, italics for faint, dull or pale and normal lower case letters as an intermediate shade. A further catalogue was presented to the Royal Astronomical Society in 1886 and contained 1730 stars [66].

Soon after this time Franks modified his colour scale to a system of six colours (R, Or, Y, G, B, V) with four shades (1 to 4) for each, a scheme based closely on that in Smyth's *Sidereal Chromatics* [67]. In addition the colour white O was added in an arrangement which placed white in the centre of a circle with six primary colours around the circumference. Two primary colours across a diameter should be complementary and produce white, an idea which had originated with Newton in his *Opticks* [68]. As a guide to standardizing the six colours, Franks suggested the colours of the nearest Fraunhofer lines as follows:

Colour	red	orange	yellow	green	blue	violet
Symbol	R	Or	Y	G	B	V
Nearest line	a, B	α	D_1, D_2	b_1, b_2	d	G, g

The idea of using spectral lines to standardize colours in fact goes back to Father Angelo Secchi, who in 1856 had proposed using the emission lines of a spark spectrum for this purpose [69, see pp. 135–7]. This was the system used for Franks' third catalogue of 758 stars in 1888 [70]. All of these catalogues were brought together into one compendium, and a total of some 6500 star colours was published by Father Hagen in 1923. Hagen's colours on the Schmidt scale were listed together with those by Franks, based essentially on his notation of 1887 [71].

Franks was one of the observers of stellar colours who studied the relationship between colour and spectral type. Using data from his two-dimensional colour system for 1360 bright stars in both hemispheres he concluded in 1907 that 'there is undoubtedly a striking agreement between the colours and spectra of the stars' [72], yet he also found there was considerable scatter in the relationship, comparable to that found later by Zinner from Potsdam data [10].

Of the one-dimensional star colour schemes used in Germany, one that came to some prominence was devised by Hermann Carl Vogel (1841–1907), the first director of the new Astrophysical Observatory at Potsdam, together with Gustav Müller. They introduced a seven-point colour scale as part of their spectral type survey of all stars to magnitude 7.5 in the zone −1° to +20° [73]. White, yellow and red were the three basic colours represented by W, G and R (German: weiß, gelb, rot) and four intermediate classes were used to give the sequence:

W, GW, WG, G, RG, GR, R.

The colours of 4051 stars were estimated on this system together with spectral types using Vogel's spectral classification scheme, which allowed Vogel and Müller to demonstrate a clear relationship between these two parameters. They concluded:

> A white or bluish white star which displays a spectrum with numerous absorption bands has not been found, while reddish-yellow or reddish coloured stars always have spectra with many absorption bands or the bands are very broad [73].

This was not the first time that colour and spectral type had been shown to be related, as Angelo Secchi (1818–78), as early as 1866, had shown this on the basis of just three colours and three spectral types [74]. However, the Potsdam observers established this fact statistically using thousands of stars, based on a sophisticated scheme of spectral classification and a more refined colour scale.

Later the Potsdam colour scale was extended by Müller and Kempf for the colour estimates made for the *Potsdamer Durchmusterung* (abbreviated PD) [75]. Here the symbols were subdivided by adding + (a little redder) or − (a little bluer) after the letters. The observations were no longer pure estimates, but made with a Zöllner photometer, which could also act as a kind of comparison colorimeter – see section 3.3.3). Seventeen colour classes were in practice used and over 14 000 northern stars had their colours determined. The scale from W to GR was calibrated in terms of the Schmidt scale by Osthoff and the data thus permitted an analysis of the colour equations of the different Zöllner photometers used at Potsdam and also of the *Harvard Photometry* (i.e. of the systematic effects of colour on the measurement of stellar magnitude) – see [75, p. i]. For the PD colour data Ernst Zinner was able to reinvestigate the relationship with spectral type [10]. Although the correlation is very obvious, the data show that a Potsdam colour determination was not as precise as a coarse Harvard spectral type without decimal subdivision. For example, stars assigned to colour GW were found among B, A, F and G spectral types with a broad maximum at type F. Zinner ascribes this rather disappointing precision to small apertures (135 mm or less) used for the Potsdam work, together with the rapid decrease in the eye's colour sensitivity for fainter images.

Heinrich Osthoff (1857–1931) in Cologne, using mainly a 4-inch Steinheil refractor, was one observer of stellar colours who employed the Schmidt scale from 0 to 10, but who defined the colour of each class more carefully than hitherto [76]. He even proposed extending it in both directions (from −1 to 12), though in practice star colours nearly all fell in the range from 1 (yellowish white) to 8 (yellowish red, red dominating). His catalogue of 1009 bright (to $m = 5$) stars claimed a colour precision of $\pm0^c_.4$ for the probable error of a single estimate, which would correspond to about $\pm0^m_.1$ to $\pm0^m_.15$ (p.e.) in $(B - V)$. (This compares with a recent result of $\pm0^m_.24$ for a typical standard deviation of a visually estimated $(B - V)$ colour index, which corresponds to about $\pm0^m_.16$ (p.e.) [50]). As a result of an accident in his youth, Osthoff had lost the use of one eye. Yet through his remarkable perseverance he acquired a leading reputation for the accuracy and care with which his colour observations were undertaken.

Osthoff was the first to consider thoroughly systematic errors in stellar colour estimates. He emphasized that only bright stars could be reliably estimated, the limit being about $2^m_.5$ for the naked eye, but fainter when progressively larger telescopes were employed. An aperture-dependent colour term still arose for the stars he observed. The effects of moonlight, atmospheric dust or haze, star altitude, eye adaptation and eye fatigue were all considered. He found night-to-night differences and long-term effects ascribed to the observer's age (stars appeared redder over the years). For double stars he investigated the effects of contrast (white stars appear too white, red ones too red when seen in close juxtaposition). The physiological effects were of particular importance. Thus a given star appeared progressively redder (by about $0^c_.7$) over the first 45 minutes of a night, during which time the eye became dark-adapted, but for the next several hours eye fatigue caused the colour estimates to become steadily more blue, by about $0^c_.5$ after about 100 estimates. The mutual effects of magnitude and colour on the estimates of these quantities are related. Just as the Purkinje effect results in a colour equation for magnitude estimates, a similar effect gives rise to a magnitude equation in colour estimates [76, 77, 78]. Indeed, it was the need for a more objective method of determining stellar colours that was a major reason for the eventual demise of the visual estimation technique.

Osthoff recorded over 2500 stellar colours, which were published in 1916 by the Vatican Observatory with the assistance of Father Hagen [78]. The catalogue is complete to magnitude 5.5 for northern stars, and the data were used by Carl Wirtz (1876–1939) to investigate the distribution of stars of different colours with galactic latitude [79]. Osthoff was also interested in colour changes in variable stars, and in this regard his colour curve for Nova Persei 1901 was of some note [80]. The observations were made over nearly ten weeks, and Osthoff showed that the colour of the nova correlated with its magnitude.

Friedrich Krüger (1864–1916) was another German astronomer who employed the Schmidt scale from 0 to 10. His catalogue from the Kiel Observatory was a compendium of colours and Secchi spectral types for 2153 stars north of −23° [81]. The colours were taken from a variety of sources, including his own observations. Krüger's later observations were from Aarhus in Denmark, where he became director of the Ole Römer Observatory. His second catalogue gave his estimates for the colours of 5915 stars using his 10-cm refractor. Some objects as faint as $m = 9$ were included. Here Krüger carefully studied the relationship between colour and Harvard spectral type and the effect of apparent magnitude on the colour estimates [82]. He showed that for stars of the same spectral type his estimates were progressively redder for the fainter magnitudes, the effect amounting to about $0°.1$ per magnitude. Krüger's *Index Catalogue* for the colours of northern and some southern stars was posthumously published by Father Hagen in 1917, and brought together an additional 2316 stars observed from Aarhus to form a compendium of mean star colours determined by Hagen, Osthoff and Krüger on the Schmidt scale [83].

Several other observers made contributions to colour estimates using the Schmidt scale, but none with the extensive coverage of Hagen, Osthoff and Krüger. Johannes Möller (1867–1957) was one of the few who reported colours of southern stars (south of −20°) made from a sailing ship with opera glasses or by naked eye [84]. Hans Emil Lau (1879–1918), a Danish amateur astronomer, reported colour estimates for 774 stars observed with his 95-mm refractor [85]. Like Osthoff, he claimed a probable error of $±0°.4$, and he explored the relationship between colour and the Maury spectral type. Lau found a larger physiological dependence of estimated colour on apparent magnitude than Krüger, which amounted to $0°.3$ apparent reddening for each fainter magnitude for stars of a given early spectral type.

In the United States, Seth Chandler (1846–1913) also adopted a numerical colour scale which ran from 0 (white) to 10 (deepest red), and used this for his three catalogues of variable stars, many of which were listed with colour estimates [86, 87, 88]. For example the third catalogue of 1896 listed 393 variables known at that time, with colours given for over 200 of them, these being mainly Chandler's own observations with his $6\frac{1}{4}$-inch refractor. Although his scale was superficially similar to that of Schmidt and Osthoff, Chandler emphasized the independence of his own colour estimates. Thus index 2 corresponded to yellow for Chandler, whereas the same colour was assigned index 4 by Schmidt. Chandler's scale had finer divisions at the red end, where most variable stars are found, and the relation between the two scales is therefore non-linear, as Chandler himself pointed out [89]. Several observers were interested in observing the colours of variable stars with the aim of detecting colour changes, and spurious reports were not uncommon. One such was that of the Czech chemist and astronomer Adalbert Šafařík (1829–1902), who observed from Prague with a 160-mm silvered mirror reflector. His colours were based on the Schmidt scale, and he claimed to have detected colour variability in the red giant star α Ursae Majoris (Dubhe) [90].

Colour estimation in astronomy was practised for over a century, and flourished especially for several decades around the turn of the century. But after about 1920 this type of observation fell out of favour. Colour estimates were less precise than the Henry Draper spectral types as an indicator of temperature, while the first photographic colour indices were obtained with the *Yerkes Actinometry* from 1912 – see section 4.8.2. The improvement in precision was shown graphically by Parkhurst when he plotted his photographic colour index against spectral type [91]. The scatter about the mean line was only about $\pm 0^{m}.05$. On the other hand his plot of colour index against the colour estimate of Müller and Kempf gave a much larger scatter. Müller and Kempf made a similar comparison which showed the mean error of their colour estimates, when expressed in terms of a photographic minus visual colour index, was as much as $\pm 0^{m}.29$ [92]. In addition to this lack of precision, colour estimates were also highly susceptible to systematic errors, especially those of physiological origin. The photographic technique avoided such problems, though not without introducing a new batch of difficulties peculiar to the photographic process.

References

[1]   Herschel, W., *Phil. Trans. R. Soc.*, **74**, 437 (1784).
[2]   Herschel, W., *Phil. Trans. R. Soc.*, **75**, 213 (1785).
[3]   Herschel, W., *Phil. Trans. R. Soc.*, p. 166 (1796).
[4]   Herschel, W., *Phil. Trans. R. Soc.*, p. 452 (1796).
[5]   Herschel, W., *Phil. Trans. R. Soc.*, p. 293 (1797).
[6]   Herschel, W., *Phil. Trans. R. Soc.*, p. 121 (1799).

[7]   Pickering, E.C., Searle, A. and Wendell, O.C., *Ann. Harvard Coll. Observ.*, **14** (Part 2), 325 (1885).

[8]   Peirce, C.S., *Ann. Harvard Coll. Observ.*, **9**, 1 (1878).

[9]   Pickering, E.C. and Wendell, O.C., *Ann. Harvard Coll. Observ.*, **23** (Part 2), 137 (1899).

[10]   Zinner, E., *Veröff. der Remeis-Sternwarte Bamberg*, **2**, 1 (1926).

[11]   Herschel, J., *Results of astronomical observations made during the years 1834, 5, 6, 7, 8, at the Cape of Good Hope*, Smith, Elder and Co., London (1847).

[12]   Baily, F., *Mem. Astron. Soc., London*, **2**, appendix (1826) – *The Astron. Soc. Catalogue*.

[13]   de Lacaille, N.-L., *Caelum Australe Stelliferum*, Paris (1763).

[14]   Doberck, W., *Astrophys. J.*, **11**, 192 and 270 (1900).

[15]   Doberck, W., *Ann. Harvard Coll. Observ.*, **41** (No. 8), 213 (1902).

[16]   Argelander, F., *Uranometria Nova*, Berlin (1843).

[17]   Herschel, J., *Mon. Not. R. Astron. Soc.*, **27**, 213 (1867).

[18]   Struve, F.G.W., *Catalogus Novus Stellarum Duplicium et Multiplicium*, St Petersburg (1827).

[19]   Struve, F.G.W., *Catalogus Duplicium et Multiplicium Mensurae Micrometricae*, St Petersburg (1837).

[20]   Lewis, T., *Mem. R. Astron. Soc.*, **56**, 1 (1906).

[21]   Pogson, N.R., *Mon. Not. R. Astron. Soc.*, **17**, 12 (1856).

[22]   Herschel, J., *Mem. R. Astron. Soc.*, **3**, 177 (1829).

[23]   Smyth, W.H., *A Cycle of Celestial Objects*, (1844).

[24]   Knott, G., *Proc. Manchester Literary and Phil. Soc.*, **5**, 187 (1866).

[25]   Knott, G., *Proc. Manchester Literary and Phil. Soc.*, **6**, 13 (1867).

[26]   Hassenstein, W., *Handbuch der Astrophys.*, Chap. 6: *Visuelle Photometrie*, p. 519, Springer-Verlag, Berlin (1931).

[27]   Argelander, F.A., *Aufforderung an Freunde der Astronomie: H. C. Schumacher's Jahrbuch für 1844*, p. 122, Stuttgart and Tübingen (1844). See p. 185 for section on magnitudes and colours of the stars.

[28]   Argelander, F.A., *Astron. Nachr.*, **19**, 393 (1842).

[29]   Baily, F., *The Catalogue of Stars of the British Assoc. for the Advancement of Sci.*, London (1845).

[30]   Baily, F., *A Catalogue of Stars in the S. hemisphere for the beginning of the year 1750 from the observations of the Abbé Lacaille, made at the Cape of Good Hope in the years 1751 and 1752*, London (1847).

[31]   Argelander, F.A., *Astron. Beobachtungen auf der Sternwarte zu Bonn*, **1** (1846); **2** (1852); **6** (1867).

[32]   Argelander, F.A., *ibid.* **1**, see p. xxiv (1846).

[33]   Argelander, F.A., *Astron. Beobachtungen auf der Sternwarte zu Bonn*, **3** (1859); **4** (1861); **5** (1862).

[34]   Pickering, E.C., *Ann. Harvard Coll. Observ.*, **70**, 1 (1909).

[35]   Pickering, E.C., *Ann. Harvard Coll. Observ.*, **72** (No. 6), 1 (1913).

[36]   Pannekoek, A., *Publ. Astron. Inst. Univ. Amsterdam*, **1**, 1 (1924).

[37]   Hopmann, J., Inaugural dissertation, Bonn (1914).

[38]   Schönfeld, E., *Astron. Beobachtungen der Sternwarte zu Bonn*, **8**, 1 (1886).

[39]   Heis, E., *Atlas Coelestis Novus*, Köln (1872).

[40]   Behrmann, C., *Vierteljahrschr. Astron. Ges.*, **2**, 238 (1867).

[41]   Behrmann, C., *Atlas des südlichen gestirnten Himmels*, Leipzig (1874).

[42]   Houzeau, J.-C., *Ann. Observ. R. Bruxelles* (nouv. sér.), **1** (1878).

[43]   Houzeau, J.-C. and Lancaster, G., *Bibliographie Générale de l'Astronomie* (1882).

[44]   Houzeau, J.-C., *Ann. Observ. R. Bruxelles*, **1** (Part 2) (1878).

[45]   Gould, B.A., *Result. Observ. Nac. Argentino Córdoba*, **1**, 1 (1879).

[46]   Gould, B.A., *Proc. American Ass. Advancement of Sci.*, **23**, 115 (1874).

[47]   Thome, J.M., *Result. Observ. Nac. Argentino Córdoba*, **16** (1892); **17** (1894); **18** (1900).

[48]   Pickering, E.C., *Ann. Harvard Coll. Observ.*, **72** (No. 7), 233 (1913).

[49]   Perrine, C.D. *Result. Observ. Nac. Argentino Córdoba*, **21** (Part 5) (1932).

[50]   Murdin, P.G., *Quart. J. R. Astron. Soc.*, **22**, 353 (1981).

[51]   van Gent, R.H. *Observatory*, **109**, 23 (1989).

[52]   Sestini, B., *Mem. dell'Osserv. del Coll. Romano: Memoria Primo*, (1845).

[53]   Sestini, B., *Mem. dell'Osserv. del Coll. Romano: Memoria Seconda*, (1847).

[54]   Hagen, J.G., *Specola Astron. Vaticana*, **3**, i (1911).

[55]   Sestini, B., *Astron. J.*, **1**, 88 (1850).

[56]   Smyth, W.H., *Sidereal Chromatics*, London (1864).

[57]   Pickering, W.H., *Pop. Astron.*, **25**, 419 (1917).

[58]   Kincaid, B., *Mon. Not. R. Astron. Soc.*, **27**, 264 (1867).

[59]   Klein, H.J., *Astron. Nachr.*, **70**, 105 (1868).

[60]   Schjellerup, H.C.F.C., *Astron. Nachr.*, **67**, 97 (1866).

[61]   Schmidt, J.F.J., *Astron. Nachr.*, **80**, 9 (1872).

[62]   Schmidt, J.F.J., *Astron. Nachr.*, **80**, 81 (1872).

[63]   Schmidt, J.F.J., *Astron. Nachr.*, **94**, 55 (1879).

[64]   Franks, W.S., *Mon. Not. R. Astron. Soc.*, **38**, 486 (1878).

[65]   Pickering, E.C., Searle, A. and Wendell, O.C., *Ann. Harvard Coll. Observ.*, **14** (Part 1), 1 (1884).

[66]   Franks, W.S., *Mon. Not. R. Astron. Soc.*, **46**, 342 (1886).

[67]   Franks, W.S., *Mon. Not. R. Astron. Soc.*, **47**, 269 (1886).

[68]   Newton, I., *Opticks* (1704).

[69]   Secchi, A., *Mem. dell'Osserv. del Coll. Romano 1852–55*, p. 1 (1856).

[70]   Franks, W.S., *Mon. Not. R. Astron. Soc.*, **48**, 265 (1888); Franks' 3rd catalogue of 758 stars was introduced here, and a copy was deposited with the R. Astron. Soc., London.

[71]   Franks, W.S. and Hagen, J.G., *Specola Astron. Vaticana*, suppl. to **3** (No. 15), i (1923).

[72]   Franks, W.S., *Mon. Not. R. Astron. Soc.*, **67**, 539 (1907).

[73]   Vogel, H.C. and Müller, G., *Publ. Astrophys. Observ. Potsdam*, **3** (No. 11), 127 (1883).

[74]   Secchi, A., *Comptes Rendus de l'Acad. des Sci.*, **63**, 364 (1866).

[75]   Müller, G., and Kempf, P., *Publ. Astrophys. Observ. Potsdam*, **17**, 1 (1907).

[76]   Osthoff, H., *Astron. Nachr.*, **153**, 141 (1900).

[77] Osthoff, H., *Astron. Nachr.*, **205**, 1 (1918).
[78] Osthoff, H., *Specola Astron. Vaticana*, **3** (No. 8), i (1916).
[79] Wirtz, C., *Vierteljahrschr. Astron. Ges.*, **54**, 2 (1919).
[80] Osthoff, H., *Astron. Nachr.*, **157**, 117 (1901).
[81] Krüger, F., *Publ. der Sternw. in Kiel*, Nr **8** (1893).
[82] Krüger, F., *Specola Astron. Vaticana*, **3** (No. 7), i (1914).
[83] Krüger, F., *Specola Astron. Vaticana*, **3** (No. 9), i (1917).
[84] Möller, J., *Astron. Nachr.*, **166**, 305 (1904).
[85] Lau, H.E., *Astron. Nachr.*, **205**, 49 (1918).
[86] Chandler, S.C., *Astron. J.*, **8**, 81 (1888).
[87] Chandler, S.C., *Astron. J.*, **13**, 89 (1890).
[88] Chandler, S.C., *Astron. J.*, **16**, 145 (1896).
[89] Chandler, S.C., *Astron. J.*, **8**, 137 (1888).
[90] Šafařík, A., *Vierteljahrschr. Astron. Ges.*, **14**, 367 (1879).
[91] Parkhurst, J.A., *Astrophys. J.*, **36**, 169 (1912).
[92] Müller, G. and Kempf, P., *Astron. Nachr.*, **194**, 219 (1913).

3   Visual photometric measurements

3.1   Early experiments in astronomical photometry

The work described in the previous chapter was based on visual magnitude estimates. Stars were at first placed into pigeon-holes which were labelled as magnitude classes, on the basis of the visual sensation to the observer's eye. Later the scale became more quantitative, in that the magnitude was regarded as a continuously varying parameter in which fractions were permissible, yet it was still based entirely on visual estimates, not measurements.

The concept of stellar photometry, or the measurement of starlight, is much more recent than that of the estimation of stellar magnitudes. The earliest photometry was still visual, in that the human retina was the only light receptor. However, the technique relied on diminishing the intensity of a light beam by a measurable amount, either so as to extinguish the rays just to the point of invisibility, or so as to change the intensity so that the brightness of two sources to be compared is made equal. This is the basis of visual photometry, whether it be by extinction or by comparison.

The earliest attempts at astronomical photometry were all comparisons of the intensities of light from the sun, moon and bright stars, sometimes using a terrestrial source, usually a candle, as an intermediate reference. Christian Huyghens (1629–95), in his posthumously published *Cosmotheoros* [1], was the first astronomical photometrist. Here he described his attempts to measure the brightness ratio of Sirius to the sun, by passing sunlight through a small hole in the end of a long tube, and further diminishing its intensity by placing a small glass ball in the hole so as to spread the transmitted beam. He went on: 'And when I then looked at the sun through the tube ,.. its brightness appeared no less than the brightness of Sirius'. Huyghens now supposed that the stars are all sun-like objects distributed at differing distances throughout space, a bold innovation that Kepler had also considered but not adopted. On this basis, from an application of geometrical optics to his instrument, he deduced that Sirius must be 27 664 times more distant than the sun.

Huyghens' work came before the true birth of photometry by Pierre Bouguer (1698–1758) in France and Johann Lambert (1728–77) in Germany. He did not explicitly convert his result to an intensity ratio using the inverse square law, and in fact the intensity ratio implied by Huyghens' result was 17 times too small. Given the crude instrument and the fact that the two objects compared were necessarily observed at very different times, such an error may not be surprising.

Bouguer was the founder of the science of photometry. Unlike Huyghens, he was certainly aware of the inverse square law. He devised the first laboratory photometers using the comparison principle and studied the decrease in the intensity of light rays travelling through an absorbing medium, including the extinction of moonlight in its passage through the terrestrial atmosphere [2]. Lambert's work came after Bouguer's, but apparently he was unaware of the latter's achievements. In his *Photometria* [3], which was published in the same year as Bouguer's posthumous work, Lambert rediscovered several of the principles used by Bouguer, including the exponential decrease with distance in the intensity of a beam of light in its passage through an absorbing medium.

Bouguer applied his photometry to the measurement of light from the sun and moon in 1725, in order to determine the brightness ratio of these two bodies. He did this by studying the illumination on a screen due to the images of the sun and the full moon produced by a concave mirror, and in turn compared these with the illumination produced by a candle. He repeated the experiment on four nights and wrote:

> I believe that one might conclude from all this, that the sun
> illuminates us about 300,000 times more than does the moon; but the
> great difficulties in determining such a ratio mean that I dare not
> consider it as exact.

In fact his result was, perhaps fortuitously, quite close to the modern value of about 400 000 [4] (see also [2]).

It is interesting that the English clergyman and astronomer, the Rev. John Michell (c. 1724–93) attempted to determine the brightness ratio of the sun to the fixed stars using Saturn as an intermediary [5]. He reasoned from geometrical principles that Saturn must be 48.4×10^9 times less bright than the sun, assuming that it reflects all the sunlight that it receives. Because Saturn and the brightest fixed stars are of comparable magnitude, these latter must likewise be less bright than the sun by a similar factor, from which the distance to the brightest stars may be found using the inverse square law. His result was about 220 000 astronomical units, or about $3\frac{1}{2}$

light years, a very plausible value by modern standards. Michell's figure
was based more on geometrical optics than photometry. Yet this was the
first reasonably reliable distance estimate to any star, and it also represents
the earliest application of the photometric distance method, so important
in modern astronomy.

William Wollaston (1766–1828) commented on Michell's calculations. He
found it

> ... surprising that no astronomer has been incited by these remarks to
> devise a method of making the requisite observations, and that now, so
> many years after Mr Michell's suggestion was made public, so much
> remains to be effected in this branch of photometry [6].

Wollaston then goes on to describe experiments he made in 1799 to find
the brightness of the sun relative to that of the moon, by comparing the
shadows they cast with that from a candle [6]. His result of just over 800 000
for the brightness ratio is the only one, apart from Bouguer's, found in the
literature up to the early nineteenth century. Wollaston's failure to take
atmospheric extinction into account (unlike Bouguer, who observed both
objects at the same altitude) is probably the main reason for his figure being
too large (see comments by Müller [7, p. 308]).

Later Wollaston devised an ingenious method of comparing the sun to
Sirius, by reflecting the light of the sun and of a candle in small spherical
glass bulbs filled with mercury, to render star-like images visible in a
telescope. Sirius observed directly through a telescope was compared with
such an artificial star produced by a candle, as was also the reflected image
of the sun, and geometrical principles then gave the intensity ratios. The
essence of the method was to make the candle image equal in brightness to
that of the astronomical body. His result for the sun's brightness relative to
that of Sirius was 2×10^{10}, which is, however, affected by an over-correction
for the loss of light on reflection from mercury. Compared to a modern
value of 1.3×10^{10} for this ratio, Wollaston's figure of 1826–27 represents
the first reasonable result based on visual photometry for the brightness of
a star relative to the sun.

3.2   Experiments of Celsius and Tulenius, the Herschels and Humboldt in measuring the relative brightness of stars

The experiments in stellar photometry described in the last section were greatly hampered by the extreme disparity in the brightness of

the sun and the stars. As Michell had pointed out, such photometry, in which the brightness of stars was referred to that of the sun, was essential if photometric stellar distances were the purpose. But there were good reasons for studying the relative brightness of the stars themselves, such as the investigation of stellar variability, as William Herschel had advocated.

At Uppsala in Sweden, Anders Celsius (1701–44), famous for his thermometric scale, was the first astronomer to attempt to improve on simple magnitude estimates by photometric measurements to determine the relative brightness of the stars. The work was undertaken with his pupil, A. Tulenius, who reported it in his thesis [8]. The technique was to insert glass plates into the light path of a star seen through a small telescope of length 30 cm. Each plate was considered to produce half a magnitude of absorption, and plates were inserted until the light from a star was extinguished, or at least rendered invisible to the observer. The number of plates required thus measured the magnitude. Sirius required 24 plates to be extinguished, and was taken to be of magnitude $m = 1$.

Using this method, 64 stars in Aries were measured, the faintest being given as $m = 12$, though in reality they were about 6.9 on a modern photometric scale. Zinner [9] states that Celsius' magnitude 5 corresponds to 4.3 on the Pogson scale, while Celsius' 8 is Pogson's 6. Hence the intensity ratio for a Celsius magnitude corresponds to a factor of 1.69 for these stars of medium brightness, far from the Pogson value of 2.512. The precision corresponded to a mean error of $\pm 0^{m}\!.38$ for the medium bright stars observed, which was actually no better than visual estimates. Tulenius may well have been aware of this circumstance, for his later work on stars in Taurus, undertaken after the premature death of his supervisor, reverted to using magnitude estimates. Yet his work was a significant first step in extinction photometry, whose principle more than a century later was used in the wedge photometer.

William Herschel experimented with comparison photometry to estimate the relative brightness of two stars. In 1817 he described a method in which two identical telescopes were directed towards two stars of unequal brightness. By stopping one of the telescopes down with a circular aperture plate, its light gathering power could be diminished so as to render the two images equal [10]. The relative stellar brightness of the two stars could then be found from the unobstructed mirror areas. Herschel proposed converting such intensity ratios into magnitude differences and using the results to investigate stellar distances within the Milky Way. He made observations on a number of bright stars, but unfortunately adopted the wrong relationship between intensity and magnitude, which led him to believe that a star's distance was in direct proportion to its magnitude. Such a relationship in turn results in a spurious increase of the spatial density of stars with distance from the solar system.

The German naturalist and explorer, Alexander von Humboldt (1769–1859) also made a few photometric observations of bright stars during his travels in South America around 1803. He used both aperture stops and pieces of coloured glass to equalize the brightness of two stellar images in his telescope. The intensities of sixteen bright stars relative to Sirius were deduced, based on a scale in which Sirius was set at 100 and second magnitude stars were in the range 60–80. Evidently the scale was far from linear, and the results were quite unreliable [11, 12].

Apart from William Herschel's and Alexander von Humboldt's brief experiments in photometric measurement, John Herschel can be regarded as the first stellar photometrist after Celsius to intercompare successfully the brightness of the stars. This work was undertaken on 19 nights during his stay at the Cape of Good Hope in the year 1836, using his so-called 'astrometer' [13]. This instrument used a prism to reflect the light of the moon into a very small lens of short focal length (about 0.23 inches), whose position could be translated on a pole, so as to be a variable distance from the observer's eye. The moon thus formed a star-like image whose apparent brightness could be varied by sliding the lens further away from or towards the observer, until equality with a star, observed directly with the unaided eye, was achieved. Application of the inverse square law to the distance from the eye to the real image of the moon thus allowed relative stellar brightnesses to be deduced.

Herschel was unsuccessful in obtaining the relative brightnesses of stars observed on different evenings, because he used Euler's incorrect formula for the change in lunar brightness with phase. However, his results within an evening for bright stars had a mean probable error of $\pm 0^m.09$ [9], which represents exceptional precision for a visual method. In fact it is equal to the best visual photometry made with considerably more sophisticated instruments in the late nineteenth century.

In 1916 Henry Norris Russell (1877–1957) undertook a reanalysis of Herschel's raw observations [14]. The principal aim was to determine the magnitude of the full moon, using the best photometric data then available for Herschel's stars. Russell carefully corrected for atmospheric extinction as well as for absorption in Herschel's lens and prism. He obtained −12.79 as the magnitude of the full moon, thus making Herschel's the first observations from which a reliable value for the apparent magnitude of the moon was obtained. Zinner inverted the problem by determining magnitudes for Herschel's stars using the correct values for the lunar magnitude on each of Herschel's nights [9], and he has given an analysis of the random and systematic errors in the final data.

3.3   New visual photometers in the nineteenth century

The second half of the nineteenth century was an extraordinarily fertile period in the physical sciences, not least in the design of new instruments and the devising of new measurement techniques. This was the era that saw the birth of astrophysics, which received its impetus especially from the advent of stellar spectroscopy. But stellar visual photometry was also put on a much firmer basis from about the 1860s onwards, though with some isolated but significant developments from the 1830s.

Visual photometers, whether for laboratory or astronomical use, can be broadly divided into two categories. Those based on the reduction in the brightness of an image or an illuminated scene by a known factor such as to render it invisible are called extinction photometers. The second category makes use of the visual comparison of the brightness of two images or illuminations, and entails changing the intensity of at least one of them in order to achieve apparent equality in brightness. Instruments operating on this principle are comparison photometers.

Both types of photometer require the dimming of a light source by a measurable factor, whether it be to achieve extinction or equality. A wide variety of techniques has been used or proposed for this purpose. These include aperture stopping, both before and after the telescope objective, the use of varying thicknesses of absorbing media, the application of the inverse square law to displacements from point sources, methods based on rotating sectors of known geometry which interrupt a beam at a high chopping frequency and those based on polarization, which invoke Malus' law† for the reduction in the intensity of polarized light once it has traversed an analyser.

Both types of photometer, extinction and comparison, have played significant roles in the development of astronomical photometry. However, only four variants saw extensive use. One was a wedge photometer that uses the extinction principle, while three were types of comparison photometer, being the instruments associated with Steinheil, Zöllner and Pickering.

---

† The law of Etienne Louis Malus, 1809, states that the intensity of light after traversing the analyser falls off as the square of the cosine of the angle through which the analyser is rotated.

3.3.1   The development of wedge photometers

The idea of using absorbing materials to extinguish a light source as a photometric aid was mentioned by Bouguer in his *Traité d'Optique* [2, p. 46], and was used in astronomy by Celsius in Sweden in 1740 – see section 3.2. However, a continuously variable amount of extinction could be produced by means of a wedge of dark, partially absorbing glass, as first proposed by Count Xavier de Maistre in 1832 [15], and soon afterwards by the Belgian astronomer, A. Quetelet (1796–1874) [16].

Charles Piazzi Smyth (1819–1900), who was later to be the Astronomer Royal for Scotland, also proposed using a wedge for stellar photometry during the time of his assistantship to Maclear at the Cape [17]. He went on to bemoan the fact that nothing had come of the Royal Astronomical Society's proposal of 1822 to award a prize

> ... to any person, who shall contrive and have executed an Instrument, by which the relative magnitudes of the stars may be measured or determined, and the utility of which for this object shall be sufficiently established by numerous observations and comparisons of known stars [18].

A later arrangement of the wedge photometer, which gave neither deviation nor dispersion to the transmitted light, comprised two wedges glued together, one of transparent and the other of absorbing glass. This was first suggested by E. Kayser in Danzig in 1862 [19]. He proposed placing such a compound wedge in the focal plane of his telescope objective, and trailing stars across the wedge so that the absorption increased with time. The time interval required to achieve extinction is then a measure of a star's magnitude, the relationship between this time interval and the magnitude being linear. In England William Dawes (1799–1868) experimented with a similar device, although his description is extremely brief [20].

The astronomer who made by far the greatest contribution to wedge photometry was Charles Pritchard (1808–93) at the University of Oxford. He described his instrument in 1882 [21] and in more detail in the following year [22]. Pritchard's equipment consisted of a wedge which was mounted between the eyepiece of a small refractor and the observer. The wedge was translated laterally to cause the disappearance of a star and the reading taken of its position. The main wedge used was $6\frac{1}{2}$ inches long and made by Grubb of Dublin. It had a linear coefficient of about 1.9 magnitudes for every inch of displacement, and was used on a 4-inch refractor. In addition, a smaller 4-inch long wedge on a 3-inch telescope was also sometimes used.

Pritchard's observing programme, which resulted in the *Uranometria Nova Oxoniensis* [23], is described in section 3.6.2. It is interesting that all of

Pritchard's main scientific work was carried out after his reaching the age of 60. He was already 73 when he embarked on the major programme of wedge photometry for which he is best remembered.

The Oxford wedge photometry had numerous critics for a variety of technical reasons. Thus Wilsing (1856–1943) at Potsdam published a detailed discussion on the effects of variable background illumination, on measuring coloured stars and on the changes in eye sensitivity in relation to wedge photometry [24], while in France Maurice Loewy (1833–1907) abandoned the development of this type of instrument, because he was unable to find a truly neutral absorbing glass – that is, one for which the wedge constant was independent of a star's colour [25]. E. Spitta cast doubt on the accuracy of Pritchard's wedge calibrations [26] and Henry Parkhurst at Harvard disputed the reliability of wedge photometry in bright moonlight [27]. Pritchard defended his method against all these criticisms [28, 29, 30, 31, 32], yet the results of his work show that the accuracy was disappointing, and could not compete with the comparison photometers being used at Harvard and Potsdam.

3.3.2 Early comparison photometers

Carl von Steinheil (1801–70) designed and built one of the earliest of the comparison photometers used in astronomy. Steinheil was professor of mathematics and physics in Munich and well known for the optical workshops he founded there in 1854. His photometer was described in a prize-winning essay submitted in 1836 to the Royal Bavarian Academy of Sciences entitled *Elemente der Helligkeitsmessungen am Sternhimmel* [33].

Steinheil's instrument was known as a prism photometer, and was the first astronomical photometer to make use of extra-focal images of stars, so that surface brightnesses rather than points were compared. For this purpose a small refractor with a split objective lens was constructed, each half of the lens being able to slide independently along the tube's axis. Light from two stars was sent to each half lens by means of internally reflecting prisms and the semicircular out-of-focus images were thus observed simultaneously and side-by-side in the common eyepiece. The position of each half lens was adjusted so as to achieve equality of surface brightness of their respective images, and the ratio of stellar brightnesses then came from the fact that the surface brightness observed decreases as $1/\delta^2$, where δ is the displacement of each half lens from the in-focus position. At equality, the images could of course be of different sizes. But so this would not unduly influence the observer, the two stars could be observed through an aperture, so that equal areas of the out-of-focus images were visible.

Fig. 3.1   Steinheil's prism photometer, 1836, as used by Ludwig Seidel for his
photometric catalogue of 1862.

Steinheil only observed about 30 stars with this instrument, but its accuracy was later demonstrated by Seidel – see section 3.4. Its main drawback was the limitation to bright stars, a consequence of using extra-focal images.

Apart from designing the prism photometer, Steinheil made a photometric comparison of the full moon with Arcturus, also using the extra-focal method. For this measurement, Arcturus was observed extra-focally through a small refractor by pulling out the eyepiece, while the moon was viewed in focus through the same instrument, but with the objective stopped down until the surface brightness equalled that of Arcturus [33]. Seidel rereduced these observations and derived a result of 20 000 for the ratio of the full moon to Arcturus, a value which was at least a factor of five too small [34].

Also of interest is a completely different type of experiment in comparison photometry undertaken by George Bond (1825–65) at Harvard, as a method of determining the brightness ratio of the sun to the full moon [35]. Here Bond made use of the virtual starlike image of the sun or moon produced by a large glass sphere with a silvered reflecting surface. The apparent brightness of such an image obeys the inverse square law, and can therefore be compared with an artificial source, for which Bond used a 'Bengola light'. According to Bond, the colour of such a flame closely matched that of the moon. The flame was compared with the image of the celestial source by reflecting both in a second small sphere whose distance from the two sources was adjusted to give equality in brightness of the two images observed. The first experiment was the comparison of the sun with the Bengola flame, then the procedure was repeated for the moon, thus allowing a ratio for the brightnesses of these two celestial bodies to be deduced.

Bond's result was that the sun's brightness is 470 980 times that of the moon, a figure much nearer the correct value than either Bouguer or Wollaston had obtained. Bond's photometry was strongly criticized by Zöllner [36], because the light from Bond's fireworks could not be considered as even roughly constant, even if ' ... those of the same size and manufacture were used throughout, and a fresh one burned for each comparison' (quoted from H. N. Russell [14]). Zöllner went on:

> In any case, the whole of Bond's photometric studies, with the exception of those relating to the chemical [i.e. photographic] intensities of a few heavenly bodies, have so much the character of just occasional dabbling, that at first I very much hesitated to describe them here at all [36, p. 117].

3.3.3   Zöllner's photometer

In 1857 the Imperial Academy of Sciences in Vienna offered a prize for stellar photometry (one of several offered by different societies and academies on this topic in the nineteenth century). The conditions were as follows:

Fig. 3.2   Friedrich Zöllner.

> It is required to present photometric determinations of the brightness
> of the fixed stars which are as numerous and as accurate as possible, in
> such a way and extent that our present knowledge of the stars makes a
> significant step forwards.

Friedrich Zöllner (1834–82) was then studying in Basel and was a candidate for the prize. His contribution consisted of the design for a new stellar photometer based on the principle of the dimming of the light from an artificial star by means of a crossed polarizer and analyser, as well as accompanying measurements on 226 stars which were compared with the artificial source.

Fig. 3.3   Zöllner's astrophotometer, 1861.

Although the prize was not awarded on the grounds that not enough stars had been measured, the article was nevertheless published in 1861 under the title *Grundzüge einer allgemeinen Photometrie des Himmels* [37]. Zöllner's photometer proved to be one of the most reliable and accurate types in astronomical use in the late nineteenth century. The design consisted of light from a kerosene lamp which was dimmed by passing it through two Nicol prisms, the second of which was a rotatable analyser. The reduction in intensity of light by polarization as a photometric technique had been proposed earlier by François Arago (1786–1853) in France [38]. After leaving the analyser, the light from the artificial star then entered the side of a small refractor (Zöllner's telescope was 41 mm in aperture), where it was reflected into the telescope's optical axis by a 45° glass plate, thus enabling its brightness to be compared directly with that of a real star seen in close proximity in the eyepiece. In order to match the colour of lamplight to starlight, it was also possible to change the colour of the former. This was accomplished with a birefringent quartz plate about 5 mm thick and a third Nicol prism placed between the lamp and the polarizer. The possibility of using this as a colorimeter was also mentioned by Zöllner, though few observers with this photometer appear to have attempted to measure star colours with it.

In using Zöllner's photometer, the lamp must of course be intrinsically brighter than the stars observed, as only its intensity is reduced, not that of the real star. The observations are made by rotating the Nicol prism analyser to obtain equality between real and artificial stars.

The instrument was duplicated by the firm of Ausfeld in Gotha, and copies were thereby acquired by several observatories, notably by Wolff in Bonn, by Müller in Potsdam, by Peirce at Harvard, by Lindemann at Pulkovo, by Tserasky in Moscow and by Fesenkov in Kharkov, all of whom made important contributions to photometric astronomy with the Zöllner photometer – see sections 3.4 and 3.6.

3.3.4   Pickering's meridian photometer

Photometry at Harvard was commenced in 1871 by Charles Peirce, during Winlock's term as director of Harvard College Observatory. Peirce's work was with a Zöllner photometer – see section 3.4. When Edward Pickering (1846–1919) came to Harvard as observatory director in 1877 he quickly decided to continue a vigorous programme of photometry

> ... as offering a field in which the results promised to be of much value, and in which there seemed to be no danger of duplicating work in progress elsewhere ... [39, see p. iii].

It is clear from the outset that Pickering was not happy with the Zöllner instrument:

> The great difficulty is the want of similarity in the two objects to be compared, especially when the star is bright. In this case, the real star presents a much smaller disk, is much brighter intrinsically, and is continually varying or twinkling. It is therefore very difficult to compare with a paler, larger, and steadier object. The lamp also varies, not only from night to night, but from minute to minute; and no correction can easily be applied for the changes in the opacity of the air, which affect the star but not the artificial light [39, see p. iii].

Fig. 3.4 Edward Pickering, during the early years of his directorship at Harvard.

For these reasons Pickering began to develop new photometric instruments for the 15-inch Harvard refractor, which were still based on the polarization method, but used the comparison of two stars instead of a star with a lamp.

It is from these early Harvard photometers, described in detail in 1879 [39], that the famous meridian photometer at Harvard was developed. The first such instrument was completed in the spring of 1879 and was described in Pickering's *Harvard Photometry* of 1884 [40]. It consisted of a horizontal telescope with two similar objectives of 4-cm aperture (1.6 inches, although this instrument was frequently referred to as the '2-inch meridian photometer' at Harvard), installed side-by-side in a common tube, which was mounted in a fixed E-W direction. Starlight entered these lenses via rotatable reflecting prisms, one for each objective. The northerly objective always observed the Pole Star (α UMi), while the other could be directed so as to receive the light from any star on or close to the meridian.

Fig. 3.5   Drawing of the 2-inch Harvard meridian photometer.

Near the common focus of both objectives the light from the stars passed
through a double-image prism of Iceland spar, a birefringent material which
divides each of the pencils into two. Hence each star produced two images,
one consisting of ordinary and the other of extraordinary rays in orthogonal

states of plane polarization. Only the ordinary rays from one objective and the extraordinary rays from the other were used. These were received by a common eyepiece in front of which was a rotatable Nicol prism. The two stars were thus seen in close juxtaposition, one being from ordinary rays, the other extraordinary. The Nicol prism was now rotated so as to render these two images of equal brightness. Both images were dimmed by the Nicol, but by different factors. A total of four readings of the Nicol orientation (that is four settings) was taken for any pair of stars, and then the intensity ratio of the two stars, and their magnitude difference, followed quite simply from the application of Malus' law for the transmission of polarized light through a polarizing filter. It was with this meridian photometer that Pickering observed all the naked-eye stars north of −30° to produce the famous *Harvard Photometry* − see section 3.6.1).

Later a larger meridian photometer with 4-inch aperture objectives was built, and this was used from 1882 to observe stars down to ninth or tenth magnitude, and also, from 1891, for the well known *Revised Harvard Photometry* for the brighter stars in both hemispheres. The design of the 4-inch instrument was very similar to the smaller photometer, except for the use of 45° mirrors instead of prisms to reflect the light into each objective lens [41].

Although the 4- and 1.6-inch photometers were the main instruments with which most of the Harvard photometric observations were undertaken, the need on occasions to reach fainter stars meant a larger visual photometer was necessary for certain work. In 1898 a 12-inch meridian photometer was constructed for observations down to 13th magnitude. This photometer was somewhat different in operating principle from its predecessors. It employed a single 12-inch aperture refracting telescope mounted E-W, and light from a meridian star was directed into the tube from a 45° plane mirror. However, for this instrument, comparison was made with an artificial star whose brightness was controlled by means of a wedge, similar to that used by Pritchard for the Oxford photometry. The real star itself was therefore not dimmed at all, thus enabling the faintest possible objects to be reached [42]. Pickering sent a photometer of this type to John Parkhurst at Yerkes Observatory in 1901, to enable the faintest possible stars to be reached on the Yerkes 40-inch refractor [43].

3.4   Photometry of Seidel, Zöllner, Wolff and Peirce

Ludwig Seidel (1821–96) in the years 1844–48 in Munich made the first reliable photometric observations, using a Steinheil prism photometer. His first paper [44] was a preliminary investigation of the capabilities of the Steinheil instrument, and also included a careful study of the effects of atmospheric extinction. In making comparisons of the intensities of two stars with this photometer, Seidel was able to correct the intensity ratio for extinction and express the results as the logarithm of the intensity ratio which would apply if the stars had been observed at the zenith.

This work was later extended to a catalogue of 744 comparisons between 208 stars, the observations being undertaken with the assistance of E. Leonhard [45]. From 1857 Seidel's plan was to observe systematically all northern stars to magnitude $3\frac{1}{2}$. A network of frequently used stars distributed over the sky was used to provide secondary standards, while the primary standard was Vega, to which all intensities were reduced.

The result was one of the earliest visual photometric catalogues of stars of any importance, and certainly the first where atmospheric extinction was corrected for, using the formula that the change in a star's magnitude is proportional to the secant of its zenith distance. The accuracy of Seidel's observations was remarkably high. Zinner has estimated a probable error of $0^{m}.05$ for the magnitudes he derived from Seidel's catalogue [9]. As for Seidel, he described his work as follows:

> These observations undertaken with the Steinheil objective-photometer
> ... to the best of my knowledge form the first and at present still the
> only sequence of measurements which encompass systematically and
> completely the stars of one hemisphere down to a given brightness
> (namely to Argelander's class 3 · 4 inclusive), while they also include
> the brightest of those visible in the southern hemisphere as well as a
> number of fainter ones in the north (among them most of
> Argelander's stars of magnitude 4 · 3) [46].

Zöllner's photometry of 226 stars [37] has already been mentioned (section 3.3.3). His observations were primarily undertaken to test his instrument and demonstrate its capabilities. The results were presented as logarithmic intensities relative to the brightest star in each short series. Each series of observations generally comprised between three and six stars, and to be more useful, these different series would have to be merged into a single body of data in which the relative brightness of all the stars was explicitly given. This Zöllner himself did not accomplish, but such a reduction was later attempted by F. J. Dorst, but with only partial success [47]. He tried to link together the different series by assuming the constancy of Zöllner's lamp and by using stars they contained in common. Zinner also re-reduced Zöllner's observations, and estimated that the mean error of the magnitudes he obtained was $0^{m}.04$ when based on several independent settings of the analyser Nicol prism in the photometer [9].

In 1862 Zöllner moved to Leipzig, and here he published his detailed treatise *Photometric Studies, with special attention to the physical constitution of the heavenly bodies* [36]. In this work he concentrated largely on solar-system photometry, using his photometer, for example, to estimate the brightness ratio of the sun to the moon to be 618 000 (which was considerably too high). He also attempted a comparison of the sun with Capella (α Aurigae) and found a ratio of 5.576×10^{10}.

From Zöllner's figure for the ratio of the sun to Capella Müller later deduced a solar apparent magnitude of $m_\odot = -26.60$. He pointed out that, as the parallax and hence distance of Capella are fairly reliably known, the sun would be at a magnitude of $m_\odot = 6.5$ if it were at the same distance. Capella itself has $m = 0.27$, and so he concluded that 'the sun is a much smaller heavenly body than is α Aurigae' [7]. This is an early (but not the first) indication of the difference in magnitude between a giant (Capella) and a dwarf star (the sun), at a time before such differences became generally accepted through the work of Hertzsprung and others in the early twentieth century.

Among the earlier pioneers of stellar photometry, Julius Wolff (1827–96), the son-in-law of Argelander, also deserves a brief mention. He used a Zöllner photometer of 37-mm aperture to observe bright stars during the years 1869–83, at first from Palermo in Sicily, but later from his private observatory in Bonn. His two publications of 1877 [48] and 1884 [49] comprise the photometric results for respectively 475 and 1130 stars to magnitude about $5\frac{1}{2}$. These catalogues expressed the data as logarithmic intensities relative to the lamp in the photometer. According to Zinner, the results, when converted to magnitudes, have probable errors of $\pm 0^{\mathrm{m}}16$, which is not very precise and is about twice as large as Wolff himself had estimated. There are also substantial systematic errors in the sense that Wolff's brighter stars are too faint and his fainter ones too bright, which Müller ascribed to poor observational technique.

Finally we come to Charles Peirce (1839–1914), the American philosopher, astronomer and United States Coast Survey sea captain. Peirce observed at Harvard, also with a Zöllner photometer. He can be regarded as the first major American stellar photometrist, if the relatively less important contributions of G. P. Bond (see section 3.1) and George Searle (1839–1918) [50] at Harvard in 1860–61 are for this purpose ignored. Peirce made his pioneering photometric observations at Harvard and in Washington in the years 1871–75, when Winlock was the director of the Harvard College Observatory. His plan was to observe all the stars in Argelander's *Uranometria Nova* in the zone $+40°$ to $+50°$, and his catalogue contained magnitudes for 494 such objects.

Peirce's catalogue is notable in being the first photometric catalogue in which stellar magnitudes are explicitly obtained from the measured intensities, and it is also significant that he adopted a constant intensity ratio for a difference of one magnitude. His value corresponded to $\log R = 0.409$, chosen so as to give a good accord with the bright stars in the *Bonner Durchmusterung*. Peirce's value of the ratio is close to Pogson's proposal of $\log R = 0.400$, to which Peirce, however, makes no reference – see section 3.5.5.

Peirce claimed a probable error for his magnitudes of $\pm 0^m.09$. Zinner found a somewhat worse value of $\pm 0^m.13$ from an analysis of Peirce's data [9].

3.5   The development of the magnitude scale from visual photometry

3.5.1   *The concept of the intensity-magnitude relationship*

Early in the twentieth century visual photometry became practically an obsolete pursuit in the major observatories, while the use of photographic methods for stellar photometry rapidly increased. Today's astronomers make essentially no use of the many thousands of visual photometric magnitudes derived from the huge programmes at Harvard and Potsdam. But this era in astronomy still left what was at that time regarded as a useful and practical legacy – this was the development of the magnitude scale.

Although the magnitude scale was originally subjective and ill-defined, it had remained the principal tool for the estimation of the brightness of stars for about two thousand years, from the time of Ptolemy and possibly as early as Hipparchus, right through to the great works of the Bonn and Córdoba *Durchmusterungen*. The advent of visual photometry necessitated some refinements in the last few decades of this time span. These refinements were:

1. the recognition that the magnitude system could and should be a quantitative scale, not merely labels to categorize stars of differing lustre,
2. the consequent use of decimal subdivisions in the numerical magnitude estimates, and
3. the extension of the scale to telescopic stars of 9th or 10th magnitude, but with no guarantee that the intensity ratio pertaining to a one magnitude interval for naked-eye stars would be reliably preserved in the extrapolation to fainter objects.

In the later nineteenth century this arbitrary magnitude system, used in the *Bonner Durchmusterung* and elsewhere for simple visual estimates, was transformed into a relatively precisely defined quantitative scale relating the magnitudes assigned to any star to the intensity of the starlight received on earth. This was the most lasting achievement of the visual photometry.

To be sure, some astronomers (for example Wolff [51]) argued that this was not a necessary step, or that it was even a hindrance to progress. But they were a minority, soon swamped by the tide of what the overwhelming majority practised. What seems clear now in hindsight is that it is hard to imagine how photographic photometry, which is far more susceptible to systematic errors than is visual photometry, might have developed if the visual magnitude scale had not first been established, and a large number of stars measured using this system.

The essence of a magnitude system is the mathematical relationship between the magnitude m and the intensity of the starlight I, or strictly speaking the stellar flux received at the earth in the visual wavelength band.

The system of stellar magnitudes was of course introduced by Hipparchus and Ptolemy as an arbitrary scale of visual sensation. In his *Traité d'Optique* Bouguer had considered that a relationship between sensory visual perception and intensity might exist, but he was not able to specify its form [2]. However, some evidence that the relationship might be logarithmic is implicit in the eighteenth century observations of both Flamsteed and Celsius. Flamsteed in his *Historia Coelestis Britannica* of 1725 found the same magnitude difference between two stars observed telescopically as for these stars observed with the naked eye, the value being independent of the telescope aperture [52]. A similar result was obtained by Celsius and his pupil Tulenius [8] when they inserted absorbing glass plates into the optical path of their telescope, and found that one plate corresponded to half a magnitude, irrespective of the brightness of the star – see section 3.2. Both these experiments imply a relationship in which magnitude is a logarithmic function of intensity, though this was not explicitly stated.†

There also exists a remarkable statement by Edmund Halley (1656–1742) in 1720 that at first sight appears to be prescient of the Pogson ratio proposed over a century later. For Halley clearly stated that sixth magnitude stars are one hundred times fainter than those of first magnitude, when he considered the effect of placing a star at ten times its actual distance,

---

† If the relationship is written $m = f(I)$ then $\Delta m = m_1 - m_2 = f(I_1) - f(I_2)$. If the intensity is changed by a given factor k then $\Delta m' = f(kI_1) - f(kI_2)$. The observation that $\Delta m = \Delta m'$ implies that f is a logarithmic function of the form $m = A \log I + B$ or $I = cR^{-m}$, where R is the intensity ratio of two stars whose magnitudes differ by one.

> ... which distance may perhaps diminish the light of any of the Stars
> of the first magnitude to that of the sixth, it being but the hundredth
> part of what, at their present distance, they appear with [53].

This statement was written even before the principles of practical photometry were enunciated by Bouguer and at a time when the concept of an intensity-magnitude relationship was nebulous or non-existent.

3.5.2   The Herschels and the intensity-magnitude relationship

Both William and John Herschel had tried to deduce the form of the magnitude-intensity relationship. William Herschel investigated this empirically by stopping down the aperture of his telescope by a known amount and then comparing the bright stars so observed with fainter ones with the full aperture. But his result was $I \propto 1/m^2$. This law implies that stars of magnitude m are m times as far away as those of first magnitude. Herschel soon saw that this relationship, together with the different numbers of stars observed at each magnitude, would give an implausible distribution of stars in space, the stellar density increasing with distance [10].

The question of the magnitude-intensity relationship was taken up again by John Herschel in his *Outlines of Astronomy* [54]. He wrote that

> ... astronomers had not yet agreed upon any principle by which the
> magnitudes may be photometrically classed *a priori*, whether for
> example a scale of brightnesses decreasing in geometrical progression
> should be adopted [equivalent to a logarithmic law], ... or whether it
> would not be preferable to adopt a scale decreasing as the squares of
> the terms of an harmonic progression [the $I \propto 1/m^2$ relation].

He decided that the actual magnitude scale in use lies somewhere between these two suggestions. But, in spite of his father's apparent difficulties with the harmonic progression, he concluded:

> We have no hesitation in adopting, and recommending others to
> adopt, the latter system in preference to the former. The conventional
> magnitudes actually in use among astronomers ... conforms [sic]
> moreover very much more nearly to this than to the geometrical
> progression [54, pp. 521–2].

John Herschel's own views on the matter had changed since 1829, when he came to the opposite conclusion to that expressed in the *Outlines of Astronomy*, preferring then the geometrical progression (that is, logarithmic law) over the the $1/m^2$ relation [55]. In practice neither Herschel had adequate photometrically measured intensities at his disposal to resolve the issue of how the visual magnitude scale was related to the stellar intensities.

3.5.3 Steinheil's logarithmic law

Steinheil in 1836 was certainly the first person explicitly to deduce the logarithmic form for the magnitude-intensity relation, which he was able to do from secure photometric observations [33]. With his prism photometer (see section 3.4) he measured the diameters of out-of-focus stellar images in his telescope, which were adjusted for equal surface brightness. He then showed that the logarithm of the diameters is a linear function of stellar magnitude, and gave the linear coefficients. From this relation he was able to derive the first empirical value for R, the intensity ratio for two stars that differ by one magnitude, using the fact that I was proportional to the area of the out-of-focus images in his photometer. His result was $R = I_m/I_{m+1} = 2.831$, a value which, however, he did not regard as being reliably determined [33].

3.5.4 The Weber-Fechner psychophysical law

The logarithmic law's physiological basis was explained by G. T. Fechner (1801–87) in Leipzig in the 1850s. Fechner extended the experiments of his senior colleague E. H. Weber (1795–1878) (brother of the renowned physicist of electromagnetism) from the aural and tactile senses to that of visual perception. Weber and Fechner were thus the founders of psychophysics, and the Weber-Fechner law relates the just perceptible differences in a stimulus to the stimulus itself. When applied to the visual sense, the stimulus is the intensity I. The law then states that $\Delta I/I$ is a constant, implying that the smallest just perceptible intensity increment is itself proportional to the intensity.

Fechner applied this law explicitly to stellar magnitudes [56]. It follows that $\Delta I/I$ must be proportional to Δm, the smallest perceptible magnitude increment. On integration this becomes a logarithmic relation between the sensation (in the stellar case this is the magnitude) and the intensity, namely

$$m = -k \log I + c,$$

where k and c are constants.

The basic principles of the new science of psychophysics were expounded in Fechner's treatise *Elemente der Psychophysik* in 1860 [57]. In this book he attempted to deduce the value of the scaling constant k in the magnitude-intensity relationship, which is related to the intensity ratio R corresponding to a one magnitude step by $\log R = 1/k$. Fechner's value for k was 2.854, resulting in $R = 2.241$.

Although the Weber-Fechner law appeared to give a physiological explanation for the logarithmic relationship between magnitudes and intensities found by Steinheil, it should still be remembered that the law is nonetheless no more than an empirical statement derived from laboratory observations of illuminated surfaces rather than star-like points. Its applicability to the astronomical situation is therefore not automatically guaranteed. Even the fundamental basis of the law itself has been criticized, on the grounds that the concept of a visual sensation has never had an adequate quantitative definition for its use in an exact mathematical relationship.

3.5.5   Pogson's proposal

Norman Pogson (1829–91) will always have a special place in the history of astronomical photometry, even though his fame has arisen from relatively peripheral addenda to two papers, one on the history of light variations in 53 known variable stars [58, see p. 295], the other on magnitude predictions for 36 minor planets [59]. In both of these papers he proposed adopting a light ratio R of 2.512 for two stars that differ in brightness by one magnitude.

In the first paper he wrote:

> I adopted 2.512 for convenience of calculation, the reciprocal of
> +log.R, a constant continually occurring in photometric formulae,
> being in this case exactly 5. There is also another advantage in this
> ratio; for in a common table of logarithms, if the natural numbers are
> supposed to represent the aperture of a telescope, expressed in inches,
> five times the corresponding logarithm, will be the excess of
> penetration of such aperture, over an aperture of one inch [58].

He further justified his use of this ratio by citing the earlier attempts to determine it, due to M. J. Johnson, C. A. von Steinheil, S. Stampfer and others (see Table 3.1). The mean of all these earlier references is given by Pogson as 2.545, a value very close to the one that he adopted for reasons of computational convenience. Pogson's second paper [59] essentially repeats the same proposal without adding further substance to it.

Pogson thereafter continued to use the $\log R = 0.4$ value for his calculations – see for example [67]. Christie referred to it briefly in 1874 [68]. But it was not until Pickering used it from 1879 (which he did so with even less discussion or justification than Pogson had done), that the Pogson value became generally accepted into astronomical photometry [39, see p. vi].

However, the strongest support for Pogson came from Müller at Potsdam:

> Astronomers since the time of Ptolemy have been used to express
> intensities in magnitudes. In addition we will be dependent for a long
> time yet for the majority of stars on the magnitude estimates of the

Fig. 3.6 Norman Pogson.

BD and other catalogues, so the introduction of a completely new scale would have met objections. It therefore meets with all approval, that Pickering has retained the stellar magnitude system. According to his proposals, one understands by one photometric magnitude the intensity difference of two stars for which the logarithm of the intensity ratio is equal to 0.4 [7, see p. 446].

Table 3.1. *Determinations and proposals for the light intensity ratio R*

Date	Author	R	k	D or P	Reference	Remarks
1829	J. Herschel	2.551	2.458	D	[55]	
"	"	2.00	3.321	P	"	Adopted for telescopic stars
1836	C. A. von Steinheil	2.831	2.213	D	[33]	
1837	F. G. W. Struve	2.890	2.170	D	[60]	
"	"	4.00	1.661	P	"	Adopted for telescopic stars
1851	S. Stampfer	2.494	2.520	D	[61]	
1853	M. J. Johnson	2.358	2.684	D	[62]	78 stars $m = 4$ to 10
1856	N. R. Pogson	2.512	2.500	P	[58, 59]	Pogson's proposal
1857	R. C. Carrington	2.747	2.279	D	[63]	
1860	G. T. Fechner	2.241	2.854	D	[57]	
1862	P. L. Seidel	2.8606	2.1908	D	[45]	
1862	K. Bruhns	2.718	2.303	P	[45]	Reported by Seidel (1862)
1865	F. Zöllner	2.755	2.272	D	[36]	293 stars $m = 1$ to 6
1866	P. L. Seidel and E. Leonhard	2.203	2.915	D	[46]	For bright stars, $m = 2$ to 4
"	"		2.857	2.193	D	"	For fainter stars to $m = 6$
1870	P. G. Rosén	2.470	2.546	D	[64]	110 BD stars, $m = 5$ to 9.5
1878	C. S. Peirce	2.339	2.710	D	[65]	Recalculation of Rosén's value by least squares with same data
1888	E. Lindemann	2.421	2.604	D	[66]	BD stars $m = 3$ to 9

Note: D: determination; P: proposal.

The adoption of Pogson's proposal at both Harvard and Potsdam, the two most prominent observatories in the new field of astrophysics, took the steam out of much of the debate on the magnitude scale. A general desire for uniformity between different observers must have been a major motive. However, Pogson's was not the only proposal for adopting a universal value of R. Karl Bruhns (1830–81) is reported to have favoured setting R equal to e, the base of natural logarithms, which would at least have conferred a certain mathematical elegance to stellar photometry! (reported by L. Seidel [45] – see also [69]).

On the Pogson scale adopted by Pickering and others the relationship $m = -2.5 \log I + c$ contains a minus sign, which signifies that higher intensities correspond to smaller magnitudes. This legacy from Ptolemy did not meet with universal favour. In particular Fechner wanted no such complications, and he criticized

> ... the inverted direction in which stellar magnitudes and intensities progress in relation to each other, which has proved to be extremely uncomfortable for the determination of the relationship between these two quantities [56].

Even as late as 1920 the eminent British physicist Oliver Lodge (1851–1940) was asking 'whether it is not time to overhaul and improve the conventional specification of stellar magnitudes?' [70]. His objections were typical of the physicist who preferred a more rational system, in which fainter stars would be represented by smaller numbers, and he derided the astronomers' use of negative values for the brightest stars. But nothing ever came of such pleas.

In view of the comparative obscurity of Pogson, a few remarks concerning him are appropriate. He worked as an assistant at the Radcliffe Observatory, Oxford under Manuel Johnson for eight years from 1852 before taking up a brief appointment as director of Dr John Lee's Hartwell House Observatory in 1859. By 1860 Pogson had accepted a position as director of the Madras Observatory and he spent the years 1861–91 continuously in India until his death. His interests were in variable stars and minor planets, and he added about 20 new discoveries of the former and eight of the latter to astronomical knowledge. A brief discussion of his work on the magnitude scale was given by Derek Jones in 1968 [71].

In addition to this proposal, there have been numerous attempts to measure the ratio R, as well as several suggestions advocating the adoption of different values from that of Pogson. Table 3.1 summarizes this work. The values in the table differ widely, because different samples of stars and estimated magnitudes for different catalogues were used and compared with photometric intensities from different observers and instruments.

Even after the Pogson ratio had been adopted at Harvard, Oxford and Potsdam, this did not signal an end to determinations of the value of the ratio R. A discussion by Seth Chandler from Harvard in 1886, for example, showed large variations in $\log R$ for the magnitudes in Argelander's *Uranometria Nova*, depending on whose photometry was used for the intensities. All analyses, however, found $\log R$ to fall from about 0.7 for the brightest stars to about 0.3 at $m = 6$ [72].

As fainter stars were observed, especially using photography, it was important to ensure that the extrapolation of the magnitude scale adhered closely to the Pogson ratio. Systematic errors dependent on magnitude represent deviations from the Pogson scale, and their elimination became a matter of vital concern to stellar photometrists. As recently as 1969 E. E. Mendoza and T. Gomez published an extensive analysis of Harvard and Potsdam visual photometries in comparison with photoelectric magnitudes, and found that the deviation from the adopted Pogson scale was not large in either case [73].

3.5.6   The zero-point of the magnitude scale

The benefit of unifying all photometry on the Pogson scale was two-fold. First, all future photometric magnitudes from different observatories should be at least approximately comparable. Secondly, the utility of magnitude results from past work, especially those of the BD, was more or less preserved for posterity, because the Pogson scale did not differ greatly from that already used by most observers.

Apart from the value of R, which in turn fixes k $(= 1/\log R)$ in the equation $m = -k \log I + c$, the other important parameter is the constant c. This too can have any arbitrary value, and was normally fixed by referring the magnitudes to that of a standard star. In Pickering's early Harvard photometry, this was taken to be Polaris, the Pole Star, fixed at $m_0 = 2.0$, giving $(m - m_0) = -k \log(I/I_0)$, where the zero subscript refers to the standard.

On the other hand, Müller, instead of using just one star, linked his zero-point to the BD scale, by ensuring that the mean magnitudes of the 144 PD standards were 6.0 in both the BD and PD photometries. He wrote:

> It is not to be doubted, that the BD, as by far the most complete catalogue of stellar magnitudes, will be the indispensable source for brightness data for a long time yet. It is therefore desirable, that newly appearing photometric catalogues which are planned as replacements of the BD, should in so far as possible be linked to the BD system [74, p. 116].

Pickering's choice of the magnitude of the Pole Star at $m = 2.0$ was later revised to $2^{m}\!.15$ [40], then $2^{m}\!.12$ [75]. These values, however, resulted in agreement of the BD and HP scales at approximately $m = 4$ and $m = 8$ [76]. The Pole Star was only used as the primary standard for the early work at Harvard. The scale of the *Harvard Photometry* was in practice tied to a zero-point defined by 100 circumpolar stars of around fifth magnitude, so that any variability in the Pole Star itself would have negligible effect on the results for other stars [40, see p. 35]. The fact that Polaris is indeed a variable went undetected during the Harvard visual observations; its variability was suspected by L. Seidel in 1852 [44] and confirmed by E. Hertzsprung in

1911 [77], who discovered a $0^m.171$ photographic amplitude for the sinusoidal variation of period 3.96 days.

D. B. Herrmann has given a table of Polaris magnitudes derived from different sources of visual photometry [69]. Thus Ptolemy and Flamsteed both assigned this star to magnitude 3^m, Argelander (in the BD) to $2^m.0$, Pritchard to $2^m.05$ and Müller and Kempf (in the PD) to $2^m.34$.

3.6 Three great photometric catalogues of the late nineteenth century

The pioneering observations of Seidel, Zöllner, Wolff and Peirce established visual photometry as a viable method of acquiring data on stellar intensities and showed that the random errors of magnitude estimates could be reduced by a factor of 2 or 3 using these new techniques. The work that followed by Pickering, Pritchard and Müller turned visual stellar photometry into a major astronomical industry. It was nevertheless a short-lived one, as the new methods of photographic photometry were to be increasingly used in the final years of the century.

3.6.1 Pickering's Harvard Photometry

The *Harvard Photometry* was Pickering's first major programme after becoming director of Harvard College Observatory in Cambridge, Massachusetts in February 1877. His whole subsequent astronomical career was to be dominated by huge programmes of data collection, in visual photometry, in spectral classification and in photographic photometry. During his forty-two years in the Harvard directorship he never compromised his belief that it was first necessary to assemble the facts relating to a large number of stars, so that subsequently the statistical basis might exist from which sound theories could be built.

The aim of the *Harvard Photometry* was to observe all the naked-eye stars north of $-30°$ with the 4-cm (1.6-inch) meridian photometer [40]. The total was 4260 stars, and the observational programme comprised nearly 95 000 comparisons of these objects with the Pole Star. A major observational effort was required. Pickering himself undertook most of this, with the assistance of Oliver Wendell (1845–1912) and Arthur Searle (1837–1920) between October 1879 and September 1882.

The main features of the programme were as follows:

    1. All stars were compared directly with the Pole Star, which was

initially assumed to be of magnitude 2.0. Subsequently this was corrected to 2.15 at the zenith, as a result of taking atmospheric extinction into account and in order to bring the magnitude scale into good accordance with that of Argelander's visual estimates.

2. To check the constancy of the Pole Star, 100 circumpolar stars between declinations $+60°$ and $+75°$ were used as secondary standards.

3. Atmospheric extinction was taken into account using a constant extinction coefficient of $0^m\!.25$ per unit air mass. All magnitudes were thereby reduced to unit air mass or zenith values. The circumpolar stars at upper and lower culminations were used for deriving the extinction coefficient.

4. The Pole Star was also compared with itself at the beginning, middle and end of each series of observations, in order to correct for the differences between the two objectives and reflecting prisms.

5. Perhaps the most important innovation was the adoption of the Pogson scale of magnitudes, in which a difference of one magnitude corresponds to a fixed intensity ratio R, with $\log R$ exactly equal to 0.4. Pickering had in fact used the 0.4 factor as early as 1879 in the reduction of the photometry with the early polarizing photometers on the 15-inch refractor [39, see p.vi], and this became the standard for all subsequent photometric work at Harvard and elsewhere.

According to Zinner, the precision of the *Harvard Photometry* (hereinafter HP) was $\pm 0^m\!.08$ (probable error) for the mean magnitude quoted for the brighter stars ($m < 4$) and $\pm 0^m\!.10$ for the fainter ones [9]. The corresponding values for single observations were respectively $\pm 0^m\!.23$ and $\pm 0^m\!.22$. It is true that the precision of one observation was not much better than a good naked-eye magnitude estimate. The advantage of the Harvard measurements over estimates lay in the elimination of subjective factors leading to systematic errors. Successive independent measurements on the same star can be averaged to improve the precision of the mean, whereas magnitude estimates are not so amenable to such processing, as the errors tend to be statistically correlated.

The second part of the *Harvard Photometry* [41] contained extensive comparisons of the HP magnitudes with those in the ancient catalogues of Ptolemy and al-Sûfi, with the work on sequences by both the Herschels and with all the important bright star magnitude estimates made in the nineteenth century, including those of Argelander, Heis, Behrmann, Gould and Houzeau, as well as the early photometry of Seidel, Zöllner, Wolff and Peirce and some of the preliminary wedge photometry of Pritchard in Oxford.

Such was the size and scope of these comparisons that Pritchard's assistant at Oxford, William Plummer, wrote:

> The publication of the entire work is complete; and a careful
> examination of the whole ... will show that the reputation this
> observatory had acquired under the direction of Bond, Winlock, and
> Peirce has been sustained and extended. The scheme of the director,
> assisted by a staff of unusual extent, has apparently not only embraced
> the production of a *Uranometria* the most complete and the most
> elaborate that has yet appeared, but to collect within a moderate
> compass the results of all that is most valuable and interesting yet
> accomplished in this branch of astronomy [78].

Thomas Lewis at the Royal Greenwich Observatory also praised Pickering's great industry and considered that the work 'must henceforth be regarded as at once the foundation and treasury of scientific stellar photometry' [79]. On the other hand Gustav Müller at Potsdam was more critical of the Harvard measurements:

> The *Harvard Photometry* includes all the stars to sixth magnitude and
> also a large number of fainter ones between the North Pole and about
> 30° southern declination. The principle of the instrument employed is
> that intensities are deduced during meridian passage of the stars by
> comparison with the Pole Star. This procedure is so simple, and as a
> result the reduction of the observations is made so easy, that the
> method is not to be fully recommended if attaining the highest
> accuracy is the aim. This comes mainly from the difficulty in
> determining the influence of the extinction, which results ... not only
> from the different altitude of both the stars being compared, but also
> arises from their azimuth difference. It happens not infrequently, that
> on apparently quite clear nights, the transparency is substantially
> different in different regions of the sky, such that local effects can play
> a major role. A condition for the very best photometric measurements
> is the close proximity of the two objects under comparison, and it is
> just this condition which is completely ignored in Pickering's procedure
> [7, see p. 446].

A little further on Müller remarked on the rather high proportion of discrepant observations in the *Harvard Photometry*, revealed by stars whose individual measurements diverged widely from the mean:

> It is hardly to be wondered that such mistakes occur frequently, given
> the very great speed with which the Cambridge photometric
> measurements have been undertaken. This is a criticism which cannot
> be withheld from works of such influence, and unfortunately it
> somewhat detracts from the trust in its reliability [7].

He is, however, full of praise for Pickering's choice of the Pogson scale (see section 3.5.5), which Müller and Kempf also adopted in their Potsdam photometry. Extensive criticisms of Pickering's work were also expressed by J. T. Wolff, who went one step further and refused to accept the use of magnitudes at all in photometric astronomy [51].

3.6.2   *Pritchard's* Uranometria Nova Oxoniensis

Professor Charles Pritchard, with his assistants W. E. Plummer (1849–1929) and B. C. Jenkins began a programme of wedge photometry of the naked-eye stars from Oxford in 1881 using two wedge photometers on 3- and 4-inch telescopes. The observations were made between December 1881 and October 1885 from Oxford and Cairo, mainly by Plummer and Jenkins, and encompassed 2784 of the bright stars north of −10° which had appeared in Argelander's *Uranometria Nova*. The choice of Egypt for the more southerly stars was to avoid observing at greater than 60° zenith distance. The site chosen was at Abbaseeyeh, on the border of the desert, about three miles from Cairo, and Pritchard remarked that 'a more advantageous, and I may add a more pleasant, place for astronomical observation it would scarcely be possible to find' [22]. The productivity of the Egyptian site proved to be more than three times that of Oxford as a result of the clearer skies.

Pritchard published a preliminary catalogue of 535 stars in 1883, a year in advance of Pickering's *Harvard Photometry* [22]. The main catalogue, with the title *Uranometria Nova Oxoniensis*, followed in 1885 [23]. Like Pickering, he adopted the Pogson magnitude scale ($\log R = 0.400$) and he also used Polaris as a primary standard. However, the zero-point corresponding to m(Polaris) = 2.05 (at the zenith) was chosen, which is a tenth of a magnitude brighter than Pickering's value. Atmospheric extinction was carefully allowed for to reduce all magnitudes to their zenith values. At Oxford the mean extinction coefficient of $0^m.253$ per unit air mass was measured and used for all the reductions of the Oxford observations, while at Cairo it was less at $0^m.187$, a result which Pritchard ascribed to 'a real difference in climate' [22].

At Harvard Pickering made a careful study of the magnitude differences between the *Harvard Photometry* and the Oxford photometry. Although the Pole Star was adopted by Pritchard as being $0^m.1$ brighter than Pickering's value, the Oxford magnitudes were nevertheless on average $0^m.05$ fainter for those stars in common to both works. This systematic difference depended somewhat on the brightness of the stars considered, being greatest at third and fourth magnitude [80].

Once again, much harsher criticism of the Oxford work came from Müller at Potsdam:

> This whole observing procedure would at first glance appear to evoke trust, especially because the influence of the personal equation, as well as possible errors in the determination of the wedge constant, have been substantially reduced. Nevertheless it is much to be regretted that

Fig. 3.7 Rev. Charles Pritchard.

by far the greatest part of the stars has been observed on only one evening (of 2786 stars in this catalogue, only 262 were measured more than once) [81].

Pritchard claimed a precision for his whole catalogue of less than a thirteenth of a magnitude, a result not supported by the more recent analysis of Zinner, who could ascribe a probable error of no better than $\pm 0^{m}.19$ for the Oxford results [9].

Fig. 3.8   Gustav Müller.

3.6.3   *The* Potsdamer Durchmusterung

Gustav Müller (1851–1925) at the Potsdam Astrophysical Observatory began observations with his Zöllner photometer as early as 1877. This is in the same year as Pickering began his experiments with photometry at Harvard and it was also several years before Pritchard began his photometric work. However, Müller's early investigations from 1877 to 1888 were concentrated on observations of the brightness of planets and asteroids [82]. By the time he commenced a systematic survey with Paul Kempf (1856–1920) of all the brighter ($m < 7.5$) northern *Bonner Durchmusterung* (BD) stars in 1886, both the *Harvard Photometry* and the *Uranometria Nova Oxoniensis* had already been published.

The *Potsdamer Durchmusterung* (PD) which resulted was the most extensive of these three catalogues, comprising 14 199 stars in the *Bonner Durchmusterung*. It was also the most precise, as Müller and Kempf had gone to extraordinary care to minimize random errors. The work was published in four volumes in 1894, 1899, 1903 and 1906 [74, 83, 84, 85] as the observations progressed (over the years 1886 to 1905), with a final *General Catalogue* being published for all the stars in 1907 [86]. Yet even by the time of publication of the first of these volumes, Pickering

Fig. 3.9 **Paul Kempf.**

and Wendell at Harvard had issued a meridian photometric catalogue containing measurements on nearly 21 000 BD stars [87] – see section 3.7.2. Although the Potsdam observers had achieved a superior level of precision and although their work was generally characterized by a greater degree of care and thoroughness than found in the Harvard photometry, the quantity of Pickering's photometric output and the overall scientific scope that his work encompassed consistently outperformed his German competitors.

For the *Potsdamer Durchmusterung* four objectives of various sizes were used in conjunction with the Potsdam Zöllner photometer, which was made by the firm of Wanscheff in Berlin. The apertures were between 67 and 135 mm. A network of 144 standard stars across the sky was established. Stars were observed in blocks of twelve closely neighbouring objects by comparing each of these with at least two standard stars within a short time span. Every star was observed independently by both Müller and Kempf and elaborate procedures were adopted to ensure that any effects due to the personal equation of the observers were minimized. Extreme care was also taken with the atmospheric extinction corrections (magnitudes were all reduced to the zenith), and in addition the colours of all the stars were estimated on a seven-point scale, so that the colour equation of the observers could be carefully studied. The Müller-Kempf colour scale placed, stars in the categories W, WG, GW, G, RG, GR and R (corresponding to white, whitish-yellow, yellowish-white ... red), with the additional suffixes of + (a bit redder) or − (a bit bluer) to indicate intermediate positions on the scale.

The PD was, like the other major catalogues, based on the Pogson scale ($\log R = 0.400$). Whereas Pickering had first implemented this scale in 1879 with the sole justification that 'the computation is simple and the true brightness is readily determined from it' [39, see p. i], Müller and Kempf on the other hand went to some pains to explain the use of this scale and to place its use in an historical context. They wrote:

> Now it is becoming urgently necessary to strive for a uniformity of notation and to fix once and for all the concept of the photometric magnitude. The *Harvard Photometry* and the *Uranometria Nova Oxoniensis* have shown the way by their good example and have introduced throughout their work the number 0.4, as proposed earlier by Pogson, for the logarithm of the brightness ratio of two consecutive photometric magnitudes. This is about the mean value of all determinations cited above, and on account of its ease of computation, it is especially to be recommended. Since there is no reason to replace any one concept of photometric magnitude so defined with any other, we have therefore likewise made use of this same value. It is to be hoped to the utmost degree, that this concept from now on be definitively introduced into all photometry [74].

The zero-point of the PD scale, however, differed significantly from either the HP or Oxford measurements, and was chosen so that the mean magnitude of the 144 PD standard stars, which had BD magnitudes lying between 4.5 and 7.3, was for both the PD and BD scales equal to 6.0. This convention placed the Potsdam values significantly fainter than those from Harvard, according to Zinner by amounts ranging from $0^{m}_{.}13$ to $0^{m}_{.}21$, the mean difference being about $0^{m}_{.}17$ [9].

If Müller was most complimentary to Pickering on the latter's choice of the Pogson scale, he was less kind when it came to discussing the precision of the Harvard photometry. First he noted that 53 stars measured at Harvard differed by more than half a magnitude from the Potsdam measurements [74, see p. 501]. Pickering, who was only on rare occasions provoked into polemics with his peers, was unfortunately tempted into publishing a rebuttal in the first volume of the *Astrophysical Journal* [88]. From an analysis of only the most discrepant stars he concluded that the Harvard photometry was actually more precise than that from Potsdam. His statistical reasoning was decidedly suspect, and he was also unwise to point out that on average only 18 stars per night were observed at Potsdam as against more than 100 at Harvard, implying a yet greater increase in the precision of the Harvard magnitudes when these were based on the mean magnitude of a star measured many times.

Müller and Kempf had the last word in this acerbic exchange [89]. Having demolished Pickering's faulty statistical analysis they went on:

> The most reliable criterion for the excellence of photometric observations is afforded by the agreement by the values obtained on different evenings for the brightness of the same star. That the probable error $0^{m}.15$ of one observation in the *Harvard Photometry* is rather large may be seen from the fact that the same error for the Potsdam measures is $0^{m}.06$. The number of observations for each star at Cambridge is not so much greater than at Potsdam as to reduce the large uncertainty of the separate measurements to approximate equality in the final results. The average probable error of a catalogue brightness is for Cambridge $\pm 0^{m}.075$ and for Potsdam $\pm 0^{m}.040$ [89].

They then went on:

> We must again emphasize the opinion which we have already expressed in our *Durchmusterung* that the Cambridge measurements have been made in far too great haste to exclude the possibility of frequent erroneous identifications of stars ... We cannot regard as advantageous the measurement by one and the same observer of 63 stars in 59 minutes ... it is quite unavoidable that when observations are made with such haste as this, the quality of the results must suffer in a not inconsiderable degree [89].

These values for the precision were admittedly changed slightly in the fourth volume of the PD, where Müller and Kempf quote $\pm 0^{m}.052$ as the probable error of a mean magnitude in their catalogue. Zinner has compared the probable errors in the HP, the PD and Pritchard's *Uranometria Nova Oxoniensis* (UNO), both for one observation and also for the mean published magnitudes [9]. His results were:

Catalogue	p.e. (one observation)	mean error
HP	0.22	0.10
PD	0.086	0.052
UNO	—	0.19

There seems little doubt about who won this particular argument.

3.7   From the HP to the *Revised Harvard Photometry and beyond*

3.7.1   *Summary of main visual photometric programmes at Harvard*

The *Harvard Photometry* (HP) of 4260 stars in 1884 was no more than the first major catalogue of a huge programme in visual stellar photometry directed by Pickering and carried out between 1876 and 1913. This programme absorbed as much time and manpower as the equally extensive Henry Draper Memorial in spectral classification, and Pickering was personally involved on many nights as a photometric observer. In this programme he was assisted principally by Arthur Searle, Oliver Wendell and Solon Bailey (1854–1931).

The photometric programmes directed by Pickering can be classified into several distinct phases. The first phase was largely experimental and involved polarizing photometers on the 15-inch refractor [39]. Then followed from 1879, the meridian photometry, first with the 4.0-cm instrument (usually called the 2-inch meridian photometer at Harvard), which was used for the *Harvard Photometry*, but after 1882 the larger 4-inch meridian photometer was used. Zinner [9] has classified the various catalogues compiled from observations with these two meridian photometers in tabular form as shown in Table 3.2.

In order to reach fainter stars than those of tenth magnitude, Pickering built a 12-inch meridian photometer in 1898. The principle of operation was somewhat different from the earlier meridian instruments. The light from an artificial star was dimmed by an optical wedge to bring it to equality with that of the real star – see section 3.3.4. The major work with this instrument was the observation of selected BD and SD stars in order to recalibrate the faint end of the Bonn magnitude scale [42].

For 12 years Pickering was the sole observer with the 12-inch meridian photometer. Between October 1898 and September 1910 he personally put in over 1500 nights of photometric observing, an incredible endurance record considering the major work-load he carried as director of one of the world's leading astrophysical institutions.

Finally, a modification of the 12-inch meridian photometer was a wedge photometer suitable for mounting on other telescopes. It operated in a similar manner to the 12-inch instrument in that it comprised an artificial star dimmed by a movable wedge. This instrument, known as the Rumford photometer, was used for a number of small programmes by Bailey in Peru from 1902–08 and at the Cape in 1909 [96].

Table 3.2. *Harvard meridian photometry, 1879–1906*

Designation	Principal observers	Years	Dec. range	Aperture	Comp. star	Ref.
PiI	Pickering	1879–82	+90° to −30°	4.0 cm	α UMi	[40, 41]
PiII	Pickering and Wendell	1882–88	+90° to −40°	10.5 cm	λ UMi	[90, 87, 76]
PiIII	Pickering	1891–94	+90° to −47°	10.5 cm	λ UMi	[91, 92]
PiIV	Pickering	1895–98	+90° to −47°	10.5 cm	λ UMi	[93]
BaI	Bailey	1889–91	−30° to −90°	10.5 cm	σ Oct	[94]
BaII	Bailey	1899	0° to −90°	10.5 cm	σ Oct	[95]
BaIII	Bailey	1900–02	+90° to −40°	10.5 cm	λ UMi	[95]
BaIV	Bailey	1902–06	+50° to −90°	10.5 cm	σ Oct	[75]

Because of the multiplicity of visual photometric programmes at Harvard between 1878 and 1910, the following table (Table 3.3) has been drawn up to show the principal publications appearing in the *Annals of the Harvard College Observatory* on this subject by Pickering and his colleagues.

3.7.2 The revision of the BD with the 4-inch meridian photometer

The small 1.6-inch meridian photometer was unsuitable for observations on stars fainter than about magnitude 7 and hence the larger 4-inch instrument was built and mounted early in 1882 in order to reach ninth or tenth magnitude. The method of observation with the 4-inch was very similar to that of the 1.6-inch, except that λ Ursae Minoris was now used as the comparison object. This was a $6^{m}_{\cdot}4$ red star about a degree from the celestial pole and more suitable than the Pole Star for comparisons with the fainter stars now planned [87].

One of the major programmes with the new photometer between 1882 and 1888 was the revision of the *Bonner Durchmusterung* (BD) by Pickering and Wendell [87]. This work comprised the photometric observation of nearly 21 000 stars in the *Bonner* and *Bonn Southern Durchmusterungen* between the pole and −20°. The stars were selected in narrow zones every 5° in declination and the results were used for a careful analysis of the scale of the BD [76]. Atmospheric extinction was treated in the same way as in the *Harvard Photometry*, using a constant coefficient of $0^{m}_{\cdot}25$ per unit air mass and correcting all stars to the zenith. The title *Revision of the BD* is possibly

Table 3.3. *Visual photometry in the Harvard Annals published 1878–1913*

	Author	Reference	*Harvard Ann.*	Notes
1.	C. S. Peirce	[65]	**9**, 1 (1878)	Observations with Zöllner photometer, 1872–75
2.	E. C. Pickering, A. Searle and W. Upton	[39]	**11** (Parts 1 and 2), 1 (1879)	Early observations with Nicol prism photometer
3.	E. C. Pickering, A.Searle and O. C. Wendell	[40]	**14** (Part 1), 1 (1884)	*Harvard Photometry* (PiI), observations with 1.6-in meridian photometer 1879–82
3a.	"	[41]	**14** (Part 2), 325 (1885)	Compares HP with earlier mags. in literature
4.	E. C. Pickering and O. C. Wendell	[90]	**23** (Part 1), 1 (1890)	4-inch meridian photometry 1882–88 (PiII)
4a.	"	[87]	**24**, 1 (1890)	Observations for *Revision of the BD* (PiII)
4b.	"	[76]	**23** (Part 2), 137 (1899)	Compares 4-inch meridian photometry with photometry by Gould, Argelander, Wm. Herschel
5.	S. I. Bailey and E. C. Pickering	[94]	**34**, 1 (1895)	Catalogue of 7922 S. stars observed 1889–91 (BaI)
6.	E. C. Pickering	[91]	**44** (Part 1), 1 (1899)	Photometric revision of the HP 1891–94 (RHP = PiIII)
6a.	"	[92]	**44** (Part 2), 111 (1902)	4-inch meridian photometry 1892–98
6b.	"	[75]	**50**, 1 (1908)	*Revised Harvard Photometry*, uses observations by Bailey to extend the RHP to 9110 stars brighter than 6.50 over whole sky. Gives positions, visual magnitudes and spectral types (BaIV)
7.	E. C. Pickering	[93]	**45**, 1 (1901)	A photometric Durchmusterung including all stars $m \leq 7.5$, dec N. of $-40°$ (PiIV)
8.	S. I. Bailey	[95]	**46** (Part 1), 1 (1903)	4-inch meridian photometer observations by Bailey in both hemispheres (BaII, BaIII)
8a.	E. C. Pickering	[97]	**46** (Part 2), 121 (1904)	Observations of variable stars, 1892–98

Table 3.3. *continued*

Author	Reference	Harvard Ann.	Notes
9. E. C. Pickering	[98]	**54**, 1 (1908)	Catalogue of 36 682 stars fainter than 6.50 observed with 4-inch meridian photometer, supplement to RHP
10. E. C. Pickering	[99]	**64** (No. 1), 1 (1912)	Meridian photometric observations 1902–06
10a. "	[100]	**64** (No. 4), 91 (1912)	Discussion of RHP
10b. "	[101]	**64** (No. 6), 159 (1912)	Magnitudes of double star components
10c. "	[102]	**64** (No. 7), 191 (1912)	Meridian photometric observations 1907–08
10d. "	[103]	**64** (No. 8), 201 (1912)	Discussion of use of Pole Star and of other circumpolar stars as photometric standards
11. O. C. Wendell	[104]	**69** (Part 1), 1 (1909)	Photometric observations with 15-inch refractor 1892–1902
11a. O. C. Wendell	[105]	**69** (Part 2), 99 (1913)	Photometric observations with 15-inch refractor 1903–12
12. E. C. Pickering	[42]	**70**, 1 (1909)	Observations with 12-inch meridian photometer of BD stars in selected zones
12a. E. C. Pickering	[106]	**74**, 1 (1913)	Catalogue of 16 300 stars observed with 12-inch meridian photometer
13. E. C. Pickering	[96]	**72** (No. 4), 79 (1913)	Observations with Rumford wedge photometer
13a. E. C. Pickering	[107]	**72** (No. 6), 191 (1913)	Scale of the BD
13b. E. C. Pickering	[108]	**72** (No. 7), 233 (1913)	Scale of the CoD

a misnomer, considering that only some 5 per cent of all BD and SD stars were reobserved in order to provide the statistical base for a revision of the BD magnitude scale to that of the *Harvard Photometry*.

Further work with the new meridian photometer was reported in volume 24 of the *Harvard Annals*, which contained photometry for 166 variable stars, 86 of them being fainter telescopic objects. This short paper became the source of considerable friction between Pickering and Seth Chandler, an expert in variable stars who was at that time employed as a voluntary research associate at the Harvard College Observatory.

In 1894 Chandler pointed out that 15 of the 86 telescopic variable stars had been incorrectly identified by Pickering, as shown by large magnitude discrepancies, sometimes amounting to several magnitudes [109]. He was thus

> ... led to the inference that misidentification prevails on so liberal scale in the work with the meridian-photometers ... as to deprive the photometric catalogues executed in this manner, of any scientific value whatever.

Pickering attempted to defend the results obtained for over 20 000 stars that form the revision of the BD, but was forced to concede the identification errors for the variable stars [110].

A second article by Chandler implied that Pickering's undue haste was the cause of the errors:

> Such tumultuous haste is conducive only to quantity, at a sad expense as to quality, in the results; and is in defiance of the principle that the amount of work attempted in any scientific undertaking must be regulated by the condition of its being done properly [111].

Such a frank exchange in print in a leading scientific journal and coming as it did from within the Harvard ranks cannot have done Pickering's reputation any good. It is clear that his results were susceptible to considerable error due to misidentifications, as Müller had already suggested (see sections 3.6.1 and 3.6.3). Yet Pickering was generally revered, except at Potsdam, and his stature was such as to survive such criticisms with only minor damage. Chandler, as editor of the *Astronomical Journal* from 1896, was also well respected for his knowledge of variable stars. The reader of Chandler's criticisms will generally agree that Pickering's work contained an unacceptable incidence of misidentified stars owing to the haste of observing at a rate in excess of one star a minute, although few would go as far as Chandler in stating that the meridian photometry was devoid of all scientific value.

3.7.3 Bailey's southern hemisphere photometry and the Revised Harvard Photometry

In 1889 Solon Bailey travelled to Peru with the 4-inch meridian photometer, in order to extend the photometric programme on bright stars to the south pole, especially all those stars with magnitude estimates observed in Gould's *Uranometria Argentina* [112], as well as those estimated by Behrmann [113] and by Houzeau [114]. Much of the observing was at Arequipa, eventually selected as the permanent site for Harvard's Boyden Station. The principal comparison star was σ Octantis. Bailey was in Peru for over two years for this work. These were the first photometric observations from the southern hemisphere since John Herschel's photometric measurements at the Cape a half century earlier, and they resulted in an important catalogue (Table 3.2, BaI) of photometry for 7922 southern stars [94].

In November 1891 Pickering began a large new programme with the 4-inch meridian photometer, the revision of the *Harvard Photometry* undertaken a decade earlier with the smaller instrument. This included the observation of all the stars brighter than 6^m2 and north of $-30°$ [91]. A second programme was also started, to observe all stars to magnitude 7.5 north of $-40°$ [93]. Pickering was himself the observer for nearly all this work, until the photometer went to Peru for a second time with Solon Bailey in 1898, in order to extend these programmes to the south pole. In the years 1891–98 Pickering had made nearly half a million photometric settings as part of these two marathon programmes, for which almost 30 000 stars were observed.

Meanwhile, during 1899 Bailey continued the observations from Arequipa in Peru, and was able to complete the programme of obtaining magnitudes of all stars to $m = 7.0$ south of $-30°$ [95]. This work covered a total of 5332 stars, including the remeasurement of the bright ones observed during his first visit to Peru nearly a decade earlier. From 1900 the meridian photometer was again in Cambridge and a programme was started to observe 839 fifth magnitude early-type stars with the greatest possible care to see if a higher precision than hitherto might be attainable (Table 3.2, BaIII) – the result was negative. This programme was continued in the southern hemisphere when Bailey went to Peru for a third time from 1902–06 (Table 3.2, BaIV) where he observed a further 866 stars.

The photometric programmes with the 4-inch photometer saw their climax in 1908 in the publication of the *Revised Harvard Photometry* (RHP) as volume 50 of the *Harvard College Observatory Annals* [75]. Here the mean magnitudes of 9110 stars brighter than magnitude 6.5 and distributed over the whole sky were brought together in one volume. The data were based on observations with both the 1.6- and 4-inch meridian photometers from 1879 to 1906, during which time over one million photometric settings had been recorded on the RHP stars as well as on fainter objects by five different observers. The accuracy claimed for the magnitudes was a mean error of $\pm0^m07$.

Pickering recommended the notation HR preceding the running index number as an abbreviation for the *Revised Harvard Photometry*, in order to designate any of these bright stars. This convenient notation has survived to the present day, long outliving the usefulness of the photometric data themselves.

The RHP was followed by a second compendium bringing together all the 4-inch meridian photometry on stars fainter than magnitude 6.50 that had so far been undertaken in Cambridge and Peru. This was published in 1908 as *A Catalogue of 36 682 Stars* [98].

In a sense the RHP was Pickering's finest memorial. Although the Henry Draper programme of spectral classification at Harvard, which Pickering directed, brought him more renown than the concurrent visual photometry, it was nevertheless the meridian photometric programme to which Pickering personally directed his greatest efforts. Thus he reported having made his one millionth photometric setting in May 1903 with the meridian photometers [115], of which nearly 700 000 were with the two smaller instruments. From this can be deduced that at least two thirds of the observational programme for the RHP and its associated *Catalogue of 36 682 Stars* was undertaken by Pickering himself, with no more than the assistance of a recorder, responsible for keeping the observational journal of each nightly observing run.

3.7.4   Pickering's 12-inch meridian photometry

When Bailey was undertaking much of the observational programme with the 4-inch meridian photometer, the 12-inch instrument was meanwhile being used by Pickering from October 1898 until 1910. The main programme was the observation of all the BD and SD (*Bonn Southern Durchmusterung*) stars in 10 arc minute wide zones situated every 5° from 84° to −19° [42].

The purpose of this large programme was the determination of the scale of the BD and SD, especially for the fainter stars [107]. This thorough analysis supplemented the earlier *Revision of the BD* from the 4-inch photometry reported in *Harvard Annals* volumes 23 and 24 – see Table 3.3. It was the stars with BD magnitudes from 9.0 to 9.5 that received especial attention in the 1913 work, so as to obtain their photometric magnitudes on the Pogson scale. The result for these stars ranged from about 9^m3 to 10^m5, although the relationship between the two systems was quite strongly dependent on declination. But apart from this programme, some 16 300 faint stars (some to magnitude 13) were also observed for a variety of reasons with the 12-inch photometer [106]. Many of these were comparison stars for known variables or they formed photometric sequences for the calibration of photographic plates.

The achievements of a quarter of a century of Harvard visual photometry were summarized by Pickering in his 1904 Annual Report [116]:

Fig. 3.10   Wedge photometer on the Yerkes 40-inch telescope, 1901.

The observations with the various forms of meridian photometers have
furnished a scale of photometric magnitudes, and measures of large
numbers of standard stars of various degrees of brightness. The first
meridian photometer had apertures of two inches. Between 1879 and
1882, nearly a hundred thousand measures were made with it of four
thousand stars, including all those of the sixth magnitude and brighter
north of declination −30°. The second photometer had apertures of
four inches, and has been in nearly continuous use since 1882. More
than a million measures, of about sixty thousand stars of the ninth
magnitude and brighter, have been made with it. This instrument has

been sent three times to Peru, and thus stars in all parts of the sky have been measured according to the same system. Since 1898, the 12-inch Meridian Photometer has been in regular use, and the observations have furnished large numbers of standards of the twelfth magnitude and brighter. Stars however bright can now be measured with this instrument, as well as with the smaller meridian photometers, by reducing the light of the real star, instead of that of the artificial star, by means of a wedge of shade glass. The continuous work of twenty-five years, including more than a million and a half observations, has thus furnished a standard scale of magnitudes, which has been extended systematically to fainter and fainter stars.

By 1906 no further work was undertaken with the 4-inch photometer, which was returned in that year from Peru and retired. The end of all visual photometry was even foreseen by Pickering:

In view of the improved method of determining the magnitudes of very faint stars photographically, it may be a question whether it will be worth while to undertake an extensive series of measures of them visually ... [117].

In the event 12-inch meridian photometry was continued at Harvard until 1910, by which time Pickering had made over 700 000 settings with this instrument, and some 1 400 000 meridian photometer settings over all.

3.8　　Visual photometry in Russia

Some notable visual photometry with Zöllner photometers was undertaken in Russia at about the same time as the developments in this field took place at Harvard and Potsdam. In the autumn of 1867 the Pulkovo Observatory acquired two Zöllner photometers, one of which was suitable for mounting on a large telescope for the observation of faint stars. It is this instrument that was used by the visiting Swedish astronomer Per Rosén (1838–1914) on the 126-mm Steinheil refractor at Pulkovo. The object of this work was to determine the light intensity ratio for unit magnitude interval of the *Bonner Durchmusterung* scale. Rosén observed 110 BD stars in 1868, going as faint as $m_{\mathrm{BD}} = 9^{\mathrm{m}}.5$, in order to calculate a value for R. His mean result was $\log R = 0.3927$ for stars between magnitudes 5 and 9.5 [64].

Eduard Lindemann (1842–97) continued this photometric research at Pulkovo from September 1870. His papers make no reference to working with Rosén, and presumably the two were not therefore collaborators. Lindemann can be regarded as the father of Russian visual photometry.

He was also the scientific secretary of the Pulkovo Observatory, and as a consequence much of his time was absorbed by administrative duties.

In his earliest photometric work Lindemann compared the performance of his Zöllner visual photometer on the 5-inch telescope with the results of the step estimation method developed by William Herschel and Argelander [118], and concluded that the precision with the photometer was no better than with the step estimation method. Lindemann also compared the BD magnitudes with his photometric measurements. He found, in agreement with other investigators, that the faintest BD stars, although given as 9^m5 by Argelander, were in fact of magnitude 10.0 on a photometric scale [66]. Another programme that Lindemann undertook at this time was the observation of stars in the galactic cluster h Persei to magnitude 10, using the photometer on the 126-mm Steinheil refractor [119].

Vitold Tserasky (also transliterated Ceraski) (1849–1925) was also one of the early Russian pioneers in stellar photometry, which he developed at Moscow Observatory from 1876 – see for example [120] on Tserasky's early experiments with his recently acquired Zöllner photometer from the firm of Ausfeld in Gotha, Germany. His best known researches included a photometric study of the stars in the cluster χ Persei [121], undertaken at the same time as Lindemann's work on the twin cluster, h Persei. Another study by Tserasky was on the Coma Berenices star cluster [122, 123]. For these observations he had adapted the Zöllner photometer to be mounted on the 10-inch refractor. This enabled him to reach magnitude 13.5 in χ Persei and about 14.0 in the Coma cluster on the Pogson scale, the faintest visual photometry being undertaken at that time at any observatory.

Tserasky is also remembered for a photometric catalogue of 466 circumpolar stars which was published posthumously in 1953 in a memorial volume [124].

Zöllner visual photometry was continued in the Soviet Union by V. Fesenkov (1889–1972), who produced in 1926 a photometric catalogue of 1155 stars observed from the Kharkov Observatory [125]. The observations were made with a Zöllner photometer on a 10-cm telescope, and included all stars to ninth magnitude from $+79.5°$ to the north pole. A total of 266 standard stars was used to tie the magnitude scale to that of the *Yerkes Actinometry* (photovisual scale), as well as to the Zöllner visual photometry of polar stars by Müller (the *Potsdam Polar Durchmusterung*) [126] (see section 3.10) and by Tserasky.

3.9   Visual colorimetry, filter photometry and spectrophotometry

3.9.1   Colorimetry

Visual estimates of stellar colour were always subject to errors, one of which was the need for the observer to memorize an arbitrary colour scale when estimating the colour of a given star. In principle better precision would be forthcoming if an artificial source, whose colour could be altered at will, could be compared directly and simultaneously with a star. A number of such astronomical colorimeters were proposed in the mid-nineteenth century. Evidently their operation in all cases was difficult and cumbersome, for such observations never became popular in comparison with the simple colour estimates discussed in section 2.8.

One such proposed colorimeter was described by Sidney Kincaid in 1867 [127]. His 'metrochrome' was a device for producing an artificial star of any desired colour in the telescopic field of view. The metrochrome light source was an electrically heated fine platinum wire whose light was collimated and then passed through a rotating cylinder with three clear apertures and three further apertures fitted with filters made from liquid solutions of different but unspecified colours. The light then entered the telescope to produce an artificial star. Rapid rotation of the cylinder produced a coloured light whose hue was adjusted by varying the sizes of the various apertures until the colour matched that of a star under simultaneous observation. The relative aperture sizes would then be a measure of the star's colour. No observations were reported.

The colorimeter used by William Christie (1845–1922), the future Astronomer Royal, was also based on the principle of combining light of three colours in different proportions to achieve any desired hue [68].

In his case he adapted Maxwell's colour box [128] which entailed separately dispersing the light from three paraffin lamps and bringing together the blue light of one spectrum with the green of the second and red of the third into a single aperture. The wavelengths of these three components were fixed but their relative intensities were independently variable through a system of adjustable slits so as to synthesize any desired colour. The perceived colour of the final aperture could therefore be matched to that of a star. The three slit widths gave an objective measurement of the star's colour.

Christie used this colour-box colorimeter on the great equatorial refractor at Greenwich in 1873 and reported colour observations of 19 stars over ten nights. The results were expressed as the relative intensities of red, green and blue light that, when mixed, gave the same colour as the star. In practice different results for the same star appear quite discordant. One problem with this device is that relative amounts of red, green and blue light from the lamps were not necessarily the relative amounts of light of the same wavelengths in the star, as a given visual colour sensation has no unique solution in terms of the mix of its monochromatic components. The starlight itself was not dispersed, and at least for bright stars, more reliable results might have come from spectrophotometry in which the intensity of each wavelength was estimated independently.

The one visual stellar colorimeter that was used successfully was the Zöllner photometer – see section 3.3.3. Although this instrument received widespread use for visual photometry, most notably by Müller and Kempf at Potsdam, it was only Zöllner himself who exploited its colorimetric capability for which it was designed. The instrument is described in Zöllner's essay *Grundzüge einer allgemeinen Photometrie des Himmels* [37]. A paraffin lamp provided the light for an artificial star whose colour was adjusted using a birefringent rock crystal plate placed between two polarizing Nicol prisms. Rotation of one of the Nicols allowed light of different colour to pass, which could be set to any colour from bluish-white through yellow to red, and the corresponding angle was then simply read off on a scale. Zöllner envisaged both matching of brightness and colour when real and artificial stars were viewed through the telescope, which was an integral part of the instrument.

Zöllner published his colorimetric results for 37 stars and planets in 1868, deduced from observations made from 1860 to 1868 [129]. Each observation entailed taking the mean angle from three successive settings of the Nicol prism and the stellar colours were simply expressed as the angle of the Nicol that matched star to lamp. Zöllner attempted to correct for the atmospheric reddening at greater zenith distances and for possible nightly changes in the state of the atmosphere. As with the photometry, the long-term stability of the paraffin lamp was essential for reliable colorimetry, and Zöllner attempted to check this by comparing it with the light emitted by a platinum wire at its melting point.

Zöllner obtained a clear increase in Nicol angle with colour index for his stars: the setting for Vega was 12°, Polaris 22°, Arcturus 31° and Betelgeuse about 42°, but variable. A plot of his settings against modern $(B - V)$ values shows considerable scatter, with Zöllner's error bar in angle corresponding to about $\pm0^{m}.2$ (standard deviation) in $(B - V)$, similar to the figure of $\pm0^{m}.24$ quoted by Murdin for visual colour estimates [130]. Nevertheless these sparse results must rate as some of the most precise colour observations in the nineteenth century and it is regrettable that more extensive observations were not undertaken either by Zöllner or by others with this instrument.

3.9.2   Visual filter photometry

The important idea of using a filter as an aid for stellar colour determinations came from Seth Chandler in 1884 in connection with his colour determinations of red variable stars [131]. It is to this paper that the present-day concept of the colour index, so pervasive in modern astronomy, owes its humble origin. The concept even predated the more concise ideas on colour indices in the work of Schwarzschild in 1900 [132] – see section 4.8.1.

Chandler, who had been making visual colour estimates on an arbitrary decimal scale, described his new idea as follows:

> In casting about for some simple means of verifying the decimal scale estimates, after making various desultory and unsatisfactory estimates, with a direct-vision prism, and otherwise, I finally hit upon what seems to be an effective way of easily recognizing differences of colour, and of numerically estimating their relative amount with great certainty – although upon an entirely arbitrary scale. The accuracy with which the relative value of moderate differences of brightness can be estimated by Argelander's [step estimation] method, suggested the idea of converting the difference of color between two stars into the difference of brightness, thus changing the element to be directly observed from a very uncertain, to a very certain one. This conversion was effected in a simple manner, by interposing a shade of colored glass, which, by its selective absorption, alters the apparent relative brightness of stars of different colors. Thus, a red star which appears exactly equal to a white one, when viewed in the ordinary way, appears fainter than the latter when a blue shade-glass is applied to the eyepiece, and brighter when a red shade-glass is used. These differences, which can be estimated very precisely by Argelander's method, thus become measures of the difference of color, of course on an entirely arbitrary scale, depending on the amount and character of the selective absorption of the shades employed.
>
> By this simple method were made the series of measurements whose results are presently to be given under the name of "Relative-Diminution Estimates" [131].

His method entailed the use of a single filter of weak blue tint which gave about half a magnitude diminution in the brightness of reddish stars. The magnitude difference between two stars was estimated without the filter and then with it, and the difference of the two gave a value for the colour difference between the stars, which Chandler called the 'relative diminution' (in modern parlance, a colour index difference).

Chandler applied his filter method to 77 red variables and compared the

Fig. 3.11   Charles Nordmann, at Versailles.

results with direct colour estimates on his decimal scale. A good correlation
between the two different methods of colour determination was found [131].

The benefits of using filters to determine stellar colours were exploited far
more fully when Charles Nordmann (1881–1940) at the Paris Observatory
began using a three-filter visual photometer [133]. This instrument was
clearly based on the principle of Zöllner's colorimeter in that it comprised
a white light source (in Nordmann's case an osmium-tungsten filament 4-
watt incandescent electric lamp) whose brightness was adjusted, using the
rotation of two polarizing Nicol prisms, to equal that of a star. However,
both lamp and starlight were passed through a colour filter consisting of a
coloured solution in a flat glass container, thus rendering the hue of both
sources identical. Nordmann claimed that after four settings of the Nicol in
different quadrants, probable errors of $\pm 0^{m}\!.4$ could be achieved, a precision
he believed to be superior to that from a visual spectroscope employing
a slit and dispersing element [134]. Three filters were used in turn, which
isolated broad bands in the red ($\lambda > 590$ nm), green (490–590 nm) and blue
($\lambda < 490$ nm).

Fig. 3.12   Charles Nordmann's filter photometer, 1909.

The earliest observations were made from Paris on the 23-cm equatorial
coudé telescope during 1905–06, and then from Biskra in Algeria in 1907–08.
At first the aim was to observe the light curves of variable stars at different
wavelengths in order to confirm the Tikhoff effect [135]. Here Nordmann
sought to explain the lack of simultaneity in the minima of variable stars
obtained in different colours by a supposed dispersion in the velocity of
propagation of light in space – see section 8.6.2. Such a dispersion might arise
from the presence of an interstellar medium. Evidence for this (later usually
referred to as the Tikhoff-Nordmann effect) was at best marginal and later
discredited. Nevertheless the results from Nordmann's filter photometry
soon suggested the possibility of obtaining stellar temperatures.

The new observations for obtaining the temperatures of stars involved
using only the red and blue filters [136]. The intensity ratios of red to
blue light were calibrated with ovens at different temperatures and with an

electric arc, and the calibration extrapolated to the higher temperatures of stars by assuming Planck energy distributions. Nordmann gave his results for thirteen bright stars and the sun as $\log(R/B)$, a kind of $(B - R)$ colour index which he found correlated well with spectral type and could be used to obtain temperatures, which were nevertheless much too hot for the early-type stars. He recalibrated his colours two months later [137], which more than halved his highest temperatures, yet they are still systematically in error (due mainly to the incorrect assumption that stars radiate like black bodies).

The effective wavelengths of his red and blue filters were respectively 640 and 460 nm. A comparison of Nordmann's $\log R/B$ with modern $(B - R)$ photoelectric colour indices on the Johnson system shows that the precision of Nordmann's results corresponds to about $\pm 0^m\!.3$ (standard deviation) in $(B - R)$. This is roughly comparable to the results from visual colour estimates – see section 2.8.

3.9.3   Visual spectrophotometry

The possibility of undertaking visual spectrophotometry, in which the relative brightness of a star would be obtained in a series of monochromatic bands within the optical spectrum, was first attempted by H. C. Vogel (1841–1907) during his early years at Potsdam. However, the concept of spectrophotometry itself goes right back to Fraunhofer, who in 1817 published his celebrated drawing of the apparent intensity distribution of light in the solar spectrum [138].

Vogel's work at Potsdam was no doubt also inspired by another earlier suggestion by Zöllner, who in 1873 had remarked that

> the relative intensities [of light in a spectrum] which hereby occur are functions of the temperature ... This method, when applied to the stars, would allow us at least to determine qualitatively their relative temperatures, that is, to decide which of two stars possesses the higher temperature [139].

Believing stellar temperatures were within his grasp, Vogel began his experiments using a prism spectroscope which was equipped with a kerosene lamp as a comparison source to determine relative intensities. The first observations were of sunlight [140]. Seven wavelengths from the blue (444 nm) to the red (633 nm) were chosen and the results recorded for six stars, Sirius, Vega, Capella, Arcturus, Aldeberan and Betelgeuse. These data were quite crude and the observer encountered many practical difficulties, especially the spectrum being too faint or of fluctuating intensity. But they showed that Sirius was clearly stronger in the ratio of blue to red light than either Aldeberan or Betelgeuse, by a factor of about four [140].

Vogel's preliminary experiments developed into a much more sophisticated series of observations by Johannes Wilsing (1856–1943) and Julius Scheiner (1858–1913) on the Potsdam 80-cm refractor from 1905. Observations were made at five wavelengths (448, 480, 513, 584 and 638 nm) with a flint glass prism spectroscope. Light from an electric comparison lamp was used to form an artificial star whose spectral intensity was matched to that of the real star using the rotation of two Nicol prisms [141]. The arrangement was therefore quite similar to Nordmann's (see section 3.9.2) except for the replacement of the coloured liquid filters by a prism to isolate the required spectral intervals.

The spectral energy distributions for 109 stars were measured with this visual spectrophotometer and the results were calibrated in the laboratory using an electric oven of known temperature which was assumed to be a black-body radiator. The whole work was characterized by an elaborate observing procedure with corrections for the wavelength-dependent absorption of the objective, for chromatic aberration, for the personal equation of the two observers, for atmospheric extinction (the corrections were to outside the atmosphere and not to the zenith) and for current variations in the comparison lamp. The typical probable error was about ± 0.05 in the logarithmic intensities at any wavelength.

Observations were continued by Wilsing and W. H. J. Münch (1879–1969) at Potsdam from 1908–13 when a further 90 stars were added to the programme, and for this work ten passbands from 451 to 642 nm were chosen [142]. All 199 stars were then reduced on a uniform scale.

The principal object of this whole programme was to obtain stellar temperatures, and in this respect the results were not very successful. The incorrect assumption that stars radiated like black bodies vitiated all the early stellar temperature determinations based on colours or spectral gradients. This problem was not resolved until the 1930s when the first non-grey stellar model atmospheres were computed by William McCrea (b. 1904) [143] – see section 7.7. However, even before this Charles Abbot (1872–1973) at the Smithsonian Astrophysical Observatory had criticized the Potsdam results for their limited spectral wavelength range of less than 200 nm, and for the possibility that Planck's black-body formula might be inapplicable to the stars [144].

3.10   The achievements of visual photometry

The era of visual photometry enjoyed its most active hey-days from around 1860 to 1910, a half century which opened with the invention of the Zöllner photometer and closed with the completion of several major catalogues, in particular the *Revised Harvard Photometry* of 1908, the *Potsdamer Durchmusterung* (the final volume was published in 1907) and Pickering's 12-inch meridian photometric catalogue which appeared in 1909. The demise of the visual technique after 1910 was not quite total, but its decline was certainly abrupt.

One of the last major visual catalogues was in fact the *Potsdam Polar Durchmusterung*, for which the observers were Gustav Müller, Erich Kron and Arnold Kohlschütter (1883–1969) between 1907 and 1920. The whole work was edited and published by W. Hassenstein in 1926 [126]. A modified Zöllner photometer with an electric lamp as the artificial star was mounted on the 30-cm refractor for most of the observations, which encompassed about 5000 stars north of +80° brighter than about $m_{vis} \simeq 11.5$, including 26 stars in the Harvard North Polar Sequence. Some visual Zöllner photometry was also undertaken at the Kharkov Observatory in the 1920s by Fesenkov (see section 3.8), while at Princeton various observers (including R. S. Dugan, N. L. Pierce, B. W. Sitterly and F. B. Wood) were using a Zöllner photometer on the 23-inch Clark refractor to observe eclipsing binary light curves throughout the 1920s and 1930s. The last of these was Frank Bradshaw Wood (b. 1915), who completed visual observations for his doctoral thesis under Russell early in 1942 [145]. Yet another programme of visual photometry after 1910 was undertaken at Mt Wilson by Edison Pettit, who used a wedge comparison photometer on the 20-inch telescope in the mid-1940s. This instrument dimmed the light from an artificial star using a photographic wedge until equality with a real star was reached [146]. Observations of Nova Puppis 1942 were made with this photometer over six years, during which time the star faded from first to nearly twelfth magnitude [147]. It was one of the last programmes of visual photometry to appear in the literature.

What had been achieved in this vigorous half century (1860–1910), which also saw the birth of astrophysics and of stellar spectroscopy? The prizes of stellar visual photometry were altogether more modest than its spectroscopic counterpart. If anything, the effort which the world's major observatories put into photometry was greater than into spectroscopy, but the rewards were more elusive and the results were less spectacular. The data obtained in photometry lent themselves less readily to astrophysical interpretations than did the results of spectroscopy, which abounded in ideas concerning stellar compositions, temperatures, evolutionary sequences and space motions.

For some who now look back on a half century of unremitting toil in visual photometry with the benefit of over an additional half century of hindsight, the accomplishments of the visual photometrists may well seem extremely meagre. Hundreds of thousands of laboriously obtained stellar visual magnitudes were catalogued and published, only to be rendered obsolete and largely forgotten as a consequence of technological progress. But for those who adopt a more sanguine view, the achievements of visual photometry were important nevertheless, in laying the groundwork for the photometry yet to come.

The main achievements during the age of visual photometry can be summarized as follows:

1. **The universal adoption of the Pogson scale**: Although the scale was in fact arbitrary, its acceptance by Pickering, Pritchard and Müller almost simultaneously in the 1880s ensured a uniformity of practice in photometry which in turn allowed stellar magnitudes from different institutions to be intercompared.

2. **The extension of photometric measurements to faint telescopic stars**: This extrapolation using visual photometry could be made with the Pogson 2.512 ratio being preserved for each magnitude below the naked-eye limit, in some cases going as faint as magnitude 13. On the other hand, magnitude estimates through the telescope, as made for example by Flamsteed, William Herschel and Argelander, had not only often diverged widely from the Pogson scale, but also from each other.

3. **The correction of photometric magnitudes for atmospheric extinction**: The practice of obtaining zenith magnitudes, which had been done first by Seidel in 1852 [44], became an essential feature of the reductions in all major photometric catalogues in the period from 1860. In particular Pritchard and initially Pickering both adopted constant extinction coefficients for all nights, the corrections varying in proportion to the secant of the zenith distance, while Müller and Kempf, and also Pickering from 1894, determined extinction on a nightly basis.

4. **The photometric cataloguing of all stars to magnitude 7.5** to an accuracy of approximately a tenth of a magnitude (probable error), as published in the major catalogues of the RHP, the PD and *Harvard Annals* volume **54**, as well as of many thousands of fainter objects, including stars in selected zones to tenth magnitude in

the *Bonner Durchmusterung* and some other stars to magnitude 13. This great body of data was useful for calibrating photographic photometry, as a basis for the future detection of possible variability in stars, for providing comparison stars for known variables, for corrections to the magnitude scales of earlier magnitude estimates (especially the BD, SD and CoD) and for the statistical analysis of the distribution of stars in space and in the different magnitude classes.

5. **The discovery of new variable stars**: As a result of visual photometry the number of known variable stars made noteworthy increases during the period 1860 to 1910, though certainly not with the spectacular results produced by photographic methods. Thus Argelander in 1844 listed 18 known variables [148], Pogson in 1856 gave 53 [58], Chambers in 1865 gave 113 [149] as did also Schönfeld in that year [150], while Chandler's three variable-star catalogues of 1888, 1890 and 1896 listed respectively 225, 260 and 393 stars [151, 152, 153].

On average the number of new visual discoveries was doubling every 12 years in the second half of the nineteenth century. By 1907 Annie Cannon (1863–1941), in her second variable star catalogue, recorded nearly 2000 variables in our Galaxy (about a quarter of which were in globular clusters) [154]. However, the big increase here was almost entirely due to photographic discoveries. This fact alone illustrates the power of astronomical photography and does much to explain the demise of visual photometry.

References

[1] Huyghens, C., *Cosmotheoros*, The Hague (1698).
[2] Bouguer, P., *Traité d'Optique sur la gradation de la lumière*, Paris (1760).
[3] Lambert, J., *Photometria sive de mensura et gradibus luminis*, Augsbourg (1760).
[4] Bouguer, P., *Essai d'Optique sur la gradation de la lumière*, Paris (1729).
[5] Michell, J., *Phil. Trans. R. Soc. London A*, **57**, 234 (1767).
[6] Wollaston, W., *Phil. Trans. R. Soc. London A*, **119**, 19 (1829).
[7] Müller, G., *Photometrie der Gestirne*, Leipzig (1897).
[8] Tulenius, A., *Dissertatio astronomica de constellatione Arietis*, Stockholm, Holmiae (1740).
[9] Zinner, E., *Bamberg Veröff. der Remeis-Sternw. Bamberg*, **2**, 1 (1926).
[10] Herschel, W., *Phil. Trans. R. Soc. London A*, **107**, 302 (1817).

[11]   von Humboldt, A., *Recueil d'Observations Astronomiques*, **1**, 71 (1810).

[12]   von Humboldt, A., *Astron. Nachr.*, **16**, 225 (1839).

[13]   Herschel, J., *Results of observations made during the years 1834, 5, 6, 7, 8 at the Cape of Good Hope*, London, Smith Elder and Co. (1847).

[14]   Russell, H.N., *Astrophys. J.*, **43**, 103 (1916).

[15]   de Maistre, X., *Bibl. Univ. de Genève*, **51**, 323 (1832).

[16]   Quetelet, A., *Bibl. Univ. de Genève*, **52**, 212 (1833).

[17]   Smyth, C.P., *Mon. Not. R. Astron. Soc.*, **6**, 13 (1843).

[18]   Baily, F., *Mem. R. Astron. Soc.*, **1**, 507 (1822).

[19]   Kayser, E., *Astron. Nachr.*, **57**, 17 (1862).

[20]   Dawes, W.R., *Mon. Not. R. Astron. Soc.*, **25**, 229 (1865).

[21]   Pritchard, C., *Mon. Not. R. Astron. Soc.*, **42**, 1 (1882).

[22]   Pritchard, C., *Mem. R. Astron. Soc.*, **47**, 353 (1883).

[23]   Pritchard, C., *Uranometria Nova Oxoniensis: Astron. observations made at the Univ. of Oxford Observ.* No. II (1885).

[24]   Wilsing, J., *Astron. Nachr.*, **112**, 265 (1885).

[25]   Loewy, M., *Mon. Not. R. Astron. Soc.*, **42**, 91 (1882).

[26]   Spitta, E.J., *Mon. Not. R. Astron. Soc.*, **50**, 319 (1890).

[27]   Parkhurst, H.M., *Sidereal Messenger*, **4**, 273 (1885).

[28]   Pritchard, C., *Mon. Not. R. Astron. Soc.*, **42**, 223 (1882).

[29]   Pritchard, C., *Mon. Not. R. Astron. Soc.*, **43**, 1, 100 (1883).

[30]   Pritchard, C., *Mon. Not. R. Astron. Soc.*, **46**, 2 (1885).

[31]   Pritchard, C., *Observatory*, **9**, 62 (1886).

[32]   Pritchard, C., *Mon. Not. R. Astron. Soc.*, **50**, 512 (1890).

[33]   von Steinheil, C.A., *Elemente der Helligkeitsmessungen am Sternhimmel: Denkschr. der K. Bayer. Akad. der Wiss., Math.-phys. Classe, II*, München (1836).

[34]   Seidel, P.L., *Abhandl. der K. Bayer, Akad. der Wiss., II. Classe*, **6**, 623 (1852).

[35]   Bond, G.P., *Mem. Nat. Acad. Arts Sci.* (New Series), **8**, 287 (1861). See also Bond, G.P., *Mon. Not. R. Astron. Soc.*, **21**, 197 (1861).

[36]   Zöllner, J.K.F., *Photometrische Untersuchungen mit besonderer Rücksicht auf die physische Beschaffenheit der Himmelskörper*, Leipzig (1865).

[37]   Zöllner, J.K.F., *Grundzüge einer allgemeinen Photometrie des Himmels*, Berlin (1861).

[38]   Arago, F., *Oeuvres*, **10**, 261. *Sixième mémoire sur la photométrie: constitution physique et photométrie des étoiles* (1858).

[39]   Pickering, E.C., Searle, A. and Upton, W. *Ann. Harvard Coll. Observ.*, **11** (Parts 1 and 2), 1 (1879).

[40]   Pickering, E.C., Searle, A. and Wendell, O.C., *Ann. Harvard Coll. Observ.*, **14** (Part 1), 1 (1884).

[41]   Pickering, E.C., Searle, A. and Wendell, O.C., *Ann. Harvard Coll. Observ.*, **14** (Part 2), 325 (1885)

[42]   Pickering, E.C., *Ann. Harvard Coll. Observ.*, **70**, 1 (1909).

[43]   Parkhurst, J.A., *Astrophys. J.*, **13**, 249 (1901).

[44]   Seidel, P.L., *Untersuchungen über die gegenseitigen Helligkeiten der Fixsterne erster Grösse: Abhandl. der kaiserl. Bayer. Akad. der Wiss., II. Classe*, **6** (Part 3), 539 (1852).

[45]   Seidel, P.L., *Resultate phot. Messungen an 208 der vorzüglichsten der Fixsterne: Abhandl. der kaiserl. Bayer. Akad. der Wiss. II. Classe*, **9** (Part 3), 419 (1862).

[46]   Seidel, P.L. and Leonhard, E., *Helligkeitsmessungen an 208 Fixsternen: Abhandl. der math.-phys. Classe der kaiserl. Bayer. Akad. der Wiss.*, **10** (Part 1), 201 (1866).

[47]   Dorst, F. J. *Astron. Nachr.*, **118**, 209 (1888).

[48]   Wolff, J.T., *Photometrische Beobachtungen an Fixsternen*, Leipzig (1877).

[49]   Wolff, J.T., *Photometrische Beobachtungen an Fixternen*, Berlin (1884).

[50]   Searle, G.M., *Astron. Nachr.*, **57**, 141 (1862).

[51]   Wolff, J.T., *Vierteljahrschr. Astron. Ges.*, **19**, 259 (1884).

[52]   Flamsteed, J., *Historia Coelestis Britannica*. London (1725).

[53]   Halley, E., *Phil. Trans. R. Soc. London*, **31**, 22 (1720).

[54]   Herschel, J., *Outlines of Astronomy*, London (1849).

[55]   Herschel, J., *Mem. R. Astron. Soc.*, **3**, 177 (1829).

[56]   Fechner, G.T., *Abhandl. der math.-phys. Classe der konigl. Sachs. Ges. der Wiss.*, **4**, 455 (1858).

[57]   Fechner, G.T., *Elemente der Psychophysik*, Leipzig (1860).

[58]   Pogson, N.R., *Radcliffe Observations*, **15**, 281 (1856).

[59]   Pogson, N.R., *Mon. Not. R. Astron. Soc.*, **17**, 12 (1856).

[60]   Struve, F.G.W., *Catalogus Duplicium et Multiplicium Mensurae Micrometricae*, St Petersburg (1837). See pp. xlii and lxix.

[61]   Stampfer, S., *Sitzungsber. der Akad. der Wiss.*, Wien, **7**, 756 (1851).

[62]   Johnson, M.J., *Mon. Not. R. Astron. Soc.*, **13**, 278 (1853).

[63]   Carrington, R.C., *Cat. 3735 Circumpolar Stars*, London (1857).

[64]   Rosén, P.G., *Bull. de l'Acad. Imp. des Sci., St Pétersbourg*, **14**, 95 (1870).

[65]   Peirce, C.S., *Ann. Harvard Coll. Observ.*, **9**, 1 (1878).

[66]   Lindemann, E., *Astron. Nachr.*, **118**, 125 (1888).

[67]   Pogson, N.R., *Astron. Nachr.*, **47**, 289 (1858).

[68]   Christie, W.H.M., *Mon. Not. R. Astron. Soc.*, **34**, 111 (1874).

[69]   Herrmann, D.B., *Die Sterne*, **48**, 113 (1972).

[70]   Lodge, O., *Nature*, **106**, 438 (1920).

[71]   Jones, D.H.P., *Astron. Soc. Pacific Leaflet*, No. **469** (1968).

[72]   Chandler, S.C., *Astron. Nachr.*, **115**, 145 (1886).

[73]   Mendoza, E.E., and Gomez, T., *Bol. Observ. Tonantzintla y Tacubaya*, **5**, 111 (1969).

[74]   Müller, G. and Kempf, P., *Publ. Astrophys. Observ. Potsdam*, **9**, 1 (1894).

[75]   Pickering, E.C., *Ann. Harvard Coll. Observ.*, **50**, 1 (1908).

[76]   Pickering, E.C. and Wendell, O.C., *Ann. Harvard Coll. Observ.*, **23** (Part 2), 137 (1899). See Chapter 8.

[77]   Hertzsprung, E., *Astron. Nachr.*, **189**, 89 (1911).

[78]   Plummer, W.E., *Observatory*, **8**, 240 (1885).

[79]   Lewis, T., *Observatory*, **8**, 49 (1885).

[80] Pickering, E.C., *Ann. Harvard Coll. Observ.*, **18** (No. 2), 15 (1890).

[81] Müller, G., *Vierteljahrschr. Astron. Ges.*, **21**, 241 (1886).

[82] Müller, G., *Publ. Astrophys. Observ. Potsdam*, **8**, 193 (1893).

[83] Müller, G. and Kempf, P., *Publ. Astrophys. Observ. Potsdam*, **13**, 1 (1899).

[84] Müller, G. and Kempf, P., *Publ. Astrophys. Observ. Potsdam*, **14**, 1 (1903).

[85] Müller, G. and Kempf, P., *Publ. Astrophys. Observ. Potsdam*, **16**, 1 (1906).

[86] Müller, G. and Kempf, P., *Publ. Astrophys. Observ. Potsdam*, **17**, (1907).

[87] Pickering, E.C. and Wendell, O.C. *Ann. Harvard Coll. Observ.*, **24**, 1 (1890).

[88] Pickering, E.C., *Astrophys. J.*, **1**, 154 (1895). See also: Pickering, E.C. *Astron. Nachr.*, **137**, 65 (1895).

[89] Müller, G. and Kempf, P., *Astron. Nachr.*, **137**, 225 (1895). See also *Astrophys. J.*, **1**, 428 (1895) for English translation.

[90] Pickering, E.C. and Wendell, O.C. *Ann. Harvard Coll. Observ.*, **23** (Part 1), 1 (1890).

[91] Pickering, E.C., *Ann. Harvard Coll. Observ.*, **44**, 1 (1899).

[92] Pickering, E.C., *Ann. Harvard Coll. Observ.*, **44** (Part 2), 111 (1902).

[93] Pickering, E.C., *Ann. Harvard Coll. Observ.*, **45**, 1 (1901).

[94] Bailey, S.I. and Pickering, E.C., *Ann. Harvard Coll. Observ.*, **34**, 1 (1895).

[95] Bailey, S.I., *Ann. Harvard Coll. Observ.*, **46** (Part 1), 1 (1903).

[96] Pickering, E.C., *Ann. Harvard Coll. Observ.*, **72** (No. 4), 79 (1913).

[97] Pickering, E.C., *Ann. Harvard Coll. Observ.*, **46** (Part 2), 121 (1904).

[98] Pickering, E.C., *Ann. Harvard Coll. Observ.*, **54**, 1 (1908).

[99] Pickering, E.C., *Ann. Harvard Coll. Observ.*, **64** (No. 1), 1 (1912).

[100] Pickering, E.C., *Ann. Harvard Coll. Observ.*, **64** (No. 4), 91 (1912).

[101] Pickering, E.C., *Ann. Harvard Coll. Observ.*, **64** (No. 6), 159 (1912).

[102] Pickering, E.C., *Ann. Harvard Coll. Observ.*, **64** (No. 7), 191 (1912).

[103] Pickering, E.C., *Ann. Harvard Coll. Observ.*, **64** (No. 8), 201 (1912).

[104] Wendell, O.C., *Ann. Harvard Coll. Observ.*, **69** (Part 1), 1 (1909).

[105] Wendell, O.C., *Ann. Harvard Coll. Observ.*, **69** (Part 2), 99 (1913).

[106] Pickering, E.C., *Ann. Harvard Coll. Observ.*, **74**, 1 (1913).

[107] Pickering, E.C., *Ann. Harvard Coll. Observ.*, **72** (No. 6), 191 (1913).

[108] Pickering, E.C., *Ann. Harvard Coll. Observ.*, **72** (No. 7), 233 (1913).

[109] Chandler, S.C., *Astron. Nachr.*, **134**, 355 (1894).

[110] Pickering, E.C., *Astron. Nachr.*, **135**, 217 (1894).

[111] Chandler, S.C., *Astron. Nachr.*, **136**, 85 (1894).

[112] Gould, B.A., *Uranometria Argentina: Result. Observ. Nac. Argentino Córdoba*, **1** (1879).

[113] Behrmann, C., *Atlas des südlichen gestirnten Himmels*, Leipzig (1874).

[114] Houzeau, J.-C., *Uranometrie Générale: Ann. de l'Observ. R. de Bruxelles (Nouvelle série)*, **1** (1878).

[115] Pickering, E.C., *Fifty-eighth Annual Report of the director of Harvard College Observatory* (1903).

[116]   Pickering, E.C., *Fifty-ninth Annual Report of the Director of Harvard
        College Observatory* (1904).
[117]   Pickering, E.C., *Sixty-first Annual Report of the Director of Harvard
        College Observatory* (1906).
[118]   Lindemann, E., *Bull. de l'Acad. Imp. des Sciences de St.-Pétersbourg*,
        20, 387 (1875).
[119]   Lindemann, E., *Bull. de l'Acad. Imp. des Sciences de St.-Pétersbourg
        (Sér. 5)*, **2**, 55 (1895).
[120]   Tserasky, V., *Ann. de l'Observ. de Moscou*, **2** (Part 2), 98 (1876).
[121]   Tserasky, V., *Ann. de l'Observ. de Moscou (2nd series)*, **3** (Part 2), 1
        (1896).
[122]   Tserasky, V., *Ann. de l'Observ. de Moscou (2nd series)*, **4**, 87 (1902).
[123]   Tserasky, V., *Ann. de l'Observ. de Moscou (2nd series)*, **6**, 33 (1917).
[124]   Podobed, V.V., *V. K. Tserasky: Selected Works on Astronomy*, ed. by
        V.V. Podobed, Moscow (1953) – catalogue ed. by G.A. Manova.
[125]   Fesenkov, V., *Photometric Catalogue of 1155 Stars*, State Editorial
        Office of the Ukraine, Kharkov (1926).
[126]   Hassenstein, W., *Publ. Astrophys. Observ. Potsdam*, **26** (Part 1), 1 (1926).
[127]   Kincaid, S.B., *Mon. Not. R. Astron. Soc.*, **27**, 264 (1867).
[128]   Maxwell, J.C., *Phil. Trans. R. Soc., London A*, **150**, 57 (1860).
[129]   Zöllner, J.K.F., *Astron. Nachr.*, **71**, 321 (1868).
[130]   Murdin, P., *Quart. J. R. Astron. Soc.*, **22**, 353 (1981).
[131]   Chandler, S.C., *Astron. J.*, **8**, 137 (1888).
[132]   Schwarzschild, K., *Sitzungsber. der königl. Akad. der Wiss., Wien*, **109**,
        1127 (1900).
[133]   Nordmann, C., *Bull. Astron.*, **26**, 5 (1909).
[134]   Nordmann, C., *Bull. Astron.*, **26**, 158 (1909).
[135]   Tikhoff, G.A., *Comptes Rendus de l'Acad. des Sci.*, **148**, 266 (1909).
[136]   Nordmann, C., *Comptes Rendus de l'Acad. des Sci.*, **149**, 557 (1909).
[137]   Nordmann, C., *Comptes Rendus de l'Acad. des Sci.*, **149**, 1038 (1909).
[138]   Fraunhofer, J., *Denkschr. Münchener Akad. Wiss.*, **5**, 193 (1817).
[139]   Zöllner, J.K.F., *Berichte der königl. Sächs. Ges. der Wiss.*, 21 Feb 1873,
        p. 36 (1873).
[140]   Vogel, H.C., *Monatsbericht. der königl. Preuss. Akad. der Wiss. zu
        Berlin*, p. 801 (1880).
[141]   Wilsing, J. and Scheiner, J., *Publ. Astrophys. Observ. Potsdam*, **19**
        (No. 56), 1 (1909).
[142]   Wilsing, J., Scheiner, J. and Münch, W.H.J., *Publ. Astrophys. Observ.
        Potsdam*, **24** (Nr 74), 1 (1919).
[143]   McCrea, W.H., *Mon. Not. R. Astron. Soc.*, **91**, 836 (1931).
[144]   Abbot, C.G., *Astrophys. J.*, **31**, 274 (1910).
[145]   Wood, F.B., *Contr. Princeton Observ.*, No. **21**, 1 (1946).
[146]   Pettit, E., *Publ. Astron. Soc. Pacific*, **61**, 25 (1949).
[147]   Pettit, E., *Publ. Astron. Soc. Pacific*, **61**, 41 (1949).
[148]   Argelander, F.A., *Aufforderung an Freunde der Astronomie:
        H. C. Schumacher's Jahrbuch für 1844*, p. 122, Stuttgart and Tübingen
        (1844). See p. 214 for section on variable stars.

[149]   Chambers, G.F., *Mon. Not. R. Astron. Soc.*, **25**, 208 (1865).
[150]   Schönfeld, E., *Astron. Nachr.*, **64**, 161 (1865).
[151]   Chandler, S.C., *Astron. J.*, **8**, 81 (1888).
[152]   Chandler, S.C., *Astron. J.*, **13**, 89 (1890).
[153]   Chandler, S.C., *Astron. J.*, **16**, 145 (1896).
[154]   Cannon, A.J., *Ann. Harvard Coll. Observ.*, **55** (Part 1), 1 (1907).

4 The early days of photographic photometry (1839–1922)

4.1 The origins of astronomical photography

When the illustrious French 'savant' François Arago addressed the Académie Française on 7 January 1839 concerning a new invention by Louis Daguerre (1789–1851), he had the vision to foresee a new era for astronomy [1]. He took the closest interest in the development of the photographic process by Daguerre, with the assistance until 1833 of Joseph Niépce (1765–1833), and he encouraged Daguerre to attempt to record an image of the moon. The result was 'a clearly visible white impression' on the resulting daguerreotype.

Arago presented a detailed account of Daguerre's process to the Academy in August of that year [2], ostensibly because Daguerre was too ill, nervous or shy to be present himself. Here he described the daguerreotype process. A polished film of silver on a copper plate was subjected to iodine vapour to give a thin layer of silver iodide. The action of light at least partially reduced this layer back to the metallic element. After exposure the plate was subjected to the vapour of mercury (by warming the liquid) which formed a white amalgam on the bright parts of the image. The unused iodide was removed by fixing the plate in a solution of sodium thiosulphate (hypo), leaving a positive and permanent impression on the plate, which was finally rinsed in hot water. Fixing was initially undertaken in a solution of common salt, but hypo was soon preferred, following its use by Sir John Herschel (who himself was one of the early pioneers of photography) as early as March 1839 [3].

Even in these early days of photography (the word was first used by Sir John Herschel), Arago saw that the method had a potential for photometry. He predicted that physicists would not simply compare intensities visually when undertaking photometric measurements, but would in future be able to measure the intensities of luminous sources absolutely, and he gave a full account of how this might be achieved by controlling both the exposure time and the brightness of the image reaching the plate [2].

Such ambitious photometric goals were not to be achieved so simply, if at all, but Arago's vision of a revolution in astronomical imaging was largely correct. Thanks to Arago's account of the daguerreotype, knowledge of the technique spread rapidly, and the first successful astronomical photograph, an image of the moon, was recorded by John Draper (1811–82) on 23 March 1840 after exposing a daguerreotype for 20 minutes [4] – see also [5]. Draper later became the second person to photograph the solar spectrum [6], shortly after Edmond Becquerel in France [7].

Meanwhile, in Paris, at the instigation of Arago, H. Fizeau and L. Foucault made the first attempt at photographic photometry when they compared the intensity of the sun's light with that from a carbon arc and from a hydrogen and oxygen blowpipe [8, 9]. The first of these papers explicitly made use of the reciprocity law, in which the photographic impression is taken to be a function of the product of intensity and exposure time. The validity of this law was investigated and found to hold for a range of exposure times over a factor of ten (that is, the same chemical effect on the daguerreotype could be achieved by exposing light for ten times as long provided the light was one tenth the intensity), but there was evidence of the law failing for ratios as high as 60 to 1. Nevertheless it was the faith in the reciprocity law that was a guiding principle in photographic photometry for nearly all of the remainder of the nineteenth century, a faith which turned out to be a major factor thwarting the success of early attempts at reliable stellar photometry using the photographic method.

The second paper by Fizeau and Foucault remarked on the phenomenon of solar limb darkening, which had been discovered visually by Bouguer [9]. The decrease in solar brightness towards the limb was shown very clearly in a later solar photograph by the same authors on 2 April 1845, sometimes cited as the first successful solar daguerreotype. It also showed two sunspot groups. The confirmation of solar limb darkening was one of the early triumphs of photography and of qualitative astronomical photometry. It was to have great significance for the theory of solar atmospheric structure from the 1920s onwards.

By 1863 Henry Roscoe (1833–1915) in Manchester had made quantitative photometric measurements of solar limb darkening [10]. He did this by the visual comparison of the amounts of blackening produced on photographic paper by different parts of the image of the sun's disk, with the degrees of blackening of the same paper in a pendulum-photometer. The latter instrument had an oscillating mask that alternately covered and exposed a piece of the photographic paper to sunlight in such a way as to produce a strip of calibrated variable exposure.

4.2   The advent of stellar photography

In the 1840s and '50s many observers successfully photographed the moon and the sun, both from Europe and the United States. The more difficult task of stellar photography was not tackled until after the first decade of photographic endeavour. In view of the very low efficiency of daguerreotype plates, both a large telescope and long exposure times would be necessary. Long exposure times in turn demanded a telescope with a first class mechanical drive in order to keep the stellar images stationary in the telescope's field of view.

In 1847 the director of the Harvard College Observatory, William Bond (1789–1859), invited the well known Boston daguerreotypists John A. Whipple and J. Wallace Black to attempt celestial photography through the Harvard 15-inch refractor. The telescope had been installed at Harvard that same year and was at that time one of the two largest refractors in the world (the other being the Pulkovo telescope). The first attempts were apparently unsuccessful. However, by December 1849 Whipple had obtained the best lunar daguerreotypes yet made (for this he was awarded a prize medal at the 1851 Great Exhibition of the Crystal Palace in London where the daguerreotypes of the moon were displayed) [11].

On 17 July 1850, Whipple, with the assistance of George Bond, the director's astronomer son, obtained the first successful daguerreotype of a star. William Bond reported:

> With the assistance of Mr. Whipple, daguerreotypist, we have obtained several impressions of the star Vega (α Lyrae). We have reason to believe this to be the first successful experiment of the kind ever made, either in this country or abroad. From the facility with which these were executed, with the aid of our great equatorial, we were encouraged to hope that the way is opening for further progress. If it should prove successful when applied to stars of less brilliancy than α Lyrae, so as to give us correct pictures of double and multiple stars, the advantages would be incalculable [12].

However, Polaris gave no impression, indicating the extreme slowness of the plates used [13].

The experiments in stellar photography were resumed in 1857, by which time two major improvements were available. The first was the regulation of the telescope's drive with a spring governor, the second the use of the wet collodion plates, which had a speed advantage over daguerreotypes by a factor of 10 to 100. The wet collodion process had been proposed by G. Le Gray in France in 1851. The glass plates had to be exposed immediately after dipping into silver nitrate solution to sensitize them.

Fig. 4.1   The Harvard College Observatory 15-inch refractor.

They were exposed while still wet, hardly a convenient process for the astronomer, but the advantages of increased speed and the possibility of printing multiple copies from the resulting negatives led to their being favoured for astronomical work.

At the time of the renewed experiments in stellar photography at Harvard,

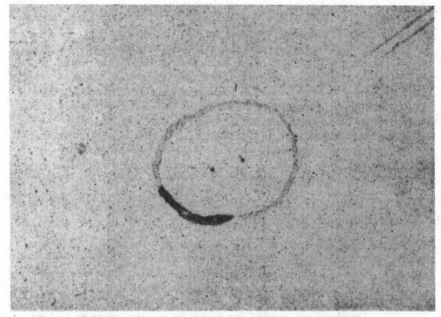

Fig. 4.2   Mizar and Alcor, photographed by George Bond at Harvard, 27 April 1857.

George Bond was the driving force that brought this new science to fruition. With Whipple and Black in April 1857, he obtained the first stellar collodion plate of the visual binary Mizar (ζ Ursae Majoris), with the nearby optical companion Alcor as a third star [13, 14]. George Bond reported the success to the *Astronomische Nachrichten*:

> On the 27th of April of the present year, impressions were first obtained of the double star Mizar (ζ Ursae Majoris) and Alcor (*g* Ursae Majoris) in its immediate vicinity all at a single exposure by the collodion process, in eighty seconds. We have however since ascertained that the principle [*sic*] star requires but two or three seconds only to afford a decided image [13].

This was the first stellar photograph of unqualified success. Many more collodion photographs of Mizar were secured during the summer of 1857, and 86 of these were used by Bond, Whipple and Black for astrometry of the two stars in the binary [13, 15, 16]. In the last cited article Bond spoke of the 'diffusion and uncertain definition characterizing the photographic discs of stars, compared with their appearance viewed directly through the telescope'. In spite of this nature of the photographic images, astrometry in excellent accord with that of F. G. W. Struve was achieved. He concluded the paper with an interesting reference to the possibility of stellar photographic photometry:

> The comparison of images of stars of different brightness so as to ascertain the relation between the diameters and intensity of their images and the quantity of light and time of exposure, I have not found time to complete. It is certain that the difference in magnitude manifests itself in two independent ways. In the diameters of images of different stars with the same exposures and in the length of time necessary to produce the first visible trace of chemical action. Whether in either of these there is the requisite sensitiveness and certainty, remains to be ascertained from the experiments which we have already made for the purpose [16].

In July 1857 George Bond wrote to his friend William Mitchell describing the merits of astronomical photography:

> Of the beauty and convenience of the process you will scarcely form a correct idea without witnessing for yourself ... On a fine night the amount of work that can be accomplished, with an entire exemption from the trouble, vexation, and fatigue which seldom fail to attend upon ordinary observations, is astonishing.
>
> The plates once secured, can be laid by for future study by daylight and at leisure. The record is there, with no room for doubt or mistakes as to its fidelity. As yet, however, we obtain images only from stars to the sixth magnitude, inclusive. To be of essential service to astronomy, it is indispensable that great improvements be yet made, and these, I feel sure, will not be accomplished without a deal of experimenting. To do this properly we need for at least a year to come the services of the excellent artists who have hitherto literally given us their assistance, expensive materials and instruments. They should be liberally remunerated, and feel at liberty, when the prospect is good for a fair night, to give up their day's business and come to the work fresh and fit to spend the whole night at the telescope. As matters are at present they come to the observatory thoroughly exhausted, for it generally happens that the best nights are preceded by their busiest days.
>
> ... We should soon be able to say what what we can and what we cannot accomplish in stellar photography – the latter limits we certainly have not reached as yet. At present the chief object of attention must be to improve the sensitiveness of the plates, to which I am assured by high authorities in chemistry there is scarcely any limit to be put in point of theory. Suppose we are finally to obtain pictures of seventh magnitude stars. It is reasonable to suppose that on some lofty mountain and in a purer atmosphere we might, with the same telescope, include the eighth magnitude. To increase the size of the telescope threefold in aperture is a practicable thing if the money can be found. This would increase the brightness of the stellar images, say eightfold, and we should be able then to photograph all the stars to the tenth and eleventh magnitude, inclusive. There is nothing then so

extravagant in predicting a future application of photography to stellar astronomy on a most magnificent scale. It is even at this moment simply a question of finding one or two hundred thousand dollars to make the telescope with and to keep up the experiments ....

P.S. I find I have forgotten to allude to two important features in stellar photography – one is that the intensity and size of the images taken in connection with the length of time during which the plate has been exposed measures the relative magnitudes of the stars. The other point is, that the measurement of distances and angles of position of double stars from the plates, we have ascertained by many trials on our earliest impressions, to be as exact as the best micrometric work. Our subsequent pictures are much more perfect, and should do better still [17].

Bond's letter to Mitchell shows he had a clear vision of the future potential of the new technique for astronomical research, and his plans clearly included stellar photometry. In July 1858 Bond sent his third paper on stellar photometry to the *Astronomische Nachrichten*, this time with an investigation of the photometric properties of the collodion plates [18]. It was the first paper to be published in a new field which was, by the turn of the century, to become a major astronomical industry.

The paper commenced with an optimistic statement of the benefits of photographic photometry over the then current visual method:

Photographs of Stars of unequal brightness present marked peculiarities in size and intensity, when their images formed in equal exposures are compared together, at once suggesting the possibility of classifying them according to a scale of photographic or chemical magnitudes, analogous to the common optical scale, but differing from it essentially, in the fact of its being based upon actual measurements, in place of the vague and uncertain estimates to which astronomers have hitherto resorted in attempting to express with numbers the relative brightness of different stars.

There are three particulars in which the proposed system will have an unquestionable advantage over that in common use, provided that the chemical action of the starlight is found to be energetic enough to furnisch [sic] accurate determinations of its amount. It will be less liable to be affected by individual peculiarities of vision. There will be less room for discordance between different observers, or for disagreement between the conclusions of the same observer at different times, as to the qualities or proportions constituting the various grades of magnitude. – Lastly it will meet perfectly the greatest of the many difficulties of the problem of the comparison of stars exhibiting diversity of colour [18].

Bond then deduced a relationship between image diameter y and exposure time t of the form $Pt + Q = y^2$. Here Q was a negative constant for a plate, being related to the time t_0 required before the first (zero-size) image of a star appeared. Thereafter, stellar images increased in size at a rate such that an equal area was added in equal times, the rate of increase of area depending on each individual star through the parameter P, which Bond called the photographic power of a star, in reality the relative stellar intensity for photographic light.

George Bond's first experiments in stellar photography were greatly curtailed after his father died in 1859 and George became the director of Harvard College Observatory. The year 1857 remained easily his most successful year in this new endeavour, with photographs of several stars, Saturn and Jupiter being recorded.

When George Bond died in 1865 it was the end of the first short era of photographic stellar photometry. From 1857 to 1882 there was a quarter century of relative inactivity in stellar photographic work. In England Warren de la Rue (1815–89) made his reputation from his lunar and solar photography. In 1858 he obtained photographs of Castor (α Gem) showing the two components of the visual binary as 'round discs distinctly separated' [19]. He again made some stellar exposures in 1860 when he photographed the Pleiades and the Orion constellation [20], but undertook no photometry. The success of his photography can in part be ascribed to his use of a reflecting telescope, thus avoiding the troublesome chromatic aberrations of visual refractors for the blue photographic range [21].

In New York, Lewis Rutherfurd (1816–92) was another of the notable pioneers of astronomical photography who was influenced by the earlier successes of the Bonds at Harvard. Rutherfurd reported photographing ninth magnitude stars in 1863 in only 3 minutes in the cluster of Praesepe [22]. For these observations he had an $11\frac{1}{4}$-inch objective doublet lens constructed for photographic work, whereas achromatic refractors were hitherto adjusted for optimum performance in visual light (to which the plates were insensitive). He wrote: 'The power to obtain images of the 9th magnitude stars with so moderate an aperture promises to develop and increase the application of photography to the mapping of the sidereal heavens, and in some measure to realize the hopes which have so long been deferred and disappointed' [22]. Presumably he was referring to the poor results he had obtained with a visual refractor and with a reflector in his earlier experiments since 1858.

Rutherfurd's work in turn impressed Benjamin Gould of the power of celestial photography, and Gould made astrometric measurements on three Rutherfurd plates of the Pleiades [23]. After Gould went to Argentina in 1870 to found the Argentine National Observatory in Córdoba, he had a research assistant, Carl Schultz-Sellack, trained by Rutherfurd in

Fig. 4.3   The Pleiades, photographed by Lewis Rutherfurd, c. 1864 with his $11\frac{1}{4}$-inch refractor, with annotations by Benjamin Gould.

photographic techniques for several weeks (see [24]). Rutherfurd sent his photographic doublet to Argentina with Sellack, but unfortunately the flint glass component was mysteriously cracked in two during transit. Success was achieved by holding the two halves together with metal clasps, and ninth magnitude stars were thereby recorded in 8 minutes, and images of some 27 star clusters were photographed. These were the very first experiments in stellar photography in the southern hemisphere [25, 26]. Unfortunately Sellack chose to publish without Gould's 'permission or even knowledge, results which were in no sense whatever his own' [27], an act which soured the success of this early venture in southern hemisphere photography. However, a new Fitz object glass was received by Gould in 1873, a new assistant hired in 1874 and Gould went on to obtain many excellent photographs of southern star clusters [28].

The photographs of de la Rue, Rutherfurd and Sellack and Gould were nearly all made on wet collodion plates, which were slow and awkward to use. The introduction of the first dry silver bromide gelatine emulsions on glass plates was in 1871. These were used by Gould in Argentina for the latter part of his work on southern clusters, and also by Henry Draper (1837–82), when he photographed the Orion nebula in 1880 [29] with his 11-inch Clark photographic refractor with an exposure of 51 minutes.

By March 1881 Draper had more than doubled the exposure time for his Orion nebula photographs and announced that the pictures showed minute stars down to magnitude 14.7 on Pogson's scale [30].† The magnitude given was presumably a visual one, as it came from the photometry by Pickering at Harvard [34]. Draper noted that 'The variation in size of the stellar images gives an idea of the relative magnitude of the stars, though that estimate requires correction for the colour of the stars' [30]. This was the same year that Edward Pickering began his first photographic trials at Harvard, and it is from this time that the remarkable possibilities offered by photography for celestial mapping and photometry really captured the imagination of the astronomical world. Suddenly many astronomers were initiating photographic programmes and the whole course of astronomy was to be changed in the enthusiasm of the 1880s decade for the new technique.

But even before Pickering had experimented sufficiently with celestial photography to devise the best method of obtaining stellar magnitudes

† A reproduction of this famous photograph appears in Fig. 4.4 and was published by Draper in a monograph by E. S. Holden on the nebula [31]. Soon afterwards the Orion nebula photography was repeated by Ainslie Common (1841–1903) who had been experimenting with dry plate celestial photography from 1879 [32]. His most successful photograph of the nebula was obtained in 1883 using his 36-inch reflector at Ealing near London [33]. He concluded that long exposures with dry plates were able to record stars invisible to the eye in the same telescope.

Fig. 4.4   The Orion nebula photographed by Henry Draper in 1882 in a
137-minute exposure on the 11-inch Clark equatorial refractor with a
dry plate, showing stars to magnitude 14.7.

from the plates, the Reverend T. E. Espin (1858–1934), as an amateur
observer for the Liverpool Astronomical Society, had mounted a Grubb
$4\frac{1}{2}$-inch compound photographic lens at West Kirby in the Wirral near
Liverpool in 1883 [35]. The following year he had devised a technique for
deriving stellar magnitudes from trailed images of stars on the dry Wratten
and Wainwright plates. On each plate the Argelander visual magnitudes

Fig. 4.5   Jules Janssen.

of two or more stars were used as standards and the magnitudes of the other stars then obtained by visual inspection of the trails. A catalogue of 500 photographic magnitudes was published in 1884, the most extensive photographic magnitude catalogue of its time, although it was based on a relatively primitive technique of magnitude estimation [36]. Espin estimated his limiting magnitude to be about 9.8 on untrailed plates exposed for one hour with this lens.

Both Espin and later Pickering favoured trails for photographic stellar photometry, but another method was also proposed in 1881 by Jules Janssen (1824–1907), director of the newly founded astrophysical observatory at Meudon near Paris. Janssen's suggestion was to spread the light into circular discs by placing the plate outside the telescope's focus and comparing what he called the 'degree of opacity' (that is density) in such images:

> A star gives on a photographic plate placed at the focus of the
> instrument a point which is black or dark and more or less regular in
> outline. But because of the small dimensions of this point, it is not
> suitable for photometric measurement. However the situation is quite
> otherwise if, instead of placing the plate in focus, it is placed just
> outside. One then gets a circle of very small diameter and roughly
> uniform blackening (if the objective is of good quality), and it is
> possible to compare the degree of opacity with other circles of similar
> origin. It is necessary to take care to control the action of the light so
> that the blackening within the circle does not become too dark, but
> instead corresponds to those instants of time when the light produces

the greatest possible change [on the plate] with increasing exposure time.

The respective degrees of opacity of two circles so obtained can be compared by photometric methods, but one has to be careful only to take the equality of blackenings into account, so as to avoid the use of tables giving the changes in opacity as a function of luminous intensity ... [37].

At this time Janssen was taking photographs of the Orion nebula with his 50-cm f/3.2 astrograph, but no data were presented using the out-of-focus method.

4.3 Early photographic photometry at Harvard

After an interval of 25 years, research in stellar photography was again resumed at Harvard College Observatory by Professor Edward Pickering in 1882, in collaboration with his younger brother William (1858–1938). At that time William Pickering was making experiments with dry plates in his photographic laboratory at the Massachusetts Institute of Technology – a nice example of his MIT work is a paper examining the relative sensitivity of dry plates from 15 different American and European manufacturers using a sensitometer [38]. Although George Bond at Harvard had favoured measuring the diameters of stellar point-like images for his photometry, Edward Pickering immediately experimented with trailed images using cameras with the sidereal drive disengaged. He first explained the technique in a lecture to the Royal Astronomical Society in June 1883 entitled 'On the determination of the light and colour of the Stars by Photography' [39, 40].

By 1885 Edward Pickering had acquired an 8-inch f/5.6 Voigtländer photographic doublet lens which was mounted by Alvan Clark and Sons in a fork-mounted equatorial astrograph known as the Bache telescope. It was to play a major role in the early Harvard photographic programmes of photometry and objective prism spectroscopy. The plates were 8 × 10 inches, covering 10° × 12° of sky with good images in the central 5° × 5° [41].

Although Pickering considered the possibility of photographic photometry from stellar images recorded as points, trails or surfaces (either out-of-focus circles or widened spectra), his initial work concentrated on trails in which the telescope drive was disengaged. He estimated magnitudes from the trails by choosing a single primary standard star (BD +85° 226, $m_{vis} = 9.5$) and recording for it a series of trails with six different telescope apertures which diminished the light in successive steps of about one magnitude. All other trails were then estimated by reference to the standard trails on a single plate, after making a correction of $2.5 \log \cos \delta$ for a star's declination. This correction is based on the fact that stars near the pole trail more slowly, as well as on an implicit assumption of the validity of the reciprocity law.† In fact the correction proved to be up to a factor of two too large, a result that was one of the earliest indications of reciprocity law failure. Trails on other plates taken at other times were still referenced to the standard by ensuring that the mean magnitude of twenty selected circumpolar stars was always 6.0, a procedure intended to allow for changes in factors such as seeing, plate sensitivity, atmospheric transparency, and development conditions. His approach thus differed markedly from the qualitative diameter measurement of stellar points used by Bond.

This work on trails was undertaken from 1885 with the collaboration of Williamina Fleming (1857–1911), and a major contribution to photographic photometry was published in 1890 in which magnitudes were presented for 1009 stars within $1°$ of the pole (m brighter than 15), for 1131 bright equatorial stars (the polar trails were exposed on the same plates to transfer the photographic scale to the equator) and for 420 stars in the Pleiades [42]. In the case of the Pleiades stars, point images rather than trails were used, and the calibration was by multiple images of different exposure time on a standard reference plate, with the telescope displaced slightly between exposures. Pickering estimated from his early work on polar trails that the probable error of the determination was around $\pm0^{m}.12$ [41]. According to Harold Weaver, the method of trails gave unsatisfactory results, because the compressions of trails with increasing declination led to an uncertain correction. 'These corrections, unfortunately, could not be determined by fundamental means then available, and, moreover, very probably varied from exposure to exposure owing to the effects of seeing' [43].

The zero-point of this early photographic photometry was established by requiring that on average the visual and photographic magnitudes of stars would be equal. Many of the early investigators found stars which were either unexpectedly bright or absent on the photographs. However, Pickering was among those who clearly saw this not so much as a problem but an advantage of the photographic method, as it provided a means of determining stellar colour:

> The fact that the photographic intensity will vary greatly with the color can scarcely be called an objection. We wish to know the true relative intensities of the light of the stars, and not merely their relative brightness as judged by the eye. As long as the spectra of the

---

† The reciprocity law states that the photographic blackening depends on the product of intensity and exposure time.

objects compared are the same, that is, as long as the light of any given wave-length emitted by each bears the same proportion to the whole, all methods of measurement will give the same result. In other words, the relative intensity will appear to be the same, whether it is measured by the eye or by the sensitive plate. This is the more precise statement which is commonly expressed by saying that the color is the same. When the spectra differ, and the colors are unlike, no single number will properly express the ratio of the two lights. The only true comparison is by a series of numbers which express the ratio of the light for each different wave-length. When, therefore, we say that a red and a blue star appear equally bright, we merely indicate that the entire radiation affects the eye equally. The visual result will not in general differ much from what would be attained if all the light had a wave-length .00006 cm., or 6000 ten-millionths of a millimetre. The photographic plate gives a more precise summing up of all the radiations, since no difference of color appears in the final picture, but the mean wave-length is not far from 4000 ten-millionths of a millimetre. Accordingly, blue stars will appear comparatively much brighter in the photograph, and red stars brighter to the eye. Their relative light can be determined only by comparison of the spectra [41, pp. 202–203].

Indeed, the importance of spectrophotometry and of specifying the wavelength at which the brightness of a star was measured was put into practice in the *Draper Memorial Catalogue of Stellar Spectra* in which the spectral types and photographic magnitudes at 432 nm of 10 351 stars were presented from trailed objective prism spectra taken with the Bache telescope [44] – see also [45, 46]. For the spectrophotometry a graduated and calibrated photographic density wedge was used to estimate the spectral intensities from the blackening of the plates at 432 nm. In addition a standard laboratory light source was used to expose a calibration spot on every plate, so that 'the quality of the plate and the excellence of the developer' could be monitored [45, p. 7].

One aspect of Pickering's work is that in addition to carrying out enormous programmes of stellar photometry and spectroscopy, he was at the same time always experimenting with new observational techniques. For example, to obtain photographic magnitudes from Orion nebula exposures made by Henry Draper and Ainslie Common, he calibrated the magnitude scale using a photographic sequence in which the stars were placed in order of brightness, a method analogous to the visual technique used a century earlier by William Herschel (see section 2.1) [47]. The small differences between consecutive stars were estimated in 'grades', each grade or step corresponding to just over a tenth of a magnitude. Another method applicable to stellar point images entailed cementing a small circular prism

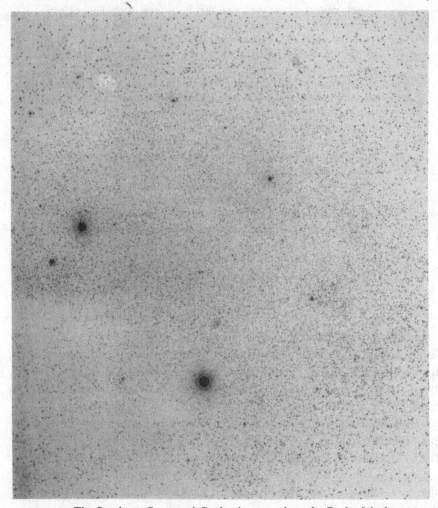

Fig. 4.6   The Southern Cross and Coalsack exposed on the Bache 8-inch
telescope at the Boyden Station in Peru, May 1893, in a 127-minute
exposure. A small prism has been cemented to the objective to give
secondary images, slightly displaced from each primary image and 5
magnitudes fainter.

(diameter 2 cm) of very small (10 arc min) angle to the centre of the Bache
objective. This refracted about 1 per cent of the light, giving secondary
stellar images just 5 magnitudes fainter than the primary images for each
star [41, pp. 183–4] (see also [45, p. xiv]) and hence enabled the magnitude
scale of the plate to be calibrated.

When William Pickering joined his brother at Harvard College Observatory in 1887 this allowed him to continue his photographic researches and to apply the results to astronomical photometry. He was interested in what he called 'quantitative photography', especially the practice of exposing small squares on plates from a standard lamp, and the investigation of the relation between density and time of exposure [48]. He was one of the early investigators who explicitly discounted the reciprocity law [48, p. 21], which states that photographic density is a function of the product of intensity and exposure time. This law had originated much earlier from the work of Bunsen and Roscoe [49], and faith in its essential validity dominated nearly all photographic photometry in the nineteenth century.

The work of William Pickering in quantitative photography came at about the same time as a similar programme in England by Captain William Abney (1843–1920), who investigated the relationship between the transparency of the image and the exposure [50]. Soon afterwards Ferdinand Hurter and Vero Driffield, of the United Atlantic Co., brought in the mathematical concept of density as a measure of the blackening on a photographic plate (defined as density $D = -\log T$, where T is the optical transmission), and they presented characteristic curves (D versus logarithm of the exposure) for various emulsions under different conditions of development [51] – sometimes since referred to as HD curves.

William Pickering applied his experience in quantitative photography to the problems which his brother was undertaking in stellar photometry. It is likely he influenced Edward Pickering in the choice of the method, using a calibrated photographic scale rather than that of image diameter [48, p. 32]. He also advocated fixing the zero-point of the photographic magnitude scale by requiring the visual and photographic magnitudes to be equal, not for all stars, but only for those of Secchi's first spectral type (that is for A stars on the later MK system). This ensured that the influence of different star colours was largely eliminated [48, p. 31], though he admitted that discrepancies of a few tenths of a magnitude (between m_{vis} and m_{pg}) could still arise for individual stars of this type.

William Pickering's principal contribution to stellar photometric data was a study he made of stars in or near the Orion nebula which complemented the visual work of George Bond [52]. The photographic magnitudes of about 670 stars were determined by comparison with 22 standard stars in the same field, whose magnitudes were in turn derived by reference to the same scales as used by Edward Pickering to determine magnitudes in the Pleiades [48, p. 36]. In establishing these scales, Pickering decided that if two exposures were made in the ratio of 3 to 1 in exposure time, then stars differing by 1 magnitude would make the same photographic impression on the plate. The three-to-one ratio appears to be an empirical rule based on experience rather than exhaustive measurements, and was adopted to correct for the effects of failure in the reciprocity law.

4.4   The *Cape Photographic Durchmusterung*

The 1880s decade was a time of extraordinary optimism in stellar astronomy, arising from a belief that photography would herald undreamed of advances in the charting of faint stars as well as in stellar astrometry, photometry and spectroscopy. The optimism was justified; tremendous advances were made in all these fields and unexpected discoveries (such as that of nebulosity around the brightest stars in the Pleiades [53] – see section 4.5) were made. Certainly expectations exceeded the results, as is now well-known, and disappointments followed, especially so in the difficult field of stellar photometry, where many intractable problems at first lay hidden for the unwary astronomer. Systematic errors plagued most early photographic photometry because the photometric properties of the plates were at first only poorly understood. These problems were slowly unravelled between 1880 and the 1920s as a result of much painstaking effort at observatories and in laboratories.

Nevertheless, several large stellar photometric programmes were initiated in the optimism of the 1880s. The work of Pickering and Mrs Fleming resulted in the first major catalogue of photographic stellar magnitudes [42] and as early as 1883 Pickering had announced his intention to undertake 'the construction of a photographic map of the whole heavens' [54]. Meanwhile, similar ambitions were being formulated at the Cape and in Paris. It was David Gill (1843–1914) at the Cape who undertook one of the most successful large scale photographic programmes of celestial mapping in this era – the *Cape Photographic Durchmusterung* (CPD).

The idea of embarking on this great programme, to complement the work of Argelander and Schönfeld for stars visible from Bonn, came to Gill in November 1882 after he had commissioned a local photographer, Mr Allis, to record images of the comet of 1882 using a $2\frac{1}{2}$-inch f/4.4 Ross lens:

> Apart from their scientific interest as representations of the Comet itself, these photographs appeared to have a still wider interest from the fact that, notwithstanding the small optical power of the instrument with which they were obtained, they showed so many stars, and these so well defined over so large an area, as to suggest the practicability of employing similar, but more powerful, means for the construction of star-maps, on any required scales and to any required order of magnitude [55].

Fig. 4.7   Sir David Gill.

Six of the Allis photographs, including one of 140 minutes exposure, were presented by Gill to the Academy of Sciences in Paris [56] and prompted Admiral Mouchez, director of the Paris Observatory, to remark that 'it is now no longer permissible to doubt that it will soon be possible to make excellent celestial maps by means of Photography' [57].

Gill moved quickly to implement his plan, writing immediately to John

Fig. 4.8   The *Cape Photographic Durchmusterung* telescope.

Dallmeyer (1832–83), the noted English manufacturer of photographic lenses. Eventually he acquired a Dallmeyer 6-inch f/9 lens and in January 1885 he received a £300 grant from the Royal Society for celestial photography. With this grant Gill employed a photographic assistant, Ray Woods, and after some preliminary experiments, he commenced the observing programme for the CPD in April 1885. This was five months before

Thome initiated visual observing for the *Córdoba Durchmusterung* for which the aims were similar, although the technique was quite different.

The CPD plates covered $6° \times 6°$ and each of 613 areas between $-18°$ and the south pole was photographed at least twice. Initially the exposures were one hour and gave measurable images to magnitude 9.5, but the exposure times were reduced to 45 or 30 minutes when more sensitive plates were used from October 1887. The whole project required over 3000 exposures (about half of which were eventually used) and the observational work was completed by the end of October 1891, in only six and a half years.

The Royal Society grant in 1885 and again the following year permitted the plates to be exposed. But the plan was to obtain positions and magnitudes of all stars south of $-18°$ to at least magnitude 9.2. For the reduction of the plates Gill lacked the resources. The solution to this problem eventually came unexpectedly from Jacobus Kapteyn (1851–1922), the director of the Astronomical Laboratory at the University of Groningen. Kapteyn wrote to Gill in December 1885 offering his services to reduce the plates in Groningen using Dutch funds and assistants:

> I would gladly give up some years of my life to this work, which would disburden you a little, as I hope, and by which I would gain the honour of associating my name with one of the greatest undertakings of our time.

Gill's correspondence to Kapteyn was published in [55]. Kapteyn estimated the reductions would take six or seven years – in the end they required nearly thirteen, mainly because the southern heavens were found to contain nearly twice as many stars per square degree as anticipated [58, p. 17]. The total number of stars in the CPD between $-18°$ and the pole was 454 875, or 32.66 per square degree, compared with only 15.19 recorded by Argelander at Bonn [58, p. 19]. The number of stars was, however, substantially less than in the rival *Córdoba Durchmusterung*, which contained 579 000 stars south of $-22°$ – see section 2.7.

So was born one of the most fruitful collaborations in the early history of astrophysics, and probably the first major programme in which institutions in different countries collaborated as equal partners. Later Arthur Stanley Eddington (1882–1944) commented on how this joint endeavour between Groningen and the Cape came about:

> At the end of 1885 there began his [Kapteyn's] partnership with Sir David Gill in the *Cape Photographic Durchmusterung*, by which Kapteyn took over the laborious task of measurement and reduction of the plates. This catalogue for the southern sky between $-18°$ and the south pole fills the same position that the *Bonn Durchmusterung* does for the northern heavens, but it reaches a somewhat fainter limit

of magnitude; it includes 450,000 stars. In this task Kapteyn generally had the services of two or three assistants; but they were for the most part unskilled (if I remember rightly, some of the work was done by prison-inmates), and the amount of individual work and attention falling on him was very heavy. Referring to the drudgery of the work, Kapteyn wrote to Gill: "However, I think my enthusiasm for the matter will be equal to (say) six or seven years of such work." It took not seven years but thirteen; his enthusiasm did not fail, and the *Cape Durchmusterung* was completed with a thoroughness and accuracy to which many have borne testimony [59].

Kapteyn's participation and support undoubtedly saved Gill's programme from an embarrassing financial difficulty, given that the Royal Society grant was not renewed in 1887 because of the then apparently more rewarding prospects of the *Carte du Ciel* and *Astrographic Catalogue* programme for which Gill himself had been a leading advocate. The result was that the Cape activities for the CPD had to be funded from Gill's own resources, to which he committed about half of his annual salary [60]. No funds were, however, available from this source for the measurement of the plates and the production of the catalogue.

Kapteyn received the first plates for the circumpolar stars early in 1887. His method of obtaining positions was unusual. He placed a small theodolite telescope at a point 54 inches in front of the plate (the focal length of the Dallmeyer lens) and obtained equatorial coordinates directly to a precision of about six arc seconds.

For the photographic photometry Kapteyn followed George Bond and measured the stellar diameters. These were converted to magnitudes using the empirical interpolation formula $m = B/(\text{diam.} + C)$, where the constants B and C were calibrated for each plate using the visual magnitudes for about a hundred stars on that plate. The principal source of the visual magnitudes was Gould's *Zone Catalogue* [61], for which the estimated values reached to about magnitude $9\frac{1}{2}$. Given the differences between visual and photographic magnitudes which Pickering had drawn attention to, the Kapteyn procedure appeared less than satisfactory. However, it was undertaken in the belief that the discrepancies of individual stars could be overcome by adopting the mean relationship for a large number of objects.

The whole problem of the calibrations was complicated by Kapteyn's discovery that the mean colours of stars depended on their galactic latitudes:

> Even considering only stars of one and the same spectral type the stars of the Milky Way are in general bluer than the stars in other regions of the sky [62, see p. 22] – see also [63].

He attempted to provide corrections (sometimes larger than half a magnitude) obtained statistically for this effect and which depended on magnitude and declination as well as on galactic latitude, but in the end he had to conclude that 'the system of photographic magnitudes of our catalogue cannot be regarded otherwise than as a first approximation to a really irreproachable system' [62, see p. (50)].

Apart from these troublesome and often large systematic errors in the CPD magnitudes, Kapteyn found the random probable errors to be mainly between $\pm 0^{m}\!\!.07$ and $\pm 0^{m}\!\!.10$, the mean value being $\pm 0^{m}\!\!.075$, a precision comparable to the best visual photometry [62, see p. 54] – see also [64].

The whole work of the CPD took Kapteyn and his assistants 13 years to complete. The work had been begun in October 1886 and it was not till the end of the century when the third and final volume of the great catalogue appeared in print [65]. Gill acknowledged that Kapteyn's share of the work had been much greater than his own and paid tribute to the accuracy of the printed catalogue:

> Probably no work of the kind of like extent has ever been issued so
> free from typographical and other errors. It is impossible to
> overestimate its value to southern sidereal astronomy, and still more
> impossible to adequately express the gratitude which is due to Kapteyn
> for his self-sacrificing labours [66, see p. lviii].

4.4.1   Later analysis of the CPD magnitudes

That the CPD contained systematic errors in its magnitude scale was recognized by Kapteyn. But the serious nature of these errors was emphasized as a result of the work of Jacob Halm (1866–1944) who had joined the Cape Observatory staff in 1907 shortly after Gill's retirement. Halm set about establishing a fundamental system of southern photographic stellar magnitudes for 78 stars near the south pole, which comprised a south polar sequence comparable to that in use in the northern hemisphere [67]. He used these fundamental magnitudes which had been calibrated with a wire objective grating (see section 4.9) to determine the magnitudes of fainter CPD stars in the −45° declination zone. Halm's standard scale coincided with the CPD at magnitude 7.5, but the two diverged rapidly and differed by nearly 2 magnitudes for $m_{CPD} = 9.5$. He concluded that although the CPD scale represented a true magnitude system, the scale constant R was considerably larger than the Pogson value of 2.512. A difference of 1 magnitude on the CPD scale corresponded to 1.82 magnitudes on Halm's photographic standard scale.

In addition Halm found substantial zero-point differences in the CPD scale as a function of right ascension in the −45° zone [67]. He related these to the changes in the mean colour of stars in this zone with right ascension, and hence concluded that 'an intimate connection between the differences (standard-C.P.D.) and the position of the area in relation to the Milky Way is undeniable' [67], a problem which Kapteyn had suspected but not quantified.

Both these systematic effects were further explored by Halm in 1918 when he recalibrated his standard magnitude scale for south polar stars [68]. Meanwhile Edward Pickering of Harvard had made an even more extensive investigation of CPD magnitudes. The Harvard and CPD scales coincided at $m = 6.0$, but differed by 1.7 magnitudes at $m_{CPD} = 10^m.5$ [69, 70]. In addition the systematic errors in the CPD with right ascension were tabulated by giving corrections for each plate (ranging from $+0^m.4$ to $-0^m.6$). Application of both corrections enabled any CPD magnitude to be reduced to the Harvard scale, which was similar to that established by Halm.

The systematic errors in the CPD magnitudes presumably arose partly from the errors in the visual magnitude estimates of Gould's *Zone Catalogue* which were used to calibrate the plates, and partly from the problems of using visual magnitudes for photographic calibrations and the question of the photographic magnitude scale zero-point that this raises, but was not dealt with, in Kapteyn's reductions.

In spite of these problems the *Cape Photographic Durchmusterung* remains as a fine tribute to the determination and efficiency of Gill and Kapteyn. Given the primitive state of the art of photographic photometry in 1885, the surprising thing is not that large systematic errors were committed, but that such a large programme should have been launched at all and brought to a successful completion in less than 15 years.

4.5   The *Carte du Ciel* and *Astrographic Catalogue*

In June 1884 at the Paris Observatory, the brothers Paul and Prosper Henry – respectively (1848–1905) and (1849–1903) – began experiments in celestial photography using a 16-cm achromatic objective lens. On showing the results to Rear-Admiral Ernest Mouchez (1821–92), director of the observatory, his comment was:

> I was so struck by the exceptional beauty of this first trial and by its extreme importance for the future of Astronomy that, in spite of several administrative difficulties, I did not hesitate to accept their proposal to have a large instrument built specially for photography of 33-cm aperture ... [71].

Fig. 4.9   Admiral Ernest Mouchez.

The new 33-cm astrograph (focal length 343 cm) was operational by April 1885 and allowed stars of about fifteenth magnitude to be reached in an exposure of about one hour [53]. The aim was to produce photographically a chart and catalogue of faint stars in the zodiac, a task which Chacornac and then the Henrys had already embarked upon from visual observations. It is with this instrument that the Henrys discovered nebulosity around the bright star Maïa in the Pleiades [72], although the existence of nebulosity around the bright stars in this cluster had been reported earlier from visual observations.

The success of the Henry photographs came to the attention of David Gill who wrote to Mouchez and 'suggested that the time had now come when steps should be taken to make a systematic international effort to apply like instruments and methods to the complete mapping of the sky' [66]. Mouchez concurred, whereupon Gill proposed in June 1886 that an international congress in Paris be organized [73]. Mouchez was at

Fig. 4.10   Paul and Prosper Henry with their astrograph at the Paris Observatory.

once the persuasive champion of this cause. He circulated a 'Proposal for Photographing the Heavens', including a copy to the Royal Society, which declared

> ... the moment has come ... to undertake the complete map of the celestial vaults by establishing an understanding between 6 or 8 observatories well situated in the two hemispheres ... Six, eight or ten years at most will allow this vast project to be realised and to be a legacy to future centuries showing a very exact picture of the sky at the end of the nineteenth century. The very high importance of such a project and the numerous discoveries that it promises for astronomers of the future, bring me to beg you to have the plan scrutinized by your illustrious Society as to find the means of coming to an agreement to prepare for and carry out the project, if it is thought to be at all feasible [74].

In a very short time interval the famous International Astrographic Congress was organized by the Académie des Sciences and took place in Paris in April 1887. Fifty-six astronomers from 18 countries attended, although these included only three astronomers from the United States and four from the southern hemisphere. This was the first international conference in astronomy and one of the earliest in any science.

Otto Struve (1819–1905) of Pulkovo Observatory became the president of the Congress. The congress resolved

> ... to prepare a general photographic map of the sky for the present epoch, and to obtain data which will allow the positions and the magnitudes of all the stars down to a given level to be determined with the greatest possible precision (the magnitudes being understood in a photographic sense yet to be defined) [75, p. 101].

Both a *Carte du Ciel* (map) to magnitude 14 and an *Astrographic Catalogue* to magnitude 11 were agreed upon, with 3 half-hour exposures being required on each plate for the *Carte*, and of a few minutes for the *Catalogue*.

All plates were to be taken on identical refracting astrographs of 33-cm aperture of the type already in use in Paris. The plates covered $2° \times 2°$ of sky and were 16-cm square. Because of the need for separate exposures for the *Carte* and *Catalogue* programmes and the requirement for overlapping plates, a total of 44 108 plates was envisaged by the Astrographic Congress by the time of the third meeting in 1891 [76, p. 135]. The work was divided among 18 observatories (of which 6 were in the southern hemisphere) – each observatory being assigned a declination zone and agreeing to take an average of about 1200 plates in each programme. Several months after the first Astrographic Congress, Gill wrote to Mouchez with concise details of the proposed organization for the two projects [77]. For the *Catalogue* alone he estimated 17 to 25 years and 6 250 000 French francs would be needed to undertake the whole programme comprising 20 627 plates and about 2 million stars down to magnitude 11. The time estimate was based on all the work of reductions being undertaken by a central bureau. In the event the reductions were made by each participating observatory in a most inhomogeneous manner, yet it still took three times longer than Gill had anticipated! (Further discussions of the programme and on Gill's estimates for the time and cost were published by R. Radau [78]; English translation in [79].)

None of the participating observatories was in North America. Pickering, the world's most illustrious stellar photographer during all these years, never attended a congress. He had written to Mouchez prior to the 1887 meeting generally offering his services and advice, but in practice he kept Harvard's involvement to a minimum [80]. Indeed, the Harvard astronomer D. Norman, with the benefit of hindsight in 1938, ascribed the success of many American observatories in new areas of astrophysics to their complete abstention from the *Carte du Ciel* and *Astrographic Catalogue* programmes.

Pickering's subsequent action of obtaining a bequest in 1889 of $50 000 from Miss Catherine Bruce (1816–1900), the astronomical benefactor, for the construction of a large 24-inch photographic telescope to make a 'Chart of the Heavens' did not endear him to the members of the Astrographic Congress. Indeed, Herbert Turner (1861–1930) and Ainslie Common, editors of *the Observatory* in England, bitterly complained in print of the 'scant courtesy' shown by Pickering towards the congress, believing that the Astrographic Congress in Paris

> ... may reasonably expect to hear from him why he has determined to set up a rival scheme to the one on which they have expended so much thought, without more particularly pointing out the relative merits and demerits of the two [81].

Pickering politely responded that he had been the first to propose photographing the whole sky, which he had done as early as June 1883 in an address to the Royal Astronomical Society [39], and that 'duplication by instruments of different forms hardly seems objectionable' [82].

On the other hand it would seem that the Astrographic Congress was reliant on Pickering and the work at Harvard to resolve the difficulties they found themselves in over the determination of photographic magnitudes. The Harvard work on the North Polar Sequence, which defined primary standards for photographic magnitudes, as well as a procedure for transferring this magnitude scale to other regions of the sky, was eventually adopted by the Congress for the work of the *Astrographic Catalogue* in 1913 [83] – see section 4.9.1.

The success of the Bruce photographic telescope fully justified Pickering's action. On the other hand, the *Carte du Ciel* programme posed a severe burden on all participating institutions, stifling new research initiatives for many decades and causing great financial hardships. One of the greatest international scientific programmes ever devised was also one of the greatest failures, and the eventual demise of several of the observatories was no doubt due to the strain imposed by participation. Five of the original observatories gave up the work before completion, while further institutions were co-opted to continue the programme.

Pickering himself later commented on the problems of the *Carte du Ciel* programme:

> The great work of a chart of the entire sky, undertaken by the Paris Observatory in cooperation with several others, is a sad example of the danger of undertaking a work on too large a scale. Although several observatories have been continually at work upon it for a quarter of a century, it is predicted that at least fifty years must elapse before it is completed, and no positions of any southern stars have yet been published. In striking contrast to this is the early completion of the *Cape Photographic Durchmusterung* which gives the positions and magnitudes of nearly half a million stars south of −19° [84].

The *Astrographic Catalogue* was completed in 1962, 75 years after the first Astrographic Congress, but in a very inhomogeneous manner so far as the different institutions were concerned. The *Carte du Ciel* was never completed; four observatories failed to take the plates required while only about half the exposures envisaged were copied and distributed – see discussion by P. Couderc [85].

The 1880s was a period of unparalleled optimism in photographic astronomy. A splendid future was foreseen for stellar astrometry, photometry and spectroscopy using the new technique. Many major successful programmes were started at this time, such as the *Draper Memorial Catalogue of Stellar Spectra*, the Potsdam photographic radial velocity, spectral classification and spectral line wavelength programmes, the Harvard photographic photometry and the *Cape Photographic Durchmusterung*. The *Carte du Ciel* and *Astrographic Catalogue* programmes alone were the major casualties.

What went wrong? By the time of the sixth congress in 1909 Mouchez, both Henry brothers and the congress president, Otto Struve, had all died, and Gill had retired – these were the main figures who had devised the original plan. Several observatories were never properly funded, including Santiago, La Plata and Rio de Janeiro, all of which were forced to withdraw. But it was the complexities of photographic plates themselves, problems little understood in 1887, which was the main cause of the difficulties. No-one had a full picture of how to derive magnitudes from *Catalogue* plates in 1887 and few foresaw the many problems. Pickering was aware of some of these, but his major memoir of 1888 was still in press at the time of the first congress.

As a major source of photometric data the *Astrographic Catalogue* was a failure. But the stimulus of the international congresses and the need to tackle the *Catalogue* programme resulted in a widespread study of photographic photometry. It took some 25 years for these problems to be properly understood by which time the Great War intervened. And after the ravages of war, Mouchez's grandiose project was never really given a second chance.

4.6　　The quest for photographic magnitudes from focal images

The Astrographic Congress of April 1887 had one very beneficial influence. Suddenly astronomers had to find ways of measuring photographic magnitudes for millions of faint stars to magnitude 11, yet it soon became evident that there was no clear picture of how to undertake this photometry. There was no agreed definition of a photographic magnitude scale and very few stars had been measured visually to such faint limits. Even the exposure time to reach magnitude 11 was uncertain. At the second congress in 1889 Prosper Henry had maintained that increasing the exposure time by a factor of 2.5 resulted in stars one magnitude fainter being recorded, and after much discussion it was therefore decided that the *Catalogue* plates should be exposed 6.25 times longer than required for stars of visual magnitude 9 [86]. At this time no-one challenged the reciprocity law on which this resolution was based. Both Janssen at Meudon [87] and Lohse at Potsdam [88] before the first congress had strongly asserted its correctness.

By 1891 the reciprocity law had been challenged by several workers. The first doubts came from Edward Pickering at Harvard [42, 45] followed in quick succession by Pritchard [89], Scheiner [90, 91] Abney [92, 93], William Pickering [48] and Dunér [94, 95].

All these observers found that progressively fainter stars required increasingly longer exposure times to record them than predicted by the Pogson 2.5 factor per magnitude. For example, Scheiner estimated an exposure 2.5 times as long gained only between 0.5 and 0.75 of a magnitude [90]. The hopes of defining a scale of photographic magnitudes based simply on the validity of the reciprocity law, as had been proposed for example by Dunér at the 1891 Congress [96], were therefore dashed.

Table 4.1. *Empirical formulae for magnitude m
vs image diameter d*

m	$=$	$A - B\sqrt{d}$	W. H. M. Christie	[97]
			H. H. Turner	[99]
m	$=$	$A - B\log d$	C. Pritchard	[89]
m	$=$	$A - B\log d$	C. V. L. Charlier	[100]
d	$=$	$a + b(m_0 - m)$	J. Scheiner	[101]
d	$=$	$-a\log m + b$	C. Pritchard	[102]
m	$=$	$A/(d + B)$	J. C. Kapteyn	[62]
m	$=$	$A - Bd + Cd^2$	K. Schwarzschild	[103]

To confuse the issue, some observers continued to publish results confirming that the reciprocity law was satisfied by their data, among them the Astronomer Royal, Sir William Christie [97]. Even when the evidence was overwhelmingly against the reciprocity law, the Henry brothers and their French colleague, Charles Trépied (from the Algiers Observatory), were stubbornly insisting on its validity and usefulness as a basis for photographic photometry [98].

From the outset the first Astrographic Congress had resolved to record focal images of stars, which renders the stellar images as nearly point-like. Magnitudes were to be obtained from the measurement of diameters, no doubt as a result of the influence of Gill and Kapteyn and their work on the *Cape Photographic Durchmusterung*. The relationship between image diameter and visual magnitude therefore became a matter of considerable interest, and many observers proposed different empirical interpolation formulae that could be used, so it was claimed, to convert image diameters to stellar magnitudes. Bond in 1858 [18] and Kapteyn for the CPD [55] had both adopted empirical formulae for stellar image diameters. Table 4.6 lists some of the formulae proposed at this time.

The question of the relationship between image diameter and exposure time is a related problem, but not identical in view of departures from the reciprocity law. This property of photographic plates was also explored in detail (see Table 4.2). One of the most thorough of these investigations was that of Carl Charlier (1862–1934) at the Lund Observatory in 1889. This work was published to celebrate the Pulkovo Observatory jubilee and was cited by many of those who subsequently entered the same field [100] – see also E. S. Holden [109] for an English summary.

Charlier adopted the $m = a - b\log d$ relationship between magnitude m and diameter d. In addition he found that the diameter increased with

Table 4.2. *Empirical formulae for image diameter d vs exposure time t*

d^2	$=$	$Pt + Q$	G. P. Bond	[18]
$d - d_0$	$=$	$P \log(t/t_0)$	W. H. M. Christie	[97]
d	$=$	$P + Q \log A + R.A. \log t$	J. M. Schaeberle	[104] (*A* is objective aperture)
d	$=$	$d_0 t^{\frac{1}{4}}$	C. Pritchard	[102]
d	$=$	$d_0 t^{\frac{1}{4}}$	C. V. L. Charlier	[100]
d	$=$	$d_0 t^{\frac{1}{4}}$	H. H. Turner	[105]
d	$=$	$d_0 t^{\frac{1}{2}}$	J. Scheiner	[106]
d	$=$	$P + Q \log t$	M. Wolf	[107, 108]

exposure time t according to the fourth root of t. The average value for b from the Stockholm Observatory plates (exposed on the 81-mm Steinheil refractor) was 6.75, whereas the value implied by the reciprocity law in conjunction with $d \propto t^{\frac{1}{4}}$ would be 10.

Charlier used his empirical formula to derive photographic magnitudes for 571 stars in the Pleiades cluster which had already been observed visually by Max Wolf (1863–1932) in Heidelberg. From these results he derived the difference $(m_{pg} - m_{vis})$ which showed a substantial trend with magnitude, ascribed by Charlier to errors in Wolf's visual scale, but in practice an indication of the colour change of stars along the Pleiades main sequence. The first cluster colour-magnitude diagram could have been plotted from the tabular data presented, but the opportunity was missed [100]. Scheiner also derived differences $(m_{pg} - m_{vis})$ for Pleiades stars and treated the result as a true colour index [110] but was unable to determine any correlation with the unreliable visual colour estimates of the same stars.

With the failure of the reciprocity law, the possibility of calibrating photographic plates by multiple but slightly displaced exposures of the same field on the same plate, using a given ratio of exposure times, had to be abandoned. Nearly all observers therefore tried to establish empirical formulae based on visual magnitude, either estimated or measured photometrically. The assumption was that if enough stars were used then the differences in colour from star to star would average out. For this purpose Kapteyn and Pritchard proposed establishing visual magnitude sequences for faint stars from magnitude 9 to 11 in ten standard regions distributed in right ascension and about 8° north of the equator [89] – see also [111].

Pritchard used his wedge photometer to undertake this work in the last years of his long life, and Charles Trépied used the magnitude data for these

Kapteyn-Pritchard areas for photographic calibrations [112]. Like Kapteyn [63, 62] – see section 4.4 – Trépied concluded from this work that the stars nearer the Milky Way were bluer, and hence photographically brighter, than those away from the galactic plane. Such effects largely vitiate attempts to calibrate photographic photometry by visual means.

Kapteyn anticipated such problems and proposed at the 1891 Astrographic Congress making absolute calibrations of plates by using a wire mesh screen placed over the telescope objectives. Such screens would be designed to give a reduction of exactly two Pogson magnitudes in the intensity of the light when used for a second displaced exposure on the same plate. A proposal for the distribution of identical screens to all participating observatories was adopted [76]. Unfortunately the screens were never made or distributed, a circumstance which Weaver later considered to be a major lost opportunity of standardizing the photometric work of the *Astrographic Catalogue* [43]. At the 1895 Astrographic Congress no better suggestion could be made than to leave the method of magnitude determination, whether by measurement or estimation, to the whim of each individual participating observatory [113].

4.7   Photographic photometry at longer wavelengths

A chance discovery by Hermann Wilhelm Vogel (1834–98) in Berlin in 1873 led to the advent of plates sensitive to green, yellow and orange light as well as to the normal 'chemical' rays (the term for the blue-ultraviolet spectral region) [114]. Vogel was using commercial dry silver bromide emulsion plates from Wortley in England which had been treated with a yellow dyestuff to prevent halation. He found the dyestuff gave a sensitivity well into the green, and his subsequent experiments led to the discovery of dyes which made plates sensitive into the orange and red regions of the spectrum.

This work was soon followed up by Captain William Abney in London. He reported using dye-sensitized plates to photograph the red part of the solar spectrum in 1876 [115, 116] and by 1880 he had produced superb solar grating spectrograms to a wavelength of about 1 μm [117].

4.7.1   *Photovisual magnitudes*

Vogel's discovery did not have an immediate impact on astronomy. By the turn of the century some photographic companies, such as Cramer, Seed and Lumière, were supplying the new dye-sensitized or

Fig. 4.11   Sensitivity function for Cramer Isochromatic plates relative to an untreated Seed 27 plate, according to Robert Wallace.

orthochromatic plates, and it was from about 1904 that these were first used for astronomy at the Yerkes Observatory. In an extensive series of papers, Robert James Wallace (1868–1945) at Yerkes explored the spectral sensitivity functions of orthochromatic plates [118] and showed how a yellow 'Tartrazine' gelatine filter used in conjunction with such a plate on a reflecting telescope could reproduce a visual response function peaking at 558 nm [119]. Photographic photometry through such a filter was termed 'photovisual'. He also investigated plate sensitometry [120], the sensitization of the emulsions with different dyestuffs [121] and the use of filters for photovisual work with refractors [122]. One of his aims was to produce a truly isochromatic plate, one which responded equally to blue and visual rays. Wallace spent four years at Yerkes after being in the employ of the Cramer Dry Plate Company. As a result Cramer Isochromatic plates were those frequently used for the early photovisual photography at Yerkes and elsewhere.

Parkhurst and Jordan at Yerkes were soon using the new emulsions for photography on the Yerkes 24-inch reflector [123]. The images for red stars, such as the very red carbon star U Cygni, showed dramatic differences between normal photographic plates and filtered photovisual ones. The first photovisual magnitudes and corresponding colour indices were derived at Yerkes about this time, and the magnitudes were shown to follow quite closely the photometric visual scale of the *Potsdamer Durchmusterung* [124,

125], which was widely accepted as providing the most reliable visually measured magnitude system. The work developed into the well-known *Yerkes Actinometry* of 1912 [126] for 630 stars brighter than visual magnitude 7.5 – see section 4.8.2.

Relatively few observers ventured into this new field in the early decades of the century. Edward King at Harvard began experimenting with the Cramer Isochromatic plates in 1918 [127] and by 1923 he had produced a catalogue of photovisual magnitudes for 100 bright northern stars [128] using the same out-of-focus technique as he had developed for photographic magnitudes – see section 4.8.3. The work was extended to the southern hemisphere using the 13-inch Boyden telescope in Peru, but the observing was curtailed with the closure of Harvard's Arequipa station at the end of 1926 [129]. King's photovisual magnitudes with the Bache telescope at Harvard showed a small colour equation compared to visually measured values, in the sense that red stars were estimated slightly too bright.

Meanwhile interest in dye-sensitized emulsions at Mt Wilson dated from 1912. Both Seares and van Rhijn were using isochromatic plates with yellow filters for photovisual photometry from 1913 [130]. This work developed into Seares' calibration of photovisual magnitudes for the North Polar Sequence in 1915, [131] which gave magnitudes for 339 stars to $m_{pv} = 17.5$ from in-focus images – see section 4.10.1.

Seares' work from 1915 really set the standards for photovisual photometry for the next three decades, simply because of its precision, extension to faint magnitudes and careful calibration. Nevertheless, Seares constantly made corrections to the scale. The photovisual North Polar Sequence magnitudes he presented to the IAU in 1922 [132] he described as provisional, yet at the second IAU General Assembly in 1925 he wrote:

> A photographic photometry has many advantages over visual methods, and there can be little difference of opinion as to the desirability of a photovisual system as a standard to which all visual and photovisual measures shall be reduced. The Mount Wilson photovisual magnitudes of stars at the North Pole have been adopted provisionally as such a standard system. These magnitudes have not yet been confirmed by published data obtained elsewhere, but indirect evidence shows that the scale can scarcely be seriously in error [133].

4.8   Photographic photometry from extrafocal images

4.8.1   Photographic photometry of Schwarzschild

It was Karl Schwarzschild (1873–1916) who, more than any of his predecessors, was able to transform photographic photometry from a mysterious and poorly understood art to a quantitative science. On his appointment as an assistant to the private von Kuffner Observatory in Vienna in 1896, Schwarzschild devoted the greater part of his time there to photometric work.

Two major articles were published as a result of the nearly three years Schwarzschild spent in Vienna on photographic studies. The first considered the photometry of stars from extrafocal images on photographic plates [134]. Here the technique of extrafocal photography was developed, following an earlier suggestion of Janssen [37, 87]. Janssen noted that, if the plate is just outside the focal plane,

> ... one then gets a circle of very small diameter and roughly uniform blackening (if the objective is of good quality), and it is possible to compare the degree of opacity with other circles of similar origin [37].

Schwarzschild used this principle on the 6-inch photographic refractor at Kuffner Observatory, the plates being displaced inside the focus so as to give images as circular disks 1.5 mm in diameter irrespective of stellar magnitude. The advantage of the method was to avoid the aberrations of the lens and the effects of an unsteady atmosphere which made the diameter method difficult, especially far from the plate's centre. Although longer exposures were required for faint stars, the determination of the degree of blackening gave more precise magnitudes than the uncertain measurements of diameter from focal images. Generally probable errors of $\pm 0\overset{m}{.}05$ were attainable.

Much of this paper was devoted to an investigation of the 'blackening law' of the plates, which gave the photographic response as a function of stellar intensity and exposure time. Quantitative results showing reciprocity failure were obtained, and this was developed further in the second paper [135] in which the blackening is taken to depend on the quantity $I t^p$ (here I is the intensity, t the exposure time and p the Schwarzschild index). A strict reciprocity law required $p = 1$, whereas Schwarzschild obtained values around 0.85 for the plates then in common astronomical use. A summary of these results also appeared in a short research note the previous year [136] – see [137] for an English translation.

A further major study of the blackening law for photograph plates was published by Erich Kron (1881–1917) at Potsdam, in which he showed that reciprocity failure also occurs for high intensity exposures – for each plate there exists an optimum intensity that produces a given blackening for a minimum of incident photon energy [138]. This major work on the properties of photographic plates appeared shortly before the outbreak of the war in which Kron, the youngest of the Potsdam observers, was not to survive.

Schwarzschild's quantitative statement concerning the reciprocity failure allowed the photographic intensities of stars to be obtained from the visually estimated blackening of the stellar disks from multiple exposures on the same plate. The blackening was determined by means of a Hartmann microphotometer. This was a device designed by Johannes Hartmann (1865–1936) at Potsdam for comparing the blackening in different photographic images using a photographic density wedge [139, 140]. The microphotometer was based on the principle that 'two sources of light are photographically equally bright when they produce equal blackening on one and the same plate with equal exposures' [140].

These techniques were applied to stars in the open clusters h and χ Persei, the Pleiades and Praesepe as well as to an investigation of the light variability of η Aquilae and β Lyrae [135]. For the Cepheid η Aql, Schwarzschild found the photographic amplitude to be $1^{\rm m}.29$, just twice the visual value, and he interpreted this as probably a result of a temperature change in the outer layers of the star. An explanation due to eclipses was untenable. Such conclusions predated Baade's pulsation hypothesis for Cepheids by nearly three decades [141].

One problem of the extrafocal method was to achieve completely uniform blackening in an extrafocal image, which inhomogeneities in the objective lens and diffraction at the telescope aperture prevented. Schwarzschild became director of the Göttingen Observatory in 1901 and it was here that he sought to improve the extrafocal method with the invention of his 'Schraffierkassette' or jiggle-camera [142, 143]. In this device the plate was held close to the focal plane but displaced sideways during the exposure on a two dimensional zig-zag path of duration 225 seconds, so as to render each stellar image as a uniformly exposed square of side 0.25 mm.

The calibration of the photographic images could be reliably undertaken using a 'half-grating', a device originally proposed by Kapteyn in his *Plan of Selected Areas* [144]. It comprised a parallel wire grating placed just in front of half the photographic plate, dimming stars by a known factor. Comparison of stars of the same magnitude in each half of the plate allowed the blackening law to be calibrated [145, 146]. This was in fact a development of a grating method that Schwarzschild had devised in Vienna and Göttingen for plate calibration, in which an objective wire grating covered the full aperture of the telescope and successive exposures

Fig. 4.12   Hartmann microphotometer, c. 1899.

were made of equal duration [147]. Such a technique was first used at the Kuffner Observatory both by Carl Wirtz [148] and later by Alexander Wilkens [149], the latter after training as a student of Schwarzschild's in Göttingen (1903–05).

Fig. 4.13   Karl Schwarzschild's 'Schraffierkassette', 1910.

The jiggle-camera technique was used by Schwarzschild to produce the *Göttinger Aktinometrie*, a catalogue of the photographic magnitudes of 3522 stars in the zone 0° to +20° to magnitude 7.5 [150]. Schwarzschild's declared aim was:

> ... to produce a photographic complement to the *Potsdam Photometric Durchmusterung*, that is, to determine the photographic magnitudes for

the stars to magnitude 7.5 of the *Bonn Durchmusterung* which have
been measured [visually] by Müller and Kempf, and to do this with a
similar accuracy as has been achieved at Potsdam [150].

This was not the first photographic catalogue of stellar magnitudes, but it
was highly influential because of the care with which it was executed.

The material was 100 jiggle-camera plates exposed through a 4.5 mm
aperture Zeiss-Tessar lens between 1904 and 1908. A Hartmann microphotometer [139, 140] was used for estimating densities. Three exposures were
made on each plate in the ratio 1 to 3 to 9 and these were used to calibrate
the plates by assuming a factor of three in exposure had the same effect as
a magnitude in intensity. In this way preliminary magnitudes were obtained
with a probable error of the mean values of $\pm 0^{m}034$.

The second part of the *Göttinger Aktinometrie* [151] contained a rigorous
discussion of the errors of the photometry, and applied corrections to
the catalogue, in particular a correction depending on right ascension, a
correction based on grating calibrations to bring the magnitudes to the
Pogson scale, and a correction of $-0^{m}29$ to bring the zero-point of the
magnitude scale onto the International System – see section 4.9.1. In part
A a correction had also been applied for the distance of the stars from the
plate centre, amounting to $0^{m}12$ at the edge of the field.

Apart from these numerous corrections, Schwarzschild also undertook an
extensive statistical study of the data [151]. He formed a colour index using
the Göttingen photographic and Potsdam visual magnitudes, and hence
investigated the relationship between this colour index and the Harvard
spectral types (the index ran from $-0^{m}6$ to $1^{m}9$ in going from types B
to Ma) and also between the colour index and visually determined colour
estimates of Osthoff [152] – see section 2.8.

Although Scheiner and Charlier had earlier derived magnitude differences ($m_{pg} - m_{vis}$) (see section 4.6), it was Schwarzschild in 1900 who was
the main promoter of the new concept of colour index, which he called
'Farbentönung' [153]. He furthermore calibrated the colour indices using
black-body flux distributions to obtain stellar temperatures, although he
recognized that a scale free of systematic errors was at that stage not possible [151]. Nevertheless Schwarzschild's results had a profound influence,
if only because his was one of the first attempts to apply photometry to
the problems of stellar astrophysics. The *Göttinger Aktinometrie* was the
product of one of the leading theoretical astronomers of the early twentieth
century, who also had a rare talent for taking great pains over careful and
accurate observational work.

Fig. 4.14   John Parkhurst.

4.8.2   *The* Yerkes Actinometry

No sooner had Schwarzschild published part B of the *Göttinger Aktinometrie* than another major photographic catalogue was published, this time by John Parkhurst (1861–1925), an astronomer at Yerkes Observatory with no lesser a reputation for the meticulous care with which he undertook observational work.

The *Yerkes Actinometry* [126] by Parkhurst comprised 630 stars in the polar zone north of +73° to magnitude 7.5, photographed with a Zeiss 14.5-cm photographic doublet. Two important features of the work deserve comment. First, this was a photometric catalogue in two colours. The origins of the photographic work at visual wavelengths at Yerkes go back to the period 1904–06 when the first experiments were undertaken by James Wallace (1868–1945) with plates sensitized using dyes for longer wavelengths and with a visual filter [119]. These techniques were developed further by Parkhurst and Frank Jordan (1865–1941) [123] when they showed the advantages of determining stellar colours using a difference in the magnitudes photographed at different wavelengths with the same instrument. This work was the earliest to exploit the colour index as a tool for astrophysical analysis, although the photometry was still based on focal images (see also section 3.9.2 on visually determined colour indices

Fig. 4.15 Zeiss camera used by John Parkhurst for the *Yerkes Actinometry*.

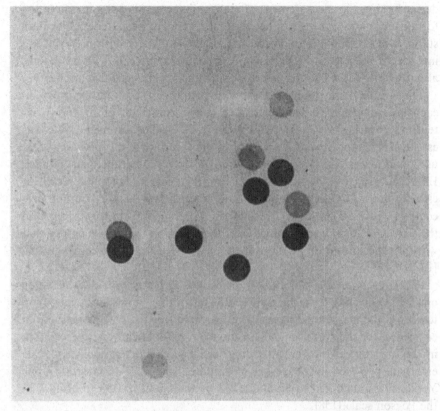

Fig. 4.16   Extrafocal images of the Pleiades, obtained by John Parkhurst,

introduced by Chandler in 1888 [154]). Parkhurst's *Yerkes Actinometry* in turn grew from this two-colour program, the main change being the decision to use extrafocal photography for the blue plates and to measure densities rather than diameters, in the hope of achieving a higher precision.

Parkhurst used the latest orthochromatic plates from the Cramer company together with a yellow filter to reproduce as closely as possible the visual passband ($\lambda_{\text{eff}} = 560$ nm), as well as taking photographic exposures (that is blue, $\lambda_{\text{eff}} = 400$ nm) on Seed plates.† The photovisual magnitudes were

---

†   The 'effective wavelength' is a mean wavelength of the passband, and has been defined by King [155] in terms of the first moment of the instrumental response function. It is independent of the stellar flux distribution. Golay, however, uses the term 'effective wavelength' for a flux-weighted mean for a photometric passband [156], which therefore depends on the flux distribution or colour of a star, and he refers to the flux-independent wavelength as the 'mean wavelength'. Golay's definitions are preferred for the modern literature, but are not adopted

derived using the measurement of stellar diameters and the interpolation formula $m_{pv} = a - b\sqrt{d}$ (calibrated using the standard magnitudes of Pleiades stars), while the photographic magnitudes were derived from extrafocal images. In the event, the precision was comparable in the two passbands, about $\pm 0^{m}_{.}04$ for the probable error in the mean catalogue magnitudes.

The second innovation introduced by Parkhurst was the exposure on each blue plate of a spot sensitometer scale from light of 20 known intensities covering a 4 magnitude range [157]. The sensitometer scale was established simply from the apertures that admitted the blue sky light used, and it was employed for calibrating all the photographic magnitudes. Like Schwarzschild, Parkhurst also used a Hartmann microphotometer for estimating the blackening in the photographic images. This calibration procedure Schwarzschild himself recognized to be superior to that adopted in the *Göttinger Aktinometrie*, which had been based in the second part of that work on the known diminution of the intensity using an objective grating [158].

Parkhurst applied a number of corrections to his magnitudes, including one for the distance from the plate centre, one for the atmospheric extinction to reduce the magnitudes to zenith values, and (for the blue magnitudes) a correction for the stellar colour arising from residual chromatic aberration in the objective. However, according to Schwarzschild, a significant scale error still persisted in the Yerkes magnitudes, such that an interval of one Yerkes magnitude had to be multiplied by the factor of 0.94 to bring it to the Pogson scale [158].

Like Schwarzschild, Parkhurst explored the relationship between colour index $(m_{pg} - m_{pv})$ and spectral type, the latter having been determined from his objective prism plates taken as part of the same programme. A linear relationship between colour and spectrum from spectral types B to M resulted. However, the carbon stars were found to be much redder, as Parkhurst had shown in a slightly earlier paper [159].

4.8.3   Edward King's extrafocal photometry

Edward King (1861–1931) at Harvard was a third pioneer of the extrafocal method who made substantial progress in overcoming the difficulties of photographic photometry in the early years of the twentieth

---

here. Alternative uses for the term 'effective wavelength' have been used in the literature. In particular, the parameter introduced by Comstock in 1897 – see section 4.11.2 – is a measure of a star's colour, and should not be confused with the term referred to above.

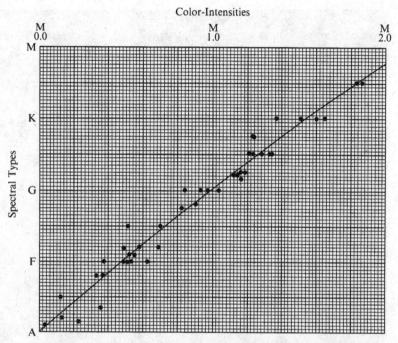

Fig. 4.17   The relation between colour index and spectral type according to Parkhurst and Jordan in 1908 – the first from purely photographic measures.

century. From 1896 Pickering had assigned King to undertake a monthly test of photographic plates [160]. The effect of emulsion age, time between exposure and development, pre-exposure and temperature were explored as part of a lengthy programme, one of the first to consider so many influences that together determine the density [161]. The result of these tests led King to the conclusion that

> photography ... has disadvantages peculiar to itself ... and the reduction of the plates used in this investigation has shown many sources of error causing discordant results. Temperature, humidity, and other influences affect the sensitive film either temporarily or permanently, and make the quantitative use of photography a problem of great difficulty [162].

In spite of these problems he devised an out-of-focus method for comparing the magnitudes of bright stars with that of Polaris using the 11-inch Draper refracting telescope. Seven extrafocal plate positions were chosen and the relative surface intensities of the light from a given star determined by comparison with a calibrated photographic wedge. The aim was

Fig. 4.18   Edward King.

to record extrafocal images of Polaris and of bright stars such that equal photographic blackening was recorded in equal 60-second exposures but with different plate positions. Knowing the law between plate position and surface intensity, which was close to an inverse square law, allowed a difference in focal positions to be converted to a magnitude difference.

King initially applied this technique to find photographic magnitudes of 33 bright stars north of −30° [163]. His zero-point was based on the adopted photographic magnitude of Polaris being $m_{pg}(\alpha$ UMi$) = 2^m_\cdot62$, a value chosen to achieve equality of photographic and visual magnitudes for A stars. The programme was then extended to include 76 stars mainly of photographic magnitude brighter than 4.0 [164], and then to 153 stars brighter than m_{pg} of 5.5 [165]. Finally 79 bright and mainly southern stars were included in the programme between 1911 and 1914 when King obtained plates on the 13-inch Boyden telescope at the Boyden Station at Arequipa, Peru [166].

Overall, the King extrafocal programme was smaller in scope and restricted to brighter stars than those undertaken by either Schwarzschild or Parkhurst at this same time. However, King also formed a colour index given by the difference between his photographic and the Harvard visual magnitudes from the meridian photometer, and he was able to demonstrate a fairly tight and nearly linear relationship between the colour index and a star's Harvard spectral type [163, 164]. In fact Pickering was able to derive photographic magnitudes for many bright stars using the King relationship between colour and spectrum together with the results of visual meridian photometry [167].

One interesting conclusion of King's investigation was the announcement of the presence of an absorbing medium in space, based on his finding of a positive correlation between the colour (defined as a magnitude difference) and the distance of a star based on trigonometric parallax [165]. Kapteyn had earlier considered the same question by exploring the dependence of stellar colours on other parameters through the equation

$$m_{pg} - m_{vis} = a + bm + cM + d\Delta.$$

Here b, c and d are constants to be determined while a is a function of spectral type [168]. Δ is a star's distance. The important constant is d, for which Kapteyn had found a value of about $0^m_\cdot66$ per kiloparsec for stars near the Milky Way (subsequently Kapteyn revised this value downwards to about $0^m_\cdot31$ /kpc [168]). On the other hand King's value was as high as $1^m_\cdot9$ /kpc.

Unfortunately all such early attempts to demonstrate the presence of an interstellar medium, by its presumed effect of increasingly reddening the more distant stars, were flawed. In practice, the whole question was complicated by the then poorly understood relationship between intrinsic stellar colour and luminosity, the more luminous stars being both intrinsically redder and also more distant. What is more, King was not aware that the reddening effect can only be reliably demonstrated if the colours of distant early-type stars in the galactic plane are analysed.

Soon after King's work Harlow Shapley asserted that interstellar selective absorption in the Galaxy must be negligible, because some blue stars could still be found in distant globular clusters such as M13 [169]. Even Kapteyn is known to have become convinced by 1915 that interstellar matter had a negligible influence on stellar magnitudes. With two such formidable opponents, King's early result was soon suppressed. Yet the concept of interstellar space absorption was never fully laid to rest in the time before Trumpler triumphantly revived it in 1930 (see section 8.6.1).

4.8.4   Fabry's method

Another method of extrafocal photometry was devised in the years 1908–10 in Marseille by Charles Fabry (1867–1945), originally for the purpose of photographic measurements of the brightness of the starlit night sky [170, 171]. The technique involved placing a short focal length lens immediately behind the focal plane of the objective, and imaging the entrance pupil, defined by the objective aperture, onto the plate a short distance beyond the Fabry lens. The result is a small circle of uniform illumination recorded on the photographic plate. Although originally devised for area photometry of extended sources, Fabry noted that the method could be used to advantage for stellar photometry, because the disks so produced would be more uniform than is generally the case when the telescope is simply put out of focus.

The Fabry method appears to have been largely neglected for some three decades. Struve and Elvey used it at Yerkes for photographic photometry of nebulae in 1936 [172]. The first stellar photographic photometry by the Fabry method was at the Radcliffe Observatory, Pretoria, where E. G. Williams (1905–40) and H. Knox-Shaw (1885–1970) obtained photographic and photovisual magnitudes for 181 southern O and B stars with a small refractor (in fact the finder telescope for the still incomplete 74-inch Radcliffe reflector!) [173]. Alan Cousins (b. 1903) subsequently obtained accurate photovisual stellar magnitudes using Fabry's technique at the Durban Observatory [174] and a full discussion of the method was then published by R. O. Redman [175] – see section 7.8.2 – and by Fabry himself [176].

In view of the long interval before the method was widely introduced into astronomical photography, it is surprising that the Soviet photoelectric stellar photometer built in Leningrad from 1936–37 for the Abastumani Observatory in Georgia was the first such instrument to employ a Fabry lens to give a uniform and stable illumination of starlight on the photocathode [177] – see section 5.4.5.

4.9   The origins of the North Polar Sequence

The North Polar Sequence, a concept which was to dominate stellar photographic photometry during the first half of the twentieth century, had its origins at Harvard from about 1907. The basic philosophy was to establish a sequence of carefully calibrated standard photographic magnitudes for stars near the pole, which, by comparison, could be used for determining relative magnitudes for stars in other regions of the sky without resorting to absolute photometric methods, such as the use of diaphragms or objective gratings. The transfer of the polar magnitude scale to other regions could, Pickering asserted, be readily undertaken by photographing the two regions on the same plate at the same altitude and with equal exposure times [178]. To facilitate this procedure a list of ten polar standards was initially proposed in 1907 [179] with magnitudes from $m_{pg} = 6.4$ to 13.3.

The choice of polar standards is interesting and can be clearly traced back to Pickering's early experiments in visual photometry at Harvard. In 1879 he had proposed the same ten stars as faint visual standards, with Polaris itself as the primary standard for all visual photometry [180]. The reasons given at that time included the visibility of the polar region at all times of the year for northern observers. The constancy of the air mass at the pole would have been another apparent advantage for extinction corrections, though in practice lower latitude observatories later found this to be a source of major difficulty, as the correction was then always large and uncertain. As for southern stars and observatories, the plan was to establish secondary standards in each of the Harvard Standard Regions as well as at the south pole [181] which would be tied to the fundamental North Polar Sequence. These 48 Standard Regions, which were centred on bands of declination at intervals of 30° from +75° to −75° (labelled from A to F), had likewise been established years earlier for the purposes of applying stellar statistics to the data from visual photometry [182].

Pickering assigned the work of determining photographic magnitudes of stars in the North Polar Sequence to Miss Henrietta Leavitt (1868–1921), one of his most trusted assistants, who became head of the Department of Photographic Stellar Photometry at Harvard. In 1909 Pickering reported on the progress of this work: 47 polar stars had by then been selected as standards and their magnitudes were being obtained on an absolute photographic scale using a variety of different telescopes and methods [183]. The aim was to

> ... determine the magnitudes of the stars of the Polar Sequence with
> an uncertainty of less than a tenth of a magnitude. If these magnitudes
> are adopted by astronomers, a basis will be established for standard

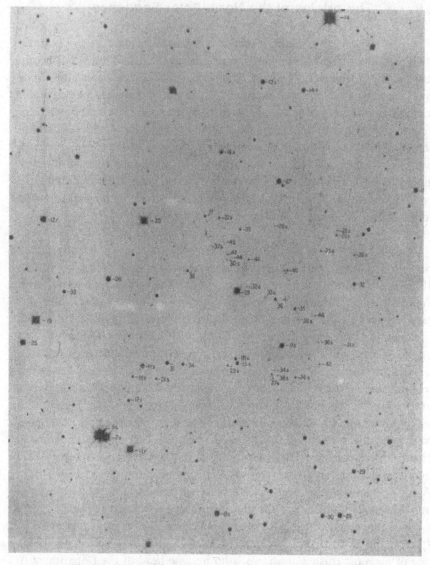

Fig. 4.19   The North Polar Sequence, from a print annotated by Henrietta
Leavitt, 1917

photographic magnitudes, on a scale which will be the same in all
parts of the sky [183].

The timing of this circular one month before the April 1909 Astrographic
Congress in Paris was no coincidence. The congress determined that all

Chapter 4

The CEO and the Orchestra Conductor

The real power of a leader is in the number of minds reached, hearts touched, souls moved, and lives changed.

Matshona Dhliwayo, Canadian philosopher and entrepreneur

Purpose

To explore the role of the chief executive officer (CEO) as the conductor of the orchestra.

In this chapter, the reader will explore

- The new role of the CEO in value orchestration
- The parallels between the CEO and the orchestra conductor
- Changes in mindset, leadership thinking, and culture required for digital health, connected care, and population health management
- The three value orchestration pillars that support mission and future purpose

The New Role of the CEO

As mentioned in Chapter 1, healthcare's transformation requires that key healthcare stakeholders come together to create value, much as performers in an orchestra come together to play a musical composition. The journey to high-value healthcare will change everything and leave no part of the organization untouched. The pace, specifics of the strategy, needs of the community, and capabilities of the players will vary—there will be no "one size fits all." The healthcare value chain will be disrupted. Soon all medical devices will be monitored with sensors, as will patients. Remote monitoring of pulse, blood chemistry, hormone levels, blood pressure, temperature, and brain waves will connect to digitized electronic health records (EHRs) and genome sequences. With artificial intelligence (AI), disease onset can be accurately predicted and prevented, and best medical practices will be more uniformly applied.[1] Visionary CEOs, individually, will be the engines of this massive transformation. Jeff Immelt, former chairman and CEO of GE, indicates: "CEOs must rethink virtually everything about how their companies work.[2] Digital is the next gateway for quality, growth and productivity but it takes a complete transformation that can't be scattered across an organization. It must be led by the CEO and engage the entire enterprise."[3]

Many parallels exist between the skills needed to be an effective orchestra conductor and the skills needed to be an effective CEO. Both the conductor and the CEO deal with great complexity and must lead, direct, and unify multiple instruments. Both leaders must ensure alignment and passionately lead to become one with their vision. Both must manage a diversity of personalities, interaction styles, and backgrounds to promote a rich, unique orchestral character or culture.[4]

THE MAESTRO OR ORCHESTRA CONDUCTOR

The Maestro (conductor) serves as a guide to the orchestra, even before it plays its first note, by choosing the works to be performed, making adjustments, working out an interpretation, and relaying the vision to the musicians. Having articulated a vision for the orchestra and its desired sound, the conductor listens to the performance of the entire orchestra, as well as by instrument group, and in some cases by instrument where passages require solos, duets, or other subgroups of the orchestra to play a prominent role. Leading 100+ musicians, the conductor establishes the tempo, timbre, balance of sound, and overall musicality to control the interpretation and pacing of the music. Conductors are there to bring musical scores to life, communicating their own highly refined sense of the works through an individual language of gestures, which might sculpt the musical line, tease out nuances, emphasize certain musical elements while controlling others, and essentially reimagine an old piece anew.[5] More than anything, the conductor will listen for passion, feeling, and commitment in the performance of the music, which will bring a collective focus to realizing the musical vision for the orchestra.[6]

Only CEOs have the power to resolve the inherent conflicts between the old industrial-age business and the emerging digital health– and value-based care future. When the future is so uncertain, there will be pushback both internally and externally to investments in value creation activities. CEOs must manage trade-offs in the traditional health system and focus on operational excellence to improve quality, safety, revenue, and margin management while simultaneously creating the future through investments in innovation, population health, talent development, and digital capabilities. CEOs must balance their tenure in their role with the tenure of the healthcare organizations they lead, particularly since the return on investment of this future will not be fully evident until after the CEO is long gone.[7]

As the conductor for the journey to high-value healthcare, the CEO must embrace the First Law of Digital Transformation:

> *Technology changes quickly, but organizations change much more slowly.*
>
> **George Westerman, coauthor of the award-winning book**
> *Leading Digital: Turning Technology into Business Transformation*

As each CEO evaluates the current environment, one filled with uncertainty, surprises, and unforeseen events, where the destination of the journey is not always clear, the CEO has two distinct options. They are:

- Protect legacy fee-for-service revenues for as long as possible, or
- Plant the seeds of change and begin to orchestrate the creation of the next-generation health and healthcare enterprise

Craig Cordola, who previously served as president and CEO of Ascension Texas and is now executive vice president and chief operating officer (COO) of Ascension, commented:

> Change is hard for all of us. The onus is on leadership to put context around "the why" and to challenge the status quo. We have to approach healthcare differently than we have in the past.[8] I don't believe we can improve healthcare by doing what has

already been done. We need to be revolutionaries and appropriately challenge some of the outmoded approaches we have grown accustomed to.[9]

There are many moving parts to this change–both human and technological. Orchestration will require the CEO to view the enterprise and the community as a series of interconnected parts. While digital health and connected care will involve change at every level of the organization, successful organizations will make change manageable. Big ideas will be broken down into well-defined waves of practical, achievable stepping-stones, offering steady, incremental progress. Prioritized ideas will be nurtured, tested, and ultimately scaled into game-changing concepts. Collective waves of innovation will build super performance over time without overwhelming the organization.[10] Technology systems, a key contributor to innovation, will largely do what they are designed to do. Human systems, on the other hand, are very different and harder to control. Therefore, the most important job for the CEO as the orchestra conductor is to define the culture of the organization—one that keeps the mission close, embraces change, encourages experimentation and collaboration, and empowers stakeholders from a variety of subgroups and partners.

Dr. Ninfa M. Saunders, FACHE, president and CEO of Navicent Health, suggests:

We must reimagine the business and the way we think about the business. I like to think of it as a peg board [see Figure 4.1]. In the past we put one peg in one hole and solved an individual problem. Today, we must think of the peg board as a whole, and the CEO must connect change to purpose—sometimes vertically, but more often horizontally and diagonally. The CEO's role is alignment of all the moving parts (strategy, operations and people–culture) across the organization and community.[11]

Figure 4.1   The CEO's role.

Orchestrating Leadership Thinking, Mindsets, and Culture

Most healthcare organizations have an overabundance of ideas for digital and population health. Proposals for new digital apps, innovation initiatives, artificial intelligence and analytics algorithms, social determinants of health programs, etc. abound. Rather than focusing on "what technology we should implement" or the "newest clinical program we should deploy," value orchestration should start with culture and make sure everyone is on the same page. The CEO should start with a coherent, systematic approach that

- Ensures that senior leadership and the rank-and-file are bought in and aligned
- Identifies the opportunities and harnesses the initiatives with the greatest potential impact
- Coordinates efforts across boundaries within the organization and across the community
- Invests in the right operating models and digital capabilities to ensure meaningful gains in performance

Cultural transformation must be intentional, with strategies focused on mindset change and new thinking, as seen in Figure 4.2.

Figure 4.2 Value orchestration pillars.

Mission and Future Purpose

While the mission and purpose of most health systems have been focused on the provision of medical care, many health systems are taking a broader population health stance. Guided by growing evidence that health and prevention of disease can be influenced by social, behavioral, and environmental factors, many organizations are defining their target populations to include not only their patients but everyone within their communities, both geographic and virtual. Through close collaboration with employers, community agencies, governmental organizations, payers, and other partners, health systems are working to create access to housing, availability of healthy food, improved education, and other programs—often with relatively small financial investments to improve community health.[12] Chirag Patel, MD, associate vice president for Population Health at Wellstar Health System in Atlanta, indicates: "We are in a high growth community, and have recognized a large portion of our community works in the construction industry. We are developing programs to target the unique needs of this population."[13]

Health is more than what happens in a doctor's office or in the hospital. Clinical care, the quality of and access to care, contributes 20% to health outcomes. The root causes of health problems occur outside the healthcare system—think education, income, community safety, housing, and discrimination.[14] Don Lovasz from CommonSpirit indicates:

> We have to learn to be adaptive. If I could have only one thing on my wish list, it is a change in the business model. Your market will tell you what it wants, then you must build the business plan and PHM operating model to support it. Routinized systems of care with data to measure total medical spend will be essential.[15]

Change the Vision—Articulate the Value That Change Will Bring and Invest Accordingly

Vision and a forward-looking perspective have long been the CEO's responsibility. But today, the ability to anticipate market trends and guide decision makers in their response to those trends takes on new significance. Establishing alternative PHM and competitive scenarios at the highest level, positioning the enterprise within the broader ecosystem, and defining the level of aggressiveness in platform development help set the stage and prepare for the future. Figure 4.3 depicts three possible scenarios.

Figure 4.3 Three PHM strategic scenarios.

The potential scenarios are defined as

■ Most Aggressive—Population Health Management
Platform Developer: Ability to provide and/or contract for
a full continuum of services across all populations and
develop care management, data, and technology infrastructure. Well positioned to own insurance products and/
or manage full provider risks.
■ Middle Tier—Population Health Management Platform
Partner: Clinically integrated regional providers who build
capabilities to form value-based delivery system and digital health. Capable of participating in PHM and risk-bearing arrangements in a delegated and/or direct fashion.
■ Least Aggressive—Population Health Management
Participant: Defined set of services for a targeted population within government or commercial agreements con-
tracted to support clinically integrated networks or to
co-manage attributed patients within specific market(s).

The importance of this decision will be discussed in more
detail in Chapter 6.

There are many approaches to planting the seeds of cultural change. Some CEOs launch innovation labs or venture
units, while others explore digital successes in adjacent sectors or other industries with their teams. Other CEOs focus
on improving the digital literacy of board members, executive team members, and employees, and others embrace a
decidedly different future vision. One health system CEO we
worked with stated: "We are a population health company."
Explanation of the "why" and value of change is essential.
Investment in activities to equip team members' mindset
changes, culture, and thinking demonstrate commitment.
During times of uncertainty, "Work on things that are likely to
be relevant to many possible futures," says John Glaser, senior
vice president of Population Health at Cerner. "Tell me a future
in which engaging patients to manage their own health is a

bad idea, because I don't see that future at all. So, I may not know how it's going to play out, but under almost under any conceivable circumstance, this will be relevant."[16]

Change the Leadership—Get the Right People on the Bus

In his best-selling book *Good to Great*, Jim Collins noted that great firms have the right people "on the bus." In 1.0, that probably meant functional experts, specialists, command-and-control decision makers, day-in-and-day-out operational managers, and leaders who were risk averse and patient. In 2.0 and beyond, we need designers, strategists, and change agents. Some of the people on the bus will have to move seats, and some will ultimately exit the bus. A strong mandate from the top and agreement on strategic priorities are not enough. The CEO must ensure that the team is set up for success—with both top-down and bottom-up efforts.

Dr. Saunders indicates: "This is not groupthink, we don't like to hear from those with different views, they rain on our parade. We have a tendency to look for approval and concurrence. What we need is affirmation and strengthening of our strategy, that is very different."[17] New behaviors and capabilities will be needed, specifically:

- Historically, healthcare executives typically focus on their own divisional agendas. Tensions frequently arise between corporate functions and geographically dispersed operating units. New governance methods and decision-making structures should be focused on creating common understanding of the mission and vision, supporting agile, cross-functional teams as they collaborate to solve problems differently, and adapting to address frequent market changes.
- Anchor hires, or outside leaders with deep expertise in digital transformation, innovation, population health,

analytics, and change leadership, can provide needed
expertise and perspective. Most importantly, however,
these new leaders help the CEO re-envision how communication occurs within the organization. Frontline
leaders help establish an environment for success by
enabling employees to learn new skills and innovate
day-to-day work practices. "That's the beauty of leadership," says Craig Cordola, "the ability to build on the
collective of the team, everyone has their own background and understanding. Honest, transparent discussions with a diversity of thinking are needed to move an
organization forward. Leaders should communicate that
the thoughts, opinions and experiences of others are
valued."[18]

Dr. Saunders has reversed the pyramid by spending one-on-
one time with employees, having over 60 town hall meetings,
and establishing a CEO Advisory Council where employees
are recommended by their peers. She indicates:

> I tell them what I'm thinking, why I am thinking it,
> what we will do and how we will begin the process
> of executing on it. I focus on activation and engage-
> ment. Ninety percent of the time, if they are fully
> activated, they will become engaged and tell me "that
> doesn't mean anything." My job as CEO is not to
> convince them but reframe the decisions I have made
> based on vetting it with them.

Change Planning Methods—Cultivate a Culture of Experimentation

Traditional healthcare strategic planning engrained in leadership that they must study all the pieces on the chessboard,
develop a multi-year road map, and deploy the new program

or service all at once, in a sequential and linear manner. Healthcare executives were trained that they had one chance to get it right, resulting in the perfect becoming the enemy of good enough. Future change will require that teams try new things, learn from them, refine, and scale. In order to institutionalize a culture of experimentation, healthcare CEOs will have to help their teams overcome engrained tendencies to

- *Apply "A to Z" Thinking:* "As healthcare leaders we are trained to jump from A to Z, to know the right answer. Often data insights tell us something very different," shares Robin Barca, RN, MS, recently retired senior vice president and COO, Baptist Health.[19] Our teams often have the desire to do what they know is right rather than fully vet the nature of the problem or opportunity.
- *Get Stuck in Analysis Paralysis:* The sheer volume of healthcare data today can result in data blindness and confusion rather than clarity. Bottlenecks and choke points are often created; data is not conclusive or analyzed according to functional perspectives.
- *Take Orders:* Information technology and data analytics teams frequently manage requests from the business without a clear sense of prioritization or clear definition regarding the value and/or return on investment. They must think in a deep and nuanced way about the human factors, organization design, operating model, and other factors in addition to the data and technology implications.
- *Failure Is Not an Option:* Viewing failed hypotheses or proofs-of-concept as a waste of money and resources when in reality, they are an opportunity for organizational learning and mitigation of significant expense and failure.

"It's really not that important if the experiments succeed or fail; it's what [the organization] learns from it. Good, bad, or indifferent—it is the intelligence that [the organization] can lay claim to. Maybe it didn't work out the way we thought it would, but we learned X, Y and Z, and we're not embarrassed by the fact that our initial assumptions were wrong. There are no failures. We tried something, and we learned something,"

Richard Gingras, vice president of Google News.[20]

Conclusion

Ultimately, value must be orchestrated through a coherent system that identifies the opportunities, harnesses those with the most potential impact, leads the change in culture and thinking, coordinates efforts across boundaries, and invests in the right operating models and digital capabilities to ensure meaningful gains in performance. The CEO, as the orchestra conductor, will help the organization answer questions such as

- "What is the problem we are trying to solve and why?"
- "What is the value we expect from solving this problem?"
- "What changes in culture are needed to gain necessary buy-in and commitment?"
- "What combination of operating model and technology will make this happen?"
- "How will we measure success?"

Notes

1. Siebel, Thomas. "Why Digital Transformation Is Now on the CEO's Shoulders." McKinsey & Company, December 2017. www.mckinsey.com/business-functions/digital-mckinsey/our-insights/why-digital-transformation-is-now-on-the-ceos-shoulders.

2. Govindarajan, Vinjay, and Jeffrey Immelt. "The Only Way Manufacturers Can Survive." *MIT Sloan Management Review*, 3, 60 (2019): 24–33.
3. Immelt, Jeffrey. "Digital Transformation Requires Leadership." LinkedIn, August 6, 2018. www.linkedin.com/pulse/digital-transformation-requires-leadership-jeff-immelt/.
4. Lawson, Peter. "Lessons for the CEO from the Orchestra Conductor." Stanton Chase, December 2018. www.stantonchase.com/lessons-for-the-ceo-from-the-orchestra-conductor/.
5. Hopkins, Brian, Ted Schadler, and James McCormick. "The Insights-Driven Business." "Insights-Driven Businesses Set the Pace for Global Growth." *Forrester*, July 27, 2016. www.forrester.com/report/InsightsDriven+Businesses+Set+The+Pace+For+Global+Growth/-/E-RES130848.
   "Conducting." Wikipedia. Wikimedia Foundation, July 29, 2019. https://en.wikipedia.org/wiki/Conducting.
6. Westerman, George. "The First Law of Digital Innovation." *MIT Sloan Management Review*, April 8, 2019. https://sloanreview.mit.edu/article/the-first-law-of-digital-innovation/.
7. Govindarajan, Vinjay, and Jeffrey Immelt. "The Only Way Manufacturers Can Survive." *MIT Sloan Management Review*, 3, 60 (2019): 24–33.
8. Arlotto, Pam, and Craig Cordola. "Orchestrating Value: Population Health in the Digital Age." Telephone Interview, August 29, 2019.
9. Cordola, Craig. "Benchmarking Limits Healthcare Innovation." LinkedIn, March 6, 2019. www.linkedin.com/pulse/benchmarking-limits-healthcare-innovation-craig-cordola/.
10. Baculard, Laurent-Pierre, Laurent Colombani, Virginie Flam, Ouriel Lancry, and Elizabeth Spaulding. "Orchestrating a Successful Digital Transformation." Bain, November 22, 2017. www.bain.com/insights/orchestrating-a-successful-digital-transformation/.
11. Arlotto, Pam, and Ninfa Saunders, PhD. "Orchestrating Value: Population Health in the Digital Age." Telephone Interview, August 22, 2019.
12. Chen, Melinda, Mark Unruh, Michael Pesko, Hye-Young Jung, Yesenia Miranda, Meagan Cea, Jacqueline Garcel, and Lawrence Casalino. "Hospitals' Engagement in Population Health: Moving Past the Medicine and into the Community." *Health Affairs*, April 5, 2016. www.healthaffairs.org/do/10.1377/hblog20160405.054312/full/.

13. Arlotto, Pam, and Chirag Patel MD. "Orchestrating Value: Population Health in the Digital Age." Telephone Interview, August 27, 2019.
14. "Health Care: How Can Health Care Professionals Continue to Expand Their Thinking about Health?" County Health Rankings & Roadmaps. University of Wisconsin Population Health Institute & RWJF. Accessed September 2, 2019. www.countyhealthrankings.org/take-action-to-improve-health/partner-center/health-care.
15. Arlotto, Pam, and Don Lovasz. "Orchestrating Value: Population Health in the Digital Age." Telephone Interview, August 28, 2019.
16. Kane, Gerald C., Anh Nguyen Phillips, Jonathan Copulsky, and Garth Andrus. "How Digital Leadership Is(n't) Different." *MIT Sloan Management Review* 60, 3 (2019): 34–39.
17. Arlotto, Pam, and Ninfa Saunders, PhD. "Orchestrating Value: Population Health in the Digital Age." Telephone Interview, August 22, 2019.
18. Arlotto, Pam, and Craig Cordola. "Orchestrating Value: Population Health in the Digital Age." Telephone Interview, August 29, 2019.
19. Arlotto, Pam, and Robin Barca. In Person Interview. Fall, 2018.
20. Kane, Gerald C., Anh Nguyen Phillips, Jonathan Copulsky, and Garth Andrus. "How Digital Leadership Is(n't) Different." *MIT Sloan Management Review* 60, 3 (2019): 34–39.

Chapter 5

Healthcare Silos and the Leadership Pivot in Decision Making

If you don't think healthcare is about power, you haven't been paying attention.

**Don Berwick, MD, president emeritus
and senior fellow at the Institute
for Healthcare Improvement**

Purpose

To examine the impact of healthcare, clinical care, and organizational silos on decision making and the leadership pivots needed along the journey to high-value healthcare.

In this chapter, the reader will consider

- The definition of a leadership pivot and why pivots are needed
- The impact of the silos that defined 1.0: Brick and Mortar Healthcare

- The challenges of the organization chart and the silo mentality
- The pivot to next-generation decision-making models and the collaborative network

The Leadership Pivot

The uncertainty of the journey to high-value healthcare becomes the new normal as organizations enter 2.0: The Transition. Venkat Venkatraman, professor at Boston University Questrom School of Business, indicates:

> We are at an inflection point where old definitions of industries, competition, and organization do not make much sense, but we do not yet have a new way to define and demarcate pockets of value created by digital technologies. The old rules of strategy and management—experimented and perfected in the industrial age—do not appear useful, yet we do not have new rules of management or value creation[1]

To thrive, during 2.0: The Transition and beyond, leaders must be willing to start down one path, learn, quickly adapt, and make changes along the way. The term *pivot*, synonymous with transformational change, is a familiar strategy in the startup world. Made popular in Eric Ries's book *The Lean Startup*, a pivot is the art of recognizing that the pursuit of a specific idea, direction, or leadership principle is no longer the correct path to follow. For many healthcare leaders, this pivot may mean altering or abandoning management and decision-making approaches that were successful in the past.

Intentional cultural change must be a priority as healthcare leaders blend digital and population health strategies and begin the hard work of

- Streamlining cost structures and improving agility
- Consolidating existing clinical, business, or financial operations
- Discovering opportunities to reinvent the consumer experience
- Transcending traditional competitive boundaries and collaborating with partners to identify and solve problems
- Reconfiguring business and clinical architecture (business and operating models) to create value

Leaders must guide the organization in knowing what to do and what not to do, including practices, values, and assumptions about their work.[2] Culture, one that is deeply understood and connects specific behaviors to specific results, must be demonstrated by leadership. Leadership pivots will be necessary. The first, and most difficult, pivot is to change the way organizational decisions are made.

The Impact of 1.0 Silos on Decision Making

Across healthcare organizations, large and small, decisions are disconnected, localized, and silo based. Occurring within clinical care teams and healthcare enterprises (i.e., functional departments, service lines, and cross-continuum), within medical trading areas, and across other segments of the market, including within payers and partners, silos have proliferated, resulting in extreme fragmentation of the healthcare industry, as illustrated in Figure 5.1.

Today, patients receive care through a patchwork of provider and ancillary silos—primary care practices, specialty clinics, hospitals, and others—which often don't communicate. Gaps in care are inevitable, and opportunities to intervene before problems arise are often missed. According to a RAND 2017 Report, "Sixty percent of Americans have at least one chronic condition, and 42 percent had multiple chronic

Figure 5.1   Healthcare silos.

conditions."[3] The sheer volume of unique disciplines and the complexity of patient conditions; coupled with misaligned incentives, has resulted in silo-based cultures that seek to retain the status quo. Thus, change has been difficult.

For example, the American Cancer Society (ACS) lists over 60 different clinical professionals that may be involved in the cancer patient's care on their website (www.cancer.org). "It is common to have different specialists or healthcare professionals as part of your cancer care team. Some of these professionals have had extra training focused on a certain type of cancer, a type of cancer treatment, a specific area, system, or part of the body, health problems related to cancer and coordination of the cancer patient's care," explains the ACS.[4] In addition to these silos of care, cancer patients with additional chronic conditions (i.e., high blood pressure, cardiac disease, kidney disease, diabetes, mental health problems, etc.) must also see specialists outside the cancer care community.

Organization Charts and the Silo Mentality

Silos also exist within the administrative, business, and financial side of healthcare. Work is divided by function (i.e., human resources, finance and accounting, supply chain, quality and

Figure 5.2 Hierarchical organization design.

performance improvement, information technology, etc.). Organization structures further define the decision-making processes within the silos. Roles, responsibilities, and relationships, as well as the hierarchy or authority, are clarified by organization charts. Accompanied by position descriptions, position control, performance review, wage and salary, and other supporting systems and documentation, the organization chart explains how each position fits within the overall enterprise and defines

- How positions are grouped and what people do
- Who each employee reports to and the leader's span of control
- Who owns specific decisions, assets, or capabilities

A typical organization structure is illustrated in Figure 5.2.

Historically, the organization chart was a static document that did not change very much. During times of stability, there were a number of pros to the organization chart and the organizational silos it represented, including:

- The workforce specialized in their specific functional subject matter expertise.

- High performers followed a vertical career path and typically rose quickly within their silo.
- Processes, information systems, and communications were optimized for the needs of the silo.
- Decisions were made based on the functional experience or expertise of leadership.

The cons, however, become more apparent during times of transition or transformation. Today, organizational charts often are obsolete before they are published. While healthcare leaders have experimented with a variety of nontraditional organizational structure designs (i.e., matrix, dyads and triads, hub and spoke, etc.) in an attempt to eliminate some of the cons, the silo mentality is alive and well. A cultural phenomenon, the silo mentality is defined as "a mindset present when certain departments or sectors do not wish to share information with others in the same company. This type of mentality reduces efficiency in the overall operation, reduces morale, and may contribute to the demise of a productive company culture."[5] "Silos create an environment where sharing and collaborating for anything other than one silo's special interests is virtually impossible," says Vijay Govindarajan, the Earl C. Daum 1924 Professor of International Business at the Tuck School of Business at Dartmouth.[6]

The silo mentality is often compounded by decision-making approaches within and across many healthcare enterprises. Decisions are made in one of two ways, with

- Someone with authority making a pronouncement or calling the shots, or
- Everyone providing input in hopes of gaining consensus

Authority-driven decisions provide accountability and responsibility but are often problematic. In today's world, many of healthcare's most pressing issues require multiple perspectives to address effectively. Consensus, on the other hand, may sound appealing based on the desire to have everyone onboard. Yet, it is not always effective and often gives everyone veto-power. "We have a vote of 100 to 1, and we call it a tie," exclaimed one healthcare executive. Additionally, consensus-based decision making can be frustrating in that decisions are slow, hard to reach, risk averse, and rely on groupthink.

The Pivot to Next-Generation Decision-Making Models

The real problem is not the silo itself but the lack of connection and integration of the silos, their decision processes, and their cultures. The hierarchical, bureaucratic structure so common for healthcare organizations was designed for the stable environments of the past. This structure kept the organization working like a well-oiled machine when change was slow, incremental, and planned. Executives led through command-and-control decision making and expected efficiency and predictability.

On the other hand, today, we are in an environment of uncertainty and disruption, not stability. Change comes fast and from multiple directions. The industry is facing large-scale, transformational change that requires collaboration and coordination from multiple silos. Strong leaders will not "own resources" but will be able to convene, facilitate, and orchestrate networked teams. Agile decision making, rapid iteration and experimentation, performance orientation, and information transparency will be the order of the day. It is becoming increasingly difficult to define relationships in a simple organization chart. Reasons include:

■ High-performing networks require the democratization of data and information. Transparency requirements and data access result in data exchange, connectivity, and sharing that bypasses hierarchical structure.

■ Escalation for the purposes of authorization slows down decisions that should be made at the point of care or by agile teams working to solve operational problems.

■ Multiple solid and dotted lines result in unclear account-ability, delays in decision making, increased numbers of meetings or committees, increased uncertainty and conflict, and added cost.

■ It becomes harder to document the fluid relationships across affiliates, partners, and communities on one page of paper.

Healthcare leaders are learning to pivot their thinking, avoiding reliance on organization charts and bypassing common missteps. For example,

■ Organization charts do not explain strategy or serve as a guide for day-to-day operations. They do not explain how the enterprise creates value (*what* gets done) or operates (*how* things get done).

■ The decision-making processes of the legacy enterprise are layered onto new ventures (i.e., clinical integration network [CIN], accountable care organization [ACO], alliance, innovation partnership, etc.), starving the new venture of resources and adding bureaucracy, management focus, and the flexibility needed to achieve its potential.

■ Technology or data is viewed as a "silver bullet," and the organization moves full steam ahead with implementation without thinking through the operational, cultural, or change implications.

■ Individuals who know how to "operate" existing clinical or business units are responsible for the new venture rather than leaders who know how to "design" new strategies, processes, platforms, and roles.

■ Best practices from the traditional industry—which often represent the old way of doing things—are applied instead of emerging practices, incorporating new and different ways of working.

■ New organizational structures are established but follow traditional command-and-control decision-making cultures, are risk averse, and are not agile. Experiments are viewed as pilots of a bigger implementation.

Table 5.1 depicts siloed thinking versus collaborative thinking and the associated leadership pivots in decision-making processes associated with each.

Through clinically integrated networks, accountable care organizations, health information exchanges, and collaborative partnerships established as part of 2.0: The Transition, extended enterprises are created. Defined as a group of companies that operate independently but come together to offer a service or product to the market, some extended enterprises operate informally, and others cooperate through contracts

Table 5.1 Leadership Pivots in Decision Making

Siloed Thinking	Collaborative Thinking
Hierarchy and organization charts	Networks and governance processes
Focus on efficiency, effectiveness, and incremental improvement	Focus on transformation and innovation
Information hoarding	Connectivity and information sharing
Command-and-control leadership	Orchestration and influence
Functional groupings and task alignment within departments	Cross-disciplinary/cross-boundary teams and projects
Slow, methodical, big-bang change	Agile, fail-fast, learning-focused, waves of experiments prior to scaling
Culture of exclusion	Culture of inclusion

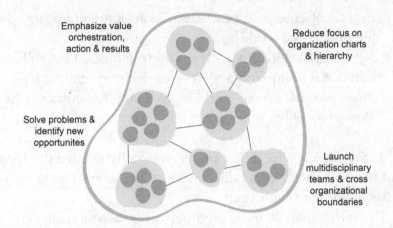

Figure 5.3 The network organization.

and agreements. Still others work through interconnected networks of affiliates, alliances, and communities as part of the broader healthcare ecosystem in their local market, regionally, or at a national level, as seen in Figure 5.3, where

- The focus is on solving problems, identifying new opportunity and orchestrating value.
- Success is defined as action and results, not organization charts and hierarchy.
- Agility and collaboration skills provide leadership power.
- Teams are multidisciplinary and cross organizational boundaries.

TRANSFORMATIONAL CHANGE AND THE NETWORK

John Kotter, author of the book *Leading Change*, states: "The successful organization of the future will have multiple organization structures: a hierarchy for optimizing traditional work and networks for big change (large-scale organizational change, such as a company redesigning its entire business model, or accomplishing its most important strategic objectives of the decade, or changing its portfolio of product offerings) ... the network is a system of teams with representatives from many divisions and levels, who leave formal titles at the door to participate in a decidedly anti-hierarchical forum. As the environment changes in various ways, this system senses and responds to it, and in turn creates more and more teams ... to address the discrete parts of a larger change ... Potential opportunities and changes are identified, urgency around tomorrow's possibilities is fostered and maintained, strategies for organization-wide changes are formed, barriers are identified and addressed, and change is achieved. To clarify, I am not talking about a cross-unit "task force" or a new "initiative" built into this year's plans. I am talking about a whole new system that is much bigger, more powerful and involves far more people. Over the past few years, I've started to see many high-performing organizations use a network-like structure outside their traditional hierarchy to lead change, and with great results."[7]

Conclusion

Dr. Ninfa Saunders, president and CEO of Navicent Health, defines the network she is building as an "up link and a lateral link"—the up link is with an organization that is bigger than her own, and the lateral link is within the community. Rather than making decisions within the vacuum of the enterprise, healthcare organizations will extend to become networks, and from these networks they will build out new ecosystems of value creation. Through partnerships with complementary and sometimes competitive players, new digital platforms will emerge that are much more than the digital technologies that drive them. New business and operating models will reduce the challenges that inhibit population health and other barriers in healthcare today. But, first, most leaders will have to pivot and change their mental model.

Notes

1. Venkatraman, Venkat. *The Digital Matrix New Rules for Business Transformation Through Technology.* Lifetree, 2017.
2. Staniland, M. *What Is Political Economy? A Study of Social Theory and Underdevelopment.* New Haven: Yale University Press, 1985.
3. Buttorff, Christien, Teague Ruder, and Melissa Bauman. *Multiple Chronic Conditions in the United States.* RAND Corporation, 2017.
4. "Health Professionals Associated with Cancer Care." American Cancer Society. Accessed September 16, 2019. www.cancer.org/treatment/finding-and-paying-for-treatment/choosing-your-treatment-team/health-professionals-associated-with-cancer-care.html.
5. Gleeson, Brent, and Megan Rozo. "The Silo Mentality: How to Break Down the Barriers." *Forbes Magazine*, October 2, 2013. www.forbes.com/sites/brentgleeson/2013/10/02/the-silo-mentality-how-to-break-down-the-barriers/#527548188c7e.
6. Govindarajan, Vijay. "Breaking Down Silos in Your Organization (Harvard Business Review)." Dartmouth News, August 15, 2011. https://news.dartmouth.edu/news/2011/08/breaking-down-silos-your-organization-harvard-business-review.
7. Kotter, John P. "Hierarchy and Network: Two Structures, One Organization." *Harvard Business Review*, May 23, 2011. https://hbr.org/2011/05/two-structures-one-organization.html.

Chapter 6

Collaborate, Create, and Innovate: Platform Thinking

The future is already here. It's just not widely distributed yet.

William Gibson, science fiction writer

Platform Thinking: A New Mental Model

Mental models are the lens through which we see the world, attribute cause and effect, and make sense of the vast amount of information we receive each day.[1] To understand the power of mental models, one doesn't have to go outside healthcare to find a great example. In Vienna, in the 1840s, a physician, Dr. Ignaz Semmelweis, observed that the death rate for puerperal fever fell tenfold when doctors washed their hands before treating patients. He shared his findings with his colleagues to introduce hand washing as a standard practice. Despite the data, his fellow doctors dismissed his findings. In fact, his colleagues and even his own wife thought he was losing his mind. They had him committed to a mental institution, where he died shortly thereafter.[2] Hand washing as a standard practice was not widely accepted until the 1980s, when the first national guidelines on hand hygiene were published. Today, Dr. Semmelweis is recognized as an early pioneer of antiseptic procedures. For the purposes of transformation, an even greater lesson learned from his work is that Dr. Semmelweis imposed a system change (the use of chlorinated lime solutions) without consulting the opinion of his peers.[3] In other words, he missed the reality that in order to change behavior, one must change the way people think.

Participation in clinical integration networks, accountable care organizations, and a variety of new innovation partnerships is beginning to change the conversation from "fix me when I'm broken" to "keep me healthy as long as possible."[4] Yet for many, due to the gravitational pull of silo mentalities, incentives inherent in traditional revenue models, and the friction of changing legacy technology, it often becomes easier to stick with business as usual. In order to orchestrate value at scale, key stakeholders must change not only what they think but also how they think. Without the right mental model, they will not see the problem, understand the benefits, or make the change.

The industrial age conditioned enterprise leaders to think linearly about work. In healthcare, one provider diagnoses and treats one patient, a hospital treats a patient during an inpatient stay, an emergency department or clinic sees a patient during one visit, etc. Most work occurred within a facility, entity, practice, or other venue of care. Services were provided and scaled by adding headcount, clinical technology, and physical space. In the digital age, through the rise of the Internet, cloud solutions, smart devices, and artificial intelligence, work can be coordinated outside the enterprise. Through networks and digital ecosystems, the cost of coordination is reduced, and value is created.

This shift in the mental model for the digital age can be referred to as *platform thinking*. Rather than thinking about assets owned, resources controlled, and market position, innovative healthcare leaders will think about becoming holistic integrators of consumer-centric, 24/7 services. These new offerings will be based on new business models that combine unique combinations of talent, technology, and information to solve problems or create new value.

PLATFORM BUSINESS MODELS

A platform is a business model that creates value by facilitating exchanges between two or more interrelated groups. In healthcare, potential participants include health consumers and patients, caregivers and families, providers, health systems, payers, suppliers, researchers, and other key stakeholders. Platforms create communities and markets with network effects to allow participants to collaborate, create, and innovate. Scale comes not from assets added but by cultivating an external network on top of your existing business. Data and technology are critical to the platform business model but not sufficient alone. Platform design is about creating the whole solution and orchestrating value for the consumer and the network. Successful platforms facilitate exchanges by reducing transaction costs and/or by enabling externalized innovation. With the advent of connected technology, these ecosystems enable platforms to scale in ways that the traditional healthcare system cannot.

Dan Michelson, chief executive officer (CEO) of Strata Decision Technology, summarized in a January 2019 Becker's Healthcare post "It's the platform, stupid," referring to his own *aha moment* at a J. P. Morgan Stanley Healthcare Meeting:

> for healthcare providers, there is a major shift taking place. They are moving from a traditional strategy of buying and building hospitals and simply providing

care into a new and more dynamic strategy that focuses on leveraging the platform they have in place to create more value and growth via new and often more profitable streams of revenue. Simply stated, the healthcare delivery systems of today will increasingly leverage the platform and resources that they have in place to become a hub for both health and healthcare in the future. There is a level of urgency to move quickly. Many feel that if they don't expand the role that they play in both health and healthcare in their community, someone else will step in.[5]

So, who would step in? We all know the players. Platform companies are redefining all industries—Google dominates searches, Amazon controls e-commerce, and Facebook rules social media. Uber and Lyft have redefined transportation, and Airbnb has reinvented the travel and rental marketplace. And, of course, Apple created the smart device as a platform. All have a role to play in healthcare, including

- Applying current solutions to health and healthcare in a new way
- Solving health and healthcare problems for their own employees
- Partnering with healthcare incumbents to reposition the delivery system
- Empowering consumers to act on their own behalf using their own health information

Michael Jacobides, Associate Professor of Strategy and Entrepreneurship at London Business School, indicates that these companies think not only "what does the customer really want?" but also "how can I connect with other participants, linking them to my platform so that together we can create real value?"[6] Healthcare ventures between Amazon, J. P. Morgan and Berkshire Hathaway, CVS and Aetna, and more traditional health systems such as Aurora Health Care and Advocate Health Care, Catholic Health Initiatives and Dignity Health, all have major ramifications. "Not every organization should assume a leadership role in a business ecosystem; however, every organization needs a digital platform strategy," said Don Scheibenreif, Gartner vice president. The digital platform strategy will vary from company to company. Some organizations will design and develop the platform, and others will participate in its network. Each organization's strategy integrates business and information technology (IT) and establishes a collective leadership vision of the organization's role in digital platforms in order to share critical assets.[7]

Opportunity abounds for Big Tech, incumbents and start-ups, to create new platforms that are designed to connect health consumers and clinical care teams as part of an innovation ecosystem (see Figure 6.1).

The innovation ecosystem consists of technology, expertise, and services. It supports participants as they build relationships, collaborate on designing new ways of working, and deploy new digital operating capabilities. New operating models may result in a focus on platforms that aggregate and mobilize

■ Transactions: Facilitating exchange of information, services, or products between different participants
■ Relationships: Consolidating a broad array of pertinent resources and helping participants connect with the most appropriate resources, building and reinforcing those relationships over time
■ Data and Insights: Providing algorithms and analytics for consumer, operational, financial, human resource, research, etc., insights
■ Integrated Technology: Streamlining cost of technology services, tools, and infrastructure

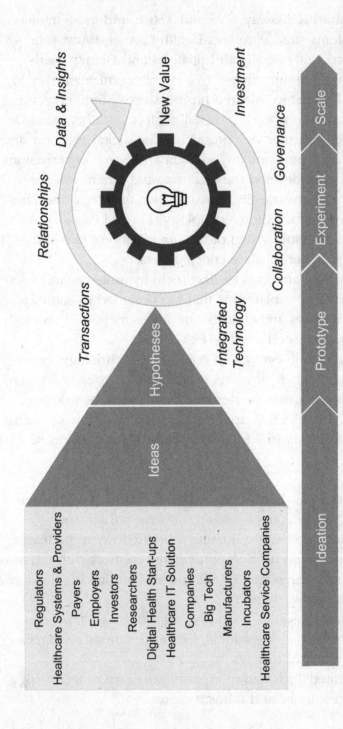

Figure 6.1   The innovation ecosystem.

- Collaboration: Shared learning; expanded know-how, competencies, and capabilities; and performance improvement
- Governance: Steering effective decision-making processes across multiple network participants
- Investment: Combining funding, expertise, experiences, and assets for the purpose of building an active platform strategy

Platform thinking will require a mental model that shifts from

- Resource control to resource orchestration
- Provider centricity to consumer and patient centricity, and eventually, consumer partnerships
- Enterprise optimization to ecosystem value creation

Role of the Platform Players

Innovation ecosystems and the platforms they launch will depend on the collaboration of multiple stakeholders. While the resulting value obtained through platform participation may vary the identities and roles of the key platform players, four types of participants exist.

- The platform owner is responsible for the vision and overall viability of the platform. As mentioned in Chapter 4 and depicted in Figure 4.3, the CEO can establish this strategic vision and direction early along the journey to high-value healthcare. The platform owner actively engages participants in platform co-creation, stimulates activity through the appropriate incentives and member experiences, and provides unique value such as know-how, technology, processes, data, research, access to consumers or delivery channels, etc. Depending on the specifics of the platform strategy, the owner could be a local or national healthcare delivery system, a payer, a public/private partnership, a commercial solutions company (e.g., software, pharma, services, manufacturing, etc.), an alliance of multiple stakeholders, etc. The platform owner should also:

- Ensure development of platform governance structures and processes.
- Ensure engagement and buy-in of collaborative markets.
- Establish structures for co-opetition.
- Invest in trust and loyalty to the ecosystem.

In Section III, the care management platform will be examined as a detailed example of a specific platform strategy. In this example, the owner would probably be a health system or payor.

■ The platform producer provides the core value offered through the interactions, relationships, and transactions of the platform. In the instance of care management, participants could include physicians and other care team members, health coaches, social workers, care managers, and a number of other health professionals.

■ The platform partner seeks strategic benefit through access to customers or producers by participating in the platform. Generally, these players are indirectly involved with the value exchange and provide additional services or products that support the platform producer. In the example of care management, the health plan, non-owner health systems and affiliates, solutions companies, etc. often partner to support the platform consumer.

■ The platform consumer uses the core value provided by the platform ecosystem. Depending on the platform strategy, the consumer may include healthy individuals seeking information, patients with multiple chronic conditions, or caregivers and families seeking help and logistical support. Platforms may support consumers seeking specific clinical or social support services, quality outcomes, experiences, expertise, etc. In the care management example, the consumer may be an attributed patient in a value-based contract or a consumer seeking digital health services.

Figure 6.2 depicts the players in the platform ecosystem and demonstrates potential participants in each role.

The platform owner has a variety of options relative to platform scope and openness. Today, many clinically integrated networks operate closed networks and base membership on health system employment or contractual agreements with payers, affiliated providers, and partners. In other environments, platforms may be established to support communities and are more open. In the instance of an open platform, the platform owner may share in the benefits in order to seed interest, increase value, and expand collaboration across the ecosystem.

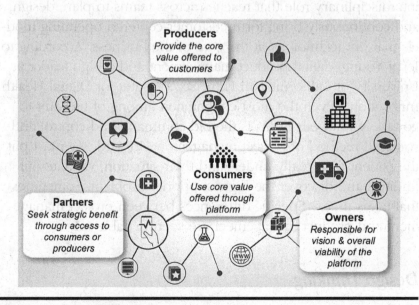

Figure 6.2 Platform players.

Platform Innovation and Design Techniques

Product Management

Project management is pervasive in healthcare today. Large enterprises have PMOs focused on managing large IT programs or enterprise initiatives. Project management is focused on output, or reaching certain milestones in a given time period, and the costs of resources consumed. Product management is a fundamentally different approach. The primary difference is that products have a primary customer and expected value. Focused on outcome, rather than output, it is more difficult to put constraints on delivery.

The role of product managers in platform innovation, design-leading ideation, and discovery sessions is to understand the customer's perspective, pain points, and expectations. Through collaborative and autonomous teams, they investigate and design value-driven solutions. While traditionally, IT has focused on implementing technology, and the business has focused on optimizing operations, product management is an interdisciplinary role that reaches across teams to plan, design, and continuously bring forth customer-centered operating models that put technology at the core of the business. According to Jerry Young, digital product management and design leader at University of California San Francisco's Center for Digital Health Innovation, "Even the most enlightened among of us want to go fast. Within our DNA, is the old command-and-control and waterfall method of project management. Instead, we must put the patient first, really understand their situation, validate our findings and discover the highest priority problem. Sometimes that takes time."[8] Specific differences between project management and product management are seen in Table 6.1.

Design Thinking

Successful platforms require strong upfront design and deep understanding of the consumers we are designing the platform

Table 6.1   Project Management versus Product Management

Project Management	Product Management
Short term–duration teams	Long-term teams
Build once and implement	Prototype, test, and learn
Waterfall methodology with final deliverable	Agile iteration with continuous releases
Key metrics: on time and on budget	Key metrics: value and customer results
Scope is single thread—IT, performance improvement, process design, etc.	Scope is multi-thread—user design, operating model, process design, etc.

to serve. Design thinking, sometimes referred to as *outside-the-box-thinking*, is an iterative process that challenges mental models and encourages one to look at problems with fresh eyes. Extremely useful in tackling problems that are ill defined or unknown, design thinking helps reframe the business model by questioning: questioning the problem, questioning the assumptions, and questioning the implications. Design thinking uncovers new ways of improving the product, service, or experience; prototyping and testing the design; and generating holistic, innovative solutions. Don Norman, author of "Rethinking Design Thinking," states:

> Designers resist the temptation to jump immediately to a solution to the stated problem. Instead, they first spend time determining what the basic, fundamental (root) issue is that needs to be addressed. They don't try to search for a solution until they have determined the real problem, and even then, instead of solving that problem, they stop to consider a wide range of potential solutions. Only then will they finally converge.[9]

Figure 6.3 illustrates an iterative design thinking process for platform design.

Empathize	**Define**	**Ideate**	**Prototype**	**Test**
Understand the consumer-pain points & what matters to them	Re-evaluate the problem based on customer priorities	Push beyond traditional answers & boundaries to solve the problem	Create hypotheses & minimum viable product	Experiment, test & learn from consumers. Refine prototype

Figure 6.3   Design thinking.

Jobs-to-be-Done Framework

Harvard Business School professor Clayton Christensen and coauthors articulated the *Jobs-to-be-Done* (JTBD) concept in a *Sloan Management Review* article (Spring 2007) as follows: "Most companies segment their markets by customer demographics or product characteristics and differentiate their offerings by adding features and functions. But the consumer has a different view of the marketplace. He simply has a job to be done and is seeking to 'hire' the best product or service to do it."[10] For platforms, there are the following JTBD:

- *Main jobs to be done,* which describe the tasks that the four participant types want to achieve
- *Related jobs to be done,* which describe the tasks the participants want to accomplish in conjunction with the main jobs to be done

Then, within each of these two types of JTBD, there are

- *Functional job aspects:* the practical and objective participant requirements
- *Emotional job aspects:* the subjective participant requirements related to feelings and perception, both personally and socially

Key considerations for platform design include

- Who are the platform participants, and what interactions will they have?
- What disconnects and problems need to be overcome?
- What opportunities exist to add or create value?
- Can the platform change the participant touchpoints, access, or relationships?
- What data do we have, or could we collect, for specific platform participants?
- Can we shift from historic, to real-time, to predictive and prescriptive data to support platform activities?
- Are there closed-loop system opportunities to reduce waste, streamline processes, and remove barriers?
- What regulatory or regional pain points may be impacted?
- What operational capabilities are needed to support the platform?
- What rules of participation are needed to define how the various participants interact?
- What incentives and rewards are necessary to ensure network effects from all participants?
- Is a closed or open model preferred, and will this change over time?
- Will the platform be primarily digital, physician, or a combination?

Conclusion

Platform thinking is a new mental model for the health and healthcare industry. While the transition to value requires a new mindset and culture, leaders must also build new competencies and capabilities to

- Understand that digital strategy will revolve around solving existing problems in new ways and recognizing new opportunities to create value.

- Create partnerships to extend the enterprise and interact across key communities.
- Design new operating models with data and technology at the core through product management, design thinking, and JBTD.

Section III will detail the specifics of the care management platform to support population health management and change across the current delivery system.

Notes

1. Bonchek, Mark. "Don't Sell a Product, Sell a Whole New Way of Thinking." *Harvard Business Review*, February 27, 2015. https://hbr.org/2014/07/dont-sell-a-product-sell-a-whole-new-way-of-thinking.
2. Ibid.
3. "Historical Perspective on Hand Hygiene in Health Care." WHO Guidelines on Hand Hygiene in Health Care: First Global Patient Safety Challenge Clean Care Is Safer Care. U.S. National Library of Medicine, January 1, 1970. www.ncbi.nlm.nih.gov/books/NBK144018/.
4. Johnson, David, and Amy Compton-Phillips. "Platforming Healthcare (TM): Owning Hospitals Is So 2015." 4sight Health, February 21, 2018. www.4sighthealth.com/platforming-healthcare-owning-hospitals-is-so-2015/.
5. Michelson, Dan. "The No. 1 Takeaway from the 2019 JP Morgan Healthcare Conference: It's the Platform, Stupid." *Becker's Hospital Review*, January 11, 2019. www.beckershospitalreview.com/hospital-management-administration/the-no-1-takeaway-from-the-2019-jp-morgan-healthcare-conference-it-s-the-platform-stupid.html.
6. "The Future Is Platforms." London Business School, November 1, 2018. www.london.edu/lbsr/the-future-is-platforms.
7. Kasey, Panetta. "Every Organization Needs a Digital Platform Strategy." Smarter With Gartner, November 8, 2016. www.gartner.com/smarterwithgartner/every-organization-needs-a-digital-platform-strategy/.

8. Arlotto, Pam, and Jerry Young. "Orchestrating Value: Population Health in the Digital Age." Interview at Rock Health Summit, September 25, 2019.

9. Dam, Rikke, and Teo Siang. "What Is Design Thinking and Why Is It So Popular?" The Interaction Design Foundation, September 2019. https://www.interaction-design.org/literature/article/what-is-design-thinking-and-why-is-it-so-popular.

10. Silverstein, David, Phil Samuel, and Neil DeCarlo. "Technique 1 – Jobs to Be Done." Innovator's Toolkit, March 3, 2016. http://innovatorstoolkit.com/content/technique-1-jobs-be-done.

THE CARE MANAGEMENT PLATFORM

> *The big-picture reason that a lot of these tech companies are getting into health care now is because the market is too big, too important and much too personal to their users for them to ignore.*

> **John Prendergass, associate director of Health Care Investment at Ben Franklin Technology Partners, a nonprofit organization in Philadelphia**

New Platforms, New Services

As the authors were putting the final touches on this book in late September 2019, Amazon unveiled a virtual care platform, dubbed Amazon Care, to bring telemedicine services to some of its Seattle-based employees. Amazon Care lets users chat, video call, or receive an in-person visit from a Mobile Care nurse seven days a week through a partnership with Washington state-based Oasis Medical Group. The service also offers two-hour prescription delivery for many prescriptions—a service that could potentially be bolstered by Amazon's $750 million acquisition of digital pharmacy startup PillPack. While Amazon Care is currently restricted to Amazon employees, it seems likely that it's destined for expansion to the general public, based on Amazon's decidedly consumer-facing release. And with over 100 million Prime members in the United States alone, the company possesses a solid launching pad for the new service.[1]

Indu Subaiya, MD, MBA, cofounder and president of Catalyst @ Health 2.0 and senior advisor to the Healthcare Information and Management Systems Society, indicates: "We're really excited about new approaches to health with tailored, outcome-based platforms. There's this phrase 'health happens everywhere' which is the idea that providers have to find new ways to partner outside their own walls, because care needs to be delivered wherever people are."[2] Multiple value propositions will be addressed through platform-driven business and operating models. Examples are illustrated in Figure III.1.

Multiple opportunities exist to reinvent broad swaths of the healthcare industry. Examples include but are not limited to

- Disease treatment and therapeutics: Interventions, treatment, or the management of a specific clinical condition
- Clinical decision support and precision medicine: Augmenting clinical decision making with continuous clinical intelligence, predictive, and prescriptive analytics to support the care process
- Fitness and wellness: Supports healthy behaviors, including fitness, nutrition, and sleep
- Disease monitoring: Remote or wearable technology that provides ongoing data regarding a specific clinical condition
- Clinical trials and research: Enables administration and management of drug discovery, clinical trial management, and other research and development processes

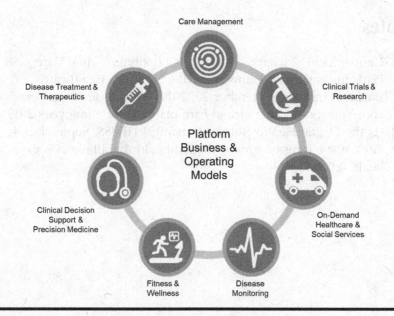

Figure III.1 Platform business and operating models.

- On-demand healthcare and social services: Delivers immediate or near-real-time health coaching, physician visits, telemedicine, and social support services ·
- Care management: Supports population health management and value-based care

Platform business and operating models are relatively new concepts to healthcare delivery organizations. As previously mentioned, the journey to high-value healthcare and development of scale in the transition to 3.0: Digital Health and Connected Care has been difficult with traditional healthcare business and operating models as the core. The chapters in this section will present the concept of the care management platform in detail—its definition, history, capabilities, and future as a potential next step along the journey. Readers should use this framework as a guide and should focus on the portions of this section that impact their own situation.

Notes

1. Hendrickson, Zachary. "Amazon Is Piloting a Virtual Care Platform as the Company's next Big Step into Healthcare." Business Insider, September 26, 2019. www.businessinsider. com/amazon-piloting-virtual-care-platform-for-employees-2019-9.
2. "Is the Digital Health Bubble Bursting?" HIMSS, September 4, 2019. www.himss.org/news/digital-health-bubble-bursting-health-20-weighs-in.

Chapter 7

The Care Management Platform, Its Layers and Hubs

A care management platform must sit at a level higher than an individual EMR. It must pull data from every system and be the platform where communication takes place.

Russ Staheli, senior vice president, Population Health & Care Management, Health Catalyst

Purpose

To explore the layers of the care management platform (CMP) and to understand how it supports healthcare delivery organizations in their transition to digital health, connected care, and population health management.

In this chapter, the reader will discover

- The definition of care management
- The layers of the CMP, including foundational systems, health information exchange, knowledge management

and analytics, advanced care management, and consumer and patient engagement
■ The CMP stakeholders and Jobs-to-be-Done (JTBD)
■ From electronic health records (EHRs) and portals to care team– and patient-centric hubs

Defining the Care Management Platform

Patients with complex healthcare needs account for a disproportionately high percentage of our nation's annual medical expenditures. Care management is defined as a range of activities intended to improve patient care and reduce the need for medical services by enhancing coordination of care, eliminating duplication, and helping patients and caregivers more effectively manage health conditions. Across the healthcare industry, these efforts have demonstrated potential to improve quality and control costs for patients with complex conditions.[1] Yet, many organizations struggle to scale or break even using traditional healthcare business and operating models.

The CMP meets the definition of a platform business model described in Chapter 6 and leverages the capabilities of clinical integration networks, accountable care organizations, and community population health initiatives. By providing tools, technologies, information, people, and care processes, the CMP supports the interactions of consumers of health and healthcare, their clinical care teams, and other ecosystem stakeholders. The CMP facilitates powerful new value propositions that extend beyond traditional industry boundaries by aggregating core care delivery services across the continuum and connecting key industry partners. The CMP framework[2] identifies foundational systems (i.e., EHRs, revenue management and practice management systems [RCM], and enterprise resource management systems [ERP]) implemented during 1.0: Brick and Mortar Healthcare. Generally built to support a specific entity or venue of care (i.e., hospitals, primary care/ patient-centered medical homes, specialists, post-acute providers, etc.), additional layers are needed to orchestrate value across the platform. These layers include health information exchange, knowledge management and analytics, advanced care management, and consumer and patient engagement, as illustrated in Figure 7.1.

The CMP framework has many implications for the transformation of healthcare. The CMP is

- Focused on the creation of new value, including new answers to old problems, development of new interactions between platform participants, and support of micro-services and experiences.
- Not implemented within one enterprise but enables networks and communities as they address market, specialty, service line, process, and consumer challenges.
- Enabled by the cloud and highly configurable, robust infrastructure.
- Designed to support the convergence of legacy business and operating models found in health plans, health systems, ambulatory care, and other components of the broader healthcare industry.
- Data driven in order to support personalized, evidence-based health management interventions.

While large EHR vendors increasingly provide the data and technology capabilities needed for each CMP layer, no one vendor can provide it all. Many organizations are becoming more open to hybrid strategies that leverage the benefits of stable legacy applications combined with the offerings of enhanced flexibility and innovation promised by digital health and cloud-based solutions. Each layer of the care management platform has distinct capabilities and tools needed to manage

CONSUMER & PATIENT ENGAGEMENT

24/7 Access via Unified Portal, Self Service Scheduling, Branded Call Centers, Customer Relationship Management, Patient Self Reported Data, Linguistic Services, Remote Monitoring, Patient Education, Telehealth/mHealth & Telemedicine, etc.

ADVANCED CARE MANAGEMENT

Health Risk Assessment, Care Management, Case Management, Care Planning, Adherence Alerts, Disease Management, Risk Management, Referral Management, Rules Based Workflows, etc.

KNOWLEDGE MANAGEMENT & ANALYTICS

Data Governance, Business Intelligence, Care Protocols, Claims Data, Point of Care Clinical Decision Support, Metrics, Data Mining, Predictive Modeling, etc.

HEALTH INFORMATION EXCHANGE

Master Patient Index, Secure Messaging, Standards based Interoperability, Communication Tools, Referral Tracking, Community Health Record, Registries, etc.

FOUNDATIONAL SYSTEMS

PCMH   Specialists   Hospitals   Post Acute Providers   Diagnostics   Rx   Payers

Figure 7.1   The care management platform.

the health of many types of populations successfully. The layers of the CMP include

- Foundational Systems: Basic transactional systems that document delivery of care. The foundational system layer includes EHRs, RCM, ERP, diagnostic data, pharmacy data, and claims data.
- Health Information Exchange: Exchange of data across care delivery sites and entities to inform care delivery. Interoperable systems, processes, and language that includes network administration, that is, connecting members of the care network to each other.
- Knowledge Management and Analytics: Ability to assimilate data from disparate sources to drive informed decision making.
- Advanced Care Management: Tools and workflows to ensure care is delivered in the appropriate setting with the desired outcomes.
- Consumer and Patient Engagement: Tools and workflows that enable the patient and their family to participate in their care.

Each of these layers will be discussed in depth in the following chapters.

A CMP supports the transition from encounter-based clinical care to episodic-based care and ultimately, population health management. To scale from 2.0: The Transition to 3.0: Digital Health and Connected Care, healthcare organizations should transition their view of the EHR and other foundational systems to consider their role in a larger platform strategy. Specifically, the capabilities needed to support key stakeholders and JTBD include

- Management of attributed and community populations and the specific needs of healthy, rising risk and highly complex patients with multiple chronic conditions
- Orchestration of the right care at the right time in the right setting for the best outcomes for the patient

Figure 7.2 depicts key platform stakeholders and their various roles. A design thinking process that explores their various pain points, experiences, and desired outcomes helps set the stage for the next-generation platform beyond today's foundation systems.

Figure 7.3 illustrates the JBTD to provide care management across the healthcare ecosystem to support population health and value-based care.

STRATEGIC

Owner - Health System, Payer, Community Partners or ACO, etc.

MEZZANINE

Care Managers, Pharmacists, Nutritionist, etc. working across multiple provider panels, care teams & entities

FRONTLINE

Clinicians, Health coaches & staff delivering care interacting with patients, care givers and families

PATIENT

Health consumers, patients, care givers, families, etc.

Figure 7.2   The CMP stakeholders.

STRATEGIC
- Population risk management
- Financial risk management
- Network leakage analysis
- Cost-of-care insights
- Organizational performance benchmarking & improvement

FRONTLINE
- Workflow-based care management
- Care gap closure
- Patient outreach
- Team care planning
- Condition focused measure & reporting

MEZZANINE
- Population identification & risk assessment
- Care management
- Care coordination & transition management
- Patient outreach
- Team care planning

PATIENT & FAMILY
- Review of all relevant health, medical & cost data
- Informed consumer & selection of health services based on cost & quality
- Selt management & condition monitoring
- Contribution of health information

Figure 7.3   JTBD for key CMP stakeholders.

The Hubs That Help Define the CMP

The next-generation CMP will gain traction through design thinking and JTBD efforts focused on two stakeholder-centric hubs – one for the care team and one for the consumer/patient.

Care Team Hub

The care team hub supports the clinical team and their interactions with patients, caregivers, and family members. The entire patient story is understood, coordinated, and managed from prevention to primary care to specialist, with specific services and interventions to result in improved experience and outcomes.

As presented in Figure 7.4, the care team hub has many capabilities. Some are available in today's EHR, such as clinical

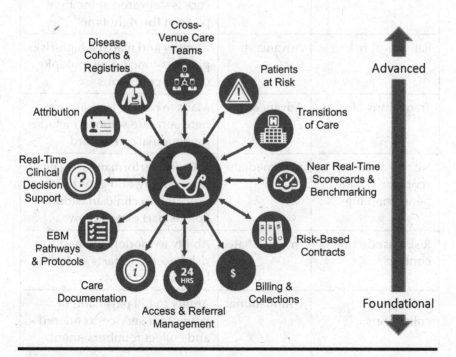

Figure 7.4 The care team hub.

documentation, and available for all patients. Others are considered more advanced. Examples include risk identification and management for specific populations, real-time alerts integrated into clinical workflow, ambient voice technologies that reduce clinician charting time, clinical content and dashboard that augment clinician decision making—all driven by cognitive computing, machine learning, and advanced analytics algorithms. The key components of the care team hub are described in Table 7.1.

Table 7.1 The Care Team Hub Components

Capability	Level	Description
Cross-venue care teams	Advanced	Processes and tools for multidisciplinary teams who coordinate care and services across the continuum and community to ensure the right care is delivered at the right place at the right time
Patients at risk	Advanced	Identify and manage high-risk patients—including multiple chronic conditions
Transitions of care	Advanced	Manage patient transitions between care settings; includes longitudinal care record
Near real-time scorecards and benchmarking	Intermediate	Current performance (quality, productivity, and gaps in care) reported to clinician within Epic as part of workflow
Risk-based contracts	Intermediate	Ability to model and monitor risk-based contracts including bundles and APMs
Billing and collections	Foundational	Ability to bill payer and/or patient for services rendered and collect reimbursement

(Continued)

Table 7.1 (Continued)   The Care Team Hub Components

Capability	Level	Description
Access and referral management	Foundational	Ability to provide earliest available appointment and keep referrals in network
Care documentation	Foundational	Electronic documentation in the EHR—history and physical, visit summaries, problem lists, care plans, etc.
Evidence-based medicine (EBM) pathways and protocols	Foundational	Use of EBM to drive order sets, protocols, and clinical pathways
Real-time clinical decision support	Intermediate	Integration of order sets and workflow-based rules, alerts, and triggers; Best Practice Alerts
Attribution	Advanced	Determining which patients are assigned to a provider's panel for care and for outcomes measurement
Disease cohorts and registries	Advanced	Identifying specific populations and using registries where appropriate to manage and track care and outcomes

The Consumer and Patient Hub

The consumer and patient hub, as illustrated in Figure 7.5, is what the community (patients and caregivers) needs to access care, access information about their care, and participate in their care on a day-to-day basis as well as over the course of their lives. Tomorrow's consumer engagement tool will be either untethered or tied to the patient, not the EHR/institution. An array of technologies will move

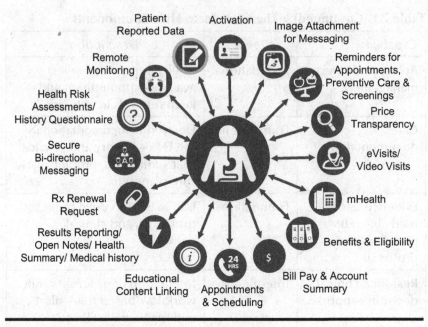

Figure 7.5 The consumer and patient hub.

the patient from engagement, to activation, to behavior change. This patient hub is also the essence of the digital consumer experience and must be fully functional, ensuring that access and engagement are seamless for the consumer. Two-way information sharing can occur, customer relationship management and other capabilities support outreach efforts, and remote capabilities ranging from telehealth to remote monitoring to mobile applications are available. The key components of the consumer and patient hub are defined in Table 7.2.

Table 7.2 Consumer and Patient Hub Components

Capability	Level	Description
Patient activation	Foundational	Patients signing up for and using their patient portal
Image attachment for messaging	Advanced	Ability for patients to create and forward image to patient health records (PHR) (e.g., dermatology)
Reminders for appointments, preventive care, and screenings	Intermediate	Ability to automatically generate correspondence in the patients' preferred method to remind them of appointments and needed screenings/preventive care
Price transparency	Advanced	Ability for consumer to see expected cost (payer and out-of-pocket) for a specific diagnostic or treatment
eVisits/video visits (virtual health)	Advanced	Ability to conduct nonurgent visits via telephone or video
mHealth	Intermediate	Mobile health applications for patients/consumers
Benefits and eligibility	Intermediate	Ability for consumers to understand what is covered under their plan; ability for consumer to edit their status
Customer service for billing; bill payment and account summary	Foundational	Ability for consumers to check their balance and pay bills online
Appointments and scheduling	Intermediate	Ability for patients to make appointment requests, direct scheduling, open scheduling, and appointment cancellation
Educational content linking	Foundational	Ability for patients to access digital education content based on their care needs and health status

(Continued)

Table 7.2 (Continued)   Consumer and Patient Hub Components

Capability	Level	Description
Results reporting/ open notes/health summary/medical history	Foundational	Ability for patients to see lab results, visit summary, and other information in their personal health record
Rx renewal request	Foundational	Ability for patients to electronically request prescription renewals
Secure bidirectional messaging	Foundational	Ability for patients to communicate in a secure electronic fashion such as email or texting
Health risk assessments/ history questionnaire	Intermediate	Pre-visit questionnaires that patients complete electronically and the providers incorporate into the visits and care planning
Remote monitoring (eHealth)	Advanced	Allows data from monitors and medical devices to report data into PHR
Patient experience data	Advanced	Ability for patients to self-report data such as activity levels, weight, pain, mood, etc.

The Hubs Combine to Create the Next-Generation Platform

While both the care team hub and the patient hub are essential for care delivery, their impact becomes more powerful in an ecosystem focused on transformation and innovation. New paradigms in health and healthcare will

■ Focus on prevention, wellness, managing risk factors, and coordinating care for those with chronic conditions.

- Make the patient experience more personal, more affordable, more convenient, and more responsive.
- Take advantage of the explosion of new technologies
  such as artificial intelligence, blockchain, the Internet of
  Things (IoT), etc.
- Expect high degrees of interoperability, connectivity, and
  data flow enabled via open APIs and population-level fast
  healthcare interoperability resources.
- Augment human decision making with artificial intelligence, machine learning, and real-time dashboards to
  facilitate personalized, comprehensive, and longitudinal
  prevention, health maintenance, and treatment.
- Dissolve boundaries between providers, systems, and
  geographies, and collaboration will be the order of
  the day.

The EHR as it is known today will recede into the background, cease to be an obstacle, and become an enabler of
the connection between patient and provider. New capabilities such as ambient voice, wearable devices, and genomic
and social determinants of health data are available and
being deployed today. Patients and their care teams will
play an active role by contributing information and changing
behaviors.

Conclusion

Where is the CMP today? What do we know about the CMP's
adoption across the market? First, while EHR vendors have
made substantial progress in developing CMP capabilities, Big
Tech and digital health startups are growing their healthcare
influence daily, and many healthcare systems have innovation
capabilities; no one approach offers all the needed capabilities.
The majority of healthcare stakeholders, including health systems, payers, and providers, have yet to develop a formal CMP

strategy. Only about 20% of health systems have the financial resources needed to build and own the CMPs—for the remaining 80%, the ability to deploy the CMP will depend on partnerships. Chapters 8–12 define, in detail, the purpose, current state, and next generation of each of the layers of the CMP.

Notes

1. Goodell, S., T.S. Bodenheimer, and R. Berry-Millet. "Care Management of Patients with Complex Health Care Needs." RWJF, December 2009. www.rwjf.org/en/library/research/2009/12/care-management-of-patients-with-complex-health-care-needs.html.
2. Arlotto, Pam W., and Susan P. Irby. *Beyond Return on Investment: Expanding the Value of Healthcare Information Technology.* Boca Raton: CRC Press, 2019.

Chapter 8

The Value of EHRs as Foundational Systems

Healthcare organizations are the most complex form of human organization we have ever attempted to manage.

Peter Drucker

Purpose

To explore electronic health records (EHRs) as the foundational layer of the care management platform (CMP) and to understand how it supports healthcare delivery organizations in their transition to digital health, connected care, and population health management,

In this chapter, the reader will review

- The evolution of clinical information systems and EHRs
- How EHRs form the foundation of the CMP
- Value derived from foundational systems
- Critical success factors for EHRs and other foundational components
- Next-generation EHR

The Clinical Information System and EHR Journey

In the early 1900s, Dr. Henry Plummer of the Mayo Clinic is credited with developing the modern dossier system where every patient had a separate medical folder to allow retrieval of patient information.[1] As the automation of these records began, in the 1960s, the patient's encounter was documented for the purposes of billing for services rendered. Early pioneers in clinical information systems included academic medical systems with their own self-built applications, Lockheed and El Camino Hospital's development of the commercial system eventually deployed by Technicon, University of Utah-3M collaboration clinical decision support system (Health Evaluation through Logical Processing or HELP), Massachusetts General Hospital with COSTAR (Computer Stored Ambulatory Record),[2] etc.

In the 1980s and early 1990s, the Institute of Medicine began to build the case for converting from paper records to an automated format. Its breakthrough publication *The Computer-Based Patient Record: An Essential Technology for Health Care*[3] set forth the argument for EHR use, identified barriers to successful adoption, and made the case for funding the advance development and adoption of the EHR. In 2004, President George W. Bush highlighted the need for adoption of EHRs in his State of the Union Address. In 2006, the Certification Commission for Healthcare Information (CCHIT) was formed and started certifying EHR vendors as compliant with certain standards. But the push that resulted in almost universal adoption was from the HITECH (Health Information Technology for Economic and Clinical Health) Act of 2009, which laid forth standards for meaningful use of EHR technology accompanied by incentives for successful use. Today, almost 86% of providers and 96% of hospitals have deployed EHRs.[4]

EHRs as the Foundation of the Care Management Platform

The EHR serves as the system of record for each patient. The Healthcare Information and Management Systems Society (HIMSS) defines the EHR as follows.

THE ELECTRONIC HEALTH RECORD (EHR)

The EHR, a longitudinal electronic record of patient health information generated by one or more encounters in any care delivery setting, includes patient demographics, progress notes, problems, medications, vital signs, past medical history, immunizations, laboratory data, and radiology reports. The EHR automates and streamlines the clinician's workflow. The EHR has the ability to generate a complete record of a clinical patient encounter—as well as supporting other care-related activities directly or indirectly via an interface—including evidence-based decision support, quality management, and outcomes reporting.[5]

The EHR helps inform the patient's story, and today's integrated EHR generally includes

- Single system implementation
- Single database of records
- Single supplier support for ease of management
- Standardized technology across the enterprise, including hospital, ambulatory, and post-acute venues of care
- Single user-interface experience for user acceptance, ease of training
- Integrated data across multiple processes, including clinical care and patient accounting
- Improved end-to-end process support

In summary, the foundational systems for the CMP consist of the EHRs or systems of record for the following:

- Patient-Centered Medical Home (PCMH): Record for the primary care practice
- Specialists: Record of treatment for specialty consults and interventions
- Hospitals: Record of treatment for inpatient stays and ambulatory procedures that are hospital based (e.g., interventional radiology procedures)
- Post-Acute Providers: Record of treatment and care for venues such as skilled nursing facilities, rehabilitation hospitals, hospice, home health, and others
- Diagnostics: Orders, results, images (where applicable), and differential diagnosis as appropriate for diagnostic ancillaries such as lab, imaging, cardiology, etc.
- Pharmacy/Prescriptions: Record of order as well as filling of both electronic and paper prescriptions (such as for controlled substances)
- Payers/Claims: Record of paid claims including provider, procedure/treatment, and billed claims

Each provides transactional data critical to the management of the individual patient as well as defined patient cohorts and the patient population as a whole.

Value of the EHR

Literature suggests that several benefits can be attributed to the adoption of an electronic health record.[6] Vendors tout advantages that will help providers improve efficiency and reduce costs. This claim is highly dependent on the success of the actual EHR implementation. What is widely accepted through several studies and publications as value associated with the EHR based on actual experience includes the following:

- Timeliness and completeness: The EHR will reflect the clinician's most recent documentation of encounters with a patient. In addition, depending on the degree of interoperability (examined in Chapter 9), it will include real-time data from other care delivery sites/providers so that complete information regarding the patient can be shared across the care continuum.

- Improved legibility and understanding: Handwritten documents are subject to misspellings and illegible handwriting. They also can include abbreviations, strikeouts, or comments not in chronological order. While these documents may not present a problem for a single practitioner, others viewing the records may not be able to interpret the documentation properly.

- Standard nomenclature: In paper records, there may be a high degree of variability in describing a diagnosis or treatment; for example, "AMI" (acute myocardial infarction) versus "Heart Attack." EHRs (regardless of vendor) use standard code sets to describe problem lists, diagnoses, procedures, lab results, prescriptions, and others. Standard code sets include ICD-10, CPT, SNOMED, LOINC, and RXNORM. These codes provide the ability to have structured data in the EHR, which allows communication of information in a standardized format and mining of data on the back-end for reporting and analytic purposes.

- Ability to track quality of care more easily: In the past, monitoring and reporting of quality outcomes, whether internal to the organization or required by certification or regulatory bodies, required significant manual effort. Typically, nurse quality abstractors would pore through patient records to find appropriate patient cases to review. Information gathered on paper, in spreadsheets, or in registries documented outcomes and was reported as appropriate to regulatory agencies, to professional groups, and to payers.

■ Avoidance of errors: The clinical decision support (CDS) framework that is enabled by EHRs helps clinicians avoid medical errors. Behind-the-scenes rules about drug–drug, drug–food, and drug–lab interactions help alert the clinician if there are allergies or other contraindications so that medical errors can be avoided. The clinician must override the alert to proceed. Here, a fine balance must be maintained between critical alerts and important information in order to avoid alert fatigue, which can contribute to clinician burnout.

■ Avoidance of cost: Similarly, advanced CDS capabilities can assist with guiding the clinician when ordering. Which lab panel is most cost effective? Are there alternative drugs on the formulary that will meet treatment needs, or in the ambulatory setting, are there drugs that are more affordable for the patient? Finally, there are tools within most EHR workflows, whether through order sets, flowsheets, or other means, that will allow (with the input of informatics or other subject matter experts) additional smart use of the information in the EHR to make cost-effective clinical decisions. One example is around antibiotic stewardship; if lab values over time indicate patient progress, high-cost antibiotics can be discontinued without impacting patient outcomes.

■ Privacy and security of data: News headlines every day recount security breaches and other lapses of security associated with EHRs, but in the paper world, medical records were easily accessible by anyone. Few controls were in place, and records often left the provider site and were discovered in nonsecure places. Today, the Health Insurance Portability and Accountability Act (HIPAA) and other legislation provides stringent standards for data storage, encryption, and access far beyond any controls in place for paper records.

■ Coordination of care: EHRs can share patient history, allergies, interventions, and a variety of pertinent clinical information. The care team can develop care plans based on the most appropriate evidence and clinical guidelines, assimilate information from across care settings, and determine future actions to coordinate and transition care.

■ Effective risk stratification: Clinical information regarding patient problems, diagnoses, and treatments can be combined with claims data to provide insight regarding existing conditions and severity of conditions. Improvements in clinical documentation allow more exact risk scoring, especially for those patients who are associated with risk-based contracts.

■ Ability to view remotely: Modern technology allows clinicians to view critical patient information remotely. This technology allows the physicians or other providers not only to complete documentation off site but also to obtain the most recent clinical information about their patients, thus allowing additional interventions (ordering of tests or medications, etc.).

Challenges with Today's Foundational Systems

While many organizations viewed the EHR with great anticipation, many have been disappointed with the return on investment (ROI). Most implemented the system rapidly and planned to revisit the system after stabilization and optimize the EHR at a later time. Unfortunately, many organizations do not have the resources or bandwidth to engage in this activity, and clinicians and others become frustrated with their tools and develop workarounds. EHRs are often blamed for physician burnout, and user satisfaction continues to be a challenge. An American Medical Association (AMA) and Dartmouth-Hitchcock Medical Center study found that for every hour of face-to-face time with patients, physicians spend nearly two additional hours on EHR and clerical tasks.[7] Additional research by the AMA and RAND Corporation identified key challenges physicians face with current EHRs, including

- Interference with the patient visit
- Lack of system-design support for team-based care
- Issues with care coordination due to lack of interoperability
- Increased cognitive workload for physicians
- Lack of data liquidity and high switching costs
- Lack of product modularity to support unique physician practices and population needs
- Difficulty communicating with patients in a changing digital landscape
- Insufficient support for incorporating end-user input into product design and post-implementation feedback for product improvement[8]

The Arch Collaborative (a service of KLAS) is a provider-led effort established to understand how to unlock the potential of EHRs. Healthcare organizations collaborate, and through standardized surveys and benchmarking, they uncover best practices for improving the satisfaction, use, and value of EHRs. Through their research, the collaborative has determined three key measures for EHR success:[9]

- Mastery: Effective initial training as well as continuing education—in essence, clinicians are confident in their ability to use the EHR both efficiently and effectively.
- Personalization (as opposed to customization): Ensuring the EHR meets the unique needs of the clinician without creating the maintenance and interoperability nightmares of customized software. Clinicians must invest the time to make sure the system functions in a more usable and effective fashion.
- Governance and decision-making processes: Structures that allow a forum for clinician exchange, as well as the means to prioritize EHR refinements in an agile fashion.

For example, the Mayo Clinic spent $1.5 billion on deploying their new enterprise EHR. Through the collaborative, they identified a need to revise their physician ordering process. The EHR implementation resulted in customization for various specialties and created confusing order sets and flow sheets. By revising order panels and streamlining orderable items, procedures, and consultations into a single catalogue, leadership has been able to guide the clinician to the appropriate choice.[10]

Other tactics that organizations are employing to realize the value of their EHR better include[11]

- EHR training sprints—concentrated two-week sprints either to bring new practices/departments online or to retrain areas that need updated education
- Varying length of training based on providers' needs to ensure enhanced ROI
- Integration of training and help desk functions to allow identification of training gaps while providing timely service
- SWAT teams to provide personalization of the EHR and improve clinician experience for targeted practices and other audiences
- Monthly meetings of engaged practitioners to focus on workflows and ensure consistency across locations and specialties
- Representation of practitioners on leadership teams to help alleviate burnout
- Focus on nursing with frequent assessment of clinician needs and adjustment of workflows and content to help staff with EHR proficiency
- Rounding of information technology analysts, trainers, help desk, and informaticists to clinics and departments on a periodic basis
- Providing every clinical service line with access to both physician and nurse informaticists familiar with that clinical area

The Next-Generation EHR

While the traditional EHR solutions focused on automating specific tasks or transactions, today's EHR is foundational to a broad array of transformational care delivery models and consumer experiences. The EHR of the future will include genomic, proteomic, and social determinants and predictive analytics that will enable highly personalized approaches to health maintenance and treatment of disease. It will become a truly unified and portable record of health and illness that is accessible to patients and providers in all locations at all times. In fact, the future of healthcare demands an EHR platform that is designed to connect health consumers with clinical care teams within an innovation ecosystem as described in Chapter 6. In the instance of the CMP, this ecosystem will extend the flow of information from patient to provider regardless of the care setting. As shown in Figure 8.1, the next-generation EHR platform will need to include the following capabilities:

- ■ Virtual network development: Extend the clinical enterprise from hospital and physician practice to connect patients/caregivers, community services, and care teams across the continuum.
- ■ Data activation and intelligent services: Combine standardized, evidence-based care with personalized approaches based on genomics, predictive analytics, and social determinants of health.
- ■ Workflow design and enablement: Leverage smart technology to reach consumers wherever they are in their journey, identify risk, and design personalized interventions.
- ■ Content strategy: Present healthcare information and retail experiences to consumers in an engaging, accessible, and dynamic way.

Figure 8.1   The next-generation EHR.

- Care management: Provide coordination across care teams with engagement by patients and their caregivers for a joint focus on optimized outcomes.
- Clinical research: Enable more effective clinical trial recruitment, data capture, registry automation, stakeholder engagement, etc.

Conclusion

EHRs automate many essential care delivery tasks, provide for the collection and storage of clinical data, and are critical to telling the patient's story. For successful EHR deployment and value realization, understanding the organizational factors that drive adoption and mastery of the EHR, including the patient population, culture, care delivery model, teaching and research environment, and organizational strategic direction, is important. As organizations design their next-generation EHR, it is essential that it continues to support the enterprise while serving as the foundation for value orchestration through the CMP.

Notes

1. Holmes, Richard. "Londonderry Family of Doctors Make History." *Londonderry News*, February 17, 2013. www.londonderrynh.net/2013/02/londonderry-family-of-doctors-make-history-2/60351.
2. Amatayakul, M. *Electronic Health Records: A Practical Guide for Professionals and Organizations.* 3rd ed. Chicago: American Health Information Management Association, 2007.
3. Dick, R.S., E.B. Steen, and D.E. Detmer, eds; Institute of Medicine. *The Computer-Based Patient Record: An Essential Technology for Health Care.* 2nd ed. Washington, DC: National Academies Press, 1997.
4. "Office-Based Physician Electronic Health Record Adoption" and "Non-Federal Acute Care Hospital Electronic Health Record Adoption." The Office of the National Coordinator for Health Information Technology. Accessed August 2019. https://dashboard.healthit.gov/quickstats/quickstats.php.
5. "Electronic Health Records." HIMSS, June 5, 2019. www.himss.org/library/ehr/.
6. "What Are the Advantages of Electronic Health Records?" The Office of the National Coordinator for Health Information Technology (ONC). Accessed August 2019. www.healthit.gov/faq/what-are-advantages-electronic-health-records.
7. "Improving Electronic Health Records." American Medical Association, October 4, 2018. www.ama-assn.org/practice-management/digital/improving-electronic-health-records.
8. Ibid.
9. KLAS Research, The Arch Collaborative. Accessed August 21, 2019. https://klasresearch.com/arch-collaborative.
10. Drees, Jackie. "Mayo Clinic Plummer Project Co-Chair Dr. Steve Peters on EHR Customization, Innovation." August 19, 2019, Becker's Health IT & CEO Report. Accessed August 26, 2019. www.beckershospitalreview.com/healthcare-information-technology/mayo-clinic-plummer-project-co-chair-dr-steve-peters-on-ehr-customization-innovation.html.
11. KLAS Research. "The Arch Collaborative." Accessed August 26, 2019. https://klasresearch.com/archcollaborative/casestudies.

Chapter 9

Interoperability and High-Performing Networks

We continue to have a systematic problem in making data available for patients and the clinicians who take care of them. This is not a problem that any single institution can solve.

It is not a problem that any single vendor can solve.

This is a problem that requires that we extract very complex and large amounts of data from one system and find a way to insert it into another system.

Christopher Ross, chief information officer, Mayo Clinic

Purpose

To explore interoperability as it relates to the care management platform (CMP) and to understand how it supports healthcare delivery organizations in their transition to digital health, connected care, and population health management (PHM).

This chapter will address

- The definition of interoperability
- The history of interoperability
- The role of standards
- Key components of the interoperability layer
- Challenges with interoperability
- The future of interoperability and integrated networks

Definition of Interoperability

Interoperability describes the extent to which systems and devices can exchange data and interpret that shared data. The Healthcare Information and Management Systems Society (HIMSS) defines interoperability as "the ability of different information systems, devices or applications to connect, in a coordinated manner, within and across organizational boundaries to access, exchange and cooperatively use data amongst

Foundational

Allows data from one information technology to be received by another but does not require the ability for the receiving information technology to be able to interpret the data

Structural

Defines the message format standards to allow uniform movement of healthcare data from one system to another to ensure the clinical or operational meaning of the data is preserved and unaltered

Semantic

Allows two or more systems or elements to both exchange and use the information that has been exchanged. By using both the structure of the data and common vocabularies the receiving information technology systems can interpret the data

Figure 9.1   Three types of interoperability.

stakeholders, with the goal of optimizing the health of individuals and populations."[1] As can be seen in Figure 9.1, there are three types (or levels) of interoperability: foundational, structural, and semantic.

Each has implications for the effectiveness of data exchange among providers, between providers and patients, and with the healthcare ecosystem. Foundational interoperability provides the technical infrastructure for data to flow from a source to a destination. Additional levels of structural (standard data structures) and semantic (common language) interoperability are required so that the data can be interpreted and used.

Interoperability—A Short History

Interoperability has several threads of history: the technology itself, associated standards, regulatory and legislative mandates, and organizations that have used/promoted it. Figure 9.2 depicts three distinct types of organizational frameworks associated with interoperability and data exchange.

Public health information exchanges originated in the 1990s. These community health management information systems (CHMIS)[2] were transaction-based systems used for information exchange, primarily around billing and patient eligibility information. Followed by community health information networks (CHINs), regional health information organizations (RHIOs), state designated entities through the Health Information Technology for Economic and Clinical Health (HITECH) Act, and a variety of not-for-profit and commercial models, public exchanges have been challenged to survive due to security and privacy concerns from patients, control and usage concerns from providers, and a lack of cooperation and consensus between competing health systems. As they often relied on grant funding, financial sustainability was a problem for many.

Over time, private enterprise data sharing plans evolved. For many, this meant implementation of a single integrated

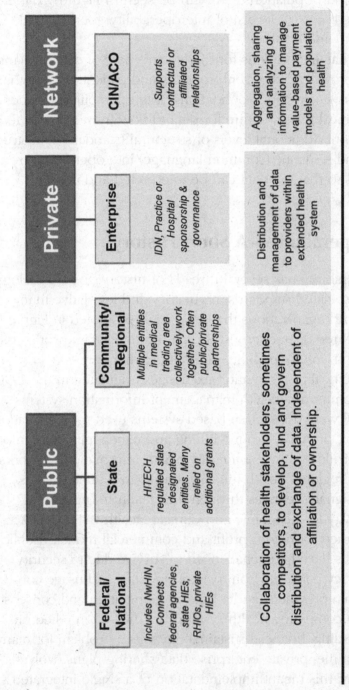

Figure 9.2 Organizational frameworks for data exchange.

electronic health record (EHR) platform across all sites of care, since EHR vendors had focused on interoperability within their individual platforms (e.g., Allscripts to Allscripts). Eventually, as clinical integration networks (CINs), accountable care organizations (ACOs), and high-performing networks grew, so did the need for data sharing across a variety of venues and vendors. In 2013, CommonWell was formed to bring together EHR vendors (Athena, Cerner, eClinicalWorks, Evident/CPSI, Greenway, and Meditech, among others). A not-for-profit trade association, whose vision is for "ubiquitous health data interoperability,"[3] CommonWell facilitated collaboration for the purpose of developing a standard way to exchange information from EHR platform to EHR platform without regional or national health information exchange (HIE) involvement to complete the transactions. To date, CommonWell is supporting providers in all 50 states.

In 2015, the Sequoia Project was created to focus on large-scale data exchange, collaboration, education, and research. Intended to serve as a neutral convener to advance healthcare interoperability, the Sequoia Project partnered with public and private sectors to launch Carequality. All major EHR vendors are participating, as are Surescripts and CommonWell. Over 600,000 providers, 1700 hospitals, and 40,000 clinics are connected, with over 36 million records exchanged monthly.[4]

Numerous roadmaps for interoperability have been created over the years. The most recent include eHI Initiative, created by the eHealth Initiative; the JASON Report, developed by Mitre Corporation; and the HIMSS EHR Association Roadmap. Of particular interest is the ONC's Shared Nationwide Interoperability Roadmap. Created in 2015, it lays out a plan in multiple-year increments to achieve the interoperability needed to enable what the Institute of Medicine calls a "learning health system." The plan has a set of guiding principles, standards, and building blocks to drive interoperability with processes to test and certify that health IT systems are implementing standards consistently.

The 21st Century Cures Act, signed in 2016, promotes and funds a number of initiatives, including several provisions to improve healthcare IT. Specifically, it promotes nationwide interoperability, prevents/reduces information blocking, and continues the push for adoption of EHRs. It places particular emphasis on providing patients with access to their electronic health information in a format that is easily understandable, secure, and timely. A major component of the Act is the Trusted Exchange Framework and Common Agreement (TEFCA).[5] This framework outlines a common set of principles, terms, and conditions to support and enable the scalable exchange of electronic health information across disparate health information networks. TEFCA is specifically designed to help ensure that HIEs, healthcare providers, health plans, individuals, and many more stakeholders have secure access to their electronic health information when and where it is needed.

Standards for Interoperability

Standards for interoperability exist to ensure that each layer of interoperability (functional, structural, and semantic) has a common way for data to move from point to point and for that data to be consumed.

There are several types of standards (typically five) needed to achieve interoperability.[6]

■ Vocabulary/terminology standards: Often unique to healthcare and use-case specific (e.g., codes to represent prescriptions cannot be also used for laboratory tests).
■ Content/format standards: Can also be unique to health-care and are often specific to a particular use case, clinical workflow, or domain (e.g., the content/format standard used to indicate a diagnosis would not be used to order a medication).

observatories participating in the *Astrographic Catalogue* refer their magnitudes to primary polar standards. A subcommission was appointed with eight members (including Kapteyn, Gill and Pickering) on the best way of achieving this goal. In the meantime Pickering's NPS of 47 stars would serve as the primary standards of photographic magnitude [184]. Pickering himself did not attend the congress but he made sure that Kapteyn was apprised of the Harvard work on the North Polar Sequence in advance of the meeting.

At this stage Miss Leavitt's work was far from complete, but the progress using 11 telescopes from apertures of half an inch to 60 inches (the Mt Wilson reflector) was described in 1910 [181]. The first detailed results were published in 1912, by which time the number of stars had been increased to 96, ranging in photographic magnitude from 2.7 to 21 [185]. Those brighter than $m_{pg} = 11.3$ were, with one exception, of spectral type A, while many of the others were judged to be white stars from their colour indices. However, a sequence of 12 red stars to magnitude 13.3 (spectral types found to be G, K or M if they were measured at all) were also included. Nearly all 96 stars were within 90 arc minutes of the pole, with the exception of a few of the brightest objects. The most remarkable aspect of this paper is the sudden quantum leap in the magnitudes of the faintest stars being measured, from 13th magnitude in 1907 to 21st in 1912, a factor of 1000 times fainter in just five years.

The task of obtaining accurate photographic magnitudes for all these stars was a major one that occupied Miss Leavitt for several years – in fact the question of revisions to the North Polar Sequence magnitudes was one that continued to occupy her up to her death in 1921. Thirteen telescopes were used for this large programme, from small astrographic refractors (the smallest being of half an inch aperture) to the large reflectors at Mt Wilson (60-inch) and Lick (36-inch Crossley) Observatories, and the observations were recorded on 255 photographic plates [186].

A wide variety of methods was used to obtain an absolute calibration of the photographic magnitude scale. All required multiple images on the same plate, such that the relative intensities of the light forming the images of a given star could be calculated. The methods included

1. the extrafocal technique of King with equal exposures at different focus settings,
2. a polarization method with birefringent plates of Iceland Spar producing for each star four images whose relative intensities depended on the angle between the two plates,
3. light reduction using a screen which was variously a wire screen

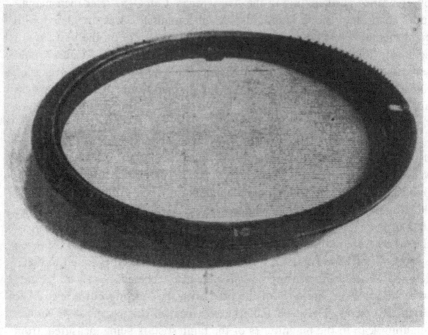

Fig. 4.20   Objective diffraction grating used for the calibration of stellar
photographic photometry.

placed either over the objective or just in front of the plate, a
perforated tin screen over the objective, a shade glass (or neutral
filter) in front of the plate, or a photographic film (also acting as a
neutral filter) in front of the plate,

4. decreasing the telescope aperture in a variety of different ways, such
   as covering one half of the objective or using a circular diaphragm,
   or

5. using a small auxiliary prism in the centre of the objective to produce faint secondary images or using a coarse objective diffraction
   grating consisting of parallel wires to give faint secondary diffraction images alongside each primary stellar image.

The last method using the prism had been used by Pickering since
the mid-1880s [41] (see section 4.3).   Only methods 2 and 5 required a
single exposure to obtain multiple images.   All the other techniques needed
sequential exposures of equal duration and normally on the same plate.
Corrections to the magnitudes were applied for the distance of a star from

the plate centre and for the colour equation of the different instruments used [186].

4.9.1   The zero-point of the magnitude scale and the International System

At the 1909 Astrographic Congress a subcommittee for photographic photometry had been established to recommend a way of fixing the zero-point and the interval of the photographic magnitude scale [184, p. B103]. The subcommittee was recommended by the congress to adopt a magnitude scale which was independent of the visual scale. At the outset the provisional use of the Harvard North Polar Sequence, at that time comprising 47 stars, was suggested. The subcommittee members were Backlund (Pulkovo), B. Baillaud (Paris), Gill (Cape), Hale (Mt Wilson), Kapteyn (Groningen) E. C. Pickering (Harvard), Scheiner (Potsdam) and Turner (Oxford) [184, p. B103]. Schwarzschild (Potsdam) later became a member.

The subcommittee met both in 1910 in Pasadena and 1913 in Bonn at the time of the fourth and fifth meetings of the International Solar Union. After the 1910 meeting in California, agreement was reached on the zero-point of the photographic magnitude scale [187], but a full report was not issued until after the Bonn meeting [83]. As might be expected, the Pogson scale with intensity ratio $10^{0.4} = 2.512$ was formally adopted for photographic photometry and the zero-point was defined so that stars with Harvard visual magnitudes between 5.5 and 6.5 and Harvard spectral types of A0 should have equal visual and photographic magnitudes. Furthermore the Harvard North Polar Sequence (then only published in preliminary form but believed to be accurate to a few hundredths of a magnitude [185]) was to form the basis for determining photographic magnitudes in other regions of the sky, using the technique of two exposures on the same plate as advocated by Pickering. Stars in the 48 Harvard Standard Regions would provide useful secondary standards for the *Astrographic Catalogue*. Furthermore Pickering agreed to establish further secondary standards in one-degree-wide declination zones, which would be chosen to correspond to the zones allocated to the eighteen participating observatories in the *Astrographic Catalogue* and *Carte du Ciel* projects.

Overall the report can be seen as a triumph for Pickering, who essentially imposed the preferred Harvard techniques of photographic photometry on the Astrographic Congress, an organization in whose grandiose programmes he had hitherto consistently declined to become an active participant. It was a major coup which brought Harvard considerable prestige for being seen to extricate the *Astrographic Catalogue* magnitude determinations from the difficult tangle into which they had found themselves, yet which required Harvard to commit itself to only a limited amount of additional observational work in setting up secondary standards – certainly a far less daunting programme than that in which the 18 participating observatories themselves were engaged.

The report of 1913 defined the so-called 'International System of Photographic Magnitudes'. It also officially recognized the term 'colour index' as the difference ($m_{pg} - m_{vis}$). In reality it proposed little that was new or not already in common practice so far as scale and zero-point go, but it gave official sanction to these practices. What the report did not do is give any guidelines as to the wavelength dependence of the photographic passband, the type of plates to be used or how to use them, nor on the type of telescope or extinction correction procedure, all of which have a bearing on precise stellar photometry and were to be sources of future difficulties. Even as the report, which had been drafted in 1910, went to press in 1913, an indication of unforeseen trouble was hinted at by Pickering in an appendix to the *Carte du Ciel* bulletin [188]: when consecutive exposures were made on the same plate, the images of the second exposure were up to a quarter of a magnitude fainter than was the case if the order of exposures had been reversed, an effect due to the difference of pre- and post-exposures by sky background light on the stellar images.

4.9.2   *Miss Leavitt's work on standard photographic sequences*

When the 1913 report was published, the work at Harvard of providing secondary photographic standards for the stars in the 48 Harvard Standard Regions and at the south pole was already well under way. Plates had been taken in all these regions to obtain photographic magnitudes and the preliminary reductions carried out for about a thousand stars in the more northerly regions designated A to D. Miss Leavitt continued this work, obtaining photographic magnitudes either by direct comparison with the primary North Polar Sequence standards, or by absolute calibration based on the various methods of prismatic companions, wire screens, secondary diffraction grating images or diaphragmed apertures. The work included observations from the large reflectors at Mt Wilson and Lick as well as a variety of Harvard telescopes based in Massachusetts, Arequipa (Peru) and South Africa.

The final compendium was published in 1917 by Pickering, at the same time as the results for the North Polar Sequence [189]. It comprised data for 2042 stars from 905 plates with a mean probable error estimated to be

±0.10 magnitudes. Each region included stars to at least magnitude 15, and in some cases went as faint as 19th magnitude.

The other commitment made by Pickering in 1913 was to provide further secondary standards in 1°-wide zones at the boundaries between the zones allocated to the 18 different observatories undertaking the *Astrographic Catalogue*. Seventeen such zones from +64.5° to −64.5° were thus defined, and once again Miss Leavitt was assigned to this work. Twelve areas were specified for each zone, at different right ascensions, and between 15 and 22 stars chosen in each area, with magnitudes mainly between m_{pg} of 7.0 and 15.5. The data for nine zones north of the equator were published in 1919, based on observations with the Metcalf 16-inch telescope at Harvard [190]. On Miss Leavitt's death in 1921, the reductions for the southern zones were only partially complete, but the whole programme was brought to a conclusion by Miss A. D. Walker working under the direction of Harlow Shapley [191, 192]. For these southern zones the 8-inch Bache telescope was used, and the magnitudes derived by comparison with the secondary standards in the Harvard C-regions at +15°. South of −30° these sequences went down to typically $m_{pg} \sim 13.5$, a brighter limit than was reached for the northern zones.

Miss Leavitt was associated with one other major programme in determining photographic magnitudes of secondary standards. In 1906 Kapteyn had published an important document, his *Plan of Selected Areas* [144]. The proposal was to obtain stellar data of all kinds in each of 206 areas distributed over the whole sky, including photographic and visual magnitudes for an anticipated 200000 stars. This huge undertaking required standards to be determined for the subsequent photographic photometry in each area. Miss Leavitt determined these standard magnitudes for up to about 20 faint stars down to about photographic magnitude 15.5 on the International System in each of 115 of Kapteyn's northern selected areas, by comparison with the primary standards of the North Polar Sequence. For this programme the polar stars and the selected areas were photographed on different plates from the same box and then developed together, thus avoiding the errors arising from multiple exposures on the same plate [193].

Well before Miss Leavitt died in 1921 it was clear that systematic effects had entered her standard magnitudes for the North Polar Sequence which depended on star colour, as well as scale errors for both the brightest and faintest stars [194]. Using the Mt Wilson 60-inch reflector, Seares found that the bright stars in the Harvard North Polar Sequence ($m_{pg} < 8$) were in error by up to $0\overset{m}{.}24$ and the faint ones (m_{pg} from 16 to 20) by up to one magnitude. In addition the colour equation (systematic errors depending on the stellar colour index, C) were especially marked for data from certain

Harvard telescopes in relation to the Mt Wilson reflector, amounting to a huge $0.33C$ term in the colour equation for the 16-inch Metcalf telescope. In a report to the National Academy of Sciences by a committee of American astronomers on the establishment of the International Astronomical Union, Seares (the American committee's chairman), after pointing out the discrepancies already existing in the polar standards deduced by different observers and instruments, advised as follows:

> In the present state of the question it seems undesirable that any particular set of standard magnitudes be designated by the adjective "international". Such an action on the part of an International Committee would necessarily convey the impression of an authoritativeness and finality of decision which it would be difficult to justify in view of the present outstanding differences in the results of different observers [195, p. 381].

This was a direct challenge to the adoption of Pickering's North Polar Sequence as international standards, a challenge that came just a year after Pickering's death and less than a year from Miss Leavitt's own demise. Seares himself was not to become the detractor of the concept of the North Polar Sequence as a system of international photometric standards; on the contrary, he was its greatest champion, one who devoted much of his working life to successive refinements of the published North Polar Sequence magnitudes so as to comply with the International System that had been first defined in 1913.

4.10　Further work on the North Polar Sequence to 1922

4.10.1　Photographic photometry of Seares at Mt Wilson

From the time of his arrival at Mt Wilson Observatory in 1909, it was the methods of photographic photometry to which Frederick Seares (1873–1964) turned his attention. The North Polar Sequence became Seares' major preoccupation for over three decades and he published numerous papers in which he sought that elusive goal of a reliable and usable set of standard magnitudes for photographic photometry. Sadly that goal was never realized, not because of any shortcomings in Seares' painstaking work, but because of the limitations in the International System itself, its lack of explicit information on the type of telescope, wavelength, passbands, colour equations and extinction corrections to be used. Seares was the pre-eminent worker in an extremely difficult field of observational research, who nevertheless was to see the North Polar Sequence system of standards virtually abandoned within his lifetime. According to one biographer, he

Fig. 4.21   Frederick Seares.

was a man 'of uncommon qualities, of remarkable patience and persistence, of a rather austere mind ... tending to mathematical rather than physical thought', and who 'quickly realized that the subject of star magnitudes was in a deplorable muddle and that the methods of in-focus photographic photometry needed the most thorough examination and development' [196].

Seares' observations were nearly all made on the 60-inch reflector, which had been recently completed at the time of his Mt Wilson appointment. His first publication on the North Polar Sequence with this telescope in 1913 outlined his techniques of photometric calibration using either circular diaphragms or wire gauze objective screens to diminish the light [197]. Successive in-focus exposures were made on the same plate and the images were compared visually with those of an arbitrary reference scale (see also [198] for a full discussion of the technique). Random errors of about $\pm 0^m.085$ were achieved. A major difficulty with the 60-inch photometry was the application of a correction depending on the angular distance of a star from the central optical axis. This distance correction varied with the use of different diaphragms, and also showed unexpected changes from plate to plate, which were probably due to sudden thermal changes in the figure of the primary mirror.

The 1913 paper immediately drew attention to the major discrepancies between the Harvard [185] and Mt Wilson North Polar Sequence magnitudes. If the scales agreed in the range 10.5 to 15.5 then the Harvard magnitudes were progressively fainter (by up to half a magnitude) than Mt

Wilson ones as one went to brighter stars (from $m_{pg} = 9$ to 2). If, on the other hand, the zero-point of the Mt Wilson scale was forced to satisfy the International System definition at magnitude 6, then the Mt Wilson values were $0^m.4$ fainter than the Harvard results between 10.5 and 15.5 [131]. The discrepancies were partly traced to the different colour equations of the numerous telescopes used at Harvard. The problem arose through the very wide passband of the unfiltered photographic magnitude system and the differing efficiencies of different telescopes to ultraviolet light. Seares was able to reduce all the Harvard data to the colour system of the Mt Wilson reflector, which decreased the discrepancies for the intermediate stars from $0^m.40$ to $0^m.24$. The residual discrepancy remained unexplained. Nevertheless a revised Harvard scale of North Polar Sequence magnitudes involving a correction of about $0^m.25$ for these stars of intermediate brightness ($m_{pg} = 10.5$ to 15.5) was published in 1922 by Pickering's successor at the Harvard College Observatory, Harlow Shapley (1885–1972) [199]. This brought the Harvard scale into line with the 1922 Mt Wilson scale to magnitude 16. Fainter than that, Shapley rejected all Miss Leavitt's results.

Problems also arose for the faint stars in the North Polar Sequence ($m > 15.5$), which Seares showed to be mainly redder objects [200] of colour index at least 0.5, whereas the bright stars were mainly white (colour index around zero). Discrepancies of up to a magnitude occurred between Mt Wilson and Harvard for the faintest objects [194]. Incidentally the North Polar Sequence contained no O or early B-type stars, a circumstance which made the photographic photometry of these hot stars very difficult.

The major paper by Seares in 1915 [131] not only placed the North Polar Sequence photographic magnitudes on a much more secure basis than hitherto over the whole range from $2^m.5$ to $20^m.0$, but also extended the North Polar Sequence to 617 stars from Miss Leavitt's 96. Moreover, photovisual magnitudes using isochromatic plates and a yellow filter were obtained for 329 of these stars, from $m_{pv} = 2.0$ to 17.5, which enabled colour indices to be obtained for many of them (an essential step for reducing the Harvard magnitudes to a homogeneous scale). The photovisual magnitudes were designed to reproduce the Harvard scale of visual photometry. They generally showed a much smaller colour equation than the photographic magnitudes, because a filter was used which defined a consistent passband. This was also narrower than the photographic passband, which was instead defined by the photographic emulsion, telescope and terrestrial atmosphere.

Although nearly all Seares' photometry was on the 60-inch reflector, refractors had been used almost exclusively at other observatories. In order to allay any fears of systematic errors from this cause, Seares and Milton Humason (1891–1972) also obtained many North Polar Sequence magnitudes with the Mt Wilson 10-inch Cooke refractor [201]. After correcting for the different colour equation of these refractor magnitudes, no systematic differences were found between the final scales from the two different telescopes. On combining the 10-inch and later 60-inch results in order to reduce random errors, a new set of North Polar Sequence magnitudes (m_{pg} and m_{pv}) was published in 1922 for 92 polar stars [202]. The reductions were in part undertaken by Miss Mary Joyner, who became Seares' tireless research assistant and, in later years, his second wife.

When the International Astronomical Union was established in 1919, Seares became the inaugural president of Commission No. 25 for Stellar Photometry. The North Polar Sequence corrections of 1922 were incorporated into his report presented at the first General Assembly at Rome in 1922, which was formally adopted at that time. In practice the International System thenceforth referred to these 1922 NPS magnitudes by Seares, even though this label was not explicitly used in the published transactions of the General Assembly. Nineteen-twenty-two can therefore be seen as a landmark year when photographic photometry finally came of age. In spite of many remaining difficulties in obtaining photographic magnitudes for stars in any part of the sky, the North Polar Sequence standards were known to a few hundredths of a magnitude over a wide magnitude interval, and the basic techniques for transferring this scale to other parts of the sky had been established.

Indeed a massive programme, initiated in 1909, had as its aim to obtain photographic magnitudes of faint stars in 139 of the Selected Areas proposed by Kapteyn for special detailed investigation [144]. This work was still in progress at the time of the Rome General Assembly, and the results were not published until 1930. The major photometric catalogue that resulted was one of Seares' largest undertakings and most significant achievements [203]. It is discussed further in section 7.2.

4.10.2   Other work on the North Polar Sequence

So great was the interest in the goal of reliable photographic photometry in the early years of this century, that several observatories were simultaneously working on the same problems. Apart from Miss Leavitt at Harvard and Seares at Mt Wilson, the principal work from about 1910 came from Dziewulski using Potsdam plates and from Chapman and Melotte at Greenwich.

Wladyslaw Dziewulski (1878–1962) was a Polish astronomer at the Cracow Observatory who had studied under Schwarzschild at Göttingen in 1908. His work on the North Polar Sequence made use of long exposure plates (mostly 90 minutes) obtained on the Potsdam 80-cm refractor by Schwarzschild or W. H. J. Münch from 1910 to 1912 [204]. Although all these were focal plates, Dziewulski measured the blackening of the central part of the images with a microphotometer. The stars were all faint, between $m_{pg} = 10$ and 15 (a few to 16), and his object was to increase the number of stars in the Harvard North Polar Sequence within this magnitude range. Calibration was by means of a wire half grating of the type used by Schwarzschild [145], placed 100 mm in front of half the plate so as to give faint first order diffraction images ($\Delta m \simeq 2^m$) on each side of the central image of each star. On the other hand the zero-point was tied to the Harvard scale using 34 North Polar Sequence stars observed by Miss Leavitt. Therefore the rather large systematic error for these same stars found by Seares was inevitably transferred to the Dziewulski results.

The programme carried out by Sydney Chapman (1888–1970) and Philibert Melotte (1880–1961) was quite similar in scope to that of Dziewulski. The 26-inch refractor at Greenwich was used and a wire objective grating gave the scale calibration [205]. The technique was described in detail in a separate paper [206]. The grating gave secondary images with $\Delta m = 2^m7$ fainter than the primary. The images were measured by direct visual comparison with an arbitrary scale of stellar images. The choice of grating in this work makes for an interesting discussion. Too coarse a wire spacing gives too small a magnitude interval between primary and secondary images, and also the physical separation of these images on the plate may be inadequate to avoid them touching or even merging. On the other hand a finer grating increases Δm to beyond 2^m5 (considered ideal), and gives a wider separation of images, but suffers from lower optical throughput and the secondary images start to become noticeably elongated as a result of dispersion [206]. In the grating used the wires (diameter 1.7 mm) were placed every 7 mm, giving practically circular secondary images with a separation from their primaries of 0.45 mm (about 14 arc seconds) on the plate.

Chapman and Melotte's final catalogue contained 262 stars within 25 arc minutes of the pole to about magnitude 15.5. Typical errors for a single long exposure (1 hour) plate were $\pm 0^m08$. The zero-point was tied to the Harvard scale.

Because the Potsdam and Greenwich programmes were mainly based on fainter North Polar Sequence stars, they were unsuited to check the important discrepancy between the Harvard and Mt Wilson scales for stars brighter than about tenth magnitude. A new observational programme to resolve this issue was undertaken by Harold Spencer Jones (1890–1960) at the time he was chief assistant at the Royal Greenwich Observatory [207]. He used the 13-inch astrographic telescope, calibrated with a wire objective grating. The primary and secondary diffraction images were used for calibrating a magnitude scale against which all images were compared. The work concentrated on the 39 brightest North Polar Sequence stars above magnitude 13.3, and showed a remarkably good agreement with the results obtained by Seares [131]. The zero-point was on the International System and therefore agreed with the Harvard scale at magnitude 6.0, but the Harvard stars were shown to be around $0\overset{m}{.}25$ too bright for the fainter stars. Furthermore the colour equation of these Greenwich observations was small compared to the Mt Wilson scale using the 60-inch reflector, in other words the red North Polar Sequence stars had the same magnitude determined at Greenwich by Spencer Jones and at Mt Wilson by Seares to within $0\overset{m}{.}12$ or better.

4.11 Stellar colours from photographic photometry

4.11.1 Photographic colour indices

As early as 1888 Pickering recognized the potential of photography to reveal information on stellar colours:

> The photograph furnishes an excellent test of the color of a star, since on comparison with the visual brightness, the stars which are faint photographically may be assumed to be red, and the bright ones blue. As the difference amounts to several magnitudes, it furnishes a test much more sensitive than that of the eye. Again, the method is applicable to the faintest stars visible, when the difference in color is imperceptible by any other means [41].

Both Charlier at the Lund Observatory and Scheiner at Potsdam considered the differences between photographic and visual magnitudes for Pleiades stars in 1889–90 [100, 110] (see section 4.6), but were unaware of the significance of their results. By 1900, however, Schwarzschild in Vienna had concisely defined the meaning of colour index, or 'Farbentönung' as he called it, by the relationship $F = -2.5 \log A$, where A is the ratio of a star's photographic to its visual brightness [153] – see section 4.8.1.

Schwarzschild at once recognized the astrophysical significance of his 'Farbentönung' or colour index which he then exploited in the *Göttinger Aktinometrie* in 1912 [151]. Here he used the difference between his photographic (blue) magnitudes and those obtained visually at Potsdam. The resultant colour index was found to correlate with spectral type and with visually estimated colour – see section 4.8.1. Similar results were obtained in the same year by Edward King at Harvard [163, 164] – see section 4.8.3. These programmes, which all relied on visually determined magnitudes in conjunction with the photographic ones, led to the official recognition of the term 'colour index' by the international subcommittee for photometry established by the *Carte du Ciel* [83] – see section 4.9.1.

The use of Cramer orthochromatic plates at Yerkes by Parkhurst and Jordan to determine photovisual magnitudes was the next important advance [123], which enabled Parkhurst to undertake the first major two-colour catalogue, the *Yerkes Actinometry* [126] – see section 4.8.2. The programme developed into the extensive photographic and photovisual photometry of the North Polar Sequence by Seares [131] in which colour indices for faint stars (to $m_{pv} = 17.5$) were obtained for the first time – see section 4.10.1.

Seares was one of the pioneers in the investigation of stellar colours. In addition to using the colour index as a magnitude difference, he invented a somewhat unorthodox index from the ratio of the exposures required to give equal images in unfiltered photographic and filtered photovisual impressions on a single isochromatic plate. The logarithm of this ratio could be calibrated empirically with colour index so as to overcome the effects of reciprocity failure and to give, so he claimed, a value with smaller uncertainty than the direct determination of the photographic and photovisual magnitudes on different plates [208, 202]. Furthermore, he considered a star's colour index could be written as the sum of three terms which depended on spectrum, absolute magnitude and distance. The first term dominated, as shown by the tight relationship between spectral type and colour. This fact enabled stellar colour classes to be defined photometrically with the notation b, a, f, g, k, m corresponding to the mean colours of stars of spectral types from B to M [209]. Decimal subdivision of the colour classes (e.g. a0, f5 etc.) could also be used, each subdivision corresponding to about $0^{m}04$ in colour index. The concept was used by Shapley (who had been a student of Seares') in some of his early work on the magnitudes and colours of stars in globular clusters [210].

These various programmes which developed the concept and use of the colour index as an astrophysical tool are described in more detail in the earlier sections cited. In the next section a quite independent photographically determined colour parameter is described which was pioneered by Bergstrand and by Hertzsprung from about 1908.

4.11.2   The effective wavelength

The idea of measuring effective wavelengths as a stellar colour parameter had a gestation period of some fifteen years. In 1896 Schwarzschild had proposed using a coarse objective grating to produce a linear series of low dispersion diffraction spectra either side of a central zero order image as an aid to the visual measurement of the components of visual binary stars [211].

The concept of effective wavelength was introduced by George Comstock (1855–1934), director of the Washburn Observatory in Wisconsin, in 1897. He defined it to be the wavelength of the brightest part of the visual spectrum and he measured this from the angular separation of the brightest parts of the two spectra of the same order produced from just two parallel slits mounted in front of the objective lens of the Washburn 40-cm refractor [212]. He determined visual effective wavelengths for 51 stars and was able to demonstrate a correlation with both visually estimated colour and the Secchi spectral type. His values ranged from 559 to 581 nm.

Comstock reported further observations in 1902 using several different objective gratings and again found a correlation with Krüger's colour estimates [213]. A similar series of visual observations was also undertaken by Hans Lau in Denmark. He obtained effective wavelengths for 70 stars with a 10-inch telescope and found that the values correlated with the Harvard spectral type [214].

Prosper Henry in Paris applied this method to a photographic determination of effective wavelengths in 1900 [215]. His interest was to demonstrate that the effective wavelength of the minor planet Eros was about the same as the stars in the field used for the Eros astrometry. In this case atmospheric refraction should affect the apparent positions of the stars and Eros equally.

When Östen Bergstrand (1873–1948) at Uppsala and Ejnar Hertzsprung (1873–1967) independently adopted this photographic technique about 1908, they were also primarily interested in atmospheric dispersion and the influence of stellar colour on astrometric measurements [216, 217]. Hertzsprung at this time was still in Denmark, where he worked at the private Urania Observatory in Copenhagen. Here he benefited from the contact with H. E. Lau who was interested in the use of objective gratings. Both Hertzsprung and Bergstrand independently recognized the value of photographic effective wavelengths as an indicator of stellar colours. Hertzsprung observed the Cepheid variable S Sagittae on the 81-mm refractor at the Urania Observatory and found that the effective wavelength changed in phase with the light curve with an amplitude of 62 Å [218]. His grating was made from a series of parallel wires of thickness 1.4 mm whose centre-to-centre spacing was 2.8 mm.

Meanwhile Bergstrand observed 92 bright stars both at Uppsala and on the 1-metre reflector at Paris-Meudon (diaphragmed to 40 cm to increase the size of the useable field). His extensive investigation showed that the λ_{eff} parameter changed by about 30 nm (from 420 to 450 nm) in going from spectral type B to M, while the values for carbon stars (N-type) were a further 10 to 20 nm larger [219]. At the same time he demonstrated an intrinsic weakness in the usefulness of effective wavelengths, for they were relatively insensitive to spectral type for the hottest stars; the best sensitivity of λ_{eff} to spectral type was for late F to G stars (or Potsdam colour WG−). This result was emphasized again in 1916 by Bergstrand and Lindblad using Uppsala observations with the Zeiss triple objective astrograph [220].

In 1909, soon after commencing his researches on effective wavelengths, Hertzsprung left Copenhagen to take up appointments with Karl Schwarzschild, first at Göttingen and then, later that year, at Potsdam. He took with him the photographic material from Urania for his classic 1911 paper on effective wavelengths, which laid the basis for the first colour-magnitude diagrams [221]. In this work he measured the distances on the plate between the apparent 'centres of gravity' in the density of the two symmetrically disposed first order spectra with an accuracy of about $\pm$ 2.0 nm, which was equivalent to measuring a colour index to about $\pm$ 0^{m}.1. The λ_{eff} and photographic colour index determinations were therefore of comparable precision, although effective wavelength reductions were simpler to carry out. However, both Hertzsprung and Bergstrand [217] found that the measured value of λ_{eff} depended on the exposure of the spectrum (a kind of photographic Purkinje effect) and the measured result had to be corrected (by up to 5.0 nm) to a standard value of the circular zero-order image diameter, a complicated procedure which was prone to systematic error. Hertzsprung also corrected for atmospheric extinction (about 3.5 nm per unit air mass).

The technique allowed Hertzsprung to reach stars of about tenth magnitude, and the results were applied to stars in four open clusters, the Pleiades, the Hyades, Praesepe and the Coma Berenices cluster. Hertzsprung summarized his most important conclusion as follows:

> The application of the method to the Pleiades showed that the stars which have common proper motion with Alcyone form a continuous sequence when arranged according to brightness and colour, and show an increase of the effective wavelength with decreasing brightness by about 50 Å from 5^{m} to 9^{m}. The majority of the Hyades stars that belong physically to the cluster behave similarly ... there are however individual stars such as γ, δ, ϵ and θ^1 Tauri which with their strong yellow colour diverge widely from the [main] sequence [222].

This, in 1911, was the first published colour-magnitude diagram, although it is known that Hertzsprung had prepared an unpublished version of the plot for the Pleiades as early as 1908. The earlier plot was later published and discussed by Alex Nielsen [223].

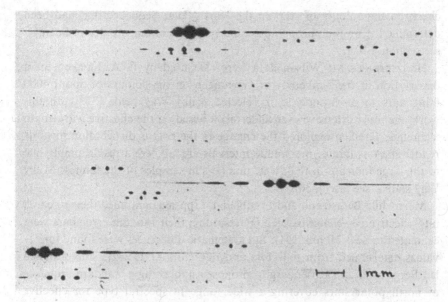

Fig. 4.22   Grating spectra of part of the Pleiades recorded by Ejnar Hertzsprung, Dec. 1907.

With these results the effective wavelength technique bore some early and very productive fruit from which much of our knowledge of stellar evolution has, in the long run, been derived. For Hertzsprung recognition took many years to come and the parallel work of Russell on field stars using trigonometric parallaxes and Harvard spectral types was at first acknowledged as representing the main pioneering advance. It was only in 1933 that the term 'Hertzsprung-Russell diagram' came into common use (see [223]).

The effective wavelength technique became a popular stellar colour parameter during the early 1920s. Hertzsprung continued his research in this field while at Potsdam. When he visited Mt Wilson in 1912 he was able to secure extensive observational material for the Pleiades using the 60-inch reflector and an objective grating [224] and for the open cluster NGC 1647 [225]. He found that lower luminosity field dwarf stars were progressively yellower in colour (in the range $-2 < M_V < +8$), but fainter than $M_V \simeq 8^m$ the colour was about constant [226]. The white dwarf star o^2 Eri B, for which Walter Adams had found an A spectral type [227], was at that time a 'very strange' exception. Hertzsprung's 1922 paper on the colours of stars near the North Pole was also based on 60-inch objective grating observations from his 1912 visit to California [228]. They provided a useful check on the colours of stars in the North Polar Sequence that had been determined from the photographic and photovisual magnitudes of Seares – see section 4.10.1.

Hertzsprung's Mt Wilson data were also used by E. A. Kreiken for a dissertation at the University of Groningen on the colours of about 4000 faint stars to magnitude 15 in selected Milky Way fields [229]. In this work, the most extensive ever undertaken based on the effective wavelength technique, Kreiken explored the change in the colour distribution towards redder stars as fainter magnitude intervals are studied, a result mainly due to the large increase in red-dwarf numbers in samples of the faintest Milky Way stars – see also [230].

Meanwhile Bergstrand and Lindblad at Uppsala continued their research into effective wavelengths. Like Hertzsprung, their random error bars were estimated to be ± 2.0 nm [231]. But systematic differences were found for λ_{eff} values determined from reflectors and refractors [231, 232]. This problem led Bergstrand and Rosenberg to propose establishing a standard sequence of north polar stars covering a wide range in spectral type for effective wavelength determinations [233], similar to that already established for photometry. The 25 stars proposed were unfortunately not all in the same field and were rather bright. The proposal never became widely accepted, in spite of the efforts of C. R. Davidson and E. Martin at Greenwich [234] and of H. von Klüber in Berlin [235] to establish standard values for the stars in the Bergstrand-Rosenberg polar sequence.

In Heidelberg Max Wolf undertook a careful study of the causes of systematic errors in effective wavelength determinations [236]. Numerous instrumental and reduction procedure effects were explored in an attempt to account for the scale differences between different observers. His paper was largely inconclusive, which led Eberhard in Potsdam to caution against comparisons between the results of different observers and to support the proposal for a sequence of λ_{eff} standard stars [237]. By the mid-1920s it was realized that the problems of establishing a reliable photographic λ_{eff} scale were at least as intractable as those pertaining to a scale of photographic magnitudes. This was a major reason for the decline in popularity of the method. Moreover the precision of λ_{eff} measurements was no longer able to compete with the $(m_{pg} - m_{pv})$ colour indices. Nevertheless in the early 1920s the determination of effective wavelengths had been widespread. Programmes were established at Pulkovo [238] and at Greenwich [239]. At Pulkovo I. Balanowsky was one observer who claimed to find larger effective wavelengths for red giants than for dwarfs of the same spectral type. The Greenwich programme by Davidson and Martin on the 30-inch reflector was an extensive one, directed towards stars brighter than magnitude 10.5

within a few degrees of the north pole, and was one of several detailed studies of the relationship of λ_{eff} to spectral type [239].

References

[1]   Arago, F., Comptes Rendus de l'Acad. des Sci., **8**, 4 (1839).
[2]   Arago, F., Comptes Rendus de l'Acad. des Sci., **9**, 250 (1839).
[3]   Herschel, J.F.W., Proc. R. Soc., **4**, 131 (1839).
[4]   Draper, J.W., Phil. Mag. (3), **17**, 217 (1840).
[5]   Draper, H., Smithsonian Contributions to Knowledge (No. 180), **14**, 1 (1864).
[6]   Draper, J.W., Phil. Mag. (3), **22**, 360 (1843).
[7]   Becquerel, A.E., Bibl. Univ. de Genéve, **40**, 341 (1842).
[8]   Fizeau, H. and Foucault, L., Comptes Rendus de l'Acad. des Sci., **18**, 746 (1844).
[9]   Fizeau, H. and Foucault, L., Comptes Rendus de l'Acad. des Sci., **18**, 860 (1844).
[10]   Roscoe, H.E., Proc. R. Soc., **12**, 648 (1863).
[11]   Bond, W.C., Ann. Harvard Coll. Observ., **1**, cli (1856).
[12]   Bond, W.C., 'Report of the director of the observatory of Harvard University, 1850', Ann. Harvard Coll. Observ., **1**, cxl (1856). See page cxlix.
[13]   Bond, G.P., Astron. Nachr., **47**, 1 (1857).
[14]   Bond, W.C., Mon. Not. R. Astron. Soc., **17**, 230 (1857).
[15]   Bond, G.P., Mon. Not. R. Astron. Soc., **18**, 71 (1858).
[16]   Bond, G.P., Astron. Nachr., **48**, 1 (1858).
[17]   Bond, G.P., to Wm. Mitchell, 6 July 1857. The letter is quoted in E.S. Holden, Memorials of W.C. Bond and of his son G.P. Bond, San Francisco and New York (1897) pp. 154–159. See also D. Norman, Osiris, **5**, 560 (1938) = Harvard Coll. Observ. Reprint No. **153** (1938) and ibid., Publ. Astron. Soc. Pacific, **2**, 300 (1890).
[18]   Bond, G.P., Astron. Nachr., **49**, 81 (1858).
[19]   de la Rue, W., Mon. Not. R. Astron. Soc., **18**, 54 (1858).
[20]   de la Rue, W., Mon. Not. R. Astron. Soc., **21**, 89 (1861).
[21]   de la Rue, W., Mon. Not. R. Astron. Soc., **19**, 352 (1859).
[22]   Rutherfurd, L.M., American J. Sci. Arts (2), **39**, 304 (1865).
[23]   Gould, B.A., Astron. Nachr., **68**, 183 (1867).
[24]   Peirce, B., American J. Sci. Arts (3), **3**, 157 (1872).
[25]   Schultz-Sellack, C., American J. Sci. Arts (3), **6**, 15 (1873).
[26]   Schultz-Sellack, C., Astron. Nachr., **82**, 65 (1873).
[27]   Gould, B.A., American J. Sci. Arts (3), **6**, 399 (1873).
[28]   Gould, B.A., Observatory, **2**, 13 (1878).
[29]   Draper, H., American J. Sci. Arts (3), **20**, 433 (1880).
[30]   Draper, H., Mon. Not. R. Astron. Soc., **42**, 367 (1882).
[31]   Holden, E.S., Astronomical & Meteorological Observations made during 1878 at the USNO, Washington (1882) Appendix 1: Monographs on the Central Parts of the Nebula of Orion. See addendum p. 226 by Henry Draper.
[32]   Common, A.A., Mon. Not. R. Astron. Soc., **45**, 22 (1885).
[33]   Common, A.A., Mon. Not. R. Astron. Soc., **43**, 255 (1883).

[34] Draper, H., *Comptes Rendus de l'Acad. des Sci.*, **92**, 964 (1881).
[35] Espin, T.E., *Observatory*, **7**, 247 (1884).
[36] Espin, T.E., *Trans. Liverpool Astron. Soc.*, **3**, 1 (1884).
[37] Janssen, J., *Comptes Rendus de l'Acad. des Sci.*, **92**, 261 (1881).
[38] Pickering, W.H., *Proc. American Acad. Arts Sci.*, **20**, 159 (1885).
[39] Pickering, E.C., *Observatory*, **6**, 199 (1883).
[40] Pickering, E.C., *Astron. Register*, **21**, 149 (1883).
[41] Pickering, E.C., *Mem. American Acad. Arts Sci.*, **11**, 179 (1888).
[42] Pickering, E.C. and Fleming, W.P., *Ann. Harvard Coll. Observ.*, **18** (No. 7), 119 (1890).
[43] Weaver, H.F., *Pop. Astron.*, **54**, 287 (1946).
[44] Pickering, E.C., *Ann. Harvard Coll. Observ.*, **27**, 1 (1890).
[45] Pickering, E.C., *Ann. Harvard Coll. Observ.*, **26** (Part 1), 1 (1891).
[46] Pickering, E.C., *Ann. Harvard Coll. Observ.*, **26** (Part 2), 193 (1897).
[47] Pickering, E.C., *Proc. American Acad. Arts Sci.*, **20**, 407 (1885).
[48] Pickering, W.H., *Ann. Harvard Coll. Observ.*, **32** (Part 1), 1 (1895).
[49] Bunsen, R.W. and Roscoe, H.E., *Ann. Phys. (2)*, **108**, 193 (1859).
[50] Abney, W. de W., *Brit. J. Photography*, **29**, 243 (1882).
[51] Hurter, F., and Driffield, V., *J. Soc. of Chem. Industry*, **9**, 455 (1890).
[52] Bond, G.P., *Ann. Harvard Coll. Observ.*, **5**, 1 (1867).
[53] Henry, P. and Henry, M., *Nature*, **34**, 35 (1886).
[54] Pickering, E.C., *Ann. Rep. of the Director of Harvard College Observatory, presented Dec. 19, 1883* (1884). See p. 11.
[55] Gill, D. and Kapteyn, J.C., *Ann. Cape Observ.*, **3**, ix (1896).
[56] Gill, D., *Comptes Rendus de l'Acad. des Sci.*, **95**, 1342 (1882).
[57] Mouchez, E., *Comptes Rendus de l'Acad. des Sci.*, **95**, 1343 (1882).
[58] Kapteyn, J.C., *Ann. Cape Observ.*, **5**, 19 (1900).
[59] Eddington, A.S., *Observatory*, **45**, 261 (1922).
[60] Warner, B., *Astronomers at the Royal Observ., Cape of Good Hope*, A.A. Balkema: Cape Town and Rotterdam, p. 93 (1979).
[61] Gould, B.A., *Result. Observ. Nac. Argentino Córdoba*, **3**, 1 (1884); *ibid.*, **4**, 1 (1884).
[62] Kapteyn, J.C., *Ann. Cape Observ.*, **3**, 1 (1896).
[63] Kapteyn, J.C., *Bull. Com. Int. Perm. de la Carte du Ciel*, **2**, 131 (1895).
[64] Kapteyn, J.C., *Vierteljahrschr. Astron. Ges.*, **24**, 213 (1889).
[65] Kapteyn, J.C., *Ann. Cape Observ.*, **5**, 1 (1900).
[66] Gill, D., *A History and Description of the Royal Observatory, Cape of Good Hope*. In *History of the Cape Observ.*, p. v. Publ. by His Majesty's Stationery Office, London (1913).
[67] Halm, J., *Mon. Not. R. Astron. Soc.*, **74**, 600 (1914).
[68] Halm, J., *Mon. Not. R. Astron. Soc.*, **78**, 199 (1918).
[69] Pickering, E.C., *Ann. Harvard Coll. Observ.*, **76** (No. 12), 243 (1916).
[70] Pickering, E.C., *Ann. Harvard Coll. Observ.*, **80** (No. 13), 231 (1917).
[71] Mouchez, E., *Ann. du Bureau des Longitudes*, 755 (1887).
[72] Henry, P. and Henry, P., *Comptes Rendus de l'Acad. des Sci.*, **102**, 848 (1886).
[73] Gill, D., *Bull. Astron.*, **3**, 321 (1886).
[74] Mouchez, E., *Mon. Not. R. Astron. Soc.*, **46**, 1 (1885).
[75] *Congrès Astrophotographique International pour le levé de la Carte du Ciel*, Paris (1887). See p. 101.
[76] *Réunion Com. Int. Perm. pour l'exécution de la Carte Photographique du Ciel*, Paris (1891).
[77] Gill, D., *Bull. Com. Int. Perm. de la Carte du Ciel*, **1**, 7 (1888).

[78]   Radau, R., *Revue des deux Mondes*, **92**, 626 (1889).
[79]   Radau, R., *Ann. Rep. Smithsonian Inst. to July 1889*, 469 (1890).
[80]   Pickering, E.C., *Congrés Astrographique International*, Annexe No. 5, 93 (1887).
[81]   Turner, H.H. and Common, A.A., *Observatory*, **12**, 308 (1889).
[82]   Pickering, E.C., *Observatory*, **12**, 375 (1889).
[83]   *Bull. Com. Int. Perm. de la Carte du Ciel*, **6**, 391 (1913).
[84]   Pickering, E.C., *Science* (new series), **39**, 1 (1914).
[85]   Couderc, P., *Trans. Int. Astron. Union*, **14B**, 172 (1971).
[86]   Henry, P., *Réunion Com. Int. Perm. de la Carte Photographique du Ciel*, (1889). See pp. 39 and 52 and resolution 18, p. 108.
[87]   Janssen, J., *Comptes Rendus de l'Acad. des Sci.*, **92**, 821 (1881).
[88]   Lohse, W.O., *Astron. Nachr.*, **111**, 147 (1885).
[89]   Pritchard, C., *Mon. Not. R. Astron. Soc.*, **51**, 430 (1891).
[90]   Scheiner, J., *Astron. Nachr.*, **128**, 113 (1891).
[91]   Scheiner, J., *Réunion Com. Int. Perm. de la Carte du Ciel*, 81 (1891).
[92]   Abney, W. de W., *Mon. Not. R. Astron. Soc.*, **54**, 65 (1893).
[93]   Abney, W. de W., *Proc. R. Soc.*, **54**, 143 (1893).
[94]   Dunér, N.C., *Bull. Com. Int. Perm. de la Carte du Ciel*, **2**, 107 (1895).
[95]   Dunér, N.C., *Réunion Com. Int. Perm. de la Carte du Ciel*, p. 64 (1896).
[96]   Dunér, N.C., *Bull. Com. Int. Perm. de la Carte du Ciel* **1**, 453 (1891).
[97]   Christie, W.H.M., *Mon. Not. R. Astron. Soc.*, **52**, 125 (1892).
[98]   Trépied, C., Henry, P. and Henry, P., *Bull. Com. Int. Perm. de la Carte du Ciel*, **2**, 110 (1895).
[99]   Turner, H.H., *Mon. Not. R. Astron. Soc.*, **65**, 755 (1905).
[100]   Charlier, C.V.L., *Publ. Astron. Ges.*, **19**, 1 (1889).
[101]   Scheiner, J., *Astron. Nachr.*, **121**, 49 (1889).
[102]   Pritchard, C., *Proc. R. Soc.*, **41**, 195 (1886).
[103]   Schwarzschild, K., *Astron. Nachr.*, **174**, 133 (1907).
[104]   Schaeberle, J.M., *Publ. Astron. Soc. Pacific*, **1**, 51 (1889).
[105]   Turner, H.H., *Mon. Not. R. Astron. Soc.*, **49**, 292 (1889).
[106]   Scheiner, J., *Bull. Com. Int. Perm. de la Carte du Ciel*, **1**, 227 (1889).
[107]   Wolf, M., *Astron. Nachr.*, **126**, 81 (1891).
[108]   Wolf, M., *Bull. Com. Int. Perm. de la Carte du Ciel*, **1**, 389 (1891).
[109]   Holden, E.S., *Publ. Astron. Soc. Pacific*, **1**, 112 (1889).
[110]   Scheiner, J., *Astron. Nachr.*, **124**, 273 (1890).
[111]   Gill, D., *Bull. Com. Int. Perm de la Carte du Ciel*, **2**, 127 (1895).
[112]   Trépied, C., *Bull. Com. Int. Perm. de la Carte du Ciel* **2**, 383 (1895).
[113]   *Réunion Com. Int. Perm. de la Carte du Ciel*, resolution 6, p. 85 (1895).
[114]   Vogel, H.W., *Ann. der Physik und Chemie*, **150**, 453 (1873).
[115]   Abney, W. de W., *Mon. Not. R. Astron. Soc.*, **37**, 276 (1876).
[116]   Abney, W. de W., *Nature*, **13**, 432 (1876).
[117]   Abney, W. de W., *Phil. Trans. R. Soc.*, **171** (Part 2), 653 (1880).
[118]   Wallace, R.J., *Astrophys. J.*, **22**, 153, 350 (1905).
[119]   Wallace, R.J., *Astrophys. J.*, **24**, 268 (1906).
[120]   Wallace, R.J., *Astrophys. J.*, **25**, 116 (1907).
[121]   Wallace, R.J., *Astrophys. J.*, **26**, 299 (1907).
[122]   Wallace, R.J., *Astrophys. J.*, **27**, 106 (1908).
[123]   Parkhurst, J.A. and Jordan, F.C., *Astrophys. J.*, **27**, 169 (1908).
[124]   Müller, G. and Kempf, P., *Publ. Potsdam Astrophys. Observ.*, **9**, 1 (1894).
[125]   Müller, G. and Kempf, P., *Publ. Potsdam Astrophys. Observ.*, **13**, (1899); **14**, (1903); **16**, (1906); **17**, (1907).

[126]   Parkhurst, J.A., *Astrophys. J.*, **36**, 169 (1912).
[127]   King, E.S., *Ann. Harvard Coll. Observ.*, **81** (No. 4), 201 (1919).
[128]   King, E.S., *Ann. Harvard Coll. Observ.*, **85** (No. 3), 45 (1923).
[129]   King, E.S., *Ann. Harvard Coll. Observ.*, **85** (No. 10), 181 (1928).
[130]   Hale, G.E., *Ann. Rep. of the Director of Mt Wilson Solar Observatory for the year 1913* (1914). See pp. 214 and 221.
[131]   Seares, F.H., *Astrophys. J.*, **41**, 206 (1915).
[132]   Seares, F.H., *Trans. Int. Astron. Union*, **1**, 69 (1922).
[133]   Seares, F.H., *Trans. Int. Astron. Union*, **2**, 83 (1925).
[134]   Schwarzschild, K., *Publ. der von Kuffner'schen Sternw.*, **5**, B1 (1900).
[135]   Schwarzschild, K., *Publ. der von Kuffner'schen Sternw.*, **5**, C1 (1900).
[136]   Schwarzschild, K., *Photographische Korrespondenz*, **36**, 109 (1899).
[137]   Schwarzschild, K., *Astrophys. J.*, **11**, 89 (1900).
[138]   Kron, E., *Publ. Potsdam Astrophys. Observ.*, **22** (No. 67), 1 (1913).
[139]   Hartmann, J., *Zeitschr. für Instrumentenkunde*, **19**, 97 (1899).
[140]   Hartmann, J., *Astrophys. J.*, **10**, 321 (1899).
[141]   Baade, W., *Astron. Nachr.*, **228**, 359 (1926).
[142]   Meyermann, B. and Schwarzschild, K., *Astron. Nachr.*, **170**, 277 (1906).
[143]   Meyermann, B. and Schwarzschild, K., *Astron. Nachr.*, **174**, 137 (1907).
[144]   Kapteyn, J.C., *Plan of Selected Areas*, Groningen (1906).
[145]   Schwarzschild, K., *Astron. Nachr.*, **183**, 297 (1909).
[146]   Schwarzschild, K., *Réunion Com. Int. Perm. de la Carte du Ciel*, B101 (1909).
[147]   Schwarzschild, K., *Astron. Nachr.*, **172**, 65 (1906).
[148]   Wirtz, C.W., *Astron. Nachr.*, **154**, 317 (1901).
[149]   Wilkens, A., *Astron. Nachr.*, **172**, 305 (1906).
[150]   Schwarzschild, K., Meyermann, B., Kohlschütter, A. and Birck, O., *Göttinger Aktin.*, Teil A, *Abhandl. der königl. Ges. der Wiss. zu Göttingen, Math.-physik. Klasse*, Neue Folge **6** (No. 6), Berlin (1910).
[151]   Schwarzschild, K., Meyermann, B., Kohlschütter, A., Birck, O. and Dziewulski, W., *Göttinger Aktin.*, Teil B, *Abhandl. der königl. Ges. der Wiss. zu Göttingen, Math.-physik. Klasse*, Neue Folge **8** (No. 4), Berlin (1912).
[152]   Osthoff, H., *Astron. Nachr.*, **153**, 142 (1900).
[153]   Schwarzschild, K., *Sitzungsber. der kaiserl. Akad. der Wiss. in Wien, Mathem.-naturwiss. Classe*, **109**, 1127 (1900).
[154]   Chandler, S.C., *Astron. J.*, **8**, 137 (1888).
[155]   King, I.R., *Astron. J.*, **57**, 253 (1952).
[156]   Golay, M., *Introduction to Astronomical Photometry*, D. Reidel, Dordrecht (1974).
[157]   Parkhurst, J.A. and Jordan, F.C., *Astrophys. J.*, **26**, 244 (1907).
[158]   Schwarzschild, K., *Vierteljahrschr. Astron. Ges.*, **47**, 356 (1912).
[159]   Parkhurst, J.A., *Astrophys. J.*, **35**, 125 (1912).
[160]   Pickering, E.C., *Harvard Coll. Observ. Circ.*, **50**, 1 (1900).
[161]   King, E.S., *Ann. Harvard Coll. Observ.*, **59** (No. 1), 1 (1912).
[162]   King, E.S., *Ann. Harvard Coll. Observ.*, **59** (No. 2), 33 (1912).
[163]   King, E.S., *Ann. Harvard Coll. Observ.*, **59** (No. 4), 95 (1912).
[164]   King, E.S., *Ann. Harvard Coll. Observ.*, **59** (No. 5), 127 (1912).
[165]   King, E.S., *Ann. Harvard Coll. Observ.*, **59** (No. 6), 157 (1912).
[166]   King, E.S., *Ann. Harvard Coll. Observ.*, **76** (No. 5), 83 (1916).
[167]   Pickering, E.C., *Ann. Harvard Coll. Observ.*, **71** (No. 1), 1 (1917).
[168]   Kapteyn, J.C., *Astrophys. J.*, **30**, 284 (1909).
[169]   Shapley, H., *Astrophys. J.*, **45**, 123 (1917).

[170] Fabry, C., *Comptes Rendus de l'Acad. des Sci.*, **150**, 273 (1910).
[171] Fabry, C., *Astrophys. J.*, **31**, 394 (1910).
[172] Struve, O. and Elvey, C.T., *Astrophys. J.*, **83**, 162 (1936).
[173] Williams, E.G. and Knox-Shaw, H., *Mon. Not. R. Astron. Soc.*, **102**, 226 (1942).
[174] Cousins, A.W.J., *Mon. Not. R. Astron. Soc.*, **103**, 154 (1943).
[175] Redman, R.O., *Mon. Not. R. Astron. Soc.*, **105**, 212 (1945).
[176] Fabry, C., *Ann. d'Astrophys.*, **6**, 65 (1943).
[177] Nikonov, V. and Kulikovsky, P., *Astron. Zhurnal – Astron. J of the Soviet Union*, **16** (Part 4), 54 (1939).
[178] Pickering, E.C., *Harvard Coll. Observ. Circ.*, 108 (1906).
[179] Pickering, E.C., *Harvard Coll. Observ. Circ.*, 125 (1907).
[180] Pickering, E.C., *Astron. Nachr.*, **95**, 29 (1879).
[181] Pickering, E.C., *Harvard Coll. Observ. Circ.*, **160**, 1 (1910).
[182] Pickering, E.C., Searle, A. and Wendell, O.C., *Ann. Harvard Coll. Observ.*, **14** (Part 2), 325 (1885).
[183] Pickering, E.C., *Harvard Coll. Observ. Circ.*, **150**, 1 (1909).
[184] *Réunion Com. Int. Perm. de la Carte du Ciel*, resolution 7, B103 (1909).
[185] Pickering, E.C., *Harvard Coll. Observ. Circ.*, **170**, 1 (1912).
[186] Leavitt, H.S., *Ann Harvard Coll. Observ.*, **71** (No. 3), 47 (1917).
[187] Schwarzschild, K., *Astron. Nachr.*, **186**, 37 (1911).
[188] Pickering, E.C., *Bull. Com. Int. Perm. de la Carte du Ciel*, **6**, 395 (1913).
[189] Pickering, E.C. *Ann. Harvard Coll. Observ.*, **71** (No. 4), 233 (1917).
[190] Leavitt, H.S., *Ann. Harvard Coll. Observ.*, **85** (No. 1), 1 (1919).
[191] Leavitt, H.S., *Ann. Harvard Coll. Observ.*, **85** (No. 7), 143 (1925).
[192] Leavitt, H.S., *Ann. Harvard Coll. Observ.*, **85** (No. 8), 157 (1926).
[193] Pickering, E.C. and Kapteyn, J.C., *Ann. Harvard Coll. Observ.*, **101**, vii (1918).
[194] Seares, F.H., *Astrophys. J.*, **41**, 259 (1915).
[195] Seares, F.H., Bailey, S.I., Jordan, F.C., Parkhurst, J.A. and Stebbins, J., *Proc. Nat. Acad. Sci.*, **6**, 349 (1920). See p. 381.
[196] Redman, R.O., *Quart. J. R. Astron. Soc.*, **7**, 75 (1966).
[197] Seares, F.H., *Astrophys. J.*, **38**, 241 (1913).
[198] Seares, F.H., *Astrophys. J.*, **39**, 307 (1914).
[199] Shapley, H., *Harvard Coll. Observ. Bull.*, 781 (1922).
[200] Seares, F.H., *Astrophys. J.*, **39**, 361 (1914).
[201] Seares, F.H. and Humason, M.L., *Astrophys. J.*, **56**, 84 (1922).
[202] Seares, F.H., *Astrophys. J.*, **56**, 97 (1922).
[203] Seares, F.H., Kapteyn, J.C., van Rhijn, P.J., Joyner, M.C. and Richmond, M.L., *Mt Wilson Catalogue of Photographic Magnitudes in Selected Areas 1–139*, Carnegie Inst. of Washington Publ. No. 402 (1930).
[204] Dziewulski, W., *Astron. Nachr.*, **198**, 65 (1914).
[205] Chapman, S. and Melotte, P.J., *Mon. Not. R. Astron. Soc.*, **74**, 40 (1913).
[206] Chapman, S. and Melotte, P.J., *Mon. Not. R. Astron. Soc.*, **74**, 50 (1913).
[207] Jones, H.S., *Mon. Not. R. Astron. Soc.*, **82**, 21 (1921).
[208] Seares, F.H., *Proc. Nat. Acad. Sci.*, **2**, 521 (1916).
[209] Seares, F.H., *Proc. Nat. Acad. Sci.*, **1**, 481 (1915).
[210] Shapley, H., *Proc. Nat. Acad. Sci.*, **2**, 15 (1916).
[211] Schwarzschild, K., *Astron. Nachr.*, **139**, 353 (1896).
[212] Comstock, G.C., *Astrophys. J.*, **5**, 26 (1897).
[213] Comstock, G.C., *Astron. Nachr.*, **160**, 69 (1902).
[214] Lau, H.E., *Astron. Nachr.*, **173**, 81 (1906).

[215]   Henry, P., *Conference astrographique int. de juillet 1900*, (No. 8), 41, Paris (1900).
[216]   Hertzsprung, E., *Bull. Astron.*, **25**, 5 (1908).
[217]   Bergstrand, Ö., *Astron. Nachr.*, **177**, 241 (1908).
[218]   Hertzsprung, E., *Astron. Nachr.*, **182**, 289 (1909).
[219]   Bergstrand, Ö., *Nova Acta Soc. Scientiarum Upsaliensis, Ser IV*, **2** (No. 4), 1 (1909).
[220]   Bergstrand, Ö. and Lindblad, B., *Ark. Mat. Astron. Fysik*, **11** (No. 17), (1916).
[221]   Hertzsprung, E., *Publ. Potsdam Astrophys. Observ.*, **22** (Nr 63), 1 (1911).
[222]   Hertzsprung, E., *Astron. Jahresbericht*, **13**, 330 (1911).
[223]   Nielsen, A., *Centaurus*, **9**, 219 (1963).
[224]   Hertzsprung, E., *Mem. de l'Acad Royale des Sci. et des Lettres de Danemark, Section des Sciences, 8ème sér.*, **4** (No. 4), (1923).
[225]   Hertzsprung, E., *Astrophys. J.*, **42**, 92 (1915).
[226]   Hertzsprung, E., *Astrophys. J.*, **42**, 111 (1915).
[227]   Adams, W.S., *Publ. Astron. Soc. Pacific*, **26**, 198 (1914).
[228]   Hertzsprung, E., *Astrophys. J.*, **55**, 370 (1922).
[229]   Kreiken, E.A., 'On the colours of the faint stars in the Milky-Way and the distance of the Scutum-group.' Inaug.-Dissertation, Groningen (1923).
[230]   Kreiken, E.A., *Mon. Not. R. Astron. Soc.*, **87**, 196 (1927).
[231]   Lindblad, B., *Ark. Mat. Astron. Fysik*, **13** (No. 26), (1918).
[232]   Bergstrand, Ö, *Festschrift für Hans Seeliger*, p. 386., Springer-Verlag, Berlin (1924).
[233]   Bergstrand, Ö. and Rosenberg, H., *Astron. Nachr.*, **215**, 447 (1922).
[234]   Davidson, C.R. and Martin, E., *Mon. Not. R. Astron. Soc.*, **84**, 425 (1924).
[235]   Klüber, H. von, *Astron. Abh. Kiel*, **5** (No. 1), 1 (1925).
[236]   Wolf, M., *Astron. Nachr.*, **213**, 49 (1921).
[237]   Eberhard, P.A.J.G., *Festschrift für Hans Seeliger*, p. 115, Springer-Verlag, Berlin (1924).
[238]   Balanowsky, I., *Bull. de l'Observ. Central de Russie à Pulkovo*, **10** (No. 94), 7 (1924).
[239]   Davidson, C. and Martin, E., *Mon. Not. R. Astron. Soc.*, **82**, 65 (1921).

5 The origins of photoelectric photometry (1892–1945)

5.1 An Irish beginning

A new era in astronomy, which in time was completely to revolutionize stellar photometry, had a rather inauspicious beginning in Ireland in 1892. George Minchin (1845–1914), an Irishman who was professor of mathematics at the Royal Indian Engineering College at Coopers Hill in London, had been experimenting with selenium photovoltaic† cells since 1890. These devices, first discovered by Edmond Becquerel (1820–91) in 1839 [1], produce an electromotive force when a photosensitive surface is under illumination. Minchin's cells comprised a photocathode which consisted of an aluminium substrate onto which a thin layer of selenium had been deposited [2]. The anode was a platinum wire. Both electrodes were mounted in a glass capsule filled with an electrolyte, initially acetone. Light was admitted to the cathode through a quartz window close to the selenium surface, and the electromotive force (emf) generated was detected with a sensitive quadrant electrometer.

The first experiments were in Dublin at the private observatory of the amateur astronomer William Monck (1839–1915) in August 1892 on a $7\frac{1}{2}$-inch Clark refractor with the collaboration of Professors George Fitzgerald (1851–1901) of Dublin and Stephen Dixon (1866–1940), both of them being Irish physicists of some note‡ [3, 4]. Unfortunately, Minchin had to return

---

† Photocells can be classified into the photovoltaic, photoconductive or photoemissive categories, depending on whether they produce a voltage, a change in conductivity or electron emission under the action of light. The word *photoelectric* is sometimes used to refer to any of these three, or it may refer to just the photoemissive cells. The latter meaning will generally be used here. Nevertheless, the early astronomical experiments with photovoltaic and photoconductive cells presaged the use of the photoelectric cell in astronomy; therefore the introductory sections of this chapter describe these early photovoltaic and photoconductive observations.

‡ Fitzgerald was best known for his hypothesis of space contraction to account for the null observations in the Michelson-Morley experiment; Dixon had taken up the engineering chair at the University of New Brunswick in 1892, but was on a visit home to Dublin. His family lived next door to Monck.

Fig. 5.1   George Minchin.

to England before the weather cleared; he was therefore absent when Monck used his cell for the first electrical detection of starlight. The experiments were not very successful. No certain detection of the light of the fixed stars

Fig. 5.2   William Monck, c. 1896.

was made, but voltages produced by the light from Jupiter, Venus and the moon were reported.

By 1894 Minchin had improved the design of his cells. The electrolyte was now oenanthol (an alcohol derived from the distillation of castor oil) and the sensitivity was higher. New observations were made on a 24-inch reflector at Daramona House, County Westmeath in central Ireland in January of that year. The voltages produced by Venus, Jupiter and Sirius were successfully recorded, though for Sirius the signal amounted to only 0.02 V [5].

A further improvement in the cells was made in the following year when observations were resumed in April at Daramona. Electrometer deflections of several millivolts were successfully recorded for Regulus, Arcturus, η Boötis and Saturn on the first night, and for several further

Fig. 5.3   Minchin's photovoltaic cell used at Daramona House, 1894.

stars and planets over the next few nights [6, 7]. Observations were resumed in January 1896 with results being reported for ten stars and Jupiter [8].

Minchin commented on the unexpectedly large signal obtained for Betelgeuse, which, together with its small parallax (and hence large distance) implied that Betelgeuse 'must be possessed of tremendous energy' [8]. This is an early reference to the high luminosity of this star. Minchin was probably influenced by the contemporary work of his colleague Monck in Dublin, who had first pointed out the dichotomy for solar-type stars between those of high and low luminosity [9].

Minchin found that the relative strengths of the signals he recorded for Arcturus, Regulus and Procyon were in good agreement with those expected from the visually determined magnitudes and he concluded that

the experiments prove conclusively that there is little difficulty in obtaining fairly accurate measurements of the light of stars of the first and second magnitudes [6].

Biographical notes on the early Irish pioneers of stellar photometry were published by C. J. Butler and I. Elliott in the proceedings of a photometric conference to mark the centenary of the work of Minchin and Monck in Ireland [10].

5.2   Photoconductive cells at Illinois

It is doubtful that the experiments made by Minchin had much influence on the future course of stellar photometry. When a photocell was next used for detecting starlight the type of cell was quite different, being based on the phenomenon of photoconductivity in selenium. The players were Joel Stebbins (1878–1966), who was to become one of the most notable of the early pioneers in stellar photoelectric photometry, with his colleague Fay Cluff Brown. The place was Urbana, at the University of Illinois, and the year was 1906 when Brown first introduced Stebbins to the photoconductive selenium cell. Stebbins later recalled his introduction to selenium cells as follows:

> At an exhibit of the Department of Physics a young man, F. C. Brown, was demonstrating a so-called selenium cell. After explaining the properties of the element selenium he would turn on an ordinary electric light at a distance of a foot or two from a selenium cell, and automatically the response was indicated by the ringing of a bell. Right then and there I got the idea that if an ordinary light will ring a bell why would not the light from a star at the focus of a telescope produce a measurable electric current? [11].

The Illinois selenium cells were mainly acquired from the firm of J. W. Giltay in Delft, Holland and consisted of a layer of crystalline selenium which formed a coating over two wires wound round a flat insulator. The decrease in resistance of the selenium between the two wires caused by the action of starlight was measured with a Wheatstone bridge equipped with a sensitive galvanometer.

The pioneering work of Stebbins and Brown from 1907 [12] was recalled by Stebbins himself half a century later:

> I soon made friends with Brown, and in due time we had a selenium cell on the 12-inch refractor; I operated the telescope and a shutter while Brown looked after the battery, galvanometer, and scale. The first trial was on Jupiter – no response; several more trials, still no response. I said to myself, "I'll fix him." The moon was shining

Fig. 5.4   Stebbins' selenium photocell at Illinois, 1910.

through a window; I took the cell with attached wires off the telescope
and exposed it to the moon. The galvanometer deflection was
measurable with plenty to spare. Result: We spent a couple of months
measuring the variation of the moon's light with phase [13].

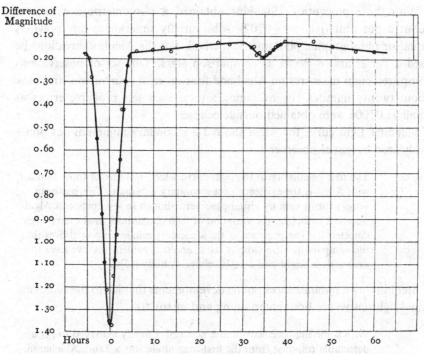

Fig. 5.5 Stebbins' photoconductive photocell light curve for Algol, 1910.

Further laboratory tests on the spectral response of four different selenium cells now followed. They showed wide differences from cell to cell, though in each case with a maximum in the far red around 700 nm. Some also had a secondary maximum near 590 nm [14].

Stebbins' best known work with the selenium cell came from the observations he made in 1909 on Algol (Brown had by then left Illinois) [15]. By this time many of the idiosyncrasies of the photoconductive cells had been discovered by trial and error at the telescope, and the light curve Stebbins obtained for this eclipsing binary is recognized as an outstanding and pioneering accomplishment (see Fig. 5.5).

In his Algol paper Stebbins outlined the precautions necessary for reliable results with the photoconductive cell. The cell was cooled to 0 °C and its temperature was controlled by a thermostat. The passage of the current through the cell to monitor the resistance was continuous, while the exposures to light were intermittent and limited to durations of about 10 seconds, with at least a minute of dark time for recovery.

With these precautions Stebbins obtained a photometric accuracy of about 2 per cent (p.e. = $\pm 0^{m}\!.02$), substantially superior to any previous visual or photographic photometric method. For the Algol observations he used α Persei and δ Persei as comparison stars. One set of observations comprised eight measures on Algol and four on each comparison, and took about twenty minutes. By averaging several such sets probable errors as small as $0^{m}\!.006$ were obtained outside eclipse.

Stebbins' light curve for Algol showed a secondary minimum not previously seen by visual observers:

> The first peculiarity of the light-curve which will attract those familiar with Algol is the existence of a secondary minimum. This has been sought for in vain by visual observers, though in my opinion if Algol were not so bright, the variation of 0.06 magnitudes might have been detected ... The presence of the secondary minimum now proves that the companion is not wholly dark, and it is evident that we have to deal with a bright and a relatively faint body [15].

Stebbins' own reminiscences on the developments that led to the successful Algol light curve are both entertaining and instructive:

> With some improvements and a new cell, I finally managed to get a detectable response from the first-magnitude star α Tauri, Aldebaran. The mean galvanometer deflection was 1.4 mm; I am sure of the 1.4 because it was the first nibble, scarcely a bite. Time went on with little change when all at once I got an idea. On a clear, cold night after a blizzard – I remember that the water pipes had been frozen at home – I tried a few measures of bright stars. Strange to say the cell had doubled in sensitivity from room temperature down to zero degrees Fahrenheit, but more important, the irregularities in the circuit had decreased some tenfold, and here at one jump was a favourable increase of possibly 20 times. The printed report said 50 times, but I am older now and will settle for 20.
>
> But the end was not yet. After an exhibit at a meeting I wrapped a cell in a handkerchief for safety and put it in my pocket. Later I forgot about the cell, pulled out the handkerchief, and dropped the cell on a hard floor. It had been a good cell, but now I had two cells each twice as good as the original. Since the extra area of two square inches had only produced irregularities, a smaller cell was all to the good. With this much to go on, I got up my nerve, placed our best cell in a vise, and with a hammer and chisel gave it a whack to break off about a quarter of it to make a really good cell.
>
> By the next summer, Brown and I had installed this fragment, properly insulated, in an icepack on the 12-inch refractor. We found we could measure second-magnitude stars with some accuracy, and that autumn our first star was Algol... We got a good light curve, including the secondary minimum which had not been detected before [13].

Further observations with the selenium cells were undertaken of Halley's Comet during 1910–11 [16], and of two further eclipsing binaries, β Aurigae [17] and δ Orionis [18], both of which were spectroscopic binaries with known orbits but not previously known to be eclipsing variables.

In spite of these early successes, Stebbins did not continue his work with selenium cells after 1911. In the autumn of that year Jakob Kunz (1874–1939) joined the Physics Department at Illinois, and he suggested to Stebbins that the new photoelectric cell might be of use for stellar photometry. A whole new technology was about to be introduced into observational astrophysics which, at least for several decades, displaced the photoconductive method.

It is interesting that Stebbins was not the first to experiment with a selenium cell for astronomical photometry. Stebbins reported apparently unpublished attempts by Edward Pickering, possibly in 1877, to perfect a selenium photometer [11] while in Germany, Ernst Ruhmer (1878–1913) had used a selenium cell to observe solar and lunar eclipses in 1902 and 1903 [19, 20].

5.3   The photoelectric cell

The photoelectric effect was first observed by Heinrich Hertz (1857–94) when in 1887 he showed that ultraviolet light was able to increase the strength of a spark from a discharging inductor [21]. Although Hertz conducted this experiment with considerable thoroughness and described his results in detail, he did not pursue this line of research further. But in the following year Wilhelm Hallwachs (1859–1922) made an even more important discovery. He showed that ultraviolet light was able to dissipate the negative charge on a zinc plate when it illuminated the plate. But a positive charge could not be dissipated in this way [22]. However, the full interpretation of these findings in terms of the ejection of electrons from the metallic surface by light had to await the discovery of the electron and the introduction of the quantum theory, concepts which Hallwachs' discovery helped bring to fruition.

Above all, it was the pioneering researches of Julius Elster (1854–1920) and his life-long colleague Hans Geitel (1855–1923) at Wolfenbüttel near Brunswick from 1889 that brought the photoelectric effect to the point where it could be used for practical photometry. Elster and Geitel found that the alkali metals showed the effect the most strongly of the different elements they investigated. By 1892, only four years after the discovery by Hallwachs, they had produced the first photoelectric cells in which the

Fig. 5.6   Jakob Kunz.

photocathodes were amalgams of sodium or potassium, and they demonstrated the possibility of using the new devices for laboratory photometry of ultraviolet light [23]. This was followed by an important discovery in 1910 that the hydrides of sodium or potassium were more sensitive to light than the metals themselves [24, 25]. This in turn quickly led to the first potassium (or sodium) hydride photoelectric cells, and it was these devices that were used for the first astronomical photoelectric photometry from 1912.

As it happened, three groups embarked upon photoelectric photometry almost simultaneously. This was not a coincidence, since Elster and Geitel had been urging astronomers at this time to undertake experiments in photoelectric astronomy. The advent of the potassium and sodium hydride cells was the stimulus that set these experiments in motion. Two of these groups were at the observatories in Berlin and Tübingen. All the early research on the photoelectric effect had been German, and Elster and Geitel had provided these two German observatories with their cells for testing, as well as advice and assistance for their use. The astronomers were Paul Guthnick (1879–1947) in Berlin and Hans Rosenberg (1879–1940) and Edgar Meyer in Tübingen. Apparently each group was initially unaware of the others experiments.

Meanwhile Jakob Kunz joined the Physics Department at the University of Illinois in 1911. He was a Swiss-born physicist who had been educated in Britain and Germany, and he suggested to Stebbins that a photoelectric cell should be tested for stellar photometry. Stebbins was able to visit the Berlin Observatory in 1912 while on sabbatical leave in Europe. He met Guthnick there who was then installing his first photoelectric apparatus. Kunz meanwhile proceeded to manufacture potassium hydride (KH) cells of a similar type to those of Elster and Geitel, and soon afterwards Kunz's student at Illinois, J. G. Kemp, was able to demonstrate more than a hundredfold increase in the sensitivity of the potassium hydride cells over those with metallic potassium cathodes [26]. He claimed that such a cell was able to detect a candle at 2.7 miles without the aid of a telescope, and concluded: 'This indicates that it is highly probable that a photoelectric cell could be used in astrophotometric work'. As a result a Kunz cell was tested on the Illinois telescope in December 1912 while Stebbins was still in Europe. Thus all three groups embarked on photoelectric investigations with very similar apparatus at about the same time.

The minute photocurrents produced by the early photoelectric cells were too small to be detected by a galvanometer. All the early observers therefore chose a sensitive string electrometer. In this instrument a fine gilded quartz or platinum wire connected to the cell's anode was charged by the photocurrent. The wire was under mechanical tension and was deflected in an applied electric field by an amount depending on the acquired charge, and which was observable in a microscope. Rosenberg reported being readily able to measure currents as small as 10^{-13} amps with this device, from the rate of deflection of the wire [27]. The string electrometers had to be in close proximity to the cells. They were extremely delicate, often showed troublesome zero-point drifts, and they only worked in a vertical orientation, necessitating their suspension from gimbals immediately below the cell housing at the end of a telescope.

5.3.1   Guthnick's photometry in Berlin

Guthnick's first experiments in 1912 were published in the annual report of the Berlin Observatory for that year [28]:

> Although the cell was made in a hurry and only as a prototype, and had only a low sensitivity, I was nevertheless successful in getting without difficulty a clear photoeffect from bright stars when the cell was used on the 12-inch refractor. The relative signals were determined by measuring the charge produced [with an electrometer], because suitable resistances were lacking. The results obtained showed that the photoelectric brightness of α Lyrae was very nearly three times greater than that of α Cygni, which ... also approximately corresponds to the visual brightness ratio.

Fig. 5.7   Paul Guthnick.

A fuller description of Guthnick's work was given in a paper in December 1913 after observations had been resumed in July of that year [29]. A commercially produced Elster and Geitel sodium cell from the Brunswick firm of Günther and Tegetmeyer (see [30]) was the main detector, and a study was made of the short-period (4.6 hours) low-amplitude (only 0^m086) early B-type variable star, β Cephei, for which Edwin Frost at Yerkes Observatory had earlier discovered radial-velocity variations. This was the first photometry of any star of this interesting class of pulsating variables, which Guthnick, however, incorrectly classified as a cluster variable (RR Lyrae star).

In the summer of 1913 the Berlin Observatory moved to a new site at Babelsberg on the outskirts of the city, and the photoelectric programme on the 30-cm Repsold refractor was continued there with, from early 1914, the collaboration of Richard Prager (1883–1945). During the years of the Great War a major photoelectric observing programme on variable stars was undertaken at this well-equipped new institution [31, 32]. The photometric properties of potassium, sodium, caesium and rubidium cells were investigated, including their wavelength sensitivities and linearity of response to light. The last two elements gave photocathodes that responded to yellow-red light as well as to the blue and violet.

All these cells were filled with argon at a low pressure, as it was found that such an inert gas greatly increased the sensitivity as a result of collisional ionization in the gas, which in effect amplified the photocurrent. The sodium cell was chosen for the principal observations, because it had

Fig. 5.8   Richard Prager.

the highest sensitivity. The voltage between cathode and anode was 100 volts. Atmospheric extinction was taken into account in the photometric reductions, including its dependence on stellar spectral type, which for these unfiltered rather broad-band observations was quite a marked effect.

In 1933 Guthnick recalled the pioneering days of photoelectric photometry at Berlin:

> In the summer of 1932 it was twenty years that had elapsed since the first attempts at photoelectric photometry, which were carried out at the old Berlin Observatory at Enckeplatz. At that time the writer of these lines made the first measurements on a 31-cm refractor using a home-made and highly primitive photoelectric apparatus. The cell, electrometer and battery had been borrowed from physicist colleagues. I was immensely pleased when I obtained from the measurements the correct value for the brightness ratio of α Lyrae to α Cygni, which was already precisely known from other work. This favourable result, together with the freely offered advice from the very distinguished physicists, Elster and Geitel, for the development of the photoelectric techniques, led to the construction of the first photoelectric stellar photometer at the observatory. This was used to investigate the short

Fig. 5.9   Guthnick and Prager's photoelectric photometer on the 30-cm refractor at Berlin-Babelsberg.

period spectroscopic binary star β Cephei [actually a pulsating star in a spectroscopic binary system] during the following summer at Neubabelsberg, to where the observatory had in the meantime been moved. This star was the first variable to be discovered by photoelectric means ... The Babelsberg photoelectric photometer has in its essential features served as a pattern to be copied not only by later Neubabelsberg photoelectric photometers, but also since then by a whole series of instruments installed at American and European observatories [33].

From 1916 Guthnick and Prager experimented with colour filter photometry by inserting a yellow filter into the beam. They thereby defined a colour index as the difference in the apparent magnitudes so obtained with and without the filter. The results from the colour index showed a clear correlation with Harvard spectral type, although the scatter was large [32].

By the end of 1917 nearly 67 000 photoelectric measurements had been obtained on about fifty stars and planets. The mean error for the magnitude difference of a variable and comparison star based on a set of consecutive measurements was claimed to be about $0^{m}\!.005$ in the best cases [32]. This was the random probable error within one night, but undoubtedly much larger systematic errors occurred from night to night, and spurious variability was therefore reported for several stars. Nevertheless five periodic light curves were obtained for several real variables, notably for β Cephei and for the peculiar A-type star, α Canum Venaticorum.

One of the stars studied by Guthnick was the first magnitude Nova Aquilae of 1918. The star was monitored for over three months to obtain the first photoelectric light curve for a nova, together with the colour-index curve using the yellow filter [34]. In addition colour indices for 67 stars were presented to recalibrate the relation between colour index and spectral type.

5.3.2   Later photoelectric work at Berlin-Babelsberg

The pioneering work in photoelectric colour-index photometry at Berlin-Babelsberg was developed further by Kurt Bottlinger (1888–1934), who had joined the observatory staff shortly after the war. From 1920–22 Bottlinger, with the collaboration of Guthnick, introduced a blue glass filter in addition to the yellow one, and thereby obtained two-filter colour indices for 459 stars using a potassium hydride cell [35]. The maxima of the filters' transmission functions were at about 440 and 460 nm, and the bands were some 60 nm wide (full width half-maximum). The probable error of an individual colour index was stated to be $0^{m}\!.013$. These were the first two-filter photoelectric colour indices in the literature, although colours

Fig. 5.10   Diagram of Guthnick and Prager photometer, Berlin, 1915.

Fig. 5.11 Photoelectric light curve for β Cephei obtained by Guthnick and Prager in Berlin, 1917.

based on a combination of photographic and visual measurements (e.g. by Karl Schwarzschild [36] and by Edward King [37]) or on photographic and photovisual photometry [38] were already familiar to astronomers. Because of the small wavelength baseline of Bottlinger's photometric system, he was unable to observe the colour difference between late-type giant and dwarf stars.

At this time the spectral and photometric differences between stars of different luminosity was a very topical subject. Walter Adams (1876–1956) at Mt Wilson, for example, pointed out that low proper motion stars (mainly more distant giants) of a given spectral type were generally redder than those of higher proper motion (mainly nearby dwarfs) [39]. There were two possible solutions, as J. C. Kapteyn explained: either the colour difference was due to the selective absorption of starlight in interstellar space, making the more distant giant stars redder, or it was an intrinsic difference between stars of different luminosity [40].

What Bottlinger did show from his colour indices was that in the diagram plotting colour index against spectral type, some stars were abnormally red. He defined a colour excess E as the increase in colour index for these stars above the majority of stars of the same spectral type. He showed that the few stars with large colour excesses were all supergiants with very small proper motions and concentrated near the plane of the Milky Way. However, not all supergiants were abnormally reddened.

This was one of the early indications for the presence of an absorbing medium distributed through space, though especially in the galactic plane. Bottlinger's work was not the earliest to suggest interstellar reddening of starlight. But in 1923 his photoelectric filter photometry was giving the most reliable stellar colours then available. His photometric data lent themselves readily to astrophysical interpretation, and the ancient science of stellar photometry became a major astrophysical tool only from about this time.

Bottlinger's pioneering work on stellar colour indices was extended by Wilhelm Becker (b. 1907) at Berlin-Babelsberg in 1930–31. His photometer with a KH photocell on the 31-cm refractor was practically identical to Bottlinger's, except that a different yellow glass filter was used and the photocell was new. The effective wavelengths of his blue and yellow passbands were at 425 and 475 nm.

Becker observed a further 356 stars with this equipment, covering a wide range of spectral types. He also rereduced with new extinction coefficients the stars observed by Bottlinger. Of these, 79 were in common to both observers, enabling Becker to derive the relationship between the colour indices on the two systems. His final catalogue presented colour indices for 738 stars on this revised Berlin-Babelsberg system from observations by both observers [41].

An analysis of these data followed in 1935 [42]. The main results were a calibration of the colour indices to obtain colour temperatures, which were nevertheless seriously in error for early-type stars because of the assumption that such objects radiate like black bodies. (The large departure in stellar spectra from the Planck energy distribution of black bodies, due to the Balmer jump of atomic hydrogen absorption, was only fully realized during the 1930s). Becker also investigated the dependence of colour index on spectral type, and he defined a colour excess which depended on luminosity. The higher luminosity early-type stars were bluer, while those of later spectral type were redder than the corresponding low luminosity objects. The former effect is due to the removal of blue and ultraviolet flux by the strong wings of Balmer series hydrogen lines of dwarf stars, while the colour difference for the cool stars is caused by a temperature difference between giants and dwarfs. In addition Becker further explored the phenomenon of selective interstellar absorption and deduced a mean reddening for distant B stars in the galactic plane of 0^m095 per 1000 parsecs on his colour system.

Bottlinger's photometric programme at Babelsberg was continued by Miss Margarethe Güssow, who obtained photoelectric colour indices for 94 stars of all spectral types from 1931–35 [43]. Her filters were not the same as used by Becker. The effective wavelengths of her passbands were at 420 and 449 nm, resulting in an index with an uncomfortably short wavelength baseline.

5.3.3   Rosenberg at Tübingen

Hans Rosenberg with Edgar Meyer at Tübingen also began photoelectric experiments in 1912. Their potassium hydride cell was obtained directly from Elster and Geitel and used on the 13-cm refractor of the university's Oesterberg Observatory at Tübingen. The first results were briefly reported to the August 1913 meeting of the Astronomische Gesellschaft in Hamburg, at which Stebbins also participated. Measurable photocurrents were obtained for stars of magnitude 5 to 6 using a string electrometer [44]. An accuracy of 3 or 4 thousandths of a magnitude was claimed to be feasible.

Although the tests with the Tübingen photometer were fully described, no quantitative data were reported. During the war years that followed, the astronomical work at Tübingen was greatly curtailed. It was not until 1920 that Rosenberg was able to report once again putting considerable effort into his photoelectric equipment. His investigations at this time were

Fig. 5.12   The Tübingen photometer of Hans Rosenberg.

directed into finding a more sensitive method of detecting photoelectric currents of around 10^{-14} amps. For this he experimented with a d.c. amplifier comprising a thermionic triode valve which gave an amplification of over 600 000.

The main advantage of the new method consisted in the use of a galvanometer instead of an electrometer, the latter being difficult to handle on the moving end of a telescope. With such a needle galvanometer, Rosenberg was able to measure the photocurrents from a fourth magnitude star [45].

The significance of these early experiments was not to be realized for over a decade, when in 1932 Albert Whitford at the Washburn Observatory, Wisconsin, also used a d.c. thermionic amplifier, which finally brought about the demise of the electrometer method in astronomical photometry – see section 5.3.4.

In spite of his noteworthy contribution of introducing the technique of thermionic amplification into astronomical photometry, Rosenberg still undertook no major observational programmes with his photometer. His singular lack of observational results did not go unnoticed in Berlin, for Guthnick remarked that: 'It is much to be regretted that extended observational stellar data have never been obtained with this instrument' [33].

The Tübingen photoelectric equipment was not fully described until 1929 when Rosenberg contributed a review article to the *Handbuch der Astrophysik* on photoelectric photometry [27]. This was the most thorough review of the instrumental aspects of the subject at that time, and concentrated especially on the manufacture and properties of photoelectric cells and the techniques of measuring very small photoelectric currents.

The Tübingen programme had ended by 1933 when Rosenberg migrated to the United States, where he accepted a position at the University of Chicago. In 1938 he was appointed director of the University Observatory in Istanbul, where he died in 1940.

5.3.4   Joel Stebbins and photoelectric photometry at Illinois and Wisconsin

With Stebbins temporarily in Europe during 1912 to 1913, the work of putting a photoelectric cell to use for astrophotometry at Illinois, in place of the earlier used photoconductive cells, fell to Jakob Kunz and his colleague W. F. Schulz. The cells were made at Urbana in the university's Physics Department, but according to the Elster and Geitel prescription. The photocathodes were potassium hydride, and the cells were filled with helium to increase the photocurrents by collisional ionization at cell voltages of about 300 V. The first tests in December 1912 gave a measurable current for Capella on the 12-inch telescope [46]. The successful detection of Arcturus followed in April.

Stebbins described these early days of photoelectric photometry in a later review:

> It was in the autumn of 1911 that Dr. Jakob Kunz, who had joined the Physics Department at Illinois, suggested that we might use a

photoelectric cell instead of the selenium cell in stellar photometry. At that time I knew very little about photoelectric cells, but Kunz promised to make one in a week or so. The week grew into months and then into a year, and then in 1912–13 I spent a sabbatical leave in Europe. The first summer, I visited Guthnick at the old observatory in Berlin, where he was installing a photoelectric cell on the telescope. The following year, at the Hamburg meeting of the Astronomische Gesellschaft, Rosenberg reported on some similar experiments by Meyer and himself at Tübingen. In the meantime Kunz and W. F. Schulz were carrying on at Illinois, and their results were published by Schulz in what I believe was the first paper showing results from observations of stars. The work of Guthnick, Meyer, and Rosenberg, and Kunz and Schulz was all independent, and in fact connected with that of Elster and Geitel, who constructed cells from the alkali metals and made many applications beginning in the early 'nineties [11].

Stebbins immediately collaborated with Kunz on his return to Illinois. His main work was the photoelectric photometry of known spectroscopic binary stars to detect light variations, possibly due to eclipses. The photometer made use of cells made by Kunz, those with hydrides of potassium, sodium, caesium and rubidium all being tested, but only the first of these was used for regular observing [47, 48]. The wavelength dependence of the response of different photocathodes of various Kunz cells was investigated by T. Shinomiya in the Physical Laboratory at Illinois [49] as well as by Eleanor Frances Seiler [50]. The rubidium cells had a response extending into the green region to about 540 nm, whereas potassium and sodium cells were limited to the blue and violet parts of the spectrum. Innovations adopted at Illinois were the use of an earthed platinum guard ring fused into the glass envelope around the cathode [47], and the change from glass to quartz envelopes for the cells from 1916 [51, 52]. Both of these developments greatly decreased the dark current, arising from electrical leakage between the electrodes through the cell envelope in the absence of illumination.

In all this work Kunz was the laboratory physicist and Stebbins the astronomer, and a productive collaboration between the two was forged. It was a collaboration which was to last a quarter of a century, until Kunz's death in 1939. In particular Kunz continued to supply Stebbins (as well as other American photometrists) with photocells for astronomical photometry long after Stebbins had left Illinois for Wisconsin. Kunz described the details of his methods of cell production in articles published in 1916 and 1917 [53, 54].

In the summer of 1915 Stebbins took his photometer to the 12-inch Lick refractor, where he obtained a light curve for β Lyrae in the superior photometric conditions of that site. The cells were more sensitive than those used earlier, enabling fifth magnitude to be reached with one per cent precision or better [48, 51]. The visit to Lick was the first of regular summer observing trips by Stebbins to California, which included ten summer observing runs at Mt Wilson on the 60- and 100-inch telescopes up to 1940 [11].

From 1920 a series of important papers appeared in the *Astrophysical Journal* in which the light curves of eclipsing binaries were presented with hitherto unattainable precision, including papers on λ Tauri [52], a new photoelectric study of Algol [55] and of the ellipsoidal variable b Persei [56]. This last star had a light curve amplitude of only $0^{m}06$, and Stebbins ascribed the variations not to eclipses but to the change in surface brightness of a tidally distorted star in a close binary.

At this time Charles Clayton Wylie took an active part in the photoelectric observations of variable stars under the supervision of Stebbins. Wylie's light curve for σ Aquilae showed it also to be an eclipsing system with ellipsoidal variations due to tidal distortion occurring outside eclipse [57]. Wylie also produced a definitive photoelectric light curve for the pulsating Cepheid variable η Aquilae [58].

Stebbins became director of the Washburn Observatory in Wisconsin in 1922 and he continued his photoelectric work there on the 15.6-inch refractor. A new photometer was built in 1922 with a Kunz cell and string electrometer for this telescope, although later, in 1927, a Lindemann electrometer replaced the very delicate string instrument [11]. The Lindemann electrometer had the advantages of being more robust and being usable in any orientation on a moving telescope – see [59] and section 5.4.1.

The new Washburn photometer was in use from 1923. Stebbins continued to work on eclipsing binaries and other variable stars. His techniques and scientific programme in the earlier Washburn years were fully described in 1928 [60]. Light curves for further eclipsing binaries were presented in this paper. Stebbins also gave a compilation of 29 certain eclipsing variables, of which 15 had been discovered in the course of his photometric programme and a further 5 by Guthnick in Berlin. Only one was discovered photographically.

On the subject of the sensitivity and precision of his photometry, Stebbins noted a hundredfold increase in the sensitivity of his photoelectric equipment over the photoconductive selenium cell of 1910, but in this time the probable errors of the photometry decreased from $0^{m}006$ to $0^{m}003$, only by a factor of two:

> It is true that the present more accurate measures are secured more quickly and easily than the old ones, but a probable error of one or two thousandths of a magnitude is still beyond reach... So long as we observe stars consecutively rather than simultaneously we shall be at

Fig. 5.13   Stebbins' photoelectric photometer at Wisconsin, c. 1928.

Fig. 5.14   Kunz quartz envelope potassium hydride photocell, 1928.

Fig. 5.15   Washburn Observatory staff, Madison, 1935. (l. to r.: rear, Ed Burnett (student technician), G.E. Kron, A.E. Whitford, front, C.M. Huffer, departmental secretary, J. Stebbins.)

the mercy of the atmosphere, and at an ordinary station this is an obstacle which can not be well overcome [60].

5.3.5   Wisconsin photoelectric photometry in the 1930s

The 1930s saw several major changes in the technique of photo-electric photometry as well as new research directions for Stebbins' group at the Washburn Observatory. When Albert Whitford (b. 1905) joined the observatory in 1931, he recalled that his

> ... task as research assistant was to carry forward Stebbins' long campaign to find something better than the electrometer. Vacuum tube amplification appeared to be a promising approach. Amplifier tubes ... had been developed in industrial laboratories. Yet for reasons then not understood, when the tube was connected to a photoelectric cell

Fig. 5.16 Albert Whitford, c. 1938.

there were fluctuations in the output many times larger than the theoretical expectations. I found the source to be cosmic-ray-generated ions in the ambient air; some of these were being collected on the lead from the photoelectric cell to the amplifier tube. Mounting the cell and the tube in a vacuum took away the air, and there was a marked reduction in the fluctuations. A test on the Washburn telescope in the spring of 1932 showed that stars of magnitude 9.0 were now measurable. The system soon went into regular use on the observing programmes then in progress [61].

Whitford thus resumed the experiments in thermionic amplification in astronomical photometry that Rosenberg had initiated more than a decade earlier – see section 5.3.3. For this he used a commercial FP-54 Pliotron tube for his d.c. amplifier. The output was recorded by a simple galvanometer in a stable location off the telescope. Currents as small as 1.1×10^{-16} amps could be detected with the new amplifier and galvanometer, which represented a gain of 2 200 000 times [62]. On the 100-inch at Mt Wilson 16th magnitude stars could now be reached, some 25 times fainter than was possible with the electrometer in use before 1931.

Fig. 5.17   Photocell with thermionic amplifier, designed by Whitford, 1932.

Going to fainter stars and using thermionic amplification inevitably introduced more noise. Harold Weaver (b. 1917) discussed noise sources in the photometry of the 1930s. Noise due to the atmospheric 'seeing' and extinction still dominated for bright stars, but photon (shot) noise, amplifier noise and dark current in the cell all became relatively more important for fainter stars [63].

Gerald Kron at Lick, one of those who adopted the Whitford techniques for his own photometry, commented in 1940 on the advantages of d.c. amplification:

> The introduction of the low-grid-current "Pliotron" type of vacuum tube made it possible to remove the mechanically delicate parts of the equipment from the telescope itself, and furthermore made practical the removal of air from the vicinity of the sensitive photocell circuit. The use of direct-current amplification with photocell and amplifying tube in a vacuum has resulted in a more stable, more sensitive, and more reliable photometer. Readings have been changed from a measurement of a rate by means of a stop watch into the more straightforward measurement of a distance, namely the galvanometer deflection. The galvanometer itself, a delicate current-measuring device in the plate circuit of the amplifying tube, can if necessary, be mounted at some distance from the telescope, and may therefore be used under optimum conditions. With such a device at his disposal, the astronomer can, under certain conditions, measure stellar brightnesses with an accuracy limited by the quality of the "seeing" alone [64].

Whitford also described the Kunz potassium hydride cells, which were still in use at Washburn during the 1930s:

> All of the potassium hydride cells used by Stebbins had been made by Jakob Kunz in the physics laboratory at the University of Illinois. I witnessed the process in the late 1930s; it was still an art, dependent on Kunz's instinct and skill. These cells were prized because of their extremely low dark current. Though considered very sensitive at the time, they were far short of the ultimate. Their quantum efficiency was about 1% at their peak response in the blue†, and the bandwidth, down to 10% of peak, was 1300 Å [61].

An important photometric programme was commenced by Stebbins in 1926 to observe 190 red giant stars of spectral type M with Charles Morse Huffer (1894–1981), another of Stebbins' younger collaborators at Wisconsin [65, 66]. This work showed for the first time that a large proportion of these objects were small amplitude irregular variables, unlike the K-type giants, which tended to be constant in light. The possibility that all M giant stars exhibit such light fluctuations on time scales of several months was raised.

---

† The printed version erroneously gave a figure of 10%.

From the early 1930s Huffer became Stebbins' main collaborator on the application of photoelectric photometry to the study of interstellar reddening, or 'space' reddening as it was then known. At the time this was one of the most intensely researched and topical subjects in astronomy, and the photoelectric photometer proved to be an indispensable tool for its investigation.

In 1933 Stebbins had shown that the globular star clusters lying within 10° of the galactic equator were substantially redder than those at higher galactic latitudes [67]. For this work two filters were used in the photometer on the 100-inch telescope at Mt Wilson. The result clearly indicated the power of photoelectric colour indices for studies of the interstellar material presumed to cause the reddening.

The two filters used by Stebbins gave passbands with effective wavelengths at 426 and 477 nm, practically the same as employed by Becker in Berlin, who was researching similar problems at this same time. One of the problems of filter photometry with the potassium hydride cell was to have a large enough wavelength baseline to derive a meaningful colour index. In the Washburn and Berlin instruments the passbands of the two filters were necessarily at the short and long wavelength edges of the photocathode response, whose total useful range was from about 380 to 500 nm. The limiting magnitude was about 12.5 on the 100-inch telescope, about a magnitude brighter than when no filters were used.

After the work on globular cluster colours, a major programme was started by Stebbins and Huffer on the colours of B stars in the Galaxy. In 1930 Robert Trumpler (1886–1956) at Lick Observatory had found evidence for a substantial space absorption of the light from galactic star clusters, from observations of the angular sizes of the clusters and of the magnitudes and spectral types of the stars they contain [68] – see section 8.6.1. Although the presence of dark absorbing matter in interstellar space had long been suspected, it was Trumpler's work which became the catalyst for the intense interest that this subject aroused among astronomers. Discussions between Stebbins and Trumpler led to the Wisconsin programme on the colours of B stars, which were much the best type of object for studies of space reddening.

In addition, a similar though less extensive programme was already underway at Yerkes Observatory. This was undertaken by Christian Elvey (1899–1972) [69] using the photoelectric photometer that Stebbins had designed for the 40-inch telescope of that observatory [70] – see section 5.4.3. Stebbins and Huffer observed the colours of 733 B-type stars brighter than $m = 7.5$ on the 15-inch Wisconsin telescope [71]. From a study of the colour excesses of reddened stars, they were able to confirm the presence of a selectively absorbing interstellar material in the plane of the Galaxy. Moreover the results indicated that the material was distributed irregularly throughout the plane, and not in a uniform stratum.

This work by Stebbins and Huffer also showed that the most distant reddened B stars observed were fainter by about 2 magnitudes as a result of interstellar absorption, and hence some 2.5 times nearer than previously believed. The same reasoning could be applied to the globular clusters, from which Stebbins and Whitford were able to reduce the implied overall dimensions of the Galaxy from some 60 000 parsecs in diameter to only half this figure [72]. In a stroke the discrepancy between the size of our Galaxy and the great spiral in Andromeda had disappeared.

The photoelectric observations of B stars to study space reddening and absorption as well as the programme on diffuse objects, especially galaxies, were continued by Stebbins, Huffer and Whitford during the 1930s and '40s – see section 5.5.2. Although the brilliant results that came from the Wisconsin Observatory were based entirely on photoelectric work, it is interesting that Stebbins recognized that photographic photometry could have produced the same conclusions:

> In fact we do not quite understand why the results in the present paper were not all secured by photography long ago; but we have been expecting photography to put us out of business ever since we began using the photoelectric cell [71].

His assessment of the potential of photoelectric photometry proved to be far too modest. The rapid advances in photoelectric and electronic instrumentation in the 1930s and '40s, together with the advantages of high quantum efficiency and linearity of response, were the factors contributing not to the total demise of photographic work, but at least to its partial eclipse. A review article by DeVorkin discusses the rise in photoelectric photometry after the war [73].

5.4   Some further pioneers of the photoelectric cell

Very few astronomers ventured into photoelectric stellar photometry before 1930, and only Guthnick and Stebbins can be said to have had outstanding success. As early as 1913 Guthnick commented on the apparent reluctance of astronomers to undertake photoelectric observations, in spite of the offer of both tubes and assistance from Elster and Geitel:

> The apparently low level of interest which has been shown by the astronomical community towards the new method up until the most

recent times can indeed only be explained by the fact that the overwhelming physical and technical difficulties have scared non-physicists away, or at least made it appear that success seemed questionable [29].

Hans Rosenberg echoed similar thoughts in his review on photoelectric photometry in 1929:

> The astrophysicist who, as a consequence of his special astronomical training, is usually not sufficiently familiar with the handling of the most sensitive galvanometers and electrometers, therefore sees himself as compelled to seek out the necessary knowledge and skills from a widely scattered and often difficult to comprehend literature, with which he is only slightly familiar. A further difficulty is found in the fact that ready to use photoelectric instruments for astrophysical purposes are at present not commercially available. Instead the user is frequently forced to see to the construction of the necessary instruments himself, and once again he will find himself unaccustomed to this work [27].

After 1930 a dozen or so more observatories ventured into the new field of photoelectric work, but with very mixed fortunes. The extreme delicacy of the instrumentation, its liability of being disturbed by moisture or vibration and the idiosyncrasies of each individual photoelectric cell were factors mitigating against productive research. Until the Second World War, a training in observational astronomy had entailed an expertise in optics and mechanics for the design and use of astronomical instruments. Detector technology equated largely with photography. The astrophysical observatory of the early twentieth century rarely required even to use electricity (except for the occasional spark or discharge for spectroscopic work), let alone electronics.

Between 1922 and 1938 six General Assemblies of the International Astronomical Union took place. The reports of Commission 25 for Photometry in the transactions for these meetings are full of the tedious complexities of photographic photometry, of the zero-point of magnitude scales and systematic errors in the North Polar Sequence. A brief mention of photoelectric solar spectrophotometry by T. Dunham (1897–1984) occurs in the 1938 Stockholm transactions (see [74]) as well as a passing reference to John Hall's photoelectric spectrophotometry of stars with the new Cs-O-Ag red- and infrared-sensitive photocathode [74].

For some three decades it was Stebbins' group at Illinois and then Wisconsin that showed the way for photoelectric research. Of those observatories that endeavoured to initiate photoelectric programmes in the 1930s (see section 5.6), relatively few succeeded to the point of providing the Wisconsin group with serious competition. Nevertheless several observers new to the field did produce useful astronomical results, and this section describes their achievements in the new world of astronomical electronics.

5.4.1   The Lindemanns

Adolf Lindemann (1846–1931) was born in Germany but he moved to Britain after the Franco-Prussian War, eventually becoming a British citizen. He settled at Sidmouth in Devon in 1884, where he established his private Sidholme Observatory. He was an electrical engineer of independent means, and he equipped his observatory with instruments he himself had designed and built. Lindemann's son was Professor Frederick Lindemann (1886–1957), who from 1919 was professor of physics at the University of Oxford. Later he became Lord Cherwell and scientific advisor to Churchill's wartime cabinet. From this remarkable father-son combination, with talents in electrical engineering, physics, machine-shop construction and astronomy, came one of the most advanced astronomical photoelectric photometers of the early decades of this century.

The first version of the Lindemann photometer was completed in 1918 and tested from the end of that year to observe bright stars on a 6-inch telescope [75]. The potassium hydride cell was home-made and filled with helium to about 0.75-mm pressure to enhance the photocurrent by collisional ionization. The voltage used was 150 V. On the 6-inch telescope the current was 10^{-11} amps from a zero magnitude star. The apparatus differed in one respect from its predecessors, in that the string electrometer was no longer suspended from gimbals but attached rigidly to the cell-box. The whole assembly was rotatable about the telescope's principal axis so that the string's displacement when charged was always in a horizontal direction.

Details of the observing procedure are interesting for the care that clearly had to be exercised:

> Measurements were usually carried out in the following manner. All connections were made, and the instrument allowed to remain in the dark for about an hour. There was often a considerable shift of the zero for the first half hour, possibly owing to induction from charges, which gradually accumulated on the glass cell walls, or more probably due to the settling down of the accumulators, which were sometimes used. The cell was then tested for leak, *i.e.* the electrometer observed for, say, ten minutes. The leak in ten minutes was seldom more than one division, *i.e.* less than 0.02 volt or about $4 \cdot 10^{-16}$ amperes.
>
> The telescope was now set on the desired object, the electrometer levelled, the mirror put into position for observing through the eyepiece, and the iris closed until all extraneous light was cut off. The mirror was then turned until the light could reach the cell and a

stop-watch started. After an appropriate interval, depending on the
luminosity of the object to be measured, the light was again cut off by
turning the mirror and the stop-watch stopped. The electrometer was
levelled and read and the fibre earthed and read, the clock being
thrown out of gear if this operation took more than a minute or so.
The standard voltage was now switched on and the electrometer read,
which completed the measurement [76].

In this paper only three stars were measured (Sirius, β And, Polaris)
relative to Capella. But the physical insights (presumably due to Frederick)
into the future potential of photoelectric photometry were remarkable. These
included the possibility of measuring stellar temperatures if magnitudes with
both potassium hydride (effective wavelength 440 nm) and caesium hydride
(550 nm) cells could be made to derive a 'caesium minus potassium' colour
index, which in turn was to be calibrated theoretically against a black-body
spectrum. For spiral 'nebulae' or galaxies, their magnitude was an indication
of their stellar content provided the distance was known. Measurements
were accordingly made on the Andromeda nebula. The blue magnitude
obtained was 3.33 (within a diameter of 40 arc minutes), from which the
Lindemanns estimated a distance of 350 kpc on the assumption of 10^{10} stars.
They concluded: 'It is clear that there is nothing inconsistent, therefore, in
regarding this nebula as a galaxy very similar to our own' [76]. Although
a factor of two too small, the distance agreed quite well with that derived
by Hubble in 1925 from the photographic magnitudes of Cepheid variables
[77], which finally conclusively established the extragalactic nature of the
nebulae.

Other proposed uses for the photometer in this visionary paper were
the surface photometry of comets, planets, the solar corona, the zodiacal
light, sunspots, aurorae and the day-time sky, with many further perceptive
insights into the physics involved.

In 1924 the Lindemanns designed a new type of quadrant electrometer
explicitly for use with the astronomical photometer, in that its operation was
independent of orientation [59]. The Lindemann electrometer carried a fine
needle mounted at right angles to a torsion fibre. The needle was deflected
when charged by photoelectrons in an electric field produced between the
quadrant plates. The essential innovation was to fix the torsion fibre (4
cm long, 4 μm thick) at both ends, rather than simply suspend it, as in
earlier laboratory versions of the instrument. The new electrometer was
miniaturized, robust and very sensitive, being able to measure charging
rates down to 10^{-14} amps. It was one of the principal innovations in a
new photoelectric photometer at Sidmouth in 1926 [78], and became the

Fig. 5.18 Lindemann photometer, 1926.

standard for current detection at other observatories, including Washburn in 1927.

Other improvements were incorporated into the new photometer, including the provision for monochromatic filters, for an electrically operated shutter in front of the cell and for a cell-box containing three different photocells, light being directed to any one of them by means of a rotatable mirror, with the intention of making multicolour photometry a possibility. No observations were reported with this device, yet it was undoubtedly the most advanced astronomical photoelectric photometer of its day. It is interesting to note that Guthnick also attempted to build a multicolour photometer comprising four alkali cells with sodium, potassium, rubidium and caesium photocathodes, which were sensitive to increasingly longer wavelengths. However, it too was never successfully used for observational work [33].

5.4.2   Edith Cummings at Lick

A photoelectric photometer was made for the 12-inch refractor at the Lick Observatory by Edith Cummings in 1920, under the direction of Elmer Dershem at Berkeley, who had collaborated earlier with Stebbins [79]. The instrument was therefore very similar to that used by Stebbins at Illinois. A potassium-hydride argon-filled photocell with a quartz envelope was provided by Jakob Kunz, and a platinum wire string electrometer was built for the project. As in most earlier photometers, the Lick photometer was suspended from gimbals to preserve its vertical orientation [80].

Edith Cummings worked on this project as a Lick fellow at the University of California at Berkeley from 1919 until her doctoral graduation in 1922. She made observations with the new photometer during 1920 and 1921. Initially 13 B stars in the Pleiades were observed to test the response of the instrument and to compare the results with the photographic magnitudes of these stars. The estimated probable error of one observation was 0^m012. The main observing programme was devoted to the short-period variable star β Cephei, the same object which Guthnick and Prager had observed with their photometer in Berlin in 1913–14. The new Lick observations were made over 16 nights from June to September 1921 and were used to construct a new light curve. This was found to have changed shape significantly from that published earlier in Berlin, with a clearly defined secondary hump during rising light, whereas only weak indications of such a feature were present before.

At this time β Cephei was generally classified along with δ Cephei as a member of the Cepheid variables, in spite of its early-type (B1) spectrum. Cepheids were then usually thought to be binary stars. Miss Cummings was able to demonstrate both the dissimilarity of the light curve to those of Cepheids and, using in addition published radial-velocity observations, that the binary hypothesis for this star was an implausible explanation for the light variations [80].

The photometer box of this early Lick photometer was used again by Edward Fath when he visited Lick in 1931, but in conjunction with the Lindemann electrometer and a new Kunz photoelectric cell from the Goodsell Observatory [81] – see section 5.4.5.

5.4.3 The Yerkes photometer

A photoelectric photometer was completed for the Yerkes Observatory in 1929. The new instrument was constructed at Madison according to the design of Stebbins, and incorporated a Kunz potassium hydride quartz cell, a Lindemann quadrant electrometer and a provision for coloured glass filters [70]. Stebbins himself installed the Yerkes photometer on the 40-inch refractor and was able to reach to about ninth magnitude. However, the cells varied widely in performance, with the result that this figure was critically dependent on the particular cell used. Indeed, the 15-inch telescope and its photometer at Madison initially outperformed the new Yerkes photometer on the 40-inch telescope because of an inferior cell in the latter instrument.

Christian Elvey used the Yerkes photometer on the 40-inch telescope to obtain the colour indices of 153 early-type stars [69]. The filters he used had effective wavelengths of 385 and 510 nm, which are near the extreme limits of the response of the potassium hydride photocathode. This work was the first photoelectric filter photometry at any American observatory, and continued the techniques developed by Bottlinger at Potsdam a decade earlier. In his investigation, Elvey plotted colour index against spectral type and found a considerable scatter in the colours for objects of the same type. He ascribed this partly to the intrinsic differences in the stars themselves, as well as to the selective interstellar absorption by matter lying between the stars, to which Trumpler had recently drawn attention [68]. The intrinsic differences he correctly interpreted as the result of the changes in the wings of the hydrogen Balmer lines as one goes from dwarf to giant then to supergiant stars. The last named were known to have the weakest wings (see for example papers by Cecilia Payne [82] and by Adams and Joy [83]) which therefore altered the colour index the least from the theoretical value applicable to a black-body radiator. It was just these bright supergiant stars, such as α Cygni (Deneb) and β Orionis (Rigel), that had the smallest observed colour excesses. The excess was defined as the difference between the observed colour and the theoretical colour of a black body whose temperature corresponded with the star's spectral type, for which Elvey used the latest calibration of spectral type with stellar temperature.

This early work by Elvey using filters in conjunction with a photoelectric cell was soon taken up by Stebbins and Huffer in Wisconsin – see

Fig. 5.19   Yerkes photometer of Stebbins and Elvey, 1931.

section 5.3.4. Elvey, however, was able to use a longer wavelength baseline than either Stebbins and Huffer or Bottlinger, because his large telescope overcame the relative cell inefficiency at wavelengths both shortwards and longwards of the photocathode's peak efficiency (at 460 nm). Thus the slope of the Yerkes colour index scale was 3.2 times that derived by Bottlinger, which made the Yerkes results less influenced by the random errors of the colour determinations.

In a second paper on early-type reddened stars, Elvey and T. G. Mehlin obtained data for 49 stars in Cepheus where extensive visual obscuration by dust was evident [84]. Some of the stars observed were as faint as the ninth magnitude, and these fainter ones also tended to be those with the larger colour excess, as might be expected. Yet the colour excesses of these objects reddened by interstellar dust showed no correlation with the strengths of the interstellar calcium K line in their spectra, which is due to calcium ions in the interstellar gas. Hence Elvey and Mehlin concluded that 'the material producing selective scattering of the star's light is not coexistent with the calcium atoms' [84].

5.4.4   Kron's photometer at Lick

Gerald Kron (b. 1913), one of the great pioneers of photoelectric photometry, began his research in this field as a graduate student working at the Lick Observatory. Here he designed and built a new photoelectric photometer for the 36-inch refractor which made use of a thermionic d.c. amplifier similar to that introduced by Whitford in 1932. Kron's photometer was first used in July 1937. The cell was a Kunz potassium hydride tube, although by 1939 a red-sensitive cell with the new CsO on silver photocathode (see section 5.5) was also available. The cell and amplifier tube were housed in an evacuated metal container to provide electrostatic shielding and keep out moisture [85, 86].

A novel feature of the new instrument was the use of a so-called photocomparator which enabled the photometer to be set on one or other of two closely neighbouring stars in quick succession without moving the telescope. This idea had been proposed by Stebbins as a means of increasing the observing efficiency for variable star work in which a nearby star served as a comparison. It is also noteworthy that Kron introduced a strong negative-power lens just in front of the photocathode, the purpose being to spread the light over a fairly large area of photosensitive surface, and hence to reduce the effects of variable surface sensitivity characteristic of most photocathodes. Other observers had simply placed the cell well outside the telescope focus to achieve a similar result. The use of a positive

Fig. 5.20   Gerry Kron with his photometer on the Lick 36-inch refractor, 1938.

Fabry lens, apparently first applied in the Abastumani Observatory's photometer of 1936 (see section 5.4.5), became commonplace after the Second
War. Its purpose was to make the telescope exit pupil coincident with the
photocathode, and was a considerable improvement on the negative lens or
extra-focal method. The new Lick photometer was able to reach $m_{pg} = 11$,
while for brighter stars ($m_{pg} \sim 6$) Kron was able to achieve probable errors
of only 0^m002 for the magnitude difference of a variable and a comparison
after six minutes' observing time [86].

As part of his dissertation Kron presented the results of observing the
fifth magnitude eclipsing binary star YZ Cassiopeiae with the blue-sensitive
Kunz cell [87]. The system has a $4\frac{1}{2}$-day orbital period and comprises an
A star with a fainter F-type companion. It was also observed a decade
earlier by Huffer at Washburn [88]. The observations by Kron in 1937–38
resulted in an accurately determined light curve. In the analysis of this
curve six elements were treated as free parameters and their best values
obtained by an iterative least squares procedure. Two of the parameters
were the limb darkening coefficients for the primary and companion stars,

Fig. 5.21   Readout station of Kron's photometer, below the floor of the 36-inch telescope at Lick. The items visible are the battery case, galvanometer, desk with galvanometer scale and control box, as well as a vacuum pump on the floor for maintaining the vacuum in the photometer receiver.

and this represents the first reliable determination of limb darkening for an eclipsing system (Rosenberg had earlier obtained limb darkening coefficients for U Cephei, but from less reliable photographic data [89], while Antonie Pannekoek (1873–1960) and Elsa van Dien were unsuccessful in obtaining a limb darkening solution for YZ Cas, because they used Huffer's observations which lacked the necessary precision [90]).

Kron repeated his YZ Cas analysis using observations with the red-sensitive cell on the photometer in 1939–40, and was able to obtain almost the same solution for the light curve at 670 nm as found earlier in the blue spectral region [91] – see section 5.5.

5.4.5   Other photoelectric photometers before 1940 with alkali cathodes

The Washburn Observatory group under Stebbins was by far the most productive of the early pioneers in photoelectric photometry. Next came Guthnick's team in Berlin, while Edith Cummings at Lick, Christian Elvey at Yerkes and Gerald Kron, also at Lick, all produced new astrophysical results using the new technique. Rosenberg and the Lindemanns produced significant technical innovations. At least nine other observatories in the 1920s and '30s constructed photoelectric photometers, but reported few or no observational results.

Among these other early photoelectric observers were Gilbert Rougier (1886–1947) at the Strasbourg Observatory [92], who published a general review of photoelectric photometry which made only brief reference to his own instrument. The photometer used argon-filled KH cells of Rougier's own manufacture, and it was attached to the 16-cm telescope at Strasbourg and the photocurrent measured with a string electrometer. In 1926 a new photometer with a Lindemann electrometer had been constructed at Strasbourg, and Rougier used this instrument both in Strasbourg and at the Pic du Midi Observatory, for the photometry of stars, of the moon and of the solar corona. He presented a doctoral thesis for this work in 1933 [93].

After Stebbins left Illinois for Wisconsin in 1922, photoelectric astronomy did not completely cease there. In 1928 Robert Baker (1883–1964) described a new photometer with a string electrometer built for the Illinois 30-inch reflector. It comprised two Kunz cells (one caesium, and the other potassium or sodium) for the stated purpose of measuring stellar colours [94].

The first Canadian photoelectric photometer was built for F. C. P. Henroteau (1889–1951) at the Dominion Observatory in Ottawa by a French firm in Paris. It too used a potassium cell and string electrometer [95]. Henroteau announced that he had used the instrument to obtain the light curves of pulsating variable stars, including Cepheids and those of the β Cepheid (or β CMa) type, with this instrument, but the data were not presented. The French design was influenced by the photometers of Guthnick and Rougier.

Meanwhile, at Mt Wilson Sinclair Smith developed a photometer for use at the coudé focus of the 60-inch telescope. The instrument was presumably constructed with the assistance of Stebbins who made regular summer visits to Mt Wilson in the 1920s and '30s. The Mt Wilson photometer also used a Kunz cell and was able to detect photocurrents as low as 500 electrons per second (about 10^{-16} amps) from stars of blue magnitude 14 [96].

In the early 1930s a photometer was in operation at the Goodsell Observatory belonging to Carleton College in Minnesota. Here the observatory director Edward Fath observed variable stars on the 16-inch telescope, including ζ Geminorum [97]. A Lindemann electrometer was mentioned in a later note [98]. The photometer and observing procedure were also discussed in a note in 1934 where an accuracy of $0^{m}_{.}01$ for variable star photometry was claimed [99]. Fath made several visits to Lick from 1931 and used the Goodsell photometer there on the 12-inch refractor [81]. His observations of low-amplitude pulsating variables enabled him to carry out period analyses, leading to the discovery of multiple periods in δ Scuti [100] and also the β Cepheid star, 12 Lacertae [101, 102]. In both these cases the multiple periods gave rise to beat phenomena in the light curves.

The only British photoelectric photometer before 1940, apart from the Lindemann instrument, was built for the Sheepshanks equatorial coudé at Cambridge [103]. The cell-box contained four photoelectric cells from the German firm of Günther and Tegetmeyer, any one of which could be illuminated. A string electrometer was later replaced by one of the Lindemann design. Early observations were made by William Smart (1889–1979) in 1929 of two B stars (ζ Persei and 9 Cephei) with anomalously red colours, as determined by the difference between the blue photoelectric and visually determined magnitudes. The possibility that selective interstellar absorption was the cause of the anomaly was not cited [104].

In the 1930s Smart used this photometer, mainly with an argon-filled potassium cell, for observations on several variable stars, including ζ Aurigae (during the 1934 eclipse) [105], δ Cephei, β Lyrae [106] and Algol [107]. He noted that a potassium cell with 180 volts across the electrodes could be used to observe A0 stars to magnitude 5.5. Apparently a number of unspecified difficulties were encountered with the photometer as Smart wrote in April 1930 to his Italian colleague Maggini:

> We have had a very disappointing experience with the photoelectric photometer and I sincerely trust you will be spared all the disappointments and trials which we have had [108].

Fig. 5.22   Response functions of five alkali photocathodes, as measured by
Mentore Maggini in Italy, 1934.

It was Mentore Maggini (1890–1941) who at the Collurania-Teramo
Observatory in Italy built two photoelectric photometers from 1930 to 1931
[109]. One of these had a single argon-filled potassium photocell from the
firm of Günther and Tegetmeyer in Brunswick, Germany, and a suspended
string electrometer. The second photometer used two cells of sodium and
rubidium by Kunz and a Lindemann electrometer. In a second paper
Maggini presented the response functions of different alkali photocells and
discussed the possibility of determining stellar temperatures from the colour
indices with the two-cell photometer [108].

In 1937 Maggini presented observations of the eclipsing binaries β Persei
and λ Tauri using the two-cell photometer, for which the passbands had
effective wavelengths of 408 and 580 nm. He was thus able to study
the reflection effect through the variation of the surface colour (due to
temperature variations) using these photoelectric observations [110].

At Harvard photoelectric photometry was commenced in 1931 by William
Calder using Kunz potassium hydride cells [111]. Initially this instrument
used a Lindemann electrometer, but this was later changed to a d.c. amplifier

Fig. 5.23   Photoelectric photometer on the 13-inch Abastumani Observatory
telescope in Soviet Georgia, 1934.

and galvanometer. Observations were made on the 61-in Wyeth reflector
at Oak Ridge Observatory, which led to several notes appearing in the
Harvard Bulletins on the photometry of variable stars [112].

At Potsdam W. Hassenstein undertook photoelectric observations on the
30-cm refractor in the years 1935–38. His photometer was based on that used
by Guthnick at the neighbouring Babelsberg Observatory except he used
a Lindemann electrometer. Magnitudes for 102 north polar stars brighter
than $m = 6.7$ were obtained with this instrument [113] and the mean
error was $0^m_{.}021$. An elaborate reduction procedure to minimize systematic
errors was devised and the final results were carefully compared with
photographic magnitudes. The Potsdam photoelectric photometry bears
the hallmark of painstaking care and attention to detail in the photometric
tradition established earlier at Potsdam by G. Müller. Of the lesser known
photoelectric observers before 1940, Hassenstein was perhaps the most
meticulous. No doubt he would have achieved much more in this field had
political events not intervened.

A photoelectric photometer built by the German firm of Günther and

Tegetmeyer was acquired for the new Abastumani Astrophysical Observatory in Soviet Georgia in 1934, where it was used for observations of variable stars by V. B. Nikonov (b. 1905) [114]. This photometer was a copy of the four-cell instrument used by Guthnick at Berlin-Babelsberg. It was mounted on the Nasmyth focus of the 13-inch reflector and observations were made with a potassium hydride cell and string electrometer.

A completely Russian photometer designed by V. B. Nikonov and P. G. Kulikovsky was built at the Astronomical Institute in Leningrad in 1936–37, and this replaced the German instrument at Abastumani from 1937 [115, 116]. It used a d.c. amplifier with Pliotron FP-54 tube and a galvanometer. The photocell and amplifier tube were housed in an evacuated tank following the example of the Wisconsin observers. This Soviet photometer employed a Fabry lens just in front of the photocell, and it was apparently the first photoelectric instrument to do so [116]. The Fabry was a short focus converging lens designed to image the primary mirror onto the photocathode, thereby producing a steady illumination. Such a lens had been proposed in 1910 by the French astronomer Charles Fabry for photographic photometry of extended sources such as the night sky [117, 118, 119]. The effects of atmospheric seeing and guiding errors were greatly reduced with such a lens.

Photoelectric observations by Nikonov and Kulikovsky with these photometers were made of a number of variable stars, including P Cygni, λ Tauri and δ Scuti. In 1939 Nikonov and Kulikovsky were among the early pioneers with the CsO infrared cell [120]. A detailed account of this Soviet photoelectric work, which is little known in the West, was published by Kulikovsky in 1941 [121].

5.5   A new red-sensitive photocathode

5.5.1   John Hall and the Cs-O-Ag photocathode in astronomy

The various alkali photocathodes all suffered from a narrow spectral response which was limited to the blue region of the spectrum. A typical KH cell had a peak response at 440 nm, but the useful range of wavelengths was only from 360 to 540 nm where the response had fallen to 10 per cent of the maximum. Several physical laboratories carried out research programmes to find a red-sensitive photocathode. The first successful report came from Lewis Koller, who in 1929 at the General Electric Company laboratories produced a red-sensitive photocathode comprising a layer of caesium oxide deposited on silver. To obtain a cell of high

Fig. 5.24   Colour response of the Cs-O-Ag (S1) cathode compared to that of
           KH, presented by John Hall in 1934.

sensitivity into the infrared region, a thin layer of metallic caesium over
the CsO layer was required. A carefully monitored process was necessary,
in which oxygen was first adsorbed by the silver, and then a caesium layer
was deposited in a vacuum. This was then heated to oxidize it except for
the outermost skin which remained metallic [122]. The resulting photocell
had a double peak in its sensitivity function, with maxima at 350 and 730
nm and a useful range from the ultraviolet to beyond one micron in the
infrared.

Photoelectric cells with the new cathode (generally described as Cs-O-Ag
and later given the technical designation of S1) were produced by Charles
Prescott at the Bell Laboratories. Some of these were quickly acquired late
in 1930 by John Hall (1908–91), who was then researching for his doctorate
at Yale University. The early cells had a very high dark current, making
them unsuitable for astronomical photometry. But experiments made by
Hall at the suggestion of Prescott soon showed that the source of this dark
current was thermionic emission from the cathode, and not leakage through
the soda-lime glass envelope (a thermionic dark current vanishes on voltage
reversal whereas one due to leakage does not). By January 1931 Hall
had shown that cooling greatly reduced the thermionic emission, no doubt

Fig. 5.25   Cooled near-infrared (S1) photometer of John Hall, 1934.

influenced by Koller's finding from experiments at higher temperatures, that the dark current was temperature-sensitive [123] – see also [124].

A practical photometer incorporating a Cs-O-Ag photocell cooled to −40°C by dry ice in a Thermos bottle was constructed in 1931 and tested on the 15-inch Loomis coelostat refracting telescope at Yale. The dark current using the best tube was less than 5×10^{-16} amps with an operating voltage of 135 volts on the cell, and this allowed the light from red stars down to about sixth magnitude to be satisfactorily measured by determining the rate at which a Lindemann electrometer was charged [125].

Albert Whitford described the technological advance of the new photocathode in astronomy that Hall had initiated:

John Hall's introduction of cells with cesium-oxide-on-silver cathodes at Yale University in 1932 brought the advantage of a useful spectral response from 3500 to 11,000 Å. Spectrophotometric observations could now be made over a much broader range of wavelengths than had been possible with the Kunz potassium hydride cell. There was no improvement in quantum efficiency; in the red and infrared region it was not over 0.5 %. Hall was the first to use refrigeration by dry ice to reduce to a very low value the thermal emission at room temperature from the cathode; for this new red-sensitive surface, it was many times that from fairly bright stars [61].

A series of ten now classic research papers by Hall appeared in the *Astrophysical Journal* from 1934 – 42, giving the results of this first photoelectric stellar photometry in the red and infrared spectral regions with a cooled photocell. During this time Hall, having graduated from Yale, spent a brief period at Columbia University, before accepting appointments at Sproul Observatory in 1934 and then at Amherst College in 1938. The refracting telescopes at all four institutions were used for this work. The highlights of his research are mentioned here.

Essentially two types of observation were carried out. First, there was the colour index photometry, based initially on observations through Wratten gelatine filters [126], but from 1934 at Sproul, Jena glass filters were used (BG17 red and RG9 infrared) to define passbands with effective wavelengths near 680 and 830 nm [127]. From these observations the first photoelectric red–infrared colour indices were derived.

The second type of observation was photoelectric spectrophotometry. This work was initiated at Sproul Observatory from April 1935 by mounting an objective grating comprising a series of closely spaced fine parallel wires placed over the objective lens of the 24-inch refractor [127]. Light from both first-order spectra was sent to the photocell after passing through narrow slits that could be moved so as to scan through the spectra. In the first observations of this type the spectrum of the M giant star β Pegasi relative to Vega was recorded at 24 wavelengths from 454 to 1007 nm [127].

The filter photometry was used for extensive programmes at Sproul on later-type stars, first for those of type K [127] and then two years later for G stars [128]. The colour indices showed a correlation with luminosity in the sense that the higher luminosity stars of a given spectral type were redder. Hall's observations thus extended to the red spectral region the earlier finding of F. H. Seares [129, 130], based mainly on photographic spectrophotometry at Potsdam in the blue to yellow regions, that red giant stars were up to about 500 K cooler than dwarfs with the same spectral classification – see section 8.8.2.

One of the first problems Hall studied with the grating spectrophotometry

Fig. 5.26   John Hall with his near-infrared photometer, cooled with dry ice, on the 40-inch US Naval Observatory telescope in Washington, DC, c. 1933.

was that of the abnormally red B stars. He observed two B1 stars, ζ Persei and ε Persei, the first with an anomalous colour excess while the second had a normal colour for its spectrum [131]. Objective grating spectrophotometry, at 15 wavelengths from the blue to over 1 micron, was undertaken on the

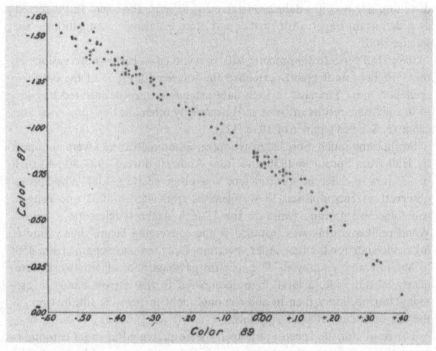

Fig. 5.27   Hall's two-colour diagram, based on near-infrared colours, 1934.

Sproul refractor. The results were presented as monochromatic magnitude differences Δm_λ between the two stars, plotted against wavelength.

By this time it was generally accepted that interstellar absorption was responsible for the abnormal colours of certain distant stars in the Galactic plane, being the result of a selective effect, in which the shorter wavelength blue and ultraviolet light was more effectively dimmed by its passage through the intervening medium. However, the wavelength dependence of the absorption was generally believed to obey a λ^{-4} law of Rayleigh scattering by particles much smaller than the wavelength. In this case interstellar reddening should be negligible in the infrared. The wavelength dependence of the absorption was thus a topic of considerable interest.

In Hall's paper on ζ and ϵ Persei he made the premise that the abnormal colour of ζ Per was due to an interstellar absorption in which $\Delta m_\lambda \propto \lambda^{-\alpha}$. The spectral index that best fitted the observations was quite close to unity, and certainly far from the Rayleigh scattering index of 4.

This was therefore some of the early observational evidence for a $1/\lambda$ interstellar scattering law, though it was neither the first evidence in this direction, nor was it a definitive statement to settle the issue. But it served as a significant impetus for further and more extensive investigations – see section 8.6.1.

John Hall's spectrophotometry was an advance on earlier observations of this type because it greatly extended the wavelength range of the data for reddened stars. The lack of such data extending into the infrared had led to inconclusive results in some of the work by others at this time – see, for example, Schalén's paper of 1936 [132].

Further and much more extensive spectrophotometric data were obtained by Hall from Sproul in 1938 and from Amherst during 1939–40. A total of 67 stars of different spectral type was observed [133, 134]. The Sproul observations encompassed 13 wavelengths from 456 to 1032 nm using a wire objective grating, while on the 18-inch Amherst telescope a blazed Wood replica grating was installed in the converging beam, thus giving a high efficiency for the first order spectrum. Only ten wavelengths from 450 to 881 nm were employed. The spectral passbands for all this work were nearly 50 nm wide, a large figure compared to the narrow bands in use today, but necessary then to allow enough light to pass the slit, in view of the low sensitivity of Hall's photocell.

The results of the spectrophotometry were presented as monochromatic magnitudes relative to the mean magnitudes for A0 stars, and had probable errors of $\pm 0^{m}\!.02$ to $\pm 0^{m}\!.03$ at most wavelengths [133]. The flux distributions, when plotted against frequency or $1/\lambda$, were practically linear (although the Paschen lines of the hotter stars produced a significant departure from linearity in the infrared). The slope of each star's flux distribution could therefore be characterized by a single parameter, the relative gradient. This was defined by $\phi = \mathrm{d}(\ln F_{\lambda})/\mathrm{d}(1/\lambda)$ and was shown to be in excellent agreement with the photographic gradients determined at the Royal Greenwich Observatory [135] and at the Göttingen Observatory [136].

Hall's spectrophotometry of 67 stars consisted of flux gradients relative to the mean of nine A0 stars, a spectral type also selected as a standard by the Greenwich and Göttingen observers. The task of obtaining absolute stellar fluxes was much more difficult and entailed observing a standard lamp carefully calibrated in the laboratory, which served as an artificial star. John Hall, together with Robley Williams (b. 1908) at Ann Arbor, was able in this way to measure the absolute fluxes for Vega, an A0 star that they chose as the primary standard 'because of its constancy, spectral type and accessibility' [137]. This was the last paper John Hall published in this great series based on photometry with the caesium oxide photocell before he joined the MIT Radiation Laboratory in 1942 for war-related research.

5.5.2 *Further use of Cs-O-Ag cells and the advent of multicolour photometry*

The cooled Cs-O-Ag photocell offered the advantage of a wide spectral response but the drawback of a low sensitivity. Only a few observers attempted to use such cells for astronomical photometry before the advent of the caesium oxide photomultiplier, which Kron applied to astronomical photometry in 1948 [138].

At Yale Arthur Bennett (b. 1904) continued to observe with John Hall's photometer on the Loomis telescope, using the same cell as Hall, but with different filters whose effective wavelengths were at about 690 and 880 nm [139]. Hall's Lindemann electrometer was replaced by a vacuum tube employed as an electrometer to record the small changes in voltage, which achieved a considerably higher sensitivity and allowed stars 1^m5 fainter to be recorded. A catalogue of colour indices for 254 stars was published from these observations made at Yale from 1934–35. Nearly all were fainter objects between visual magnitude 6 and 9. The average probable error was $\pm 0^m010$.

Bennett's paper appeared in the same volume of the *Astrophysical Journal* as John Hall's work on ζ Persei, which suggested a $1/\lambda$ reddening law was close to the truth. Bennett included three reddened B stars in his observations and reached practically the same conclusion as Hall. Clearly a $1/\lambda$ law could give a much better fit than the λ^{-4} Rayleigh law. He commented that: 'Scanty as the data are, they nevertheless strengthen the growing evidence that the reddening of the B stars is not due to Rayleigh scattering' [139].

At Lick Gerald Kron had from the outset designed his new photometer to take either a blue-sensitive alkali tube or a red-sensitive Cs-O-Ag one. In 1939–40 he used a refrigerated Western Electric red cell to repeat the observations and limb darkening analysis of the eclipsing binary star, YZ Cas [91]. The result confirmed the earlier analysis he had made in blue light. Photometry with the caesium oxide cell was also attempted in the Soviet Union by V. B. Nikonov at the Abastumani Observatory in Georgia in 1939. He used a photocell of Russian origin, and rather surprisingly operated it without any cooling. Yet the room temperature dark current was reported to be only 3×10^{-14} amps. A light curve for the W UMa-type eclipsing binary 44 i BooB was obtained with this cell on the 13-inch Abastumani reflector [120].

However, the most significant development came from the work of Joel Stebbins and Albert Whitford at Wisconsin. Following the success of John Hall with the Cs-O-Ag cells, the Wisconsin astronomers began using a photometer built around one of the new devices from 1937 for their observing programme at Mt Wilson. They used a commercially available Western Electric tube (type D97087) and, as with John Hall's photometer, the tube was refrigerated with dry ice and enclosed in an evacuated tank which excluded all moisture [140]. However, unlike Hall, Whitford chose to amplify the photocurrent with a thermionic valve amplifier whose output was sent via a shielded cable to a galvanometer some distance from the telescope. A current amplification of 1.3 million times was achieved. This arrangement, used earlier with the alkali cells, undoubtedly greatly simplified the observing procedure.

Some technical details of the red cells are interesting. A fourth magnitude star observed with the 60-inch telescope gave a photocurrent of 3.4×10^{-12} amps, whereas a Kunz KH cell gave 23×10^{-12} amps for the same star, as well as having a dark current typically ten times smaller than the cooled red cell produced.

The greatest innovation by Stebbins and Whitford was to introduce a system of multicolour filter photometry [140]. Six glass filters were chosen to make use of the entire available wavelength range from the Cs-O-Ag tubes. These filters were designated by their colours as follows:

Name	ultraviolet	violet	blue	green	red	infrared
Symbol	U	V	B	G	R	I
Effective λ (nm)	353	422	488	570	719	1030

Thus V and B approximately corresponded to the two filter passbands used in the KH photometry, while the G filter closely corresponded to the old visual photometry. The R and I passbands were at longer wavelengths than the ones used by Hall [127], while the U filter, centred just below the Balmer jump in early-type stars though still straddling this feature, represented the first use of ultraviolet light in photoelectric work.

A series of seven papers concerning multicolour photometry of stars and galaxies appeared in the *Astrophysical Journal* by Stebbins with the coauthorship of Whitford in most cases. The first concerned the photometry of 69 O and B stars, and exploited the wide wavelength baseline now available in order to investigate the wavelength dependence of interstellar extinction. A $1/\lambda$ interstellar law was found to fit the observations fairly well, as Hall and Bennett among others had earlier suspected. However, even a λ^{-1} law was not a perfect fit to the new observations. Otto Struve later commented on this work:

> Stebbins' photoelectric measures established beyond doubt that the Rayleigh type of absorption was not effective and that a law involving

the inverse first power of the wave length more nearly represented his observations. His greatest contribution in this field, and perhaps of his entire career, was the recognition that even the λ^{-1} relation is not entirely correct and that the true form of the absorption coefficient is a more complicated function of the wavelength [141].

A later paper presented six-colour photometry for 238 stars of different spectral types based on Mt Wilson observations from 1940–44 on the 60- and 100-inch telescopes [142]. This enabled the relation between the spectral type and $(V - I)$ colour index to be calibrated for stars of different luminosity and in particular the colour differences between cool dwarfs, giants and supergiants were clearly demonstrated. Colour temperatures were derived from these results by comparing them with those derived theoretically from black bodies. By this time it was known that black bodies gave rather poor fits, especially to B and A stars, because of the large Balmer discontinuity in the ultraviolet region of their spectra. However, the filters at longer wavelengths allowed satisfactory temperatures to be obtained – for type A0 these were about 11 000 K, which is about 10 per cent too high.

Other pioneering work with the new cells involved observations of Cepheid variables, still a favourite topic for Stebbins [143, 144, 145], an attempt to detect radiation from the galactic centre in the infrared [146] and an extension of the earlier KH cell programme [147] on extragalactic 'nebulae' to observe these extended objects in six colours [148], a task for which the photometer had been explicitly designed.

The programme on the centre of the Milky Way galaxy was undertaken by scanning the area over several degrees using the R and I filters. A large area with a considerable colour excess was detected, indicating light emitted from a large number of reddened late-type stars in the Galaxy's central bulge, but the dust obscuration even at a wavelength of 1 μm prevented direct observation of any central source or Galactic nucleus – a goal only achieved with a PbS cell at 2.2 μm wavelength by E. E. Becklin and G. Neugebauer in 1966 [149].

5.6 Concluding remarks on photoelectric photometry before the photomultiplier

The progress of stellar photoelectric photometry before 1940 can be characterized by just a few groups making considerable progress into the new and difficult field of astronomical electronics, while (especially from 1930 onwards) a rather large number of observers tried to emulate this work. Those who did try often encountered technical difficulties and their

Table 5.1. *Observatories engaged in photoelectric stellar photometry before 1940*

Observatory	Observers	Year	Ref.
Berlin	Guthnick, Prager, Hügeler,	1912	[31]
	Bottlinger, W.Becker, Güssow		[35, 41]
Tübingen	Rosenberg, Meyer	1912	[44]
Urbana, Illinois	Stebbins, Schulz, Kunz,	1912	[46]
	Dershem, Wylie		[53]
"	Baker	1928	[94]
Lick	Stebbins	1915	[150]
"	Cummings	1920	[80]
"	Fath	1931	[81]
"	Kron	1937	[86]
Sidholme, Devon	A.F. and F.A. Lindemann	1918	[75]
Washburn, Wisconsin	Stebbins, Whitford, Huffer	1922	[60]
Strasbourg	Rougier	c. 1925	[92]
Yerkes	Elvey, Stebbins, Mehlin	1929	[70, 69]
Dominion, Ottawa	Henroteau	c. 1929	[95]
Cambridge, UK	Smart, Green	1929	[104, 103]
Mt Wilson	Stebbins, Whitford	1930	[67]
"	Smith	c. 1933	[96]
Collurania, Teramo	Maggini	1930	[109]
Goodsell, Minnesota	Fath	1931	[97]
Harvard	Calder	1931	[111]
Yale	Hall	1931	[125]
"	Bennett	1935	[139]
Rutherfurd, Columbia	Hall	1933	[127]
Pulkovo	Nikonov	1933	[121, p. 41]
Sproul, Swarthmore	Hall, Delaplaine	1934	[127]
Abastumani, Georgia	Nikonov, Kulikovsky	1934	[114, 116]
Potsdam	Hassenstein	1938	[113]
Amherst	Hall	1938	[151]
Steward	Roach, Wood	1938	[152, 153]

Notes
1. Observers separated by commas were collaborators.
2. The year is the year of initial involvement.
3. In each case the reference is selected as being an example of a major or an early reference from the observers cited.
4. From 1913 the Berlin Observatory was resited at Berlin-Babelsberg.

output of published results was zero or sparse. In the former category Stebbins at Washburn, Guthnick at Berlin-Babelsberg and Hall at Yale and Sproul were all pre-eminent.

Table 5.1 shows that at least 22 observatories (9 in Europe and 13 in

Fig. 5.28   Five photoelectric photometrists at the first symposium for the use of the photoelectric cell in astronomy, Seattle, June 1940. (l. to r.: Hall, Kron, Stebbins, Whitford, Beals.)

North America) engaged in photoelectric photometry at some time or other prior to 1940. As many as 37 observers participated in the development and use of photoelectric photometers in astronomy, and over 200 articles were published giving observational results (see bibliographies by A. P. Linnell [154] and by P. Kulikovsky [121]). It would therefore be quite mistaken to suggest that the groups of Stebbins, Guthnick and Hall were the only observers who attempted photoelectric photometry before the advent of the photomultiplier, or even that Washburn was the only active American centre for photoelectric research in astronomy before the Second World War – see for example [73]. What is true is that just a few groups had much greater success and productivity than all the others, that to get good results from an early photoelectric photometer was as much an art as a science, and that the vast majority of all stellar photometry in the 1920s and 1930s continued to be photographic.

The very first conference of photoelectric photometrists was a *Symposium on the photoelectric cell in astrophysical research* held in June 1940 in Seattle, as a workshop of the Astronomical Society of the Pacific meeting at that time. There were just five participants at this workshop, and five papers were presented. Yet in this group were severàl of the most successful photoelectric photometrists in North America. Those present were Stebbins, Whitford, Kron, Hall and Carlyle Beals (who used a photocell for microphotometry), and the papers published constitute a valuable summary of the past history (by Stebbins [11]) and current practice of pre-photomultiplier photoelectric photometry.

It must be significant that the two most successful observatories with potassium hydride cells had the direct and close support from physicists actively engaged in cell research and manufacture: Guthnick from Elster and Geitel, Stebbins from Kunz. This was also the case for John Hall, who had the assistance of Charles Prescott at Bell Labs with the Cs-O-Ag photocells. Collaboration of this sort between physicists and astronomers was a key element for success. The reader of the early papers by Stebbins in photoelectric photometry will at once notice the emphasis on astrophysics as the driving force which motivated his research. His early papers were full of the details of eclipsing binary light curves and their analysis, not the technical details of how to get a photoelectric photometer to work – problems which he certainly would have had, and which with Kunz's help he evidently solved. This picture is not the same for the less successful observers who tackled similar instrumental problems, but without the same level of technical support.

It is also not surprising that the major advances in astrophysics in the area of photometry came soon after advances in instrumental technique. Before 1940 the major technical breakthroughs were the hydrogenated photocathode, the Lindemann electrometer, the thermionic valve amplifier, the caesium oxide on silver infrared-sensitive photocathode and the use of dry ice for cooling. In each case these developments resulted in fainter stars or a wider wavelength baseline being reached. The SbCs photocathode, the use of photomultiplication and the advent of pulse-counting were further major advances that had important consequences for astronomical photometry after 1940.

Stellar photometry was by no means the only branch of astronomical research in which photocells were employed prior to 1940. For example, Kunz and Stebbins made photoelectric measurements of the brightness of the solar corona as early as 1918 [155]. And Bengt Strömgren (1908–87), whose introduction to the photocell in astronomy came from none other than Guthnick at the Berlin-Babelsberg Observatory in the early 1920s, used a cell in Copenhagen for astrometry. He recorded the accurate times of meridian passage, by allowing the image of a star being monitored to cross a grid of parallel wires in the focal plane of the telescope [156, 157].

References

[1] Becquerel, E., *Comptes Rendus de l'Acad. des Sci.*, **9**, 561 (1839).
[2] Minchin, G.M., *Phil. Mag.*, **31**, 207 (1891).
[3] Monck, W.H.S., *Astron. Astrophys.*, **11**, 843 (1892).
[4] Dixon, S.M., *Astron. Astrophys.*, **11**, 844 (1892).
[5] Minchin, G.M., *Nature*, **49**, 270 (1894).
[6] Minchin, G.M., *Proc. R. Soc.*, **58**, 142 (1895).
[7] Minchin, G.M., *Nature*, **52**, 246 (1895).
[8] Minchin, G.M., *Proc. R. Soc.*, **59**, 231 (1896).
[9] Monck, W.H.S., *J. Brit. Astron. Assoc.*, **5**, 418 (1895).
[10] Butler, C.J. and Elliott, I, *Proc. IAU Coll.*, **136**, 3 (1993).
[11] Stebbins, J., *Publ. Astron. Soc. Pacific*, **52**, 235 (1940).
[12] Stebbins, J. and Brown, F.C., *Astrophys. J.*, **26**, 326 (1907).
[13] Stebbins, J., *Publ. Astron. Soc. Pacific*, **69**, 506 (1957).
[14] Stebbins, J., *Astrophys. J.*, **27**, 183 (1908).
[15] Stebbins, J., *Astrophys. J.*, **32**, 185 (1910).
[16] Stebbins, J., *Astrophys. J.*, **32**, 179 (1910).
[17] Stebbins, J., *Astrophys. J.*, **34**, 112 (1911).
[18] Stebbins, J., *Astrophys. J.*, **42**, 133 (1915).
[19] Ruhmer, E., *Weltall*, **3**, 63 (1902).
[20] Ruhmer, E., *Weltall*, **3**, 200 (1903).
[21] Hertz, H., *Ann. der Physik*, **31**, 983 (1887).
[22] Hallwachs, W., *Ann. der Physik*, **33**, 301 (1888).
[23] Elster, J. and Geitel, H., *Ann. der Phys.*, **48**, 625 (1893).
[24] Elster, J. and Geitel, H., *Physik. Zeitschr.*, **11**, 212 (1910).
[25] Elster, J. and Geitel, H., *Physik. Zeitschr.*, **12**, 609 (1911).
[26] Kemp, J.G., *Phys. Rev. (2)*, **1**, 274 (1913).
[27] Rosenberg, H., *Handbuch der Astrophys.*, **2** (Part 1), 380 (1929).
[28] Struve, H., *Jahresbericht der Berlin Sternw., 1912* in *Vierteljahrschr. Astron. Ges.*, **48**, 56 (1913).
[29] Guthnick, P., *Astron. Nachr.*, **196**, 357 (1913).
[30] Elster, J. and Geitel, H., *Physik. Zeitschr.*, **13**, 739 (1912).
[31] Guthnick, P. and Prager, R., *Veröff. Sternw. Berlin-Babelsberg*, **1** (Heft 1), 1 (1914).
[32] Guthnick, P. and Prager, R., *Veröff. Sternw. Berlin-Babelsberg*, **2** (Heft 3), 1 (1918).
[33] Guthnick, P., *Die Sterne*, **13**, 2 (1933).
[34] Guthnick, P. and Hügeler, P., *Astron. Nachr.*, **210**, 345 (1920).
[35] Bottlinger, K. F., *Veröff. Sternw. Berlin-Babelsberg*, **3** (Heft 4), 1 (1923).
[36] Schwarzschild, K., *Abhandl. der königl. Ges. der Wiss. zu Göttingen, Math.-phys. Klasse*, **8** (No. 4) (1912).
[37] King, E.S., *Ann. Harv. Coll. Observ.*, **76** (No. 6), 107 (1916).
[38] Parkhurst, J.A., *Astrophys. J.*, **36**, 169 (1912).
[39] Adams, W.S., *Astrophys. J.*, **39**, 89 (1914).
[40] Kapteyn, J.C., *Astrophys. J.*, **40**, 187 (1914).

[41]   Becker, W., *Veröff. Universitätssternw. Berlin-Babelsberg*, **10** (Heft 3) (1933).

[42]   Becker, W., *Veröff. Universitätssternw. Berlin-Babelsberg*, **10** (Heft 6) (1935).

[43]   Güssow, M., *Zeitschr. für Astrophys.*, **20**, 25 (1940).

[44]   Meyer, E. and Rosenberg, H., *Vierteljahrschr. Astron. Ges.*, **48**, 210 (1913).

[45]   Rosenberg, H., *Vierteljahrschr. Astron. Ges.*, **56**, 126 (1921).

[46]   Schulz, W.F., *Astrophys. J.*, **38**, 187 (1913).

[47]   Kunz, J., Schulz, W.F. and Stebbins, J., *Pop. Astron.*, **22**, 631 (1914).

[48]   Kunz, J. and Stebbins, J., *Pop. Astron.*, **23**, 603 (1915).

[49]   Shinomiya, T., *Astrophys. J.*, **49**, 303 (1919).

[50]   Seiler, E.F., *Astrophys. J.*, **52**, 129 (1920).

[51]   Kunz, J. and Stebbins, J., *Pop. Astron.*, **25**, 657 (1917).

[52]   Stebbins, J., *Astrophys. J.*, **51**, 193 (1920).

[53]   Kunz, J. and Stebbins, J., *Phys. Rev.*, **7**, 62 (1916).

[54]   Kunz, J., *Astrophys. J.*, **45**, 69 (1917).

[55]   Stebbins, J., *Astrophys. J.*, **53**, 105 (1921).

[56]   Stebbins, J., *Astrophys. J.*, **57**, 1 (1923).

[57]   Wylie, C.C., *Astrophys. J.*, **56**, 232 (1922).

[58]   Wylie, C.C., *Astrophys. J.*, **56**, 217 (1922).

[59]   Lindemann, F.A., Lindemann, A.F. and Keeley, T.C., *Phil. Mag.* (6) **47**, 577 (1924).

[60]   Stebbins, J., *Publ. Washburn Observ.*, **15** (Part 1), 1 (1928).

[61]   Whitford, A.E., *Ann. Rev. Astron. Astrophys.*, **24**, 1 (1986).

[62]   Whitford, A.E., *Astrophys. J.*, **76**, 213 (1932).

[63]   Weaver, H.F., *Pop. Astron.*, **54**, 504 (1946).

[64]   Kron, G.E., *Publ. Astron. Soc. Pacific*, **52**, 250 (1940).

[65]   Huffer, C.M., *Pop. Astron.*, **35**, 487 (1927).

[66]   Stebbins, J. and Huffer, C.M., *Publ. Washburn Observ.*, **15** (Part 3), 137 (1930).

[67]   Stebbins, J., *Proc. Nat. Acad. Sci.*, **19**, 222 (1933).

[68]   Trumpler, R., *Lick Observ. Bull.*, **14** (No. 420), 154 (1930).

[69]   Elvey, C.T., *Astrophys. J.*, **74**, 298 (1931).

[70]   Stebbins, J., *Astrophys. J.*, **74**, 289 (1931).

[71]   Stebbins, J. and Huffer, C.M., *Publ. Washburn Observ.*, **15** (Part 5), 215 (1934).

[72]   Stebbins, J. and Whitford, A.E., *Astrophys. J.*, **84**, 132 (1936).

[73]   DeVorkin, D.H. *Proc. I.E.E.E.*, **73**, 1205, (1985).

[74]   Pannekoek, A., *Trans. Int. Astron. Union*, **6**, 293 (1939).

[75]   Lindemann, A.F. and Lindemann, F.A., *Mon. Not. R. Astron. Soc.*, **79**, 343 (1919).

[76]   Lindemann, A.F. and Lindemann, F.A., *Mon. Not. R. Astron. Soc.*, **79**, 350 (1919).

[77]   Hubble, E.P., *Pop. Astron.*, **33**, 252 (1925).

[78]   Lindemann, A.F. and Lindemann, F.A., *Mon. Not. R. Astron. Soc.*, **86**, 600 (1926).

[79]   Stebbins, J. and Dershem, E., *Astrophys. J.*, **49**, 344 (1919).

[80]   Cummings, E.E., *Lick Observ. Bull.*, **11**, 99 (1923).

[81]   Fath, E.A., *Lick Observ. Bull.*, (No. 474) **17**, 115 (1935).

[82]   Payne, C.H., *Proc. Nat. Acad. Sci.*, **14**, 296 (1928).

[83]   Adams, W.S. and Joy, A., *Astrophys. J.*, **57**, 294 (1923).

[84]   Elvey, C.T. and Mehlin, T.G., *Astrophys. J.*, **75**, 354 (1932).

[85] Kron, G.E., *Publ. Astron. Soc. Pacific*, **50**, 171 (1938).
[86] Kron, G.E., *Lick Observ. Bull.*, (No. 499) **19**, 53 (1939).
[87] Kron, G.E., *Lick Observ. Bull.*, **19**, 59 (1939).
[88] Huffer, C.M., *Publ. Washburn Observ.*, **15**, 103 (1928).
[89] Rosenberg, H.O., *Astrophys. J.*, **83**, 67 (1936).
[90] Pannekoek, A. and van Dien, E., *Bull. Astron. Inst. Netherlands*, **8**, 141 (1937).
[91] Kron, G.E., *Astrophys. J.*, **96**, 173 (1942).
[92] Rougier, G.H., *Bull. Soc. Astron. France*, **39**, 58 (1925).
[93] Rougier, G.H., *Ann. de l'Observ. de Strasbourg*, **2** (Fasc. 3), 205 (1933).
[94] Baker, R.H., *Pop. Astron.*, **36**, 86 (1928).
[95] Henroteau, F.C.P., *Pop. Astron.*, **37**, 267 (1929).
[96] Smith, S., *Phys. Rev.(2)* **43**, 211 (1933).
[97] Fath, E.A., *Publ. Astron. Soc. Pacific*, **43**, 292 (1931).
[98] Fath, E.A., *Publ. Astron. Soc. Pacific*, **46**, 234 (1934).
[99] Fath, E.A., *Astron. Soc. Pacific Leaflet*, No. **63** (1934).
[100] Fath, E.A., *Lick Observ. Bull.*, (No. 501) **19**, 77 (1940).
[101] Fath, E.A., *Pop. Astron.*, **46**, 241 (1938).
[102] Fath, E.A., *Astron. J.*, **52**, 123 (1947).
[103] Smart, W.M., *Observatory*, **56**, 76 (1933).
[104] Smart, W.M., *Mon. Not. R. Astron. Soc.*, **89**, 545 (1929).
[105] Smart, W.M. and Green, H.E., *Mon. Not. R. Astron. Soc.*, **95**, 31 (1934).
[106] Smart, W.M., *Mon. Not. R. Astron. Soc.*, **95**, 644 (1935).
[107] Smart, W.M., *Mon. Not. R. Astron. Soc.*, **97**, 396 (1937).
[108] Maggini, M., *Mem. Soc. Astron. Italia*, **8**, 47 (1934).
[109] Maggini, M., *Mem. Soc. Astron. Italia*, **6**, 5 (1932).
[110] Maggini, M., *Mem. Soc. Astron. Italia*, **10**, 229 (1937).
[111] Calder, W.A., *Harvard Coll. Observ. Circ.*, **405**, 1 (1935).
[112] Calder, W.A., *Harvard Coll. Observ. Bull.*, **907**, 23 (1938).
[113] Hassenstein, W., *Astron. Nachr.*, **269**, 185 (1939).
[114] Nikonov, V.B., *Bull. Abastumani Astrophys. Observ.*, **1**, 38 (1937).
[115] Nikonov, V.B., *Bull. Abastumani Astrophys. Observ.*, **2**, 27 (1938).
[116] Nikonov, V.B. and Kulikovsky, P., *Astron. Zhurnal*, **16** (Part 4), 54 (1939).
[117] Fabry, C., *Astrophys. J.*, **31**, 394 (1910).
[118] Fabry, C., *Comptes Rendus de l'Acad. des Sci.*, **150**, 273 (1910).
[119] Fabry, C., *Ann. d'Astrophys.*, **6**, 65 (1943).
[120] Nikonov, V.B., *Bull. Abastumani Astrophys. Observ.*, **4**, 11 (1940).
[121] Kulikovsky, P., *Publ. Sternberg State Astron. Inst.*, **17** (Part 2), 2 (1941).
[122] Koller, L.R., *Phys. Rev. (2)*, **36**, 1639 (1930).
[123] Koller, L.R., *Phys. Rev. (2)*, **33**, 1082 (1929).
[124] Kingsbury, E.K. and Stilwell, G.R., *Phys. Rev. (2)*, **37**, 1549 (1931).
[125] Hall, J.S., *Proc. Nat. Acad. Sci.*, **18**, 365 (1932).
[126] Hall, J.S., *Astrophys. J.*, **79**, 145 (1934).
[127] Hall, J.S., *Astrophys. J.*, **84**, 369 (1936).
[128] Hall, J.S., *Astrophys. J.*, **88**, 319 (1938).
[129] Seares, F.H., *Publ. Astron. Soc. Pacific*, **30**, 99 (1918).
[130] Seares, F.H., *Astrophys. J.*, **55**, 165 (1922).
[131] Hall, J.S., *Astrophys. J.*, **85**, 145 (1937).
[132] Schalén, C., *Nova Acta Reg. Soc. Sci. Upsal.*, Ser. IV, **10**, (No. 1), 1 = *Medd. Astron. Observ. Upsala*, No. **64** (1936).
[133] Hall, J.S., *Astrophys. J.*, **94**, 71 (1941).

[134]   Hall, J.S., *Astrophys. J.*, **95**, 231 (1942).
[135]   Greaves, W.M.H., Davidson, C.R. and Martin, E.G., *Mon. Not. R. Astron. Soc.*, **100**, 189 (1940).
[136]   Kienle, H., Strassl, H. and Wempe, J., *Zeitschr. für Astrophys.*, **16**, 201 (1938).
[137]   Hall, J.S. and Williams, R.C., *Astrophys. J.*, **95**, 225 (1942).
[138]   Kron, G.E., *Harvard Coll. Observ. Circ.*, **451**, 37 (1948).
[139]   Bennett, A.L., *Astrophys. J.*, **85**, 257 (1937).
[140]   Stebbins, J. and Whitford, A.E., *Astrophys. J.*, **98**, 20 (1943).
[141]   Struve, O., *Pop. Astron.*, **56**, 287 (1948).
[142]   Stebbins, J. and Whitford, A.E., *Astrophys. J.*, **102**, 318 (1945).
[143]   Stebbins, J., *Astrophys. J.*, **101**, 47 (1945).
[144]   Stebbins, J., *Astrophys. J.*, **103**, 108 (1946).
[145]   Stebbins, J., Kron, G.E. and Smith, J.L., *Astrophys. J.*, **115**, 292 (1952).
[146]   Stebbins, J. and Whitford, A.E., *Astrophys. J.*, **106**, 235 (1947).
[147]   Stebbins, J. and Whitford, A.E., *Astrophys. J.*, **86**, 247 (1937).
[148]   Stebbins, J. and Whitford, A.E., *Astrophys. J.*, **108**, 413 (1948).
[149]   Becklin, E.E. and Neugebauer, G., *Astrophys. J.*, **151**, 145 (1968).
[150]   Stebbins, J., *Lick Observ. Bull.*, **8**, 186 (1916).
[151]   Hall, J.S., *Astrophys. J.*, **90**, 449 (1939).
[152]   Roach, F.E., *Astrophys. J.*, **89**, 669 (1939).
[153]   Wood, F.B., *Contrib. Princeton Univ. Observ.*, **21**, 1 (1946).
[154]   Linnell, A.P., *Astron. Photoelectric Photometry*, ed. by F.B. Wood, Washington, American Assoc. Advancement of Sci. (1953).
[155]   Kunz, J. and Stebbins, J., *Astrophys. J.*, **49**, 137 (1919).
[156]   Strömgren, B., *Astron. Nachr.*, **226**, 81 (1925).
[157]   Strömgren, B., *Vierteljahrschr. Astron. Ges.*, **68**, 365 (1933).

6 Photometry at longer wavelengths

6.1   Introduction to infrared photometry

If the story of astronomical photometry is the story of detector technology, then this is demonstrated most clearly by the development of infrared astronomy. Here a remarkable variety of both thermal and non-thermal detectors has been devised. The former rely on detecting a small temperature rise by the heating effect of the incident radiation, while the latter make use of chemical or electronic transitions induced directly by the individual incoming photons. In the nineteenth century these included liquid-in-glass thermometers, thermocouples, pyrometers, bolometers and radiometers as well as the tasimeter, photographic plates and phosphorescent screens. Much useful information was obtained on the properties of heat radiation, its intensity distribution in the sun, on its wavelengths and on the presence of strong telluric absorption bands superimposed on celestial spectra, which in turn dictate the wavelengths at which ground-based photometry could be undertaken.

The first really useful stellar photometry at wavelengths beyond one micron was made with radiometers and thermocouples in the first half of the twentieth century, but was limited to bright stars observed with large telescopes, so inefficient and noisy were the detectors and so bright was the sky in relation to the stars.

Today astronomers might be forgiven for believing infrared astronomy only began in 1947 when Kuiper first used a Cashman lead sulphide photoconductive cell for stellar observations. This was certainly the start of a new era which really expanded after Low's germanium bolometer was developed from 1961. But one message of this chapter is to remind us that in fact a century and a half of essential and painstaking groundwork had been put in before this, which has made infrared astronomy in recent times the flourishing subject that it now is.

6.2   **William Herschel's discovery of IR rays**

In a single volume of the *Philosophical Transactions of the Royal Society* for the year 1800 William Herschel published four classic papers on the emission of heat rays from the sun. In all of these papers he used mercury-in-glass thermometers with blackened bulbs as his detectors. In the first paper he produced a solar spectrum with a prism and used three thermometers, only one of which was in the spectrum. The others served as controls [1]. With this simple apparatus he recorded the temperature difference of the bulb in the spectrum from those to the side, after about 10 minutes illumination. The result was 7 °F for the red rays, $3\frac{1}{4}$ °F for green rays but only 2 °F when the thermometer was in the violet part of the spectrum.

The next paper extended these results beyond the red in the visible spectrum. He made the important discovery that the sun's rays were present beyond the last visible red rays and continued to have a heating effect in this infrared region [2]. When the first thermometer was a quarter inch beyond the last visible illumination, the heating power was a maximum†, giving a 9-°F temperature rise. He concluded that 'there are rays coming from the sun, which are less refrangible than any of those which affect the sight. They are invested with a high power of heating bodies, but with none of illuminating objects; and this explains the reason why they have hitherto escaped unnoticed' [2].

In the next two papers [3, 4] Herschel stressed the similarity of the light and heat rays from the sun and laboratory sources, including their common properties of reflection and refraction, and he performed a large number of carefully conducted experiments for the absorptive properties of different materials to heat and light. In the last paper he also drew two separate curves for the distribution of the heating and illuminating powers of the two types of ray. The heat rays could be detected to $2\frac{1}{4}$ inches beyond the visible red. No wavelength calibration was attempted by Herschel, his experiments preceding by two years those of Thomas Young and the theory of light and colours, which resulted in the first reliable optical wavelengths [5]. However, his optical spectrum was about 3 inches in length so it is certain that he detected radiation well beyond 1 micron.

Herschel was not the first person to observe heat rays coming from the sun. Several investigators in the late eighteenth century had already demonstrated this. He was the first, however, to show the presence of

---

† That the maximum apparently lay beyond the visible region was in part due to the lower dispersion of a prism in the near infrared than in the visible.

heat rays of lower refrangibility than visible ones. His experiments on the different absorptive properties of heat and light rays by different media led him to conclude that heat and light rays were quite separate entities in spite of many similar physical properties, and not different manifestations of a single type of ray [4].

Herschel's conclusions on the presence of 'ultra-red' radiation, as it was at first designated, caused some controversy. But he found early support from Henry Englefield (1752–1822) who repeated Herschel's experiments but using a lens after the prism and a slit to isolate narrow regions of the solar spectrum [6, 7]. Many others, such as C. E. Wünsch [8] and Henry Meikle [9], had less success, and published accounts which discounted Herschel's findings.

6.3   Further early observations of solar infrared radiation

Following William Herschel's discovery of infrared heat radiation from the sun, three topics dominated the study of the solar infrared at different times during the nineteenth century. First, there was the controversy concerning the nature of the new radiation and its relation to visible light, secondly there arose the problem of measuring the wavelength of these rays, and finally the mapping of the solar spectrum and the associated absorption features was a topic of great interest, especially the related question of its maximum extent to longer wavelengths.

As early as 1814 Jean Baptiste Biot (1774–1862) had proclaimed that heat, light and the chemical (ultraviolet) rays were all of the same type of radiation, but still different rays [10]. Essentially he accepted Herschel's finding that the heat rays corresponded to invisible radiation and were not simply an attribute of visible light rays. This view was disputed by David Brewster (1781–1868), who believed all three types of ray invariably occurred together. The separate nature of heat and light rays was largely confirmed by the experiments of Melloni in Italy from 1832 – see section 6.4.

Meanwhile, Claude-Servais Pouillet (1790–1868) in France undertook a remarkably thorough study of solar heat radiation in 1838 [11]. This included the first attempt to measure the flux of solar heat radiation reaching the earth's surface, using a simple instrument called a pyrheliometer – essentially a small waterbath (10 cm in diameter) in a blackened container and equipped with a thermometer to record the rate of temperature increase. By calibrating this temperature rise he deduced that a flux of 1.7633 calories cm^{-2} min^{-1} (= 1.44 kW m^{-2}) was received by the earth from the sun if the atmosphere were to absorb nothing. Pouillet's work was thus the first to attempt to measure the solar constant (cf. the modern value of 1.37 kW m^{-2}). It is also remarkable for its careful allowance for the absorption in the terrestrial atmosphere, long before extinction corrections became commonplace in visual stellar photometry.

Pouillet went on to estimate the heat flux from the sun's surface, which he found to be 85 kcal cm^{-2} min^{-1} (69.3 MW m^{-2}), enough, he wrote, to melt nearly 17 km of ice a minute at the sun! He also found the temperature of the sun to be at least 1461 °C based on his value for the solar surface flux, a result remarkable not for its accuracy but for the fact that it was arrived at over four decades before Josef Stefan's (1835–93) law of 1879 [12], which related the total flux of radiation emitted by a body to the fourth power of its temperature.

Soon after Pouillet's solar pyrometry, John Herschel devised an ingenious technique to record the sun's infrared. A paper blackened with soot and soaked in alcohol had a solar spectrum focussed upon it. The alcohol dried beyond the visible spectrum in a series of bands separated by four deep troughs [13]. This was the first evidence for the existence of deep absorption features in the infrared, later to be ascribed to telluric water vapour. However, the initial evidence was doubted by Lord Rayleigh (1842–1919) [14] and by John Draper [15] who were unable to reproduce this experiment.

Nevertheless, by 1847 Hippolyte Fizeau (1819–96) and Léon Foucault (1819–68) also found broad absorption bands in the solar infrared spectrum lying beyond the A band in the red [16]. For this work they used sensitive alcohol thermometers with miniature bulbs such that a 1-degree temperature rise gave as much as an 8-mm rise of the fluid in the stem.

In this paper it was furthermore shown that infrared rays could display the same interference, polarization and diffraction phenomena as visible light, which could in principle be used to determine their wavelengths. Johann Müller in fact determined the first infrared wavelengths in 1858 (see section 6.4) and Fizeau did so himself in 1878 [17]. He found the strongest absorption to be at 1.445 μm while the solar infrared ceased (so he believed) at 1.940 μm. These results were only extended to longer wavelengths (5.3 μm) when Langley used his bolometer with a grating in the 1880s (see section 6.5). The telluric water vapour bands were later to have a marked influence on the practice of infrared stellar photometry from the ground.

Observations of the solar infrared at much higher spectral resolution, which revealed many more weaker absorption features, were made by means of photography, first by Edmond Becquerel in France in 1842 [18], and then by John Draper in New York in 1843 [19]. However, these very early photographic plates, which provided the first non-thermal infrared detector, could only record the region immediately beyond the visible to about 1μm. Section 7.4 discusses later developments in red and infrared photography.

Another non-thermal infrared detector was provided by the phenomenon of phosphorescence, and this was explored extensively by Edmond Becquerel from 1843. He used phosphorescent screens with layers of powdered calcium or barium sulphide. These would phosphoresce after exposure to ultraviolet light, but he found that infrared radiation destroyed the phosphorescence of a screen previously exposed to shorter wavelengths [20, 21]. Focussing a solar infrared spectrum on a preflashed screen therefore allowed the absorption bands to be studied. Becquerel later measured the wavelengths in the solar spectrum to about 1.8 μm using this detector [22, 23].

Perhaps one of the most unusual infrared detectors of the nineteenth century was Thomas Edison's (1847–1931) tasimeter, a device which relied on the change in electrical resistance of powdered carbon when under compression from a vulcanite rod onto which heat rays had been focussed [24]. Edison believed temperature rises in the rod as small as 10^{-6} °F could be detected with this device (superior to the best thermopiles of that time), and he set out to measure the heat from the solar corona at the time of the 1878 solar eclipse in Wyoming. The experiment was inconclusive.

But perhaps Edison was the first person to envisage making a survey of the sky in the infrared, if the tasimeter could be mounted on a large telescope [25], a vision that arose from his claim to have detected heat from Arcturus using his 4-inch solar telescope (see also Lockyer's report on these observations [26]). But according to Nichols, the Arcturus results were also spurious [27]. It seems likely that the tasimeter experiments, which have been described recently by J. Eddy [28], were not the success that Edison had hoped or claimed for them.

In this section various thermal and non-thermal infrared detectors of the nineteenth century have been described. Some made a contribution to scientific knowledge. In practice all were exceedingly inefficient and unable to compete with the thermocouple or the platinum bolometer, the two instruments with which real progress was made. These are discussed in sections 6.4, 6.5 and 6.7.

6.4   The thermocouple as infrared detector

When Thomas Seebeck (1770–1831) at Jena discovered the phenomenon of thermoelectricity in 1822 this gave experimenters a much more convenient heat detector than the liquid-in-glass thermometer used by Herschel [29]. His first simple thermocouple was constructed from metallic strips of bismuth and copper and he demonstrated the flow of a current when one of the two junctions was heated. A wide variety of other pairs of materials was also studied.

Macedonio Melloni (1798–1854) exploited Seebeck's discovery for a thorough investigation of the nature of radiant heat. He developed the thermopile as a heat detector, comprising an array of thermocouples connected to a galvanometer. His experiments were commenced in Paris in 1831 and continued in Naples from 1839 until about 1853. He explored the transparency of different materials (including water) to heat, the position of the maximum of heat intensity in the solar spectrum and the influence on this maximum of the material of the prism used. Melloni's results were published in a long series of papers in *Comptes Rendus* and *Annales de Chimie et de Physique*, some of the more important ones being in 1831 [30] on the solar heat maximum, and in 1833 [31] on the heat transparency of media. He showed that rocksalt was transparent to the infrared (heat) rays and therefore well suited for the construction of prisms and lenses for experiments on these rays.

Melloni's principal result was to demonstrate the many identical physical properties of heat and light rays which led him to conclude they were indeed the different manifestations of the same phenomenon [32]. His detection of the heating power of the moon made in 1846 with his thermocouple from his meteorological station high on Mt Vesuvius was also a classic astronomical observation, the first in the infrared for a celestial body other than the sun [33, 34].

This observation of the moon was repeated a decade later by Charles Piazzi Smyth, Astronomer Royal for Scotland, during his pioneering investigation of mountain-top astronomical observing from near the summit of Mt Guajara in Teneriffe. Here in 1856 Piazzi Smyth compared the heat of the moon with that from a nearby candle, using a Gassiot thermopile, and he devised the technique of pointing his thermopile alternately at the moon and then at the sky 20° distant each side of the moon to eliminate radiation from the sky background [35]. In addition Piazzi Smyth took extraordinary care to avoid the heat of his own body influencing his observations, by ensuring that he was clad 'in non-conducting flannel'. He was one of the notable early pioneers of infrared astronomy.

Although Melloni believed heat to be an ethereal vibration of the same nature as that postulated for light rays, it was not until 1858 that Johann Müller (1809–75) in Freiburg made the first rough estimate of the wavelength of these vibrations. In one experiment Müller used a rocksalt prism to observe the solar infrared with a thermopile. He estimated the refractive index for the extreme rays observed to be 1.506 and from this attempted to obtain the wavelength. The most realistic estimate came from a graphical extrapolation of the dispersion $n(\lambda)$ formula and gave about 1.8 μm [36]. Recognizing the effect of a non-linear dispersion on the observed solar intensity distribution of heat rays, he corrected his observed distribution to a normal (i.e. linear) wavelength scale, which shifted the true peak to shorter visible wavelengths.

The development of more sensitive multi-element thermopiles allowed the infrared solar spectrum to be studied in greater detail and wavelengths to be measured more reliably. Angelo Secchi in Rome, who was later to become the noted stellar spectroscopist, used a thermopile in 1852 to study the phenomenon of solar limb darkening in the infrared [37]. His experiments were able to demonstrate nearly a factor of two in the intensity of undispersed solar heat radiation between the disk centre and the limb. Two of the pioneers of solar thermopile infrared spectroscopy were Lamansky and Mouton. In 1871 Sergei Lamansky obtained a solar prismatic spectrum in which the maximum in the infrared had three broad absorption bands superimposed on it, which he interpreted as being of telluric origin [38]. Shortly afterwards Louis Mouton (1844–95) in France repeated this experiment and obtained four absorption dips, for which he gave the wavelengths as 0.85, 0.985, 1.23 and 1.48 μm [39]. The first weak band was evidently missed by Lamansky; although Mouton's wavelengths are slightly overestimated, his bands can be readily identified with well known water vapour absorptions in the earth's atmosphere. His infrared wavelengths came from a study of interference phenomena in a thin birefringent quartz plate of known thickness when viewed with a spectroscope and using polarized light [40]. Such a method had in fact been pioneered in France by Fizeau [17] using a small alcohol thermometer instead of a thermopile, with similar results. Both Fizeau and Mouton concluded that the intensity of solar heat radiation fell to zero shortly before a wavelength of 2 μm with no emission beyond that point (see section 6.3), a result which was to be dramatically reversed by the work of Langley from 1881 (see section 6.7).

The thermocouple was the first instrument to be used to detect the infrared radiation from stars. These historic observations were made by William Huggins (1824–1910) at his private Tulse Hill observatory in London in 1866–67, and mark the birth of infrared stellar photometry [41]. Huggins'

Fig. 6.1   William Huggins.

thermopiles comprised no more than one or two pairs of elements. The output was detected by a sensitive galvanometer. The thermopile was carefully insulated from extraneous heat sources by placing it inside a tube lined with cotton wool, and the instrument was mounted on his 8-inch refractor using wood to eliminate conduction from the brass of the telescope. Huggins described how he directed the telescope a short distance from a bright star, waited four or five minutes for the galvanometer needle to settle, then carefully moved the telescope onto a star using the finder telescope.

The needle was then watched during five minutes or longer; almost always the needle began to move as soon as the image of the star fell upon it. The telescope was then moved, so as to direct it again to the sky near the star. Generally, in one or two minutes, the needle began to return towards its original position. In a similar manner twelve to twenty observations of the same star were made [41].

The results were a 3° deflection of the needle for Regulus and Arcturus, 2° for Sirius, $1\frac{1}{2}°$ for Pollux and no recordable effect for Castor. Thirty years later Huggins remarked that this larger deflection for Arcturus than for Sirius was in accord with the heat observations of E. F. Nichols at Yerkes using a sensitive radiometer [42].

Similar observations were made in the following year, 1868, by Edward Stone (1831–97) using the $12\frac{3}{4}$-inch equatorial telescope at the Royal Greenwich Observatory, with an antimony-bismuth thermocouple and galvanometer [43]. Stone noted brighter stars were readily detected, but like Huggins, he was troubled by zero-point drifts and changes in sky conditions. It often took some ten minutes for the needle to settle. Nevertheless from his observations of Vega and Arcturus he noted that

> from the whole of these observations I think we can conclude that Arcturus gives to us considerably more heat than α Lyrae; that the amount of heat is diminished very rapidly as the amount of moisture in the air increases; that nearly the whole heat is intercepted by the slightest cloud [43].

These extremely difficult observations by Huggins and Stone can hardly be described as photometry, as their main achievement was the detection of stellar heat radiation rather than its measurement, even though both observers apparently found that the red stars were stronger infrared radiators relative to their visual brightness. Neither Huggins nor Stone continued this work, and the only other astronomical observations employing the thermopile from this same period came from Laurence Parsons, the Fourth Earl of Rosse (1840–1908) (formerly Lord Oxmantown). He was able to make some high quality observations from 1868 using the 36-inch reflector at Birr Castle in Ireland showing the dependence of heat radiation from the moon on lunar phase and that heat was extinguished in the terrestrial atmosphere according to a similar law to that for starlight [44, 45, 46]. He also used his thermopile to determine the temperature of the lunar surface [47, 48]. One instrumental detail of note was his use of two opposing thermopiles connected side-by-side to the same galvanometer, such that one received radiation only from the background sky. The galvanometer reading thus automatically gave a differential value for the lunar signal above the background [44].

In order to improve the sensitivity of the thermocouple the British physicist, Charles Vernon Boys (1855–1944), designed an instrument he called a radiomicrometer. In this instrument the circuit of a light weight thermocouple was completed by a small loop of copper wire, and the loop was suspended by a fine torsion wire in a magnetic field [49, 50]. The radiomicrometer thus incorporated a thermocouple as part of the moving coil of a galvanometer.

Boys made repeated observations with the radiomicrometer from 1888 to 1890 in an attempt to detect infrared stellar and planetary radiation using his $15\frac{5}{8}$-inch alt-azimuth reflecting telescope in central England [51]. All these attempts failed in spite of his belief that his instrument was about one thousand times as sensitive as the thermocouples of Huggins or Stone. The heat from distant candles and the moon was detected. Boys' failure to record the stellar infrared from even the brightest stars led him to doubt the reliability of the Huggins and Stone results.

6.5   Langley's bolometer

The work of Samuel Pierpont Langley (1834–1906), at the Allegheny Observatory in Pittsburgh from about 1880 and then at the Smithsonian Institution in Washington from 1889, represents a major milestone in the history of infrared astronomy. He was by far the most important infrared astronomer of the nineteenth century and his work over nearly two decades resulted in our knowledge of the solar spectrum being extended by nearly a factor of ten in wavelength.

Langley was director of the Allegheny Observatory from 1867 and from about 1870 his interest was directed towards the study of solar radiation using thermopiles. During the 1870s he studied the phenomena of solar limb darkening and the radiation from sunspots in the infrared [52, 53]. During this time he became acutely aware of the shortcomings of the thermopile for infrared work, even for such a bright source as the sun, especially on account of its slow response, low sensitivity and large sensitive detector area (making it unsuitable for spectroscopic work). Langley saw the need for an instrument which 'should be an advance over the thermopile, as the latter had been over the thermometer' [54, see p. 10] and from 1879 to 1881 he set about the design of a new infrared detector to satisfy these goals.

The instrument devised by Langley was the bolometer, whose operation involved the measuring the increase in resistance of a thin strip of blackened platinum when its temperature is raised. It thus employed the same principle as the platinum resistance thermometer, which had been devised three decades earlier by Adolph Svanberg (1806–57) in Uppsala [55]. Like all other infrared detectors used in the nineteenth and earlier twentieth centuries (except for photographic plates and phosphorescent screens), the bolometer relied on a thermal response to the incoming infrared photons. The resistance change of the heated platinum was detected by means of a Wheatstone bridge, in which an unexposed control strip was placed in an adjacent arm of the bridge, and a sensitive galvanometer used to measure the infrared signal.

The earliest such actinic balance or bolometer, so-called by Langley because he believed it responded to radiation over the entire electromagnetic spectrum, was described by Langley in 1881 [56]. The platinum strips were only a few microns in thickness. Their small thermal capacity gave a high sensitivity and fast response, enabling readings to be taken in a few seconds instead of after minutes with the best thermopiles. Langley was able to measure temperature changes of 10^{-4} °C in the platinum, and the detection limit was about a factor of ten smaller still.

Langley's researches in infrared astronomy were entirely directed towards solar spectrobolometry. He was the first to use a diffraction grating for the solar infrared, and here the linear or normal dispersion at once showed the maximum of thermal radiation in the solar spectrum to be in the orange (near the sodium D lines) and not in the infrared [56, 57], as Müller had earlier found – see section 6.4. This finding concurred with the recognition by this time of the identity of heat and light radiation, which implied that the solar intensity maximum must necessarily be the same in both cases.

Langley's principal interest at this time was a determination of the total amount of solar radiation received on earth from above the terrestrial atmosphere, from the integration of his bolometric spectra. By 1882 he had extended the observed solar spectrum from its previous limit of about 1.8 μm to a new value of 2.8 μm, with some three quarters of the solar energy being found at invisible wavelengths. Langley's solar constant was 2.84 calories $cm^{-2} min^{-1}$ [57], considerably higher than modern values (presumably as a result of errors in calibrating the bolometer in terms of absolute units). The study of the absorption of solar radiation by the earth's atmosphere was always a central theme of Langley's work. He showed that the continuous absorption was much less in the infrared than the visible, even though the former region was also broken up by deep and wide absorption bands of telluric origin [58].

Recognizing the need for high-altitude observations to obtain the best values for the solar constant, Langley undertook in 1883 an expedition to Mt Whitney in southern California. Here he used the bolometer at an altitude of about 3600 m to measure solar radiation to the longest possible wavelengths. For this work he dispersed the sunlight with a prism spectrograph, in which the optical elements were made from infrared-transmitting rocksalt. He wrote:

> It was in the course of these observations, and on this mountain, at an altitude of 12,000 feet, that the writer, after carrying the bolometer to the end of the then known prismatic spectrum (near what is now known as Ω), was rewarded for all past pains by first discerning beyond this "end" a new region of almost indefinite extent in which physicists have subsequently found a fertile field [54, see p. 14].

The results of the expedition were reported the following year [59] in a publication described by Charles Abbot as 'a monument to the energy, perseverance, originality, and skill in observation of Mr. Langley' [60].

By 1886 Langley had improved the sensitivity of the bolometer and was able to extend the solar spectrum to 'hitherto unrecognised wavelengths' [61]. Here he achieved a limiting wavelength of 5.3 μm. The measurement of these infrared wavelengths was undertaken by determining in the laboratory the refractive index of the rocksalt prism, $n(\lambda)$, by using the emission lines from a bright carbon arc. Light from the arc was diffracted by a grating before passing into the prism spectrometer. The diffraction grating law, $n\lambda$ = constant, enabled the infrared wavelength to be determined in terms of the known value for the D_2 line in the visible spectrum. Solar radiation itself was too feeble in this infrared region to be detected by the bolometer after dispersion by a grating.

In 1887 Langley took up a new position at the Smithsonian Institution in Washington, where he soon became that institution's third secretary. In 1890 he founded the Smithsonian Astrophysical Observatory and it was here he continued his bolometric researches. The installation, in 1892, of an automatic recording solar spectrobolometer, fed by a heliostat, was a major advance [62]. Numerous improvements in the sensitivity of this instrument were made from 1892 to 1895, which helped isolate the galvanometer from extraneous vibrations and thermal drifts, with the result that the most precise bolographic records of the sun's infrared radiation could be obtained by the winter of 1896–97 [54]. The principal aim at this time was to map the absorption lines in the solar infrared to 5.3 μm. About 700 lines were observed and accurate wavelengths for 222 were recorded. The resolving power of the spectrobolometer ($\lambda/\Delta\lambda$) was about 2000 in the near infrared to 1.2 μm, but because wider slits were needed to obtain a measurable signal at longer wavelengths, the resolving power was reduced to only a few hundred. Line positions from six bolographic records were obtained to about 1 arc second (angle of deviation from prism) corresponding to about

Fig. 6.2   Bolographs of the infrared solar spectrum by Samuel Pierpont Langley

0.2 nm in the near infrared ($\lambda < 1.2$ μm) or to about 1 nm at the longer wavelengths.

After 1897 Langley's energies were increasingly taken up by his equally pioneering experiments in heavier-than-air flight, following his first successful flight of a model powered aircraft in 1896. However, the research in solar infrared radiation was continued at the Smithsonian by Charles Abbot (1872–1973) and Loyd B. Aldrich (1884–1965) with the assistance of

Frederick Fowle (1869–1940) [63]. The latter station marked a return to that site 25 years after Langley had undertaken his solar radiation measurements there in 1883. In addition a solar expedition to Algeria was undertaken in 1911–12. Further high-altitude stations were set up in Chile from 1918 and in Arizona a few years later [64] for measurements of the solar spectrum, the solar constant, solar limb darkening and the absorption of solar radiation by molecules in the terrestrial atmosphere.

Abbot's spectrobolometry resulted in an improved and much quoted solar energy distribution based on prismatic bolometry at Washington, Mt Wilson and Mt Whitney [65]. Here he tabulated solar intensities between 0.30 and 3.00 μm and deduced a solar effective temperature of 5830 K and also determined a new value for the solar constant. A later version of the solar energy distribution was published in 1923 [66].

6.5.1   Abbot's stellar spectrobolometry at Mt Wilson

Although the spectrobolometer was used almost exclusively for measurements of solar radiation, Abbot and Aldrich made one brief experiment with this detector in 1922 at the coudé prism spectrograph of the Mt Wilson 100-inch telescope [66]. The aim was to determine optical and infrared energy distributions for ten of the brightest stars, using a very sensitive galvanometer able to detect currents as small as 5×10^{-2} amps. However, numerous instrumental difficulties were encountered and reliable energy curves were not obtained. Nevertheless, this was the earliest stellar spectrophotometry in the infrared, and although the ultimate goal of measuring stellar temperatures was not realized, the general systematic trend of the curves with spectral type was evident. The authors described their pioneering stellar observations as follows:

> Though we have not concealed the shortcomings of these stellar observations, they cost a great deal of effort. Fatalities seemed to lurk about the work to surprise us so that we were almost ashamed to meet any one on Mount Wilson lest he should ask what new things had gone wrong that day. We made a list of all the serious mishaps, and they numbered nearly 30, some requiring a whole week to repair. But we feel after all that, a decided step was made to have gotten from 10 to 30 millimeters deflection in the fairly extended spectra of four of the brightest stars. For it was not many years ago that Boys failed to recognize stellar heat and Nichols observed one or two millimeters in the total radiation of such stars [66].

Later Abbot used a Nichols radiometer at Mt Wilson for his stellar spectrophotometry and more reliable results were soon forthcoming (see section 6.7).

6.6   The radiometer

6.6.1   Origin of the radiometer

The last quarter of the nineteenth century was a period of extensive experimentation in developing new detectors for the infrared. In addition to the thermopile which had already seen its début in astronomy, this was the era of infrared photography, of the radiometer, the radiomicrometer and of the Langley bolometer, all of which were tried as astronomical detectors.

As a completely non-electromagnetic device, the radiometer was quite different in principle from the other detectors of the infrared (beyond 1.1 μm). The instrument was devised by William Crookes (1832–1919) from 1875 when he constructed a radiometer consisting of four thin mica vanes, black on one side, white on the other, which rotated in an evacuated glass tube when acted upon by radiation [67]. A variant of this device was the torsion radiometer in which two vanes with the blackened surface on the same side were suspended from a fine torsion fibre whose deflection, owing to an excess of radiation on one vane (relative to the other), was measured by a light beam directed to a small mirror attached to the vane supports. Crookes used such a torsion radiometer to explore the distribution of solar energy in a prismatic spectrum [68]. Like earlier investigators he found the maximum apparently to be in the infrared. The physical principle of the radiometer's operation was at first not apparent, though George Stoney's (1826–1911) explanation in terms of the kinetic theory of gases was eventually accepted [69]. The theory postulated non-adiabatic collisions of gas molecules from the heated black vane surfaces, thus transferring momentum to the vanes. Crookes investigated the effect of gas pressure on the radiometric effect after this theory was announced [70] and found a maximum sensitivity at about 5×10^{-5} atmospheres.

6.6.2   Stellar radiometry by Ernest Nichols

The torsion radiometer was developed into a sensitive infrared detector by Ernst Pringsheim (1859–1917) in Berlin for his doctoral thesis published in 1883 [71]. He used the detector together with a grating to measure wavelengths in the infrared solar spectrum [72]. The American physicist Ernest Fox Nichols (1869–1924) spent the years 1894–96 at the Physical Institute in Berlin where he further perfected Pringsheim's instrument [73, 74]. The total suspended weight was only 7 mg, including the two mica vanes each only 2 mm in diameter, and a very fine quartz fibre was used for the torsion. Although less portable than a bolometer, it was also less sensitive to disturbing influences causing drift in the latter instrument, and the compensation for background radiation, using one vane for the source radiation and the other only for background, was a useful attribute of the device. Nichols used the radiometer to study the infrared properties of quartz between 4 and 9 μm wavelength [73, 74].

On his return to the United States, Nichols accepted a professorship in physics at Dartmouth College in 1898. At the invitation of Hale, he brought his radiometer to Yerkes Observatory in the summer of that year, where it was installed in the heliostat room and received light from a stationary 24-inch f/8 mirror. It was in August 1898 that Nichols made the first reliable quantitative infrared stellar photometric measurements of Arcturus and Vega. Arcturus gave a mean deflection of 0.60 mm, six times that estimated for a candle at 15 miles, and the mean ratio for the heat emission of Arcturus to Vega was 2.1 [75].

After returning to Yerkes in August 1900, Nichols produced just one major paper as his contribution to infrared astronomy. He reported radiometric measurements on Vega, Arcturus, Jupiter and Saturn, and after correcting these for atmospheric absorptions (measured experimentally by observing distant candles) he deduced thermal intensities for these objects in the ratios 1 : 2.2 : 4.7 : 0.74 at the zenith [27]. He also gave absolute thermal values in units of 10^{-8} metre candles.

The similarity of Nichols' infrared ratio for Arcturus to Vega with the value for this same quantity obtained thirty years earlier by Huggins prompted a comment by Huggins to the effect that his early result had been confirmed [76, 42]. However, this was not the view of Nichols himself who believed, like Boys, that the observations of both Huggins and Stone were spurious and that his was the first instrument with sufficient sensitivity to detect the stellar infrared. Subsequently Coblentz used a thermocouple (see section 6.7) to obtain a similar value to that of Nichols [77], and he took the view that this vindicated Huggins and Stone's results, meagre though they were.

Although the results obtained by Nichols were also meagre, his paper showed some foresight in the application of infrared astronomy to astrophysics. Using the new radiation laws of Wien [78] and of Stefan [12], (the latter had been deduced theoretically by Boltzmann in 1884 [79]), Nichols showed how it would be possible in principle to deduce stellar angular diameters. He reasoned that Arcturus probably had a larger angular size than Vega, which would be the most plausible cause of its greater infrared intensity [27].

6.6.3 Abbot's stellar spectroradiometry at Mt Wilson

The first attempt at determining stellar energy distributions in the infrared by Abbot in 1922 had used the bolometer on the Mt Wilson coudé spectrograph, but with unsatisfactory results – see section 6.6.1. In the following year (October 1923) Abbot returned to Mt Wilson, hoping to improve these observations using a radiometer constructed by Nichols as the detector [80]. The instrument consisted of two small mica vanes each 0.5 × 1.5 mm, separated by 2.5 mm and on a torsion fibre suspension. Deflections were detected with a 5-m optical arm. Given the larger telescope, better sky conditions and more sensitive radiometer than that of Nichols, Abbot estimated a possible gain of a thousand-fold over the Yerkes radiometry.

For this first attempt at stellar spectroradiometry nine bright stars were selected and the radiometer replaced the bolometer on the 100-inch coudé spectrograph. The spectra were measured from 437 nm to 2.224 μm at 15 prism settings, including 4 for wavelengths greater than 1 micron. The procedure was to allow starlight to strike one vane of the radiometer for 15 s, before the shutter was closed for 15 s, alternating between open and shut eight times. Readings of the deflection were recorded at the end of each 15-s interval. The observations were reduced relative to the sun (observed by passing sunlight through small holes in an objective mask on the 100-inch telescope).

The resulting stellar energy spectra, covering both visible and infrared regions, represent the first successful spectrophotometry of stars over such a large wavelength baseline and enabled Abbot to determine temperatures by fitting black-body curves to his data. The values ranged from 2500 K for α Herculis to 16 000 K for Rigel. Abbot furthermore applied the analytical method used by Nichols to obtain angular diameters for his stars, from which, in conjunction with their trigonometric parallaxes (which provide a direct measure of distance), he was able to deduce their radii. Whereas Procyon was found to have a radiometric radius only 10 per cent greater than that of the sun, the values for Rigel and α Herculis exceeded the solar radius by several hundred times, results which were generally in agreement with the Michelson interferometry for supergiant stars at that time being attempted by F. G. Pease at Mt Wilson [81, 82].

A major challenge for stellar radiometrists was to build an instrument with greater sensitivity, which entailed a lower mass of the vanes and their supporting structure, a reduced thermal conductivity through the vanes, a lower torsional modulus from the fibre suspension, optimizing the pressure of the gas to achieve high sensitivity and sufficient damping and the elimination of stray electric fields. In 1926 Abbot constructed a new radiometer whose vanes were made from flies' wings in order to minimize their moment of inertia. The final version of this radiometer had vanes comprising 3 laminated wings separated by 0.1 mm to prevent heat conduction. The area was 0.4×1.0 mm and the front surface of the vane was coated with lampblack [83]. The fly wing vanes had a combined mass of only 35 μg and the whole moving system was less than 1 mg. It was, according to Harold Weaver, 'undoubtedly one of the most unusual instruments to be found anywhere in the history of photometry' [84].

A fly-wing radiometer was taken to Mt Wilson in 1928 and used on the 100-inch coudé by Abbot with the assistance of Walter Adams to determine the energy curves of 18 bright stars and two planets [83]. Most of these spectral observations were in the wavelength range 0.589 to 2.224 μm, although a few went further to the blue. The results were still not very precise, the average probable error of one deflection on Rigel being 10 per cent, comparable to the precision reached with the mica radiometer in 1923.

Nearly two decades later Abbot returned to experimenting with radiometers for stellar spectrophotometry. His 1945 instrument had composite vanes made from fly wings and foil and was especially designed to be electrostatically shielded to prevent stray fields giving spurious deflections [85]. The moving system mass was only 0.40 mg and the radiometer was 20 times as sensitive as that of 1928.

Abbot and Aldrich again observed several bright stars on the 100-inch coudé with the new radiometer in September 1947 [86]. The spectrograph had a combined crown and flint prism to give a more uniform dispersion. However, observations only extended to 817 nm. The precision of the spectroradiometry was not high, being around 10 per cent for each observation both in 1947 and in 1923. The results of the two runs for stars in common were generally concordant. The authors noted that: 'the curves show a progressive displacement of the maxima toward the red for advancing spectral types'. This must be regarded as a weak qualitative conclusion from all the effort put into radiometry.

The novel fly-wing detector was unable to compete with the Cs-O-Ag (S1) photoelectric cell which could deliver very useful spectrophotometric data on stars even in a small telescope, as was demonstrated by John Hall at Sproul Observatory from 1935 – see section 5.5.1. However, together with the thermocouple and the bolometer, the radiometer was one of the early infrared detectors which in the 1920s had a brief moment of note in the history of astrophysics, by showing that stars as well as the sun radiate in the infrared at least to 2.2 μm, that the energy distributions approximate those of black bodies and that such spectrophotometry, if properly calibrated (no model atmosphere fluxes were then available for this purpose), could in principle be used for determining stellar temperatures and angular diameters.

6.7   Thermocouple photometry in the early twentieth century

Although the thermocouple was the first detector to be used for observations of stellar infrared radiation (by Huggins and Stone in the 1860s), by the turn of the century the radiometer had been developed by Nichols to the point of being the preferred detector for stellar work. The bolometer was also potentially suited to stellar infrared photometry, although the bulky apparatus and its relative complexity of operation prevented it from being so used for other than solar observations until 1922 – see section 6.5.1.

Meanwhile the development of the thermocouple made rapid progress in the early twentieth century, so that by the 1920s it was easily the most suitable infrared detector. Infrared stellar photometry in the 1920s made a quantum leap forward. From the astrophysical viewpoint the most important advances in this field prior to the introduction of the lead sulphide cell were made with thermocouples at this time.

One of the first developments was the invention of the vacuum thermocouple by Peëtr Lebedev (1866–1912) in Moscow [87]. Heat losses by convection and conduction are eliminated if the junctions are in an evacuated cell, leading to a rise in sensitivity of up to 30 times. Edison Pettit in 1950 summarized the principal requirements for a sensitive astronomical thermocouple, including the optimum choice of metals to maximize the thermoelectric voltage, a small receiver mass to be heated at the thermo-junction, minimal heat losses from the junction, a well-blackened receiver absorbing over a very wide spectral range and a window to the vacuum cell transparent to infrared rays [88].

Some of these properties were discussed theoretically by E. S. Johansen in 1910 [89]. He suggested that an iron-bismuth vacuum thermocouple, designed to minimize heat conduction losses along the wires, would be suitable for detecting stellar radiation. At Johns Hopkins University, Herman Pfund (1879–1949) constructed a vacuum thermocouple with bismuth alloys using the Johansen principles, and was able to demonstrate a gain of 13 times as a result of the evacuation [90].

It was this instrument that Pfund took to the Allegheny Observatory in 1913 and with which he made observations there on the 30-inch reflector [91]. The two thermojunctions were small blackened disks in a vacuum cell

(i)

(ii)

Fig. 6.3   (i) Herman Pfund's vacuum thermocouple used at the Allegheny
Observatory, 1913. (The thermal junctions in the capsule, B, are viewed
through the eyepiece, E. H is a charcoal evacuator.) (ii) Pfund's
vacuum thermocouple showing thermal junctions, A and B. Filaments
1 and 2' were of Bi-Sn; 1' and 2 were Bi-Sb. The star was imaged on
one black disk, the sky alone on the other.

with a fluorite window and the whole cell could be inserted into the eyepiece
of the telescope, which allowed the image of a star to be focussed onto one
of the junctions. Poor weather prevented extensive observations and only
Vega, Jupiter and Altair were observed. Nevertheless, Pfund reported that:

Fig. 6.4   Thermocouple used by William Coblentz at Lick Observatory, 1914.

'In every case the deflections followed so definitely when the signal was given that not even a skeptic could have doubted the reality of the effect' [91].

6.7.1   Infrared photometry of W. W. Coblentz

Pfund had emphasized that the excellent stability of his galvanometer deflections with a thermocouple was a result of the careful compensation or balancing of the two junctions for background radiation and other extraneous effects, a point also stressed by William Coblentz (1873–1962) at the Bureau of Standards in discussing the relative merits of different infrared detectors [92]. Coblentz went on to build a thermocouple based on pure bismuth and a bismuth-and-tin alloy, and it is this instrument he used on the Crossley 36-inch reflector at Lick Observatory in July–August 1914 [77]. His instrument was a thermocouple, not a thermopile, and he pointed out the unsuitability of the multi-element pile for the observation of stellar point sources. This paper reported by far the most productive stellar observations in the infrared at that time. The data related to 105 stars to visual magnitude 6.7. By means of a water cell containing a 1-cm optical path, Coblentz was also able to make approximate estimates of the fraction of the total radiation stars of different spectral type emitted beyond about 1.4 μm. For M stars this amounted to about three quarters of their energy output, but for A stars it composed only about one third (both these figures he later revised downwards because the effects of atmospheric extinction were not taken into account). It is interesting to note that this is one of the earliest applications of a filter (water absorbs everything beyond 1.4 μm) in astronomical photometry, predating by two years the yellow glass filter employed by Guthnick and Prager in their photoelectric observations from Berlin – see section 5.3.1.

Coblentz estimated his thermocouple to be about 150 times more sensitive than a Nichols radiometer. Although its absolute efficiency for converting thermal into electrical energy was still abysmally low (around 10^{-6}), and far worse than the efficiency of selective detectors in the form of selenium photoconductive cells and potassium photoelectric cells then becoming available to astronomers (see section 5.3.1), nevertheless the very broad band (or non-selective nature) of the thermocouple still made it an indispensable instrument for the infrared region between about 1 and 10 μm, as well as a useful but not ideal detector at shorter visible wavelengths.

Coblentz made a further series of thermocouple observations in 1922, this time on the 40-inch reflector at the Lowell Observatory at an altitude of 2200 m [93]. On this occasion he observed a total of 30 objects including Venus and Mars. The main innovation was the use of transmission screens or filters to isolate five broad-band spectral regions between 0.30 and 10 μm. Sixteen stars were observed through such screens. Coblentz calibrated the relative signals observed through his filters theoretically using the Planck energy curves for black bodies at different temperatures. He was thereby able to estimate temperatures of 3000 °C for M stars and 9000–10 000 °C for B stars. These results were quite crude and added little to what was already known of stellar temperatures from visual and photographic spectrophotometry. The main result was the demonstration that stars radiated approximately like black bodies not only in the visible region but in the infrared as well.

Coblentz published a more popular account of his work with thermocouples in 1923, including a discussion of his extensive planetary photometry, which was a major interest [94]. The thermocouple and water cell were well suited to studies of the thermal radiation from planetary surfaces which was entirely in the infrared, whereas scattered solar radiation was mainly at shorter wavelengths and transmitted by the water cell. A major paper on planetary surface temperatures was the result of this work [95].

6.7.2   Thermocouple photometry of Pettit and Nicholson

Edison Pettit (1889–1962) and Seth Nicholson (1891–1963) from the early 1920s continued the work pioneered by Coblentz, and became the principal observers to apply the thermocouple to stellar astronomy during the inter-war years. They overcame the low efficiency of even their best detectors by using the light-gathering power of the 100-inch Hooker telescope. Like Coblentz they used a water cell to derive a water-cell index, and in addition they defined a heat index based on a combination of visual and radiometric (i.e. with the thermocouple) photometry. Both these indices

Fig. 6.5   A: Vacuum thermocouple of Edison Pettit and Seth Nicholson, 1922.
B: Junction of the thermocouple as seen by the observer looking into
the eyepiece.

gave information on stellar temperatures and angular diameters. They made
a special study of long-period variable stars and, like Coblentz, they also
devoted much time to the determination of planetary surface temperatures.
In short, they pushed the thermocouple observations and their interpretation
to the limit of this detector's capabilities and showed that some interesting
astrophysics could be undertaken in this new spectral region.

The first paper in 1922 [96] by Pettit and Nicholson gave a detailed
discussion of the design and manufacture of vacuum thermocouples for
stellar astronomy. The typical conversion efficiency from thermal to electrical energy was 4.5×10^{-7}, fully a hundred times below the limit imposed
by the second law of thermodynamics for a temperature differential and
about $2 \times 10^{-2}\,°C$ between the junctions. Nevertheless their junctions were
both sensitive (typically a temperature difference of $1.6 \times 10^{-4}\,°C$ per mm
deflection) and fast acting (response time a few milliseconds). Their most
successful couples were from bismuth and a bismuth-tin alloy (as used by
Coblentz) and red stars down to $V \sim 8^m$ could be observed, for which the

Fig. 6.6   Atmospheric transmission in the infrared, determined by Pettit &
Nicholson, 1928.

temperature difference was as small as 10^{-5} °C (e.g. the red dwarf Boss 4342
gave $\Delta T = 9 \times 10^{-6}$ °C [97]).

The thermocouple was mounted at the newtonian focus of the telescope
and the observer set a star alternately with 20-second intervals on each of
the two receivers, which were small blackened disks attached to each junction. The deflections were recorded on a sensitive D'Arsonval galvanometer
placed on a lower level. The deflections of an 8-m light beam by the
galvanometer were recorded photographically with a moving plateholder.

This arrangement allowed precisions of about $\pm0^{m}\!.1$ to be obtained in
good conditions. Observations were normally made at night when the
seeing was better, although full daylight had no disturbing influence on
the deflections, the two junctions being carefully compensated for the sky
background.

In a major programme from late 1921 to 1927 Pettit and Nicholson
observed 124 bright stars with their thermocouples [97]. An interesting
part of this work was the analysis of their data to derive a heat index
(HI $= m_v - m_r$) from the radiometric thermocouple magnitudes m_r. Like
the colour indices used by photographic photometrists, the heat index was
set equal to zero for A0-type stars and was expressed in magnitudes on a
Pogson scale.

The 1-cm water cell effectively blocked all radiation beyond 1.4 μm and
the absorption produced was expressed as a WC index also in magnitudes.
Both HI and WC were broad-band colour indices based on the radiometric

measures. Their data showed good correlations of either index with spectral type, which also indicated the temperature difference of red giants from red dwarfs of the same spectral type, an effect already known from photometry at shorter wavelengths – see section 8.8.2.

More interesting was their plot of the heat index HI versus the water cell index WC, an early representation of a two-colour diagram. Pettit and Nicholson computed the theoretical locus of black bodies in this diagram and showed the cooler M stars to diverge progressively from the black-body line, presumably as a result of molecular line blocking in the visual band which made the heat index larger than that of a black body at the same temperature as the star.

If one of these indices could be used to obtain temperatures (using a theoretical calibration for black bodies) then stellar angular diameters could be derived from the temperature and m_r magnitude reduced to outside the earth's atmosphere. This relationship can be regarded as a forerunner of the much more recent Barnes-Evans relationship for stellar angular diameters from photometry [98], the main difference of substance being Pettit and Nicholson's use of Planck curves to derive implicitly stellar surface fluxes from their photometry, instead of calibrating this quantity from data pertaining to actual stars, as done by Barnes and Evans. Nevertheless they went on to derive angular diameters for most of their stars and to compare these with those from Pease's interferometric programme. In this respect the analysis was quite similar to the spectroradiometry being undertaken at this time by Abbot from the Smithsonian Astrophysical Observatory at the coudé focus of the Mt Wilson 100-inch [80]. Indeed with both these infrared programmes being undertaken at Mt Wilson from the early 1920s, it is not surprising that Abbot would have discussed the methods of analysing the data with Pettit and Nicholson. The Carnegie observers, needless to say, obtained a far more extensive data set. Their angular diameters were generally about 50 per cent greater than the interferometric ones by Pease, a discrepancy which was ascribed to departures from black-body radiation for the stars analysed by the method of Pettit and Nicholson. Nevertheless the remarkable achievement was that by two completely independent methods, stellar angular diameters could be determined which agreed so well. This was surely one of the major triumphs of stellar astrophysics in the 1920s, given that the values being determined were no more than a few milli-arc seconds in most cases. (Their result for Betelgeuse of 75 milli-arc seconds was the largest value obtained; most were much smaller.)

Apart from their use of the thermocouple to determine stellar temperatures and angular diameters for cool stars, other work undertaken by Pettit and Nicholson was a study of the infrared light curves of six long period variable stars [99, 100], a determination of the spectral energy distribution and temperature of sunspots [101] and a survey of the distribution of surface temperature over the planet Mars [102].

The only other observers of note to use the thermocouple for radiometric observations of stars were Theodore Sterne (1907–1970) and Richard Emberson (b. 1914) using the 60-inch Wyeth telescope of Harvard's Oak Ridge Observatory in 1938. Their vacuum thermocouple was based on an antimony-tungsten junction, these wires being soldered to a small blackened copper disk in a vacuum, less than half a millimeter in diameter, which was the receiver of the stellar radiation [103].

A total of 82 bright non-variable stars were observed in this programme, to about fourth visual magnitude and covering all spectral types. The reductions obtained radiometric magnitudes m_r and heat indices $m_{pv} - m_r$ and $m_{pg} - m_r$. The behaviour of these indices with spectral type was explored and a comparison made with the results of Pettit and Nicholson. Small discrepancies of up to $0^m\!.25$ were found in m_r only for the reddest N-type stars.

The Sterne and Emberson data were less extensive than those of Pettit and Nicholson. Nevertheless it was a useful and carefully executed contribution to early infrared photometry and a confirmation of the stellar data obtained by the Mt Wilson observers.

6.8   New infrared photoconductive cells after World War II

Although Stebbins had used a selenium photoconductive cell as early as 1907, he soon discontinued using this type of detector in favour of photoelectric cells – see section 5.2. Photoconductive cell research meanwhile continued in the laboratory in the 1920s [104] but these devices were not used for astronomical work.

The Second World War had an important impact on infrared technology, including the development of new photoconducting materials. Charles Oxley at the US Naval Research Laboratory reported testing lead sulphide photoconductive cells of German manufacture in 1946 [105] and the British Admiralty was also researching into these detectors at this time [106]. Meanwhile Robert Cashman (1906–88) at Northwestern University was one of the pioneers of the PbS cell in the United States [107]. He began work on this type of detector in 1944, in part because of the military requirement to develop heat-seeking missiles. But the astronomical spin-off from Cashman's work followed soon after the war, when he collaborated

Fig. 6.7   Four types of lead sulphide photoconductive infrared cells from the 1950s.

.with Wallace Wilson (1851–1908) (who built the electronic amplifier) and Gerard Kuiper (1905–73) for the infrared spectrometry of bright stars and planets [108].

The PbS photoconductive cell was operated uncooled on the 82-in Mc-Donald Observatory reflector. Its sensitivity extended to about 3.6 μm, but with a peak at 2.5 μm, which nearly coincided with one of the transparent windows for infrared radiation in the terrestrial atmosphere. At the peak, the sensitivity was a thousand times that of a thermocouple. The beam was chopped at 1080 Hz with a toothed wheel to provide sky cancellation, a technique in fact proposed as early as 1929 by Herman Pfund at the Johns Hopkins University [109] to overcome the problem of detecting faint infrared sources in a bright infrared sky.

Kuiper and his colleagues observed several bright stars and planets in these early pioneering experiments, including the Mira-variable star R Leonis, which was shown to be very bright at 1.6 μm in spite of its faint visual magnitude.

Albert Whitford was another of the early infrared pioneers with the lead sulphide detector. He also used a cell provided by Cashman and made the first broad-band photometric PbS-cell observations (at 0.9 and 2.1 μm) on the 100-inch Mt Wilson reflector in 1947 [110]. His observations included distant supergiants and showed that the $1/\lambda$ interstellar extinction law could be extended to longer wavelengths, at least as a fair approximation.

At the Cambridge Observatories, Peter Fellgett (b. 1922) carried out a more extensive survey with an uncooled lead sulphide detector [111]. His survey of 51 stars on the 36-inch telescope showed that the colour index $(m_{\text{PbS}} - m_{\text{V}})$ correlated well with the thermocouple heat index of Pettit and

Fig. 6.8   PbS infrared photometer at Harvard College Observatory, c. 1957.

Nicholson [97], as well as with the photoelectric $(V - I)$ values of Stebbins and Whitford.

Although Fellgett made these pioneering observations with an uncooled detector he was fully aware of the theoretical advantages of cooling [112], because the detector's sensitivity was limited by thermal radiation received from the surroundings. This was demonstrated in practice by B. N. Watts for PbS cells at temperatures down to that of liquid air [113]. As early as 1948–49 Whitford was using a cooled Cashman PbS cell on the 100-inch telescope at Mt Wilson [114], while the following year Harold Johnson commenced his photometry at 2.2 and 3.6 μm with a liquid-nitrogen cooled PbS cell photometer [115]. About 1960 thus represents the start of the modern era of instrumentation and discovery in infrared astronomy.

6.9   Johnson's multicolour photometry

Harold Johnson (1921–80) began his infrared photometry using a cooled PbS photoconductive cell in 1959. However, by January 1961 he had changed his detector to an InSb photovoltaic device, also at 77K in a liquid-nitrogen dewar [116]. The photovoltaic detectors are also semiconductor devices, but rely on the internal field at a p-n function, generated by photoexcitations, to determine the incident photon signal. The InSb cell had the advantage of extending the wavelength coverage to 5 μm, even though the quantum efficiency at 2.2 and 3.6 μm was below that of the PbS cell.

In this first study of infrared stellar photometry Johnson observed over 50 stars of all spectral types from O5 to M6 [116]. He defined four broad-band passbands which coincided with transparent windows in the earth's atmosphere, and designated these as J (1.3 μm), K (2.2 μm), L (3.6 μm) and M (5.0 μm). The bands were defined by interference filters.

The observations were undertaken at McDonald Observatory on the 82-inch telescope, at Kitt Peak (36-inch), in the Catalina Mountains (28-inch) and, from 1963, at the Tonantzintla Observatory in Mexico. His first paper gave results for the K and L bands. The effective temperatures derived by Johnson for cool stars were down to about 3000 K for an M5 dwarf, assuming it radiated like a black body. He showed that $(V - K)$ correlated well with $(B - V)$, although the relationship was not linear.

With M-band (5 μm) InSb photometry at McDonald Observatory from October 1962, Johnson and Mitchell were able to extend these observations of stellar continua to longer wavelengths and compare $(B - V)$ with $(K - M)$ [117]. One of the earliest examples of a very red star from this preliminary work was χ Cygni, a long-period Mira variable with a colour temperature around 2000 K.

Undoubtedly the gallium-doped germanium bolometer, developed by Frank Low (b. 1933) in 1961 [118] was the major advance that allowed the longer wavelengths beyond 5 μm to be explored. The bolometer was cooled with liquid helium to 2 K. Low's bolometer was the first thermal detector based on a semiconductor device. Its operating principle is the decrease in the electrical resistance of the doped germanium as a result of a small temperature rise produced by the incident radiation. The essential feature is that electrons and holes are produced by thermal excitation rather than by photoexcitation of the photoconductive detectors [119].

At this time (1961) Low was on the staff of Texas Instruments. Even before he moved to the Lunar and Planetary Laboratory at the University of Arizona in 1965 he was active in infrared astronomy. The collaboration with Johnson allowed the 10-μm N band to be used from July 1963 [120] and the 22-μm Q band from 1966 [121].

The germanium bolometer was the principal detector used at 10 and 20 μm. However, Robert Wildey (b. 1934) and Bruce Murray at Caltech also made 10-μm observations of stars in 1963 (even before Low's bolometry), using the Hale 200-inch telescope [122]. These observations used a mercury-doped germanium photoconductive cell cooled with liquid hydrogen [123], and the 10-μm fluxes for 25 bright stars of types B8 to M7 were reported.

Johnson and his colleagues observed a large number of bright stars in the $UBVRIJKLMN$ multicolour system. Individual papers on M dwarfs [124] and on carbon stars and Mira variables [125] appeared. An important catalogue of photometric data was published at this time [126]. By fitting black-body curves over this wide wavelength range (0.36 to 10 μm), the effective temperatures and bolometric corrections of stars of different spectral type were calibrated [127, 128].

In the 1960s other observers were also active in observing stellar continuum fluxes into the infrared region. For example a programme at the Perkins Observatory in Ohio by Philip Barnhart and Walter Mitchell using a PbS photometer was commenced in 1960 to investigate the relationship between stellar effective temperatures and infrared fluxes for stars of different spectral type [129, 130].

6.10   Infrared sky surveys in the 1960s

The first infrared sky survey using a dry-ice cooled PbS photocell was made by Freeman Hall (b. 1928) at the ITT Federal Laboratories in

San Fernando, California in 1960–63. He used a 20-inch f/2.5 newtonian telescope and scanned just 18 per cent of the sky at 2.2 μm. [131, 132, 133]. Only 81 probable sources were detected in this preliminary work, and the results were compared with Fellgett's observations.

The first infrared sky survey of major significance at a wavelength greater than 1 micron was carried out by Gerry Neugebauer (b. 1932) and Bob Leighton (b. 1919) at Caltech from 1965–68. The telescope comprised a very fast (f/1) aluminized epoxy 'light-bucket' mirror of diameter 1.55 m in an equatorial mount. An array of eight liquid-nitrogen cooled PbS photoconductive cells and also a photovoltaic silicon photocell gave stellar magnitudes at 2.2 μm (K) and at 840 nm (I) over the sky from $-30°$ to $+81°$ [134].

This survey was remarkable for its reliability and completeness. Some 20 000 infrared sources were detected, of which 5612, with their K magnitude brighter than 3.0, were catalogued. The majority of these objects in the *Two-micron sky survey* catalogue could be identified with known stellar sources (for example two-thirds were identified with stars in the Smithsonian catalogue). However, the brightest objects in the Caltech survey at 2.2 μm were not necessarily prominent visually – they were generally cool late-type giants or supergiants, with temperatures from 2000 to 4000 K, and included several Mira-type long-period variable stars. However, a few objects in the survey – some 50 stars – had ($I - K$) colour temperatures corresponding to about 1000 K and these reddest objects were mostly not identified with visual sources. Indeed, Charles Hetzler at the Yerkes Observatory [135] three decades earlier had drawn attention to extraordinarily red objects from his near infrared photographic survey – see section 7.4.3. Some of the newly found very red stars were announced by the Caltech observers in 1965–66 [136, 137]. Included were objects such as NML Cygni (IRC +40 448), a late M-type supergiant with an apparent colour temperature of only 500 K. Also notable in the Caltech survey is IRC +10 216, a heavily reddened carbon star, later found to be the brightest object in the sky at 5 μm, but as faint as 18th magnitude visually. As discussed in the next section, the interpretation that these red objects were truly very cool stars was soon discarded.

During the 1960s the southern sky south of $-30°$ was not surveyed at 2 microns with the same thoroughness as achieved in the Caltech work. However, Stephen Price of the ITT Federal Laboratories continued the work of Freeman Hall and carried out a preliminary infrared survey at Mt John in New Zealand in 1967. About half the sky from $-50°$ to $-62°$ was scanned with a 30-element PbS cell array mounted on a 61-cm f/2 aluminium mirror. A total of 414 sources were catalogued of which only two were identified as abnormally red objects [138].

At longer wavelengths the infrared sky at 4, 10 and 20 μm was surveyed by Russell Walker and Stephen Price from the Air Force Cambridge Research Laboratories. This AFCRL survey was carried out in 1971–72, and the resulting catalogue comprised 3198 entries [139]. The survey made use of a helium-cooled germanium bolometer in a rocket – the darkness of the infrared sky at high altitude enabling large areas of the sky to be mapped during the short duration of the rocket flight.

Over half of these sources were already in the Caltech survey at 2.2 μm. Many of the entries, however, were spurious. A characteristic of many of the sources was that they were generally extended – only 300 were point sources.

At 20 μm the brightest object is the small nebula associated with the peculiar star, η Carinae. Other bright objects include IRC +10216 and NML Cygni. Most of the sources seen at 20 μm also appeared in the Caltech 2-μm survey, but are often faint objects at the shorter wavelength and invisible in the visual region. Many of the brightest 20-μm sources are extended H II regions, such as the Orion nebula, and correspond to warm dust clouds within the ionized hydrogen gas, the grains being at temperatures of about 250 K.

6.11   New infrared sources and their interpretation

The announcement of 2 very red stars with large $(I - K)$ colour indices by the Caltech observers in 1965 (the stars were named NML Cygni and NML Tauri after the authors of the paper) [136] and of a further 14 red objects in 1966 [137] caused tremendous interest among astronomers. Five of the stars in the second paper were known Mira variables. Many observers continued intensive observations of these objects [140, 141, 142]. At the same time the Mexican astronomer Eugenio Mendoza found the star R Mon to have a large infrared excess, from observations obtained with Johnson's apparatus in Arizona [143]. The energy distribution for this 12th magnitude (in V) T Tauri-like star peaked at about 4 μm. Frank Low and Bruce Smith extended Mendoza's photometry to 20 μm and proposed that a viable model for this and other very red stars was that of a circumstellar dust shell which both strongly absorbed the visual radiation ($\lambda < 1\mu$m) and reradiated this energy at longer infrared wavelengths [144]. In the case of NML Cygni a black body of $T \sim 700$ K would account for the large infrared excess [142], and this corresponded to the temperature of the dust grains. The circumstellar dust grain model was in accordance with a suggestion by Arcadio Poveda [145], who proposed that circumstellar material should commonly be found around young T Tauri stars (such as R Mon) as a precursor to the formation of a planetary system.

Harry Hyland (b. 1939) and his colleagues at Caltech showed that thick dust shells could explain the infrared excesses of stars such as NML Cygni and the similar Mira-type star, VY CMa [146]. As it happens, both of these objects were known to be OH microwave emitters, and a model comprising a late M-type supergiant with an expanding dust shell was shown to be in good agreement with the microwave observations.

The circumstellar dust model received widespread support from the late 1960s onwards. Evidence for the grains being composed mainly of silicates of iron and magnesium (that is olivine) came from the infrared spectrophotometry of Fred Gillett with Frank Low and Wayne Stein (b. 1937) [147]. These observers used a germanium bolometer with a rotating interference filter and found a very broad emission peak at about 10 μm superimposed on the continuum flux curve for several late-type stars, which Neville Woolf (b. 1932) and Edward Ney (b. 1920) [148] showed was probably the emission from silicate grains in cases where the dust shell was optically thin. Such a model received theoretical support from Robert Gilman at Princeton [149].

One of the most interesting objects found from infrared observations was a point (or at least unresolved) source in the Orion nebula which was found to be radiating strongly at 10 μm. The object was found by Eric Becklin and Gerry Neugebauer in 1967, originally from PbS observations between 1.6 and 3.4 μm [150], but no visible source could be identified. The black-body colour temperature was about 700 K. Because the object was in a young star-forming region, the suggestion was made that the Becklin-Neugebauer object was a protostar, still undergoing slow gravitational contraction, inside a very dense dust shell that excluded all visible radiation [150]. Douglas Kleinmann (b. 1942) and Frank Low in Tucson, in attempting to record the new object at 10 μm, serendipitously discovered a nearby small but intense infrared nebula, some half an arc minute across corresponding to an extended dust cloud at only 100 K [151]. The Kleinmann-Low nebula was located about an arc minute from the central 'Trapezium' region of the Orion nebula, which is itself an infrared source at 10 to 20 μm [152].

The small nebula (6 arc seconds across) associated with the peculiar emission-line star η Carinae is the strongest 20-μm source in the whole sky [153, 154]. Here the circumstellar dust is at about 250 K and occupies a region some 6000 astronomical units in diameter [155]. η Carinae itself is a hot nova-like star with a complex emission-line spectrum. It has an effective temperature greater than 10000 K and a luminosity of at least 2 million times that of the sun. It is an example of an early-type supergiant warming a very extensive circumstellar dusty region.

Finally, the emission-line B stars were also shown to have moderate infrared excesses (at 3.5 μm) in the late 1960s. These observations were first made by Harold Johnson [156] and continued by Woolf, Stein and Peter Strittmatter (b. 1939) [157], who showed that the emission in this case was the free-free 'Bremsstrahlung' radiation from an ionized circumstellar shell of hydrogen, rather than from dust grains.

Even sources at the centre of the Galaxy, estimated to be hidden by 25 magnitudes of interstellar extinction at visual wavelengths, were first observed in the infrared at 2.2 and 3.4 μm in 1968. These pioneering observations were made by Becklin and Neugebauer at Caltech [158]. They interpreted the extended source to be radiation from millions of unresolved cool stars in the galactic nucleus.

In the Soviet Union, Viktor Moroz at the Crimean Astrophysical Observatory was the pioneer infrared observer in that country. His observations of the Crab nebula in 1964 with a PbS photocell on the 1.25-m telescope showed it to be an extended infrared source [159]. Subsequent work has shown this to be a non-thermal synchrotron source of radiation.

It is clear that, from the early 1960s, infrared measurements added a spectacular new dimension to astronomical photometry. By the end of that decade an exciting variety of different infrared sources had been discovered. The rôle of dust grains gave new insights into the birth and evolution of stars and of physical processes in the interstellar medium. By 1970 a whole new branch of astrophysics was gathering momentum, all the while being driven by new developments in infrared technology, including new detectors, new infrared telescopes and new observation vehicles such as rockets, balloons and high-flying aircraft.

References

[1]   Herschel, W., *Phil. Trans. R. Soc.*, **90**, 255 (1800).
[2]   Herschel, W., *Phil. Trans. R. Soc.*, **90**, 284 (1800).
[3]   Herschel, W., *Phil. Trans. R. Soc.*, **90**, 293 (1800).
[4]   Herschel, W., *Phil. Trans. R. Soc.*, **90**, 437 (1800).
[5]   Young, T., *Phil. Trans. R. Soc.*, **92**, 365 (1802).
[6]   Englefield, H.C., *R. Inst. J.*, **1**, 202 (1802).
[7]   Englefield, H.C., *Gilbert's Ann. der Physik*, **12**, 399 (1803).
[8]   Wünsch, C.E., *Magazin der Ges. der naturforsch. Freunde zu Berlin*, **1**, 185 (1807).
[9]   Meikle, H., *Phil. Mag.*, **65**, 10 (1825).
[10]   Biot, Jean J.B., *Gilbert's Ann. der Physik*, **16**, 376 (1814).
[11]   Pouillet, C.-S., *Comptes Rendus de l'Acad. des Sci.*, **7**, 24 (1828).
[12]   Stefan, J., *Sitzungsber. Deutsche Akad. Wiss.*, **79** (part 2), 391 (1879).
[13]   Herschel, J., *Phil. Trans. R. Soc.*, **130**, 1 (1840).

[14]   Lord Rayleigh, *Phil. Mag.*, **4**, 348 (1877).
[15]   Draper, J., *Proc. Nat. Acad. Sci. America*, **16**, 223 (1881).
[16]   Fizeau, H. and Foucault, L., *Comptes Rendus de l'Acad. des Sci.*, **25**, 447 (1847).
[17]   Fizeau, H., *Ann. Chimie et Phys.*, (5) **15**, 394 (1878).
[18]   Becquerel, E., *Bibl. Univ. Genève*, **40**, 341 (1842).
[19]   Draper, J.W., *Phil. Mag.*, (3) **22**, 360 (1843).
[20]   Becquerel, E., *Ann. Chimie et Physique*, (3) **9**, 257 (1843) see p. 314.
[21]   Becquerel, E., *Ann. Chimie et Physique*, (3) **22**, 244 (1848).
[22]   Becquerel, E., *Comptes Rendus de l'Acad. des Sci.*, **77**, 302 (1873).
[23]   Becquerel, E., *Comptes Rendus de l'Acad. des Sci.*, **83**, 249 (1876).
[24]   Edison, T.A., *American J. Sci.*, **117**, 52 (1879).
[25]   Edison, T.A., *Sci. American*, **39**, 112 (1878).
[26]   Lockyer, J.N., *Nature*, **18**, 410 (1878).
[27]   Nichols, E.F., *Astrophys. J.*, **13**, 101 (1901).
[28]   Eddy, J.A., *J. Hist. Astron.*, **3**, 165 (1972).
[29]   Seebeck, T., *Pogg. Ann. der Phys.*, **6**, 1, 133, 253 (1826).
[30]   Melloni, M., *Ann. Chimie et Physique*, (2) **48**, 198 (1831); ibid. **48**, 385 (1831).
[31]   Melloni, M., *Ann. Chimie et Physique*, **53**, 5 (1833).
[32]   Melloni, M., *Comptes Rendus de l'Acad. des Sci.*, **15**, 454 (1842).
[33]   Melloni, M., *Comptes Rendus de l'Acad. des Sci.*, **22**, 541 (1846).
[34]   Melloni, M., *Pogg. Ann. der Phys.*, **68**, 220 (1846).
[35]   Smyth, C.P., 'Account of the astronomical experiment of 1856 on the Peak of Teneriffe' *R. Inst. Proc.*, **2**, 493 (1854–58).
[36]   Müller, J., *Pogg. Ann. der Phys.*, **105**, 337 (1858); *Phil. Mag.*, **17**, 233 (1859).
[37]   Secchi, A., *Astron. Nachr.*, **34**, 219 (1852).
[38]   Lamansky, S., *Monatsberichte der königl. Akad. der Wiss. zu Berlin*, p. 632 (1871).
[39]   Mouton, L., *Comptes Rendus de l'Acad. des Sci.*, **89**, 295 (1879).
[40]   Mouton, L., *Comptes Rendus de l'Acad. des Sci.*, **88**, 1078 (1879).
[41]   Huggins, W., *Proc. R. Soc.*, **17**, 309 (1869).
[42]   Huggins, W. and Lady M. Huggins, *An Atlas of Representative Stellar Spectra*, p. 88, William Wesley and Son, London (1899).
[43]   Stone, E.J., *Proc. R. Soc.*, **18**, 159 (1870).
[44]   Parsons, L., *Proc. R. Soc.*, **17**, 436 (1869).
[45]   Parsons, L., *Proc. R. Soc.*, **19**, 9 (1870).
[46]   Parsons, L., *Phil. Trans. R. Soc.*, **163**, 587 (1873).
[47]   Parsons, L., *Mon. Not. R. Astron. Soc.*, **34**, 197 (1874).
[48]   Parsons, L., *Nature*, **16**, 438 (1877).
[49]   Boys, C.V., *Proc. R. Soc.*, **42**, 189 (1887).
[50]   Boys, C.V., *Proc. R. Soc.*, **44**, 96 (1888).
[51]   Boys, C.V., *Proc. R. Soc.*, **47**, 480 (1890).
[52]   Langley, S.P., *Comptes Rendus de l'Acad. des Sci.*, **80**, 746, 819 (1875).
[53]   Langley, S.P., *Comptes Rendus de l'Acad. des Sci.*, **81**, 436 (1875).
[54]   Langley, S.P., *Ann. Smithsonian Astrophys. Observ.*, **1**, 1 (1900).
[55]   Svanberg, A., *Pogg. Ann. der Phys.*, **84**, 411 (1851).
[56]   Langley, S.P., *Proc. American Acad.*, **16**, 342 (1881).
[57]   Langley, S.P., *Comptes Rendus de l'Acad. des Sci.*, **95**, 482 (1882).
[58]   Langley, S.P., *American J. Sci.*, **25**, 169 (1883).

[59]   Langley, S.P., 'Researches on solar heat and its absorption by the earth's atmosphere. A report of the Mount Whitney Expedition', *U.S. Signal Service Professional Papers*, No. **15** (1884).
[60]   Abbot, C.G., *Astrophys. J.*, **23**, 271 (1906).
[61]   Langley, S.P., *American J. Sci.*, **32**, 83 (1866).
[62]   Langley, S.P., *Astron. Astrophys.*, **13**, 41 (1894).
[63]   Abbot, C.G. and Fowle, F.E., *Ann. Smithsonian Astrophys. Observ.*, **2**, 1 (1908).
[64]   Abbot, C.G., Fowle, F.E. and Aldrich, L.B., *Ann. Smithsonian Astrophys. Observ.*, **4**, 1 (1922).
[65]   Abbot, C.G., *Astrophys. J.*, **34**, 197 (1911).
[66]   Abbot, C.G., Fowle, F.E. and Aldrich, L.B., *Smithsonian Misc. Coll.*, **74**, 1 (1923).
[67]   Crookes, W., *Proc. R. Soc.*, **23**, 373 (1875).
[68]   Crookes, W., *Proc. R. Soc.*, **24**, 276 (1876).
[69]   Stoney, G.J., *Phil. Mag.*, **1**, 177 (1876).
[70]   Crookes, W., *Proc. R. Soc.*, **27**, 29 (1878).
[71]   Pringsheim, E., *Ann. der Physik*, **254**, 1 (1883).
[72]   Pringsheim, E., *Ann. der Physik*, **254**, 32 (1883).
[73]   Nichols, E.F., *Phys. Rev.*, **4**, 297 (1897).
[74]   Nichols, E.F., *Wiedemann's Ann. der Physik*, **60**, 401 (1897).
[75]   Hale, G.E., *Astrophys. J.*, **9**, 360 (1899).
[76]   Huggins, W., *Publ. of Sir Wm Huggins' Observatory*, **2**, 472 (1909).
[77]   Coblentz, W.W., *Lick Observ. Bull.*, **8** (No. 266), 104 (1915).
[78]   Wien, W., *Sitzungsber. deutsche Akad. Wiss.*, p. 55 (1893).
[79]   Boltzmann, L., *Ann. der Physik und Chemie*, **22**, 291 (1884).
[80]   Abbot, C.G., *Astrophys. J.*, **60**, 87 (1924).
[81]   Michelson, A.A. and Pease, F.G., *Astrophys. J.*, **53**, 249 (1921).
[82]   Pease, F.G., *Publ. Astron. Soc. Pacific*, **33**, 171 (1921).
[83]   Abbot, C.G., *Astrophys. J.*, **69**, 293 (1929).
[84]   Weaver, H.F., *Pop. Astron.*, **54**, 451 (1946).
[85]   Abbot, C.G., Hoover, W.H. and Clark, L.B., *Smithsonian Misc. Coll.*, **104** (No. 14), (1945).
[86]   Abbot, C.G. and Aldrich, L.B., *Smithsonian. Misc. Coll.*, **107** (No. 19), 1 (1948).
[87]   Lebedev, P., *Ann. der Physik*, **56**, 12 (1895).
[88]   Pettit, E., in *Astrophysics: a topical symposium* ed. A.J. Hynek, Chap. 6: 'The Sun and stellar radiation', Chicago Univ. Press (1951).
[89]   Johansen, E.S., *Ann. der Physik*(3), **33**, 517 (1910).
[90]   Pfund, A.H., *Phys. Rev.*, **34**, 228 (1912).
[91]   Pfund, A.H., *Publ. Allegheny Observ.*, **3** (No. 6), 43 (1913).
[92]   Coblentz, W.W., *Bull. Bur. Standards*, **9**, 7 (1913).
[93]   Coblentz, W.W., *Astrophys. J.*, **55**, 20 (1922).
[94]   Coblentz, W.W., *Pop. Astron.*, **31**, 105 (1923).
[95]   Menzel, D.H., Coblentz, W.W. and Lampland, C.O., *Astrophys. J.*, **63**, 177 (1926).
[96]   Pettit, E. and Nicholson, S.B., *Astrophys. J.*, **56**, 295 (1922).
[97]   Pettit, E. and Nicholson, S.B., *Astrophys. J.*, **68**, 279 (1928).
[98]   Barnes, T.G. and Evans, D.S., *Mon. Not. R. Astron. Soc.*, **174**, 489 (1976).
[99]   Pettit, E. and Nicholson, S.B., *Publ. Astron. Soc. Pacific*, **34**, 181 (1922).
[100] Pettit, E. and Nicholson, S.B., *Astrophys. J.*, **78**, 320 (1933).
[101] Pettit, E. and Nicholson, S.B., *Astrophys. J.*, **71**, 153 (1930).

[102] Pettit, E. and Nicholson, S.B., *Pop. Astron.*, **32**, 601 (1924).
[103] Sterne, T.E. and Emberson, R.M., *Astrophys. J.*, **94**, 412 (1941).
[104] Case, T.W., *Phys. Rev. (2)*, **15**, 289 (1920).
[105] Oxley, C.L., *J. Optical Soc. America*, **36**, 356 (1946).
[106] Sosnowski, L., Starkiewicz, J. and Simpson, O., *Nature*, **159**, 818 (1947).
[107] Cashman, R.J., *J. Optical Soc. America*, **36**, 356 (1946).
[108] Kuiper, G.P., Wilson, W. and Cashman, R.J., *Astrophys. J.*, **106**, 243 (1947).
[109] Pfund, A.H., *Science*, **69**, 71 (1929).
[110] Whitford, A.E., *Astrophys. J.*, **107**, 102 (1948).
[111] Fellgett, P.B., *Mon. Not. R. Astron. Soc.*, **111**, 537 (1951).
[112] Fellgett, P.B., *J. Optical Soc. America*, **39**, 970 (1949).
[113] Watts, B.N., *Proc. Phys. Soc.*, **62**A, 456 (1949).
[114] Whitford, A.E., *Astron. J.*, **63**, 201 (1958).
[115] Johnson, H.L. and Mitchell, R.I., *Comm. Lunar Planetary Lab.*, **1**, 73 (1962).
[116] Johnson, H.L., *Astrophys. J.*, **135**, 69 (1962).
[117] Johnson, H.L. and Mitchell, R.I., *Astrophys. J.*, **138**, 302 (1963).
[118] Low, F.J., *J. Optical Soc. America*, **51**, 1300 (1961).
[119] Low, F.J. and Rieke, G.H., in *Methods of Experimental Physics*, **12A** Astrophysics, Optical and Infrared, ed. N. Carleton, New York : Academic Press (1974).
[120] Low, F.J. and Johnson, H.L., *Astrophys. J.*, **139**, 1130 (1964).
[121] Low, F.J., *Astrophys. J.*, **146**, 326 (1966).
[122] Wildey, R.L. and Murray, B.C., *Astrophys. J.*, **139**, 435 (1964).
[123] Westphal, J.A., Murray, B.C. and Martz, D.E., *Appl. Optics*, **2**, 749 (1963).
[124] Johnson, H.L., *Astrophys. J.*, **141**, 170 (1965).
[125] Mendoza, E.E. and Johnson, H.L., *Astrophys. J.*, **141**, 161 (1965).
[126] Johnson, H.L., Mitchell, R.I., Iriarte, B. and Wisniewski, W.Z., *Comm. Lunar Planetary Lab.*, **4**, (No. 63) 99 (1966).
[127] Johnson, H.L., *Bol. Observ. Tonantzintla y Tacubaya*, **3**, 305 (1964).
[128] Johnson, H.L., *Ann. Rev. Astron. Astrophys.*, **4**, 193 (1966).
[129] Barnhart, P.E. and Mitchell, W.E., *Contrib. Perkins Observ.* (2), No. 16, 1 (1966).
[130] Barnhart, P.E. and Mitchell, W.E., Jr., *Astrophys. J.*, **71**, 378 (1966).
[131] Hall, F.F., *Proc. IR Information Symp.*, **6**, 137 (1961).
[132] Hall, F.F., *Final report subcontract No 62-151, Aerospace Corporation, ITT Federal Labs: Stellar irradiance measurements*, Jan. 1963.
[133] Hall, F.F., *Liège Mem.*, **9**, 432 (1964).
[134] Neugebauer, G. and Leighton, R.B., *Two-micron Sky Survey: a preliminary catalog. NASA Special Publication*, SP-3047, p. 309 (1969).
[135] Hetzler, C., *Astrophys. J.*, **86**, 509 (1937).
[136] Neugebauer, G., Martz, D.E. and Leighton, R.B., *Astrophys. J.*, **142**, 399 (1965).
[137] Ulrich, B.T., Neugebauer, G., McCammon, D., Leighton, R.B., Hughes, E.E. and Becklin, E., *Astrophys. J.*, **146**, 288 (1966).
[138] Price, S.D., *Astron. J.*, **73**, 431 (1968).
[139] Walker, R.G. and Price, S.D., *Air Force Cambridge Research Laboratories Infrared Sky Survey*, AFCRL TR-0373 (1975).
[140] McCammon, D., Münch, G. and Neugebauer, G., *Astrophys. J.*, **147**, 575 (1967).
[141] Wing, R.F., Spinrad, H. and Kuhi, L.V., *Astrophys. J.*, **147**, 117 (1967).

[142] Johnson, H.J., Low, F.J. and Steinmetz, D., *Astrophys. J.*, **142**, 808 (1965).
[143] Mendoza, E.E., *Astrophys. J.*, **143**, 1010 (1966).
[144] Low, F.J. and Smith, B.J., *Nature*, **212**, 675 (1966).
[145] Poveda, A., *Bol. Observ. Tonantzintla y Tacubaya*, **4**, 15 (1965).
[146] Hyland, A.R., Becklin, E.E., Neugebauer, G. and Wallerstein, G., *Astrophys. J.*, **158**, 619 (1969).
[147] Gillett, F.C., Low, F.J. and Stein, W.A., *Astrophys. J.*, **154**, 677 (1968).
[148] Woolf, N.J. and Ney, E.P., *Astrophys. J.*, **155**, L181 (1969).
[149] Gilman, R.C., *Astrophys. J.*, **155**, L185 (1969).
[150] Becklin, E. E. and Neugebauer, G., *Astrophys. J.*, **147**, 799 (1967).
[151] Kleinmann, D.E. and Low, F.J., *Astrophys. J.*, **149**, L1 (1967).
[152] Ney, E.P. and Allen, D.A., *Astrophys. J.*, **155**, L193 (1969).
[153] Neugebauer, G. and Westphal, J., *Astrophys. J.*, **152**, L89 (1968).
[154] Westphal, J.A. and Neugebauer, G., *Astrophys. J.*, **156**, L45 (1969).
[155] Pagel, B.E.J., *Astrophys. Letters*, **4**, 221 (1969).
[156] Johnson, H.L., *Astrophys. J.*, **150**, L39 (1967).
[157] Woolf, N.J., Stein, W.A. and Strittmatter, P.A., *Astron. Astrophys.*, **9**, 252 (1970).
[158] Becklin, E. E. and Neugebauer, G., *Astrophys. J.*, **151**, 145 (1968).
[159] Moroz, V.I., *Soviet Astron. J.*, **7**, 748 (1964).

7 Photographic photometry from 1922

7.1   Photographic photometry in 1922

The year 1922 can be regarded as a high point in the history of stellar photographic photometry. The first General Assembly of the International Astronomical Union had met in Rome in May of that year. Frederick Seares from Mt Wilson was the president of the Commission 25 for Stellar Photometry and his report [1] presented both photographic (blue-ultraviolet) and photovisual (green-yellow) magnitudes for 92 of the stars of the original Harvard North Polar Sequence, defined by Miss Leavitt in 1912 [2]. This report was adopted by the IAU at the Rome meeting [3], and even though the description 'International' was not applied by the IAU to Seares' magnitudes, in practice they became known as the 'International System' (notation IPg and IPv), displacing the Harvard photographic magnitudes of 1912 and 1917 [4] from this position.

All the stars in the 1922 report had appeared in Seares' more extensive polar list of 1915 [5] which had significant divergences from the Harvard scale, especially for the faintest and brightest stars [6]. Indeed, Harlow Shapley at Harvard in effect recognized the superiority of the Mt Wilson data in 1923 by revising Miss Leavitt's photographic magnitudes of bright stars to conform closely to the Seares scale, and by rejecting all her values for the faintest stars ($m_{pg} > 16.02$) [7].

The 1922 magnitudes by Seares, however, contained small corrections for many stars relative to his 1915 values, deduced by a careful comparison of the Mt Wilson 60-inch reflector and 10-inch astrograph scales with those from other observatories (Göttingen, Greenwich, Harvard, Potsdam and Yerkes). The original data on which Seares' IAU report was based were described in detail in two papers in the *Astrophysical Journal* [8, 9].

The 1922 magnitudes were undoubtedly a marked improvement on earlier magnitude scales. The random error bars were claimed to be no more than $\pm 0^{m}\!.024$ (p.e.), the magnitudes were believed to comply with the Pogson scale, and they extended to faint limits ($m_{pg} = 20; m_{pv} = 17.5$) in two spectral regions. Moreover, Seares, as the inaugural Commission 25 president, was in a powerful position to ensure their acceptance. Edward Pickering had died in February 1919, just a few months before the IAU had been formed in Brussels in July of that year. Also in 1922, Miss Leavitt, a member of the Commission (but not of the American delegation to Brussels), died just a few months before the first General Assembly in Rome. The loss of both Pickering and Miss Leavitt thus effectively removed any Harvard voice from the decision-making process on photographic photometry.

From reading the 1922 IAU report, it is easy to gain the impression that the problems of photographic photometry, after decades of struggle, had at last been solved. In practice the report gave little advice on the practical techniques of photometry, in particular how to transfer the North Polar Sequence magnitudes to other areas of the sky. That such problems existed was known to those observers in the field, as a remark by Pickering to the American Philosophical Society in 1916 made clear [10], when he spoke of 'extraordinary sources of systematic errors', especially when two exposures were made on the same plate. In addition there was a poor understanding of the rôle of instrumental response functions for the two passbands (in particular the effect of ultraviolet radiation in the photographic band), of extinction corrections and their dependence on stellar colour, as well as of nightly variations in extinction. Yet another problem came from the preponderance of A-type stars at the bright end of the North Polar Sequence, but red stars at the faint end, which could play havoc when observers used telescopes with different colour equations to that of the Mt Wilson silver-on-glass 60-inch reflector, on which Seares had based his final magnitude system.

In general, 1922 was a time of great confidence in astronomy; the advent of the IAU itself, the first applications of physical principles to solve astronomical problems (for example, the use of the Planck black-body energy distribution for stellar radiation and the application of the Saha equation to stellar spectra) and the construction of new large reflecting telescopes (in particular the 100-inch Hooker telescope at Mt Wilson) all suggested progress. Some of the intrinsic problems still lurking in stellar photography were pushed aside or ignored and new large projects of photometry were embarked upon.

In truth it was remarkable that Seares achieved the success he undoubtedly did with such simple methods. His reduction procedure was no more than the visual inspection of stellar images through a microscope and the comparison with a scale of standard images. Using aperture diaphragms and gauze screens, he was able to calibrate the relative intensities of starlight producing stellar images over a dynamic range of over 10^6 in visual light and 10^7 in the blue-ultraviolet region, using none other than the non-linear photographic plate as his detector.

7.2   Some major photometric catalogues of the 1920s and 1930s

The establishment of the North Polar Sequence at Harvard and Mt Wilson allowed photographic magnitudes for very faint stars to be obtained for the first time. Several major programmes were undertaken. One of the earlier ones, and also the largest, arose from the cooperation between Pickering and Kapteyn to determine magnitudes in the Groningen Selected Areas [11].

The observations for this programme were commenced as early as 1907 at Arequipa using the 24-inch Bruce telescope – see [12]. Miss Leavitt established secondary standards in all 206 of these Selected Areas by transferring her scale of North Polar Sequence magnitudes to about 20 stars in each area, using plates exposed from the same batch and developed together [4] – see section 4.9.2. For the northern areas the 16-inch Metcalf telescope at Harvard was used. Generally 1-hour exposures allowed stars of 16th (or occasionally 17th) photographic magnitude to be reached and the magnitudes were obtained from image diameters at Groningen. A typical probable error of a catalogue magnitude was $\pm 0\overset{m}{.}11$.

The huge programme covered all 206 Selected Areas in both hemispheres, and photographic magnitudes for about 251 000 faint stars were the result [13, 14, 15]. Unfortunately none of Miss Leavitt, Pickering or Kapteyn survived to see the project to completion and the last two volumes of the *Harvard-Groningen Durchmusterung* were published by Pieter van Rhijn (1886–1960), Kapteyn's successor at Groningen.

Meanwhile the *Astrographic Catalogue* continued to produce large numbers of stellar magnitudes based on stellar diameters, but generally not tied to the North Polar Sequence. By 1925 these amounted to about 1.4×10^6 stars, the statistics having been compiled by H. H. Turner [16] at Oxford for the different participating observatories – see also [17].

The magnitudes were generally of low quality, often tied to the visual scale of the *Bonner Durchmusterung* (even though they were based on photographic diameters), or even left as unreduced image sizes, and were very heterogeneous from observatory to observatory and also from plate to plate. Seares and Joyner attempted to bring some order into these data by publishing recommended corrections for the magnitudes or calibrations for the image diameters in 39 astrographic catalogue zones of 14 observatories, so as to reduce the values to the Mt Wilson International Scale (IPg) [18]. The method was based on star counts per square degree as a function of galactic latitude. In view of the many uncertainties that remained, the data were still of mediocre quality.

The work of Harold Spencer Jones with Jacob Halm (1866–1944) represents an attempt to improve the quality of the photographic magnitudes of stars in the Cape astrographic zone and deserves mention. The zone spanned declination $-40°$ to $-52°$ and magnitudes of 20 843 stars to $m_{pg} = 11.5$ were derived [19], by reference to a sequence established at the south pole – see [20] for details of the calibration. The probable error of a magnitude in this catalogue was $\pm 0^m19$ [21].

The third major catalogue of this era was the famous *Mt Wilson Catalogue of Photographic Magnitudes in Selected Areas 1–139* by Seares, Kapteyn and van Rhijn assisted by Mary Joyner and Myrtle Richmond [22]. This work involved the determination of photographic magnitudes for 67 941 faint stars to about magnitude 18.5 in 139 of the Selected Areas north of $-15°$. Because of the difficulty of a direct transfer of the North Polar Sequence scale through successive one-hour exposures on the same plate of the pole and a selected area, the standards for the catalogue were determined independently in each area with diaphragms and wire gauze screens. The North Polar Sequence standards were, however, used to fix the zero-point in the selected areas by means of two short (2-minute) exposures on the same plate. As with Seares' work on the North Polar Sequence itself, the star diameters were recorded against an arbitrary scale which, when calibrated with the standards, allowed the photographic magnitude of each star to be determined. A typical precision of the magnitudes from one observation was $\pm 0^m15$ for these faint stars.

The corrections for atmospheric extinction reduced all values to the zenith, as was the common practice for all photographic photometry at that time. The extinction coefficient used was 0.324 magnitudes per air mass and the same value was adopted for all nights and for stars of all colours (the colours were in any case generally unknown), a process which inevitably introduced significant systematic errors into the results. Weaver later discussed the errors introduced by this rudimentary extinction correction procedure and showed that red stars observed at the pole from Mt Wilson would be about 0^m05 too bright when reduced to the zenith [23]. In fact it was not until 1943 that Seares produced a satisfactory treatment of extinction. He calculated the extinction for stars radiating as black bodies of different temperatures, and showed that the extinction in the photographic passband for hot blue stars exceeded that for the cooler red ones [24]. Systematic differences between blue and red stars of more than 0^m1 were incurred by using a mean extinction coefficient for all NPS stars, when reducing observations at Mt Wilson to the zenith.

It is perhaps ironic that Kapteyn should have initiated rather similar programmes in his Selected Areas at both Harvard and Mt Wilson and pursued both of these simultaneously with his American collaborators. Although the Harvard programme was more extensive, covering all the Selected Areas in both hemispheres, the Mt Wilson data went some 2 magnitudes fainter and were on a scale shown to follow closely that of the International System of 1922. In 1925 Seares made a detailed comparison of the magnitudes in the *Harvard-Groningen Durchmusterung* with those in the still unpublished *Mt Wilson Catalogue*, using the many stars in common for the northern areas [25]. He found a large colour equation term arising from the use of the Metcalf telescope at Harvard, and the magnitude differences showed probable errors of about $\pm 0^{m}.20$, arising from the errors of both sets of data.

A rather more specialized catalogue from this time was the extension of the *Yerkes Actinometry*. The original survey by Parkhurst [26] covered stars brighter than $m_{pg} = 7.5$ and north of $+73°$. The extension was undertaken by Arthur Fairley at Yerkes, and went from $+75°$ to $+60°$ down to $m_{pg} = 8.25$ [27]. Only photographic magnitudes were obtained and these were from extrafocal images whose densities were compared with a series of spots of known relative intensity exposed on the same plate. The zero-point came by tying the magnitudes to the photometric visual magnitudes of the *Potsdam Durchmusterung* for stars of spectral type around A0, then applying a correction to bring this to the International System. Fairley's catalogue contained magnitudes for 2354 stars with probable errors of typically $\pm 0^{m}.033$, showing that the extrafocal method could deliver results of high precision, at least for relatively bright stars. The scale and zero-point of the second *Yerkes Actinometry* were analysed by Eberhard [28], who found the values reported by Fairley to follow closely on the scale of Parkhurst, except for the very bright stars ($m < 6$).

7.3   Plate photometers for photographic photometry

As early as 1910 Edward Pickering at Harvard suggested the benefits of being able to measure astronomical photographic plates in an objective way by passing heat or light rays through them and detecting the transmission of the plate with a thermopile or bolometer [29]. In this case the idea was not pursued further. However, a year later, Harlan Stetson (1885–1964), apparently motivated by Pickering's remarks, began

Fig. 7.1   Harlan Stetson's plate photometer, 1916.

experiments at Dartmouth College to construct a thermopile photometer
for measuring plate magnitudes [30, 31]. An illuminated pinhole diaphragm
was projected onto the plate and the change in transmission when a star's
image was centred in the light beam was detected from the deflection of
a galvanometer connected to the thermopile. The instrument was used by
Stetson at the Dearborn and Yerkes Observatories to determine photovisual
magnitudes of bright stars in the Pleiades, and for a study of the eclipsing
variable U Cephei [32], with probable errors of only a few hundredths of
a magnitude. The instrument was also proposed for measuring extrafocal
star images, though the application to focal images was the principal goal.
For either image type, the galvanometer deflections had to be calibrated
for each plate to give stellar magnitudes, using standard stars, or at least a
secondary sequence of magnitudes.

Quite independently of Stetson, Jan Schilt (1894–1982) at Groningen
designed an almost identical instrument, apparently unaware of Stetson's
work [33, 34, 35]. The aperture of the diaphragm in these photometers was

Fig. 7.2   Jan Schilt's plate photometer, c. 1922.

fixed for the measurements on a given plate, which limited the useful range
of measurement to some four or five magnitudes. Schilt obtained probable
errors of about $\pm 0^m\!.007$ [36].

The theory of the Schilt photometer was described further in a detailed
article by Frank Ross (1874–1960) at Yerkes Observatory [37] on photographic photometry. Ross became one of Seares' close collaborators and
Schilt photometers of Ross design were used at Yerkes and Mt Wilson for
a major catalogue of polar stars [38].

Another large programme based on Schilt photometry was the photographic magnitudes measured at Yale and Columbia Observatories for zones
in the *Yale Catalogue* by Schilt and Sarah Hill [39, 40, 41, 42, 43]. Schilt had
taken up a position at the Rutherfurd Observatory of Columbia University
in 1931; his photometer became widely used at American observatories
from that time. The catalogues cited included measures for nearly 89 000
stars in declination zones +10° to +60°, many of these being by Schilt
himself.

The *Cape Photographic Catalogue* (see section 7.8.2) was another vast
programme where the Schilt photometer was used, in this case for both

Fig. 7.3   Thermopile plate microphotometer by Askania, c. 1930.

photographic and photovisual magnitudes of about 70 000 southern stars [44, 45].

A major improvement to the Stetson-Schilt photometer came with the iris photometer of Heinrich Siedentopf (1906–63) in 1934. At this time Siedentopf was director of the university observatory at Jena in Germany. Instead of a fixed diaphragm, the new instrument had an adjustable iris which could be reduced in aperture until a given intensity of light was allowed to pass when centred on a stellar image [46]. This greatly improved the range of magnitudes that could be measured on a given plate, from 4 or 5 magnitudes for the Schilt photometer to a range of about 11 magnitudes for the iris instrument.

After the Second World War, numerous observatories acquired iris photometers. One described by Schilt and his colleagues at the Rutherfurd Observatory used a photomultiplier tube and a chopped comparison beam (from the same lamp but not passing through the plate) which eliminates problems due to fluctuations in lamp brightness [47]. Another was built at the Basel Observatory by W. Becker [48] with which 300 stars per hour could be measured. Magnitudes to a precision of about $\pm 0{.}^{\!m}03$ to $0{.}^{\!m}04$

could be obtained, which represents about the limit inherent in the photographic method with the emulsions then available. Other descriptions in the literature are those of the Göttingen Observatory iris photometer in 1953 (based on an earlier instrument there in 1937/38 by Kienle) [49] and the Goethe Link Observatory instrument at the University of Indiana in 1956 [50].

7.4   Photovisual and photored photometry from the 1920s

John Parkhurst, Edward King and especially Frederick Seares were the major pioneers of photovisual photometry – see section 4.7.1. For Seares, photovisual magnitudes were an important part of his 1922 IAU report which defined the International System. Seares again stressed the advantages of these photovisual standards in a paper to the *Astrophysical Journal* in 1925 [51]. For bright stars the Mt Wilson photovisual scale was essentially identical to the Potsdam visual scale apart from a zero-point difference of about a quarter of a magnitude. On the other hand the Harvard visual photometry was shown to have variable colour equations in different magnitude ranges, depending also on the instrument used. This was clearly an undesirable effect that Seares claimed to be absent from his own data.

This kind of detailed discussion of scale differences, systematic errors and colour equations was bread and butter for Seares, and it is rather astonishing that he should want to devote so much of his working life to this sort of analysis, and relatively little to the application of photometry to solving astrophysical problems, which Shapley for example had shown to be such a profitable activity with his research on globular cluster distances. Thus when the Potsdam observers published a new catalogue of Zöllner visual photometry for polar stars (the last major catalogue of visual photometry) [52], Seares made a detailed analysis of the very small departures between this new visual scale and his own photovisual one [53]. He also provided detailed transformation formulae between all the major catalogues of visual or photovisual magnitudes to the Mt Wilson scale [54, 55].

Several other observers obtained photovisual magnitudes in the 1920s and 1930s. One programme by Pieter van Rhijn and Bart Bok (1906–83) obtained m_{pv} (mainly 10^m to 13^m) for 509 stars in seven Kapteyn Selected Areas at $+75°$ [56]. The Cramer Isochromatic plates were exposed on the 26-inch visual refractor at the Leander-McCormick Observatory of the University of Virginia by H. L. Alden and P. van de Kamp, and tied to the

1922 International System by exposing polar and Selected Area fields on the same plate.

The Leander-McCormick Observatory was at this time undertaking a large proper motion survey in various regions of the sky north of −30° [57]. Cramer Isochromatic plates were exposed in two epochs (1914–24 and 1924–32) and those of the second epoch were used for the photovisual photometry. The same plates were also exposed to the North Polar Sequence in order to derive magnitudes on the International System, using a Schilt photometer. A high degree of accuracy was not claimed for this photometry; the probable errors were stated to be $\pm 0^{\mathrm{m}}.12$. The magnitudes were generally between m_{pv} values of 7.5 and 12.5 and the colour equation in this magnitude range was stated to be negligible compared with Seares' IPv values.

At Harvard Cecilia Payne (1900–79) continued the long photometric tradition of that observatory by obtaining photovisual magnitude ($m_{\mathrm{pv}} = 6.5$ to 11) for 819 stars in each of the Harvard Standard Regions [58]. The history of the programme is interesting, as the plates had been taken before 1922 and calibrated using objective gratings. Miss Leavitt had done much of the reductions before she died, but the material remained unpublished. In the present catalogue the northern A and B regions were based on Miss Leavitt's unpublished magnitudes, the southern (E, F) regions on Miss Payne's reductions, while the C and D regions relied on both investigators.

The Harvard photovisual magnitudes were not accurately on the International System, as Miss Payne herself noted. Nor were the different regions quite concordant among themselves, in spite of Miss Payne's attempts to make them so. Once again it was Seares who investigated these effects [54], though Miss Payne later gave her own calibration [59, 60].

One of the last contributions of Seares to photographic photometry, and one of his major catalogues, was published in 1941 as a joint programme with Frank Ross at Yerkes and with Mary Joyner. The *Catalogue of Magnitudes and Colors of stars north of* +80° [38] was produced in the belief that greatly increasing the number of north polar standards would help the magnitude scale be transferred to other regions of the sky. In this respect the catalogue represents a valiant effort to save the International North Polar Sequence System, which was certainly in its death throes by the 1940s. The catalogue gave m_{pg} and m_{pv} values for 2271 stars mainly brighter than visual magnitude 11. It is discussed further in section 7.8.1.

7.4.1   Photographic photometry in the red at Harvard

Commercial dye-sensitized emulsions became available in the red (to beyond the Hα line) in the early 1920s (the panchromatic plates)

Table 7.1. *Principal contributions to photovisual magnitudes (1912–1941)*

Name	Description of programme	Ref.
J. A. Parkhurst	*Yerkes Actinometry*	[26]
F. H. Seares	NPS (1915)	[5]
F. H. Seares	NPS (International System)	[1]
E. S. King	100 bright stars	[61]
J. A. Parkhurst	Selected Areas at +45°	[62]
P. J. van Rhijn and B. J. Bok	Selected Areas at +75°	[56]
F. E. Ross and R. S. Zug	m_{pg} and m_{pv} for 636 stars along the path of Eros	[63]
A. S. Fairley	*Yerkes Actinometry* (Part 2)	[27]
C. H. Payne	Harvard Standard Regions	[58]
J. Armeanca	m_{pv} for 202 stars, m_{pg} for 260 stars in $100' \times 100'$ field at N. Pole to $m_{pv} = 14.71$	[64]
E. Rybka	260 stars near N. Pole	[65]
H. Müller	Stars near N. America Nebula	[66]
A. de Sitter	Bright stars N. of +80°	[67]
E. Rybka	653 stars near N. Pole	[68]
P. van de Kamp and A. N. Vyssotsky	m_{pv} for 18 000 stars in the Leander-McCormick proper motion study	[57]
B. J. Bok and W. F. Swann	Selected Areas at +75°	[69]
F. H. Seares, F. E. Ross, M. C. Joyner	Magnitudes and colours of 2271 stars N. of +80°	[38]

and into the infrared in the 1930s, and astronomers were able to extend the wavelength range of photographic spectroscopy and photometry. These emulsions were not especially easy to use; they were slow, liable to variable fogging and gave larger magnitude errors than normal plates. The first experiments in red photographic photometry were by Edward King in 1923–24 at Harvard using the Draper 8-inch refractor and his extrafocal technique – see section 4.8.3. He used Ilford Panchromatic Special Rapid plates, which were sensitive to about 660 nm and were sometimes hypersensitized in ammonia solution to increase the speed (a practice later condemned by Cecilia Payne if reliable photometry was to be achieved [70]). A red filter eliminated the blue region below an unspecified wavelength. The chromatic technique used by Ernst Öpik in Estonia also isolated a red passband. These observations were made at the same time as King's, but were published earlier. They are described in section 7.6.

Some years later (1929–30) Ruth Ingalls, a student at Radcliffe College, continued this work for her degree using the 11-inch Draper telescope. The combined results of both observers produced red magnitudes for 37 of the brightest stars in the northern sky, from which a red–visual colour index was formed, with zero-point fixed at A0 [71]. The index correlated with spectral type and changed about a magnitude from types B to M.

These early pioneering experiments at Harvard in red photometry were continued after King's death in 1931, by Cecilia Payne-Gaposchkin and Sergei Gaposchkin from 1935. They used the 12-inch Metcalf refractor, the new Eastman I-C Special plate, developed by C. E. Kenneth Mees (1882–1960), and a Ciné red filter to eliminate blue light, giving a 630-nm effective wavelength. Their images were always focal. Their first paper, although jointly authored, had all the hallmarks of pure Cecilia, and was a masterly exposition of techniques, methods and prospects of red photometry [70]. The term 'photo-red' was introduced for the new magnitude scale, and after a careful discussion on the merits of different zero-points, they opted for that defined by just three A0 North Polar Sequence stars on the grounds that

> ... all zero points are arbitrary, and, provided that it is clearly stated exactly how the zero point is determined, it seems best to select one that combines theoretical defensibility with practical attainability [70].

The magnitude error bars in m_{pr} were typically $\pm0^m\!.15$ (p.e.) from one plate, giving colour indices $(m_{pg} - m_{pr})$ to about $\pm0^m\!.10$ from four blue and four red plates. They argued that although this was larger than for a blue–photovisual colour index, the larger wavelength baseline more than compensated, giving the new method a slight advantage. They discussed the possible future uses of photored photometry and predicted that the discovery of very red stars and the observation of red irregular variables would be prime areas of application. On the other hand photo-infrared photometry (at 830 nm), although technically feasible, was deemed unlikely to be useful, as in practice the difficulties would be too large [70].

This first paper gave magnitudes to $m_{pr} = 13.27$ for 41 stars in the North Polar Sequence [70]. A series of further observational results now followed. The blue–red colour indices of stars in the Harvard C regions (at $+15°$) gave a colour index of -0.28 for the A0 stars, further evidence for reddening at the north pole [72]. These C region results were extended using Harvard's 24-inch Bruce refractor at Bloemfontein so they could provide secondary standards for southern observers [73], and indeed a large survey to establish sequences in all the southern Kapteyn Selected Areas 140–206, comprising about one thousand stars to $m_{pr} \simeq 12.5$, was undertaken at the Boyden

Station [74]. Differential extinction corrections were made, and were much less than at shorter wavelengths, amounting to $0^{m}_{.}131$ per air mass [75].

The work on establishing sequences in the southern Selected Areas allowed a large statistical survey of red colour indices to be undertaken in eight of these areas, including two at low galactic latitudes ($b \leq 6°$) [76]. A total of 4051 stars to magnitude $m_{pr} \simeq 12.5$ was included in the programme. The paper analysed the blue–red colour indices as a function of spectral type and apparent magnitude (m_{pr}), the types coming from data supplied by Friedrich Becker (1900–85) for the *Potsdam Southern Spektraldurchmusterung*, which was then being undertaken from Bolivia [77, 78, 79]. The results showed that for late-type stars of a given spectral type, the fainter stars were bluer. The interpretation was an increasing proportion of dwarfs relative to giants in the fainter more distant samples. On the other hand the effects of reddening due to the interstellar medium were found to be marked only for the B stars (and to a lesser extent, the red giants) in the two areas near the galactic equator. This work showed just how difficult it really is to disentangle the competing effects of temperature, luminosity and interstellar reddening on stellar colours, especially given the patchy and highly variable nature which we now recognize for the interstellar reddening and the change in the relative mix of giant and dwarf stars as a function of both distance and galactic latitude.

Another programme involving red magnitudes at Harvard was the photometry of seven galactic clusters by James Cuffey (b. 1911) to derive colour-magnitude diagrams (m_{pr} *vs* $m_{pg} - m_{pr}$), generally to about $m_{pr} = 14$ [80], using the 36-inch reflector at the Steward Observatory in Arizona for some of the plates. A total of 2600 stars were measured. The programme is notable for its derivation of photometric distances for these clusters, using Robert Trumpler's technique of fitting main-sequence apparent magnitudes to mean absolute magnitudes as a function of spectral type [81] – see section 8.6.1. Three of the clusters showed substantial interstellar reddening.

Although quite independent of the Harvard red photometry in the North Polar Sequence, the work of Jason Nassau and Virginia Burger with Eastman 103aE plates and a Wratten No. 22 filter gave a very similar passband and an effective wavelength of 620 nm [82]. These observers used the Schmidt telescope in Cleveland (the first photometry on this type of instrument) to extend the scale of photo-red North Polar Sequence magnitudes by over two magnitudes to $m_{pr} = 15.35$. Their scale was essentially identical to that of the Gaposchkins, but their zero-point was defined on the assumption that ($m_{pv} - m_{pr}$) should be proportional to $m_{pg} - m_{pv}$ over the spectral type range A0 to A5. This somewhat unorthodox definition gave a $0^{m}_{.}06$ difference from the Harvard zero-point.

Eugeniusz Rybka (1898–1988) in Poland was another photometrist who obtained photored magnitudes for polar stars [83]. His effective wavelength was 610 nm using a Wratten No. 27 filter, and he obtained data for 172 stars north of +84°, including 17 stars in the North Polar Sequence, using the 10.5-cm Zeiss astrograph at the Lvov Observatory between 1938 and 1940. He claimed probable errors of only $\pm 0^{m}_{.}036$ and good agreement with both the Harvard and Cleveland data.

7.4.2   Becker's RGU system of photographic photometry

In 1933 Wilhelm Becker (b. 1907) was appointed as an assistant at the Potsdam Astrophysical Observatory, and it was in that year that he began his first experiments in red photography using Agfa Infrared 730 emulsion and a Schott RG1 filter on the 30-cm Schroeder refractor. Becker obtained red magnitudes ($\lambda \simeq 710$ nm) for 190 bright stars of a wide range in spectral type, using extrafocal exposures [84]. In this paper, extensive use was made of two-colour diagrams, by comparing $m_{vis} - m_{red}$ with $m_{pg} - m_{vis}$, as well as with the infrared heat indices obtained by Pettit and Nicholson [85] – see section 6.7.2.

The effect of interstellar reddening on different colour indices was one aspect that Becker emphasized in this paper, but the data were barely adequate to draw any firm conclusions, partly because only very bright and relatively nearby stars were observed.

Becker considered the possibilities of multicolour photographic photometry while a university teacher at Göttingen (1942–45). His first contribution on this subject from Göttingen was one of the most far-sighted and refreshing discourses on the potential of stellar photometry to be published [86]. It was also a condemnation of the outmoded and conservative practices used by most photometric observers up to that time. It is unfortunate that the original paper, which is entitled 'On the need for a reform of astronomical photometry', has not been widely read, a consequence of it being written in German in an observatory publication (rather than mainstream journal) right at the end of the war. However, its general theme and contents were reported to the International Astronomical Union by Greaves at the eighth General Assembly [87]. Becker summarized the need for change as follows:

> In contrast to astrometry and spectral analysis of the stars, there is today in astronomical photometry a definite sterility in the methods used. This has led to the situation that the results of photometric observation in most cases stimulate no further developments. This fact has its origins in the historical development of astronomical photometry and can substantially be traced back to the following three

circumstances. First, the spectral regions for photometry were never defined by relevant criteria, but rather by historical accident. The internationally recognized visual and photographic regions are defined quite independently of the properties of stellar radiation, by the colour sensitivity of the eye and of the blue plate. Staying with these regions would preclude many possibilities for photometry. Secondly, the following fact has made a further contribution to the current unprofitability of photometry: the concept of the brightness [of a star] has from the beginning been so rigidly adhered to, which stems from the continuing practice of very frequently publishing magnitudes with star positions. The inflexibility of this concept was a negative influence on ideas of stellar brightness and prevented any physical interpretation of brightness coming about. A third circumstance hampered the fruitful development of photometry, especially in central Europe. This was the severely deficient and outmoded instrumentation of the majority of observatories [86].

Becker then continues by proposing a new† system of broad-band photographic photometry, using filters to define bands in the red (638 nm), green (481 nm), blue (424 nm) and ultraviolet (373 nm), from which a variety of colour indices can be derived, suitable for studying temperature, luminosity effects and interstellar reddening. The benefits of a multicolour system for studying interstellar reddening were clearly shown. A single colour index cannot distinguish an intrinsically red K star from a highly reddened B star with the same ($m_{red} - m_{green}$) index. But using in addition $m_{UV} - m_{green}$ readily separates the two, because the reddened B star has far more ultraviolet light (relative to green) than does the K star. Similar ideas had been expressed by Becker in his earlier papers [88, 89] and also independently by Greenstein [90] – see also [91]. In view of the very strong Balmer absorption in A0 stars, Becker also recommended that B0 stars be chosen to define the zero-point of the new magnitude scales. The photometry was to be carried out only with aluminized reflectors [86].

Becker's second paper in this series gave magnitudes for 66 stars in the North Polar Sequence on his new system [92], while the third considered some of the properties of the colour indices in the new system as a function of spectral type and in two-colour diagrams [93]. Here Becker also gave R, G and U magnitudes for 154 stars in Kapteyn's Selected Area 89, down to thirteenth magnitude (the plates for this were exposed between 1935 and 1938 on the 50-cm reflector at Potsdam).

Finally Becker studied the galactic cluster M52 in the new system [94]. By observing A stars both in the cluster and in the surrounding field, he was able to show how the reddening occurred in two discrete dust clouds

---

† In fact Collmann's three-colour photometry resembled and preceded Becker's – see section 7.6.

Fig. 7.4   Wilhelm Becker's muticolour system for photographic photometry in 1946, showing five passbands.

at about 950 pc and 1650 pc along the line of sight, with the cluster itself being embedded in the second cloud. As Stebbins and Whitford had already suggested from photoelectric work [95], Becker independently showed that a $1/\lambda$ law fitted the interstellar absorption from ultraviolet to red wavelengths [94].

Later work in Becker's system was restricted to three bandpasses (red, green, ultraviolet – hence the appellation 'RGU system'). From 1960 Becker and his colleagues at Basel were undertaking RGU photometry in the Selected Areas to deduce stellar density gradients in the galactic halo, using plates from the Palomar Schmidt telescope [96, 97, 98, 99]. They showed that halo stars with ultraviolet excesses due to weak metallic absorption lines could be more readily separated in a two-colour $(U-G, R-G)$ diagram than was possible from UBV photoelectric photometry. Moreover, absolute magnitudes could also be estimated from a star's position in the diagram.

Anyone familiar with the literature of stellar photometry from say 1840–1940 will find inspiration in Becker's first Göttingen article [86]. Photometric observers were preoccupied with cataloguing, with error bars, magnitude scales, colour equations and relationships between magnitude systems. Thousands of nights at the telescope were devoted to such pursuits, and the careers of several astronomical generations† were locked into an ac-

---

† Shapley, Stebbins and Becker were a few of the notable exceptions to this trend up to this time.

tivity where the solution of astronomical problems was not the primary motivation.

Becker's *RGU* system did not release a revolution in photometry, because after the war this revolution, the application of photometry to astrophysics, was underway in any case. The *RGU* system never became widely used, probably because it was a photographic system in an era when photoelectric photometry was becoming dominant.

7.4.3 Early infrared photography

Although Abney photographed the near infrared solar spectrum in 1880, the slowness and difficulty of working with infrared plates precluded their use for photographic photometry beyond the visible spectrum until after Kodak introduced the 1-N infrared emulsion in 1933. This was based on the new tricarbocyanine dyes, for which sensitivity to 1.1 μm was possible. The detailed history of the development of new dyes for these long wavelengths to 1933 is given by Brooker, Hamer and Mees at the Kodak Research Laboratories [100].

Paul Merrill (1887–1961) at Mt Wilson was the first to use the new emulsion for astronomy in 1933; grating spectra of cool stars to 900 nm were readily recorded [101]. However, photometry was not part of this programme. The earliest photometric work was commenced at Yerkes Observatory in 1934 by Charles Hetzler [102]. Using mainly the 10-inch Bruce refractor with an infrared gelatine filter he recorded wide-angle near infrared ($\lambda_{eff} \simeq 850$ nm) photographs of Milky Way fields. Hetzler was surprised to discover quite a large number of exceptionally red stars, which were generally identified with long-period variable stars or with cool carbon stars. Defining an infrared colour index as ($m_{560} - m_{850}$), Hetzler found 102 stars with indices in the range 5.0 to 10, and wrote:

> The infrared intensity of some of these stars is so outstanding that often the variable is the only star showing on an infrared plate covering several square degrees. The inference was natural that here was a method for the discovery of new red variables and generally of stars that are too red to be recorded on ordinary plates [102].

Hetzler recognized that these objects corresponded to low temperature stars of late spectral type, and Jean Rösch at Bordeaux estimated temperatures of around 1500 K for objects with an infrared index of 5, without considering the complicating effects of line blocking in the visual band nor of interstellar reddening [103].

In the 1950s the main pioneer of near infrared surveys for cool stars was Jason Nassau (1892–1965) at the Warner and Swasey Observatory in Cleveland, Ohio. Here Nassau and his colleagues used the 24-inch Burrell-Schmidt telescope with 1-N plates and a Wratten No. 89 filter to give an effective wavelength of about 770 nm. Photometry of over 700 red M stars was reported in 1949 [104]. Later work was primarily very low dispersion objective prism surveys which allowed spectral types to be estimated from the molecular bands. Nevertheless Nassau showed that approximate infrared magnitudes could still be obtained from the objective prism spectra, and hundreds of late M and C stars were catalogued in Milky Way fields [105, 106].

7.5   The zero-points of the North Polar Sequence scales

The zero-points of Seares' North Polar Sequence magnitude scales had been fixed so that the photographic and photovisual values for A0 stars near sixth magnitude agreed with the visual magnitude, in accordance with the international agreement of 1910 – see section 4.9.1. Unfortunately the North Polar Sequence contained only two A0 stars near $m_{vis} = 6.0$ and the zero-points were in practice based on just seven early-type stars [5]. Rigorous adherence to the international zero-point was therefore not possible.

In 1930–31 the close opposition of the minor planet Eros afforded a rare opportunity of accurate astrometry to establish an improved value for the solar parallax and hence distance to the sun. In order to obtain precise positions for Eros a large international campaign was set up to establish standard reference stars along the expected path of the minor planet (this campaign is described in detail in [107]). In addition to accurate positions, colour indices for the reference stars were essential, so that the effects of differential atmospheric dispersion on measured position could be taken into account. With this aim, accurate magnitudes and colours were determined for the Eros reference stars by Frank Ross and Richard Zug at Yerkes for 636 stars north of $-17°$ [63]. Two small astrographic cameras were used, one for photographic and the other for photovisual exposures. The faintest magnitudes were about $m_{pg} = 11.0$ and $m_{pv} = 10.5$. Although the majority of stars were of later spectral type, some A stars were included.

At Mt Wilson, Seares, Bancroft Sitterly and Mary Joyner extended these observations for 374 mainly southern stars with the 10-inch refractor [108], about a third of these being in common with the Yerkes data.

Most of these stars in both programmes also had Harvard spectral types, so a unique opportunity was provided of closely re-examining the spectral type *versus* colour index relationship. Both groups essentially obtained concordant information with each other, but quite discordant with the earlier data from the North Polar Sequence. Seares and his colleagues summarized the discrepancy as follows:

> The most noteworthy features of these results, however, are, first, that both series of measures show a color index of about −0.15 mag. for A0 stars, whereas the value for the polar region is zero; and, second, that both depart widely from the accordant relations between color and spectrum found by King, Parkhurst, and Seares [108].

Seares rechecked his zero-point determination in the polar region using 64 stars close to type A0 and found a colour index of $-0^{m}\!.06$ [55], still significantly different from that for the Eros standard stars. The larger negative value for brighter A0 stars was meanwhile confirmed by F. E. Carr [109] at Yerkes. But for fainter stars his value was close to zero.

This discrepancy in the colour-index zero-point was a major embarrassment for those, including Seares, who saw the North Polar stars as providing a standard for colour as well as magnitude which could be transferred to different regions of the sky. Seares suspected that reddening of the polar stars by interstellar material (by about 0.10 magnitudes in the colour index) was the cause of the problem [55].

By the time of the sixth General Assembly of the International Astronomical Union (in Stockholm, 1938) the zero-point of the International System was a major topic of debate. Seares was still president of Commission 25 for stellar photometry, and his report recommended abandoning the 1910 zero-point based on A0 stars and accepting the actual zero-points defined by the North Polar Sequence scales themselves, which would give unreddened A0 stars a colour index of about $-0^{m}\!.14$ [110].

This proposal was circulated to members of the commission prior to the meeting and most supported abandoning the old zero-point based on A0 stars and adopting that which in practice was already widely in use, although van Rhijn and Schilt had some reservations. That A0 stars in any case make poor standards of colour was also noted, for not only are they often reddened by interstellar matter, but also the strong Balmer continuous and line absorptions in the photographic (blue–ultraviolet) region varied from star to star and this rendered the magnitudes unduly sensitive to the instrumental response.

A paper read by Seares in 1936 to the National Academy of Sciences [111] again explained the cause of the problem as being

> ... probably due to selective absorption, as many of the stars originally used are not far from the Milky Way. The important point, however, is that for A0 stars in unobscured regions the mean

color-index on the international system (i.e., $IPg - IPv$) is not zero,
but -0.14, with an uncertainty of 0.02 or 0.03 mag.

The explanation of this unexpected result ... is that the polar region
is covered by a veil of obscuration, and when the zero-point of the
international photographic scale was fixed, before there was any
evidence of selective absorption, the choice was influenced by an
unsuspected color-excess in the polar stars [111].

The mid-1930s were the early days of reliable photoelectric photometry,
and Joel Stebbins and Albert Whitford used their photometer on the 60-inch
telescope at Mt Wilson in 1935 to obtain photoelectric colour indices of the
brighter North Polar Sequence stars, as well as of A0 stars in other parts
of the sky [112]. The data, when transformed to the International System,
confirmed Seares' conclusions concerning the colours of the North Polar
Sequence stars and of A0 stars elsewhere in the sky. The high precision
and linear response of photoelectric photometry, however, at once revealed
other major problems for the North Polar Sequence magnitudes. These are
discussed in section 7.9.

Although Seares continued to maintain that the intrinsic colour of A0
stars was as blue as -0.15, even as late as 1943 [113, 114], other observers
were by this time advocating smaller values (for example, E. G. Martin at
Greenwich found -0.07 for the intrinsic colour of an A0 star [115]) or they
pointed out the presence of errors in the original Eros star photometry (a
result of faulty extinction corrections at large air mass [116]) or of classification errors in the Harvard spectral types used for North Polar Sequence
stars [117]. By 1946 William Morgan (1906–95) and William Bidelman
(b. 1918) at Yerkes had derived a colour index on the International System
of only -0.04 for unreddened A0 stars, based on accurate photoelectric
photometry and new MKK (the new Yerkes system) spectral classifications
[118].

The whole issue of the zero-point was thus seen to be largely a 'red
herring', which nevertheless did substantial damage to the reputation of the
International System of photometry at a time when its other deficiencies
were also becoming apparent. It also highlighted the vulnerability of the
photometry to systematic errors and emphasized the dangers of tying a
photometric scale to the insufficiently reliable determinations of spectral
type then available.

7.6   Ultraviolet photometry and two-colour diagrams

Although the traditional method of obtaining stellar colours by photography was to expose photographic and photovisual images on separate plates, a number of other methods or variations on this technique were devised. Seares' exposure-ratio method of 1916 has already been referred to – see section 4.10.1. This method was also used by Bohumil Šternberk (1897–1983), a student of Guthnick's, at the University Observatory of Berlin-Babelsberg in 1922–23 [119] to obtain colours for stars in the Pleiades, Praesepe and Coma star clusters.

A much more extensive application of the exposure-ratio technique was undertaken by K. G. Malmquist of the Lund Observatory in Sweden. He used the 1-m reflector at the Hamburg-Bergedorf Observatory to obtain colour indices for 3700 stars at the north galactic pole to $m_{pv} = 14$. [120]. As in Seares' work, the results were all transformed into the equivalent colour indices, the transformations coming from Seares' North Polar Sequence colours.

One of the disadvantages of the exposure-ratio method was the fairly large number of exposures needed on each plate. For example Malmquist used nine (seven blue and two yellow ones). Obviously there is some practical benefit if a stellar colour can be derived from a single exposure, and G. A. Tikhoff at Pulkovo Observatory devised a method to do this in 1916, based on the chromatic aberration of the photographically corrected astrograph [121]. The central part of the objective was blocked off and the astrograph placed out of focus so that the blue-violet image of each star on the orthochromatic plate was a ring. In the centre of the ring a yellow image was recorded more nearly in focus. The ratio of the densities in these two parts of the image is a measure of stellar colour. The procedure was also proposed quite independently by N. Tamm (1876–1957) in Sweden, using a 12-cm Zeiss astrograph [122]. Bohumil Šternberk also used this technique to obtain colours for 91 bright stars observed from Berlin-Babelsberg [119].

Ernst Öpik (1893–1985) and R. Livländer at Tartu University in Estonia developed the Tikhoff method further [123]. In 1923 they used a 16-cm astrograph with both orthochromatic and ordinary Hauff plates. The central spots on the orthochromatic plates were dominated by red light ($\lambda \simeq 630$ nm) but also had a weak component due to ultraviolet rays ($\lambda \simeq 365$ nm) which could be detected on the ordinary photographic images. The extrafocal rings corresponded on both types of plate to blue light ($\lambda \simeq 430$ nm). The ultraviolet images were used to correct the red measures for ultraviolet contamination. But more importantly they allowed ultraviolet minus blue colour indices to be determined, the first time that ultraviolet

Fig. 7.5   Extrafocal chromatic images of the double cluster h and χ Persei by
N. Tamm in Sweden, used for measuring colour indices.

radiation had been isolated for stellar photometry in a separate band. It was
also the first photographic use of the red rather than visual region, although
King at Harvard was experimenting with red photometry at the same time
– see section 7.4.1. This work preceded by a decade the better known
ultraviolet observations by Barbier and Chalonge on the Jungfraujoch [124].

What is amazing about this little known Estonian work is that the first
two-colour diagram was plotted, based on the colour indices ($m_{UV} - m_{pg}$)
and ($m_{pg} - m_{red}$). For dwarfs, this clearly showed an S-shaped sequence, the
A0 stars being at a maximum in ($m_{UV} - m_{pg}$). The explanation in terms of
the strong ultraviolet absorption in dwarfs (in fact the converging Balmer
series lines) was explicitly given by Öpik and Livländer. They also plotted
colour index against spectral type. The redder colours of the late-type giants
than dwarfs was found in both of the colour indices they used – see also
section 8.8.2.

A second paper by Öpik and his colleagues at the Dorpat Observatory in
Estonia a decade later extended the method to more stars and gave further
colour *vs* spectral type and two-colour diagrams [125].

An attempt to repeat some of Öpik's two-colour results was made by

Fig. 7.6   The first two-colour diagram, by Öpik and Livländer, 1925.

Wolfgang Collmann in Bonn in 1934 [126]. His methods relied on focal images with the 30-cm Zeiss astrograph (formerly in Bolivia for the *Potsdam Southern Spektraldurchmusterung*), and three passbands were isolated with Schott filters, centred at 384, 455 and 725 nm (the last on Agfa Infrared plates). The ultraviolet filter was designed to cover the luminosity-sensitive CN absorption bands, while the infrared one was to achieve a long base-line and hence high temperature sensitivity. The ability of his two-colour diagram to differentiate dwarfs and giants was only partially successful, but the paper is interesting for its use of filters, even in the blue, and for the choice of wavelengths. Collmann's techniques were remarkably similar to the later *RGU* system of Wilhelm Becker which was devised in 1935. The absence of references to Collmann in Becker's publications is puzzling – see section 7.4.2.

Another highly ingenious but in the event not very productive technique for obtaining stellar colours came from Yngve Öhman (1903–88) at the Stockholm Observatory [127, 128]. In this device two birefringent Iceland Spar plates (4 mm thick) have a quartz plate placed between them. The first Iceland Spar plate produces separated ordinary and extraordinary rays of orthogonal polarization. The planes of polarization are rotated by the quartz plate through about 180° for ultraviolet light, but only half this amount in the green. The second Iceland Spar plate, at 90° to the first, acts as an analyser, allowing rays of a given polarization and hence wavelength to be transmitted in each of four beams. Each exposure gave four focal stellar images, two ultraviolet ones ($\lambda \simeq 370$ nm) and two in the green region ($\lambda \simeq 510$ nm), from which an ultraviolet minus green colour index could be derived. Some results using this instrument were discussed by Öhman in 1938 [129].

7.7   Photographic spectrophotometry

In 1901 Max Planck (1855–1947) derived theoretically the energy distribution radiated by a body in thermodynamic equilibrium with its surroundings [130], usually referred to as a Planck or black-body radiation curve. He showed that the energy radiated at any wavelength depended only on the body's temperature. Almost immediately Planck's work had an influence on astrophysics. Astronomers in principle could apply photometric methods to the determination of stellar temperatures, on the assumption that they radiated like black bodies, and such programmes were initially undertaken using visual observations by Wilsing and Scheiner at Potsdam and by Nordmann in Paris – see section 3.9.3.

At the same time as Planck's theoretical work, Karl Schwarzschild in Vienna developed the principles of photographic photometry taking the failure of the reciprocity law into account [131] – see section 4.8.1. Thus the possibility arose of determining the relative energy distribution with wavelength for stars from the photographic densities measured in stellar spectra. Adolf Hnatek (1876–1960) in Vienna was the first to attempt this [132]. He chose continuum wavelengths from 398 to 498 nm and determined the flux gradients to obtain colour temperatures based on Planck's black-body curves. For all spectrophotometry a standard source of known temperature is required so that relative measurements can be made. Hnatek chose the star Altair as his standard and adopted 7100 K for its black-body temperature, in practice at least a 1000 K too cool. Thus his results for the temperatures of seven stars were also systematically in error.

Meanwhile Hans Rosenberg from Tübingen embarked on an extensive programme of photographic spectrophotometry, using plates exposed in Göttingen (where Schwarzschild was now director) during 1907–09. Seventy bright stars to third magnitude were included [133] and the energy distribution from 400 to 500 nm deduced to derive colour temperatures, using Charles Abbot's absolute intensity data for the sun to calibrate his data [134]. Rosenberg's results for early-type stars were somewhat hotter than currently accepted values (e.g. for B0 stars he obtained 30 000 K) and much hotter than the visually determined colour temperatures from Potsdam. They were strongly criticized by Wilsing [135], in part for the use of a short wavelength baseline in the blue spectral region where there are many lines. Rosenberg's different spectral region and his failure to allow for line blocking probably accounts for the major differences with Potsdam. Yet both sets of data were still based on the erroneous assumption of the validity of Planck black-body distributions for stellar radiation.

A programme carried out in Edinburgh by Ralph Sampson (1866–1939), the Astronomer Royal for Scotland, was in one sense an improvement over the earlier Rosenberg data, for Ilford panchromatic plates were used so that the spectra extended as far as the red Hα line for the cooler stars [136]. This therefore increased the wavelength baseline and utilized relatively line-free spectral regions. A novel recording microdensitometer was used to register the spectra from the objective prism plates. Two papers were published giving continuum spectral gradients for some 80 stars, which were calibrated relative to Capella, taken to be a standard black-body source at 5500 K [137, 138]. The colour temperatures of early-type stars were still too high in Sampson's system of measurement (Vega had $T = 13\,000$ K), but not as much so as in Rosenberg's work.

7.7.1 Spectrophotometry of the Balmer jump

When William Hammond Wright (1871–1959) at Lick produced an intensity plot from a photographic spectrum of Vega (A0V) in 1918, showing a high level of absorption for wavelengths below 370 nm [139, see p. 257], this was an early clue to the failure of the black-body assumption, at least for A stars. This observation of the Balmer jump was followed up by Wright's student, Ch'ing Sung Yü [140]. Yü obtained microphotometer tracings for 91 B and A stars ($\lambda = 330$ to 510 nm) observed with the Crossley reflector. These showed the Balmer series hydrogen lines merge towards their series limit, but generally the last observed line at the start of the strong ultraviolet absorption was at a longer wavelength than the series limit of 364.7 nm observed in the laboratory.

Yü's spectrophotometric survey of B and A stars clearly showed that Planck curves were poor approximations for the observed stellar energy distributions of early-type stars, especially if shorter wavelengths in the blue and ultraviolet were used, as was in fact the case for most early photographic spectrophotometry. Nevertheless he still applied the Planck law to obtain colour temperatures in the blue spectral region. As with Rosenberg, these were substantially too high for the early-type stars (e.g. Vega had $T = 16\,000$ K). The dangers of applying the Planck law were emphasized, however, by Alfred Brill when he reviewed stellar temperature determinations in 1932 [141]:

> The disagreement between the original temperature scales of Wilsing and of Rosenberg can be explained by the fact that the Planck law is no longer obeyed over the relatively wide spectral region of the visual and the photographically sensitive radiations.

Following the pioneering work at Lick on the Balmer jump, a large programme of ultraviolet stellar spectrophotometry was established by Daniel Barbier (1907–65) and Daniel Chalonge (1895–1977) from a high-altitude observing station on the Jungfraujoch in the Swiss Alps. From 1934 they made photographic observations with a quartz objective prism telescope, to record the spectra of stars from 310 to 460 nm [124]. The Barbier and Chalonge ultraviolet spectra were measured to find four parameters, which characterize the departures of the radiation from black-body spectra. These were the spectral gradients in the ultraviolet and the blue (ϕ_{UV} and ϕ_{blue}), the size of the Balmer jump D and its apparent wavelength, λ_1.

By 1939, 204 stars of spectral type B, A and F had been measured in this system [142]. The Balmer jump was found to depend on stellar temperature and luminosity, the value of λ_1, mainly on the luminosity alone (through the pressure broadening of the Balmer line wings), while the spectral gradients were essentially dependent on just the temperature. The basis of an elegant spectral classification system was thus devised, initially in two dimensions (D, λ_1) [143, 144, 145] but later in three $(D, \lambda_1, \phi_{blue})$ [146, 147]. The third dimension allowed peculiar stars such as metallic-line A stars, metal-poor subdwarfs or highly space-reddened stars to be identified from their location in the $(D, \lambda_1, \phi_{blue})$ diagram.

7.7.2 Absolute photographic spectrophotometry of the 1930s and 1940s

Given that stars are not accurately black-body radiators, then it was clear from the early 1930s that it was not valid to calibrate spectrophotometry by taking any standard star and treating it as a black-body source at some adopted temperature. Serious systematic errors for stars of temperature much different from the standard would then inevitably result. To circumvent this problem, spectrophotometry had to be relative to carefully calibrated lamps whose colour temperatures had been determined against artificial black-body sources in the laboratory. William Greaves (1897–1955) at the Royal Greenwich Observatory commenced such a programme in 1926, using at first an acetylene burner [148], but later a tungsten filament lamp [149]. A system of secondary stellar standards based on 25 B and A stars was thereby established, and absolute spectral gradients in a further 38 stars of types B to G were measured.

Other observers also embarked on this type of work, notably Hans Kienle (1895–1975) in Göttingen and Robley Williams at Ann Arbor, Michigan. Kienle's programme used objective prism spectra from 370 to 685 nm, measured at some 30 wavelengths. A calibrated tungsten filament lamp was used as an artificial star [150, 151]. The results were detailed enough to show that the colour temperature of an A0 star changes from 12 200 K at 555 nm to as high as 23 500 K at 435 nm, as a result of departures of the stellar radiation from a black-body spectrum.

The Ann Arbor observations by Robley Williams on the Michigan $37\frac{1}{2}$-inch reflector were a more limited but carefully executed programme to determine spectral gradients for A0 stars, using a tungsten lamp, which in turn was calibrated in the GEC laboratory at Nela Park in Ohio. Eleven wavelengths from 404 to 637 nm were measured from Moll microphotometer tracings of prismatic slit spectrograms [152]. In 1939 Williams took his lamp to the National Physical Laboratory at Teddington, England and to the University Observatory at Göttingen and hence was able to compare his own absolute calibrations with those of Greaves and Kienle [153]. Likewise Barbier and Chalonge in 1936 and again in 1938 also calibrated their lamp in Kienle's laboratory in Göttingen [154, 150] (a rare example of pre-war Franco-German collaboration!). As a result of these visits, all four observatories engaged in absolute spectrophotometry in the 1930s were able to show that they had adopted essentially consistent lamp calibrations on which their spectrophotometry was based.

The challenge of the 1930s was how to interpret the non-Planckian energy curves, which were especially striking for B and A type stars. The theoretical work of William McCrea (b. 1904) in 1931 in Edinburgh on the fluxes from model stellar atmospheres showed how this might be done [155]. McCrea computed the first non-grey atmospheres in which the strongly wavelength-dependent opacity of atomic hydrogen was explicitly included. The Balmer jump and the unexpectedly steep gradients just longwards of the jump for A stars were clearly shown. But the models were less successful for solar-type stars, where a Planck curve still gave a better fit to the observations. The question of the interpretation of the spectrophotometric data is discussed further in section 8.8.1.

7.8   Two major photometric catalogues of the 1940s and 1950s

7.8.1   *The* Mt Wilson Polar Catalogue

The *Mt Wilson Polar Catalogue* of Seares, Ross and Mary Joyner [38] was conceived in the 1930s in the belief that transfers of the International System from the pole to other regions of the sky required a much larger number of polar standards.

The catalogue included 2271 stars within 10 degrees of the pole and gave photographic and photovisual magnitudes on the International System. The probable errors of the catalogue values were impressively small, only $\pm 0^m.015$ in m_{pg} and $\pm 0^m.017$ in m_{pv}, and the limiting magnitudes were roughly 11.7 for the photographic and 11.0 for the photovisual. The method of observation and reduction was unusual for photometry by Seares, probably reflecting the influence of Frank Ross from Yerkes, for all the plates in both colours were slightly extrafocal, and the magnitudes were obtained with a Schilt photometer of Ross design. The observations were also obtained by Frank Ross, mainly on the 5-inch f/7 camera of his design at Mt Wilson, but also using some Yerkes and Flagstaff plates for the preliminary work. The plates were exposed between 1933 and 1937, and by 1935 a preliminary catalogue of photographic magnitudes (with photovisual data for 331 stars) was issued in mimeographed form.

As will be discussed in section 7.9, the North Polar Sequence had several fundamental problems, just one of them being the poor spectral type distribution and the change in mean colour with magnitude. Even if the new catalogue was able to address these defects of the original system, it did nothing to rectify other fundamental problems, in particular how to transfer the polar magnitudes to other distant regions of the sky. Nevertheless, it received warm and respectful reviews, as, for example, from Cecilia Payne-Gaposchkin:

> There has been some question in recent years concerning the desirability of keeping to the International System of Magnitudes as originally defined, partly because the aluminization of mirrors has changed the colour system, partly because the stars at the North Pole itself, used to establish the zero-point, are found to be obscured and therefore not of normal colour for their spectral classes. But the system has established its usefulness by the most important of all tests – accuracy and consistency – and these have made it the accepted system for pragmatic reasons. The Mt Wilson Catalogue of stars north of +80°, like the North Polar Sequence and the Mount Wilson Catalogue of Selected Areas, is a cornerstone of present-day astronomy [156].

Fig. 7.7   Fabry photometer attached to the 13-inch astrograph at the Cape
Observatory, c. 1950, as used by Alan Cousins.

Fig. 7.8 Richard Stoy.

7.8.2 *The* Cape Photographic Catalogue for 1950.0

The *Cape Photographic Catalogue for 1950.0*, or CPC50, was the last major catalogue of photographic photometry undertaken (except for the southernmost regions) without the assistance of photoelectric sequences. It was a large programme to obtain accurate photographic and photovisual magnitudes of stars in the southern sky south of −30° (but excluding the Cape astrographic zone of −40° to −52°) to about magnitude $m_{pg} = 11$, and the only major programme of southern hemisphere photometry over a large region of the sky since the *Cape Photographic Durchmusterung* of the 1890s.

Although originally conceived by Spencer Jones, the programme was initiated in 1938 and undertaken by Richard Stoy (1910–94), who was until 1950 under the direction of John Jackson (1887–1958). In-focus photographic and photovisual Ilford plates were taken on the Cape twin photometric cameras, stopped down to about 3.5-inches aperture. The original plan to tie these to the International System through E-region magnitudes obtained by Henrietta Leavitt and Cecilia Payne [157, 58] using plates from Harvard's Boyden Station, had to be abandoned by 1943 when it was concluded that these standards were hopelessly inadequate. The frustrating battle of trying to calibrate the Schilt photometer measures of these plates with the International System was described by Stoy in 1944 [158, 116, 159] using at first E-region stars, then the stars along the 1931 path of Eros and finally cluster stars in the Pleiades, Hyades and Praesepe, but all without success.

Stoy later commented that the attempts to relate the Cape measures to the International System

> ... turned out to be anything but routine and having stumbled around for some three years in the Harvard morass I had come to the conclusion that there were no reliable standard magnitudes in the southern hemisphere and that even reputedly good magnitudes in the northern hemisphere were very far from consistent. I well remember the reactions of Jackson and Redman to this conclusion. Jackson, ever the optimist, thought that a week or two would suffice to clear the matter up; Redman, the confirmed pessimist, considered that it was more likely to take six months and immediately got busy. Thus began a collaboration that was extremely helpful to the Cape and which was to involve Redman, on and off, for the next ten years [160].

From 1944–47 the twin cameras were mounted on the Radcliffe 74-inch reflector (it was waiting for its mirror during the war years) and Roderick Redman (1905–75) was the principal observer. It was decided at this stage to recalibrate the E-region standards using the extrafocal Fabry method with a rotating sector [161] – see section 4.8.4 – and thereby establish the southern SPg, SPv system of photographic photometry, with the hope of being able to link this to the International System and the North Polar Sequence at a later stage. The problems of establishing a satisfactory sequence of photometric standards in the southern hemisphere at this time illustrated the unsuitability of the North Polar Sequence as a fundamental reference system south of the equator.

In an attempt to overcome these problems Stoy circulated a letter in July 1950 to active photometric observers outside South Africa to solicit their advice on the establishment of 'key' regions with standard sequences in order to link the North Polar Sequence to the E-region standards of the Cape S-system. Most replies favoured linking the E regions to the Selected Areas or C regions at +15° and thence to the north pole [162], and in fact Redman had taken the twin cameras to Cambridge with him in 1947 in order to complete the link to the North Polar Sequence [163]. The techniques of obtaining magnitudes from focal plates in the S-system were described in 1949 [164].

Fig. 7.9   The Cape Observatory modified Schilt photometer, c. 1962, used for the CPC50 catalogue.

The S-system itself went through several modifications from the original '1948' version with updates in 1953 [165], 1958 [166] and 1962, the last based on photoelectric calibrations with the 24-inch Victoria refractor at the Cape [167]. The 1958 system (sometimes known as S') represented an attempt to remove a small residual amount of radiation shortwards of 380 nm from the SPg passband, so as to facilitate the linear transformation to the Johnson-Morgan UBV photometry.

As for the CPC50 itself, this is contained in six consecutive volumes of the *Cape Observatory Annals* [44, 45]. It contained photometry and positions for about 70 000 stars with probable errors in the magnitudes, for all but the faintest stars, of about $\pm 0\overset{m}{.}04$ in the blue and $\pm 0\overset{m}{.}05$ in the visual. A discussion of the entire programme and the relationship of the SPg, SPv magnitudes to the International System and to the photoelectric BV system of Johnson and Morgan was presented by Stoy in 1956 [168] and again in 1972 [169] at the Cambridge astrophysics conference held in honour of Professor Redman. Here Stoy commented:

All the tests that I have been able to make, including numerous comparisons with photoelectric observations, confirm the homogeneity of these magnitudes and that the probable errors originally assigned are realistic. The fact that these magnitudes and colours are so good is very largely due to the discrimination with which Redman chose the nights on which to observe and the great care he took in developing the resulting plates ... In assessing our debt to Redman for this magnificent series of observations it must be remembered that at this time he was working under difficult circumstances, completely alone, and that at least half of the 400 pairs of plates had four 15 minute exposures on them and so must have required considerably more than one hour's observing time each ...

By a happy accident the colour curve and transmissions of the Cape Photographic photometric lens is such that radiation shortwards of 3800 Å contributes very little to its in-focus images, consequently it is possible to reduce the SPg, SPv given for the 70,000 stars in the CPC50 to V and $B - V$ by simple linear corrections without any appreciable loss of inherent accuracy [170].

7.9   The demise of the North Polar Sequence

The North Polar Sequence as a definitive system of standard stars for photometry had its origins as a proposal by Pickering about 1907. It was published in preliminary form in 1912 [2] and in its final form from Harvard in 1917 [157] from the work of Miss Leavitt. After being greatly extended by Seares at Mt Wilson to fainter magnitudes and to photovisual magnitudes in 1915 [5] and then revised in 1922, this system was adopted by the International Astronomical Union. But from 1922 to 1952, between the first and eighth General Assemblies (both held in Rome) the reputation of the International System of the North Polar Sequence standards was increasingly tarnished. By 1955 it had effectively ceased to exist as a practical magnitude system.

So in the three decades from 1922 what went wrong? The decline and fall of the North Polar Sequence is in fact one of the more interesting episodes in the history of stellar photometry, because it epitomizes the conflict between the traditional concept of photometry and the more modern astrophysics. After the failure of the *Carte du Ciel* programme fully to achieve its photometric goals, the demise of the North Polar Sequence can be regarded as the second major catastrophe for astronomical photometry as an international science.

By the 1930s astronomers were thinking far more concisely about stellar spectral energy distributions, or the relative amounts of light of different

Fig. 7.10   Colours and magnitudes of stars in the North Polar Sequence

colour emitted by a star. The work of Greaves, Robley Williams, Kienle and of Barbier and Chalonge in absolute spectrophotometry is evidence for this.

Alfred Brill (1885–1949) in Berlin made a detailed study of the published data on stellar energy distributions and their relationship to temperature [171], and by 1932 he had concluded that the radiation of the stars departs significantly from that of black bodies, especially for those stars of early spectral type [141].

The relationship of spectrophotometry to broad-band integral photometry was also considered, for example by Paul Rossier at Geneva, who mathematically folded Planck's black-body energy distributions with the presumed detector sensitivity functions, be it the eye or photographic plate, to derive stellar magnitudes for stars of different temperature, after integrating the resulting function over all wavelengths [172].

Such ideas were not especially new (see for example the review articles of Lundmark and Brill in 1932 [173, 141]), but they served to emphasize the need to define the sensitivity function of the receiver and detector. Also, as pointed out by Boris Vorontsov-Velyaminov (b. 1904), stars with non-Planckian energy distributions, in particular those with strong emission lines such as Wolf-Rayet stars or emission-line B stars, can be brighter by several tenths of a magnitude (or in the extreme cases of novae, by several magnitudes) as a result of their lines [174].

When the Crossley telescope at Lick was aluminized in 1933 [175] and the two Mt Wilson reflectors in 1935, using John Strong's new vacuum coating process [176], the technique was heralded as a new advance for ultraviolet spectroscopy, because of the much higher reflectivity of aluminium over silver below 325 nm. But some calculations by Edison Pettit at Mt Wilson on the change in the colour equation in photographic photometry, resulting from the increased exposure of photographic plates to the ultraviolet, should have been taken as a dire warning for the International System [177].

In 1939 Mary Hunt at Harvard-Radcliffe (her supervisor was Cecilia Payne-Gaposchkin) also analysed the effect of aluminium mirrors on photographic magnitudes, by comparing plates taken with the Oak Ridge 24-inch reflector with aluminized mirrors (in 1938) and with silvered mirrors (in 1937). Large corrections of several tenths of a magnitude were required for the photographic magnitudes of early-type stars [178]. What is more, she showed that silvered mirrors, because they tarnish after a few months, change their ultraviolet reflectivity significantly. The implication is that a given silvered mirror telescope, including of course the Mt Wilson 60-inch on which Seares had based the International System, will have had a time-dependent colour equation as the silver tarnished over a time scale of several months. Mary Hunt also stressed the greater atmospheric extinction of ultraviolet light, which meant that the amount actually recorded on photographs with aluminized reflectors would be dependent on the zenith distance.

Seares' answer to the problems created by aluminized reflectors was to filter out the ultraviolet:

> At first this promised to be a serious difficulty; but experiments at Mount Wilson have provided a simple solution. A filter of ordinary crown glass in front of the photographic plate transforms the aluminized mirror into the practical equivalent of a silvered reflector [179].

Another related problem that became increasingly evident and hence irksome for photometry in the 1930s was the effect of the Balmer absorption lines of hydrogen and the Balmer continuous absorption ($\lambda < 364$ nm) on stellar photographic magnitudes, especially for A stars. These absorptions were right in the middle of the photographic passband and show a strong luminosity effect, the line absorption being strong for dwarfs but weaker for giants, whereas the continuous absorption in the ultraviolet was strong for giants, but weaker for dwarfs. Both types of absorption are also strongly temperature sensitive. Hertzsprung at the IAU General Assembly in 1932 spoke briefly about the merits of using a filter for photographic photometry so as to record the continuum between the Hγ and Hδ lines, but avoid the lines themselves [180].

Before the sixth General Assembly of the IAU in Stockholm, Seares, as president of Commission 25 for photometry, had circulated a memorandum soliciting comments on how to reduce observations with aluminized reflectors to the International System [110], based on the Mt Wilson 60-inch silvered-mirror telescope, which of course no longer existed in that form! The replies were interesting and diverse. For example Walter Baade (1893–1960) described how he was using a Schott GG1 filter at Mt Wilson to absorb the ultraviolet, and in effect convert an aluminized reflector to a silvered one, though at the expense of about $0\overset{m}{.}1$ in limiting magnitude [181]. Without the filter the Cepheids in the dwarf satellite galaxy IC 1613 appeared about $0\overset{m}{.}25$ too faint (in reality the comparison B stars used were too bright by this amount!). The error would make the galaxy appear over 10 per cent too distant.

On the other hand, Cecilia Payne-Gaposchkin, who often enjoyed arguing the opposite viewpoint to that of her peers, replied:

> The use of a glass filter in modifying the effects of the aluminized mirror would probably be difficult to establish as a standard procedure, unless the precise kind of glass used, and its thickness, were kept constant in different observatories. Even so, it would seem desirable to determine the "colour equation" of the aluminium-glass filter combination directly, and if that has to be done in any case, many will feel, I think, that a direct determination of the colour equation, without any glass filter, would serve the purpose equally well. An additional optical complication would be avoided, and a fainter magnitude probably obtained [182].

Again at the Stockholm meeting, Hertzsprung presented a memorandum arguing in favour of a much narrower passband for photographic blue photometry, so as to avoid the problem of different effective wavelengths for photographic magnitudes of stars of different temperature [183]. Since this would in effect entail a complete redefinition of the international photographic magnitude scale (IPg), Hertzsprung proposed the IPg magnitudes 'should be abandoned as standards as soon as possible and replaced by another system of practically monochromatic magnitudes'.

The Stockholm meeting was also the time that Seares, who must have seen the defence of his International System as one of his principal rôles as Commission 25 president, had to propose abandoning the A0 zero-point for the IPg scale, because the A0 stars at the north pole were thought to be significantly reddened – see section 7.5 and [110]. Interstellar reddening was of course yet another reason why stellar energy distributions might be non-Planckian, and such effects meant that unique transformations between the magnitudes obtained on different telescopes may not exist. Indeed this conclusion was explicitly stated quite a bit later by Harold Johnson:

> It is known that the inclusion of radiation to the violet of 3800 Å in the measurements makes the relations between different colour systems nonlinear, and, in most cases, multivalued [184].

In other words, two stars of the same colour index in the International System could have different colours in another system, including the photoelectric system that Johnson was then pioneering.

In 1938 the International System had to face another assault, this time from the much more precise photometry of the photoelectric cell. Joel Stebbins and Albert Whitford had observed magnitudes and colours of the thirty brightest stars (to $m_{pg} = 11.6$) with a photoelectric potassium hydride cell, mainly using the 60-inch reflector at Mt Wilson [185]. Their filters had effective wavelengths of 434 and 467 nm and were much narrower than the very broad photographic band at about 425 nm. After transforming their blue photoelectric index to the international photographic scale IPg, using a colour equation derived from all thirty stars, they claimed to find evidence of a systematic scale difference between the photoelectric values and those derived from photography. Between magnitude 5 and 9 (i.e. $\Delta m = 4.0$) on the international scale, the photoelectric results showed a change of $\Delta m = 4.2$.

This alarming result was not published for over a year while further tests were made and discussions with Seares were held. No significant systematic errors could be found in the photoelectric work, and the probable errors were as small as $\pm 0^{m}_{.}01$ or less. On the other hand the International System magnitudes had also been checked rigorously by many observers on different telescopes, and as Seares stated: 'That any large part of this discrepancy should be the result of observational error seems improbable' [179]. Seares was able to show that the photographic Ipg and transformed photoelectric scales actually agreed rather well from magnitude $m_{pg} = 6.6$ and fainter. The problem could be isolated to stars 1 to 5 of the North Polar Sequence which were all bright (mainly naked-eye) early A-type stars, and which appeared too bright in the photoelectric (Pe) work. First Seares introduced small revisions to his original 1922 IPg magnitudes to reduce the random errors (but not change the scale) of the original data. He called these new revised results Pg_r values [179]. He then concluded:

> Since the spectral types of these five [brightest] stars are all close to
> A0, the most promising explanation seems to lie in the influence of
> Balmer-line and hydrogen continuous absorption on the Pg_r
> magnitudes and the lack of any such influence on the Pe measures
> [179].

It is important to emphasize that neither scale was in error. They were just measuring different regions of the spectrum and expecting to get concordant results. The photographic magnitudes, however, included the region from 365 to 400 nm where the Balmer lines approach their series limit. This region was practically excluded by the filters from Stebbins' photoelectric cell. Therefore, for A0 stars with such strong Balmer lines, the photographic magnitudes are relatively fainter. Although no errors had been committed by either party, it was clear that the wide passband of the IPg magnitudes covering the strong Balmer line series limit, together with the change in the mean spectral type of the North Polar Sequence stars with magnitude, were most unfortunate properties of the International System, and the cause of the current discrepancies.

It is interesting that another series of photoelectric observations of 102 bright north polar stars was made by W. Hassenstein in the years 1935–38 on the 30-cm Potsdam refractor [186]. However, no significant scale errors for the brightest North Polar Sequence stars were evident in these data [187]. The Hassenstein measures were in a single unfiltered passband defined by the response of the potassium photocell, and therefore presumably gave a broader sensitivity function more closely resembling that of the International System.

One of the fundamental assumptions of the International System was that the scale and zero-point of the North Polar Sequence magnitudes could be transferred from the north pole to any other region of the sky, by taking two consecutive exposures under identical conditions. In the case of southern hemisphere observers, the transfer had to be via secondary standards (the Harvard C regions at $+15°$ were favoured – see [157, 58, 188]), or even tertiary ones in the E regions at $-45°$ declination (these were used for the CPC50 catalogue [158] – see section 7.8.2).

This process of photographic transfers by comparing the size of stellar images in different exposures was fraught with difficulties, with the result that errors of zero-point or scale in different parts of the sky were commonplace. In 1935 Bergstrand commented:

> It seems that in general fixing the exact zero-point in a way that is
> independent of the positions of the stars is subject to considerable

difficulties. Perhaps this is one of the weakest points in stellar photographic photometry [189].

A few years later Seares, in the introduction to the *Mt Wilson Polar Catalogue*, echoed the same thing:

> Attempts to transfer the photometric system of the brighter stars of the North Polar Sequence (NPS) to other parts of the sky have met with serious difficulty. The standards are few and scattered, B-type stars are lacking, and the red stars do not accurately define the color system. As a group, these standards can be observed only with large-field cameras which require complicated corrections depending on the color, brightness, and position of the stars, and frequently also on focus and other factors such that each plate must be treated by itself. The bright polar standards thus failed of the purpose for which they were intended. Ten years after their adoption the relation of the various photometric catalogues to the North Polar Sequence system was still mostly unknown and some of the current investigations gave little evidence that any such system existed [38].

This was an unusually frank statement from the principal architect of the North Polar Sequence. Apart from the problem of having to use wide-angle astrographic refractors for the transfer, with their large colour equations relative to the International System, other factors mitigated against a successful comparison of stellar images on two exposures. These were discussed by Harold Weaver at Lick in 1947, and included 'sky brightness, seeing, transparency and similarity of guiding and focus during the two exposures' [190]. Polar plates rarely had the same guiding errors as those nearer the equator, and changes in other conditions, such as seeing, could vitiate the transfer of the North Polar Sequence magnitudes. An increase in seeing was especially difficult, as this made the images of bright stars appear larger and hence brighter, while fainter stars appeared fainter or even disappeared below the plate limit. Weaver noted that

> ... systematic errors of as much as 0.5 mag. in the scale established by the comparison method are not unusual and that even under favorable conditions that yield apparently excellent plates, systematic errors of 0.2–0.3 mag. are common [190].

These problems of transfer were also discussed by Richard Stoy and Roderick Redman at this time [191]. They noted that 'since photometry should be carried out at as small zenith distances as possible, confining its practice to the altitude of the Pole has in the past been an unnecessary handicap to accurate work'. Obviously observers south of say latitude $+30°$ always have to observe the pole through a large air mass (if they can see it at all), which would generally be larger than for meridian plates at lower declinations.

The unfortunate distribution of stars of different spectral type in the North Polar Sequence has already been referred to. This was undoubtedly the cause of the discrepancies found by Stebbins and Whitford [185] for bright stars, and contributed to the problems of magnitude transfers with refractors and of establishing colour equations for any instrument. The distribution itself was illustrated by Redman in a report to the IAU Commission 25 in 1952 [162]. This report was from the sub-commission on magnitude sequences (established in 1938 in Stockholm), and came at a time when serious doubts on the future existence of the International System were widespread. The conclusion of this report was remarkably conservative considering the manifest failings of the North Polar Sequence and the International System: 'The general feeling of the Sub-Committee', Redman reported 'is that the time is not yet ripe for any very radical change in the standard system' [162]. He cited 'the very large amount of time and labour already invested in it [that] makes any change inadvisable except after the most exhaustive technical examination and discussion'. Yet the decision was consistent with the time-honoured practice throughout stellar photometry of striving to preserve the current magnitude scale on which so much effort had been expended for the benefit of future generations. History has also shown that future generations of observers would devise new more precise techniques of observation which would quickly render the old data obsolete.

Photoelectric photometry in 1950 was certainly the new technique that challenged yet again the photographic methods. A seminal paper by Stebbins, Whitford and Johnson [192] with the new 1P21 photomultiplier tube reported observations of stars in three Selected Areas to faint magnitude limits ($m_{pg} \leq 19.3$) using the Mt Wilson reflectors. The observations were in what came to be known as the photoelectric (P,V) system, which was designed to simulate the International System, and hence allowed comparisons to be made with the faint stars measured photographically in the *Mt Wilson Catalogue* of 1930 [22]. The results showed serious differences with the photographic magnitudes for faint stars, with the discrepancy starting between m_{pg} 12 to 14 and increasing to about $0^{m}.6$ for the faintest stars in the sense that the photographic scale was too compressed. The authors wrote: 'We are forced to conclude, therefore, that a scale error has crept into the photographic magnitudes in the Selected Areas' [192].

It will be recalled (section 7.2) that the scale of the *Mt Wilson Catalogue* was calibrated independently in each Selected Area, using the same techniques as used for the North Polar Sequence. Although the scale was not tied directly to the North Polar Sequence, Seares did check the conformity to the International System down to about magnitude 16.5 in a number of Selected Areas. He claimed no departures from the International System. Since this is fainter than the differences between the Selected Area magnitudes and the photoelectric results, one must assume that a similar scale error is also present in the International System of the type found by Stebbins, Whitford and Johnson.

The 1952 Rome meeting of the International Astronomical Union can be seen as a critical time for the International System. It was the first IAU meeting when Seares was not Commission 25 president. This post was now held by William Greaves from Edinburgh, who opened his 1952 report by reproducing a memorandum by Stoy from the Cape which emphasized once again how mathematically a system of magnitudes must have both the stellar energy distribution and the passband sensitivity function defined at the outset [193]. Neither was ever done for the International System.

Instead of abandoning the International System at this time, which Commission 25 might well have been tempted to do, they instead proposed new 'interim' values for the brighter 25 North Polar Sequence magnitudes. These new values were to force agreement in scale and zero-point with the photoelectric work (much of which was still at that time unpublished) of Redman and his Cambridge colleagues [163], of Arthur Cox [194] at the Cape and Goethe Link Observatories, of Olin Eggen at Lick [195, 196] as well as of Stebbins, Whitford and Johnson [185, 192]. In particular the 'interim' values now proposed changed the photographic magnitudes of the brightest stars to make them up to $0^{m}\!.15$ brighter. This was a curious decision, as the magnitudes were now no longer on a photographic scale that could be reproduced with unfiltered photographic plates. The Redman report referred to 'errors' in the old International System for these stars, rather than systematic differences due to different sensitivity functions. That the new 'interim' values would be unsuitable for unfiltered photographic photometry is not explicitly mentioned in the report.

At this time Harold Johnson at Yerkes had attempted to approximate the International System photographic passband by synthetically reconstructing it from photoelectric ultraviolet (U) and 'photographic' (P) measures [184]. By adding half the U signal to that of P he formed a new magnitude ($P_{0.5}$) which behaved rather like m_{pg}, and the colour index ($P_{0.5} - V$) resembled ($m_{pg} - m_{pv}$) on the International System. Because the relationship between ($P_{0.5} - V$) and ($P - V$) was non-linear and possibly multivalued (if different types of star were considered) this led Johnson to conclude that

> ... the North Polar Sequence is shown to be inadequate as a standard region, because of the absence of blue, supergiant†, heavily reddened, and red dwarf stars [184].

† In fact Polaris is a supergiant and the brightest star in the North Polar Sequence.

The Rome meeting concluded with a number of recommendations for further reform of the North Polar Sequence, not for its abolition. These recommendations were for a study of procedures needed for photographic photometry to $\pm 0^m.02$, a redefinition of the zero-points of both photographic and photovisual scales (possibly so as to bring conformity with the new photoelectric (P,V) system), to extend the scales to both fainter stars and to a greater range of stellar types and to establish secondary magnitude sequences at $-45°$ and $+15°$. Weaver also proposed the use of a filter to eliminate ultraviolet radiation from photographic work, while Becker promoted the merits of his *RGU* system. Indeed if all these reforms had been implemented, the International System might have survived as a usable system. But it is doubtful if any observers would have still wanted to use it, considering the growing prevalence of photomultipliers and the new possibilities of direct photoelectric calibrations of stellar sequences on photographic plates.

Redman concluded his 1952 IAU report to Commission 25 with a nice tribute to Seares:

> There is one final comment: on present evidence the original North Polar Sequence is extremely near a Pogson scale from about 7^m to 15^m, and some tribute should be paid to the first President of the Commission on Stellar Photometry, Dr F. H. Seares, who contributed more than any other man to this result. It is astonishing, not that a systematic error has been found over quite a limited range at the bright end of the scale, up to a maximum perhaps about $0^m.2$ pg and $0^m.1$ pv, but that his work has stood up so well to testing by the best photo-electric methods. He observed by photographic methods only, at a time when photometric standards were much lower than they are now, and his results stand in conspicuous contrast to the great volume of stellar magnitude work down to 1940 [162].

At the ninth General Assembly of the IAU in Dublin in 1955, the International System and the North Polar Sequence were finally laid to rest. If photographic photometry was to be undertaken, then observers were to use a filter such as Schott GG13 to eliminate radiation of wavelength less than 380 nm, which in turn implied that the magnitudes would not be those of the International System. By this time the Johnson and Morgan *UBV* photoelectric system [197], with its large number of equatorial standards, had already been established, and it became the preferred system for stellar photometry, as recommended by Commission 25. It is therefore appropriate to herald this new era with the remarks of Johnson on why this change came about:

> It has now become common knowledge among photometric observers that the International System of magnitudes and colors as defined by

the stars of the North Polar Sequence is too poorly defined for the standardization of highly accurate photometry. Transformations to the International System of Photographic Magnitudes of the North Polar Sequence stars are ambiguous and must always remain so for the following reasons: (1) The International Photographic Magnitudes, I_{pg}, contain an unknown amount of ultraviolet radiation on the violet side of 3800 Å that has been shown to have a detrimental effect upon the precision of transformation, and (2) the number of types of stars in the North Polar Sequence is entirely too small to permit transformations of sufficient accuracy for modern photometry [198].

7.10 Trends in photographic photometry 1950–1970

The demise of the International System was a major disaster for astronomical photometry, and the repercussions of this continued through all three IAU General Assemblies of the 1950s decade. In Rome in 1952 Commission 25 president William Greaves declared:

> ... it is clear there is a majority of opinion to the effect that the time has come for the Commission to re-examine the fundamentals of astronomical photometry.

Indeed Stoy's memorandum on 'What is a stellar magnitude' was one attempt at such a reexamination, and it became the basis for much of Greaves' report to Commission 25 [199].

The end of the International System was by no means the end of photographic photometry, which had been developed over a century into a highly refined technique. In Dublin in 1955 Greaves commented that: 'In ordinary wide-band photometry there is no serious technical difficulty in setting up a Pogson scale in any given region of the sky with standard errors not exceeding $\pm 0^{m}_{.}02$ down to 18^{m} or 19^{m}' [200]. In practice most observers did not realize this level of precision (error bars two or three times larger were typical), but this was, nevertheless, adequate for many astrophysical purposes.

Moreover, the advantages of the photographic plate, namely a wide angular field, the simultaneous recording of many thousands of images, the automatic integration of the stellar signal and an excellent long-term storage medium for the data meant that in many applications photographic work was still preferred over the photomultiplier.

The 1950s, therefore, saw more a change in direction for photographic photometry, which possibly lowered its status from a technique at the leading edge of photometric research, to that of an indispensable method for special purposes. These purposes were, in particular, the photometry of star clusters, especially the populous and crowded globular clusters, and the photometry of stars from wide-angle Schmidt telescope plates, especially of clusters or of crowded Milky Way and Magellanic Cloud fields. The photomultiplier, in fact, became the essential adjunct for the photographic photometrist, in enabling photoelectric sequences to be established for the photometric calibration of the plates. This was a significant change in the technique of photographic photometry. Another change, or at least improvement, was in the digitization and automation of iris photometers to extract the photometric data.

By 1958 Richard Stoy (the new IAU Commission 25 president), at the Moscow IAU General Assembly, reported some photographic photometry still being undertaken in the International System. But he commented in his report that

> ... there is still no unanimity about its definition. Some observers attempt to retain the original 1922 definition, some the extended polar observations of Seares, Ross and Joyner [38], some the interim definition of 1952 [162] and some modified versions of the rather limited California definition [of Stebbins, Whitford and Johnson] [192].

In these circumstances, it is not surprising that Johnson's *UBV* photoelectric photometry, as well as Becker's photographic *RGU* system, would prevail by the end of the decade.

7.10.1   Photographic photometry of clusters and the photoelectric sequence

In 1950 the great majority of photographic photometry was on the International System, although some three-colour photometry in the red, green and ultraviolet was being undertaken by W. Becker and Jurgen Stock at the Hamburg-Bergedorf Observatory. A good example of this latter work from that time was of the B-star association NGC 6913 [201]. Plates were usually calibrated by reference to photographic sequences in a different region of the sky, either to the North Polar Sequence or to secondary sequences in Harvard regions or Kapteyn Selected Areas.

The idea of calibrating plates photoelectrically came from the early observers with the 931-A or IP21 photomultipliers. Bart Bok, with his wife Priscilla, then at Harvard, was an early advocate of this technique, and he established the first photoelectric sequences from the Boyden Observatory on his visit there in 1950 [202]. His student, Uco van Wijk, established the first Magellanic Cloud photoelectric sequence from Boyden, also at that time [203] – see section 9.6.1.

Other observers of sequences soon followed, including Archibald Brown, from Yerkes and McDonald Observatories, for his study of the globular cluster M15 [204]. The photometry of this cluster was also undertaken at the same time by Harold Johnson and Martin Schwarzschild from Mt Wilson, likewise using a two-colour photoelectric calibration. These sequences were on what came to be known as the (P, V) system (see section 9.3.1), which enjoyed a relatively ephemeral existence prior to the introduction of the UBV system in 1953.

The photoelectric sequence enabled direct calibration of the reading from either an iris photometer (or a Schilt fixed aperture photometer), which in effect recorded the diameter of a stellar photographic image – see section 7.3. If the sequence stars were established in the same field as that of the plate, then the need for uncertain magnitude transfers or for photographic calibrations was at once avoided.

Southern hemisphere observers in South Africa and Australia played a significant role in establishing the early photoelectric sequences, including Arthur Cox [205, 206], Alan Cousins and Richard Stoy [207], Ivan King [208] and Pieter Oosterhoff [209]. However, two of the largest projects involved photographic photometry, with photoelectric (P, V) calibrations of over one thousand stars, in each of the globular clusters M92 and M3 by Halton Arp, William Baum and Allan Sandage at Mt Wilson and Palomar Observatories [210, 211]. These studies, from deep photographic exposures on the 200-inch telescope at the prime focus, allowed the magnitudes of faint stars to about the main-sequence turn-off point to be determined. In 1955, Arp added five further clusters to these with calibrated photographic photometry [212].

Yet another example of an early photoelectric sequence was provided by the pioneering pulse-counting photometry at Cambridge by Arthur Beer, Roderick Redman and Gilbert Yates, in order to calibrate the photographic images of nearly 1300 stars in Kapteyn's Selected Areas [163] – see section 9.2.

The UBV system of Johnson and Morgan was originally devised in 1953 as a photoelectric system, but Johnson soon added a prescription of plates and filters to enable the system to be applied in photographic work [198]. These were as follows:

Passband	Filter	Plate
ultraviolet	Corning 9863 or Schott UG 2 (2mm)	Kodak 103aO
blue	Schott GG 13 (2mm)	Kodak 103aO
visual	Schott GG 11 (2mm)	Kodak 103aD

This combination was immediately used for three-colour photographic photometry of clusters, notably by Johnson and Sandage for the old disk cluster M67 [213], for the young open cluster M11 [214] and for the globular cluster M3 [215]. In all cases Johnson undertook the photoelectric calibration on the 82-inch telescope at McDonald, while the Mt Wilson 60-inch or 100-inch telescopes (diaphragmed to smaller apertures so as to improve the image definition over the whole field) were used for most of the photographic work. It was shown that no colour equation existed in these photographic plates; in other words, the calibration curve relating photoelectric and photographic observations was independent of star colour. This is a useful condition for accurate photometry and arises when the transmission and sensitivity functions of all passbands are closely similar in both photographic and photoelectric observations.

The photoelectric sequence became an important part of accurate photographic photometry, and there was a considerable demand for faint sequences to be established around clusters or in Kapteyn Selected Areas. In 1973 Noel Argue, with the support of Bart Bok, compiled a catalogue of photoelectric sequences, following a proposal at the 1970 Brighton General Assembly of the IAU [216]. In the catalogue and its supplement, 480 sequences were cited, nearly all of them in the UBV system of photoelectric photometry.

In the 1950s and 1960s two three-colour systems of photographic photometry dominated the output in cluster research and for photometry in Milky Way fields, namely the Johnson UBV system and Wilhelm Becker's RGU system – see section 7.4.2. Although the latter system was devised about a decade before the UBV system, it never was popular among American observers. However, the large output of Becker with Jurgen Stock from Hamburg (during Becker's time there, 1945–53), and later from Basel, meant that numerous clusters were observed in the RGU system – see for example [217, 218, 219]. Meanwhile Stock was obtaining RGU plates on the Burrell-Schmidt telescope in Cleveland in 1955 [220], while the RGU plates from the Palomar Schmidt by the Basel group are discussed in section 7.4.2.

The RGU system did not have photoelectric standards, probably because the 1P21 photomultiplier was unable to reach the red band at 640 nm. Early plates had photographic standards, but later photoelectric UBV calibrations were used, together with transformations to RGU – see for example [221, 222]. The lack of photoelectric standards for RGU was perceived as a major drawback in the mid-1950s. William Greaves, in his Dublin report to IAU Commission 25, remarked:

> ... the establishment, with all modern high precision, of the modified three-colour system suggested by Becker would involve a considerable amount of labour. The system of Johnson and Morgan is immediately

available as it stands; their work as Stoy has remarked, has provided the framework of what appears to be an adequate and acceptable system of standard magnitudes and colours for a three-colour photometry ... [200].

IAU Commission 37 reports (on stellar clusters) gave lists of cluster photometry during these years. Thus at the Berkeley 1961 IAU meeting there are 28 RGU galactic cluster paper citations for the period 1958–61, compared with nearly 200 for the UBV (including $UBVR$ and U_CBV) photographic system [223]. These statistics compare with the roughly equal numbers (RGU: 12 clusters and UBV: 16 clusters) reported for photographic photometry at the Moscow IAU General Assembly for the period 1954–58 [224].

One observer in the RGU system was Noel Argue at Cambridge who exposed plates on the 17/24-inch Schmidt telescope at Cambridge and made photometric measurements to a precision of several hundredths of a magnitude (e.g. $\pm 0^m\!\!.035$ at $m_G = 11$ and twice this for stars at $m_G = 15$, the plate limit) [225]. However, he soon thereafter decided to abandon the RGU system in favour of UBV photometry and reported to the IAU meeting in Berkeley:

> So far we have confined ourselves to the R, G, U System and have been seriously handicapped by lack of standard magnitudes, intrinsic colours and so on. This system was used since it has been claimed as capable of distinguishing between intermediate- and late-type giants and dwarfs. In our Praesepe survey we have not been able to confirm this. To us the system seems little different from the U, B, V System in this respect and we are considering abandoning it in favour of U, B, V for which extensive material has now accumulated [226].

Although the photoelectric calibration of photographic exposures was, according to nearly all accounts, a major advance, a few observers maintained that more traditional methods could realize a comparable precision. One such was René Racine, who in 1969 advocated calibrating prime focus plates on the Palomar 200-inch telescope using a small prism to create secondary images [227], a technique similar to that first proposed by Edward Pickering over eight decades earlier – see section 4.3.

7.10.2 Photometry with Schmidt telescopes

Although the Schmidt telescope was devised in 1930 by Bernhard Schmidt (1879–1935) in Hamburg [228] as a wide-field photographic instrument, it was not until the 1950s that serious consideration was given to

undertaking precision photographic photometry with Schmidt telescopes.†
The first experiments at Harvard by Bart Bok and Margaret Olmstead in
1950 were not at all encouraging, and much larger random errors were reported for stellar magnitudes from Schmidt plates than from those obtained
with conventional telescopes [229].

Donald Cameron, using the Burrell–Schmidt telescope at Cleveland and
a dual beam iris photometer, also reported random errors about twice those
from conventional telescopes [230]. His was one of the early discussions on
the photometric capabilities of the Schmidt and drew attention to the need
for field corrections, as well as to the problems of vignetting and of the
colour equation in the derived magnitudes. A typical precision was $\pm0\overset{m}{.}06$.

In spite of the difficulty of achieving high photometric precision, several
observers persevered with Schmidt telescope photometry from the mid-
1950s. Table 7.2 lists some of the early workers in this field. At this time the
Palomar 48-inch Schmidt was in operation and carrying out the Palomar
Observatory Sky Survey (completed 1959). However, early attempts to
derive reliable magnitudes from film copies of this survey were not especially
successful [231, 232].

At the Moscow IAU General Assembly of 1958, Wilhelm Becker reported
to Commission 25 on the growing use of Schmidt telescopes for photometry
[257]. At this time Hans Haffner [238], using the 80-cm Hamburg-Bergedorf
Schmidt, and Noel Argue using the 17-inch Cambridge Schmidt [240, 225],
had both initiated extensive investigations of the photometric capabilities
of these instruments. The principal problems identified were the focussing
errors, from the failure to maintain the emulsion in the curved focal plane,
together with the fact that very small stellar images quickly saturated a few
photographic grains, which lowered the sensitivity of the image diameter to
the magnitude. Emulsion variations over the large plates could also cause a
problem, as could the fact that stars in different parts of the field illuminate
different areas of the spherical primary mirror.

Argue's investigation at Cambridge showed that focus had to be maintained to within 50 μm over the curved focal plane, to achieve field errors in
the photometry not exceeding $\pm0\overset{m}{.}036$. Emulsion irregularities contributed
a comparable amount of error. Overall error bars of $\pm0\overset{m}{.}05$ at $m = 11$
and $\pm0\overset{m}{.}1$ at $m = 15$ were typical. A good photoelectric calibration was
necessary to obtain such results. Argue measured his plates on a Sartorius

† Jason Nassau and Virginia Burger had earlier, in 1946, used the Burrell–Schmidt
telescope in Cleveland for the photometry of red stars [82] – see section 7.4.1.
However, they did not address the special problems that arise in Schmidt-
telescope photometry in their discussion.

Table 7.2. *Some photometric observers with Schmidt telescopes*

Observers	Observatory/Institution	Year of publication	Ref.
J. Nassau & V. Burger	Cleveland	1946	[82]
B. Bok & M. Olmstead	Harvard	1950	[229]
D. Cameron	Warner & Swasey	1951	[230]
O. Eklöf	Uppsala	1949, 1954	[233, 234]
B. Westerlund	Uppsala	1954	[235]
E. A. Müller	Basel	1955	[236]
J. Stock	Warner & Swasey	1956	[220]
K. A. Barkhatova	Engelhardt, Kazan	1956–58	[237]
H. Haffner	Hamburg	1956	[238]
J. Hardorp	Hamburg	1960	[221]
H. Schäfer	Bonn	1960	[239]
A. N. Argue	Cambridge	1960–63	[240, 225, 241]
B. A. Vorontsov-Velyaminov	Palomar	1961	[232]
G. Haro, W. J. Luyten	Palomar	1962	[242]
G. Lyngå	Boyden	1962	[243]
M. J. Smyth, K. Nandy	Boyden	1962	[244]
P. S. The, C. Roslund	Bosscha	1963	[245]
R. P. Fenkart	Palomar	1965	[246]
C. Grubissich	Palomar	1965	[247]
G. Lyngå	Uppsala-Stromlo	1965	[248]
L. C. Lawrence, V. C. Reddish	Edinburgh	1965	[249]
S. I. Kadla	Tautenberg	1966	[250]
T. L. Evans	St Andrews	1967	[251]
U. Lindoff	Uppsala-Stromlo	1966, 1968	[252, 253]
K. Nandy	Edinburgh-Monte Porzio	1971	[254]
M. T. Brück	Edinburgh-Monte Porzio	1971	[255]
W. Becker	Basel	1972	[256]

iris photometer and reduced them by means of the Cambridge EDSAC computers [258, 225].

The use of digitized and semi-automated iris photometers for measuring the diameters of large numbers of stellar images on photographic plates was practised at several observatories by 1960. Becker's group in Basel were able to measure 300 stars an hour with a skilled operator [48], while at Hamburg the iris photometer, of the type described by Haffner [49], could measure 380 stars an hour when converted to digitized output – see comments by Stoy [259]. On the other hand Argue at Cambridge achieved a lower yet still impressive rate of measurement of 125 stars an hour [240, 260]. A similarly digitized iris photometer was also developed at the

Royal Observatory, Edinburgh [261]. In the United States iris photometers of the type described by L. C. Eichner at the Rutherfurd Observatory of Columbia University [47] were duplicated at other institutions, including in Cleveland [230] and at Caltech – see for example [262].

In 1961, at the Berkeley IAU meeting, Peter Fellgett reported on his proposal for a fully automated plate measuring machine that would give stellar positions and magnitudes without human intervention during the measuring process. He reasoned that

> ... the classical Schmidt telescope is outstanding not only in its approach to theoretical perfection but also in the extent to which the high theoretical performance can be approached in practice. Its capabilities have seldom been fully exploited. Since more that 10^4 star images may be recorded on a single plate, the only practicable way to use the whole of the information is to transform it into digital form wholly automatically and to carry out the research on an electronic computer [263].

Fellgett's innovative ideas led to two such projects being undertaken, at Edinburgh and Cambridge. The Edinburgh GALAXY machine utilized a scanning light spot from a cathode-ray tube which was focussed onto a Schmidt plate so as to measure the photographic density, typically in a 16-μm-sized pixel [264, 265]. A thousand stars an hour could be located and their magnitudes measured. GALAXY was brought into service at the Royal Observatory, Edinburgh, in 1969, originally for use with the 40-cm Edinburgh Schmidt. Its initial performance was described by Vincent Reddish [266] and Richard Stoy [267]. GALAXY was soon in operation 24 hours a day and it revolutionized Schmidt telescope photometry, being in high demand from observers in Britain and from overseas – see [268, 269].

At Cambridge the automatic plate-measuring project made use of a flying laser beam guided by two computer-controlled mirrors with orthogonal axes. Work on the APM project at Cambridge was undertaken by Edward Kibblewhite, and a prototype instrument was completed in 1971 [270]. Measurement rates of ten stars a second were achieved.

Good Schmidt photometry still required a photoelectric calibration, although some purely photographic techniques have been explored. These included a number of techniques that produce double images of a fixed intensity ratio. In particular the use of birefringent calcite plates to give an ordinary and extraordinary image was tried in Edinburgh by Mary Brück [271] – see also [272].

There is no doubt that the Schmidt telescope, with its wide-field capability, has maintained and extended interest in photographic photometry long after the introduction of higher performance but much smaller area detectors,

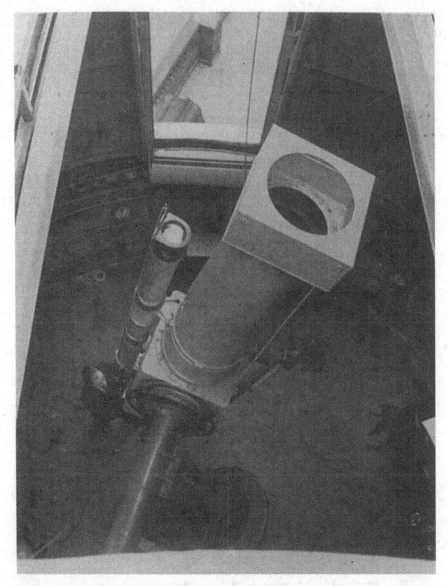

Fig. 7.11   The Edinburgh 16/24-inch Schmidt telescope, c. 1952.

notably the CCD. The use of photographic photometry for millions of stars on Schmidt plates with moderate precision has thus been undertaken at a time when photographic photometry on conventional telescopes has become virtually obsolete. Some of the results of the first two decades of Schmidt

photometry, the period covered here, were presented by Wilhelm Becker at
the Hamburg Schmidt telescope conference in 1972 [256].

References

[1]   Seares, F.H., *Trans. Int. Astron. Union*, **1**, 69 (1922).
[2]   Pickering, E.C., *Harvard Coll. Observ. Circ.*, **170**, 1 (1912).
[3]   Baillaud, B., *Trans. Int. Astron. Union*, **1**, 200 (1922).
[4]   Leavitt, H.S., *Ann. Harvard Coll. Observ.*, **71** (No. 3), (1917).
[5]   Seares, F.H., *Astrophys. J.*, **41**, 206 (1915).
[6]   Seares, F.H., *Astrophys. J.*, **41**, 259 (1915).
[7]   Shapley, H., *Harvard Coll. Observ. Bull.*, **781** (1923).
[8]   Seares, F.H. and Humason, M.H., *Astrophys. J.*, **56**, 84 (1922).
[9]   Seares, F.H., *Astrophys. J.*, **56**, 97 (1922).
[10] Pickering, E.C., *Nature*, **97**, 494 (1916).
[11] Kapteyn, J.C., *Plan of Selected Areas*, Groningen (1906).
[12] Pickering, E.C., *Sixty-second Annual Report of the Director of Harvard
      College Observatory* (1908).
[13] Pickering, E.C. and Kapteyn, J.C., *Ann. Harvard Coll. Observ.*, **101**, 1
      (1918).
[14] Pickering, E.C., Kapteyn, J.C. and van Rhijn, P., *Ann. Harvard Coll.
      Observ.*, **102**, 1 (1923).
[15] Pickering, E.C., Kapteyn, J.C. and van Rhijn, P., *Ann. Harvard Coll.
      Observ.*, **103**, 1 (1924).
[16] Turner, H.H., *Mon. Not. R. Astron. Soc.*, **85**, 610 (1925).
[17] Seares, F.H., van Rhijn, P.J., Joyner, M.C. and Richmond, M.L.,
      Astrophys. J., **62**, 320 (1925).
[18] Seares, F.H. and Joyner, M.C., *Astrophys. J.*, **63**, 160 (1926).
[19] Jones, H.S., *Magnitudes of stars contained in the Cape Zone Catalogue
      of 20843 stars for equinox 1900.0*, London (1927).
[20] Jones, H.S. and Halm, J., *Trans. Int. Astron. Union*, **2**, 88 (1925).
[21] Seares, F.H., *Trans. Int. Astron. Union*, **3**, 147 (1929).
[22] Seares, F.H., Kapteyn, J.C. and van Rhijn, P.J., *Mt Wilson Catalogue of
      Photographic Magnitudes in Selected Areas 1–139*, Carnegie Institution
      of Washington Publ. No. 402 (1930).
[23] Weaver, H.F., *Handbuch der Physik*, **54**, 130 (1962).
[24] Seares, F.H. and Joyner, M.C., *Astrophys. J.*, **98**, 302 (1943).
[25] Seares, F.H., Joyner, M.C. and Richmond, M.L., *Astrophys. J.*, **61**, 303
      (1925).
[26] Parkhurst, J.A., *Astrophys. J.*, **36**, 169 (1912).
[27] Fairley, A.S., *Astrophys. J.*, **73**, 125 (1931).
[28] Eberhard, G., *Vierteljahrschr. Astron. Ges.*, **66**, 321 (1931).
[29] Pickering, E.C., *Harvard Coll. Observ. Circ.*, **155**, (1910).
[30] Stetson, H.T., *Pop. Astron.*, **23**, 24 (1915).
[31] Stetson, H.T., *Astrophys. J.*, **43**, 253 (1916).
[32] Stetson, H.T., *Astrophys. J.*, **43**, 325 (1916).
[33] Schilt, J., *Bull. Astron. Inst. Netherlands*, **1** (No. 10), 51 (1922).
[34] Schilt, J., *Publ. Kapteyn Astron. Lab. Groningen*, **32**, 1 (1924).
[35] Schilt, J., *Bull. Astron. Inst. Netherlands*, **2** (No. 60), 135 (1924).
[36] Stetson, H.T. and Carpenter, E.F., *Astrophys. J.*, **58**, 36 (1923).

[37] Ross, F.E., *Astrophys. J.*, **84**, 241 (1936).

[38] Seares, F.H., Ross, F.E. and Joyner, M.C., *Cat. of Magnitudes and Colors of stars north of +80°, Carnegie Institution of Washington Publ.*, **532** (1941).

[39] Schlesinger, F. and Barney, I., *Trans. Astron. Observ. Yale Univ.*, **9**, 1 (1933).

[40] Schlesinger, F., Barney, I. and Gesler, C., *Trans. Astron. Observ. Yale Univ.*, **10**, 11 (1933).

[41] Schilt, J. and Hill, S.J., *Contrib. Rutherfurd Observ. Columbia Univ.*, **30** (1937).

[42] Schilt, J. and Hill, S.J., *Contrib. Rutherfurd Observ. Columbia Univ.*, **31** (1938).

[43] Hill, S.J. and Schilt, J., *Contrib. Rutherfurd Observ. Columbia Univ.*, **32** (1952).

[44] Jackson, J. and J. Stoy, R.H., *Ann. Cape Observ.*, **17** (1954); **18**, **19** (1955); **20** (1958).

[45] Stoy, R.H., *Ann. Cape Observ.*, **21** (1966); **22** (1968).

[46] Siedentopf, H., *Astron. Nachr.*, **254**, 33 (1934).

[47] Eichner, L.C., Hett, J.H., Schilt, J., Schwarzschild, M. and Sterling, H.T., *Astron. J.*, **53**, 25 (1947).

[48] Becker, W. and Biber, C., *Zeitschr. für Astrophys.*, **41**, 52 (1956).

[49] Haffner, H., *Veröff. der Univ.-Sternw. Göttingen*, No. **106** (1953).

[50] Cuffey, J., *Sky and Tel.*, **15**, 258 (1956).

[51] Seares, F.H., *Astrophys. J.*, **61**, 284 (1925).

[52] Hassenstein, W., *Publ. Potsdam Astrophys. Observ.*, **26** (Part 2), 1 (1927).

[53] Seares, F.H., *Astrophys. J.*, **74**, 131 (1931).

[54] Seares, F.H., *Trans. Int. Astron. Union*, **4**, 136 (1933).

[55] Seares, F.H., *Astrophys. J.*, **78**, 141 (1933).

[56] van Rhijn, P. and Bok, B., *Publ. Kapteyn Astron. Lab. Groningen*, No. **44**, 1 (1929).

[57] van de Kamp, P. and Vyssotsky, A.N., *Publ. Leander-McCormick Observ.*, **7**, 1 (1937).

[58] Payne, C.H., *Ann. Harvard Coll. Observ.*, **89** (No. 1), 1 (1931).

[59] Payne, C.H., *Ann. Harvard Coll. Observ.*, **89** (No. 6), 105 (1935).

[60] Payne-Gaposchkin, C.H., *Ann. Harvard Coll. Observ.*, **89** (No. 12), 191 (1938).

[61] King, E.S., *Ann. Harvard Coll. Observ.*, **85** (No. 3), 45 (1923).

[62] Parkhurst, J.A., *Publ. Yerkes Observ.*, **4** (Part 6) (1927).

[63] Ross, F.E. and Zug, R.S., *Astron. Nachr.*, **239**, 289 (1930).

[64] Armeanca, J., *Zeitschr. für Astrophys.*, **7**, 78 (1933).

[65] Rybka, E., *Publ. Astron. Observ. Warsaw Univ.*, **9**, 1 (1934).

[66] Müller, H., *Veröff. Astron. Recheninst. Berlin-Dahlem*, No. **53** (1936).

[67] de Sitter, A., *Bull. Astron. Inst. Netherlands*, **8**, 185 (1937).

[68] Rybka, E., *Acta Astron.*, **2** (Ser. b), 54 (1937).

[69] Bok, B.J. and Swann, W.F., *Ann. Harvard Coll. Observ.*, **105**, 371 (1938).

[70] Payne-Gaposchkin, C.H. and Gaposchkin, S., *Ann. Harvard Coll. Observ.*, **89** (No. 5), 93 (1935).

[71] King, E.S. and Ingalls, R., *Ann. Harvard Coll. Observ.*, **85** (No. 11), 191 (1930).

[72] Payne-Gaposchkin, C.H., *Ann. Harvard Coll. Observ.*, **89** (No. 6), 105 (1935).

[73]   Payne-Gaposchkin, C.H., *Ann. Harvard Coll. Observ.*, **89** (No. 8), 123 (1937).
[74]   Gaposchkin, S., *Ann. Harvard Coll. Observ.*, **89** (No. 9), 143 (1937).
[75]   Gaposchkin, S., *Harvard Coll. Observ. Bull.*, **904**, 22 (1936).
[76]   Payne-Gaposchkin, C., *Ann. Harvard Coll. Observ.*, **105** (No. 19), 383 (1936).
[77]   Becker, F., *Publ. Astrophys. Observ. Potsdam*, **27** (Parts 1, 2, 3) (1931).
[78]   Brück, H.A., *Publ. Astrophys. Observ. Potsdam*, **28** (Part 4) (1935).
[79]   Becker, F., *Publ. Astrophys. Observ. Potsdam*, **28** (Parts 5, 6) (1938).
[80]   Cuffey, J., *Ann. Harvard Coll. Observ.*, **105** (No. 21) 403 (1936).
[81]   Trumpler, R., *Lick Observ. Bull.*, **14** (No. 420), 154 (1930).
[82]   Nassau, J. J. and Burger, V., *Astrophys. J.*, **103**, 25 (1946).
[83]   Rybka, E., *Travaux Soc. Sci. Lettres Wroclaw (B)* No. **28** = *Contrib. Wroclaw Astron. Observ.* No. **5** (1950).
[84]   Becker, W., *Zeitschr. für Astrophys.*, **9**, 79 (1934).
[85]   Pettit, E. and Nicholson, S., *Astrophys. J.*, **68**, 279 (1928).
[86]   Becker, W., *Veröff. Univ.-Sternw. Göttingen*, **5** (Nr 79), 159 (1946).
[87]   Greaves, W.M.H., *Trans. Int. Astron. Union*, **8**, 355 (1953).
[88]   Becker, W., *Zeitschr. für Astrophys.*, **15**, 225 (1938).
[89]   Becker, W., *Astron. Nachr.*, **272**, 179 (1942).
[90]   Greenstein, J.L., *Astrophys. J.*, **104**, 403 (1946).
[91]   Becker, W., *Astrophys. J.*, **107**, 278 (1948).
[92]   Becker, W., *Veröff. Univ.-Sternw. Göttingen*, **5** (No. 80), 173 (1946).
[93]   Becker, W., *Veröff. Univ.-Sternw. Göttingen*, **5** (No. 81), 184 (1946).
[94]   Becker, W., *Veröff. Univ.-Sternw. Göttingen*, **5** (No. 82), 196 (1946).
[95]   Stebbins, J. and Whitford, A.E., *Astrophys. J.*, **98**, 20 (1943).
[96]   Becker, W., *Zeitschr. für Astrophys.*, **62**, 54 (1965).
[97]   Becker, W., *Zeitschr. für Astrophys.*, **66**, 404 (1967).
[98]   Fenkart, R.P., *Zeitschr. für Astrophys.*, **66**, 390 (1967).
[99]   Fenkart, R.P., *Zeitschr. für Astrophys.*, **68**, 87 (1968).
[100] Brooker, L.G., Hamer, F.M. and Mees, C.E.K., *J. Optical Soc. America*, **23**, 216 (1933).
[101] Merrill, P.W., *Astrophys. J.*, **79**, 183 (1934).
[102] Hetzler, C., *Astrophys. J.*, **86**, 509 (1937).
[103] Rösch, J., *Ann. d'Astrophys.*, **6**, 45 (1943).
[104] Nassau, J.J. and van Albada, G.B., *Astrophys. J.*, **109**, 391 (1949).
[105] Nassau, J.J. and Blanco, V.M., *Astrophys. J.*, **120**, 118, 129 (1954).
[106] Nassau, J.J. and Blanco, V.M., *Astrophys. J.*, **125**, 195 (1957).
[107] Jones, H.S., *Trans. Int. Astron. Union*, **4**, 194 (1933).
[108] Seares, F.H., Sitterly, B.W. and Joyner, M.C., *Astrophys. J.*, **72**, 311 (1930).
[109] Carr, F.E., *Astrophys. J.*, **76**, 70 (1932).
[110] Seares, F.H., *Trans. Int. Astron. Union*, **6**, 215 (1939).
[111] Seares, F.H., *Proc. Nat. Acad. Sci.*, **22**, 327 (1936).
[112] Stebbins, J. and Whitford, A.E., *Astrophys. J.*, **87**, 237 (1937).
[113] Seares, F.H., *Mon. Not. R. Astron. Soc.*, **103**, 281 (1943).
[114] Seares, F.H. and Joyner, M.C., *Astrophys. J.*, **98**, 261 (1943).
[115] Martin, E.G., *Mon. Not. R. Astron. Soc.*, **102**, 261 (1942).
[116] Stoy, R.H. and Menzies, A., *Mon. Not. R. Astron. Soc.*, **104**, 298 (1944).
[117] Keenan, P.C. and Babcock, H.W., *Astrophys. J.*, **93**, 64 (1941).
[118] Morgan, W.W. and Bidelman, W.P., *Astrophys. J.*, **104**, 245 (1946).

to exchange data with their EHR. They may access data through an HIE portal. Without integrated data, workflows can be inefficient, thus reducing adoption and likelihood of use.

∎ Data storage models inconsistent: When data comes from multiple sources, the data may not all be aggregated and stored in one place. The degree to which data is consumed from other EHRs, and the means by which that information is integrated into the patient record vary from provider to provider, resulting in a record that will not be complete or consistent.

∎ Data normalization: Data from multiple sources requires that the information be standardized and normalized, often resulting in time-consuming and cumbersome work. The benefits are the ability to analyze the data for a number of purposes, including risk stratification, disease management, and others, yet many are not willing to expend the effort.

∎ Matching patient data: The technology and algorithms necessary to create the MPI have been available for some time. Yet, challenges still exist in mapping and manual correction of duplicate patients. Technology vendors must continue to refine their solutions to improve matching rates and reduce matching errors.

∎ Referral Management for PHM: Availability of this technology varies from HIE to HIE, and it is not typically available on a provider-to-provider basis. As such, referrals tend to occur in network (within a clinically integrated network), where all members share the same EHR platform. Closed-loop referral management capabilities must be developed and deployed.

∎ Real-time encounter notification capability: Notification of providers when a patient presents in the emergency department or is admitted is not available as part of the core functionality of either an EHR or an HIE. Vendors emerging in the marketplace offer this as a bolt-on solution.

Future of Interoperability

New standards, technologies, and regulatory developments will continue to shape the direction of interoperability and enable access to needed data for consumer use and care delivery and to support continuous intelligence. "The future of the EHR is going to look a lot like your phone," predicts Stanley Crane, chief information officer at Allscripts.[10] By 2023, 60% of HIEs will shift the focus of their business models from information exchange to data management and analytical services, creating new opportunities to leverage data from a variety of sources.[11] There are three transformative opportunities:

- TEFCA: In 2018, the ONC proposed TEFCA as a means of implementing some of the interoperability requirements associated with the 21st Century Cures Act of 2016. TEFCA is tasked with establishing a technical and governance framework that enables nationwide patient-data sharing across the large number of HIEs that currently operate around the country and the providers that participate in the networks, resulting in
  - Consolidation: HIEs merging with other players or being absorbed by larger organizations.
  - Partnerships: HIEs complementing healthcare delivery organizations, payers, and others to leverage their collective data assets for stratifying risk and closing gaps in care.
  - Innovation: New data exchange standards and enhanced data interchange platforms will allow expanded offerings, such as semantic normalization, advanced data modeling, and predictive/prescriptive analytics.
- Fast Healthcare Interoperability Resources Specification (FHIR): HL7 has established FHIR to facilitate the exchange of healthcare information between any parties involved in the healthcare ecosystem (providers, patients, caregivers, payers, researchers, etc.). FHIR uses the Internet to connect

discrete data elements, each with a unique identifier, allow-ing developers to build applications (or apps) that could retrieve and use data from an EHR, share data through open source platforms and mobile applications, and offer patients and providers the ability to gain an incredibly rich new set of functionalities. While still in its initial stages, FHIR holds great promise for future development.

■ Blockchain: An emerging distributed database system, blockchain is gaining traction as a potential key to unlocking barriers in healthcare data sharing and enable-ment of the industry-wide shift to value-based care. In the simplest terms, blockchain is a shared record of transac-tions. It enables participants in a group to securely share data with each other without a middleman and keep track of what was exchanged and when. Instead of that record being located on a single, hackable computer, it is maintained across multiple computers, which makes the information extremely difficult to tamper with or delete. That tamper-proof characteristic, along with a process that ensures any information put into the blockchain is valid, enables trust between the group participants.[12] To date, the hype surrounding blockchain for healthcare exceeds the number of potential (realistic) applications. It remains to be seen whether blockchain can solve problems related to interoperability better than existing technologies.

Conclusion

Interoperability may be considered by some as the final frontier—the key capability to enable true population health management. By making data accessible by the provider, the patient, the payer, and all involved in the consumption and delivery of care, better decisions about delivery and consump-tion of care can be made, resulting in better access, lower cost of care, and improved outcomes.

Notes

1. "Interoperability 101," HIMSS, www.himss.org/library/interoperability-standards/101-the-basics.
2. Becker, Jonathan, Neelam Dwivedi, and Sandeep Purao. "Regional Health Information Organizations in the US." *Encyclopedia of Information Science and Technology*. 3rd ed. IGI Global, 2015. 3496-3505. Web. September 24, 2019. doi:10.4018/978-1-4666-5888-2.ch343.
3. "About CommonWell," January 23, 2019. www.commonwellalliance.org/about/.
4. "Carequality Interoperability Framework Adopters." https://carequality.org/members-and-supporters/.
5. Interoperability," "Trusted Exchange Framework and Common Agreement," April 19, 2019. www.healthit.gov/topic/interoperability/trusted-exchange-framework-and-common-agreement.
6. DeSalvo, Karen B. and Erica Galvez, Office of the National Coordinator, "Connecting Health and Care for the Nation: A Shared Nationwide Interoperability Roadmap," October 6, 2015, www.healthit.gov/buzz-blog/electronic-health-and-medical-records/interoperability- electronic-health-and-medical-records/connecting-health-care-nation-shared-nationwide-interoperability-roadmap-version-10.
7. "ASC X12 Store." X12. Accessed October 1, 2019. http://x12.org/x12org/about/asc-x12-faqs.cfm.
8. Leventhal, Rajiv. "External Data-Sharing Efforts Largely Insufficient, Healthcare Professionals Report." *Healthcare Innovation*, August 21, 2019. www.hcinnovationgroup.com/interoperability-hie/news/21093647/external-datasharing-efforts-largely-insufficient-healthcare-professionals-report.
9. Sujansky, Walter, California Health Care Foundation. "Promises and Pitfalls: A Look at California's Regional Health Information Organizations." January 15, 2019. www.chcf.org/publication/promise-pitfalls-californias-regional-health-information-organizations/.
10. Bresnick, Jennifer. "4 Basics to Know about the Role of FHIR in Interoperability." Health IT Analytics, March 22, 2016. https://healthitanalytics.com/news/4-basics-to-know-about-the-role-of-fhir-in-interoperability.

11. Runyon, Barry. "Market Guide for Health Information Exchange Platforms." The Gartner Group, April 9, 2019. www.gartner.com/en/documents/3906722/market-guide-for-health-information-exchange-platforms.
12. Livingston, Shelby. "Will Blockchain Save the Healthcare System?" *Modern Healthcare*, February 9, 2019. www.modernhealthcare.com/article/20190209/TRANSFORMATION02/190209953/will-blockchain-save-the-healthcare-system.

Chapter 10

Knowledge Management and Analytics

Hiding within those mounds of data is knowledge that could change the life of a patient or change the world.

Atul Butte, MD, PhD, Priscilla Chan & Mark Zuckerberg Distinguished Professor, University of California, San Francisco, Chief Data Scientist University of California Health System

Purpose

To explore the key role of knowledge management and analytics as it relates to the care management platform (CMP) and to understand how it supports healthcare delivery organizations in their transition to digital health, connected care, and population health management (PHM).

In this chapter, the reader will review

- A brief history of healthcare analytics
- The insight-driven decision-making process

- The knowledge management and analytics landscape and key components of the care management platform
- Challenges and key success factors
- Where data and analytics are headed

Data and Analytics for Population Health

The use of data to drive PHM decision making may have first been demonstrated by Florence Nightingale. Known to most as the founder of modern nursing, she was also one of the first statisticians and, indeed, the first female statistician on record in the field of medicine.[1] While serving on the battlefields during the Crimean War (1853–56), she catalogued the causes of soldiers' deaths. She then set about analyzing her findings and came to a revolutionary conclusion: the primary cause of death for troops was not from wounds suffered on the battle-field, nor was it from other injuries. Instead, the leading cause of death was from disease, specifically diseases caused by unsanitary conditions and poor public hygiene.

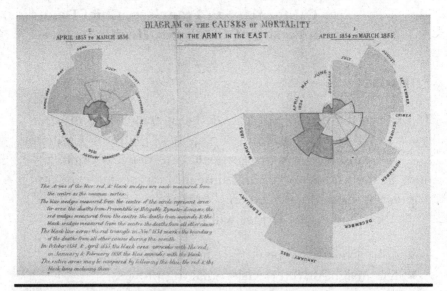

Figure 10.1 Florence Nightingale's visualization of mortality in the Crimean War.

Nightingale's polar area diagram (Figure 10.1) provided a visualization of her data and made a clear case for reform. It detailed month by month deaths from enemy fire, other battlefield casualties, and preventable conditions such as typhus, cholera, dysentery, and frostbite. The diagram on the right shows mortality before reforms were put into place, and the diagram on the left shows the effects after reforms were put into place.

Today, as the healthcare industry shifts from 1.0: Brick and Mortar Healthcare to 2.0: The Transition and then to 3.0: Digital Health and Connected Care, healthcare organizations are investing in data and analytics tools, systems, and resources. As mentioned in Chapter 2, leadership priorities shift from implementing "systems of record" to building "systems of insight," initially consisting of

- Routine daily, monthly, or annual reports from enterprise systems such as electronic health records (EHRs) and enterprise resource management systems (ERPs)
- Data repositories, data lakes, data visualization tools, and ad hoc analytics
- Point systems to analyze targeted questions
- Scorecards and dashboards for the board and senior leadership
- Performance metrics and benchmarks to compare with other organizations

Often, the impact of silos and the silo mentality on data becomes clear. Specifically, the proliferation of point systems, decentralized data analysts, and data islands (i.e., unconnected data sources) across operating units results in

- Hoarding of information
- Limited trust in data provided by others across the enterprise
- Poor data quality and conflicting data definitions
- Duplication of effort, rework, and added expense for data cleanup and refinement

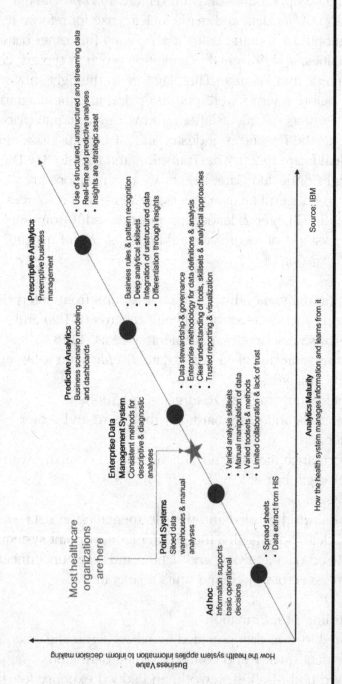

Figure 10.2 Enterprise data management system.

Progress along the journey to high-value healthcare requires consistent data and analytics strategies, governance, systems, methods, tools, and processes across the enterprise. Figure 10.2 illustrates the necessary shift from decentralized point systems to a consistent enterprise data management system to drive insight-driven decision making. With increasing levels of maturity and resulting business value, internal and external data sources will support descriptive and diagnostic analyses, eventually progressing to predictive and prescriptive analytics.

To succeed in today's volatile healthcare business environment, leadership requires data that is pertinent, accurate, and timely. Ideally, an insight-driven decision making (I-DDM) culture and capability will

- Improve the speed of decision making.
- Decrease the cost of decision making.
- Make better fact-based decisions.
- Reduce uncertainty.
- Expand organizational learning.
- Set the stage for self-service analytics and machine learning.

INSIGHT-DRIVEN DECISION MAKING (I-DDM)

Data, analytics, and actionable insights are embedded in the decision-making process at every level of the organization. These organizations transform their strategic priorities, operating models, and customer journeys to create measurable value. As part of 2.0, the organization shifts from implementing systems of record to establishing systems of insight. I-DDM is defined as the business discipline and technology to harness insights and consistently turn data into action.[2] This is not a specific technology but, rather, a business strategy, methodology, and approach to working designed to discover and apply data in a meaningful way. The I-DDM (as seen in Figure 10.3) process helps the organization clarify

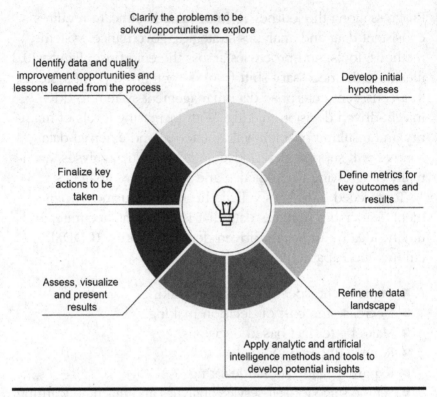

Figure 10.3   Insight-driven decision-making process.

the problems to be solved/opportunities to explore; develop initial hypotheses; define metrics for key outcomes and results; refine the data landscape; apply analytic and artificial intelligence methods and tools to develop potential insights; assess, visualize, and present results; finalize key actions to be taken; and identify data quality improvement opportunities and lessons learned from the process.

In the book *Creating a Data-Driven Organization*, Carl Anderson says: "Data-drivenness is about building tools, abilities, and, most crucially, a *culture* that acts on data."[3] For the most part, 1.0 organizations spend the majority of their time gathering (i.e., cleaning and manipulating) data prior to analyzing it. While spreadsheet and point-based departmental

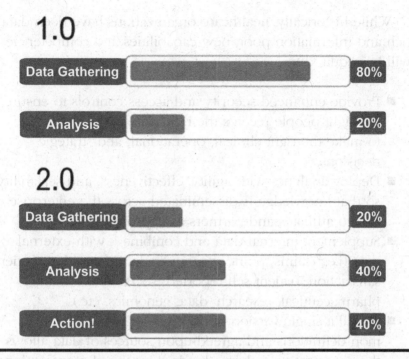

Figure 10.4 The pivot from analysis to action.

systems have historically been sufficient, the growth and complexity of issues within the healthcare industry have changed that. The pivot to 2.0 and beyond requires that the majority of effort be spent on analysis and action, as seen in Figure 10.4.

The Knowledge Management and Analytics Layer of the CMP

Design of new care models and services for patients with chronic conditions will depend on the knowledge management and analytics layer of the CMP (see Figure 7.1), as claims, clinical, and other relevant data will help define the needs of each patient population. Risk stratification, identification of gaps in care, determination of the most effective interventions (both clinical and social support), development of care plans, and outcomes measurement will depend on the organization's ability to leverage data and analytics.

While historically, healthcare organizations have been data rich and information poor, new capabilities and competencies will be required to

- Provide enhanced security and access controls to ensure the right people receive the right data at the right time to make the right clinical, operational, and strategic decisions.
- Deploy analytics with agility, effectiveness, and scalability, so that knowledge is disseminated across the enterprise and to affiliates and partners as appropriate.
- Supplement internal data and combine it with external data (i.e., claims, point of care clinical information, patient satisfaction, patient self-reported, social determinants, pharmaceutical, research, data, genomics, etc.).
- Create a single version of the truth—the use of common definitions and agreed-upon sources of data allows the organization to have standard means of representing information used for decision making.
- Present actionable, customized intelligence in a compelling way and allow the data to tell the story in a way that supports the appropriate action.

An enterprise data management system will support many strategic, operational, financial, human resource, supply chain, performance improvement, etc., knowledge management and analytics (KMA) initiatives. For the purposes of PHM and the CMP, the KMA layer uses information foundational systems, data acquired through interoperability capabilities, and data ingested from other sources. Key capabilities include

- Business intelligence (BI): The data, tools, skillsets, and techniques that allow identification, extraction, and analysis of data. Clinical intelligence can be considered a subset of BI that deals strictly with clinical data and its interpretation. Central to the concept of business intelligence is the ability to extract, transform, and load information from a variety of sources into a central repository. This repository can take the form of an enterprise data warehouse, multiple specialized data marts, or a data lake.

■ Data governance: Described as "The formulation of policy to optimize, secure and leverage information as an enterprise asset by aligning the objectives of multiple functions,"[4] effective data governance requires strong business ownership with IT support. Because of the depth, breadth, and complexity of healthcare data, governance should focus on critical data elements—those most essential to clinical and operational decision making. There should be a plan for data quality measurement and enforcement of policies around data quality. Roles and privileges for access to data must be defined. (Who can see? Who can add, edit, or delete data?) Data security must be ensured—at rest and in transit. And the lifecycle of data must be defined—at what point is data retired?

■ Care protocols: Evidence-based established standards for the prevention of illness and treatment of a patient with one or more conditions. As part of the CMP, the protocols address the longitudinal journey of the patient from pre-diagnosis or rising risk to management or reversal of disease in all the settings where care may take place, from the physician office to diagnostic facilities to the emergency room, inpatient stays, post-acute care, rehabilitation, social/community services, and palliative care. In each instance, protocols ensure that the right pathway is followed based on the patient's unique situation. In many settings today, guidelines and clinical content are being developed to address social determinants, behavioral health, and other factors that contribute to the patient's overall health.

■ Point of care clinical decision support: Relying on care protocols and other evidence-based medicine, clinical decision support (CDS) at the point of care allows rules-based workflow engines to guide the clinician. While CDS does not substitute for clinical critical thinking, it does allow the checking of multiple interactions that would either most benefit the patient or prevent harm.

■ Data aggregation and normalization: Data of a similar type may come from many sources—for example, there may be information from a number of home health agencies that needs to be aggregated to understand the totality of services being rendered. By aggregating this data, a complete picture of how patients and consumers are using home health services can be developed. Aggregation usually occurs in a centralized data repository such as an enterprise data warehouse, data marts, or data lakes. When data is loaded from disparate sources into a central data repository, there is often a difference in how various terms are expressed—for example, one data source may use the terminology "AMI," while another might use "Heart Attack." The process of normalization ensures that like terms are used for each data element. Data standards (reference Chapter 9—Interoperability) ensure that there is a common crosswalk so that when data is analyzed, the definitions are commonly understood.

■ Data mining: Selective query of one or more databases to produce analysis. Mining can occur in order to extract raw data or can occur at a summary level. For example, lab values for hemoglobin A1c (blood sugars) can be extracted at both the patient/individual test result level to allow further analysis, or summary data can be created that details the number of lab values that occur within a certain range.

As KMA competences evolve beyond descriptive and diagnostic analytics, more advanced analytics, including predictive and prescriptive analytics, will be part of data maturity, as seen in Figure 10.5.

Figure 10.5   Data maturity model.

The data maturity model includes

■ Descriptive Analytics: Standard and ad hoc reporting that answers What happened? How many? (e.g., number of patients with a certain condition), How often does a situation happen? When did it happen? Where did it happen? (e.g., what are the arrival patterns at the emergency department in key geographies?) and Who did it happen to? (e.g., demographic profile). In addition, there may be questions such as How much did it cost? Often, through additional queries and drill downs, answers to What exactly is the problem? or What is the root cause? can be addressed. For the purposes of PHM, dashboards provide key performance indicators, quality metrics, and other indicators of performance against contract or other management objectives. Reports and routine analyses are built once and used many times. Business and clinical leaders often become proficient at self-service ad hoc analyses over time.

■ Diagnostic Analytics: Answers the question, Why is this happening? Oftentimes, requiring more rigorous analysis than the pure descriptive activity, analysts slice and dice the data to gain new insights and knowledge about stratified patients and the needs of the population. Additional validation against care standards, outcome targets, and other comparative data may require further investigation or analysis of data quality issues. If there are problems with data elements composing key metrics and data findings, factors contributing to variances should be examined further.

■ Predictive Analytics: Answers the question, What might happen? Involving a combination of statistical techniques including basic trending, regression analysis, and machine learning, large amounts of data from the past are analyzed to identify patterns, identify trends, and predict the future. Analysts must be careful to ensure that predictive models reflect the needs of the patient population and consider care team workflow, and that if alerts are developed, the triggers are complementary to management of the impacted population. Embedded in real-time decision support systems, clinicians, financial experts, and administrative staff receive alerts about potential events before they happen and are able to make informed decisions regarding a course of action. Examples to support PHM include preventing a readmission, risk scoring for potential outcomes and analysis of interventional options, forecasting patient deterioration, activating patient behavioral changes, and predicting utilization.

■ Prescriptive Analytics: Responds to the question, How do we make a positive outcome happen or avoid a negative outcome? Prescriptive analytics continue to update information and demonstrate suggested actions to augment decisions. It is typically embedded within real-time workflow; the clinician will not be replaced but will be given alternatives and suggestions. The benefits will range from development of precision medicine and improved therapeutics to lowered cost of care and enhanced personalization of the patient experience.

Challenges and Critical Success Factors

According to Thomas Redmond, "the two most important instances in the life of data are the point at which data is created and the point at which data is used."[5] Done well, data can positively impact every aspect of the healthcare industry, every healthcare organization, every clinician, and every patient. Done poorly, the potential exists for patient harm, errors, poor quality, and wasted energy and money. Specific challenges and critical success factors include

■ Data quality—Dealing with problematic data can cost as much as 20% of revenue or 50% of operating expenses.[6] What happens when healthcare delivery organizations have poor-quality data? It becomes more difficult to make decisions. Professional time is wasted, departments don't trust each other's data, decisions are delayed and often made with incomplete information, and risks associated with the decision increase. In the case of population health, it makes it more difficult to prove value, reduces the effectiveness of already difficult change, and can result in scrutiny from payers and regulators. Clinical integration is more difficult, and key stakeholders are less likely to support needed changes.

Data quality should be continuously and rigorously reviewed, expected levels of quality defined, and governance processes put in place to ensure data quality at the source, including

- Relentless attention to data definitions and integrity of data sources
- Measurement of data accuracy and gaps
- Aggressive target setting for data quality improvement
- Formalized accountability for data quality

Finally, it is important to recognize that data quality issues require cultural change.

■ Addressing PHM data integration challenges—While the notion of a "single source of truth" has a certain appeal, the reality is that in order to manage the health of different populations, data will come from multiple sources, as indicated in Figure 10.6. Disparate vendors, customized systems, differing terminology, varying levels of automation, etc. will create challenges in mapping data and information across each population.

Identification of current and future sources and planning for integration through effective data governance will ensure that the value of these data assets can be leveraged and maximized.

■ Access to data and tools—The proliferation of point systems and the lack of structured data for analysis cause numerous challenges. Often, analysts have multiple data sources available for analysis, and the most appropriate

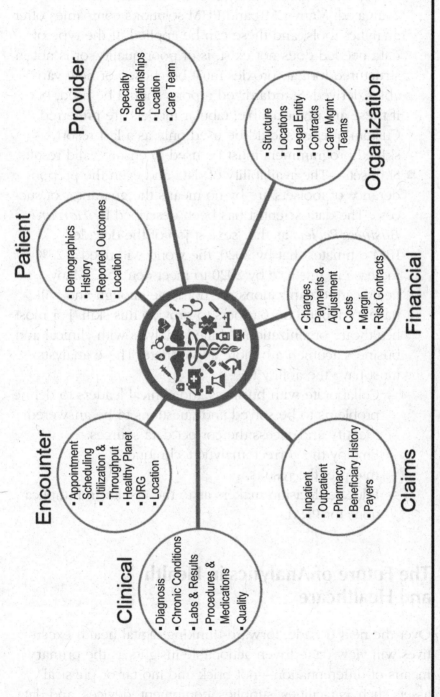

Figure 10.6 Sources of data to support populations.

source and tools for analyzing these sources must be evaluated. Many CMP and PHM solutions companies offer analytics tools, and these can be applied. If the type of data needed does not exist, is of poor quality, or is not in structured format, proxies must be chosen or new variables derived. Standardized reports should be used, but if these are not available, tabular models are preferred. Custom queries should be used only as a last resort, as skilled programmers must be used to ensure valid results.

■ Skill sets—The availability of data and even the preponderance of toolsets are by no means the guarantor of success. The data scientist has been described by *Harvard Business Review* as the "sexiest job of the decade." IBM estimates that by 2020, the world will need a 28% increase in this role by 2020 to meet demand.[7] Many healthcare organizations are not large enough and will have to depend on partners to provide this skill. For most healthcare organizations, skilled analysts with clinical and business acumen are more appropriate. These analysts must have the ability to:

- Collaborate with business and clinical leaders to define problems to be solved and questions to be answered.
- Identify and access the correct data sources.
- Employ the correct analytic techniques.
- Interpret the results.
- Educate decision makers as to the results and implications for PHM.

The Future of Analytics in Health and Healthcare

Over the next decade, forward-thinking digital health executives will view data-driven actionable insights as the primary means of differentiation—not brick and mortar or physical assets such as facilities, supplies, equipment, devices, and data centers. Changes that will propel this trend are:

- Data analysis, which is primarily historic today, will shift to real-time predictive and prescriptive analytics.
- Insight delivery will be embedded in processes and workflow and will lead to action at the point of care and empowered patients.
- Cognitive computing and artificial intelligence all but eliminate routine manual task work and augment clinical, financial, and business decision making.
- Integrated, curated data can help personalize customer experiences.
- The emergence of "citizen data scientist" or business and clinical power users who want self-service tools and capabilities.

These changes will produce significant changes in the volume, sources, and types of data available as the industry progresses toward 3.0: Digital Health and Connected Care, as seen in Figure 10.7.

As the quantity of data and the types of information available to healthcare organizations continue to grow, a shift will occur from relying primarily on descriptive and diagnostic analytics to more predictive, prescriptive, and artificial intelligence–based analytics. The "Waterfall" development cycle that traditional BI shops have deployed (requirements definition, data model build, data integration scripts, semantic layer, query) is no longer agile enough to respond to the rapidly changing analytic needs of the organization. *Forbes* magazine introduced the concept of continuous intelligence.

CONTINUOUS INTELLIGENCE

"Continuous intelligence (CI) ... enables the business to feed off continuous, high-frequency, intuitive insights from all data ... CI is an AI-based, machine-driven way to continuously interpret data, discover patterns and learn what's of value in the data. This allows business users to mash up and

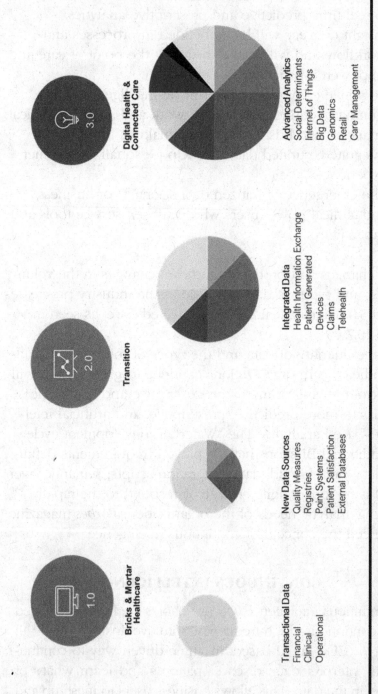

Figure 10.7 Expanding volume, sources, and types of data.

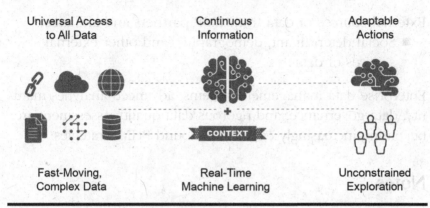

Universal Access
to All Data

Continuous
Information

Adaptable
Actions

CONTEXT

Fast-Moving,
Complex Data

Real-Time
Machine Learning

Unconstrained
Exploration

Figure 10.8 Continuous intelligence.

blend disparate data intelligently with the objective of discovering new insights constantly and revealing it as a data
story with complete context ,... a smart machine and AI that
discovers everything in your data, no matter how complex."[8]

Figure 10.8 illustrates the assimilation of complex and fast-
moving data with pervasive access. Information flow is continuous and incorporates real-time machine learning, where
actions are adaptable as the information changes and grows.
CI provides for unconstrained exploration of the data, allowing
new possibilities in problem solving. The implications for PHM
are broad and varied but suggest heightened ability to provide
better care and improved outcomes.

Conclusion

The KMA layer of the CMP is critical for

■ Integrating the large amounts of data available from foundational systems
■ Incorporating data obtained through connectivity, interoperability, and health information exchange

■ External sources of data from CMP partners and affiliates
  ■ Social determinant, demographic, and other external
    sources of data

Enterprise data management systems, advanced analytics maturity, data governance, and rigorous data quality assessment are becoming increasingly essential to sound PHM strategies.

Notes

1. Science Museum. "Florence Nightingale: The Pioneer Statistician." December 10, 2018. www.sciencemuseum.org.uk/objects-and-stories/florence-nightingale-pioneer-statistician.
2. Redman, Thomas C. "Bad Data Costs the U.S. $3 Trillion Per Year." *Harvard Business Review*, October 4, 2017. https://hbr.org/2016/09/bad-data-costs-the-u-s-3-trillion-per-year.
3. Anderson, Carl. *Creating a Data-Driven Organization*. O'Reilly Media, Inc., August 2015. www.oreilly.com/library/view/creating-a-data-driven/9781491916902/ch01.html.
4. Soares, Sunil. *The Chief Data Officer Handbook for Data Governance*. MC Press Online, 2014.
5. Redman, Thomas C. *Data Driven—Profiting from Your Most Important Business Asset*. Boston: Harvard Business Review Press, 2008.
6. Hopkins, Brian, Ted Schadler, and James McCormick. "The Insights-Driven Business." "Insights-Driven Businesses Set The Pace For Global Growth." Forrester, July 27, 2016.
7. Redman, Thomas C. "Bad Data Costs the U.S. $3 Trillion Per Year." *Harvard Business Review*, October 4, 2017. https://hbr.org/2016/09/bad-data-costs-the-u-s-3-trillion-per-year.
8. Mulligan, Sharmila. "What Is Continuous Intelligence?" *Forbes*, October 18, 2018. www.forbes.com/sites/forbestechcouncil/2018/10/18/what-is-continuous-intelligence/#540878587d25.

Chapter 11

Advanced Care Management

> *The doctor of the future will give no medicine but will interest his patient in the care of the human frame, in diet and in the cause and prevention of disease.*
>
> **Thomas Edison, 1903**

Purpose

To explore the breadth and depth of advanced care management within the care management platform (CMP) and to understand how it is essential in supporting healthcare delivery organizations in their transition to digital health, connected care, and population health management.

In this chapter, the reader will review

- Advanced care management concepts and framework
- Key advanced care management components of the care management platform
- Challenges and key success factors
- The future of care management for population health management

Advanced Care Management Concepts and Framework

According to the Robert Wood Johnson Foundation (RWJF), "Care management is a set of activities intended to improve patient care and reduce the need for medical services by enhancing coordination of care, eliminate duplication, and helping patients and caregivers more effectively manage health conditions. These efforts have demonstrated potential to improve quality and control costs for patients with complex conditions."[1] Given their incentives to reduce cost and improve quality, accountable care organizations (ACOs) often employ care management programs that follow evidence-based strategies for increasing the value of care delivered to people with complex needs. These strategies include

- Identifying people who are at high risk for adverse clinical events (often referred to as risk stratification)
- Stratifying high-risk patients into subgroups with common needs (segmentation)
- Improving care transitions across settings
- Engaging individuals and their families in care decisions
- Using programs that help patients address chronic illness[2]

Yet, care management is a delivery innovation that is difficult to implement and costly to support through traditional labor-intensive healthcare delivery processes. According to a survey of ACOs by the Commonwealth Fund, there is wide variation in evidence-based care received by patients with complex needs. Only 30% of ACOs report that most or all clinicians receive training and have processes available to them to encourage patient engagement and activation.

Effective management of population health requires new platforms to reach beyond the physician office or clinic to

- Identify patient segments with the greatest risk that would benefit from additional attention and coordination.

- Manage the high needs of complex patients with efficient, evidence-based workflows and tools that span wellness, disease prevention, and chronic care management services.
- Provide high-touch interactions as well as personalized outreach via the appropriate media and message.
- Allow the provider's electronic health record (EHR) to ingest, interpret, and manage patient-entered or device-generated data.

As seen in Figure 11.1, Advanced care management is a continuous cycle. It begins with defining the patient population to be managed and developing an understanding of relative health and associated risks.

Then, the care team must be engaged with the patient to develop a plan of care using evidence-based pathways and protocols. Embedded rules-based workflows ensure the patient gets the right care at the right time and place. Effectiveness of care (quality, cost, and access) is measured on a regular basis not only to evaluate performance but also to identify areas for

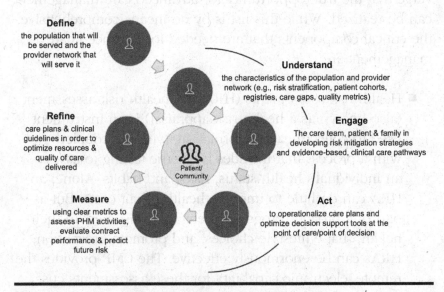

Define
the population that will be served and the provider network that will serve it

Understand
the characteristics of the population and provider network (e.g., risk stratification, patient cohorts, registries, care gaps, quality metrics)

Refine
care plans & clinical guidelines in order to optimize resources & quality of care delivered

Engage
The care team, patient & family in developing risk mitigation strategies and evidence-based, clinical care pathways

Patient/ Community

Measure
using clear metrics to assess PHM activities, evaluate contract performance & predict future risk

Act
to operationalize care plans and optimize decision support tools at the point of care/point of decision

Figure 11.1 The advanced care management cycle.

improvement. Pathways and protocols can be refined through machine learning, or as guidelines are updated, or as newly identified risks need mitigation.

Key Components of the Advanced Care Management Layer of the CMP

The advanced care management layer is truly the heart of the CMP depicted in Figure 7.1. The CMP relies heavily on the foundational EHR to document care, provide clinical decision support, and gather interoperable data to provide a comprehensive view of the patient across all providers and venues. Data and analytics provide both a retrospective view ("how well did we care for the patient?") and a prospective view ("what might happen next?") with an eye to the best course of action. Care managers, along with the multidisciplinary care teams, ensure that the right care is delivered at the right time and the right place. It is only when the three previous layers (foundational, interoperability, and analytics) of the CMP converge that the true opportunity for advanced care management can be realized. While this list is by no means comprehensive, the critical components that are needed for advanced care management are

- Health risk assessments (HRAs): A health risk assessment (also known as a health risk appraisal) is an instrument used to collect health information, typically coupled with a process that includes biometric testing to assess an individual's health status, risks, and habits. Alone, an HRA can do little to improve health or cut costs. But as part of a broader program to engage consumers in their health, shape lifestyle choices, and promote prevention, HRAs can be enormously effective. The CMP provides the remote, electronic capability for these assessments customized for patients and their conditions.

- Attribution: A key to care management, attribution identifies which patients are assigned to a provider's panel for care and outcomes measurement. In this way, a care provider can be notified when a patient is due for annual wellness visits, other screenings, and follow-up care. Other tools can alert the care team when a patient presents at the emergency department (ED) or is admitted to a hospital regardless of location, and the care team can get involved in that episode of care.
- Longitudinal care plan (LCP): Care planning requires a complete view of the patient across the care continuum and includes an LCP. The patient and care team work together to develop a plan for care visits, diet, exercise, medication, and therapies; the LCP can be documented in the EHR and accessible by the patient electronically. The care team can note progress in the record and revise the plan as they interact with the patient. A key tool in managing transitions of care, the LCP should address episodic care, such as a joint replacement, as well as chronic disease management, such as diabetes. In addition to a comprehensive clinical portrait of the patient—past illnesses, surgeries/procedures, and chronologic lab values—the LCP should include social determinants of health (SDOH) that contribute both to the patient's condition and to the actual care plan.
- Case management: Episode-based management of a patient. Traditionally part of the acute care process, case management involves understanding the diagnosis, the prognosis, the care plan, and the anticipated discharge date. Diagnosis-related group (DRG)-based contracts (Medicare, and depending on the market, Medicaid and Commercial) provide detailed planning and management to ensure the patient is discharged on time based on the expected length of stay. As population health management becomes more important, case managers help reduce readmission risk by managing appropriate discharge and follow-up care.

■ Adherence alerts: Adherence alerts let care teams know if patients are not following their care plans. This indication could include whether medication refills occurred, whether follow-up appointments were kept, and whether unplanned utilization (such as an ED visit or inpatient admission) occurred. By having real-time notification from any facility in the patient's medical trading area, the care team can interact with the patient at the earliest possible opportunity and work to get the patient back on the appropriate care pathway.

■ Disease management: Management of specific disease processes (e.g., diabetes) across the care continuum is enabled using evidence-based guidelines and supported by registries. Many times, patients will have multiple chronic conditions (e.g., hypertension, diabetes, congestive heart failure, and depression) and need extensive support mechanisms, including social worker involvement, to manage these concurrent ailments. By developing and documenting a longitudinal plan of care based on established protocols and coordinating the many resources needed to carry out the plan, caregivers and patients can work together to manage the illnesses better to create an improved quality of life.

■ Social determinants of health: SDOH include factors such as socioeconomic status, income, housing, education levels, marital status, physical environment, employment status, and social support networks, as well as access to healthcare. Addressing social determinants of health is important for improving health and reducing long-standing disparities in health and healthcare, which are often rooted in social and economic disadvantages.[3] EHRs that allow documentation of SDOH can also provide the ability to reference appropriate community resources, such as a food pantry for patients who have food insecurity issues. When incorporated into risk models (predictive modeling), SDOH can also be good predictors of outcomes and point to early intervention to prevent unfavorable results such as readmissions.

■ Risk management: Risk management occurs at the patient level as well as the panel level. The ability to identify and manage high-risk patients—including multiple chronic conditions—is key to developing customized care plans for patients. At a higher level, the ability to model and monitor risk-based contracts, including bundles and alternative payment models (APMs), is critical to being able to avoid downside risk and maximize incentives.

■ Referral management: Patient referrals indicate a change in diagnosis, escalation in care, or need for additional specialty opinion. Historically highly dependent on faxes and other analog communication methods, integrated referral management includes tools, workflows, and data to ensure appropriate transition to other care providers. In addition to other EHRs, systems such as scheduling, insurance verification and billing, and provider directories are part of the process. Structured algorithms can be developed to provide triggers or automatic initiative of the referral process based on key care management protocols, to follow up on the referral status, to analyze key outcomes metrics associated with the referral, or to ensure that the referral stays within the network.

■ Rules-based workflows: Clinical workflow has been defined as the flow of care-related tasks as seen in the management of a patient trajectory.[4] It can be for a single clinical provider, across a care team, from one care team to another within the same health system, or across multiple entities. Rules-based workflows are built upon clinical content and decision support, including guidelines, protocols or pathways. Alerts and triggers occur when a specific treatment is either indicated or contraindicated. Notification is also given when patient care diverges from the recommended workflow. Predictive models can also be incorporated into workflows to trigger interventions or augment clinical decision making.

The Future of Advanced Care Management

Digital health tools, from wearables to remote monitors to ingestible sensors, are providing continuous information about patients and their statuses. mHealth-enabled apps are linking smartphones to the EHR. Digital care management models will combine the best of traditional healthcare, such as physician-led care teams and integration with the broader health system, with

- Technology-enabled continuous remote care and augmented intelligence
- Hybrid virtual and in-person care, designed based on the specifics of the population
- New behavioral modification and activation programs
- Synchronous and asynchronous communication methods (i.e., text, video, face-to-face, etc.)
- Care models that include physicians, mid-level practitioners, health coaches, mental health professions, and other support services

Providers must embrace consumer participation and patient activation, defined as understanding one's own role in the care process. Activated patients have the knowledge, skills, and confidence to become active participants in their own care. The greatest challenge for future advanced care management models will be to help patients with both high-acuity health challenges and low health literacy become low-acuity, highly health literate populations.[5]

Conclusion

The majority of care management and coordination processes—from acute care to rehab facilities, skilled nursing facilities, home health, and hospice throughout the community—are being reimagined today. The CMP advanced care management layer will support a focus on chronic care management over the next decade while also taking important steps to prevent and reverse these conditions simultaneously. The next chapter discusses the final and most important layer of the CMP, the consumer and patient engagement layer.

Notes

1. Goodell, Sarah, Thomas Bodenheimer, and Rachel Berry-Millet. "Care Management of Patients with Complex Health Care Needs." Robert Wood Johnson Foundation, December 2009. www.rwjf.org/en/library/research/2009/12/care-management-of-patients-with-complex-health-care-needs.html.
2. Peck, Kristen A., Benjamin Usadi, Alexander Mainor, Helen Newton, and Ellen Meara. "How ACOs Are Caring for People with Complex Needs." Commonwealth Fund, December 11, 2018. www.commonwealthfund.org/publications/fund-reports/2018/dec/how-acos-are-caring-people-complex-needs.
3. "Beyond Health Care: The Role of Social Determinants in Promoting Health and Health Equity." Henry J. Kaiser Family Foundation, May 10, 2018. www.kff.org/disparities-policy/issue-brief/beyond-health-care-the-role-ofsocial-determinants-in-promoting-health-andhealth-equity/.
4. Gooch, Phil, and Abdul Roudsari. "Computerization of Workflows, Guidelines, and Care Pathways: a Review of Implementation Challenges for Process-Oriented Health Information Systems." *Journal of the American Medical Informatics Association*, 18, 6 (2011): 738–748.
5. Snell, Alan. "The Role of Remote Care Management in Population Health." Health Affairs, April 4, 2014. www.healthaffairs.org/do/10.1377/hblog20140404.038196/full/.

Chapter 12

Consumer and Patient Engagement

The words "patient-centeredness" are verbal analgesics, but they mask real pain.

Dr. Donald Berwick, Institute for Healthcare Improvement president emeritus and former CMS administrator

Purpose

To explore the consumer and patient engagement layer of the care management platform (CMP) and to understand how it supports healthcare delivery organizations in their transition to digital health, connected care, and population health management.

In this chapter, the reader will review

- The importance of consumer and patient engagement in population health management
- The components of the consumer and patient engagement layer of the CMP
- The shift from engagement, to participation, to mediation in the future

Consumer and Patient Engagement— Population Health's Missing Piece

Studies suggest that patients who are well-informed, educated about their condition, and involved in their healthcare decisions not only have greater satisfaction of care but also tend to have better outcomes and lower cost. These patients demonstrate healthy behaviors such as physical activity and good nutrition, receive routine preventative care, conduct chronic care self-management, etc. They also have fewer unplanned readmissions, medical errors, and delays in care. Unfortunately, rather than empowering patients in self-care, the current system leaves patients uninformed and disengaged, providing them with few or no resources and an abundance of frustrating tasks (e.g., duplicate requests, long waits, confusing payment programs, and fragmented care).[1]

> When it comes to value-based contracting, the biggest cultural change for provider organizations is taking a step back and thinking about care delivery on a holistic scale ... Patient engagement in a population-focused model is about understanding the consumer and their issues and being able to anticipate their needs based on the data and knowledge that you have gathered from across the system.

So indicates Sharon Hicks, senior associate at Open Minds, a national leader in market intelligence and management best practices for serving consumers with chronic conditions.[2] Effective consumer and patient engagement enables an organization to help activate patients, to steer individuals to the best site of care, and to manage outcomes and resource utilization, and consists of a robust strategy that includes

▪ Patient education and targeted approaches to improve health

- Holistic personal care plans and partnerships between patients, families, community agencies, employers, and retail health providers
- Use of mobile, telehealth, and digital tools to enable self-care, patient engagement, and behavior change
- Integration of devices, monitoring, communications, and information technology to support digital care interventions

However, many health systems are just beginning to develop and implement patient engagement strategies. In a survey conducted by *HealthLeaders*[3] magazine, the question was asked: "In which patient engagement areas is your organization investing with the intent of supporting population health management?" Not surprisingly, most had invested in patient portals and outreach programs. Fewer had developed holistic approaches that included new care models, processes, and data with digital health capabilities, as seen in Figure 12.1.

Consumers are interested in navigating the complexities of healthcare delivery as seamlessly and inexpensively as possible. A 2017 CDW survey[4] revealed patients' views of health providers' use of technology to interact with them, as seen in Figure 12.2.

The consumer and patient engagement layer of the CMP will enable the shift from 2.0: The Transition to 3.0: Digital Health and Connected Care and focus on "systems of engagement" as mentioned in Chapter 2. Health consumers and patients will be able to create a personal health and wellness cloud: one that captures and curates a lifelong narrative of health and wellness information, receives inputs from environmental and social sources, and links individuals to the broader health system care delivery process. At the same time, the CMP will function as a care navigator with tools that assist consumers in making choices regarding the services they need and the experiences they prefer.[5]

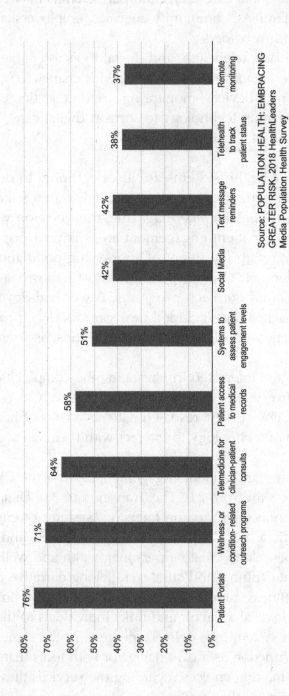

Figure 12.1 Investment in patient engagement capabilities.

Only **29%** of patients give their healthcare providers an "A" for their use of technology to interact with and engage patients

Source: CDW 2017 Patient Engagement Study

Figure 12.2   Patients who give their providers an "A."

The Consumer and Patient Engagement Layer of the CMP

The consumer and patient engagement layer of the CMP (seen in Figure 7.1) is focused on expanding the activities of the patient hub (see Chapter 7). Directing attention to the responsibilities of the patients and their caregivers, the CMP must support consumers' access to all relevant health, medical, and cost data related to themselves or those for whom they are responsible. The CMP must also support the consumer's choice through access to data that supports the selection of healthcare services based on cost and quality. Finally, through the CMP, consumers must be able to understand and monitor their own health, create a personal plan of care, make informed health-related decisions, and have access to the care team. The key consumer and patient engagement components of the CMP include

- 24/7 access to patient information: Today, many patients access their patient information through a tethered portal—an application built on the electronic health record (EHR) infrastructure of one health system or provider. The organization manages the portal and decides which information can be accessed by the patient. Most tethered patient portals hold medical information that is derived from the EHR, such as a discharge summary, a medication and allergy list, and laboratory results. Portals can include more interactive features and allow patients to send secure messages to clinical staff, schedule appointments, or request prescription refills.[6] Most patients, however, have multiple physicians they interact with. Each may provide access to a unique patient portal, often with different navigation tools and user look and feel. Two options exist to remedy this situation:

- Personal health record apps: Patients collect their own health data, and they decide whether to share the data with providers or family members.
- Unified patient portals: An EHR-agnostic portal that consolidates information across multiple provider sites and creates an improved patient experience.

The key to success is patient activation—the consumer signs up for and uses the patient portal. Open Notes, a movement dedicated to making healthcare more open and transparent, encourages doctors, nurses, therapists, and other healthcare professionals to share clinical visit notes electronically with patients, helping facilitate the patients' legal right to access to their own medical records.

- ■ Self-service scheduling: Patients/consumers have the ability to schedule appointments with their existing providers (both primary care and specialty) as well as urgent care/emergency department visits and diagnostic procedures (mammograms, colonoscopies, etc.). In addition, patients can establish new relationships through open scheduling with providers with whom they have no relationship. This ability, regardless of an existing relationship with the provider, is essential to both the patient (choice and access) and the provider (optimizing capacity).
- ■ Branded call centers: For consumers not interacting through the Internet, the call center can serve as one-stop shopping for scheduling initial appointments, diagnostic

tests, and follow-up visits. It can also serve the healthcare delivery organization through the ability to conduct outreach for addressing gaps in care (screenings and immunizations) and revenue cycle activities such as follow-up on co-pays and collection of other accounts due. Call centers can also serve as initial phone triage for patients by using evidence-based protocols to direct consumers to the most appropriate resource given the presenting conditions.

■ Customer relationship management (CRM): CRM capabilities help healthcare organizations deliver highly personalized and engaging outreach to target populations. By integrating data from a variety of sources to complete a profile, the CRM provides a 360-degree view of key consumers and patients and their individual preferences. The CRM typically reduces wait time and improves the patient experience during intake, facilitates referrals across multiple venues of care, eliminates administrative errors, and supports overall management of inbound and outbound communications.

■ Patient-reported data and remote monitoring: Patient- and consumer-directed tools, wearables, and remote monitoring are enabling data collection away from medical facilities at lower cost for a variety of conditions and health behaviors. Once collected, the information is transmitted to EHRs or data repositories. Examples include
  - Patient satisfaction with services rendered (e.g., Press-Gainey)
  - Clinical data such as weight, blood pressure, heart rate, pulse oximeter readings, blood glucose levels, etc.
  - Continuous surveillance monitors that can locate patients with conditions such as dementia and alert healthcare professionals to an event such as a fall
  - Remote infertility treatment and monitoring
  - At-home tests that can keep substance abuse patients accountable for and on track with their goals

- Plan of care elements such as medication adherence, caloric intake, exercise, and other information such as quality of life, range of motion, mood, etc.

■ Linguistic services: These services can range from bedside translators, to patient education materials published in the appropriate language, to virtual health with 24/7 remote interpretation. The last is especially effective when interpretive resources are scarce or an organization has a geographically dispersed service area.

■ Patient education: Curated content to support population groups and communities ensures that it comes from a trusted source, is appropriate in context and amount of information, is reviewed by the appropriate clinical teams, and is part of the prevention, diagnostic, treatment, and disease management process. Provided via numerous vehicles and media channels, including web content, videos, and smartphone apps, the education can be provided in a manner that most suits the patients' preferences and their unique situation.

■ Community referral management: Many consumers are not aware of the large set of resources available to them in the community. By pairing social determinants of health factors (e.g., food insecurity and transportation needs) as documented through advanced care coordination with a catalogue of available services, consumers can be matched with appropriate resources given their individual needs. This additional level of service can often make a difference between patients and their families being able to follow treatment plans, minimizing complications and risk, and attending scheduled appointments or ending up in the emergency department or being admitted as inpatients.

■ mHealth: Mobile (smartphone)-based applications for wellness, chronic disease management, and diagnostic capabilities are becoming progressively sophisticated and prevalent. mHealth can be used to conduct video visits, schedule appointments, and request prescription refills. mHealth can also be used for gamification—applications that help guide patients toward health with activities that educate patients and promote healthy behaviors. Finally, many mHealth applications focus on disease-specific situations (diabetes or behavioral health) to help patients interact via social media with other patients, navigate the health system, or find new clinical trials that address their unique needs.

■ Virtual health: The term *virtual health* refers to the gamut of capabilities for patients or consumers to interact with providers when they are not in the same geographic location. This interaction may include a spectrum of activities, from email transmissions to simple telephone consults, through face-to-face video chats, to interfaces with medical equipment. Many organizations start with virtual urgent care visits, allowing the patient on-demand access while alleviating demands on the emergency department or where primary care capacity is constrained. Other virtual health applications range from interpretive services to highly specialized services (e.g., Tele-Derm) to urgent/emergent services for facilities that do not have the local specialized staff available (e.g., Tele-Stroke).

■ Digital therapeutics: Evidence-based therapeutic interventions driven by high-quality software programs to prevent, manage, or treat a broad spectrum of physical, mental, and behavioral conditions. Digital therapeutics form an independent category of evidence-based products within the broader digital health landscape and are distinct from pure-play adherence, diagnostic, and telehealth products. These offerings have the potential to augment current medical treatment, provide novel therapy options for unmet medical needs, reduce reliance on certain pharmaceuticals or therapies, and integrate into medical guidelines. The Food and Drug Administration is working to modernize its regulatory policies and review programs to consider digital therapeutics.

The Future of Consumer and Patient Engagement

A wide range of innovators, from inside and outside the healthcare industry, are making investments, forging partnerships, and building new business to orchestrate value in tomorrow's transformed ecosystem. Rather than designing patient-centered care, Deborah Kilpatrick, CEO of Evidation Health, encourages these innovators to think differently about the consumer and patient. "Patient centric means just designing around the patient or consumer—30% of the way there," she indicates. "Patient mediated means patients are actively controlling and influencing the process ... patients have access to a data set they've never had access to before—access to their data."

Remarkable opportunities exist through the convergence of consumerism and digital capabilities such as clinical clones and avatars, virtual reality, interoperable data, machine and deep learning capabilities, and always-on biosensors. Initially, through a participatory model of care and a transformed patient–provider relationship, individuals will work with their health professional team as equal and responsible partners. Simultaneously, precision medicine will consider genetics, environment, and lifestyle to custom tailor prevention and treatment options for each person. By 2030, digital innovation will create a brighter future for the consumers of health and healthcare.

Conclusion

Today, consumer and patient engagement tools to support the CMP are still nascent across the healthcare industry. Yet, consumers continue to go digital and are now doing so not just out of curiosity or for general fitness and well-being—but with the intention to address concrete health needs. More Americans use digital health to manage diagnoses, connect with providers, and make critical healthcare decisions than ever before.[7] With much work to be done, leaders are developing thoughtful strategies to support consumers and patients, identifying the infrastructure (talent, data, processes, technologies, etc.) to execute on these strategies, and partnering to launch experiments in local markets and across the nation.

Notes

1. James, Ted A. "The Future of Patient Engagement in the Digital Age." Lean Forward. Harvard Medical School CME Online, October 15, 2018. https://leanforward.hms.harvard.edu/2018/10/10/the-future-of-patient-engagement-in-the-digital-age/.
2. Threnhauser, Sarah C. "Consumer Engagement Is the Missing Piece in Population Health." OPEN MINDS. Accessed September 27, 2019. www.openminds.com/market-intelligence/executive-briefings/consumer-engagement-missing-piece-population-health/.
3. "Population Health: Embracing Greater Risk." HealthLeaders Media Population Health Survey, August 2018. www.healthleadersmedia.com/report/intelligence/population-health-embracing-greater-risk.
4. "CDW Healthcare's Patient Engagement Perspectives." CDW. Accessed September 27, 2019. www.cdw.com/content/cdw/en/newsroom/archive/cdw-healthcares-patient-engagement-perspectives.html.
5. Roberts, David. "How the Cross-Currents of Convergence Can Deliver Participatory Health." EY, September 5, 2017. www.ey.com/en_us/health/how-the-cross-currents-of-convergence-can-deliver-participatory-health.
6. Wildenbos, Gaby Anne, Frank Horenberg, Monique Jaspers, Linda Peute, and Danielle Sent. "How Do Patients Value and Prioritize Patient Portal Functionalities and Usage Factors? A Conjoint Analysis Study with Chronically Ill Patients." BMC Medical Informatics and Decision Making. BioMed Central, November 21, 2018. https://bmcmedinformdecismak.biomedcentral.com/articles/10.1186/s12911-018-0708-5.
7. Zewig, Megan, and Sean Day. "Beyond Wellness for the Healthy: Digital Health Consumer Adoption 2018." Rock Health. Accessed September 28, 2019. https://rockhealth.com/reports/beyond-wellness-for-the-healthy-digital-health-consumer-adoption-2018/.

MAKING VALUE ACTIONABLE

Today you have to run faster to stay in the same place.

Philip Kotler, the father of modern marketing

Next Steps

To transform healthcare, leaders will have to manage change in new and different ways. Ultimately, we must change the way healthcare changes. Digital health and connected care will dramatically change the clinician-to-clinician, provider-to-patient, and consumer-driven interactions via new platform business models and ecosystems. This section provides an overview of the population health services organization, a shared-services approach to designing, experimenting with, and deploying PHM at scale. A case for digital health, the diabetic patient with multiple chronic conditions, is examined. The last chapter provides closing thoughts and a look toward the future.

Chapter 13

The Population Health Services Organization

At the end of the day, people are demanding value and people want more transparency about what's going on with the cost of care and the value that they are getting with the health care system around the country.

Bernard J. Tyson, CEO, Kaiser Permanente

Purpose

To introduce the concept of the population health services organization (PHSO) and highlight a case for digital health: the diabetic patient with multiple chronic conditions.

The reader will explore

- The definition and role of the PHSO
- The similarities to a management services organization (MSO), and the differences
- PHSO operating and maturity models
- A case for digital health: diabetic patients with multiple chronic conditions and the PHSO

The Population Health Services Organization

Over the next 10 years, the number of payers adopting value-based contracts will increase; consumer expectations for convenient, accessible, and affordable health and healthcare services will increase; the employer-driven healthcare economy will increase; and the number of healthcare providers willing to digitally transform and innovate will increase. The digital health and connected care ecosystem will simultaneously support novel approaches to disease prevention and reversal, chronic care management, value-based reimbursement and health consumers, patients, and clinician community development.

Historically, health systems have focused on *institutional management* or oversight of the facilities, infrastructure, and ancillary/support resources of healthcare delivery. Clinicians concentrated on *patient management* and episodic diagnosis and treatment. Payers emphasized *cost management* through a variety of reimbursement programs and practices. This singular focus created persistent inefficiencies and resulted in unplanned utilization of expensive healthcare resources, continued access barriers including lack of insurance coverage, healthcare quality and safety issues, lack of communication and data sharing, and difficulty managing medically complex patients. As Figure 13.1 illustrates, a PHSO helps bridge the divide between health systems, providers, payers, patients, and other community stakeholders. A PHSO is an agile, shared-services organization that provides a portfolio of people, programs, and health interventions to ensure the delivery of the right care at the right time to the right person. The PHSO will serve as the care management platform (CMP) owner's advocate and develop partnerships to deploy new care management platforms and digital health solutions. Additionally, the PHSO will

■ Establish new governance structures and decision-making models.

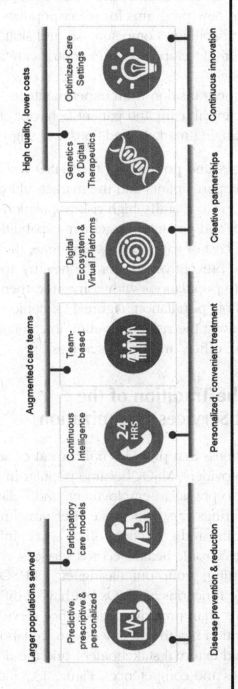

Figure 13.1 Portfolio of people, programs and health interventions.

- Leverage clinical and claims data to design and potentially operate new programs for select populations.
- Build new capabilities, competencies, and skill sets.
- Help providers develop consumer-centric care and future delivery models.
- Coordinate the transition from experiments to scale.
- Encourage clinical team and patient behavior change.
- Adapt to changing market conditions and align incentives.

While the strategies and priorities of the PHSO will vary depending on the participants and the market, ultimately, the goal of the PHSO is to identify high-risk populations, design care management and patient engagement capabilities, and manage the total cost of care. At the same time, the PHSO should encourage preventive care for the healthy and address issues pertinent to populations with rising risk, therefore impacting the whole population. Figure 13.2 depicts the population segments along the risk continuum, interventions, and the mix of virtual, office, and home services.

Founded in the Tradition of the Management Services Organization

An MSO is a business that provides nonclinical or administrative services to providers. MSOs became popular in the 1990s as an alternative to physician employment, and today, their structure and offerings vary widely (i.e., personnel management; billing, coding and collection; office space; information technology and electronic health records services; compliance and quality reporting; group purchasing; etc.). PHSOs perform many of the same functions as MSOs but have a different orientation—rather than providing back-office services, they often lead population health strategy design, collaboration across internal and external stakeholders, and the development of new capabilities and competences. Figure 13.3 illustrates an operating model for a PHSO.

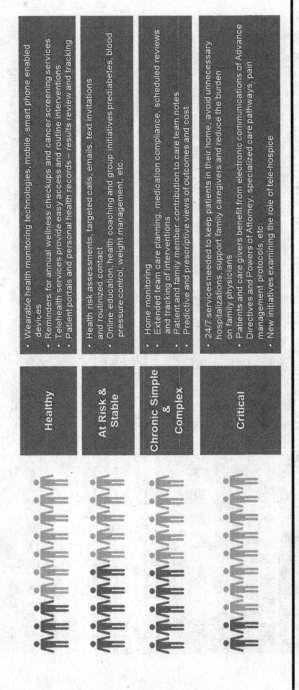

Figure 13.2 Population segments and digital health interventions.

Figure 13.3   The PHSO operating model.

Frequently, the PHSO launches in a narrow or targeted manner. With a focus on specific value-based contracts such as an MSSP or other partial risk agreements, the PHSO may work with a health system and its affiliates to complete a community health needs assessment. Once this is identified, the PHSO can serve a role in filling the identified gaps by addressing social determinants of health, post-acute, home health, primary care, and other health services. Initiatives such as stratifying high-risk patients within the population and developing referral management and transitions of care programs are typically early-stage activities. A maturity model for the PHSO is shown in Figure 13.4.

As the PHSO matures, it can provide patient navigation services and, in some instances, extended nonmedical services such as behavioral services (nutrition, exercise, lifestyle, etc.), help with transportation, home safety equipment, etc. In some instances, the PHSO leads or partners with others to design innovative new business and operating models, such as

■ Remote monitoring and patient-generated data: New technologies, such as wearables, offer healthcare providers data to monitor patients with chronic conditions constantly and to proactively manage population health needs.
■ Network utilization and management: Digital health solutions offer opportunities to track patient utilization, report and analyze profitability, improve referral management and appropriateness, and simplify scheduling, resulting in better ways to keep patients in their networks.
■ Social community support: New virtual tools provide opportunities for community partners to share data and connect with each other to support the patient through care coordination and outcomes management. These solutions play a big role in improving public health and supporting underserved populations.[1]
■ New front door to healthcare: Retail care, urgent care, telehealth and virtual care, AI and chatbots, and a variety

Full Risk

- Expand Governance to include community, public-private partnerships, agencies, etc.
- Develop programs across connected ecosystem for population health & wellness, consumer-centric care, disease management & prevention
- Explore convergency opportunities with key payer partners
- Manage health of member longitudinally, total cost of care & long-term outcomes management
- Integrate real time metrics into the clinical workflow and develop predictive & prescriptive analytics algorithms
- Transform care team and physician practice capabilities & capacity
- Personalize treatment plans based on advanced clinical decision support & artificial intelligence
- Design consumer experience to include virtual, retail, voice and other digital health technologies
- Develop innovative business & operating models in conjunction with digital health & connected care

Downside Risk

- Formalize Governance efforts to oversee collaborative improvement teams, monitor contract performance & prioritize care management platform strategy
- Develop formal leadership structure for PHM
- Manage multiple contracts across affiliates & partners
- Manage high risk populations using clinical guidelines, dashboards & care management tools
- Understand gaps in care
- Establish processes to personalize treatment & wellness plans
- Develop patient hub & robust digital infrastructure
- Integrate patient reported data
- Expand performance measurement and develop real time point of care dashboards
- Monitor regulatory issues & improve outreach to payers

Partial Risk

- Launch PHSO & Governance structure
- Focus on value-based contracts and community health needs assessment
- Educate affiliated and employed providers
- Develop referral network & monitor leakage
- Develop transitions of care program
- Expand patient-centric technologies: scheduling, assessments, portals, mobile apps, etc.
- Providers encourage more active patient participation
- Expand analytics & outcomes measurement capabilities
- Monitor regulatory issues

Provider-Centric	Network-Centric	Community & Consumer-Centric

Figure 13.4 The PHSO maturity model.

of other digital tools make it easier for consumers to access health and healthcare services conveniently.

■ Hospital at Home: Provides select patients with the option to receive acute hospital care at home. Studies have reported that treating acutely ill older adult patients diagnosed with conditions such as congestive heart failure (CHF) and chronic obstructive pulmonary disease (COPD) at home rather than in a hospital has many benefits. Hospital at Home has resulted in lower costs, shorter duration of hospital-equivalent treatment, fewer procedures, reduced geriatric complications, improved activities of daily living, and better patient and caregiver satisfaction.[2]

■ Never discharge model: A wholistic care model that connects patients and their care teams for life. Virtual and community-based services coordinate and deliver care on a 24/7 basis. Efforts include navigation of patients from acute to post-acute services, standardizing back- and front-office functions, defining standards of care, and a variety of other experiences for the patient journey. Services can assist a patient with decisions as complex as cancer care or as simple as whether to go to an emergency room or urgent care center.

■ Mobile integrated healthcare: Integration of community emergency medical services (EMS) providers, primary care, hospice, home care, palliative care teams, and community service organizations to provide comprehensive, physician-led population health management solutions across the care continuum. Community based and technologically sophisticated, these services bring together clinical, logistical, analytics, and education competencies in a collaborative effort to provide 24/7/365 interprofessional services, often incorporating a command center to receive 911 calls and match the calls to available and appropriate resources. These programs address wellness, prevention, chronic care, post-hospital discharge, social support, and patient education for a locally defined population.[3]

PHSOs can provide a wide range of administrative and population health management services to providers and the community. Because of this wide range of services, it is critical to design the services based on the needs of the specific populations, the key partners, and the community. Specific benefits of this model include

- Centralized governance and program management
- Standardized methods, tools, and resources
- Economies of scale, increased efficiency, and streamlined cost of services
- Ability to attract new partners and expand the network
- Capacity to support multi-payer contracts and agreements
- Access to capital to support CMP infrastructure
- Expanded reach to consumers requiring wellness and preventive services
- Engagement of consumers and patients in designing their preferred experiences
- Creative thinking beyond "business as usual" and ability to collaborate with "uncommon partners"

A Case for Digital Health—Diabetes

Today, in America,

- 30.3 million people, or 9.4% of the population, have diabetes.
- 86 million individuals age 18 or older have prediabetes.
- 7.2 million people with diabetes are undiagnosed.
- 1.5 million people are diagnosed every year.[4]

Chronic diseases such as diabetes require regular follow-up and therapy progression. As diabetes treatment protocols become more complex, and as patients require extensive ongoing self-management support, digital health and connected care platforms provide the opportunity to educate healthy individuals, improve the patient experience, and dramatically impact the outcomes and cost of diabetes care. The anytime-anywhere nature of digital health supports the delivery of automated outreach, individualized coaching, and remote monitoring. Patients are able to share data and connect with their health team in a variety of virtual and physical settings. In 2016, the American Diabetes Association documented the Diabetes Digital Health Ecosystem, as seen in Figure 13.5.

As of September 2019, the website Medical Startups identified 37 of the top diabetes digital startups. Livongo Health

Source: American Association of Diabetes Educators (AADE) 2016 Technology Workgroup. Based on Architecture for Integrated Mobility Framework (AIM).

Figure 13.5   The diabetes digital health ecosystem.

(LVGO), well known for its diabetes management technology, went public in late July 2019. LVGO is expanding its offerings to include programs for managing prediabetes, hypertension, weight, and behavioral health, and it points to peer-reviewed studies that show its technology's effectiveness.[5] LVGO and four other startups, Verily, ViaCyte, Omada Health, and Insulet, round out the top five of these diabetes-focused startups, and together they have raised over $2.7 billion dollars in funding.[6]

"Chronic disease has three characteristics that align well with digital health," indicates Anant Vinjamoori, MD, senior product manager at Virta Health, a clinician-led treatment program that was founded in 2014 with the goal of reversing type 2 diabetes in 100 million people by 2025. According to Dr. Vinjamoori, these characteristics include the following:

- Chronic conditions are continuous, not episodic. Patients' condition changes every day, requiring constant monitoring.
- Everyday habits make a big difference. Patient adherence to daily nutritional, behavioral, and medication regimens is required.
- Specialized medical attention is required. Skilled medical care is needed to adjust medications and care plan in response to changing biomarkers.[7]

A PHSO can work with key partners across the digital health and connected care landscape to design the components of the CMP based on the specific needs of the diabetic population, particularly those with multiple care management issues, and the capabilities of the local healthcare landscape. Figure 13.6 depicts a diabetic patient with multiple care management issues.

As part of the CMP ecosystem, the physician and care team (i.e., care manager, advance practice provider, nurse, health coach, social workers, etc.)—which includes both primary

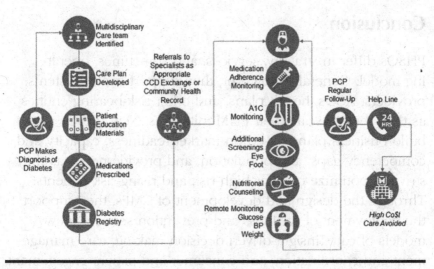

Figure 13.6   Diabetic patient with multiple care management issues.

and specialty care providers (i.e., endocrinology, nephrology, ophthalmology, etc.)—develop a care plan for the patient that includes education, health behaviors, medication, and a variety of other interventions. Digital health and connected care platforms are creating significant inroads in:

- Recognizing early warning signs and conducting earlier screening for prediabetes
- Applying analytics to result in next-generation digital diagnostic and therapeutic tools
- Preventing progression from prediabetes to diabetes
- Developing evidence-based behavioral analytics and modification tools
- Preventing short- and long-term complications
- Achieving glycemic goals and patient adherence to personalized care plans
- Real-time connectivity with consumer electronics (e.g., smartphones and smartwatches) and monitoring tools
- Reducing the cost of care through virtual visits and improving care management processes

Conclusion

PHSOs differ in strategy, services, and sometimes, operating model. Generally, however, they support health systems, providers, ACOs, health plans, and other risk-bearing entities as they seek to scale their PHM initiatives. New PHSOs must build business plans based on market readiness, capacity and competency gaps, and population, and provide needs as they strive to optimize care for high-risk and rising-risk patients. Through the design and development of CMPs, they support the deployment of wellness and prevention services, new models of care, insight-driven decision making, care management and coordination, and consumer and patient engagement and activation. Partnership opportunities exist across the spectrum for providers, the community, digital health companies, payers, and other key stakeholders to work with PHSOs.

Notes

1. Wagenen, Juliet Van. "The Top 5 Digital Innovations Transforming Healthcare Organizations." Technology Solutions That Drive Healthcare, December 11, 2017. https://healthtechmagazine.net/article/2017/12/top-5-digital-priorities-healthcare-organizations.
2. Lazare, Jaimie. "Hospital at Home: Patient Care Model of the Future?" *Aging Well*, 6, 2 (2013): 20. Accessed September 8, 2019. www.todaysgeriatricmedicine.com/archive/0313p20.shtml.
3. Clarke, Janice L., Scott Bourn, Alexis Skoufalos, Eric H. Beck, and Daniel J. Castillo. "An Innovative Approach to Health Care Delivery for Patients with Chronic Conditions." *Population Health Management*, 20, 1 (2017): 23–30. www.ncbi.nlm.nih.gov/pmc/articles/PMC5278805/.
4. Ginestro, Mark, Angelina Carvajal, and Adam Manhi. "Digital Health and Disruption in Diabetes." KPMG, 2018.
5. "Livongo Upsizes IPO to $355M in Bid to Become Netflix of Health." Xconomy, July 26, 2019. https://xconomy.com/san-francisco/2019/07/24/livongo-upsizes-ipo-to-355m-in-bid-to-become-netflix-of-health/.

6. "Top 37 Diabetes Startups." Medical Startups. Accessed September 30, 2019. www.medicalstartups.org/top/diabetes/.
7. Vinjamooori, Anant. "Rock Health Summit." In *Practicing Medicine at Scale: Effectively and Efficiently Delivering Outcomes for Chronic Disease.* San Francisco, CA, 2019.

Chapter 14

Final Thoughts

> *Imagine a model of healthcare that's always available and driven by data so you're continuously collecting data off your body, about your environment, your nutrition, and activity ... then it delivers back to you personalized health care throughout your whole life. You don't have to be in a brick-and-mortar building to get it, and you have access to the world's best experts.*
>
> **Leslie Saxon, founder and executive director, USC Center for Body Computing**

Purpose

To provide concluding thoughts on the role of digital health and connected care in supporting population health management, and to provide future considerations for value orchestration in the health and healthcare system of the future.

In this chapter, the reader will be able to contemplate

- The shift from IT as a cost center to digital as core to the business of health and healthcare.

- Moving the needle while the needle moves.
- Today's reality; we've only just begun.

Mindset Shift Redux

In January 2019, John Sculley, former CEO of Pepsi-Co and Apple, and current chairman of the board of RxAdvance, a cloud-based pharmacy benefits manager, said: "I believe healthcare will transform from a hierarchical, vertical, siloed, industry into a horizontal, platform-based, continuum-of-care industry organized around empowering consumers with amazing technology tools—giving ordinary people better control over their own wellness and preventive care. It happened in telecommunications, retailing, financial services, and there will be innovators who will lead this revolution in healthcare, too."[1] If this is true, those responsible for healthcare transformation and innovation will have to make an even great mindset shift. No longer a competition between health system, payer, and other industry incumbents with technology as an enabling function for traditional business and operating models, the digital future puts converging technologies at the core of the business (see Figure 14.1).

Big Tech has arrived. Yet, one can observe that healthcare is hard to change. The streets of the healthcare industry are paved with outsiders who tried and failed to reinvent this industry. This time, however, is different. The consumer has expectations for convenience, quality, transparency, and reasonable cost. Someone is sure to deliver.

Moving the Needle While the Needle Moves

For years, the healthcare industry has benchmarked its performance against peer groups. The Quadruple Aim—enhancing patient experience, improving population health, reducing

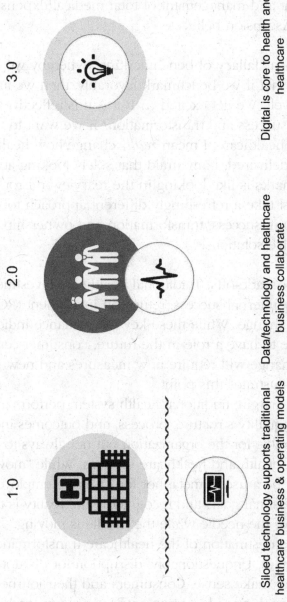

Figure 14.1 Mindset shift—The role of technology.

costs, and improving the work life of healthcare providers—
is widely accepted as a compass to optimize health system
performance. Value and risk–based agreements incent quality
improvement and management of total medical expense. Craig
Cordola of Ascension believes:

> There is a "fallacy of benchmarking" whereby we
> believe that if we benchmark favorably, then we are
> doing well. We get excited … But is this reflective
> of true success and transformation? If we want to
> change healthcare, I mean *really* change how health-
> care is delivered, I am afraid that solely looking at
> benchmarks is like looking in the rearview mirror.
> We must take a refreshingly different approach to
> truly claim success, transformation and ownership of
> innovative solutions.[2]

There will be trade-offs. Traditional healthcare investments are
measured by internal success, return on investment (ROI), and
incremental change. While these key performance indicators
will continue to have a role in the future, consumer-centric,
disruptive change will require new measures and new goals.
Figure 14.2 illustrates this point.

Revenue, margin, traditional health system performance
metrics, and quality structure, process, and outcomes indicators are desirable for the organization but not always to the
consumer of health and healthcare services. While "moving the
needle" may be a useful metaphor for inspiring employees and
achieving personal goals and recognition, the reality is that it is
hard to "move the needle while the needle is moving."

Today, the destination of the healthcare transformation journey is uncertain. Unquestionably, disruption for disruption's
sake does not make sense. Consumers and their journeys and
experiences with our silos, fragmented processes, and interoperable systems must take precedence.

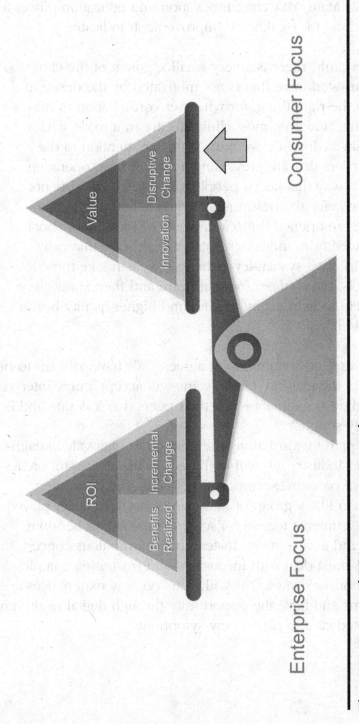

Figure 14.2 Internal ROI versus consumer value.

Kedar Mate, MD, chief innovation and education officer for the Institute for Healthcare Improvement, indicates:

> Certainly, there is a very small segment of the clinician workforce that is not motivated by the desire to do the right thing, for whatever constellation of reasons. However, most clinicians are in it to do what's right … Instead, we must shift our attention to the barriers that are preventing a system from operating in a way that keeps people safe and allows patients to receive the best possible care. When we do that, we are opened up to a universe of tools, many borrowed from industries outside healthcare that can help drive system-level change. We can take those tools, tweak them for healthcare and then apply them to help engineer safer and higher-quality health systems[3]

Don Lovasz of CommonSpirit agrees: "We have to learn to be adaptive, the majority of clinicians will accept a new intervention if they are convinced by their peers that it is safe and is clinically sound."[4]

The path forward along the journey to high-value healthcare and Industry 4.0 will be based on the successful orchestration of consumer-centric value. Today, the performers may seem like a group of musicians who have never played their instruments together. Each artist has his or her own tempo and arrangement. Instead of a harmonious concert, patients must deal with incoherent and frustrating complexity. Tomorrow's musicians will focus on new experiences and platforms and have the opportunity through digital health and connected care to play a new symphony.

Notes

1. Spitzer, Julie. "Tim Cook: Apple's 'Greatest Contribution to Mankind' Will Be about Health. Apple CEO Tim Cook Suggested That the Company's Upcoming Health-Related Work Will Be Its." *Becker's Hospital Review*, January 9, 2019. www.beckershospitalreview.com/healthcare-information-technology/tim-cook-apple-s-greatest-contribution-to-mankind-will-be-about-health.html.
2. Cordola, Craig. "Benchmarking Limits Healthcare Innovation." LinkedIn, March 6, 2019. www.linkedin.com/pulse/benchmarking-limits-healthcare-innovation-craig-cordola/.
3. Pyrek, Kelly. "The Science of Improvement: Moving the Needle on Healthcare Personnel Behavior." *Infection Control Today*, June 8, 2018. www.infectioncontroltoday.com/best-practices-compliance/science-improvement-moving-needle-healthcare-personnel-behavior.
4. Arlotto, Pam, and Don Lovasz. "Orchestrating Value: Population Health in the Digital Age." Telephone Interview, August 28, 2019.

Index

[119] Šternberk, B., *Veröff. Univ.-Sternw. Berlin-Babelsberg*, **5** (Heft 2), 1 (1924).

[120] Malmquist, K.G., *Meddelande från Lunds Astron. Observ.*, **4** (Ser II) (No. 37), 1 (1927).

[121] Tikhoff, G.A., *Izvestia Imp. Akad. Nauk*, **10** (No. 5), 299 (1916) (= *Bull. de l'Acad. Imp. des sciences, Petrograd*); German version in *Astron. Nachr.*, **218**, 145 (1923).

[122] Tamm, N., *Astron. Nachr.*, **216**, 331 (1922).

[123] Öpik, E and Livländer, R., *Publ. de l'Observ. Astron. de l'Univ. de Tartu (Dorpat)*, **26** (No. 3), 1 (1925).

[124] Barbier, D., Chalonge, D. and Vassy, E., *J. de Phys. et le Radium*, **6** (sér. 7), 137 (1935).

[125] Öpik, E., Livländer, R. and Silde, O., *Publ. de l'Observ. Astron. de l'Univ. de Tartu*, **28** (No. 2), 1 (1935).

[126] Collmann, W., *Zeitschr. für Astrophys.*, **9**, 185 (1935).

[127] Öhman, Y., *Observatory*, **59**, 335 (1936).

[128] Öhman, Y., *Arkiv vör Matematik, Astron. och Fysik*, **25B** (No. 19) (1936).

[129] Öhman, Y., *Populär Astron. Tidskrift*, **19**, 11 (1938).

[130] Planck, M., *Wiedemanns Ann. der Physik*, **4**, 553 (1901).

[131] Schwarzschild, K., *Publ. Kufner'schen Sternw. Wien*, **5**, B1 and C1 (1900).

[132] Hnatek, A., *Astron. Nachr.*, **187**, 369 (1911).

[133] Rosenberg, H., *Abhandlungen der Kaiserl. Leopold. Carol. Deutschen Akad. der Naturforscher, Nova Acta*, **101** (No. 2) (1914).

[134] Abbot, C.G., *Astrophys. J.*, **34**, 197 (1911).

[135] Wilsing, J., *Astron. Nachr.*, **204**, 153 (1917).

[136] Sampson, R.A., *Mon. Not. R. Astron. Soc.*, **83**, 174 (1923).

[137] Sampson, R.A., *Mon. Not. R. Astron. Soc.*, **85**, 212 (1925).

[138] Sampson, R.A., *Mon. Not. R. Astron. Soc.*, **90**, 636 (1930).

[139] Wright, W.H., *Publ. Lick Observ.*, **13**, 191 (1918).

[140] Yü, C.S., *Lick Observ. Bull.*, **12** (No. 375), 104 (1926).

[141] Brill, A., *Handbuch der Astrophys.*, **5** (Part 1), 128, J. Springer-Verlag, Berlin (1932).

[142] Barbier, D. and Chalonge, D., *Ann. d'Astrophys.*, **4**, 30 (1941).

[143] Barbier, D. and Chalonge, D., *Ann. d'Astrophys.*, **2**, 254 (1939).

[144] Barbier, D., Chalonge, D. and Canavaggia, R., *Ann. d'Astrophys.*, **10**, 195 (1947).

[145] Chalonge, D. and Divan, L., *Ann. d'Astrophys.*, **15**, 201 (1952).

[146] Chalonge, D. and Divan, L., *Comptes Rendus de l'Acad. des Sci.*, **327**, 298 (1953).

[147] Chalonge, D., *Ann. d'Astrophys.*, **19**, 258 (1956).

[148] Greaves, W.M.H., Davidson, C.R. and Martin, E.G., *Observations of Colour Temps. of Stars*, London, HM Stationery Office (1932).

[149] Greaves, W.M.H., Davidson, C. and Martin, E., *Mon. Not. R. Astron. Soc.*, **94**, 488 (1934).

[150] Kienle, H., Straßl, H. and Wempe, J., *Zeitschr. für Astrophys.*, **16**, 201 (1938).

[151] Kienle, H., Wempe, J. and Beileke, F., *Zeitschr. für Astrophys.*, **20**, 91 (1940).

[152] Williams, R.C., *Publ. Observ. Univ. Michigan*, **7**, 93 and 147 (1939).

[153] Williams, R.C., *Publ. Observ. Univ. Michigan*, **8**, 37 (1940).

[154]   Barbier, D., Chalonge, D. and Kienle, H., *Zeitschr. für Astrophys.*, **12**, 178 (1936).
[155]   McCrea, W.H., *Mon. Not. R. Astron. Soc.*, **91**, 836 (1931).
[156]   Payne-Gaposchkin, C.H., *Astrophys. J.*, **97**, 78 (1943).
[157]   Pickering, E.C., *Ann. Harvard Coll. Observ.*, **71** (Part 4), 233 (1917).
[158]   Stoy, R.H., *Mon. Not. R. Astron. Soc.*, **103**, 288 (1944).
[159]   Stoy, R.H., *Mon. Not. R. Astron. Soc.*, **104**, 317 (1944).
[160]   Stoy, R.H., *Mon. Not. Astron. Soc. S. Africa*, **34**, 132 (1975).
[161]   Redman, R.O., *Mon. Not. R. Astron. Soc.*, **105**, 212 (1945).
[162]   Redman, R.O., *Trans. Int. Astron. Union*, **8**, 373 (1954).
[163]   Beer, A., Redman, R.O. and Yates, G.G., *Mem. R. Astron. Soc.*, **67** (Part 1), 1 (1954).
[164]   Menzies, A., Redman, R.O. and Stoy, R.H., *Mon. Not. R. Astron. Soc.*, **109**, 647 (1949).
[165]   Stoy, R.H., *Cape Mimeogram*, No. **3** (1953).
[166]   Stoy, R.H., *Cape Mimeogram*, No. **5** (1958).
[167]   Cousins, A.W.J. and Stoy, R.H., *R. Observ. Bull.*, (ser. E), No. **49**, E1 (1962).
[168]   Stoy, R.H., *Vistas in Astron.*, **2**, 1099 (1956).
[169]   Stoy, R.H., *Observatory*, **92**, 217 (1972).
[170]   Stoy, R.H., Private communication of unpublished text delivered to the 1972 Cambridge astrophysics conference (1972).
[171]   Brill, A., *Astron. Nachr.*, **218**, 209; **219**, 353, 401 (1923).
[172]   Rossier, P., *Publ. de l'Observ. de Genève (A)*, **3**, 460 (1933).
[173]   Lundmark, K., *Handbuch. der Astrophys.*, **5** (Part 1), 210 (1932).
[174]   Vorontsov-Velyaminov, B., *Zeitschr. für Astrophys.*, **9**, 353 (1935).
[175]   Aitken, R.G., *Publ. Astron. Soc. Pacific*, **46**, 59 (1934).
[176]   Strong, J., *Publ. Astron. Soc. Pacific*, **46**, 18 (1934).
[177]   Pettit, E., *Publ. Astron. Soc. Pacific*, **46**, 27 (1934).
[178]   Hunt, M.R., *Harvard Coll. Observ. Bull.*, **910**, 18 (1939).
[179]   Seares, F.H., *Publ. Astron. Soc. Pacific*, **50**, 5 (1938).
[180]   Hertzsprung, E., *Trans. Int. Astron. Union*, **4**, 154 (1933).
[181]   Baade, W., *Trans. Int. Astron. Union*, **6**, 217 (1939).
[182]   Payne-Gaposchkin, C., *Trans. Int. Astron. Union*, **6**, 218 (1939).
[183]   Hertzsprung, E., *Trans. Int. Astron. Union*, **6**, 407 (1939).
[184]   Johnson, H.L., *Astrophys. J.*, **116**, 272 (1952).
[185]   Stebbins, J. and Whitford, A.E., *Astrophys. J.*, **87**, 237 (1938).
[186]   Hassenstein, W., *Astron. Nachr.*, **269**, 185 (1939).
[187]   Seares, F.H., *Astrophys. J.*, **94**, 21 (1941).
[188]   Greenstein, J.L., *Ann. Harvard Coll. Observ.*, **89** (No. 11), 179 (1937).
[189]   Bergstrand, Ö., *Trans. Int. Astron. Union*, **5**, 156 (1936).
[190]   Weaver, H.F., *Astrophys. J.*, **106**, 366 (1947).
[191]   Stoy, R.H. and Redman, R.O., *Observatory*, **66**, 330 (1946).
[192]   Stebbins, J., Whitford, A.E. and Johnson, H.L., *Astrophys. J.*, **112**, 469 (1950).
[193]   Greaves, W.M.H., *Trans. Int. Astron. Union*, **8**, 355 (1954).
[194]   Cox, A., *Astrophys. J.*, **117**, 83 (1953).
[195]   Eggen, O.J., *Astrophys. J.*, **111**, 65 (1950).
[196]   Eggen, O.J., *Astrophys. J.*, **114**, 141 (1951).
[197]   Johnson, H.L. and Morgan, W.W., *Astrophys. J.*, **117**, 313 (1953).
[198]   Johnson, H.L., *Ann. d'Astrophys.*, **18**, 292 (1955).
[199]   Greaves, W.M.H., *Trans. Int. Astron. Union*, **8**, 355 (1954).
[200]   Greaves, W.M.H., *Trans. Int. Astron. Union*, **9**, 338 (1957).

[201] Becker, W. and Stock, J., *Astron. Nachr.*, **278**, 115 (1950).
[202] Bok, B.J. and Bok, P.F., *Astron. J.* **56**, 35 (1951).
[203] van Wijk, U., *Astron. J.* **57**, 27 (1952).
[204] Brown, A., *Astrophys. J.*, **113**, 344 (1951).
[205] Cox, A.N., *Astrophys. J.*, **117**, 83 (1953).
[206] Cox, A.N., *Astrophys. J.*, **121**, 628 (1955).
[207] Cousins, A.W.J. and Stoy, R.H., *Mon. Not. R. Astron. Soc.*, **114**, 349 (1954).
[208] King, I., *Astron. J.*, **60**, 391 (1955).
[209] Kooreman, C.J. and Oosterhoff, P.T., *Ann. Sterrewacht Leiden*, **21**, 115 (1957).
[210] Arp, H.C., Baum, W.A. and Sandage, A.R. *Astron. J.*, **58**, 4 (1953).
[211] Sandage, A.R. *Astron. J.*, **58**, 61 (1953).
[212] Arp, H.C., *Astron. J.*, **60**, 317 (1955).
[213] Johnson H.L. and Sandage, A.R., *Astrophys. J.*, **121**, 616 (1955).
[214] Johnson H.L., Sandage, A.R. and Wahlquist, D.W., *Astrophys. J.*, **124**, 81 (1956).
[215] Johnson H.L. and Sandage, A.R., *Astrophys. J.*, **124**, 379 (1956).
[216] Argue, A.N., Bok, B.J. and Miller, E.W., *A Catalogue of Photometric Sequences*, publ. Steward Observ., Univ. Arizona, 30 pp. (1973); *ibid.*, *Supplement to a Catalogue of Photometric Sequences*, publ. Steward Observ., Univ. Arizona, 8 pp. (1973).
[217] Becker, W., *Zeitschr. für Astrophys.*, **29**, 177 (1951).
[218] Becker, W. and Stock, J., *Zeitschr. für Astrophys.*, **34**, 1 (1954).
[219] Becker, W. and Stock, J., *Zeitschr. für Astrophys.*, **45**, 282 (1958).
[220] Stock, J., *Astrophys. J.*, **123**, 258 (1956).
[221] Hardorp, J., *Astron. Abhandl. Sternwarte Hamburg-Bergedorf*, **5**, 215 (1960).
[222] Grubissich, C. *Zeitschr. für Astrophys.*, **50**, 14 (1960).
[223] Haffner, H., *Trans. Int. Astron. Union*, **11A**, 419 (1962).
[224] Heckmann, O., *Trans. Int. Astron. Union*, **10**, 575 (1960).
[225] Argue, A.N., *Mon. Not. R. Astron. Soc.*, **122**, 197 (1961).
[226] Argue, A.N., quoted by R.H. Stoy in *Trans. Int. Astron. Union*, **11A**, 241 (1962). See p. 243.
[227] Racine, R. *Astron. J.*, **74**, 1073 (1969).
[228] Schmidt, B.V., *Mitt. der Hamburger Sternwarte*, **7**, 15 (1932).
[229] Bok, B.J. and Olmstead, M., *Astron. J.*, **55**, 65 (1950).
[230] Cameron, D.M., *Astron. J.*, **56**, 92 (1951).
[231] Bajcár, R., *Bull. Astron. Inst. Czech.*, **11**, 204 (1960).
[232] Vorontsov-Velyaminov, B.A. and Savejeva, M.V., *Astron. Zhurn.*, **38**, 185 (1961).
[233] Eklöf, O., *Arkiv Astron.*, **1**, 77 (1949).
[234] Eklöf, O., *Arkiv Astron.*, **1**, 315 (1954).
[235] Westerlund, B., *Arkiv Astron.*, **1**, 567 (1955).
[236] Müller, E.A., *Zeitschr. für Astrophys.*, **38**, 110 (1955).
[237] Barkhatova, K.A., *Astron. Zhurn.*, **33**, 556, 733, 850 (1956); *ibid.*, **34**, 203 (1957); Barkhatova, K.A. and Dracklushina, L.I., *Astron. Zhurn.*, **35**, 491 (1957).
[238] Haffner, H., *Mitt. Astron. Gesell.*, p. 44 (1956).
[239] Schäfer, H., *Veröff. Univ. Sternw. Bonn*, Nr. **58** (1960).
[240] Argue, A.N., *Vistas in Astron.*, **3**, 184 (1960).
[241] Argue, A.N., *Mon. Not. R. Astron. Soc.*, **127**, 97 (1963).

[242]　Haro, G. and Luyten, W.J., *Bol. Observ. Tonantzintla y Tacubaya*, **3**, 37 (1962).

[243]　Lyngå, G., *Arkiv Astron.*, **3**, 65 (1962).

[244]　Smyth, M.J. and Nandy, K., *Publ. R. Observ. Edinburgh*, **3**, 21 (1962); see also *ibid.*, *Mon. Not. R. Astron. Soc.*, **126**, 121 (1962).

[245]　The, P.S. and Roslund, C., *Contrib. Bosscha Observ. Lembang*, No. **19** (1963).

[246]　Fenkart, R.P., *Zeitschr. für Astrophys.*, **62**, 90 (1965).

[247]　Grubissich, C., *Zeitschr. für Astrophys.*, **60**, 249 (1965).

[248]　Lyngå, G., *Acta Univ. Lund*, (ser. 2) No. **3**, 16 pp. (1965).

[249]　Lawrence, L.C. and Reddish, V.C., *Publ. R. Observ. Edinburgh*, **3** (No. 9) (1965).

[250]　Kadla, S.I., *Comm. Astron. Observ. Pulkovo*, **24** (No. 5), 93 (1966).

[251]　Evans, T.L., *Observatory*, **87**, 32 (1967).

[252]　Lindoff, U., *Arkiv Astron.*, **4**, 305 (1966).

[253]　Lindoff, U., *Arkiv Astron.*, **4**, 471, 493, 587 (1968); *ibid.*, **5**, 45, 63, 221 (1968).

[254]　Nandy, K., *Publ. R. Observ. Edinburgh*, **7**, 47 (1971).

[255]　Brück, M.T., *Publ. R. Observ. Edinburgh*, **7**, 63 (1971).

[256]　Becker, W., *ESO Conference on the Rôle of Schmidt Telescopes in Astronomy*, ed. U. Haug, p. 9 (1972).

[257]　Becker, W., *Trans. Int. Astron. Union*, **10**, 383 (1960).

[258]　Dewhirst, D.W., *Observatory*, **76**, 176 (1956).

[259]　Stoy, R.H., *Trans. Int. Astron. Union*, **11A**, 241 (1962). See p. 246.

[260]　Argue, A.N., *Observatory*, **80**, 73 (1960).

[261]　Fellgett, P.B. and Seddon, H., *Observatory*, **83**, 25 (1963).

[262]　Burbidge, E.M. and Sandage, A., *Astrophys. J.*, **127**, 527 (1958)

[263]　Fellgett, P.B., *Trans. Int. Astron. Union*, **11A**, 31 (1962).

[264]　Walker, G.S., *Publ. R. Observ. Edinburgh*, **8**, 103 (1971).

[265]　Pratt, N.M., *Publ. R. Observ. Edinburgh*, **8**, 109 (1971).

[266]　Reddish, V.C. *Phys. Bull.*, **21**, 351 (1970).

[267]　Stoy, R.H., *Coll. Int. Astron. Union*, **7**, 48 (1970).

[268]　Brück, H.A., *Quart. J. R. Astron. Soc.*, **12**, 183 (1971).

[269]　Brück, H.A., *Quart. J. R. Astron. Soc.*, **13**, 580 (1972).

[270]　Kibblewhite, E.J., *Publ. R. Observ. Edinburgh*, **8**, 122 (1971).

[271]　Brück, M.T., Nandy, K., Caprioli, G., Smriglio, F., *Astrophys. Space Sci.*, **4**, 2, 213 (1969).

[272]　Brand, P.W.J.L., *Publ. R. Observ. Edinburgh*, **7**, 35 (1971).

8   Photometry and the birth of astrophysics

8.1   Introduction

During most of the nineteenth century and in the first decade of the twentieth, astronomical photometry by visual or photographic means was a major activity. Several million magnitudes were probably obtained during this whole era. It is rather astonishing therefore that so little analysis of these data to deduce new knowledge pertaining to the stars was ever undertaken. Argelander, Gould, Thome, Müller and above all Pickering were all great cataloguers, but not analysers, of photometric data.

Early in the twentieth century this often sterile activity saw a remarkable transformation, at least in some quarters. From 1908 Wilsing and Scheiner were deriving the first stellar temperatures from their spectrophotometry using Planck black-body curves. This was the dawn of the new astrophysics. The ensuing decade saw intense interest in star clusters and variable stars and culminated in 1918 in Shapley's triumphant conclusion concerning the dimensions of our Galaxy and the sun's place within it. This was possibly the most significant conclusion ever derived primarily from stellar photometric observations.

The discussion in this chapter is essentially the author's personal selection of some of the milestones in twentieth century astrophysics based on photometry. Stellar evolution, the interstellar medium and eclipsing binaries all form major ingredients in this story, though in the final analysis the selection of topics is arbitrary. The term 'astrophysics' has been broadened to include stellar statistics and Galactic structure, because these became important research areas using photometric results.

One striking fact in the early development of the new astrophysics is that American astronomers almost exclusively filled the leading rôles, with just a handful of Europeans (for example, Wilsing, Hertzsprung, Chalonge, B. Strömgren) making important contributions based on photometry. The completion of the Mt Wilson 60-inch reflector in 1908 and the 100-inch a decade later, and the abstinence of American observatories from the

Fig. 8.1   Solon Bailey.

paralysing *Carte du Ciel* project may have been two of the factors that promoted this American dominance.

8.2   Solon Bailey and the discovery of cluster variables

When Solon Bailey discovered variable stars from photography of the globular clusters M3 and M5 in 1895, the first steps were taken for a remarkable new chapter in astronomical research. Within a quarter of a century the results from the study of these 'cluster variables', as Bailey called them [1], were to change profoundly our whole picture of the sidereal universe and of the sun's place within it.

At this time Bailey was undertaking photometric programmes, both visually and photographically, from Harvard's Boyden Station in Arequipa, Peru, which he had established as a permanent southern outstation in 1889. It was certainly fortunate that for a photographic study of globular clusters the northern objects M3 and M5 'were among the first clusters examined, and both yielded surprising results' [2]. Pickering published a note in the newly established *Harvard Circulars* [3] announcing Bailey's discovery of 87 variables in M3, as well as 46 in M5, indicating a much higher percentage of variables for cluster stars than for the general field (see also [4] for cluster variables in ω Cen and [1] for those in M5). However, in four further globular clusters Bailey found inexplicably few cluster variables (between 2 and 5 per cluster) and in five further clusters there were none at all. These were not the first variable stars to be found in globular clusters†, but they were the first to be catalogued systematically in large numbers.

By 1897 Bailey had found 310 cluster variables in 16 globular clusters; only in one (M13) could he find none, while M3 had 113. He at once recognized that these stars had short periods, in many cases only a few hours, a result confirmed, at least for one variable in M5, for which Pickering deduced a period of $0^d.4638$ [9]. Edward Barnard, using the new 40-inch refractor at Yerkes Observatory, also obtained a period of about half a day for another M5 star, yet two further variables in this cluster had periods of about four weeks [10]. These longer-period stars provided an important clue to be used by Shapley in his method of determining the distances to the globular clusters – see section 8.5.1.

Bailey continued his search for variables in most of the brighter globular clusters, and in 1898 he had recorded 509 in 21 clusters after examining 19 050 stars [11]. M3 with 132 variable stars and ω Centauri with 125 had the greatest number. However, the percentage of variables in different clusters ranged from 0 to 15 per cent. The cluster variables Bailey recorded had amplitudes of at least $0^m.5$, periods less than a day, and a great uniformity in their light curves. Bailey made a special study of the variables in ω Centauri, the nearest and brightest globular, for which he found 98 of the cluster variables with periods less than a day [11]. Although these stars showed a general similarity in their light curves, he was nevertheless able to classify them into several groups according to their amplitude and the asymmetry of the rise and fall in their light.

The Bailey classification was expounded in more detail in 1902 when a thorough study of 128 variables in ω Centauri was published [12]. The subclasses were designated 'a', 'b' and 'c', the last having the smallest amplitudes and the most symmetrical (nearly sinusoidal) light curves, whereas subclass 'a' stars were characterized by large amplitudes (over one magnitude) and the most asymmetric light curves with rapid rises and slow declines. Further detailed studies of the variables in M3 [13], M5 [14] and M15 [15] followed

---

† Pickering had found one variable in M3 in 1889 [5] and the English amateurs David Packer [6, 7] and Ainslie Common [8] discovered respectively 2 and 5 variable stars in M5 in 1890.

over the next two decades mainly using 13-inch Boyden refractor or 60-inch Mt Wilson reflector observations. These were the four clusters richest in variables and together accounted for 422 variables, over 80 per cent of all those discovered in globular clusters. Bailey, with the assistance of Miss E. Leland, obtained photographic light curves and periods for nearly all of them and found a mean period of close to $0^d.55$ for the cluster variables in each globular system [16].

For the study of variables, Bailey adapted the method of sequences of William Herschel and Argelander, by dividing the cluster up into small areas comprising sequences of about ten stars which were placed in order of brightness on each photographic plate. For magnitude determinations, the variable was first compared with an arbitrary scale of images which in turn was calibrated with a number of comparison stars between magnitudes (m_{pg}) 9 and 15 in the immediate vicinity of the cluster [12]. The comparison star magnitudes were in turn derived from visual photometry, often by making the dubious assumption of spectral type A in order to derive a colour index and hence photographic magnitude. The magnitudes so derived certainly would have been subject to systematic errors, and the random errors were typically $\pm 0^m.1$. Nevertheless such precision was entirely adequate for the purposes of variable classification and period determination.

In 1916 Bailey published a catalogue of 76 globular clusters known at the time (rather more than half the number currently known as part of our Galaxy). The catalogue summarized the data on variables in about two dozen clusters surveyed and gave a comprehensive bibliography on globular clusters [17]. Bailey had laid the groundwork for Shapley's extensive researches on globular clusters from 1914, in which the cluster variables played a pivotal rôle – see section 8.5. Shapley's work was also based on the related Cepheid variables, yet another domain in which Harvard was at this time pre-eminent.

8.3   The photometry of Cepheid variables, and their rôle in astrophysics

8.3.1   Miss Leavitt's remarkable discovery

Henrietta Leavitt's variable star work at Harvard commenced in December 1903 and the two Magellanic Clouds became objects of her special attention. She quickly discovered variables in these satellite galaxies in large numbers, 54 in the Small Magellanic Cloud (SMC) being announced in 1904 from a comparison of just two plates taken with the Bruce 24-inch

Fig. 8.2   Henrietta Leavitt.

photographic telescope in Peru [18], and just one month later 152 were discovered in the Large Magellanic Cloud (LMC) from 21 plates [19]. The number catalogued in the SMC had reached nearly 900 just a year later [20]. This work culminated in Miss Leavitt's important catalogue of 1777 variables in the Magellanic Clouds [21]. Her method of discovery was ingenious, and consisted in producing a positive copy of one of the plates and then superimposing the other negatives precisely on the positive. The images of the variable stars, when viewed through the two plates in contact, were readily identified [18]. All the new variable stars were faint, the great majority being below 13th magnitude at maximum. The Magellanic Cloud catalogue by itself almost doubled the total number of variable stars known in the entire sky at that time (Annie Cannon's second catalogue of variable stars of 1907 listed 1957 stars in our Galaxy)[22].

Of the hundreds of variables discovered by Miss Leavitt in both clouds, she obtained periods for 16 of them in the SMC, using a series of long exposure plates (2 to 5 hours). The periods found were between 1 day and 127 days, although all but three were less than 2 weeks. She briefly commented: 'It is worthy of notice that ... the brighter variables have the longer periods' [21]. This apparent relationship between period and

Fig. 8.3   Period-luminosity law for Small Magellanic Cloud Cepheids by
           Henrietta Leavitt, 1912.

magnitude, so fleetingly alluded to, had evidently made a firm impression
on Miss Leavitt. She next added a further 9 SMC variables to those with
period determinations and they followed the same pattern. When either
maximum or minimum magnitude was plotted against the logarithm of the
period, then a linear relationship resulted [23]. In her own words (but over
Pickering's name):

> The two resulting curves, one for maxima and one for minima, are
> surprisingly smooth, and of remarkable form. In Figure 2 ... a straight
> line can readily be drawn among each of the two series of points
> corresponding to maxima and minima, thus showing that there is a
> simple relation between the brightness of the variables and their
> periods. The logarithm of the period increases by about 0.48 for each
> increase of one magnitude in brightness... Since the variables are
> probably at nearly the same distance from the Earth, their periods are
> apparently associated with their actual emission of light, as determined
> by their mass, density, and surface brightness [23].

Miss Leavitt recognized the similarity between these SMC variables and
certain brighter Galactic stars (unfortunately she quoted UY Cygni as an
example, an RR Lyrae or cluster-type variable in the Galactic field which is
not strictly comparable to the Cloud Cepheids) and in expressing the hope
that parallaxes for such Galactic variables might be measured, she may
have foreseen the possibility of determining a distance to the clouds using
the magnitudes of the Cepheid variables. If she did, such a line of research
was not pursued.

8.3.2 Calibration of the Cepheid period-luminosity law and the first photometric distances

It was Ejnar Hertzsprung in Potsdam who capitalized on Miss Leavitt's discovery, both in providing the first calibration of the Cepheid period-luminosity law and as a result the first distance determination to an extragalactic object based on the calibration. The starting point for Hertzsprung's work was the *Preliminary General Catalogue of 6188 Stars* by Lewis Boss (1846–1912) [24], a fundamental catalogue containing the best data on stellar proper motions available in 1910. Thirteen Galactic Cepheids were included in this catalogue, and Hertzsprung was able to use these stars to determine their secular parallax [25]. This is a statistical analysis based on the apparent motions of the stars and on the known solar space velocity, which enables the mean parallax or distance of a number of field stars of similar type (including luminosity) to be determined. The method had been devised in 1901 by Kapteyn [26].

Hertzsprung had earlier applied the same technique to the stars with narrow spectral lines discovered by Miss Maury (the so-called c-type stars) and shown that these were distant objects of high luminosity [27, 28]. The extension of this earlier work to the Galactic Cepheids, some of which were in any case included in Miss Maury's c-type stars, was therefore an analysis he would have naturally undertaken, given the stimulus of Miss Leavitt's work in 1912.

The result of Hertzsprung's analysis was that the 13 Galactic Cepheids had a mean parallax of 0.035 arc seconds. From this the distance and luminosity at once followed. Hertzsprung expressed the result as an absolute magnitude, which was defined by Kapteyn as the apparent magnitude of a star if it were transferred to a distance from the sun corresponding to a parallax of 0.1 arc seconds [29] – or a distance of 10 parsecs. He found $M_{vis} = -2.3 \pm 0.5$ † as the mean Cepheid value.

The next step was to assume that Miss Leavitt's SMC variables were also Cepheids and hence must have the same luminosity or absolute magnitude for the same mean period. In this case their mean apparent visual magnitude of 13.0, when compared with the absolute magnitude of −2.3, gave Hertzsprung a parallax for the stars in the SMC of only 0.0001 arc seconds. This minute value corresponds to a huge distance which Hertzsprung unfortunately miscalculated at 3000 instead of 30 000 light years. But even at 3000 light years he deduced that the SMC was well above the plane of the Milky Way and separate from it. It was at that time by far the largest

---

† Hertzsprung chose to express his absolute magnitudes for a standard distance of 1 parsec, so his result was in fact −7.3.

distance that had been determined for any individual object in the universe. Furthermore the statistical parallax for the Galactic Cepheids enabled their distances in the plane of the Galaxy to be determined. They lay within an extensive but highly flattened disk some 10 000 light years in diameter [25].

Hertzsprung's distance to the SMC was about a factor of five too small, partly as a result of uncertainty in the colour of the Cepheids (used to obtain the visual magnitudes from Miss Leavitt's photographic data) but mainly because the Galactic stars used for the calibration were dimmed by interstellar dust within the Galaxy, which resulted in his mean absolute magnitudes being too faint. Nevertheless the principle of the method, in which Cepheids are used as standard candles to obtain photometric distances was generally correct. The work was a milestone in the application of photometry to astrophysics. Later application of the same technique was to influence profoundly our understanding of the distance scales within the whole universe.

Quite independently of Hertzsprung, Henry Norris Russell also calculated the mean absolute magnitude of the same 13 Galactic Cepheids in the Boss Preliminary General Catalogue. He presented the result to the Astronomical and Astrophysical Society of America in Cleveland over the 1913 New Year, six months before Hertzsprung's work. His value for their mean absolute visual magnitude was −2.4, practically identical to Hertzsprung's result [30, 31]. He therefore takes equal credit for showing that Cepheids are high luminosity stars of large dimensions and low densities. However, he did not apply this result to Miss Leavitt's data either to calibrate the Cepheids' periods in terms of luminosity or to obtain a distance for the Small Magellanic Cloud.

8.3.3   Cepheids as pulsating stars

The interpretation of the physical nature of Cepheid variability was at first a separate question to their use as standard candles for distance estimation. Later, once the concept of Cepheids as pulsating stars had become established, pulsation theory was able to give some theoretical support for the existence of a period-luminosity law on which the distances depended.

The idea of pulsating stars is not one that came easily. The discovery of the first spectroscopic binaries in 1889 by Pickering and Vogel firmly fixed in astronomers' minds the idea that periodic radial-velocity variations were caused by the orbital motion of a binary star. When Aristarch Belopolsky (1854–1934) discovered radial-velocity variations in δ Cephei in 1894, it was therefore natural for him to assume the star to be the brighter member of a binary system, for which he derived the orbit [32]. An earlier suggestion by the German theoretician August Ritter in 1879, that most periodic variable stars were pulsating, had not found favour, and was generally ignored [33]. Nevertheless Ritter had developed the mathematics of radial pulsations of homogeneous gaseous spheres and derived the result that the period varies inversely as the square root of the density, a relationship later derived by Eddington for centrally condensed stars.

The binary hypothesis had numerous problems, most notably the occurrence of the radial-velocity maximum near minimum light, which is in disagreement with a simple binary model in which the light variations are due to eclipses. A review by D. Brunt in 1913 discussed these difficulties and some of the *ad hoc* binary models devised by various authors to try and overcome them, though with limited success [34]. The whole question of Cepheid variability was tackled by Harlow Shapley in 1914. His classic paper discussed in detail the observational evidence, in particular the small irregularities in the light curves, the variation in spectral type and colour in phase with the light and the recently discovered giant (in fact supergiant) status of Cepheids which would have made these stars larger than their presumed binary separations, unless the orbits of all Cepheids were fortuitously observed at low inclination [35]. The evidence, based largely on the photometry of many observers, led to the demise of the binary hypothesis (which for example Ludendorff [36] had already foreseen as a likely outcome) and the proposal by Shapley that radial pulsations might instead be the cause. Such pulsations could not be oscillations of a star between prolate and oblate spheroids as F. R. Moulton had earlier suggested [37], because the light would then be at a maximum twice in every cycle as the star passed through its spherical state. On the other hand, the theory of radial pulsations was then barely developed, which accounts for Shapley's rather tentative formulation of his proposal: 'The explanation that appears to promise the simplest solution of most, if not all, of the Cepheid phenomena is founded on the rather vague conception of periodic pulsations in the masses of isolated stars' [35].

Shapley's suggestion was supported theoretically by Eddington in England, who considered the maintenance of radial pulsations [38] and worked out the thermodynamics of pulsating stars in two influential theoretical papers [39]. Furthermore Baade proposed an observational test of the Shapley-Eddington pulsation hypothesis [40]. His idea was to compare the radius variations deduced from integrating the radial-velocity curve with those deduced from the light and colour curves using the equation $L = 4\pi R^2 \sigma T_{\text{eff}}^4$. The test required knowing both the luminosity or mean absolute bolometric magnitudes of the Cepheids (from the statistical parallax) and also their surface temperatures (from colour or spectral type). The lack of calibrations of the photometry prevented Baade himself applying his test and also resulted in an attempt by Karl Bottlinger being unsuccessful [41], but this was finally done by several observers in the 1940s, by which time the pulsation theory was firmly established [42, 43, 44].

It should be mentioned that Shapley's paper did not lead to an immediate rejection of the binary hypothesis by all astronomers. For example Charles Perrine in Córdoba published a spirited and detailed defence of the binary hypothesis as late as 1919, though his strange failure to reference the papers of Shapley and Eddington may indicate that he was no longer in touch with the latest developments [45].

8.4   Early ideas on the structure of the Milky Way and the origins of stellar statistics

The researches of William Herschel on 'the construction of the heavens' [46, 47] from 1784 to 1818 mark the earliest attempt to apply stellar photometry to the problem of elucidating the structure of the Milky Way. His star gauges were based on the simplifying assumptions of an equal luminosity for all stars, a uniform spatial density of stars to the edge of the stellar system and the absence of an absorbing interstellar medium. Distance alone determined a star's apparent magnitude. From these assumptions Herschel deduced his disk-shaped structure for the Milky Way, some five times more extended in the galactic plane than in the perpendicular direction. 'In the sides of the stratum opposite to our situation in it [i.e. towards the galactic poles] cannot extend to 100 times the distance of Sirius' [47] while along the plane he could penetrate to a distance of 497 times that of Sirius, which we can now identify with about 1300 parsecs. The outline of the Milky Way was not elliptical but quite irregular and the sun was near, but not coincident, with the centre. In Herschel's universe the nebulae were great star systems lying outside the Milky Way. Herschel's picture of the Milky Way was modified somewhat towards the end of his life. In particular in 1818 he concluded that the Milky Way was 'fathomless', implying that the stars on the edge of the system were invisible in his telescope, though later misinterpreted by Struve to mean of infinite extent.

In the nineteenth century several astronomers developed theories of galactic structure. Notable is the conclusion of Wilhelm Olbers of Bremen that, if the stars were infinite in number, then the whole sky should shine with the brilliance of daylight. His solution to his famous paradox was to suppose space to be filled with an absorbing medium sufficient to extinguish the more distant stars [48]. A closely similar idea was also published by Jean-Phillippe de Chéseaux as early as 1744 – see [49] and section 8.6.1.

Wilhelm Struve, the first director of the Pulkovo Observatory, was influenced by Olbers' suggestion, for his galactic model comprised parallel planes of decreasing star density towards the galactic poles and which were infinite in extent within the plane of the Milky Way, but whose transparency was limited by an absorbing medium [50] – see section 8.6.1. The Struve model departed radically from Herschel's in assigning the large number of stars on the galactic equator to a true increase in spatial density, whereas for Herschel this increase in numbers simply reflected the system's greater extent in the equatorial directions.

Struve's photometric material comprised some 52 000 often poorly estimated stellar magnitudes to visual magnitude 9, taken from the transit circle observations of Bessel, Piazzi and others, and his analysis involved counting stars to find their relative numbers as a function of galactic latitude. His conclusions met with a number of objections, most especially from John Herschel, who had no sympathy for the idea of an absorbing medium [51].

Several astronomers developed during the second half of the nineteenth century a theory of the Milky Way as a ring-shaped object whose depth in the line of sight was comparable to its lateral extent. Such a model was first suggested by the amateur astronomer Richard Proctor (1837–88) [52]. This idea, which required the Milky Way to be composed of stars of a wide range of luminosity, did receive some support in Italy from Giovanni Celoria (1842–1920) [53] and Giovanni Schiaparelli (1835–1910) [54], who studied the distribution of the brighter stars in the sky. The ring model with an eccentric location for the sun was also considered by C. Easton (1864–1929) in Holland, on the basis of the distribution of stars at low galactic latitudes and the changes in brightness of the Milky Way with longitude. However, he apparently favoured a spiral structure, likewise with the sun displaced from the spiral's centre [55]. This was in fact the earliest suggestion that our Galaxy might be a spiral.

The true successor to Herschel in the science of stellar statistics was Hugo von Seeliger (1849–1924), the director of the Munich Observatory. Seeliger was the first to derive the mathematical integral equations from which he showed that the luminosity function and spatial density of the stars in the Galaxy could be derived from their distribution over apparent magnitude, that is, from counting the numbers of stars in a given area to successive magnitude limits [56]. In his second major paper he generalized the theory to include the possibility of an interstellar absorbing medium, though in practice he did not subscribe to its reality [57].

Seeliger recognized the need for accurate and complete photometric data if the density of stars throughout the Galaxy was to be deduced. He made use of the *Bonner Durchmusterung* data for this purpose, though immediately recognized their inadequacy, both because of departures from the Pogson scale and incompleteness below about magnitude 9.2. Nevertheless Seeliger found the number of stars in consecutive magnitude intervals to be less than four, the value expected for a uniform density of stars along the line of sight, and he interpreted his data as the result of the sun lying near the centre of a finite universe with density decreasing outwards in all directions. The actual dimensions of the star system depended on a knowledge of the mean parallax of stars of any given apparent magnitude. In his later work he was able to use the statistical parallaxes of Kapteyn and hence to deduce a radius of the Milky Way of less than 4 kpc in the galactic plane.

Karl Schwarzschild developed the theory of the problem further. He set no finite upper limit to the size of the Milky Way, which simplified Seeliger's integral equations and allowed analytical solutions to be found if the raw data on star numbers and mean parallaxes could be represented by simple functions of the apparent magnitude [58]. In Schwarzschild's universe the luminosity function was a gaussian and the stellar density declined exponentially with distance from the sun.

The science of stellar statistics reached its zenith with the work of Kapteyn at the Groningen Astronomical Laboratory, which he founded. Here he became the leader in the statistical investigation of stellar data of all kinds which came to him from the observatories around the world. Magnitudes, proper motions, trigonometric parallaxes, radial velocities and spectral types were all of the greatest interest to Kapteyn, and it was in order to assemble a collection of data going to the faintest limits possible that he devised his famous *Plan of Selected Areas* in 1906 [59] – see section 4.9.2. The plan divided the sky into 206 areas where the data for statistical purposes were to be obtained. A large collaborative effort was necessary and Pickering was from the start one of the main contributors to the photometric programme, using the 16-inch Metcalf and 24-inch Bruce telescopes in northern and southern hemispheres. This resulted in three volumes of the Harvard Annals being devoted to the *Durchmusterung of Selected Areas*, in which were published photographic magnitudes for faint stars in each area to about magnitude 16 [60, 61, 62].

However, long before these results were available to him, Kapteyn had commenced his great programme of deducing the structure of the stellar system from the numbers of stars in different directions between given magnitude limits, and using their proper motions to obtain the mean parallax of stars of a given magnitude. His purpose was to solve the integral equations to derive the luminosity function and the stellar density. For the parallaxes

Fig. 8.4   Jacobus Cornelius Kapteyn.

Kapteyn devised the method of secular (or statistical) parallax based on the proper motion components away from the direction of the solar velocity through space [26, 63]. He found thus the mean parallax of stars according to their apparent magnitude and proper motion, as well as the distribution of parallaxes within each group. His procedure was described in a popular lecture to the Royal Institution in 1908. From the limited data then available, he found that the sun lay near the centre of a stellar system whose density was essentially zero at a distance of 9 kpc in the galactic plane [64].

At this time the data for the fainter stars to magnitude 16 were taken from a variety of sources, including the gauges of Sir John Herschel, the *Cape Photographic Durchmusterung*, certain published zones of the *Carte du Ciel* and the visual photometry of faint stars at Harvard by Wendell and Pickering [65, 66] – see [67]. Although the analysis was performed using visual magnitudes, most of the observations were made photographically in the expectation that the systematic errors would be uniformly distributed and hence cancel, if large numbers of stars were considered.

In later years Pieter van Rhijn became Kapteyn's assistant (and later, his successor) at the Groningen Laboratory, and the statistics on the distribution over stellar magnitudes was greatly improved in van Rhijn's analysis of 1917. By this time the Harvard programme for the 65 northernmost selected areas to magnitude $m_{pg} = 15.5$ was available in advance of publication. [68]. In addition the magnitudes and statistics for many stars had been determined at Greenwich by Sydney Chapman and Philibert Melotte from the Franklin-Adams charts, and some of these data were incorporated into the latest Groningen statistics [69].

In the final years of his life, Kapteyn published two major papers in the *Astrophysical Journal* giving his latest attempts to determine the density of stars within the Galaxy and the luminosity function [70, 71]. In the latter of these he adopted a series of concentric oblate spheroids of axial ratio 5.1 to 1 for the contours of equal star density, as giving a close approximation of the structure of the Galaxy. The sun was near to but not quite at the centre of this system, and the density in successive shells diminished to be close to zero beyond the last, whose extent (semi-major axis) in the Galactic plane was 8465 parsecs and towards the Galactic pole was 1660 parsecs.

This model was 'Kapteyn's Universe', a model based on the assumption that interstellar absorption, if it existed, played a negligible rôle in stellar statistics. In reality this assumption was flawed, and although Kapteyn's data gave a reasonable representation of the galactic density towards the poles, the absorption of starlight by interstellar dust in the galactic plane completely vitiated his results for the structure and dimensions of the Galaxy at lower latitudes. In addition his assumption of a luminosity function that was the same in all parts of the Galaxy was also shown later to be untenable.

It was nevertheless Kapteyn's Universe (or the earlier versions of it going back to 1902 [29]) which became the accepted model for about the first quarter of the century. As a result of the work on stellar galactic motions by Lindblad in 1926 and Oort in 1927 it was shown that the Galaxy was rotating about a point in the direction of Sagittarius. This was one of the pieces of evidence that gave strong support to the rival scheme proposed by Shapley, described in the next section. In addition the demonstration of the extragalactic nature of the spiral nebulae by Hubble in 1924 gave a strong link between the Milky Way and the spiral in Andromeda, as being objects of similar type and dimensions – see [72] for a detailed discussion of M31.

Even after Kapteyn's universe had begun to crumble, major researches in stellar statistics were continued by van Rhijn in Groningen [73] on the luminosity function of different spectral types, by Antonie Pannekoek in

Amsterdam on the space distributions of A, K and B stars [74] and by Carl Charlier and his colleagues at Lund in Sweden on the distribution of the B stars and of stellar clusters [75]. Charlier's work in stellar statistics dates back to 1911 in a major paper discussing the fundamental integral equations of Seeliger and their solution [76]. His data for faint stars came principally from the *Carte du Ciel* charts and he deduced an equatorial extent of the Galaxy somewhere between 3 and 7 kpc.

At this time the only published photographic atlas that encompassed the whole sky was the Harvard Map produced by Pickering in 1903. The map comprised glass plate prints each 8 × 10 inches for the not unreasonable sum of $15 [77]. It went to a limiting magnitude of nearly 12. Hans Henie at Lund, working under Charlier, counted about 400 000 stars to magnitude 11 on the Harvard Map to produce charts of star surface density over the sky [78].

One of Charlier's most interesting papers pertains to the statistics of star clusters, which he undertook at the same time as Shapley was researching the same topic at Mt Wilson [79]. In this work he reached a remarkably different result from that of Shapley, in spite of using similar observational data. Charlier's work on clusters is discussed further in section 8.5.

8.5   Shapley's research on globular clusters

When Harlow Shapley completed his doctoral thesis on eclipsing binary stars under Russell at Princeton in 1913, he was fortunate in having his influential former Missouri professor, Frederick Seares, to recommend him for a post with Hale at Mt Wilson. Shapley arrived in California in April 1914, but only after he had first visited Harvard College Observatory where he was able to discuss his future research plans with Solon Bailey. Bailey saw the possibilities of using the Mt Wilson 60-inch telescope for continuing the research on globular clusters and their variables. As a result this became Shapley's great preoccupation during the seven years he spent at Mt Wilson, years of incredible energy and prodigious output in which the interpretation of data in photographic photometry was to transform our view of the sidereal universe.

Shapley's research was based on the photometry of stars, mainly brighter than fifteenth magnitude, in the brighter globular clusters. About 70 such objects were then known, and his method involved the estimation of photographic and photovisual magnitudes from focal images with the 60-inch reflector. For most of this work Shapley used a graded scale for comparison with cluster stars. The scale was in turn calibrated with stars in Seares' North

Fig. 8.5   Harlow Shapley.

Polar Sequence. However, Shapley readily admitted that high precision was not his goal. His probable errors for a magnitude determination from one plate were typically $\pm 0^{m}\!.05$ [80, 81] and for a colour index $(m_{pg} - m_{pv})$ they were around $\pm 0^{m}\!.07$. In addition the density of stellar images in the more central crowded regions of globular clusters was affected by the Eberhard effect† [82], and Shapley acknowledged this to be a source of systematic error. Nevertheless it is ironic that the interpretation of Shapley's data did not rest critically on the need for high accuracy. Photographic observers had spent over three decades of hard effort to try to eliminate systematic errors in photographic photometry and to apply these techniques to large scale photographic surveys to amass the data needed for statistical analysis. Shapley eschewed the need for high photometric accuracy and also all the photographic photometry of faint field stars, which was then available or becoming available, and which Kapteyn saw as essential for delineating the size and shape of the universe. Instead he concentrated on stars in just a

† The Eberhard effect is an adjacency effect in which the density at any point on a plate is affected by the relatively high density of closely neighbouring points.

handful of clusters and solved in a few years of intensive effort a problem whose solution had eluded his contemporaries for more than two decades.

The results of these seven years appeared in two long series of articles, the main ones being 19 papers in the *Astrophysical Journal* from 1917 to 1921, the first three being abstracts of earlier papers published as *Contributions from the Mt Wilson Solar Observatory*. A second series of 13 shorter papers was published in the *Proceedings of the National Academy of Sciences*. In general these summarized the principal results in a less technical format or gave preliminary findings. But even these two series accounted for less than half the total of papers he published while at Mt Wilson. Table 8.1 summarizes the main series of papers in the *Astrophysical Journal* and *Proceedings of the National Academy of Sciences*. Undoubtedly the most important of these papers (in the *Astrophysical Journal*) were numbers 6, 7 and 12 concerning the distances to the globular clusters and the structure of the sidereal universe.

Apart from these important conclusions, the papers also reported a large mass of photometric data based on, according to paper 7 [83], 15 000 estimates of stellar magnitude (for the results of that paper alone). Numerous other conclusions were reached by Shapley in the course of this work – information on the distribution of colour indices for stars in globular clusters†, on the absence of interstellar reddening of starlight, on the properties of cluster variables, the calibration of the Cepheid period-luminosity law and its theoretical basis, the absolute magnitudes of cluster variables and of the brightest red giants in globular clusters, the sizes, shapes and integrated absolute magnitudes of the globular clusters, the energy sources required for stellar evolution, the dynamics of globular clusters in the Galaxy and the relation of globular clusters to open clusters. Not all his conclusions were correct, most notably those pertaining to the lack of interstellar reddening and to the fate of globular clusters in crossing the galactic plane. Nevertheless the topics covered represent an amazing breadth of interest and depth of insight. According to Zdeněk Kopal 'the years 1914–21 mark, in retrospect, a high noon in the life of Harlow Shapley as an individual investigator: certainly he never published papers of greater originality and importance than during those years of full achievement' [85].

---

† In 1915 Shapley commented on the differences in the colour-magnitude diagrams and stellar contents of globular and open clusters. His work preceded Baade's discovery of stellar populations by over three decades (see Helen Sawyer Hogg [84]).

Table 8.1. *Summary of Shapley's Mt Wilson papers on photometry in star clusters*

A: Series in *Astrophys. J.* and *Contrib. Mt Wilson Solar Observ.*

No.	Ap. J. ref.	Mt Wilson contrib. no.	Title	Comments
1.	**45**, 118 (1917)	**115** (1915)	The general problem of clusters	Types of star cluster, Galactic distribution of clusters. Magnitude determination in clusters.
2.	**45**, 123 (1917)	**116** (1915)	1300 stars in Hercules	Pg and pv photometry of M13 stars. Distribution of colour classes in M13. Blue stars in M13 indicate absence of interstellar reddening. Distance to M13 from magnitudes of brightest stars.
3.	**45**, 140 (1917)	**117** (1916)	A catalogue of 311 stars in M67	Pg and pv photometry of M67 stars. Distribution of colour classes in this open cluster quite different from M13 but similar to that for field stars.
4.	**45**, 164 (1917)	**126**	The galactic cluster M11	Pg and pv magnitudes for 458 stars in the galactic cluster M11. Distribution of colours shows a peak for early type stars. Plots a colour-magnitude diagram.
5.	**46**, 64 (1917)	**133**	Colour indices of stars in the galactic clouds	Investigates distribution of colour indices in four Milky Way fields, which is found to be similar to that of solar neighbourhood.
6.	**48**, 89 (1918)	**151**	On the determination of the distances of globular clusters.	Distances to globular clusters from (i) calibration of Cepheid $P-L$ law; (ii) abs mag of cluster variables; (iii) abs mag of brightest stars; (iv) angular diameter of cluster
7.	**48**, 154 (1918)	**152**	The distances, distribution in space and dimensions of 69 globular clusters.	Application of results of paper 6. above to 69 globular clusters; for 41 of them the distance is based solely on angular diameter. Centre of globular cluster distribution is 13 kpc distant in Sagittarius. Absence of globular clusters at low galactic latitudes.
8.	**48**, 279 (1918)	**153**	The luminosities and distances of 139 Cepheid variables	Parallaxes are given for 139 Galactic Cepheids including 45 cluster-type variables in the field (RR Lyrae stars). The high proper motions of the latter due to the high space velocities of giant stars at large galactic latitudes. On other hand Cepheids ($P > 1$ day) are at low latitudes.
9.	**49**, 24 (1919)	**154**	Three notes on Cepheid variation	(i) M_V should be linear function of $\log P$ using $P^2 \propto 1/\rho$ for pulsating systems; (ii) M3 cluster variables are redder when fainter; (iii) Ultraviolet photometry of M15 cluster variables.
10.	**49**, 96 (1919)	**155**	A critical magnitude in the sequence of stellar luminosities	Distribution of pv mags in M3 as function of stellar colour shows peak at $M_{pv} = 15.50$, close to that for cluster variables.
11.	**49**, 249 (1919)	**156**	A comparison of the distances of various celestial objects	Compares distances to different types of object. In Shapley's universe the globular clusters are the most distant objects of all because of his neglect of interstellar absorption for objects in the Milky Way. Spiral nebulae are among the nearest of objects to the sun.
12.	**49**, 311 (1919)	**157**	Remarks on the arrangement of the sidereal universe	System of globular clusters forms an ellipsoidal system whose centre is 20 kpc distant in Sagittarius, but with an absence of globulars in Galactic plane. Milky Way comprises a flattened disk of stars possibly with a diameter of 100 kpc. The bright B stars constitute a local cluster in a plane tilted with respect to the overall Galaxy. Stellar evolution occurs on timescales greater than 10^5 years and requires sources of energy other than gravitational potential energy.
13.	**50**, 42 (1919)	**160**	The galactic planes in 41 globular clusters	Of 41 globular clusters, 30 show an apparent elongation while 11 have a circular outline.
14.	**50**, 107 (1919) (with Martha B. Shapley)	**161**	Further remarks on the structure of the Galactic system	17 further globular clusters are added to those of paper 7. Globular and open clusters occupy mutually exclusive regions of space. Globular distances from their integrated magnitudes.
15.	**51**, 49 (1920)	**175**	A photometric analysis of the globular system M68.	60-inch telescope used to discover 28 variables in this cluster. Properties of giant stars in globular clusters and of cluster variables are summarized.
16.	**51**, 140 (1920) (with Helen N. Davis)	**176**	Photometric catalogue of 848 stars in M3.	Pg and pv magnitudes for stars in M3. Distribution of stars with colour class investigated – maximum is near class F5.

Table 8.1. *continued*

No.	*Ap. J.* ref.	*Mt Wilson* contrib. no.	Title	Comments
17.	**52**, 73 (1920)	**190**	Miscellaneous results	(i) Discovery of 88 variable stars in 8 globular clusters. (ii) Integrated absolute visual magnitudes of globular clusters are typically $\langle M_V \rangle = -8.8 \pm 0.5$. (iii) Derivation of a theoretical *P-L* law.
18.	**52**, 232 (1920)	**195**	The periods and light curves of 26 Cepheid variables in M72.	Periods for 26 cluster variables are obtained in the range 0.33 to 0.66 days and a distance of 25.6 kpc is obtained for the globular cluster M72.
19.	**54**, 323 (1921) (with Myrtle L. Richmond)	**218**	A photometric survey of the Pleiades	Pg and pv magnitudes are obtained for 821 stars in the Pleiades, including the first data for dwarf stars in any cluster.

B: Series in *Proc. Nat. Acad. Sciences*

No.	Ref.	Title	Comments
1.	**2**, 12 (1916)	On the absorption of light in space	The presence of many blue stars (colour class b) in the globular cluster M13 means interstellar reddening must be negligible.
2.	**2**, 15 (1916)	On the sequence of spectral types in stellar evolution.	In M13 the brightest stars are increasingly red. According to Russell's theory of stellar evolution, the red giants are precursors of stellar cooling phase exhibited by dwarf stars.
3.	**2**, 525 (1916)	The colours of the brighter stars in four globular clusters.	The average colour index in different ranges of M_{pv} in the clusters M3, M13, M5 and M15 is found. In all cases the brighter stars are redder.
4.	**3**, 25 (1917)	On the colours of stars in the galactic clouds surrounding M11.	The distribution of different colour indices in the open cluster M11 is explored and a colour-magnitude diagram is plotted.
5.	**3**, 267 (1917)	Further evidence of the absence of scattering of light in space.	The presence of blue stars in or near a number of globular and open clusters implies the general absence of interstellar scattering and reddening of starlight. Globular clusters M3, M5, M13, M15 are 10 kpc or more distant if blue stars have $M_{pv} = 0$
6.	**3**, 276 (1917)	The relation of blue stars and variables to galactic planes.	M13 and ω Cen show elliptical symmetry. Shapley attempts to relate distribution of blue stars and variables to the axis of symmetry in an analogous way to that found in Milky Way.
7.	**3**, 479 (1917)	A method for the determination of the relative distances of globular clusters.	Cluster variables have the same median magnitude in each cluster and their absolute magnitudes should be the same in different clusters. This provides a method of distance determination.
8.	**4**, 224 (1918)	A summary of results bearing on the structure of the sidereal universe.	Globular clusters show the centre of the Milky Way system is 20 kpc distant. The diameter of the whole Milky Way is as much as 90 kpc. Globular clusters are not found close to the galactic plane. The brighter B stars form a local cluster inclined 12° to the plane of the Milky Way.
9.	**5**, 344 (1919)	The distances and distribution of 70 open clusters.	Distances to 70 open clusters are obtained from their angular diameters. The most distant is 16 kpc from the sun, much less than the most distant globular at more than 50 kpc. Possibility of some observation of distant open clusters is mentioned.
10.	**5**, 434 (1919)	Spectral type B and the local stellar system.	The distribution of the bright B stars in the Milky Way to form the 'local cluster' is discussed. (Now known as Gould's Belt.)
11.	**6**, 293 (1920)	Frequency curves of the absolute magnitude and colour index for 1152 giant stars.	The distribution over colour for 1143 red giant stars in 9 globular clusters is investigated. The brighter stars are redder. No star more luminous $M_{pv} = -6$ is found.
12.	**6**, 486 (1920) (with Helen N. Davis)	Summary of a photometric investigation of the globular cluster system M3.	Colours and magnitudes for 848 stars in M3 are discussed.
13.	**7**, 152 (1921) (with Beatrice W. Mayberry)	Variable stars in NGC 7006.	11 cluster variables in the globular cluster have a median photographic magnitude of 18.96 from which a distance of 69 kpc is found.

8.5.1 Shapley's calibration of the P-L law and the distances to the globular clusters

The techniques used by Shapley to determine globular cluster distances are described in paper 6 [86]. The logical steps in his reasoning

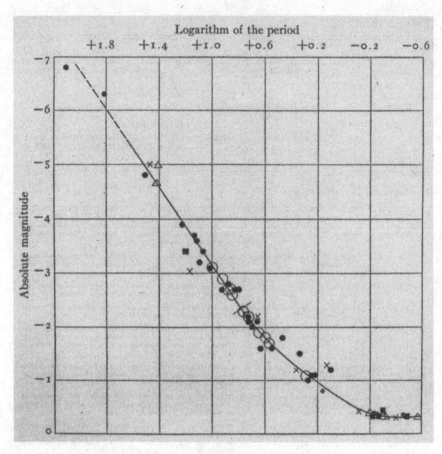

Fig. 8.6   Period-luminosity law for Cepheids according to Shapley, 1918.

are of considerable historical interest and are worth describing, especially as some reviews gloss over the critical points. His starting point was to find the absolute magnitudes of the Galactic Cepheids using the method of statistical parallax. His analysis was based on the proper motions and radial velocities of only 11 stars, two less than used by Hertzsprung or Russell† (see section 8.3.2). His mean absolute magnitude for all 11 stars was $\langle M_V \rangle = -2.35 \pm 0.19$, practically identical to the value found by Hertzsprung and Russell, which, as noted earlier, was in reality too faint as it ignored interstellar absorption.

These stars had a mean period of about 6 days, and Shapley found a few variables in the globular clusters with comparable periods, which

† He rejected the Cepheids κ Pav and ℓ Car because of their peculiar light curves.

he naturally assumed to be stars of the same type. The globular cluster ω Centauri had as many as five variables of this kind. In reality they were so-called Population II Cepheids (or W Virginis stars) which Baade in 1952 showed to be about $1^{m}.5$ fainter at a given period than the classical (Population I) Cepheids used for the calibration [87] and [88]. Only four clusters were known with these longer-period Cepheids ($P > 1$ d) so the next step was to use these clusters to determine the absolute magnitudes, first of the cluster variables, and secondly of the brightest red giants. From these absolute magnitudes distances to other clusters could be derived, provided the cluster variables and red giants were of the same luminosity in different clusters.

It so happened that Shapley's error in the zero-point of the galactic Cepheids owing to neglect of interstellar absorption roughly cancelled that from the assumption that W Virginis Cepheids have the same zero-point as the classical Cepheids in the galactic field, and Shapley's absolute magnitude for the cluster variables($M_{pg} = -0.23$ [86]) was therefore not greatly in error. The same comment applies to the red giants. Here he excluded the 5 brightest and took the mean M_{pg} of the next 25 in a given cluster. His result was about $1^{m}.3$ brighter than the cluster variables, or $\langle M_{pg} \rangle = -1.51 \pm 0.28$.

It is worth noting here that in 1916, even before Shapley had used the cluster variables as distance indicators for the globular clusters, Hugo von Zeipel obtained a distance for the cluster M13 based on a mean M_{pg} of $+0.5$. His result was 10 kpc for this cluster, very similar to the result of 11.1 kpc found by Shapley in 1918 [83]. (Von Zeipel's absolute magnitude was based on Hertzsprung's calibration of the Cepheid period-luminosity law together with Miss Leavitt's finding that cluster variables were $1^{m}.3$ fainter than the mean magnitude of the Cepheids used by Hertzsprung.)

The final step in Shapley's analysis was the calibration of the globular cluster angular diameters using 29 clusters with distances obtained from cluster variables and red giants. It might be expected that the angular size would vary inversely as the distance, but in fact Shapley discovered the further away clusters to be smaller, a result he ascribed to a photographic effect rather than anything intrinsic to the clusters themselves. In fact his neglect of interstellar absorption by dust, which is important for the more distant globulars, as well as systematic errors in Shapley's photographic magnitudes†, caused a systematic overestimate for the distances of the

---

† According to Jean Dufay (1896–1967) at the Lyon Observatory, Shapley also incurred systematic errors in his distances based on the magnitudes of individual stars in globular clusters [89]. Dufay instead used integrated cluster magnitudes as distance indicators and claimed that no dependence of linear dimensions or total luminosity of the clusters on their distance was the result. Systematic mag-

fainter clusters, yet Shapley steadfastly rejected the influence of interstellar material on his data on the grounds that blue stars were present in some globular clusters [80, 91]. The calibration of the angular diameters was now used for 41 further globular clusters where neither red giants nor cluster variables were observed [83]. Many were southern objects with angular diameters taken directly from the photographic atlas by John Franklin-Adams (1843–1912) [92]. The neglect of interstellar absorption in establishing this calibration was the third important error in Shapley's work, and resulted in the distances of the fainter globulars being substantially overestimated. Nevertheless, he obtained a distance of 20 kpc for the centre of the system of globular clusters in the constellation of Sagittarius, and at once identified this as also the centre of the Milky Way system which, according to Shapley, comprised the entire observable universe‡.

In January 1918 Shapley wrote to Eddington on his new concept for the universe:

> I have had in mind from the first that results more important to the problem of the galactic system than to any other question might be contributed by the cluster studies. Now, with startling suddenness and definiteness, they seem to have elucidated the whole sidereal structure ...
>
> The luminosity-period law of Cepheid variation – a fundamental feature in this work – is now very prettily defined. It is based on 230 stars with periods ranging from about 100 days to five hours. The measurement of the magnitudes necessary for the determination of the distances and space distribution of the clusters took a painful amount of stupid labor, but I am forgetting that for now we have the parallaxes of every one of them ...
>
> To be brief, the globular clusters outline the sidereal system, but they avoid the plane of the Milky Way ... [94]

This epoch-making discovery not only expanded the size of this universe by more than a factor of ten from that outlined by Kapteyn, but for the first time placed the sun at an eccentric location. That Shapley's result

---

nitude errors by Shapley were also investigated by Boris Vorontsov-Velyaminov in Moscow [90]. He showed that Shapley's magnitude scale was compressed, and corresponded to an intensity ratio $R = 1.615$ instead of the Pogson value of 2.512.

‡   Much later, Shapley conceded that his neglect of interstellar absorption was 'one of my blunders... I had the misfortune of finding some blue stars in the center of the Milky Way, in the northern Milky Way. On that too flimsy basis, I assumed there was no absorption in space, or very little... When I found it was false, I switched immediately to the truth – namely, that there's enough absorption in space to dim down my clusters. They were not as far away as my observations had indicated.' [93].

Fig. 8.7   Shapley's projection of globular cluster positions onto a plane
perpendicular to the Galaxy, 1918.

to the centre of the Milky Way was some $2\frac{1}{2}$ times too large† is perhaps
unimportant compared to the great significance of the new concept of
the structure of our Galaxy and our place within it, comparable to the
revolution of Copernicus with regard to the solar system. Shapley's was
easily the greatest triumph of stellar photometry, which after well over a
century from the time of William Herschel had finally come of age with the
birth of modern astrophysics.

Yet Shapley's was not the only study of the globular clusters in 1918.
At Lund Observatory Carl Charlier undertook an extensive study of the
distances of 75 globular clusters based on their angular diameters [96]. Like
Shapley he plotted their distribution in a plane normal to the plane of the
Galaxy, but unlike Shapley he considered them to be very nearby objects,
based on the spurious assumption that their dispersion above and below
the galactic plane should be the same as the B stars. On this basis Charlier's
globular clusters were all within 400 pc and the nearest, ω Centauri, was only
23 pc away, in the immediate solar neighbourhood. Charlier believed that

---

† For a modern account of the same problem see [95], where a distance of 8.5 kpc
is obtained for the centre of the globular cluster system.

the brightest stars in the globular clusters were low luminosity red dwarfs, a result diametrically opposed to Shapley's. Although his conclusions were so very wide of the mark, they illustrate the fickle nature of the data and the complexities of drawing reliable conclusions from the scant material then available.

8.6   Stellar photometry and the interstellar medium

8.6.1   The discovery of an interstellar absorbing medium

Evidence for the presence of an interstellar medium has been sought by four related lines of photometric research:

1. the general absorption of starlight in space
2. the dispersion of starlight in space
3. the reddening or selective absorption of starlight in space, and
4. the polarization of starlight in space

The first mention of the possible absorption of starlight was made by Jean-Philippe Loys de Chéseaux (1718–51) in 1744 [97] which, like the work of Wilhelm Olbers (1758–1840) some eighty years later, attempted to explain the darkness of the night sky by a general absorption of starlight in an otherwise infinite sidereal universe [48] (see also [49]).

The famous paradox named after Olbers was also discussed by Olbers in a letter to Bessel:

> I have recently sent to Bode's Jahrbuch a small essay on the transparency of cosmic spaces, in which, in my opinion, even if I have not demonstrated, but at least I have made it very probable, that the cosmic spaces are not absolutely transparent ... [98].

The question of a general absorption of starlight was taken up again by Wilhelm Struve at Pulkovo in 1847. He made a careful analysis of Olbers' paradox and concluded that light lost 1/107th of its intensity in traversing unit distance, taken to be the distance of first magnitude stars [50, see p. 87]. Struve's figure would amount to about 1^{m}/kpc absorption to account for the observed deficit of the faintest stars in the Milky Way. These references to an implicit general absorption were among the few to refer to an interstellar medium in the eighteenth and nineteenth centuries. The evidence was in any case largely spurious, as the conclusions were based on the erroneous assumption of a uniform distribution of stars in space.

The reference by William Herschel to 'vacant places' that were 'generally quite deprived of stars' [46] supported the idea that the dark nebulae of the Milky Way represented a true absence of stars. Two seldom-cited contrary viewpoints in the nineteenth century ascribed Herschel's vacant places to dark obscuring matter – one came from the future pioneer of stellar spectroscopy, Angelo Secchi in Rome in 1853 [99], the other from Arthur Ranyard (1845–94), a former secretary of the Royal Astronomical Society and editor of the journal *Knowledge* [100]. Neither generated much interest by their independent suggestions. Meanwhile Edward Emerson Barnard (1857–1923) at Lick and later Yerkes Observatories obtained long-exposure photographs of the Milky Way from 1889. He was always equivocal about the nature of the dark spaces, generally preferring Herschel's explanation, until, towards the end of his life, he found he had to accept that dark dust clouds must be obscuring the light of more distant stars [101]. Max Wolf (1863–1932) in Heidelberg had speculated that a dark region in Cygnus was probably due to obscuring interstellar material [102], a view endorsed by Heber Curtis on the grounds that stellar motions would have soon blurred the boundaries of any supposed vacancies of stars [103, 104].

If astronomers by 1920 had generally accepted that discrete dark clouds of obscuring matter must exist in the Milky Way, they were slower to agree that a general absorbing medium must pervade the plane of our Galaxy. Indeed Kapteyn had revived this idea in 1904 and from a statistical analysis he claimed to have found evidence for a general absorption of $1^{m}6$/kpc [105]. He also introduced the term 'selective absorption' for the reddening or colour excess introduced by the interstellar medium [106] and derived a value of $0^{m}66$/kpc for the increase in the colour excess with distance [107]. However, such statistical analyses of stellar colour in practice required much better data on intrinsic colours and their dependence on luminosity and metallicity than was at that time available.

Later both Jakob Halm at the Cape of Good Hope and Carl Schalén at Uppsala also attempted to derive values for the general absorption based on the statistics of faint stars. Halm found that $2^{m}1$/kpc was required to reconcile his star counts over the whole sky [108] with the apparent decrease in star density with distance from the sun. Schalén confined his study to A and B stars in the Milky Way and obtained $0^{m}5$/kpc also from photographic magnitudes [109].

By the time Sir Arthur Eddington delivered his influential Bakerian lecture to the Royal Society in 1926 on 'Diffuse matter in space' there was still no general consensus on the existence of a general absorbing medium nor of its nature [110]. Eddington believed a highly ionized gas pervaded interstellar space, but also suggested that dust particles of 'meteoric material' must be present, at least in the dark clouds to give the necessary high values of absorption that were found in these regions. Henry Norris Russell had

Fig. 8.8   Robert Trumpler.

also concluded that dust particles with size comparable to that of the wavelength of light must be present in the dark clouds [111, 112]. But in spite of these influential protagonists in favour of interstellar dust clouds, Shapley's equally influential finding that there is negligible reddening of stars in the direction of globular clusters such as M13 [80] meant that no agreement on a general absorbing medium was to be had.

The whole question of the existence of an absorbing interstellar medium in the Galactic plane was finally resolved in 1930 by Robert Trumpler (1886–1956) at Lick Observatory. Trumpler compared the photometric distances of stars in 100 open star clusters, based on their apparent magnitudes and spectral types, with distances estimated from the angular sizes of the clusters themselves [113]. The two distances could only be reconciled for the fainter clusters if a general absorbing medium in the Galactic plane were invoked, for which Trumpler derived 0^m67 of photographic extinction per kiloparsec and about half this amount for visual light. His study showed that the more distant clusters were also redder, thereby confirming that the absorption is both general and selective. He wrote:

> We are thus led to the conclusion that some general and selective absorption is taking place in our Milky Way system, but that this absorption is confined to a relatively thin layer extending more or less uniformly along the plane of symmetry of the system. Perhaps this absorbing material is related to interstellar calcium or to the diffuse nebulae which are also strongly concentrated to the Galactic plane [113].

Fig. 8.9 Trumpler's diagram showing the relation between open cluster distances from their angular diameter and those obtained by photometry.

A claim by Boris Vorontsov-Velyaminov in 1987 to have discovered the general absorption by the interstellar medium in 1929 a year before Trumpler [114] does not hold up to a close scrutiny of his paper, in which systematic errors in Shapley's globular cluster distances are demonstrated [90]. In fact Vorontsov-Velyaminov went no further than showing that reliable cluster distances are essential before any final judgement can be made on the presence of an absorbing medium.

In a second paper in 1930 Trumpler reviewed the evidence for the interstellar absorption of starlight [115]. He emphasized that the globular clusters and spiral 'nebulǽ', because they are observed at higher galactic latitudes than the open clusters, are largely unaffected by the absorbing medium, thereby accounting for Shapley's observation of no colour excess for globular cluster stars.

Robert Aitken, the Lick director, hailed Trumpler's work as 'one of the most important contributions to astronomical literature made during this year' [116]. It was a major landmark in the progress of astrophysics and based mainly on the results of photographic photometry. It is interesting to note that both van Rhijn [117] and Shapley [118] had attempted to investigate the general absorption in space using the data on the angular diameters of globular clusters – a technique practically identical to that of Trumpler, except they applied it to globular instead of open clusters. In both cases the conclusions were negative concerning an absorbing medium in interstellar space. Shapley wrote that '... the average obstruction up to distances of one hundred thousand light years is not in excess of half a magnitude, so that in these inter-stellar regions in and near our own galactic system we find space effectively clear' [118]. Had he worked with open clusters, Shapley's conclusion might have been very different.

In his second paper Trumpler had expressed some doubts that λ^{-4} Rayleigh scattering could account for the observed selective absorption, though he accepted that a layer of microscopic dust particles, a few hundred parsecs in thickness, was the most likely medium. Soon afterwards he concluded, from a study of the energy distributions in the photographic spectra of reddened and unreddened B stars, that Rayleigh scattering, which would be produced by particles much smaller than the wavelength of the light, was incompatible with his photometric data on open clusters in the Milky Way [119].

At the Pulkovo Observatory, Boris Gerasimovic (1889–1937) first proposed a $1/\lambda$ law for galactic O and B stars in 1932, though he appeared to prefer a reddening process intrinsic to the stars themselves rather than of interstellar origin [120]. The $1/\lambda$ law received support on theoretical and observational grounds from Carl Schalén at Uppsala Observatory. He applied the theory of scattering by solid spheres developed earlier by the German physicist, Gustav Mie (1868–1957) [121]. In Schalén's paper some evidence for a $1/\lambda$ law was found for dark clouds, but the data from photographic and photoelectric photometry gave no clear result for the general absorption or scattering throughout the galactic plane [122]. Theoretically, however, the $1/\lambda$ law would be consistent with Mie scattering from small metallic particles of a size comparable to the wavelength.

Further progress on the wavelength dependence of the selective absorption was made by the application of the Cs-O-Ag photoelectric cell to obtain multicolour photometry, notably by John Hall and Albert Whitford. This is discussed in section 5.5.2.

The discovery of the reddening of starlight by the interstellar medium in the Galaxy spurred interest among observers with photoelectric cells to investigate the colours of reddened stars. Those who made early contributions in this area were Wilhelm Becker in Berlin (see section 5.3.2), Stebbins and Huffer in Wisconsin (see section 5.3.5), Christian Elvey at Yerkes (see section 5.4.3), John Hall at the Sproul Observatory (see section 5.5.1), Arthur Bennett at Yale (see section 5.5.2) and above all Stebbins and Whitford at

Fig. 8.10   Trumpler's spectra of nearby and distant stars of the same (B0)
spectral type, showing the effects of interstellar extinction on the
ultraviolet.

Wisconsin (see section 5.5.2). All these programmes were undertaken in the
1930s with KH or Cs-O-Ag photocells.

8.6.2   The dispersion of starlight in interstellar space

The possibility that the presence of an interstellar medium might
be detected by its dispersive power on light rays travelling through it enjoyed
a brief and controversial airing in the astronomical literature of the early
twentieth century. The idea that the speed of light in interstellar space
might depend on its wavelength had originated with Arago, but was not
tested until 1908 when Charles Nordmann in France and G. A. Tikhoff
(1875–1960) in Russia independently claimed to have found the effect from
observations of binary stars.

Nordmann made his visual observations of eclipsing binaries through red,
green and blue filters (see section 3.9.2) and recorded the time differences
between the mid-eclipse of Algol in the three colours. The red eclipse was
claimed to occur 16 minutes earlier than that in blue light, indicating a

slower velocity (by about 150 m s^{-1}) for the latter rays [123]. λ Tau showed a three times larger time lag.

In the same year Tikhoff reported on his radial velocity studies undertaken with A. A. Belopolsky (1854–1934) at Pulkovo since 1896 on spectroscopic binary stars, including some Cepheids which were mistaken for binaries. For β Aur time lags of a given phase amounted to 10 to 20 minutes between blue (450 nm) and violet (400 nm) spectral regions [124]. Several other stars showed similar results.

Both scientists claimed their results provided evidence for a dispersing medium in interstellar space, and the wavelength dependence of the phase of light and velocity curves became known as the Tikhoff-Nordmann effect. The Russian physicist Petr Lebedev (1866–1912) at once criticized the claims of Tikhoff and Nordmann, attacking them on two separate fronts. First, he claimed that if light is dispersed in space, then it must also be absorbed, and he estimated the absorption would be so great that we would not even be able to see the sun, let alone any stars [125]! Secondly he found that the time lags between two wavelengths were not in proportion to the estimated distances, as would be expected on the dispersive-medium hypothesis. Thus RT Per was judged to be over 12 times as distant as Algol, but its time lag was nearly 3 times shorter than that reported for the nearer star. From this he concluded the dispersion theory to be invalid [126].

A lively discussion followed in the literature (see review in [127]). Henry Norris Russell at Princeton obtained the light curves of six eclipsing variables both photographically and visually, using data from Harvard [128]. Although five of these systems showed small but significant differences between the photographic and visual times of mid-eclipse, the differences in sign from one variable to another led him to reject the Tikhoff-Nordmann dispersion hypothesis. Perhaps the remarkable finding was that the speed of light was constant to within 1 part in 10^8 for the photographic relative to the visual rays.

The idea of interstellar dispersion was finally laid to rest by Shapley in 1922, from a study of the light curves of variable stars in M5 [129]. From the determination of 21 time lags between the photographic and photovisual curves, he found an insignificant time difference of 0.0004 ± 0.0008 days. He concluded:

> Radiations which differ in wave length by about twenty per cent, and in amplitude as well, can travel through space for 40,000 years without losing more than one or two minutes with respect to each other, if indeed there is any difference whatever [129].

Shapley found that the velocity of light differed by no more than 5 cm s^{-1} between these wavelengths; the sensitivity of his test arose from his use of a distant cluster and the rapid change in brightness of cluster variables. His conclusion might have been judged as less than definitive had the confinement of the interstellar medium to the Galactic plane been recognized at this time.

8.6.3   The discovery of interstellar polarization

The discovery of the polarization of starlight by interstellar particles is a fascinating example of a serendipitous event. Intrinsic stellar polarization was sought, but the unrelated and unexpected phenomenon of interstellar polarization was found.

As early as 1934 Yngve Öhman (1903–88) had suggested that non-spherical stars should have their light partially polarized [130]. He looked for such effects in the binary star β Lyrae and produced some inconclusive evidence of variable polarization of the light in the Hγ line, using a photographic spectropolarimeter on the Stockholm 40-inch telescope.

Some years later, in 1943, Öhman devised his so-called flicker photometer which incorporated a rotating polarizer in the beam of a photomultiplier photometer [131]. The amplitude of the a.c. signal from the tube at twice the rotation frequency of the polarizer measured the polarization of the source. The possibility of measuring the polarization of faint sources was discussed, but no data were reported.

Interest in the possible existence of stellar polarization was renewed in 1946 when Chandrasekhar predicted that up to 11 per cent polarization should occur from the limb of an early-type star with an electron-scattering atmosphere [132]. Such an effect might be detected in an eclipsing binary near the time of primary eclipse. At once both Edith Janssen [133] and Albert Hiltner [134] searched for this effect, in respectively U Sge and RY Per, using photographic polarimetry with a rotating Wollaston prism on the Yerkes refractor. Their results were at best marginal.

Meanwhile John Hall at Amherst was building a photoelectric polarimeter, which used a rotating analyser that produced a 30 Hz a.c. signal from a polarized light source [135]. Hall brought this instrument to the McDonald Observatory where he collaborated with Hiltner in August 1947 to search for polarization in the Wolf-Rayet eclipsing binary star CQ Cephei. The instrument was at first not entirely successful. By 1948 Hall had a position at the US Naval Observatory (with its 40-inch reflector), while Hiltner at Yerkes and McDonald had developed his own photoelectric polarimeter with a rotatable Polaroid analyser. Both observers worked independently from that time.

Two classic papers were published together in the journal *Science* in 1949,

Fig. 8.11 Albert Hiltner.

based on the separate observations of Hiltner and Hall using photoelectric polarimetry [136, 137]. Each independently found polarization of stars in the Milky Way at low latitudes. Hiltner had observed CQ Cephei and other stars. Some had polarization of up to 12 per cent and the planes of the electric vector were generally parallel to the Galactic equator. He at once concluded that 'the measured polarization does not arise in the atmospheres of these stars, but must have been introduced by the intervening interstellar medium. If this conclusion is accepted, a new factor in the study of interstellar clouds is introduced' [136].

Hall in his paper studied the colour dependence of the polarization and found this to be more or less independent of the wavelength [137]. Together with Alfred Mikesell (b. 1914) he observed over 175 early-type stars on the 40-inch reflector. It was shown that those with large interstellar reddening often had large polarization, although some reddened stars were not polarized at all; but conversely highly polarized stars were always reddened [138].

Even before this last paper had appeared, Lyman Spitzer (b. 1914) and John Tukey (b. 1915) at Princeton suggested that interstellar polarization could be associated with the alignment of needle-shaped ferromagnetic grains in interstellar dust clouds perpendicular to the Galactic plane [139]. Fields of about 10^{-5} gauss would be required.

Leverett Davis (b. 1914) and Jesse Greenstein (b. 1909) independently arrived at a similar theory involving grain alignment in a field perpendicular to the Galaxy [140]. By 1951 they had modified the theory once it was clear that a rapidly spinning grain ($\omega \sim 10^6$ rad/s owing to collisions with gas atoms) could not dissipate its energy by magnetic hysteresis losses in the time available between collisions. The theory was modified in 1951 to one in which elongated paramagnetic grains are rotating about their shorter dimensions on an axis parallel to the Galactic magnetic field in the plane of the Galaxy [141]. Small hysteresis losses were shown to dampen out the rotation about axes inclined to the field. This Davis-Greenstein mechanism thus satisfactorily accounted for the observations of polarization, and was proposed only two years after the discovery by Hiltner and Hall.

Further observations by Hiltner and Hall greatly extended the observational data pertaining to interstellar polarization. Hiltner published data for 841 stars in 1951 [142], for 41 stars towards the Galactic centre in 1954 [143] and for a further 405 mainly OB stars to 12th magnitude [144]. His observations were compiled into a polarimetric catalogue in 1956 [145]. Here it was shown that the interstellar polarization-to-extinction ratio (both in magnitudes) never exceeded 0.060 and the dependence of this quantity on Galactic longitude was plotted. A high value in the direction $\ell = 102°$ (towards Cassiopeia) indicated a line-of-sight perpendicular to the Galactic field and to a spiral arm (see also [146]).

Meanwhile John Hall in 1958 compiled a catalogue [147] giving the polarization for nearly 2600 stars. It comprised his own data and also those of Hiltner and of Elske van P. Smith (b. 1929) from Harvard, who had observed some 200 southern stars from the Boyden Station in South Africa [148].

Otto Struve, commenting on this early productive period in polarimetric photometry, wrote in 1962:

> It is regrettable, perhaps, that Hiltner and Hall did not combine their results but published them separately. Apparently their joint observation in August, 1947, was somewhat more convincing to Hall than to Hiltner. But in their subsequent, independent observations they have extended their earlier work in a most remarkable way, and reached substantially the same conclusions. The question of priority, which may seem important at the present time, no doubt will be submerged soon by the universal recognition this outstanding work deserves [149].

Other observers made significant contributions to interstellar polarization studies from the late 1950s onwards. Thus Alfred Behr (b. 1913) in Göttingen obtained the polarization data for 550 stars within 2 kpc of the sun, and estimated the increase of polarization with distance [150].

By 1972 two major programmes had been completed which included many stars in the southern Milky Way not previously observed. These were undertaken by Gerhard Klare (b. 1932) and his colleagues in Heidelberg, using the 50-cm Heidelberg reflector at the Boyden Station in South Africa to observe 1660 OB stars [151], and by Don Mathewson (b. 1929) and Vince Ford, who observed 1800 stars on the 61-cm telescope at Siding Spring Observatory in Australia [152]. These last authors combined the results for nearly 7000 stars obtained by different observers to show the distribution of interstellar polarization vectors in the Milky Way.

8.7   Galactic clusters and the HR diagram

8.7.1   Pioneering work of Hertzsprung and Russell

Henry Norris Russell (1877–1957) at Princeton and Ejnar Hertzsprung at Copenhagen and Potsdam each independently devised the diagram named after them in the years 1910–1913. Their starting points were quite different; Russell studied nearby stars, using trigonometric parallaxes (some were his own measurements from the time he visited Cambridge, England from 1902 to 1905) together with photometry and spectral types from Harvard to plot absolute visual magnitudes against the spectral type for nearly 200 stars. On the other hand, Hertzsprung's contribution was entirely photometric. He used apparent magnitudes and his own effective wavelengths (as a measure of colour) for stars in galactic clusters and plotted one parameter against the other to obtain the first cluster colour-magnitude diagram – see section 4.11.2†.

The relationship between these two astronomers is interesting. Russell presented his early ideas in August 1910 to a meeting of the Astronomical and Astrophysical Society of America at Harvard [154]. Karl Schwarzschild from Potsdam was also present and no doubt communicated the early results of his young colleague Hertzsprung to Russell. Hertzsprung's work on clusters was commenced in 1907 at the Urania Sternwarte in Copenhagen as an amateur astronomer, but he continued this work in Potsdam on taking an appointment there under Schwarzschild in 1908. It is probable that he had produced his first colour-magnitude diagrams by this time, which showed the dichotomy of red stars into those of high and low luminosity. Hertzsprung's famous paper on clusters appeared in the *Publications of the Potsdam Astrophysical Observatory* in 1911 [155] and gave the colour-

† The earlier finding by Charlier in 1889 [153] of a correlation between colour index and apparent magnitude for stars in the Pleiades was dismissed by him as being due to a systematic error in his photometry. A remarkable opportunity to plot the first cluster colour-magnitude diagram was therefore missed – see section 4.6.

Fig. 8.12   Colour-magnitude diagram for the Hyades, presented by Hertzsprung in 1911.

magnitude diagrams for four clusters: the Pleiades, the Hyades, Praesepe and the Coma Berenices cluster – see section 4.11.2. Later he extended the results on the Pleiades to magnitude 15 [156] and presented data for another cluster, NGC 1647 [157], in both cases using observations he obtained on the 60-inch telescope at Mt Wilson in 1912.

In 1913 Russell travelled to Europe. His first so-called Russell diagram (M_V versus spectral type) for nearby stars was presented at a meeting of the Royal Astronomical Society in London [158], but a published copy of the diagram did not come till the following year, after the December 1913 meeting of the American Astronomical Society in Atlanta [159].

Also while in Europe Russell met Hertzsprung for the first time in 1913, at the Bonn meeting of the International Solar Union. In his own articles relating to nearby stars, he readily acknowledged Hertzsprung's independent contribution on the colour-magnitude diagram for clusters. In spite of this, the diagram was widely known as the Russell diagram. Trumpler at times referred to the Hertzsprung-Russell diagram in 1925 [160] but it was not until 1933, when Bengt Strömgren (who, like Hertzsprung, came from Denmark) popularized the term in common use today [161, 162].

Thus by 1913 the foundations of the Hertzsprung-Russell diagram had been devised and its two most striking features were shown to be a main sequence (Hertzsprung's term) from luminous blue to intrinsically faint red stars and for late-type stars a 'collateral series' of more luminous stars, which marks the giant stars in the diagram, whereas the main sequence is populated by dwarfs. The terms 'giant' and 'dwarf' were used in 1913 by

Russell, who clearly recognized the relationship between the physical size of a star and its location in the diagram, although he erroneously ascribed these terms to Hertzsprung. At this time the relationship between colour (or spectral type) and stellar temperature was strongly suspected (from the work of Wilsing and Scheiner in Potsdam) though poorly established. A decade later, following the work of Saha on ionization, it was clearly shown that both colour and spectral type closely correlate with the temperature of a star's surface layers.

8.7.2   Trumpler and the classification of cluster HR diagrams

After Hertzsprung several observers studied galactic cluster colour-magnitude diagrams from about 1915. These included investigations by Seares for NGC 1647 [163], by Hugo von Zeipel and J. Lindgren for M37 [164], by Shapley and Myrtle Richmond for the Pleiades [165] and by K. Graff for the Pleiades [166] and, in subsequent papers, for several other clusters.

Shapley was certainly one of the most prolific observers of star clusters, although globular clusters were always his principal interest. Moreover he was surprisingly slow to recognize the significance of cluster HR diagrams for stellar evolution. In his major book *Star Clusters* [167], Shapley had broadly classified galactic cluster HR diagrams into the Pleiades and Hyades types, the former consisting entirely of main sequence stars, the brightest being of spectral type B or A, while the Hyades type of cluster contained some yellow or red stars of high luminosity. Shapley placed M67 in a separate category because of its predominance of red stars, including many red giants.

Robert Trumpler's classification of cluster HR diagrams was more comprehensive than Shapley's scheme. His interest in clusters dated from about 1918, during his time at the Allegheny Observatory [168, 169], and continued when he moved to Lick in that year. His paper of 1925 was a major contribution to galactic cluster research [160]. Here he proposed the term 'galactic cluster' for the first time as an alternative to 'open cluster' (because of their distribution close to the Galactic plane) and he introduced his two-dimensional classification of cluster HR diagrams. Class 1 had the giant branch entirely missing, while class 2 had a marked crowding of stars on the giant branch in addition to many dwarf stars (respectively Shapley's Pleiades and Hyades types). In addition classes b, a or f represented the spectral type of the brightest dwarfs and this parameter gave the second dimension in Trumpler's classification.

Trumpler noted that clusters in practice populate just four possible classes,

Fig. 8.13 Trumpler's diagram illustrating his scheme for the classification of
open clusters.

namely 1b, 1a, 2a or 2f. Typical examples were respectively the Pleiades
(1b), M34 (1a), the Hyades and Praesepe (2a) and finally NGC 752 (the
sole example of type 2f). Trumpler's paper was therefore more than a
classification, for it drew attention to the lack of red giant stars in those
clusters with early B-type stars on the main sequence.

In 1930 the scheme was extended in Trumpler's classic paper on galactic
clusters [113]. A class 3 was introduced for clusters in which giants predom-
inated over dwarfs, and intermediate classes 1–2 and 2–3 were also used.
For the second dimension the notation recognized types o, b, b–a, a, a–f
and f. In this scheme type 1b occurred the most frequently, followed by 2a
and 1–2b. He noted that

> ... open clusters which contain stars of highest temperature (types O
> and B) contain very few or no red or yellow giant stars (the few being
> generally supergiants); while clusters, in which types O and B are
> missing, most frequently contain an appreciable, or even a
> considerable number of stars in the giant branch [113].

The classifications of 100 clusters were presented in this work.

Trumpler recognized in his 1925 paper that his classification was relevant to the theory of stellar evolution. He surmised that the order of evolution was 2b → 2a → 1b → 1a → 1f. However, at this time the theory was dominated by the erroneous ideas of Lockyer and Russell. The correct interpretation of the cluster diagrams first required an understanding of nuclear processes in stellar interiors and was still some two decades in the future.

8.7.3   Clusters and the theory of stellar evolution

The development of spectral classification of the stars had a profound influence on theories of stellar evolution. Although the simplest concept involved the evolution of stars from the 'early' to 'late' spectral types, these ideas were refined by Normal Lockyer in the late nineteenth century. His scheme entailed stars forming as cool objects from 'meteoritic' material and gravitationally contracting with rising temperatures. After reaching a maximum temperature they then cooled off as they radiated away their thermal energy [170, 171].

Russell in 1913 further developed this theory [158, 172]. The youngest stars were supposed to be red giants which then evolved into more compact dwarf stars of early spectral type before descending the main sequence during the cooling stage of their evolution. The giant stars were known to be large and of low density in contrast to the small compact dwarfs, so the observational evidence provided by the new Russell diagram seemed for a time to give direct support to the theory of gravitational collapse of gaseous spheres as had been developed by Lord Kelvin, Helmholtz, Lane, Ritter and Emden.

This was the first attempt to relate stellar evolution to a star's changing position in the Hertzsprung-Russell diagram. In the event Russell considerably changed his ideas in the 1920s [173, 174] as new theories of stellar opacity, radiative transfer of energy and stellar energy generation were applied to stellar structure. Above all, it was Eddington in 1926, who, in his landmark book *The Internal Constitution of the Stars*, drew attention to the problem of the source of stellar energy [175]. Here he recognized that some form of subatomic energy must provide for the luminosity of the sun and stars, and that gravitational collapse alone was an inadequate energy source over the long time intervals required. He even considered that the annihilation of matter to produce energy might be required, but had no knowledge of how such a process might operate in stellar interiors.

Another important step came in 1926–27 when Heinrich Vogt and Russell independently deduced the theorem named after them, that the structure of a star, and hence its position in the Hertzsprung-Russell diagram, depends only on its mass and composition [176, 174]. Consequently an evolutionary track links the positions in the HR diagram of a star of given mass but different compositions which result from different ages. On the other hand stars of different mass follow different evolutionary tracks even though they start out with the same composition.

These ideas of Vogt and Russell were applied by Bengt Strömgren in 1933. He concluded that:

> One would therefore expect that the tracks of evolution in the HR diagram are the lines of constant mass. One would further expect that the hydrogen content decreases, so that the stars expand. Perhaps the simplest hypothesis that can be made is that the stars start as pure-hydrogen stars in which, in the course of time, hydrogen is transformed to complex elements, the energy radiated away in the successive equilibrium configurations being equal to the energy set free by the transformation. On this hypothesis the rate at which hydrogen is used up is given by the luminosity, and the course of evolution can be followed [162].

These theoretical ideas were applied by Gerard Kuiper to the observational data obtained by Trumpler on the HR diagrams of galactic and globular clusters [177, 178]. Kuiper produced a composite diagram for 16 clusters and transformed the coordinates into absolute bolometric magnitude (M_{bol}) and the logarithm of effective temperature ($\log T_{eff}$). He compared this work with the theoretical results of Strömgren and believed the empirical composite diagram showed the loci for clusters of different age owing to their different hydrogen content, whereas within a cluster the hydrogen content of the stars was the same. Such ideas were a significant advance, but they preceded any clear understanding of the nature of nuclear processes in stars and the fact that such processes were confined to the central core.

The two most significant advances in understanding the early stages of stellar evolution came in 1939 and 1942. First Hans Bethe (b. 1906) showed how hydrogen nuclei could be fused into helium to provide the energy for main-sequence stars [179] and then Mario Schönberg and S. Chandrasekhar (1910–95) showed that at the end of the main-sequence life of a star an isothermal helium core would form, surrounded by a hydrogen-rich envelope [180]. Such a core had a maximum mass of about 10 per cent of the star's mass if it was to support the envelope by ideal gas pressure. The restructuring of a star whose core had reached the Schönberg-Chandrasekhar limit corresponded to the rapid evolution of a more massive star across the Hertzsprung gap in the HR diagram to become a red giant on a Kelvin-Helmholtz time scale, as shown by the work of Allan Sandage and Martin Schwarzschild [181].

The first attempts to compute evolutionary tracks for stars based on hydrogen fusion processes were made by George Gamow (1904–68) [182, 183, 184], but his tracks essentially evolved up the main sequence in the HR diagram without forming red giants as evolved stars and hence were unable to account for the observations of galactic clusters. The problem arose from the assumption that main-sequence stars were fully mixed by convection and hence consumed all their hydrogen during this early phase.

The first successful post-main-sequence evolutionary tracks based on nuclear astrophysics were computed by Fred Hoyle (b. 1915) and M. Schwarzschild in 1955 and covered the evolution of low mass stars through to the stage of core helium burning [185]. For the first time a satisfactory agreement with the colour-magnitude diagrams of globular clusters was possible. At about the same time the initial evolution of more massive stars, as observed in some of the younger galactic clusters, was considered by Roger Tayler (b. 1929) [186, 187], by Sandage and Schwarzschild [181] and by R. S. Kushwaha [188].

8.7.4   Photoelectric photometry of galactic clusters in the 1950s

Even though Trumpler's work of 1925–30 was a significant milestone for galactic cluster research, the truly golden age for this work was the 1950s decade. The introduction of the photomultiplier tube was the stimulus that allowed a flood of high precision cluster photometry to be undertaken. Without doubt Harold Johnson from 1951 was the most productive observer of galactic clusters at this time, but major contributions were also made by Olin Eggen, Arthur Cox, Stewart Sharpless, Harold Weaver, Allan Sandage, Albert Hiltner, David Harris, Merle Walker, Halton Arp, James Cuffey and Nancy Roman (all Americans), as well as by Å. Wallenquist (Uppsala), by Klaus Bahnner (b. 1921) and Gerhard Miczaika (1917–89) (Heidelberg) and by Wilhelm Becker, J. Stock and G. Thiessen (Hamburg-Bergedorf) – see Table 8.2. Suddenly cluster photometry became one of the most popular branches of observational astronomy, spurred by the technical developments in photometric instrumentation on the one hand and by the theoretical breakthrough in understanding stellar evolution on the other.

The main developments in this decade were:

1. the use of three-colour photometry to determine the interstellar reddening to the cluster and the correction of colour-magnitude diagrams for the effects of reddening and absorption by interstellar dust,

Table 8.2. *Selected papers on photoelectric photometry of galactic clusters in the 1950s*

	Observer(s)	Cluster	Observatory	Reference	Notes
1.	Eggen	Hyades	Washburn, Lick	[189]	(P_{gp}, C_p) system
2.	Eggen	Pleiades	Lick	[190]	"
3.	Eggen	Coma, UMa	Washburn, Lick	[191]	"
4.	Wallenquist	Praesepe	Uppsala	[192]	
5.	Johnson, Morgan	Pleiades	McDonald	[193]	(P, V) system
6.	Eggen	Praesepe, M39	Lick	[194]	(P_{gp}, C_p) system
7.	Sharpless	Orion association	McDonald	[195]	UBV system
8.	Weaver	Coma	Lick	[196]	(P, V) system
9.	Johnson	Praesepe	McDonald	[197]	UBV system
10.	Bahner, Miczaika	Coma	Heidelberg	[198]	
11.	Johnson, Morgan	Pleiades, M36	McDonald	[199]	Defines UBV system
12.	Johnson	M39	McDonald	[200]	UBV system
13.	Johnson	NGC 752	McDonald	[201]	UBV
14.	Weaver	M39	Lick	[202]	(P, V)
15.	Harris	Pleiades	McDonald	[203]	(M_p, C_y) system
16.	Brownlee, Cox	NGC 6231	Goethe Link	[204]	
17.	Hogg	NGC 6025		[205]	
18.	Thiessen	Coma	Hamburg-Bergedorf	[206]	
19.	Johnson	M34		[207]	UBV
20.	Cox	NGC 2287	R. Observ. Cape	[208]	(P, V)
21.	Becker, Stock	11 clusters with O, B stars	Hamburg-Bergedorf	[209]	partly photographic
22.	Bappu	h and χ Per and surroundings	Lick	[210, 211]	(P, V)
23.	Harris, Morgan, Roman	IC 348		[212]	
24.	Hogg, Kron	IC 4665		[213]	UBV
25.	Roman	NGC 752		[214]	UBV
26.	Johnson, Sandage	M67		[215]	UBV
27.	Johnson, Knuckles	Hyades, Coma		[216]	UBV
28.	Johnson, Morgan	h and χ Per		[217]	UBV
29.	Cuffey, McCuskey	NGC 2169		[218]	UBV
30.	Johnson, Sandage, Wahlquist	M11	McDonald	[219]	UBV
31.	Heckmann, Johnson	Hyades		[220]	UBV
32.	Walker	NGC 2264	Lick	[221]	UBV
33.	Mianes, Daguillon	NGC 7243	Haute Provence	[222]	
34.	Walker	NGC 6530	Lick	[223]	UBV
35.	Arp, van Sant	NGC 4755	Goethe Link	[224]	partly photographic
36.	Walker	NGC 6940	Lick	[225]	UBV
37.	Arp	NGC 330 (SMC)	Goethe Link	[226]	
38.	Fernie	NGC 2547		[227]	
39.	Rohlfs, Schrick, Stock	NGC 6405	Boyden Station	[228]	UBV

2. the determination of more precise photometric distances to clusters,

3. the confirmation of stellar evolution theory from the distributions of stars in different cluster colour-magnitude diagrams, and

4. the determination of cluster ages using the results of this theory for the rates of stellar evolution.

The question of the ratio of total to selective absorption, which is the same thing as the ratio of interstellar extinction to reddening, was considered by Oort [229] as early as 1938, but using the early two-colour photoelectric photometry of Stebbins and Whitford – see section 5.5.2. Morgan, Harris and Johnson [230], Victor Blanco [231] and Hiltner and Johnson [232] all considered the ratio $R = A_V/E(B - V)$ in the UBV system and obtained values close to 3.0, notwithstanding the puzzling discovery by Stewart Sharpless (b. 1926) of an anomalously high ratio ($R \sim 6$) in the Orion association [195] – a paper published in 1952 even before the paper defining the UBV system had appeared! These authors either used the observed $1/\lambda$ reddening law combined with energy distributions and filter functions [231], or they considered the data for stars of the same spectral type and distance but different colour, due to variable reddening across the face of a given cluster, as in the double cluster h and χ Persei [232].

Knowledge of the ratio R allowed the interstellar extinction A_V to be obtained from the reddening $E(B - V)$, an essential step if the effects of interstellar dust particles on the photometry were to be corrected for. This was explicitly accomplished by Johnson for the galactic cluster M34 where the reddening of $0^{m}_{.}09$ in $(B - V)$ came from the photometry of 15 B stars [207]. In addition Johnson and Morgan showed how to define a reddening-free index $Q = (U - B) - 0.72(B - V)$ which correlated better with spectral type than either colour index separately [233].

The concept of a photometric distance (or parallax) is an old one; the method is basically the estimation of the distance of a celestial body from its apparent brightness and assumed luminosity. For stars in galactic clusters this becomes a powerful technique, given that the mean value for many stars can be obtained. Photometric parallaxes for galactic clusters were first derived in 1922 by Peter Doig (1882–1952), a British amateur astronomer and marine draughtsman, and independently by Sigfrid Raab, also in 1922, at the Lund Observatory in Sweden. Doig explicitly gave the relationship between absolute magnitude and spectral type for both dwarf and giant stars [234]. Comparison with the apparent magnitudes of cluster stars of the same type allowed parallaxes and distances to be derived. Results for fourteen galactic clusters were obtained [235] which were in excellent agreement with the parallaxes obtained by Raab [236]. Raab applied his technique to 39 galactic clusters. His method, which was less refined than Doig's, was essentially to find the mean apparent magnitude of B8–A5 stars (using Harvard spectral classifications) in these clusters. The distances then followed from the mean adopted absolute magnitude of such stars, taken to be 1.37.

Photometric parallaxes by main-sequence fitting and based on photoelectric photometry were derived from 1950, first by Olin Eggen (b. 1919) for the Pleiades [189], and subsequently by many others, most notably by Johnson [207] for M34, by Arthur Cox for NGC 2287 [208], by Johnson and

Fig. 8.14   Composite colour-magnitude diagram for clusters by Harold Johnson
and Allan Sandage, 1955.

Sandage for M67 [215] and by Johnson and Hiltner for NGC 2362, h and
χ Persei and the Orion association [237]. By 1956 Johnson had derived
photometric distances for 20 galactic clusters and given a careful summary
of the method using *UBV* photometry [238]. The probable errors in the
distances were about ±10 per cent. Johnson also showed how to correct
the photometric distances of galactic clusters for the effects of interstellar
extinction [207, 238]. A little paradoxically, a reddened cluster appeared
nearer, because the reddening made stars of a given observed colour index
appear brighter than otherwise.

Johnson emphasized that the relationship between absolute magnitude
and colour index could not be reliably established using nearby field stars
with trigonometric distances, because of a significant brightening of a star
during its hydrogen-burning main-sequence lifetime [216], which affects
the absolute magnitude of many main-sequence field stars. Johnson and
Knuckles thus introduced the concept of the 'original' or 'initial' main

sequence, later referred to as the 'zero-age main sequence' by Johnson and Hiltner [237], and which was derived by synthesizing the lower unevolved main sequences observed from several galactic clusters. Several authors produced refinements to this zero-age main sequence (e.g. Eggen using nearby stars [239] and both Sandage and Johnson using clusters [240, 238]) so that more reliable photometric distances could be obtained.

The method of photometric cluster distances is further complicated by the effect of chemical composition on the position of the zero-age main sequence, as was discussed by Sandage and Eggen [241]. This arises both because of a greater line blocking effect at shorter wavelengths, giving metal-poor stars an excess of ultraviolet light (and hence bluer colours), and because a difference in metallicity implies a different interior opacity and hence structure, which in turn is expected to make metal-poor stars have a less luminous zero-age main sequence [242, 241]. All photometric distances were measured relative to the Hyades but most clusters have at least a small ultraviolet excess relative to stars in this cluster. Sandage and Eggen showed how to correct for this presumed abundance effect to avoid a systematic error in the photometric distances for other clusters [241, 243]. A spectroscopic analysis of the metallicity of stars in the Hyades by Per Nissen in 1970 confirmed the higher value for stars in this cluster than for the sun by about a factor of two [244].

The study of galactic cluster colour-magnitude (or HR) diagrams from the 1950s provided a striking confirmation of the general predictions of stellar evolution theory. The composite HR diagram for sixteen clusters produced by Kuiper in 1936 and 1937 [177, 178] came too early for a proper theoretical interpretation. By 1952 Bengt Strömgren had summarized the main new developments in evolution theory, including the ideas of Chandrasekhar and Schönberg on core hydrogen exhaustion and post-main-sequence evolution. He cited the study of galactic cluster HR diagrams as a profitable means of confirming these ideas [242]. In particular he gave an expression for the time in years for a main-sequence star to exhaust its hydrogen in the core, which depended on mass and initial luminosity. Sandage and Schwarzschild gave the same equation a few months later [181]. Essentially this was $\tau = 1.1 \times 10^{10} \, (M/L)$ years (M, L are the mass and luminosity in solar units), which would allow cluster ages to be determined reliably for the first time, provided the mass and luminosity of the bluest main-sequence stars could be found.

The composite cluster colour-magnitude diagrams produced by Sandage and also by Eggen from 1955 were an excellent way of illustrating the observational evidence on stellar evolution [215, 245]. Each cluster provided a snapshot of the different evolutionary states found, and also ages were obtained for many of the clusters from the positions of their main sequence turn-offs. For M67 the age derived was 5×10^9 years, about the same as that of the sun [215]. At the time this was the oldest galactic cluster known.

The Johnson-Sandage composite cluster colour-magnitude diagram of 1955 displayed photometric results for seven galactic clusters as well as two globular clusters (M2, M92). The latter followed significantly different loci in the diagram owing to their greater still ages and lower metallicity than those of any galactic cluster. On the other hand the galactic clusters ranged in age from the very young double cluster, h and χ Persei (observed photoelectrically by Johnson and Morgan [217]) to the old galactic cluster M67. Johnson and Hiltner derived an age for h and χ Persei of 2–3 million years, based on the photometry of the massive upper main-sequence stars [237]. These authors also derived the same age for another young cluster, NGC 2362.

Merle Walker (b. 1926) at Lick made a special study of very young galactic clusters. His most striking result was for NGC 2264 which showed stars of type O7 to A0 on the zero-age main sequence, but later than about A0 the stars were some some 2^m above the zero-age locus [221]. He interpreted this finding as being due to the lower mass stars still gravitationally contracting to the main sequence prior to the onset of nuclear burning. During this relatively brief pre-main-sequence phase stars were predicted by Edwin Salpeter (b. 1924) to follow a track to the main sequence from above, similar to Walker's observations [246].

Sandage expanded his composite cluster diagram to ten galactic clusters in 1957 [240] and he used this to determine the main-sequence progenitors of the evolved red giants and supergiants found in many clusters, based on the evolutionary theory of Schönberg and Chandrasekhar [180]. By the late 1950s Louis Henyey (1910–70) and his collaborators at Berkeley had computed improved evolutionary tracks for main-sequence stars from which cluster loci or isochrones in the colour-magnitude diagram were predicted [247]. These early electronic computations allowed more reliable cluster ages to be determined.

Two very timely conferences, in 1957 and in 1962, brought together some of the leading astronomers active in cluster photometry and stellar evolution theory. The first was sponsored by the Vatican Observatory and discussed the subject of stellar populations [248]. Five years later at Lake Como the Italian Physical Society sponsored a meeting on stellar evolution [249]. Sandage attended both these conferences and gave succinct reviews on the latest results on the observational aspects of stellar evolution.

8.8   Physical stellar parameters from photometry

8.8.1   Stellar temperatures from photometry

The theoretical derivation of the energy distribution with wavelength for black bodies of different temperature by Max Planck in 1901 [250] opened the way for stellar colour temperatures to be obtained from photometry. The earliest results were from visual spectrophotometry by Wilsing and Scheiner at Potsdam from 1905 (see section 3.9.3) using five passbands and a prism spectroscope. This work was soon followed by the visual filter photometry of Charles Nordmann – see section 3.9.2.

Planck curves are known to give significant systematic errors for stellar temperatures, especially for early-type stars with large Balmer discontinuities. The size of the errors depended very much on the spectral regions selected and hence the early colour temperatures showed wide discrepancies between observers. The early photographic work on energy distributions by Adolf Hnatek in Vienna, Hans Rosenberg in Tübingen and Ralph Sampson in Edinburgh (see section 7.7) all incurred the same problems, as discussed in a review article by Alfred Brill in 1923 [251]. It was only after the behaviour of the Balmer jump had been fully explored that reliable stellar temperatures became possible. The main observational program in Balmer jump photometry was that of Barbier and Chalonge from 1934 (section 7.7.1), while the theoretical non-grey stellar model atmospheres first computed by McCrea in 1931 with the hydrogen photoionization opacity, showed how for A and B stars the energy distribution departed markedly from the black-body curves [252].

Thus by 1908 the fact that stars of different spectral type and colour represent a temperature sequence was generally well established and this was further confirmed in 1921 by applying Saha's equation for ionization in stellar atmospheres to the observations of line strengths in stellar spectra [253]. But a reliable and accurate scale of temperatures was not possible until new and careful photographic spectrophotometry by Greaves of Greenwich, Kienle in Göttingen and Robley Williams at Ann Arbor, Michigan during the 1930s (see section 7.7.2). In 1936 Antonie Pannekoek reviewed these results and considered that the A0 and M0 stars (in particular α Lyr, α Sco, α Ori) were the only points on the spectral-type scale where the effective temperatures (10 500 K for dA0; 3300 K for cM0) were well determined (to within 5 per cent), other than of course for the sun [254].

Gerard Kuiper's classic paper of 1938 reanalysed much of the available spectroscopic and photometric data on stellar temperatures [255]. Kuiper clearly differentiated between colour temperature (essentially a measure of the spectral flux gradient) and effective temperature, a measure of the surface brightness of a star integrated over all wavelengths. He attempted to correct the colour temperatures of W. Becker [256] and of Alfred Brill [257] to the scale of effective temperature and hence derive the mean T_{eff} values for spectral types from A to M for dwarf and giant stars. Thermocouple data from Pettit and Nicholson in the near infrared [258] (see section 6.7.2) were also included for the cooler stars, and in addition the results for six late-type giants with measured angular diameters were discussed.†

Kuiper's work gave the first reasonably accurate scale of effective temperature over a wide range of spectral type. When, nearly three decades later, Harold Johnson revised the stellar temperature scale from his multicolour $UBVRIJKLMN$ visual and infrared photometry (based on the eight available angular diameters or on black-body fits to the flux distributions), the corrections were generally no more than a few hundred degrees from the Kuiper scale, except at type A0 where Kuiper's 10 700 K compares with Johnson's 9850 K [259].

For early-type stars the interpretation of stellar colours was complicated by the presence of the Balmer jump and strong hydrogen lines in their spectra. A reliable scale of effective temperatures could only be derived after the computation of non-grey atmospheres had become sufficiently refined. Such models with the effect of the Balmer lines explicitly included were computed by Eugene Avrett (b. 1933) and Stephen Strom (b. 1942) at Harvard [260] and by Dimitri Mihalas (b. 1939) at Princeton [261]. Mihalas' work resulted in a comprehensive grid of Balmer-line-blanketed model atmospheres for spectral types B8 to F2 for which theoretical colours on the UBV system were calculated.

Thus the Kuiper effective temperature and bolometric correction scale remained as the principal calibration for these quantities for nearly three decades. The Mihalas and Johnson calibrations superseded that of Kuiper from the mid-1960s and Johnson's in turn was improved, especially for K and M giant stars, once many more stellar angular diameters by lunar occultation observations became available during the 1970s [262]. As shown in Table 8.3, the general trend has been to raise the adopted temperatures for red giant stars by a few hundred kelvin since the time of Kuiper's 1936 calibration.

---

† An angular diameter and a spectral energy distribution together allow the value of T_{eff} to be obtained.

Table 8.3. *Summary of the effective-temperature scale by Kuiper, Johnson and Ridgway et al. for late-type giant stars.*

Sp. type	T_{eff} (Kuiper)	T_{eff} (Johnson)	T_{eff} (Ridgway *et al.*)
G0	5200	—	—
G5	6420	5010	—
K0	4230	4720	4790
K5	3580	3780	3980
M0	3400	3660	3895
M5	—	2950	3420
M6	2750	2800	3250

8.8.2   Colour differences between giants and dwarfs

In 1897 Antonia Maury at Harvard drew attention to the appearance of the continuous spectra of her Group XV stars (now known as K stars) on objective prism plates. She wrote:

> The stars of this group appear to fall into two divisions, exhibiting a slight difference in the degree of absorption in the violet region … In the first, the general absorption is light; in the second it is more conspicuous … and beyond wavelength 3889 … the photographic spectrum generally appears to be suddenly cut off [263].

The effect was dismissed by Annie Cannon in 1901 as 'photographic effects, rather than real' [264], but the question was taken up by Kapteyn in 1909. He ascribed the loss of the violet region of certain K stars to the selective absorption of an interstellar medium, which rendered the more distant stars deficient in violet light [106].

By 1914 Walter Adams and Arnold Kohlschütter had found that the violet-deficient stars have small proper motions whereas those with a stronger violet spectrum were on average with larger proper motions [265, 266]. The main theme of their classic joint paper was the determination of spectroscopic absolute magnitudes. In short, they found the violet-deficient stars to be more luminous and distant giants, the others relatively nearby dwarfs. This work led to the debate on whether these differences were intrinsic luminosity effects in the stars themselves or due to an interstellar absorbing medium. The former solution was favoured by Adams and Kohlschütter, the latter by Kapteyn [267].

This problem was taken up independently by Bertil Lindblad at Uppsala and by Seares at Mt Wilson. Lindblad used effective wavelengths (see section 4.11.2) to find the colours, and concluded that

Fig. 8.15   Colour differences bewteen giants and dwarfs according to Bertil
Lindblad, 1918, using effective wavelengths as a colour index.

> ... the colour of a star is in an intimate relationship to its absolute
> magnitude; giants and dwarfs form two separate series in relation to
> colour. It's very important that the two series are so widely separated
> that, if the colour is accurately known, ... one can distinguish giants
> from dwarfs. In this way, a new method is opening up for determining
> the absolute magnitude of the stars ... [268].

A lecture by Seares, also published in the spring of 1918, based on colours
from his exposure-ratio method, came to a similar conclusion [269, 270].
The data were incorporated into a major paper by Seares in 1922 which
considered the energy distributions and colour indices of giant and dwarf
stars, the colours coming from Seares' Mt Wilson observations, the spectrophotometry from Potsdam [271]. Here Seares showed that for late-type
stars (types F5 to M) the giants were significantly redder and hence cooler
than the dwarfs. The effect was a maximum at K0, where the intrinsic
colour index difference was nearly half a magnitude. The colour index was
closely related to surface brightness and Seares wrote:

> The difference in surface brightness between giants and dwarfs is large,
> and cannot be neglected [271].

At the same time Ejnar Hertzsprung in Leiden considered a large body
of colour data (colour indices, colour estimates, spectrophotometry and

Fig. 8.16   Colour differences bewteen giants and dwarfs according to Frederick Seares, 1918, using his exposure ratio colour index. Open circles: giants; filled circles: dwarfs.

effective wavelengths) for 734 stars whose absolute magnitudes were estimated statistically from proper motions [272]. His data showed a similar dichotomy in the colours of late-type dwarfs and giants, interpreted in terms of the cooler temperatures for giants of a given spectral type. Neither of these papers ruled out interstellar reddening for more distant stars, but for the brighter relatively nearby objects used, the temperature effect was clearly dominant.

The effect of luminosity on the colour of cool stars was confirmed by other observers, including Cecilia Payne-Gaposchkin as part of her study of the colour indices of bright stars in the Harvard Standard Regions [273] and also an in-depth article by Ernst Öpik at the Tartu Observatory in Estonia [274].

A theoretical explanation for the luminosity affect was succinctly expressed by the Princeton astronomer John Q. Stewart (1894–1972) in 1923, based on Saha's ionization equation [275]. He wrote:

> ... a given degree of ionisation [on which the spectral types depend] should be reached at a lower temperature in stars of low density than of high density, and giant stars should be redder than dwarf stars of the same spectral type.

That the lower density stars were giants Seares himself had shown in his long paper in 1922 on stellar masses and densities [271]. He argued that giants are more luminous than dwarfs of the same surface brightness because they are much larger. On the other hand their masses are not much greater than those of dwarfs; therefore their densities must be much less.

8.8.3   Metallicity from photometric data

The idea that the heavy element (or 'metal') content of a star's outer layers might affect its colour is an old one. That the metallicity of the reversing layer should determine the strengths of the absorption lines in a spectrum was implicit in the early spectroscopic investigations of Kirchhoff and Bunsen in 1860 [276] on the sun, and of Huggins and Miller in 1864 [277] on bright stars. Given that the lines correspond to an absence of light at certain wavelengths, it was then a small step to surmise that a link between photometric colours and metallicity might exist. Indeed Huggins went so far as to suggest that differences in colour among the stars were due entirely to the different strengths of their absorption lines, and not at all to the influence of temperature, a conclusion which seemed concordant with the observation of many strong lines in the blue spectral region of the reddest stars.

George Ellery Hale (1868–1938) revived this idea of the effect of spectral lines on star colours in his book *The Study of Stellar Evolution* in 1908 [278]. He believed the yellow colour of the sun could be ascribed to the large number of lines at shorter wavelengths, which, if absent, would leave the sun with a bluish-white colour similar to that of Sirius.

These ideas were hardly exploited at all for nearly a century after they were first expressed by Huggins. Kapteyn recognized that star colour might depend on more than just temperature, and explicitly introduced a linear dependence of colour on absolute magnitude and distance to account for luminosity and interstellar reddening effects, but not on metallicity [106]. Given the lack of any quantitative data on stellar metal content, it is hardly surprising that no investigation of this effect was pursued.

Wilhelm Becker was one of the strong advocates for the application of multicolour photometry to problems in stellar astrophysics. His early investigation of the photographic two-colour diagram ($(m_{pg} - m_{pv})$ *vs.* $(m_{pv} - m_{pr})$) led him to discussing the departures of certain stars from the locus of normal stars in the diagram [279]. But there was no exploitation by him at that time to show the dependence of these effects on metal content, nor was there in his series of papers in 1946 proclaiming the benefits of his multicolour *RGU* system [280, 281, 282, 283].

Greenstein had also discussed the two-colour diagrams for Harvard Standard Region C4 as early as 1938, using photographic, photovisual and photored magnitudes [284]. He concluded that the deviations in colour

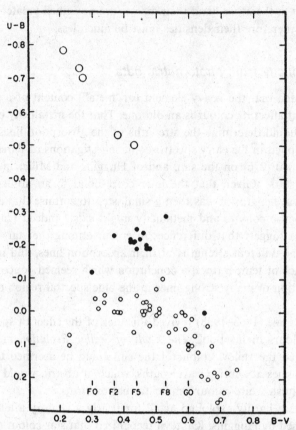

Fig. 8.17   Ultraviolet excesses of subdwarfs (filled circles) in the two-colour
diagram, shown by Nancy Roman, 1954. (The small open circles are
normal dwarf stars, while the larger open circles are heavily reddened
O or B stars.)

appeared not to be due to luminosity for the later-type stars he considered. However, it was not until 1954 that the proper interpretation of the
two-colour diagrams was made by Nancy Roman (b. 1925) at the Yerkes
Observatory [285]. She showed that a number of rare high-velocity F stars
identified as subdwarfs had ultraviolet excesses in the two-colour $(U - B,
B - V)$ diagram, and she was able explicitly to identify the cause of the
excess as being due to the weak metallic lines arising from the stars' low
metallicity.

Indeed the 1950s was the time when such an analysis for the first time
became possible, arising from the conclusion by Walter Baade that two

stellar populations exist in M31 [286], from the identification of high-velocity subdwarfs in the Hertzsprung-Russell diagram by Gerard Kuiper in 1948 [287], from the discovery of strong- and weak-lined classes among late-type stars by Nancy Roman in 1950 [288] and from the quantitative analysis of two subdwarf spectra by Lawrence Aller (b. 1913) and Joseph Chamberlain (b. 1928) in 1951. Since Kuiper, Greenstein (until 1948), Aller, Chamberlain and Roman were all at Yerkes at this time, together with Johnson and Morgan (the originators of the UBV photoelectric system and of the two-colour $(U-B, B-V)$ diagram [199]) and Bengt Strömgren (who devised a forerunner of the widely used $uvby$ system in the late 1950s while at Yerkes [289]), an extraordinarily fertile range of talented individuals, all experts in stellar photometry or spectroscopy, were interacting together in one place.

Nancy Roman's catalogue of about 600 high-velocity stars in 1955 provided further evidence for the ultraviolet excesses for members of these Population II objects, the values reaching up to about $0^{m}\!.2$ for those with the weakest lines [290]. This at once opened the way for further detailed abundance analyses of these weak-lined stars using high dispersion spectra, for example by Bodo Baschek in Kiel [291], by Aller and Greenstein (by then at Caltech) in 1960 [292] and by Arnold Heiser at Yerkes [293]. In addition George Wallerstein (b. 1930) at Caltech and later Berkeley analysed the spectra of 31 solar-type dwarfs, including some metal-poor ones, which, together with earlier analyses for subdwarfs in the literature, gave the first reliable empirical calibration of the ultraviolet excess from photometry in terms of the deficiency of heavy elements in these stars [294, 295].

The question of subdwarf colours was of wider interest than a means of demonstrating their low metallicity. Whether they truly follow a separate sequence in the luminosity *vs.* effective temperature diagram was a topic of some debate. After carefully correcting the colours for the effects of low metallicity, Martin Schwarzschild, Leonard Searle and R. Howard concluded they indeed lay about one magnitude below the main sequence for normal stars [296]. However, this conclusion was doubted by Robert Wildey and his colleagues at Mt Wilson, after carefully correcting the UBV colours for the effects of the weak subdwarf lines [297], in spite of the earlier theoretical conclusion by Anders Reiz (a Swedish astronomer working at Yerkes under Bengt Strömgren) that metal-poor stars should follow a subdwarf sequence about a magnitude below the main sequence in the HR diagram [298].

The benefits of investigating the effects of spectral line strength on photometry using narrow passbands were emphasized by Griffin and Redman at Cambridge in 1960 [299]. In this paper, the first in a series from the Cambridge Observatories, the coudé spectrograph on the 36-inch telescope was used to select narrow passbands (30 to 50 Å) centred on selected spectral features. The signal in these bands and the adjacent continuum was recorded with a photon-counting photoelectric photometer. In the first paper violet CN and CH(G) molecular bands were observed in over 700 late-type stars. In later papers by Deeming, Griffin, Peat, Scarfe and Price other lines were studied, such as Hα, NaD, Mgb and FeI (525 nm). However, the extensive data obtained were primarily sensitive to luminosity and temperature. The strong spectral features were generally too saturated to show abundance effects.

A similar photoelectric technique to that used at Cambridge was, however, exploited by Per Nissen, using a group of weak iron lines in a 0.35 nm wide band at 480.0 nm, following a suggestion by Bengt Strömgren [300]. The observations were made on the McMath solar telescope at Kitt Peak Observatory and iron abundance data were obtained for the Hyades and other F and G field stars. Hyron Spinrad and Benjamin Taylor at Lick also devised a programme of narrow-band spectrophotometry in the late 1960s, in which 16 different spectral features from 380 to 920 nm were observed, including CN, CH, CaI (427 nm), Mgb, NaD and Balmer lines and from which Ca, Mg and Na element abundances were derived for late-type stars [301].

As for more traditional filter photometry, Bengt Strömgren was one of those who was quick to realize the value of narrower passbands for studies of stellar metallicity. During his time as director of Yerkes and McDonald Observatories (1951–57) he devised a six-colour photometric system using mainly interference filters of width about 10 nm [289]. Strömgren used a violet e filter at 403 nm where there are many metallic lines in F stars. He defined a metallicity index $m = (e(403 \text{ nm}) - d(450 \text{ nm})) - (d(450 \text{ nm}) - a(500 \text{ nm}))$ as the difference of two colour indices, which was sensitive to metal content but relatively less so to effective temperature, surface gravity or interstellar reddening (see also [302]). This intermediate-band photoelectric system evolved into the $uvby$ system in the early 1960s when Strömgren was at Princeton. The index $m_1 = (v-b)-(b-y)$, after correction for reddening, was shown by Strömgren to be a good indicator of metal abundance, and especially for subdwarf stars of intermediate (F to early G) spectral type, such as HD 19445 [303].

8.8.4   Stellar populations and photometry

The years from the mid-1940s to the early 1960s were eventful and productive ones for stellar astrophysics. The concept of stellar populations, the great increase in observational data on cluster colour-magnitude

Fig. 8.18   Walter Baade's schematic Hertzsprung-Russell diagram showing the locations of stars of populations I (shaded) and II (hatched), 1944.

diagrams, the first real understanding of stellar evolution and the rôle of nuclear processes in stars and an understanding of the relationship of stars to the evolution of the Galaxy as a whole all occurred during these two decades.

Walter Baade's conclusion that stars in the Andromeda galaxy can be conveniently classified into two populations designated as I (characterized by OB stars and galactic clusters) or II (by cluster variables and globular clusters) marks the beginning of this era [286]. Baade's conclusions rested almost entirely on photographic photometry of stars in M31 and in its two dwarf satellite galaxies. His deep red plates with the Mt Wilson 100-inch telescope owe their success in part to the dark skies resulting from the war-time blackout in Los Angeles, and they enabled the absolute magnitudes and colours of the brightest stars in these systems to be derived. The extension of the classification to stars in our own Galaxy was, however, explicitly made. Indeed, much of the evidence for such a classification within the Galaxy was already available; for example, Shapley and Trumpler had both drawn attention to the very different colour-magnitude diagrams of open and globular clusters, while Oort [304] had discussed the properties of the so-called high velocity stars, noting in particular the absence of luminous blue stars from this group.

When the Vatican Observatory sponsored a conference on stellar populations in 1957, most of the leading observers and theoreticians on stellar evolution were brought together for a productive exchange of views – they included Baade, Sandage, Oort, Schwarzschild, Hoyle and Morgan. At this meeting Baade was able to draw attention to the correlation of population type with age, metallicity and interstellar dust content [305], while Jan Oort reviewed the different dynamical properties of stars in the two populations [306]. He also proposed a finer subdivision into five population categories, namely halo population II, intermediate population II, disk population, intermediate population I and extreme population I.

The discussion in 1962 by Olin Eggen, Donald Lynden-Bell (b. 1935) and Allan Sandage of the evidence for the early collapse of the Galaxy to a disk can be regarded as the culmination of this active post-war era in stellar and galactic evolution [307]. Once again photometry played a major rôle in the observational data supporting these authors' conclusions. In particular they showed how the ultraviolet excess, as determined on the UBV system, and which indicated a deficiency of heavier metallic elements in a star, correlated well with a star's galactic dynamics, including the orbital eccentricity, the velocity component at right angles to the Galactic plane and the orbital angular momentum per unit mass.

Thus the concept of stellar populations, which was introduced by Baade using a purely photometric definition, was extended to include a variety of additional kinematic, spectroscopic and photometric properties of stars. And finally all these properties were united by Eggen, Lynden-Bell and Sandage into a grand synthesis of Galactic evolution. Many astronomers had contributed to this result, yet it was probably the most significant triumph for stellar photometry since Shapley had deduced a photometric distance to the Galactic centre from his studies of globular clusters in 1918.

8.9   Russell and Shapley and the analysis of eclipsing-binary photometry

Eclipsing-binary stars provided one of the earliest and most fertile areas for the application of astrophysics to photometric data. The subject is dominated by the papers of Henry Norris Russell in the *Astro-*

physical Journal of 1912. A brief review of the early observational work on eclipsing binaries precedes a discussion of Russell's work.

8.9.1   John Goodricke and Algol

The story of the discovery of the periodicity of the magnitude changes of Algol (β Persei) by the young John Goodricke (1764–86) of York in England is one of the most celebrated in variable star history. He observed the star regularly from November 1782 to May 1783 and found that the brightness declined abruptly from second to fourth magnitude in nearly $3\frac{1}{2}$ hours, before recovering in about the same time interval, and recurring with a period of about 2 days, 20 hours and 45 minutes [308].

Although the variability of Algol was already known from the observations of Geminiano Montanari (1632–1687) in Bologna from 1667–70 [309], it was the discovery of the periodicity and its interpretation by Goodricke which represent an outstanding and very early analysis of stellar photometric observations. Goodricke wrote:

> If it were not too early to hazard even a conjecture on the cause of
> this variation, I should imagine it could hardly be accounted for
> otherwise than either by the interposition of a large body revolving
> around Algol, or some kind of motion of its own, by which part of its
> body, covered with spots or such like matter, is periodically turned
> towards the earth [308].

This bold suggestion represents the first discovery of an eclipsing binary. The alternative explanation of a rotating spotted star is, however, also interesting and was much later invoked to account for RS Canum Venaticorum and its variability. Confirmation had to await the spectroscopic velocity observations of Vogel in 1889 [310]. The second system of this type to be found, β Lyrae in 1785, was also a Goodricke discovery [311]. Meanwhile Goodricke's ideas remained largely ignored for nearly a century. Herschel apparently did not favour the eclipse hypothesis, but a fairly detailed analysis by William Sewell in Cambridge in 1791 remained unpublished until it was discovered in the Maskelyne papers at Greenwich by Olin Eggen in 1957 [312]. Sewell reasoned that Algol was most probably a double star comprising two sun-like objects in a mutual orbit seen edge-on from the earth.

This idea was revived in 1870 by Thomas Aldis (1843–1908), a recent graduate from Trinity College, Cambridge, who deduced a diameter ratio of 5 to 4 for the two objects [313], and soon afterwards by Edward Pickering at Harvard [314]. The year 1880 represents the start of the modern era for the photometric study of eclipsing binaries. Pickering, Searle and Wendell obtained visual meridian photometry on Algol and U Cephei [315], but in neither case was a complete light curve obtained. Oliver Wendell continued eclipsing binary photometry at Harvard on the 15-inch refractor using one of Pickering's early polarizing photometers in the 1890s and until about 1910, obtaining a complete light curve for U Pegasi and data for twelve additional systems [316]. Wendell's observations were analysed by G. W. Myers in Munich in 1898, but he was unsuccessful in obtaining any solution for the system's geometry [317]. Alexander Roberts in South Africa also attempted modelling the light curves of U Peg and RR Cen, but failed to obtain definitive solutions [318, 319].

8.9.2   The Russell model

Henry Norris Russell at Princeton in 1912, working in part with his doctoral student Harlow Shapley, published four classic papers on a general solution for eclipsing binary light curves [320, 321, 322, 323]. The problem is a geometrical one, but complex because of the large number of variables governing both the elements of the orbit as well as the sizes, non-spherical shapes and luminosities of both stars and also their limb darkening, gravity darkening and 'reflection' effects. The Russell model assumed tidal distortion caused the stars to be prolate spheroids aligned along their major axes, and the limb darkenings were either both zero (uniformly bright disks) or one (completely dark at the limb). With these simplifying assumptions Russell showed how in principle the light curves of binaries, provided they were not too close to each other, could be solved. Even so the solution required numerical tabulations of transcendental functions, and a rectification of the observed photometry to allow for proximity effects such as the reflection effect and the ellipsoidal shape of the stars.

The Russell model was first used by Russell for the analysis of W Del, W UMa and W Cru in 1912 [324], and this was followed a few years later by the results for 90 systems by Shapley for his doctoral thesis based on a wide variety of visual, photographic and selenium photocell photometry [325]; see also [326]. This enormous undertaking represents one of the first major applications of physical analysis to stellar photometric data, coming as it did only a few years after the first stellar temperatures were derived by Wilsing and Scheiner from stellar colours – see section 8.8.1.

The importance of the Russell model was that for the first time a direct measurement of stellar sizes became possible, and hence also of densities. Shapley's data gave clear evidence for later-type components in binary systems being either much less dense than the sun or of comparable density to the sun, a result which tied in very satisfactorily with the dichotomy in late-type luminosities found by Hertzsprung and Russell from their colour (or spectral-type) *versus* magnitude diagrams. In addition clear evidence for limb darkening, already well observed in the sun, was found for many of these systems, as well as evidence for the non-spherical shape of the stars, especially for the closer binary systems.

This highly productive era in the analysis of eclipsing binary photometry by Russell and Shapley has been eloquently described by Zdeněk Kopal in his book of personal reminiscences:

> The time when Shapley came to Princeton could not have been more opportune. Shortly before, Russell had embarked on a new approach to the problem of the analysis of the light curves of eclipsing variables for the characteristics of the constituent stars – a problem directed at the very heart of stellar astrophysics, and one which also remained closest to Russell's own heart till the evening of his life. The arrival of a research student of Shapley's calibre at this juncture was a godsend to Russell as well; and although Russell still had more than a third of a century to teach, Harlow Shapley, his junior by only eight years, remained without doubt his most distinguished pupil.
>
> Thousands of published observations of eclipsing variables were available in 1912 for analysis by the new methods. Aided by his never-absent slide-rule, and unimpeded by any excess of mathematical punctilio, Russell was the trail-blazer; but without the energy with which Shapley applied the new methods to practical cases, the new methods would not have got off the ground. Shapley's Ph.D. thesis in 1914 (*Princeton Observatory Contribution* number 3) on the orbits of 90 eclipsing binaries virtually created at a stroke a new branch of double-star astronomy [327].

8.9.3   Eclipsing-binary photometry 1912–1940

Although Russell was not an observer, he was not simply a theoretician either, but a consummate practitioner in the art of data analysis. He was able to rely on a wealth of observational material coming from Harvard (especially from Oliver Wendell and Henrietta Leavitt) and elsewhere, including from his colleague at Princeton, Raymond Smith Dugan (1878–1940). In the years from 1911 to 1940 Dugan was to become one of the best known photometric observers of eclipsing binaries, using the Princeton polarizing visual photometer. He also published the first finding list for eclipsing binaries in 1934 [328], which catalogued photometric data for 269 systems. The growth of the subject in the following years can be gauged from the second list in 1947 by Newton Lacy Pierce [329], with about twice as many objects.

Other prominent eclipsing binary observers who benefitted from the greatly increased demand for photometric data after Russell's theoretical analysis were Joel Stebbins and Albert Nijland. Stebbins' famous paper with his selenium photoconductive cell, in which he first observed the shallow secondary eclipse of Algol, is discussed in section 5.2 [330]. The secondary eclipse depth was only $0^{m}06$, showing the companion not to be a completely dark object. Indeed the companion was shown to have a reflection effect, being significantly brighter over the hemisphere facing the primary. Eclipsing-binary photometry remained a high priority for Stebbins in his later photoelectric work at Illinois and Wisconsin.

Meanwhile the director of the Utrecht Observatory, Albert Nijland (1868–1936), was a prolific observer of variable stars, providing a large number of visual estimates, which were used in Shapley's thesis for as many as 18 systems.

The observation and analysis of close binary stars was by the 1930s a large and growing area of astrophysics, which extended well beyond the field of photometric astronomy, even though photometry was an essential element in its development. One further theoretical result merits a mention here, namely the finding by Russell that a close eclipsing binary in which the stars are not point masses should display apsidal motion [331]. This is a rotation of the major axis or apse line of an eccentric orbit. Russell showed that tidally interacting stars should show this effect, which can be demonstrated from eclipse timings. In principle, information on the degree of central mass concentration of the stars should be forthcoming from the apsidal period. Russell cited some preliminary evidence for apsidal motion for the eclipsing system Y Cygni, for which he deduced a ratio of central-to-mean density of six. A decade later Thomas Cowling (1906–1990), at about the time he took up a mathematics lectureship at the University of Manchester, corrected Russell's analysis so as to take into account the changes in the tidal distortion of the stars as they moved in their elliptical orbit, which had the effect of increasing the central mass concentration required to achieve a given apsidal period [332]. Similar results were obtained by T. E. Sterne at Harvard a year later [333]. Russell then applied the refined theory to the observational data for 19 eclipsing systems for which the mass distributions were considered to be those of gaseous polytropes. For the best observed cases the ratio of central-to-mean density now came to values in the range from 48 to 460 [334].

References

[1] Bailey, S.I., *Astrophys. J.*, **10**, 255 (1899).

[2] Bailey, S.I., *History and Work of the Harvard College Observatory*, McGraw-Hill, New York, London (1931). See p. 181.

[3] Pickering, E.C., *Harvard Coll. Observ. Circ.*, **2** (1895).

[4] Bailey, S.I., *Harvard Coll. Observ. Circ.*, **33** (1898).

[5] Pickering, E.C., *Astron. Nachr.*, **123**, 207 (1889).

[6] Packer, D.E., *Sid. Messenger*, **9**, 381 (1890); *ibid.*, *English Mechanic*, **51**, 378 (1890).

[7] Packer, D.E., *Sid. Messenger*, **10**, 107 (1891); *ibid.*, *English Mechanic*, **52**, 80 (1891).

[8] Common, A.A., *Mon. Not. R. Astron. Soc.*, **50**, 517 (1890).

[9] Pickering, E.C., *Astron. Nachr.*, **140**, 285 (1896).

[10] Barnard, E.E., *Astron. Nachr.*, **147**, 243 (1898).

[11] Pickering, E.C., *Harvard Coll. Observ. Circ.*, **33** (1898).

[12] Bailey, S.I., *Ann. Harvard Coll. Observ.*, **38**, 1 (1902).

[13] Bailey, S.I., *Ann. Harvard Coll. Observ.*, **78** (Part 1), 1 (1913).

[14] Bailey, S.I., *Ann. Harvard. Coll. Observ.*, **78** (Part 2), 99 (1917).

[15] Bailey, S.I., *Ann. Harvard Coll. Observ.*, **78** (Part 3), 195 (1919).

[16] Bailey, S.I., *Harvard. Coll. Observ. Circ.*, **193** (1916).

[17] Bailey, S.I., *Ann. Harvard Coll. Observ.*, **76** (No. 4), 43 (1916).

[18] Pickering, E.C., *Harvard Coll. Observ. Circ.*, **79** (1904).

[19] Pickering, E.C., *Harvard Coll. Observ. Circ.*, **82** (1904).

[20] Pickering, E.C., *Harvard Coll. Observ. Circ.*, **96** (1905).

[21] Leavitt, H.S., *Ann. Harvard Coll. Observ.*, **60** (No. 4), 87 (1908).

[22] Cannon, A.J., *Ann. Harvard Coll. Observ.*, **55** (No. 1), 1 (1907).

[23] Pickering, E.C., *Harvard Coll. Observ. Circ.*, **173**, 1 (1912).

[24] Boss, L., *Preliminary General Catalogue of 6188 Stars for the epoch 1900*, Washington: Carnegie Institution (1910).

[25] Hertzsprung, E., *Astron. Nachr.*, **196**, 201 (1913).

[26] Kapteyn, J.C., *Publ. Astron. Lab. Groningen*, No. 8, 1 (1901).

[27] Hertzsprung, E., *Zeitschr. für Wiss. Photog.*, **3**, 429 (1905).

[28] Hertzsprung, E., *Zeitschr. für Wiss. Photog.*, **5**, 86 (1907).

[29] Kapteyn, J.C., *Publ. Astron. Lab. Groningen*, No. 11, 1 (1902).

[30] Russell, H.N., *Science*, **37**, 651 (1913).

[31] Russell, H.N., *Publ. Astron. Astrophys. Soc. Amer.*, **2**, 174 (1915).

[32] Belopolsky, A.A., *Astron. Nachr.*, **136**, 287 (1894). See also *Astrophys. J.*, **1**, 160 (1895) for English translation.

[33] Ritter, A., *Ann. Physik und Chemie*, **8** (2), 157 (1879).

[34] Brunt, D., *Observatory*, **36**, 59 (1913).

[35] Shapley, H., *Astrophys. J.*, **40**, 448 (1914).

[36] Ludendorff, H., *Astron. Nachr.*, **193**, 304 (1912).

[37] Moulton, F.R., *Astrophys. J.*, **29**, 257 (1909).

[38] Eddington. A.S., *Observatory*, **40**, 290 (1917).

[39] Eddington, A.S., *Mon. Not. R. Astron. Soc.*, **79**, 2, 177 (1918).

[40] Baade, W., *Astron. Nachr.*, **228**, 359 (1926).

[41] Bottlinger, K.F., *Astron. Nachr.*, **232**, 3 (1928).

[42] Baade, W., *Zeitschr. für Astrophys.*, **19**, 289 (1940).

[43] van Hoof, A., *Mededeelingen Koninklijke Vlaamsche Academie voor Wetenschappen*, **5** (No. 12) (1943).

[44] Wesselink, A.J., *Bull. Astron. Inst. Netherlands*, **10**, 91 (1946).

[45] Perrine, C.D., *Astrophys. J.*, **50**, 81 (1919).

[46] Herschel, W., *Phil. Trans. R. Soc.*, **74**, 437 (1784).

[47] Herschel, W., *Phil. Trans. R. Soc.*, **75**, 213 (1785).

[48] Olbers, W.H.M., *Bode's Berliner astronomiches Jahrbuch für das Jahr 1826: Über die Durchsichtigkeit des Weltraums*, pp. 110–131, Berlin (1823).

[49] Jaki, S.L., *J. Hist. Astron.*, **1**, 53 (1970).

[50] Struve, F.G.W., *Études d'astronomie stellaire: sur la voie lactée et sur la distance des étoiles fixes*, St Pétersburg, Acad. Imp. des Sciences (1847).

[51] Herschel, J., *Outlines of Astronomy*, Longman, Brown, Green and Longmans (1849). See article 798, p. 537.

[52] Proctor, R.A., *Mon. Not. R. Astron. Soc.*, **32**, 1 (1871).

[53] Celoria, G., *Pubbl. del Reale Osserv. di Brera in Milano*, No. **3**, 1 (1877).

[54] Schiaparelli, G., *Pubbl. del Reale Osserv. di Brera in Milano*, No. **34**, 1 (1889).

[55] Easton, C., *Astrophys. J.*, **1**, 136 (1900).

[56] von Seeliger, H., *Abhandl. der König. Bayer. Acad. der Wiss. in München, II. Klasse*, **19** (Part 3) (1898).

[57] von Seeliger, H., *Abhandl. der König. Bayer. Acad. der Wiss. in München, II. Klasse*, **25** (Part 3) (1909).

[58] Schwarzschild, K., *Astron. Nachr.*, **190**, 361 (1912).

[59] Kapteyn, J.C., *Plan of Selected Areas*, Groningen (1906).

[60] Pickering, E.C. and Kapteyn, J.C., *Ann. Harvard. Coll. Observ.*, **101**, 1 (1918).

[61] Pickering, E.C., Kapteyn, J.C. and van Rhijn, P.J., *Ann. Harvard. Coll. Observ.*, **102**, 1 (1923).

[62] Pickering, E.C., Kapteyn, J.C. and van Rhijn, P.J., *Ann. Harvard. Coll. Observ.*, **103**, 1 (1924).

[63] Kapteyn, J.C., van Rhijn, P.J. and Weersma, H.A., *Publ. Astron. Lab. Groningen*, No. 29 (1918).

[64] Kapteyn, J.C., *Nature*, **78**, 210 and 234 (1908).

[65] Wendell, O.C. and Pickering, E.C., *Ann. Harvard Coll. Observ.*, **37** (Part 1) (1900).

[66] Wendell, O.C. and Pickering, E.C., *Ann. Harvard Coll. Observ.*, **37** (Part 2) (1902).

[67] Kapteyn, J.C., *Publ. Astron. Lab. Groningen*, No. 18 (1908).

[68] van Rhijn, P.J., *Publ. Astron. Lab. Groningen*, No. 27 (1917).

[69] Chapman, S. and Melotte, P.J., *Mem. R. Astron. Soc.*, **80** (Part 4), 145 (1915).

[70] Kapteyn, J.C. and van Rhijn, P.J., *Astrophys. J.*, **52**, 23 (1920).

[71] Kapteyn, J.C., *Astrophys. J.*, **55**, 302 (1922).

[72] Hubble, E., *Astrophys. J.*, **69**, 103 (1929).

[73] van Rhijn, P.J., *Publ. Astron. Lab. Groningen*, No. 38 (1925).

[74] Pannekoek, A., *Publ. Astron. Inst. Netherlands*, No. **2** (1929).

[75] Charlier, C.V.L., *Nova Acta Regiae Societatis Sci. Upsaliensis (iv)*, **4** (No. 7) (1916).

[76] Charlier, C.V.L., *Medd. Lunds Astron. Observ. (Ser. 2)*, **1** (No. 8) (1912).

[77] Pickering, E.C., *Harvard Coll. Observ. Circ.*, **71** (1903).

[78] Henie, H., *Medd. Lunds Astron. Observ. (Ser. 2)*, **1** (No. 10) (1913).

[79]   Charlier, C.V.L., *Medd. Lunds. Astron. Observ. (Ser. 2)*, **2** (No. 19) (1918).

[80]   Shapley, H., *Astrophys. J.*, **45**, 123 (1917).

[81]   Shapley, H., *Contrib. Mt. Wilson Observ.*, No. **116** (1915).

[82]   Eberhard, G., *Publ. Astrophys. Observ. Potsdam*, **26** (Part 1), No. 84, 1 (1926).

[83]   Shapley, H., *Astrophys. J.*, **48**, 154 (1918).

[84]   Sawyer Hogg, H., *Publ. Astron. Soc. Pacific*, **77**, 336 (1965).

[85]   Kopal, Z., *Astrophys. Space Sci.*, **18**, 259 (1972).

[86]   Shapley, H., *Astrophys. J.*, **48**, 89 (1918).

[87]   Baade, W., *Trans. Int. Astron. Union*, **8**, 397 (1954).

[88]   Baade, W., *Publ. Astron. Soc. Pacific*, **68**, 5 (1956).

[89]   Dufay, J., *Bull. Observ. Lyon*, **11**, 59 (1929).

[90]   Vorontsov-Velyaminov, B., *Astron. Nachr.*, **237**, 381 (1930).

[91]   Shapley, H., *Proc. Nat. Acad. Sci. America*, **3**, 267 (1917).

[92]   Dyson, F.W., *Mem. R. Astron. Soc.*, **60** (Part 3), 141 (1915).

[93]   Shapley, H., *Oral History Interview with H. Shapley by C. Weiner and H. Wright*, Amer. Inst. of Phys., Niels Bohr Library, p. 55 (1966).

[94]   Shapley, H., Letter to A.S. Eddington, Harvard (8 January 1918).

[95]   Harris, W.E., *Astrophys. J.*, **81**, 1095 (1976).

[96]   Charlier, C.V.L., *Medd. Lunds. Astron. Observ.* (Ser. 1), **2**, No. 19 (1918).

[97]   de Chéseaux, J.-P.L., *Trâité de la Comète qui a paru en Déc. 1743 et en Jan., Fév. et Mars 1744: Appendix II 'Sur la force de la lumière, sa propagation dans l'Ether et sur la distance des Étoiles fixes*, pp. 223–9 (1744).

[98]   Olbers, W.H.M., *Briefwechsel zwischen W. Olbers und F.W. Bessel*, edited by A. Erman (Leipzig) **2**, 244 (1852); quoted by S.L. Jaki in *The Milky Way*, Science History Publications (1872). See p. 283.

[99]   Secchi, A., *Astronomia in Roma nel pontificate di Pio IX* (1853). See Abetti, G. and Hack, M., *Nebulae and Galaxies*, New York: T.Y. Crowell (1959), p. 20.

[100] Ranyard, A.C., *Knowledge*, **17**, 253 (1894).

[101] Barnard, E.E., *Astrophys. J.*, **50**, 1 (1919).

[102] Wolf, M., *Mon. Not. R. Astron. Soc.*, **64**, 838 (1904).

[103] Curtis, H.D., *Proc. Nat. Acad. Sci. America*, **3**, 678 (1917).

[104] Curtis, H.D., *Publ. Astron. Soc. Pacific*, **30**, 65 (1918).

[105] Kapteyn, J.C., *Astron. J.*, **24**, 115 (1904).

[106] Kapteyn, J.C., *Astrophys. J.*, **29**, 46 (1909).

[107] Kapteyn, J.C., *Astrophys. J.*, **30**, 284 (1910).

[108] Halm, J., *Mon. Not. R. Astron. Soc.*, **80**, 162 (1919).

[109] Schalén, C., *Astron. Nachr.*, **236**, 249 (1929).

[110] Eddington, A.S., *Proc. R. Soc.*, **111** (A), 424 (1926).

[111] Russell, H.N., *Proc. Nat. Acad. Sci. America*, **8**, 115 (1922).

[112] Russell, H.N., *Nature*, **110**, 81 (1922).

[113] Trumpler, R.J., *Lick Observ. Bull.*, **14**, 154 (1930).

[114] Vorontsov-Velyaminov, B., *Sky and Telescope*, **73**, 4 (1987).

[115] Trumpler, R.J., *Publ. Astron. Soc. Pacific*, **42**, 214 (1930).

[116] Aitken, R.G., *Publ. Amer. Astron. Soc.*, **6**, 395 (1931).

[117] van Rhijn, P.J., *Bull. Astron. Inst. Netherlands*, **4**, 123 (1928).

[118] Shapley, H., *Harvard Coll. Observ. Bull.*, **864**, 7 (1929).

[119] Trumpler, R.J., *Publ. Astron. Soc. Pacific*, **42**, 267 (1930).

[120]   Gerasimovic, B.P., *Zeitschr. für Astrophys.*, **4**, 265 (1932).
[121]   Mie, G., *Ann. der Physik*, **25** (4), 377 (1908).
[122]   Schalén, C., *Nova Acta Regiae Societatis Sci. Upsaliensis* (iv), **10** (No. 1), 1 (1936) = *Medd. Astron. Observ. Upsala*, No. **64** (1936).
[123]   Nordmann, C., *Comptes Rendus*, **146**, 266 and 383 (1908).
[124]   Tikhoff, G.A., *Comptes Rendus*, **146**, 570 (1908).
[125]   Lebedev, P., *Comptes Rendus*, **146**, 1254 (1908).
[126]   Lebedev, P., *Comptes Rendus*, **147**, 515 (1908).
[127]   (anonymous), *Observatory*, **31**, 359 (1908).
[128]   Russell, H.N., Fowler, M. and Borton, M.C., *Astrophys. J.*, **45**, 306 (1917).
[129]   Shapley, H., *Harvard Coll. Observ. Bull.*, **763**, 1 (1922).
[130]   Öhman, Y., *Nature*, **134**, 534 (1934).
[131]   Öhman, Y., *Arkiv Mat. Astron. och Fysik*, **29B**, No. 12 (1943).
[132]   Chandrasekhar, S., *Astrophys. J.*, **103**, 351 (1946).
[133]   Janssen, E.M., *Astrophys. J.*, **103**, 380 (1946).
[134]   Hiltner, W.A., *Astrophys. J.*, **106**, 231 (1947).
[135]   Hall, J.S., *Astrophys. J.*, **54**, 39 (1948).
[136]   Hiltner, W.A., *Science*, **109**, 165 (1949).
[137]   Hall, J.S., *Science*, **109**, 166 (1949).
[138]   Hall, J.S. and Mikesell, A.H., *Astrophys. J.*, **54**, 187 (1949).
[139]   Spitzer, L. and Tukey, J.W., *Science*, **109**, 461 (1949).
[140]   Davis, L. and Greenstein, J.L., *Phys. Rev.*, **75**, 1605 (1949).
[141]   Davis, L. and Greenstein, J.L., *Astrophys. J.*, **114**, 206 (1951).
[142]   Hiltner, W.A., *Astrophys. J.*, **114**, 241 (1951).
[143]   Hiltner, W.A., *Astrophys. J.*, **120**, 41 (1954).
[144]   Hiltner, W.A., *Astrophys. J.*, **120**, 454 (1954).
[145]   Hiltner, W.A., *Astrophys. J. Suppl. Ser.*, **2**, 389 (1956).
[146]   Hiltner, W.A., *Vistas in Astron.*, **2**, 1084 (1956).
[147]   Hall, J.S., *Publ. US Nav. Observ.*, **17** (Part 6) (1958).
[148]   Smith, E. van P., *Astrophys. J.*, **124**, 43 (1956).
[149]   Struve, O. and Zebergs, V., *Astronomy of the 20th Century*, Macmillan Co., New York (1962). See p. 371.
[150]   Behr, A., *Nachr. Akad. Wiss. Göttingen, Math.-Phys. Klasse*, **2a**, 185 (1959).
[151]   Klare, G., Neckel, T. and Schnur, G., *Astron. Astrophys. Suppl. Ser.*, **5**, 239 (1972).
[152]   Mathewson, D.S. and Ford, V.L., *Mem. R. Astron. Soc. Australia*, **74**, 139 (1971).
[153]   Charlier, C.V.L., *Vierteljahrschr. Astron. Ges.*, **19**, 1 (1889).
[154]   Russell, H.N., *Publ. Astron. Astrophys. Soc. America*, **2**, 33 (1915).
[155]   Hertzsprung, E., *Publ. Potsdam Astrophys. Observ.*, **22** (No. 63), 1 (1911).
[156]   Hertzsprung, E., *Mém. de l'Acad. Roy. des Sci. et des Lettres de Danemark, Section des Sci.*, 8ème série, **4** (No. 4) (1923).
[157]   Hertzsprung, E., *Astrophys. J.*, **42**, 92 (1915).
[158]   Russell, H.N., *Observatory*, **36**, 324 (1913).
[159]   Russell, H.N., *Publ. American Astron. Soc.*, **3**, 22 (1918); also published in *Popular Astron.*, **22**, 275 and 331 (1914) and *Nature*, **93**, 227, 252 and 281 (1914).
[160]   Trumpler, R.J., *Publ. Astron. Soc. Pacific*, **37**, 307 (1925).
[161]   Strömgren, B., *Vierteljahrschr. Astron. Ges.*, **68**, 306 (1933).
[162]   Strömgren, B., *Zeitschr. für Astrophys.*, **7**, 222 (1933).

[163]   Seares, F.H., *Astrophys. J.*, **42**, 120 (1916).
[164]   von Zeipel, H. and Lindgren, J., *Proc. Swedish Acad.*, **61** (No. 15) (1921).
[165]   Shapley, H. and Richmond, M., *Astrophys. J.*, **54**, 323 (1921).
[166]   Graff, K., *Hamburg Abhandlungen*, **2**, 3 (1920).
[167]   Shapley, H., *Star Clusters*, Harvard Coll. Observ. Monograph No. 2, McGraw-Hill Co., New York (1930).
[168]   Trumpler, R.J., *Pop. Astron.*, **26**, 9 (1918).
[169]   Trumpler, R.J., *Publ. Astron. Soc. Pacific*, **32**, 43 (1920).
[170]   Lockyer, J.N., *Phil. Trans. R. Soc. London*, (A) **184**, 675 (1893).
[171]   Lockyer, J.N., *Inorganic Evolution*, Macmillan and Co., London (1890).
[172]   Russell, H.N., *Pop. Astron.*, **22**, 275 and 331 (1914).
[173]   Russell. H.N., *Nature*, **116**, 209 (1925).
[174]   Russell, H.N., Dugan, R.S. and Stewart, J.Q., *Astronomy*, Ginn and Co., Boston (1927).
[175]   Eddington, A.S., *The Internal Constitution of the Stars*, Cambridge (1926).
[176]   Vogt, H., *Astron. Nachr.*, **226**, 301 (1926).
[177]   Kuiper, G.P., *Harvard Coll. Observ. Bull.*, **903**, 1 (1936).
[178]   Kuiper, G.P., *Astrophys. J.*, **86**, 176 (1937).
[179]   Bethe, H.A., *Phys. Rev.*, **55**, 434 (1939).
[180]   Schönberg, M. and Chandrasekhar, S., *Astrophys. J.*, **96**, 161 (1942).
[181]   Sandage, A.R. and Schwarzschild, M., *Astrophys. J.*, **116**, 463 (1952).
[182]   Gamow, G., *Phys. Rev*, **53**, 595 and 908 (1938).
[183]   Gamow, G., *Phys. Rev.*, **55**, 718 and 796 (1939).
[184]   Gamow, G., *Nature*, **144**, 575 and 620 (1939).
[185]   Hoyle, F. and Schwarzschild, M., *Astrophys. J. Suppl. Ser.*, **2**, 1 (1955).
[186]   Tayler, R.J., *Astrophys. J.*, **120**, 332 (1954).
[187]   Tayler, R.J., *Mon. Not. R. Astron. Soc.*, **116**, 25 (1956).
[188]   Kushwaha, R.S., *Astrophys. J.*, **125**, 242 (1957).
[189]   Eggen, O.J., *Astrophys. J.*, **111**, 65 (1950).
[190]   Eggen, O.J., *Astrophys. J.*, **111**, 81 (1950).
[191]   Eggen, O.J., *Astrophys. J.*, **111**, 414 (1950).
[192]   Wallenquist, Å., *Arkiv Astron.*, **1**, 101 (1950).
[193]   Johnson, H.L. and Morgan, W.W., *Astrophys. J.*, **114**, 522 (1951).
[194]   Eggen, O.J., *Astrophys. J.*, **113**, 657 (1951).
[195]   Sharpless, S., *Astrophys. J.*, **116**, 251 (1952).
[196]   Weaver, H.F., *Astrophys. J.*, **116**, 612 (1952).
[197]   Johnson, H.L., *Astrophys. J.*, **116**, 640 (1952).
[198]   Bahner, K. and Miczaika, G.R., *Zeitschr. für Astrophys.*, **31**, 236 (1952).
[199]   Johnson, H.L. and Morgan, W.W., *Astrophys. J.*, **117**, 313 (1953).
[200]   Johnson, H.L., *Astrophys. J.*, **117**, 353 (1953).
[201]   Johnson, H.L., *Astrophys. J.*, **117**, 356 (1953).
[202]   Weaver, H.F., *Astrophys. J.*, **117**, 366 (1953).
[203]   Harris, D.L., *Astrophys. J.*, **117**, 469 (1953).
[204]   Brownlee, R.R. and Cox, A.N., *Astrophys. J.*, **118**, 165 (1953).
[205]   Hogg, A.R., *Mon. Not. R. Astron. Soc.*, **113**, 746 (1953).
[206]   Thiessen, G., *Zeitschr. für Astrophys.*, **32**, 59 (1953).
[207]   Johnson, H.L., *Astrophys.J.*, **119**, 185 (1954).
[208]   Cox, A.N., *Astrophys. J.*, **119**, 188 (1954).
[209]   Becker, W.H. and Stock, J., *Zeitschr. für Astrophys.*, **34**, 1 (1954).

[210]   Bappu, M.K.V., *Mon. Not. R. Astron. Soc.*, **114**, 680 (1954).
[211]   Bappu, M.K.V., *Observatory*, **75**, 47 (1955).
[212]   Harris, D.L., Morgan, W.W. and Roman, N.G. *Astrophys. J.*, **119**, 622 (1954).
[213]   Hogg, A.R. and Kron, G.E., *Astron. J.*, **60**, 365 (1955).
[214]   Roman, N.G. *Astrophys. J.*, **121**, 454 (1955).
[215]   Johnson. H.L. and Sandage, A.R., *Astrophys. J.*, **121**, 616 (1955).
[216]   Johnson, H.L. and Knuckles, C.F., *Astrophys. J.*, **122**, 209 (1955).
[217]   Johnson. H.L. and Morgan, W.W., *Astrophys. J.*, **122**, 429 (1955).
[218]   Cuffey, J. and McCuskey, S.W., *Astrophys. J.*, **123**, 59 (1956).
[219]   Johnson. H.L., Sandage, A.R. and Wahlquist, H.D., *Astrophys. J.*, **124**, 81 (1956).
[220]   Heckmann, O. and Johnson, H.L., *Astrophys. J.*, **124**, 477 (1956).
[221]   Walker, M.F., *Astrophys. J. Suppl. Ser.*, **2**, 365 (1956).
[222]   Mianes, P. and Daguillon, J., *J. des Observateurs*, **40**, 65 (1957).
[223]   Walker, M.F., *Astrophys. J.*, **125**, 636 (1957).
[224]   Arp, H.C. and van Sant, C.T., *Astron. J.*, **63**, 341 (1958).
[225]   Walker, M.F., *Astrophys. J.*, **128**, 562 (1958).
[226]   Arp, H.C., *Astron. J.*, **64**, 254 (1959).
[227]   Fernie, J.D., *Mon. Not. Astron. Soc. S. Africa*, **18**, 57 (1959).
[228]   Rohlfs, K., Schrick, K.-W. and Stock, S., *Zeitschr. für Astrophys*, **47**, 15 (1959).
[229]   Oort, J., *Bull. Astron. Soc. Netherlands*, **8**, 233 (1938).
[230]   Morgan, W.W., Harris, D.L. and Johnson, H.L., *Astrophys. J.*, **118**, 92 (1953).
[231]   Blanco, V.M., *Astrophys. J.*, **123**, 64 (1955).
[232]   Hiltner, W.A. and Johnson, H.L., *Astrophys. J.*, **124**, 367 (1956).
[233]   Morgan, W.W. and Johnson, H.L., *Astrophys. J.*, **117**, 313 (1953).
[234]   Doig, P., *Mon. Not. R. Astron. Soc.*, **82**, 461 (1922).
[235]   Doig, P., *J. British Astron. Assoc.*, **35**, 201 (1925).
[236]   Raab, S., *Lund Observ. Medd., Ser. 2*, No. **28** (1922).
[237]   Johnson, H.L. and Hiltner, W.A., *Astrophys. J.*, **123**, 267 (1956).
[238]   Johnson, H.L., *Astrophys. J.*, **126**, 121 (1957).
[239]   Eggen, O.J., *Astron. J.*, **60**, 401 (1955).
[240]   Sandage, A.R., *Astrophys. J.*, **125**, 435 (1957).
[241]   Sandage, A.R. and Eggen, O.J., *Mon. Not. R. Astron. Soc.*, **119**, 278 (1959).
[242]   Strömgren, B., *Astrophys. J.*, **57**, 65 (1952).
[243]   Eggen, O.J. and Sandage, A.R., *Astrophys. J.*, **136**, 735 (1962).
[244]   Nissen, P.E., *Astron. Astrophys.*, **8**, 476 (1970).
[245]   Eggen, O.J., *Astron. J.*, **60**, 407 (1955).
[246]   Salpeter, E.E., *Mém. Soc. Roy. des Sci. de Liège* (sér. 4), **14**, 116 (1954).
[247]   Henyey, L.G., LeLevier, R. and Levee, R.D., *Astrophys. J.*, **129**, 2 (1959).
[248]   O'Connell, D.J. (ed.), *Stellar Populations: Proc. of the Conference sponsored by the Pontifical Acad. of Sci. and the Vatican Observatory*, 544 pp., Vatican Observatory (1958).
[249]   Gratton, L. (ed.), *Star Evolution: Proc. Int. School of Physics 'Enrico Fermi', Course 28*, 488 pp., Academic Press, New York and London (1963).
[250]   Planck, M., *Wiedemanns Ann. der Physik*, **4**, 553 (1901).
[251]   Brill, A., *Astron. Nachr.*, **218**, 209 (1923).
[252]   McCrea, W.H., *Mon. Not. R. Astron. Soc.*, **91**, 836 (1931).

[253] Saha, M.N., *Proc. R. Soc.*, **99A**, 135 (1921).
[254] Pannekoek, A., *Astrophys. J.*, **84**, 481 (1936).
[255] Kuiper, G.P., *Astrophys. J.*, **88**, 429 (1938).
[256] Becker, W., *Veröff. Berlin-Babelsberg*, **10** (Heft 6), 1 (1935).
[257] Brill, A., *Handbuch der Astrophys.*, **5** (Part 1), 150 (1932).
[258] Pettit, E. and Nicholson, S.B., *Astrophys. J.*, **68**, 279 (1928).
[259] Johnson, H.L., *Ann. Rev. Astron. Astrophys.*, **4**, 193 (1966).
[260] Avrett, E.H. and Strom, S.E., *Ann. d'Astrophys.*, **27**, 781 (1964).
[261] Mihalas, D., *Astrophys. J. Supp. Ser.*, **13**, 1 (1965).
[262] Ridgway, S.T., Joyce, R.R., White, N.M. and Wing, R.F., *Astrophys. J.*, **235**, 126 (1980).
[263] Maury, A.C., *Ann. Harvard Coll. Observ.*, **28** (Part 1), 1 (1897).
[264] Cannon, A.J., *Ann. Harvard. Coll. Observ.*, **28** (Part 2), 129 (1901). See p. 159.
[265] Adams, W.S., *Astrophys. J.*, **39**, 89 (1914).
[266] Adams, W.S. and Kohlschütter, A., *Astrophys. J.*, **40**, 385 (1914).
[267] Kapteyn, J.C., *Astrophys. J.*, **40**, 187 (1914).
[268] Lindblad, B., *Ark. för Mat., Astron. och Fysik*, **13** (No. 26), 1 (1918).
[269] Seares, F.H., *Publ. Astron. Soc. Pacific*, **30**, 99 (1918).
[270] Seares, F.H., *Proc. Nat. Acad. Sci. America*, **5**, 232 (1919).
[271] Seares, F.H., *Astrophys. J.*, **55**, 165 (1922).
[272] Hertzsprung, E., *Ann. Sterrew. Leiden*, **4** (Part 1), 1 (1922).
[273] Payne-Gaposchkin, C.H., *Ann. Harvard. Coll. Observ.*, **89** (No. 6), 105 (1935).
[274] Öpik, E., *Publ. de l'Observ. de Tartu*, **27** (No. 1), 1 (1929).
[275] Stewart, J.Q., *Pop. Astron.*, **31**, 88 (1923).
[276] Kirchhoff, G. and Bunsen, R., *Poggendorffs Ann.*, **110**, 160 (1860).
[277] Huggins, W. and Miller, W.A., *Phil. Trans. R. Soc.*, **154**, 413 (1864).
[278] Hale, G.E., *The Study of Stellar Evolution*, Chicago Univ. Press (1908).
[279] Becker, W., *Zeitschr. für Astrophys.*, **9**, 79 (1934).
[280] Becker, W., *Veröff. der Univ. Sternwarte Göttingen*, **5** (No. 79), 159 (1946).
[281] Becker, W., *Veröff. der Univ. Sternwarte Göttingen*, **5** (No. 80), 173 (1946).
[282] Becker, W., *Veröff. der Univ. Sternwarte Göttingen*, **5** (No. 81), 184 (1946).
[283] Becker, W., *Veröff. der Univ. Sternwarte Göttingen*, **5** (No. 82), 196 (1946).
[284] Greenstein, J.L., *Harvard. Coll. Observ. Bull.*, **907**, 30 (1938).
[285] Roman, N.G., *Astrophys. J.*, **59**, 307 (1954).
[286] Baade, W., *Astrophys. J.*, **100**, 137 (1944).
[287] Kuiper, G.P., *Astron. J.*, **53**, 194, (1948).
[288] Roman, N.G., *Astrophys. J.*, **112**, 554 (1950).
[289] Strömgren, B., in *Stellar Populations*, p. 385, ed. D.J.K. O'Connell, Publ. Vatican Observ. (1958).
[290] Roman, N.G., *Astrophys. J. Supp. Ser.*, **2**, 195 (1955).
[291] Baschek, B., *Zeitschr. für Astrophys.*, **48**, 95 (1959).
[292] Aller, L.H. and Greenstein, J.L., *Astrophys. J. Suppl. Ser.*, **5**, 139 (1960).
[293] Heiser, A.M., *Astrophys. J.*, **132**, 506 (1960).
[294] Wallerstein, G., *Astrophys. J. Supp. Ser*, **6**, 407 (1961).
[295] Wallerstein, G. and Carlson, M., *Astrophys. J.*, **132**, 276 (1960).
[296] Schwarzschild, M., Searle, L. and Howard, R., *Astrophys. J.*, **122**, 353 (1955).

[297]   Wildey, R.L., Burbidge, E.M., Sandage, A.R. and Burbidge, G.R.,
        Astrophys. J., **135**, 94 (1962).
[298]   Reiz, A., *Astrophys. J.*, **120**, 342 (1954).
[299]   Griffin, R.F. and Redman, R.O., *Mon. Not. R. Astron. Soc.*, **120**, 287
        (1960).
[300]   Nissen, P.E., *Astron. Astrophys.*, **6**, 138 (1970).
[301]   Spinrad, H. and Taylor, B.J., *Astrophys. J.*, **157**, 1279 (1969).
[302]   Strömgren, B., in *Stellar Populations*, p. 245, ed. D.J.K. O'Connell,
        Publ. Vatican Observ. (1958).
[303]   Strömgren, B., *Ann. Rev. Astron. Astrophys.*, **4**, 433 (1966).
[304]   Oort, J.H., *Publ. Astron. Lab. Groningen*, No. 40 (1926).
[305]   Baade, W., in *Stellar Populations*, p. 3, ed. D.J.K. O'Connell, Publ.
        Vatican Observ. (1958).
[306]   Oort, J.H. in *Stellar Populations*, p. 415, ed. D.J.K. O'Connell, Publ.
        Vatican Observ. (1958).
[307]   Eggen, O.J., Lynden-Bell, D. and Sandage, A.R., *Astrophys. J.*, **136**, 748
        (1962).
[308]   Goodricke, J., *Phil. Trans. R. Soc. London*, (A) **73**, 474 (1783).
[309]   Montanari, G., *Sopra la sparizione d'alcune stelle e altre novità celesti*,
        in *Prose di Signori Academici Gelati di Bologna* (1671). See also
        Z. Kopal, *Close Binary Systems*, Chapman and Hall (1959) p. 12 for
        further details of Montanari's discovery.
[310]   Vogel, H.C., *Astron. Nachr.*, **123**, 289 (1890).
[311]   Goodricke, J., *Phil. Trans. R. Soc. London* (A), **75**, 40, 153 (1785).
[312]   Eggen, O.J., *Observatory*, **77**, 191 (1957).
[313]   Aldis, T.S., *Phil. Mag.*, **39** (4), 363 (1870).
[314]   Pickering, E.C., *Proc. Amer. Acad. Arts & Sciences*, **16**, 1 (1881).
[315]   Pickering, E.C., Searle, A. and Wendell, O.C., *Proc. Nat. Acad. Sci.
        America*, **16**, 370 (1881).
[316]   Wendell, O.C., *Ann. Harvard Coll. Observ.*, **69** (Part 1), 1 (1909).
[317]   Myers, G.W., *Astrophys. J.*, **8**, 163 (1898).
[318]   Roberts, A.W., *Mon. Not. R. Astron. Soc.*, **63**, 527 (1903).
[319]   Roberts, A.W., *Mon. Not. R. Astron. Soc.*, **66**, 123 (1906).
[320]   Russell, H.N., *Astrophys. J.*, **35**, 315 (1912).
[321]   Russell, H.N., *Astrophys. J.*, **36**, 54 (1912).
[322]   Russell, H.N. and Shapley, H., *Astrophys. J.*, **36**, 239 (1912).
[323]   Russell, H.N. and Shapley, H., *Astrophys. J.*, **36**, 385 (1912).
[324]   Russell, H.N., *Astrophys. J.*, **36**, 133 (1912).
[325]   Shapley, H., *Contrib. Princeton Univ. Observ.*, No. 3, 1 (1915).
[326]   Shapley, H., *Astrophys. J.*, **38**, 158 (1915).
[327]   Kopal, Z., *Of stars and men*, A. Hilger, Bristol and Boston (1986). See
        p. 157.
[328]   Dugan, R.S., *Contrib. Princeton Univ. Observ.*, No. 15 (1934).
[329]   Pierce, N.L., *Contrib. Princeton Univ. Observ.*, No. 22 (1947).
[330]   Stebbins, J., *Astrophys. J.*, **32**, 185 (1910).
[331]   Russell, H.N., *Mon. Not. R. Astron. Soc.*, **88**, 641 (1928).
[332]   Cowling, T.G., *Mon. Not. R. Astron. Soc.*, **98**, 734 (1938).
[333]   Sterne, T.E., *Mon. Not. R. Astron. Soc.*, **99**, 451 (1939).
[334]   Russell, H.N., *Astrophys. J.*, **90**, 641 (1939).

9 Photoelectric photometry with the photomultiplier

9.1　The first photomultipliers

It is well known that photomultiplier tubes revolutionized astronomical photometry after 1945. Their success was on a scale that the single-stage photocells never achieved. The fact that electrons could be ejected from a solid surface not only by photoemission or thermally, but also by electron bombardment (known as secondary emission) had been known since the first decade of the twentieth century. As early as 1918 Albert Hull (1880–1966) had proposed amplifying thermionic currents using this phenomenon [1].

In 1935 researchers from RCA in New Jersey and from Philips, in Eindhoven, Holland, independently proposed using secondary emission to amplify the weak photocurrents from a photoelectric cell. The RCA device was constructed by Harley Iams (b. 1905) and Bernard Salzberg (b. 1907) [2], while a few months later Frans Penning (1894–1953) and A. Kruithof tested a similar cell in Holland [3]. These were the first photomultipliers. In both cases the first photocathode and the secondary surface or dynode were Cs-O-Ag (S1) surfaces, and a gain of six or seven was achieved with either 1 kilovolt (RCA tube) or 500 V (Philips tube) between anode and cathode, which was an amplification only slightly better than that from a gas-filled diode tube.

Other photomultipliers with multiple stages were made the following year. One was a 7-stage tube with wire-mesh screen dynodes constructed by G. Weiss of the German Post Office [4]. But the most vigorous development was undertaken at RCA in New Jersey by Vladimir Zworykin (1889–1982) and his colleagues, also from 1936. Zworykin was born in Russia and migrated to the United States in 1919. He devised the iconoscope television camera tube in 1931, and has been described as 'the father of television'. But his achievements in photoelectricity were also significant milestones. In 1936 he had produced both 9- and 12-stage magnetically focussed photomultiplier tubes with S1 cathode and dynodes, as well as

2-stage designs with electrostatic focussing [5]. The noise of these devices was shown to be dominated by the shot noise in the photocurrent from the cathode, while the gain or amplification was essentially noise-free. The performance was much superior to a thermionic valve amplifier in conjunction with a simple photocell.

The very first photomultiplier to be used in astronomy was one of Zworykin's new tubes which had been acquired by Stebbins in 1937 and was used by Whitford and Kron as an autoguider on the 60-inch telescope at Mt Wilson [6]. According to Kron:

> Stebbins knew that Zworykin was working on some kind of a device at RCA and so he wrote to Zworykin ... and sure enough Zworykin sent a laboratory constructed magnetically focussed photomultiplier. It had an S1 surface, it turned out. And that's what we used as that [auto-]guider, it actually worked [7, p. 37]

A visionary paper written by Hans Siedentopf in 1939 also advocated the use of the photomultiplier for a photoelectric spectrohelioscope [8]. The proposal was to display an image of the sun on an oscilloscope screen using a narrow spectral band, for the purpose of studying the surface brightness of the disk, including limb darkening, sunspots and faculae. Some experiments with a photomultiplier of German manufacture were made. The Whitford-Kron and Siedentopf articles were apparently the only two describing astronomical applications for photomultipliers to be published before the war.

9.1.1   The CsSb (S4) photocathode and the development of the 1P21 photomultiplier

At about the same time as the first photomultipliers were being developed at RCA and elsewhere, Paul Görlich (1905–86) in Dresden, Germany, described a new blue-sensitive photocathode comprising layers of caesium and antimony [9, 10, 11]. This new photocathode gave a peak quantum efficiency of close to 13 per cent at its maximum near 400 nm, which was far superior to the KH surface. The sensitivity extended to a threshold at about 630 nm on the long wavelength side of the peak.

The CsSb photocathode was developed at RCA where it was given the photocathode surface designation S4, and incorporated into the RCA 929 vacuum photocell in 1940 [12]. This was followed almost immediately by the RCA 931 photomultiplier, a compact nine-stage side-illuminated electrostatically focussed tube in a circular configuration in which the photocathode and dynodes were all S4 surfaces [13]. The developments in phototubes, including photomultipliers, were reviewed at this time by Alan Glover (b. 1909)

Fig. 9.1   The RCA 931-A and 1P21 photomultiplier tubes.

at RCA [14, 15]. The 931 photomultiplier, later known as the 931-A, gave a gain of about 6×10^4 with 100 V per stage, or 2.3×10^5 at 125 V per stage. The response was linear, sensitivity high and the high-frequency response far superior to the older gas-filled photocells. An immediate application was for the sound track in the motion-picture industry.

The most famous photomultiplier from RCA was the 1P21, first produced in 1943, and which became available commercially after the war. According to Zworykin, these tubes are

> ... similar to the 931-A tubes, being selected simply for very low dark current and high overall sensitivity. This selection makes them particularly suitable for the measurement of extremely small quantities of light [16].

Gains of about two million times were typical with an overall high tension voltage of 1000 V on this tube. Ralph Engstrom (b. 1914), also from RCA, discussed the 1P21 and other RCA photomultipliers in 1947 [17]. By this time the first tests of the 1P21 in astronomy had already been made by Gerry Kron at Lick [18], who wrote that 'the convenience offered by the multiplier will not fail to impress workers in the field of photoelectric photometry'. This prediction proved to be largely correct; after 1946 many observatories acquired 1P21 photomultipliers, constructed photometers for them (often based on the advice of Kron) and undertook reliable photoelectric photometry for the first time. According to Albert Whitford, himself a pioneer of the new detector, 'the advent of the 1P21 also broke a psychological barrier.

Fig. 9.2   Kron's 1P21 photometer on the 36-inch refractor, c. 1946.

Photoelectric photometry was no longer the province of a small band of specialists. Now relatively uncomplicated, the technique was taken up by quite a number of observatories ...' [19]. Whitford also explained why the 1P21 was such a success:

> There were three things that had come together... in this RCA 1P21 multiplier. One was a much higher quantum response, and that came as a result of a development in Germany by Görlich of the antimony-cesium cathode. The second was, wider spectrum response

Fig. 9.3   Diagram of the dynode structure of the RCA 1P21 photomultiplier.

than the old potassium alkali photo-cells that were in use for many years. And the third thing was an essentially noise-free system of amplification, which the multiplier train provided. It can easily be shown that the noises produced in the multiplication process don't appreciably increase the Poisson statistics of the original photoemission [20].

9.1.2   Lallemand photomultipliers

André Lallemand (1904–78) at the Paris Observatory was another early pioneer in photomultiplier technology. In 1943 he moved from Strasbourg to the Paris Observatory, where he established his Laboratory for Astronomical Physics. Photomultipliers were produced in this laboratory from 1945. They were electrostatically focussed linear photomultipliers in which the dynodes had a venetian blind structure. A variety of experimental tubes with SbCs photocathodes were produced by Lallemand, having 7, 12, 17 or 19 stages [21]. The dynode surfaces were of silver-magnesium alloy, which was found to give a high electron multiplication factor. The 19-stage Lallemand photomultiplier gave a typical gain of two million (see review article by Lallemand in 1962 [22]).

The 19-stage Lallemand photomultiplier was used for astronomical pho-

Fig. 9.4   Three early Lallemand photomultiplier tubes. From l. to r., sensitive to visible, to near infrared and to ultraviolet light.

tometry at the Observatoire de Haute Provence from 1950 [23, 24] and at several other European observatories – for example by Jan Oort (1900–92) and Theodore Walraven from Leiden in their pioneering work at Haute Provence on the optical polarization of the Crab nebula [25], by Roger Bouigue (b. 1920) and J.-L. Chapuis in Toulouse [26], and at the Turin Observatory [27].

A Lallemand photomultiplier tube with a Cs-O-Ag (S1) photocathode was also used by Kron on the Crossley telescope at Lick for his large field integrated photometry of star clusters [28]. Lallemand was in fact the first successfully to produce sensitive photomultipliers for the near infrared, and several were tested by Kron from about 1956 [29] and used for photometry [30]. Other commercial manufacturers followed, such as Farnsworth Electronics (16 M1 tube), DuMont Laboratories (K 1613) and RCA (with the RCA 7102). An early RCA red-sensitive S1 photomultiplier that preceded the RCA 7102 was the C-7050, which was tested by Kron in 1948 [31], but it proved to be noisy and lacked sensitivity.

9.2   Pulse-counting techniques in astronomical photometry

That the flux from a star consists of a stream of discrete photons had been clearly recognized since the beginning of the twentieth century. The statistical implications of this fact for stellar photometry were discussed, on the basis of Poisson statistics, by Sinclair Smith in 1932 [32]. Assuming a 60-inch telescope equipped with a photocell of 10 per cent quantum efficiency and a blue filter, Smith calculated that 21-second integrations are required for photometry to 1 per cent on a 14th magnitude star, provided photon statistics were to dominate the noise.

The practical challenge of realizing such a result was that of constructing a photon-counting detector which would be largely immune to the dark current and amplifier noise of the Kunz photocells available in the early 1930s. Photomultipliers later provided the means to achieve this, and this was first demonstrated by Zoltan Bay (b. 1900) [33] and James Allen (b. 1911) [34], using 12-stage electrostatically focussed photomultiplier tubes as a counter of X-ray photons or for α, β or γ-ray particles. Bay's tube had Ag-Mg alloy dynodes giving a gain as high as 10^8 at 3500 V.

Even before the development of the photomultiplier, astronomers had tried without success to record the pulses from individual photons. One who did so was Bengt Strömgren:

> I even tried then [in 1933] to do pulse counting, but never succeeded. You can imagine, with the amplification of 100, instead of what we have today, 10^6, you had to try to record very small voltages, of a millionth [of a volt], and the only hope was that each photoelectron event takes place in a very short time. I never managed [35].

The possibility of detecting individual stellar photons with photomultipliers became apparent soon after the Second World War. Gerry Kron was the first to draw the attention of astronomers to the possibilities this offered, in his influential 1946 paper on: 'The application of the multiplier phototube to astronomical photoelectron photometry' [18]. He explicitly stated one advantage, of not counting the smaller pulses arising from thermal electron emission from the dynodes, by having a discriminator circuit which allows mainly the larger photon-generated pulses to be recorded. Some early laboratory tests were carried out by Ralph Engstrom [17] soon afterwards.

The first pulse- (or photon-) counting stellar photometers were built by

William Blitzstein (b. 1920) at the Cook Observatory of the University of Pennsylvania [36] and by Gilbert Yates (b. 1912) at the Cambridge Observatories, both in 1948 [37, 38]. The Yates photometer was operational in November of that year and was the first to be described, though possibly the second to be built. It used a dry-ice cooled RCA 931-A photomultiplier photometer on the 15-inch Huggins refractor at Cambridge. Anode pulses of some million electrons from each recorded photon were amplified to about 35 volts and counted electronically, after discriminating against the generally smaller thermal dark pulses and the many very small pulses due to leakage current. Not only was a digital signal produced at once for further analysis, but its value was less sensitive to voltage drift on the tube than was the case for techniques of direct-current measurement. Yates presented data for a 6.9 magnitude K0 star (GC 7739). He estimated that 12th magnitude was attainable with his instrumentation.

A second version of the Cambridge pulse-counting photometer was used to calibrate the photographic measures in the $+15°$ Selected Areas by Arthur Beer (1900–80), Redman and Yates [39]. The instrument was described by Redman and Yates at the Philadelphia photoelectric photometry conference of 31 December 1951 [40]. The time resolution of the electronics was about 600 ns, which required pulse-pairing corrections for the stars brighter than about $V = 7.3$. Photometric precisions of about $\pm^{m}05$ were obtained for stars down to $V = 11$ on the Huggins refractor. A third version of the instrument was used on the Cambridge 36-inch reflecting telescope.

Blitzstein began development of his pulse-counting photometer at the University of Pennsylvania in 1947 and the first observations of eclipsing binary stars (including XZ Andromedae) were made the following year on the 15-inch siderostat refractor [36]. Another pulse counting photometer was under development at Princeton by Newton Lacy Pierce from 1948, but when Pierce died in 1950 before its completion, this instrument was acquired by Blitzstein, and parts of it were used to improve the Cook photometer. The history of the development of the Pierce photometer at the Cook Observatory was given by Blitzstein in 1953, 1958 and 1988 [36, 41, 42]. By 1955, at the now combined Flower and Cook Observatory, the Pierce photometer was a dual-channel instrument for variable-star photometry, allowing simultaneous observation of a comparison star. Automated digital printing of the time of observation and of the pulse count was a feature of the system. The tubes used were either the RCA 1P21 or 1P28, the latter being an essentially identical photomultiplier except with a quartz envelope photocathode (known as S5), allowing higher ultraviolet sensitivity.

Pulse-counting photometry was soon adopted at other observatories, for example at Radcliffe Observatory with their Cambridge-built polarimeter

Fig. 9.5 The Pierce pulse-counting photometer at the Flower and Cook Observatory, c. 1955.

(see the Radcliffe Observatory 1954 annual report [43]), and by William Baum (b. 1924) at the prime-focus photometer of the Palomar 200-inch telescope from 1953 [44, 45, 46], using an EMI 6685 photomultiplier. Photometry on objects fainter than 23rd magnitude was reported, including many faint stars on the main sequence of the globular cluster M13 [47].

Blitzstein discussed the pros and cons of pulse counting over d.c. methods at the Philadelphia meeting [36]. Discrimination against thermal dark emission from the dynodes and leakage current, insensitivity of the signal to voltage drift and the convenience of having digital data were cited. The disadvantages mentioned were the relative complexity of the electronics and the non-linearity of the signal due to pulse pairing for bright stars.

The advantages of pulse-counting were by no means universally accepted or adopted. Thus Harold Johnson in 1962 argued that 'most of the supposed advantages of the pulse-counting method over d.c. methods do not exist' [48]. In particular he claimed that discrimination against dark emission entailed the rejection of a significant fraction of the primary photoelectrons, and he claimed that d.c. amplifiers with digital recording could be essentially drift-free. Moreover, early pulse-counting electronics was subject to radio interference, and the need for corrections for pulse pairing in the photometric data for bright stars posed a problem. Therefore, for at least two decades after its first introduction, the pulse-counting technique in astronomical photometry was not in widespread use.

9.3   Photometric systems: the (P,V) and UBV systems

9.3.1   The (P,V) system

The first photometric observers with photomultipliers generally used blue and yellow filters in an attempt approximately to reproduce the photographic and photovisual magnitudes of the International System of Seares. However, there was no agreement on exactly which filters to use. Thus Eggen used Schott BG1 and GG7 filters at Madison, but Corning 5330 and 3385 at Lick [49], in both cases using refracting telescopes. On the other hand Stebbins and Whitford used Schott BG12 and GG7 with a 1P21 to observe elliptical galaxies on the Mt Wilson 100-inch reflector [50]. Unfortunately, such practices led to a multiplicity of slightly different systems for each observer, a problem later stressed by Johnson [51]. These early photometric observations were tied to stars in the North Polar Sequence using a linear transformation, and the resulting blue magnitudes and colours were known as (Pg_p, C_p) on the International System ('p' for photoelectric).

In 1951 Gerry Kron proposed a simplified notation for the new photometry, namely the (P, V) system [52]. One problem encountered early on was that the magnitudes and colours depended somewhat on the choice of NPS standards, which arose from the blue colours of the brightest of these stars. Accordingly, Stebbins, Whitford and Johnson [53] adopted just nine of the

NPS stars to serve as standards to define the system.† The same stars were also used by Kron and J. Lynn Smith [52].

On 6 July 1950 an informal meeting of photometrists was held in Pasadena. The participants were Bowen, Baade, Baum, Minkowski and Pettit (Mt Wilson and Palomar); Eggen, Kron and Weaver (Lick); Whitford (Washburn) and Johnson (Yerkes and McDonald). It was agreed to confirm the use of the nine NPS stars for all future photoelectric photometry. The Stebbins-Whitford-Johnson magnitudes for these stars would define the (P, V) system.

Almost immediately problems arose for the (P, V) system. In the 1950–51 winter, Johnson had commenced photometry in three passbands (designated U, B and Y) on the McDonald 13- and 82-inch reflectors [54]. The peak wavelengths were at 363, 426 and 529 nm and were defined with a combination of Corning and Schott filters. Ultraviolet light ($\lambda < 380$ nm) was excluded from the blue passband. The B and Y photometry could be transformed to the (P, V) system, which, however, agreed poorly, for the Pleiades cluster stars, with the earlier data of Eggen.

An important paper by Harold Johnson showed that the ultraviolet light ($\lambda < 380$ nm) made the transformation between the International System of NPS standards and photoelectric photometry non-linear and multivalued [55]. Different amounts of ultraviolet light also led to colour equations in the photoelectric data of different observers using different blue filters. Moreover, the International System could only be reproduced if about half the photoelectric U signal were added in to Johnson's B.

Eggen, who undertook photometry in Australia from April 1951 and again at Lick from the following year, had meanwhile adopted the Corning 5562 filter for his blue passband [56], which effectively also excluded the ultraviolet. This, however, resulted in non-linearities when transforming to the original (P, V) system, where some ultraviolet was included. Eggen's (P, V) system was therefore known as $(P, V)_E$, and many of his photometric data of the 1950s were based on this ultraviolet-free system – see for example [57].

The (P, V) system did not immediately die as soon as the UBV system was introduced, mainly because of its continued use by Eggen. Also Kron and Nicholas Mayall (1906–93) proposed creating a three-colour (P, V, I) system based on (P, V) and a near infrared magnitude obtained separately with a Lallemand S1 tube [58, 59] (see also [60]). However, few observations were made.

---

† They were NPS numbers 6, 2r, 10, 4r, 13, 8r, 16, 19, 12r with photographic magnitudes from 7.1 to 13.8.

Fig. 9.6   Harold Johnson.

9.3.2   The UBV system

The three-colour UBV system was devised by Johnson and Morgan at the Yerkes and McDonald Observatories in 1950 and the first observations were made in the winter of 1950–51. Its conception was a natural consequence of Johnson's work on the ultraviolet response of the International System photographic passband, and of the problems of tying a photometric system to the NPS standards, which were concentrated in a single region of the sky and contained only a small range of stellar types.

Following experiments with ultraviolet, blue and yellow three-colour photometry in 1951 [54], the UBV system was formally launched in 1953

Table 9.1. *Filters for the UBV system*

Ultraviolet	(U)	Corning 9863
Blue	(B)	Corning 5030 + Schott GG13 (2mm)
Visual	(V)	Corning 3384

[61]. The passbands had effective wavelengths of about 350, 430 and 550 nm respectively, using the prescription of Table 9.1.

Johnson also specified that a 1P21 photomultiplier and aluminized reflecting telescope at an altitude of about 7000 feet must be used. Ten bright primary standard stars, of type ranging from O9 V to K4 III, initially defined the standard UBV magnitudes. In 1954 this list was extended by adding 98 mainly equatorial secondary standards [62] which now defined the UBV system. Further standards were included in Johnson's definitive paper of 1955, together with a full account of the UBV system and its implementation [63].

The value of a multicolour photometric system for solving astrophysical problems, such as determining the luminosity, metallicity or reddening of stars, had been recognized in the earlier work of Stebbins and Whitford and of W. Becker. Johnson and Morgan in particular applied the new system to the two-colour $(U - B, B - V)$ diagram, and showed how the effects of luminosity and reddening could be analysed. A reddening-free parameter Q was defined as $Q = (U - B) - 0.72(B - V)$, which could be used to distinguish between reddened early-type stars and unreddened stars of later spectral type [61].

Although Johnson and Morgan jointly authored the original paper on the UBV system, Johnson was alone responsible for all the photometric observing, while Morgan undertook the spectral classifications to which the photometry was closely linked. Whether the idea of introducing a third ultraviolet passband was also Johnson's is debatable: according to Morgan [64], he (WWM) devised the UBV system and wrote most of the paper. Johnson was the observer and invented the Q-parameter.

The first IAU General Assembly, following the publication of the Johnson-Morgan paper, was in Dublin in 1955. By this time the inadequacies of the International System of photometry had been evident for many years, and in any case the new technology of photomultipliers rendered obsolete many of the old photometric techniques based on photography and the North Polar Sequence. Commission 25 (for stellar photometry) at the Dublin meeting formally recognized the UBV system as an official system for three-colour photometry, in spite of some adverse comments from W. Becker [65].

9.3.3   The Cape U_CBV system

A system of three-colour photometry based on the Johnson-Morgan UBV was devised at the Royal Observatory at the Cape from 1953. Here the 24-inch Victoria refractor and the 13-inch astrographic telescope (used for the Cape zones of the *Carte du Ciel*) were used extensively for photoelectric photometry from 1950. The visit of Arthur Code (b. 1923) and Theodore Houck to the Cape in 1953 resulted in tests of the ultraviolet transparency ($\lambda < 380$ nm) of the Victoria refractor objective – see [66]. Sufficient light was transmitted, but the U passband used for the Cape photometry differed significantly from the Johnson U defined for aluminized reflectors. The mean Cape U wavelength was 396 nm. Transformations were multivalued and non-linear between the systems, and hence the photometry was retained in the unique Cape refractor system, which was developed by Alan Cousins and Richard Stoy in the later 1950s [67]. These authors published catalogues of photometric data in the Cape system in the 1960s [68, 69]. The standard stars in this system were stars in the nine Harvard E-regions at about $-45°$ declination.

9.3.4   Some important photometric catalogues of the 1960s

Several important catalogues of three-colour photoelectric photometry were published in the 1960s. One was the catalogue of Harold Johnson with Richard Mitchell, Braulis Iriarte and Wieslaw Wiśniewski of $UBVRIJKL$ multicolour photometry of bright stars [70]. So far as the $UBVRI$ photomultiplier data were concerned, these were reported for 1567 stars. The observations were from the Catalina Station of the Lunar and Planetary Laboratory and from the Tonantzintla Observatory 40-inch telescope in Mexico.

The Johnson *et al.* catalogue of 1966 was included as a compendium of UBV and U_CBV photometry published by Victor Blanco (b. 1918) and others from the Warner and Swasey and US Naval Observatories. This compendium gave data for over 20 000 stars produced by all observers in these two systems up until January 1967 [71]. One of the larger publications of photometric data included in the Blanco catalogue was Olin Eggen's UBV photometry of 1008 of the nearer K and M giants [72].

Fig. 9.7   The original Cape photoelectric photometer attached to the Cape
astrographic telescope, c. 1953.

9.3.5   Deficiencies of the UBV system

Unfortunately the *UBV* system did not solve all the problems
of the International System which it replaced, in spite of its widespread
popularity. One of the problems arose from the short wavelength side of
the *U* filter being defined partly by the atmosphere, thereby making it
impossible for observers at different altitudes to obtain single-valued linear
transformations to the standard system outside the atmosphere. Systematic
errors of $0^{m}.03$ to $0^{m}.05$ in the $(U - B)$ colour index could arise as a result
– see [73, 74]. Another problem of the *UBV* system arose from a red
leak in the Corning 9863 ultraviolet filter, and the variable red response of
different 1P21 photomultipliers, which together created a problem for the
photometry of the reddest stars. Also, the fact that the initial observations
used an uncooled 1P21, but in 1952 the tube was cooled, resulted in a small
change in the *UBV* response functions. The uncooled tube had a higher
sensitivity at longer wavelengths, yet it was observations on this system
which defined the original standards [75].

In addition, the rationale of the UBV system was simply to divide the old IPg photographic passband into two photoelectric bands (U and B), given that these could be included within the range of wavelength sensitivity of the S4 cathode. Little thought was given to the astrophysical requirements. Thus the U band straddles the Balmer jump, making the $(U - B)$ colour a less sensitive parameter of the size of the discontinuity itself, and the B band includes the Balmer hydrogen lines near the limit, making the $(B - V)$ colour of A stars sensitive to luminosity as well as to temperature. Such undesirable features prompted the development of new photometric systems which responded better to the determination of the basic stellar parameters of luminosity, temperature, chemical composition and interstellar reddening.

9.4   The transfer of new photometric technology and techniques

9.4.1   The contribution of Gerry Kron

When the first photomultiplier tubes became available from RCA and from André Lallemand's laboratory after the Second World War, astronomers at once had to devise new techniques for their use in astronomical photometry, and they had to become accustomed with electron-tube electronics of a complexity unknown to most observers of the pre-war generation. The inventors of the new devices at RCA were themselves not astronomers, so the immediate problem was the transfer of the expertise in their use to the astronomical community. Gerry Kron, above all others, was the person who most promoted the new detector's use in astronomy. He was a natural instrumentalist and was skilled in machine tools since his high-school days. Before entering astronomy, Kron had studied engineering, and during the war his work on radar at MIT and on missile technology in the US Navy gave him an invaluable background in electronics.

Stebbins knew Zworykin at RCA personally, and this enabled Kron to obtain a 931 photomultiplier for photometry as early as 1941. Work on the project was interrupted by the war, but resumed by Kron in 1945 on his return to Lick, when he used a $300 grant from the American Philosophical Society to purchase two 1P21 tubes at $47.50 each (see the review article by DeVorkin for further details [76]). By this time Kron had built his first operational photometer for the 12-inch and 36-inch Lick refractors: it comprised a focal plane diaphragm, a guiding eyepiece, filters, dark

Fig. 9.8   Gerry Kron's 1P21 photometer at Lick, *c.* 1949. Note the balsa-wood case for holding dry ice.

slide, photomultiplier, batteries and a sensitive galvanometer. There was no refrigeration, no Fabry lens and no d.c. amplification.

Kron's first photometer was described in detail in 1946 [77] in an IAU publication, which was reissued by Zdeněk Kopal at Harvard as a *Harvard Circular* in 1948 [78]. In 1946 Kron was also exhorting amateur astronomers to build photoelectric photometers, based on either the 931-A or 1P21 tubes [79]. The total outlay was about $150 if the latter tube was used, or about $40 less for the 931-A. The drawings for the Kron photometer were available from Kopal for just 50 cents to all interested astronomers. The less expensive 1P22 photomultiplier (cost $9.50) was also advocated by Kron for bright star photometry [78]. It had a Cs-Bi (S8) photocathode, for

Fig. 9.9   Photoelectric 1P21 photometer with amplifier and chart recorder on
the Lick 12-inch refractor 1949.

which the peak sensitivity was considerably lower than the CsSb (S4), but
it was sensitive to longer wavelengths [17]. However, its use never became
widespread in astronomy.

At this time both Kron at Lick and Whitford at the Washburn and Mt
Wilson Observatories were also independently building photometers with

d.c. amplifiers and dry-ice refrigerated photomultipliers. The design of Kron's photomultiplier with balsa-wood cold box at Lick, which cooled the 1P21 to −78 °C using dry ice, is discussed by Whitford in his review article on photoelectric techniques [80]. A Fabry lens was used to image the objective onto the photomultiplier's photocathode. The reduction in the dark current shot noise to very low levels made thermionic valve amplification of the photocurrent advantageous [81], and also the high sensitivity galvanometer could be replaced by a less sensitive milliammeter or a strip-chart recorder. Kron's photometer with d.c. amplifier was used on the 36-inch Crossley telescope at Lick from 1948 [82]. The strip-chart recorder was obtained by Kron free from the US Navy as surplus equipment after the war. Within a decade the Brown recorder was to become the essential adjunct to every photoelectric installation for astronomical photometry. This was a self-balancing potentiometer combined with a strip-chart recorder, manufactured by the Brown Instrument Division of the Minneapolis-Honeywell Regulator Company in Philadelphia.

The future potential of the 1P21 to astronomical photometry was outlined by Kron in a paper showing considerable vision and insight, published in the *Astrophysical Journal* in 1946 [18]. The paper discussed the signal-to-noise ratio, dark currents, cooling, d.c. amplification and even pulse-counting techniques. Kron himself described this as 'a very splendid paper... That paper was so highly regarded that it wasn't published immediately, it was passed around the Yerkes and McDonald Observatories – the manuscript – before it went into the *Astrophysical Journal*' [7, p. 61].

As well as being a pioneer of the 1P21 in astronomy, Kron continued to experiment with diode photocells for a number of years, especially the red-sensitive (S1) Continental Electric CE-25 cell. He devised feedback amplifiers with a high load resistance and low input capacitance which gave a high gain but acceptably low time constant of about 2 seconds [83, 84].

9.4.2 Further improvements in the application of photomultipliers

Many observatories built photomultiplier photometers from the late 1940s and in the 1950s, based on the 1P21, on the 931-A or on a Lallemand tube. In fact the first astronomical photometer to make use of a photomultiplier was the flicker photometer of Yngve Öhman (1903–88) at the Stockholm Observatory in 1943 [85, 86]. This was really a stellar colorimeter and used an RCA 931 tube on the 24-inch Stockholm refractor. The design was unconventional in that it used a rotating polarizer followed by a quartz birefringent plate alternately to select complementary colours.

An a.c. amplifier gave a null amplitude for an analyser setting which depended on the colour of the star.

An example of an early 1P21 photometer with a d.c. amplifier based on Kron's design principles is that used on the 12-inch reflector at the Vanderbilt University by John DeWitt and Carl Seyfert (1911–60) [87]. This photometer included a regulated 1000-volt power supply to replace the bulkier batteries with their less stable voltage. The tube was cooled to −80°C using dry ice. A light curve for the 10th magnitude eclipsing variable SV Cam was produced.

Another early photomultiplier photometer was that built at the Steward Observatory in 1949 by Edwin Carpenter (1898–1963) and Frank Bradshaw Wood, also based on Kron's design [88]. Either a d.c. amplifier and milliammeter, or a sensitive galvanometer, could be used.

An interesting summary of developments in photoelectric photometry was reported by Harold Cox to the British Astronomical Association in 1948 [89]. One problem outside North America was the scarcity and high price of the RCA tubes. By about 1948 the Edison Swan Company in England was producing the equivalent of the RCA 931-A, while EMI at this time had the Emitron 440, which, according to Howard Sterling, may give a performance comparable to that of the 1P21 [90].

Later EMI tubes became widely used in stellar photometry. Indeed William Baum was using EMI photomultipliers in the United States as early as 1951 [91]. The EMI 5060 was an end-on tube used in the prime-focus photometer on the 200-inch Palomar telescope, and from 1953 the EMI 6585 was used for pulse-counting photometry to 23rd magnitude on this telescope [45]. The performance of the EMI 5060 was discussed by Noel Argue [92] and compared to that of the 1P21.

By the mid-1950s new photocathode surfaces were being developed. One was the S11 cathode, used by EMI in many of its photomultipliers of the late 1950s. It was a variant of the S4, being a semitransparent CsSb on a lime-glass window. The peak response was at 440 nm (cf. 400 nm for S4) and the peak quantum efficiency was somewhat greater than for the S4 surface [93]. The EMI 9502 photomultiplier, which was frequently used for astronomical pulse-counting applications, was a 13-stage end-illuminated tube with an S11 cathode and venetian blind dynode structure (see [94]) of the type used by Lallemand. It was in the EMI photomultiplier catalogue for 1958. The RCA 6199 was another early S11 photomultiplier, but this employed a focussed dynode configuration similar to that of the 1P21.

In 1955 Alfred Sommer at the RCA laboratories in Princeton announced a new photoemissive surface, known as a multialkali or S20 surface [95]. It consisted of successive layers of potassium, sodium and caesium on an-

Fig. 9.10 EMI photomultiplier tubes, 1959.

timony (SbKNaCs), the Cs being essentially a monatomic surface layer. The luminous sensitivity was as high as $180\mu A/\text{lm}$ (compared to $40\mu A/\text{lm}$ for the S4 surface) and the useful sensitivity extended to about 800 nm. S20 photomultipliers became available in the late 1950s (for example, the RCA C7237 and the ITT FW-130); their high quantum efficiency in the red (typically 20 per cent) made them the preferred detector over S1 photomultipliers (such as the RCA 7102) in the Hα region. Sandage and Lewis Smith were experimenting with a new $UBVR$ system of S20 photomultiplier photometry at Palomar in 1960. They used the RCA C7237 (later known as the RCA 7265) tube, and the red passband had a mean wavelength of 670 nm [96].

Another improvement in the mid-1950s was the use of the integrating d.c. amplifier, a device which allowed the output from the amplifier to charge a capacitor whose final voltage was therefore a measure of the integrated signal over a fixed time. Such integrating amplifiers were developed by Robert Weitbrecht (b. 1920) at Yerkes Observatory [97] and used for example by

Tom Gehrels (b. 1925) in 1956 [98] for asteroid photometry. This method of analogue integration was, therefore, a useful technique for photometers where pulse-counting was not employed.

The optical design of photoelectric photometers was greatly improved in the 1950s. A common arrangement was for a low power field lens to be inserted using a flip mirror just ahead of the diaphragm, while a higher power lens for centering the star in the diaphragm was provided just behind the focal plane. The optical layout was discussed by Whitford, who also gave details of an offset guiding system for observations of faint stars [80].

9.4.3   Reductions of photometric data and the use of computers in photometry

The 1950s was the era of the first electronic computers and these soon proved to be the invaluable tool for reducing the raw data of photoelectric photometry. The EDSAC computer in Cambridge was the second such machine and was used widely for numerical problems in the physical sciences from 1949 [99, 100, 101].

In the early to mid-1950s some observatories were cataloguing and sorting digital data on punched-card machines – these include the Royal Greenwich Observatory [102] and Mt Stromlo Observatory [103].

The US Naval Observatory was one of the first to move to the computerized reductions of photometric data. In 1956, work was underway by John Hall and Arthur Hoag (b. 1921) for photoelectric observations to be punched onto cards at the telescope for eventual reduction in an IBM 650 computer [104]. Shortly afterwards Halton Arp at Caltech described a successful photometric reduction program running on a Datatron Digital 204 computer, which reduced several nights of photometry in 5 to 10 minutes [105]. Other observatories soon followed: Harold Johnson at Lowell [106], Daniel Schulte (b. 1929) at Kitt Peak [107, 108] and Stewart Sharpless (b. 1926) also at the US Naval Observatory [109] all described operating programs for photometric reductions.

Automated photometers under computer control followed in the 1960s. One such instrument at the Skalnate Pleso Observatory in Czechoslovakia used a computer for automatic filter selection, timing and data output to a typewriter [110].

As for the photometric reductions, the algorithms followed the mathematical formulation outlined by Arp [111, 105] for UBV photometry, which in turn was based on the reduction methods used by Stebbins, Whitford and Johnson [53] and by William Smart in Cambridge [112]. These methods entailed the reduction of all magnitudes to zero air mass, with the extinction correction being a linear function of sec$z$ (where z is the zenith angle) and with the extinction coefficient also showing a slight but linear dependence on colour index [49]. The instrumental magnitudes and colours so obtained were then transformed through linear transformations to the standard system using the results for standard stars.† These reduction techniques were reviewed and refined by Robert Hardie (1923–89) in 1962 [113] – see also [114]. They became widespread for nearly all photoelectric reductions in the 1950s‡ by which time Stebbins was advocating that all photometry should be reduced to outside the atmosphere, because of night-to-night variations in the extinction coefficient [116]. Indeed, as early as 1949, Eggen was determining extinction on a nightly basis and observing both blue and red extinction stars, so that the colour dependence of the extinction coefficient could be found [49].

The correct treatment of atmospheric extinction, especially for broadband systems like the UBV system, was widely discussed in the literature. Seares and Joyner [117] had stressed the variation of the extinction coefficient with stellar colour in 1943. Ivan King at Harvard [118] showed how the increase in the effective wavelength§ of a filter passband with increasing air mass, sometimes known as the Forbes effect (after the Bakerian lecture by James Forbes to the Royal Society [119]) resulted in the extinction no longer being strictly linear with sec$z$. Victor Blanco also studied bandwidth effects on UBV atmospheric extinction [120] and concluded that significant errors in extinction corrections could easily arise as a result of this non-linearity, especially in the U magnitudes and $(U - B)$ colours.

9.4.4 Two influential photometric conferences

In 1951 and 1953, two influential conferences on photoelectric photometry were held in the United States. They brought together some of the leading photometric observers and served to disseminate the latest advances in photometric techniques with photomultipliers. The first conference was held in Philadelphia on 31 December 1951 and was sponsored by the American Association for the Advancement of Science. Frank Bradshaw Wood (University of Pennsylvania) was the organizer and proceedings editor [121]. The second larger, and probably more influential meeting, was

---

† Observations for Johnson's UBV standards were initially reduced with no colour term in the $(U - B)$ extinction, possibly because accuracies of a few hundredths of a magnitude in this colour index were at first deemed to be satisfactory.

‡ An exception was the Cape system of photoelectric photometry which was not reduced to outside the atmosphere – see [115].

§ Here 'effective wavelength' is a flux-weighted mean wavelength, following the definition of Golay – see the footnote in section 4.8.2

at the Lowell Observatory, Flagstaff, 31 August – 1 September 1953, and sponsored by the National Science Foundation; Whitford was chairman of the Organizing Committee, John Irwin the proceedings editor [122].

The topics under discussion at these meetings are interesting. The relative merits of d.c. and a.c. amplifiers were topical at the time, the latter being advocated by John Hall, at least for certain special applications such as polarimetry – see [123]. Pulse-counting methods had just been introduced by Blitzstein [36], by Yates [40] and shortly afterwards by Baum at Palomar [45]. Sources of noise and the limits of sensitivity and precision were discussed by Whitford at both meetings [124, 125], and Baum reported photometry of stars as faint as 23rd magnitude using the 200-inch telescope [91, 45]. The reduction of photometry to outside the atmosphere was emphasized by Stebbins [116].

This last-mentioned paper was one of several that considered the effects of the atmosphere (seeing, transparency, scintillation and sky brightness) on the choice of sites for photometric telescopes and on reduction techniques. These were all issues that had received only minimal attention from photometrists hitherto. The photometric conferences of the early 1950s set new standards for the practice of astronomical photometry at the time that the UBV system was being introduced and was soon to become the officially recognized system by the IAU [65].

9.5   New photometric systems 1950–70

The first photometric systems using photomultipliers were the by (P, V) system in the late 1940s and the UBV system in the early 1950s. Both were systems strongly influenced by the capabilities of the S4 photocathode and by the traditions of the International System of photographic photometry. The 1950s saw the demise of the International System and a growing awareness of the astrophysical importance of the careful selection of photometric passbands. With the availability of robust photomultipliers and, a little later, of new photocathode surfaces, the 1950s and 1960s decades saw a large number (several dozen) of new photometric systems being launched. Some were short-lived and experimental, some were used at only one observatory or by one observer. Only a few became well established. This section reviews the more important developments. Table 9.2 gives details of some of the new systems of photometry that appeared prior to 1970.

Table 9.2. *Table of photometric systems in photoelectric photometry to 1970*

	Designation	Founder(s)	Year	Photocathode	Type	Reference	Comments
1.	$UVBGRI$	Stebbins & Whitford	1943	S1	B	[126]	Six-colour system; used with pm tubes from 1958
2.	(P,V)	Stebbins et al.	1950	S4	B	[53]	Pe version of International System
3.	$(RI)_K$	Kron	1951	S1	B	[52]	Initial use with diode photocells
4.	$abcdef$	Strömgren	1952	S4	N	[127]	Experimental system
5.	UBV	Johnson & Morgan	1953	S4	B	[61]	
6.	$(P,V)_E$	Eggen	1955	S4	B	[56]	P band free of UV
7.	gnk	Gyldenkerne	1955	S4	N	[128]	Danish narrow-band system for late-type stars
8.	β	Crawford	1958	S4	I,N	[129]	$H\beta$ line
9.	PVI	Kron & Mayall	1960	S4 & S1, or S1	B	[59]	
10.	$VBLUW$	Walraven	1960	S11	I,B	[130]	Walraven system
11.	$RQPNMLK$	Borgman	1960	S11	N,I	[131]	Borgman system
12.	$U_C BV$	Cousins et al.	1961	S4	B	[67]	Cape system
13.	$uvby$	Strömgren	1963	S4	I	[132]	
14.	$UPXYZVTS$	Straižys	1962	S20	I	[133]	Vilnius system
15.	$UBVR$	Sandage & Smith	1962	S20	B	[96]	
16.	$UBVRI$	Johnson & Mitchell	1962	S11 & S1	B	[134]	Johnson broad-band system; also extended to $JKLMN$ in infrared
17.	$UB_1 BB_2 V_1 VG$	Golay	1963	S11	I,B	[135]	Geneva system
18.	$(102, 65, 62)$	Eggen	1967	S1	N	[136]	narrow-band system for M stars
19.	$rrg8rg9i$	Argue	1967	S1	B,I	[137]	
20.	$33–110$	Johnson et al.	1967	S11 & S1	N	[138]	Johnson 13-colour narrow-band system
21.	$gnkmfu$	Dickow et al.	1970	S11	N	[139]	Danish narrow-band system for late-type stars
22.	$(RI)_C$	Cousins	1976	GaAs	B	[140]	Cousins system

Note; B: broad-band system; I: intermediate-band; N: narrow-band

Fig. 9.11   Lallemand side-illuminated S4 photomultiplier known as the 'Simplette', with its cooling chamber. It was used for Geneva-system photometry, c. 1955.

9.5.1   Narrow- and intermediate-band systems

The use of interference filters for narrow-band photometry was one such development. Bengt Strömgren, then at the Yerkes and McDonald Observatories, was the pioneer of the experimental *abcdef* six-colour system [127, 141]. The first observations were made at McDonald in 1950, coincidentally at the same place and about the same time as Johnson and Morgan devised the *UBV* system. Strömgren showed how composite indices called *c*, *l* and *m* could be constructed, which were sensitive to respectively Balmer jump, Hβ-line strength and metallicity for B, A and F stars. Astrophysical applications therefore determined the design of the passbands for the first time in photoelectric photometry. The *abcdef* system was, however, not very practical for photometric work, partly because the interference filter passbands were too narrow (less than 10 nm) to reach faint stars, and also because of some redundancy in the filters.

Strömgren's trials with interference-filter photometry led to further tests being made by K. Gyldenkerne at the Copenhagen Observatory using a filter wheel with 25 interference filters [142], from which was developed a system of photometry for late-type stars that measured the strengths of three absorption features, namely the G-band of CH, the CN band (421.6 nm) and the CaII K line (indices respectively g, n, k) based on measurements in just five of the filters [128, 143]. In the 1960s this was further developed into the Danish $gnkmfu$ system for late-type stars [139].

After Strömgren left Yerkes for Princeton in 1957 he developed the widely used intermediate-band $uvby$ system [132, 144]. This was based on $abcdef$, but employed wider passbands and, as with the earlier system, interference filters were used except in the ultraviolet. Composite indices m, and c, were sensitive to metallicity and the Balmer jump for B and F stars.† The passbands were about 20 nm wide (except for u which was 30 nm).

The $uvby$ system has become closely associated with the β system of Hβ-line photoelectric photometry, which was devised by David Crawford (b. 1931) during the time of his doctoral thesis research at Yerkes and McDonald Observatories, under the supervision of Strömgren [129]. Crawford and Strömgren improved on the original l index of the $abcdef$ system, and devised two photometers which would simultaneously measure the flux of the Hβ line in narrow- and intermediate-band filters. These were 1.5 and 15.0 nm wide in the final version of this system, used at McDonald Observatory from October 1957. The β-index was then defined as for a colour index in these two filters.‡ This index is sensitive to luminosity and temperature for B stars, but essentially only to temperature for F stars; on the other hand, the c_1 index is largely a temperature indicator for B stars, but is sensitive to both temperature and luminosity for F types. A complete discussion of the properties of $uvby\beta$ photometry and its use for stellar classification was given by Strömgren in a review article in 1966 [145].

The $uvby\beta$ system has become the most widely used intermediate-band system in astronomy. By 1970 some 50 papers annually were being published in this system [146], and by 1976 the grand total was 775. The first printed photometric catalogue of $uvby\beta$ photometry was compiled by E. Lindemann and Bernard Hauck (b. 1937) in 1971 and contained data for 7603 stars [147].

A number of photometric systems were devised around 1960 and some of these used intermediate or narrow bands for several of their filters. In fact, the $uvby$ system was not the first to be described in the literature. These included the Borgman system (1960), the Walraven system (1960), the Geneva system (1963) and the Vilnius system (1963), where the dates refer to the year of the first major publication in which each system was

---

† These were $m_1 = (v - b) - (b - y)$ and $c_1 = (u - v) - (v - b)$. The subscripts distinguish these indices from similarly defined m and c in the $abcdef$ system.

‡ $\beta = 2.5\log I(15.0) - \log I(1.5) +$ constant.

described. These four systems have certain properties in common; they were multicolour intermediate-bandwidth photomultiplier systems, using mainly the near-ultraviolet to yellow spectral regions, and designed to separate stars of different effective temperature, luminosity, metallicity and interstellar reddening which occurred in different regions of the Hertzsprung-Russell diagram.

Jan Borgman's system from Groningen [131, 148] used seven interference filters $RQPNMLK$. It was a development of an earlier five-filter system devised by Borgman with Strömgren and Morgan at Yerkes, for the separation of population types among later-type stars [149].

In 1967 Harold Johnson extended the Borgman system to a 13-colour narrow-band system by adding six additional filters from 630 to 1100 nm using an RCA 7102 (S1) photomultiplier [138]. This system was used over the next decade by Johnson and Mitchell to obtain photometry on bright stars in both hemispheres [150].

The Walraven $WULBV$ system was devised by Theodore Walraven (b. 1916) and his wife at the Leiden Southern Station; U, B and V were similar to, though narrower than, the corresponding Johnson filters (B avoided the Hβ and Hϵ lines), while W and L were still narrower ultraviolet filters each side of the Balmer Jump [151]. The light in all four filters was measured simultaneously. The Walraven system was designed explicitly for reddening studies of early-type stars, but has also been used for Cepheids and other F and G supergiants [152, 153].

The Geneva system was devised by Marcel Golay (b. 1927) at the Geneva Observatory, and has been in use since 1959. It has seven glass filters $UB_1BB_2V_1G$; here UBV are similar to the Johnson UBV, while B_1, B_2, V_1 and G are narrower, about 40 nm wide [135]. The system has been described extensively by Golay [154, 155] and it was designed to give the temperature, luminosity, metallicity and reddening of a wide range of spectral types, and also to detect fast-rotating stars, stars with spectral peculiarities and also binary systems. The early observations were made at Geneva, Haute-Provence and on the Jungfraujoch, and catalogues were produced by F. Rufener and his associates [156, 157]. In 1971, just 1406 mainly brighter stars were in Rufener's catalogue, but the amount of high-precision photometry in this system increased enormously after that date when observing was undertaken from La Silla in Chile. In many ways the Geneva system was the first really comprehensive system of stellar photometry, with carefully chosen and calibrated passbands designed to analyse a wide range of stellar types and of astrophysical phenomena.

The Vilnius system was first devised in 1962 by Vytautas Straižys in Lithuania and has some features in common with the Geneva system. It has seven filters ($UPXYZVS$), although occasionally (in 1965–66) an eighth red filter (T) has been used [133]. Unlike the other intermediate-band systems described, it was devised for an S20 multialkali photomultiplier, originally one of Soviet manufacture (an FEU-79). The filters are glass, except for T and S, which are interference filters. Like the Geneva system, it can be regarded as a comprehensive system in that it was designed for the study of all spectral types and a wide range of spectral peculiarities. Not all filters are needed for any given spectral type – for example $UPXYZ$ are used for early-type stars, and $XYZTS$ for late types. A detailed discussion has been given by Straižys [73].

The Vilnius system is still in active use, but not nearly so many stars have been observed as for Geneva photometry. The catalogue of Kazimieras Zdanavičius (b. 1938) *et al.* in 1972 gave data for 600 bright stars [158], while several hundred other stars of various types had been reported in the literature prior to that date.

9.5.2   Broad-band systems in the red

The original broad-band multicolour photoelectric system was the six-colour $UVBGRI$ system of Stebbins and Whitford [126, 159]. It was devised primarily for reddening studies on B stars, and the original detector was a Western Electric S1 diode photocell (type D 97087). A notable series of papers by Stebbins, Whitford and, later, Kron was produced using this system at Mt Wilson from 1940 and on the Crossley reflector at Lick from 1949 (e.g. [160]).

In the mid-1950s Kron received five S1 photomultipliers from Lallemand in Paris [29], and one of these with 12 stages was used by Kron to transform the six-colour system to the new photomultiplier [30]. This system was continued to be used by Richard Sears (b. 1931) at Lick from 1959; after 1961 an RCA 7102 S1 photomultiplier was used [161]. The original standards were those of the North Polar Sequence, but new standards were later proposed by James Breckinridge (b. 1939) and Kron [162].

The six-colour system has continued to be in use, notably by P. Mianes and his associates at the Lyon Observatory in France, who observed with a 20-stage Lallemand S1 tube at Haute Provence and on La Silla as recently as December 1970 [163, 164].

In the 1960s the six-colour system appears to have lost favour to the multicolour $UBVRIJKLMN$ system, devised by Johnson from 1959 as an extension of the UBV system [134, 165]. Of these ten bands, R and I were observed with an ITT FW-118 (S1) photomultiplier; the mean wavelengths were given by Johnson as about 670 and 870 nm (though in practice wavelengths considerably longer than these appear more likely – see the comments by V. Straižys [73]). The reasons for Johnson $UBVRI$ photometry overtaking the six-colour system are not obvious – it appears to be mainly the greater amount of published material and the existing popularity of the by UBV system.

An extensive catalogue of Johnson multicolour photometry obtained in Arizona, Mexico and at the McDonald Observatory was published in 1966 [70]. The properties of the system were reviewed by Johnson, also in 1966 [166], and its application to determining effective temperatures and bolometric corrections for cool stars was discussed.

The photomultiplier passbands of the Johnson system ($UBVRI$) required two photomultipliers for their realization (S4 or S11, and S1); this inconvenience limited many observers to just UBV, given the low sensitivity of S1 tubes. The S20 photocathode was at first unable to record the Johnson I band. Only in the early 1970s did an extended S20R (or S25) photomultiplier make five-filter Johnson photometry a possibility [167], followed shortly afterwards by tubes with the new GaAs photocathode [168, 169].

The Kron RI system is another broad-band system originally based on a diode S1 photocell (type Continental Electric CE-25) and glass and gelatine filters [52]. This system was first used on the Crossley and 36-inch refractor telescopes at Lick in 1949. The mean wavelengths were 680 and 825 nm. Kron took his photometer to Australia in 1951 and continued the (RI) photometry of bright stars at Mt Stromlo Observatory with Ben Gascoigne (b. 1915), using standard stars in the Harvard C regions [170]. For the Australian work an interference filter was used for the R band. A paper with $(R, I)_K$ photometry for 282 parallax stars was the principal outcome, and the colour vs. red absolute magnitude (M_R) diagram was investigated [171]. Olin Eggen in Australia continued observing in the Kron system, using Kron's original filters but an ITT FW-118 (S1) photomultiplier [172, 173].

The Cambridge astronomer Noel Argue (b. 1922), observing at Kitt Peak in 1964, used his own system of red photometry with an RCA 7102 (S1) photomultiplier [137]. He had four filters: r (broad-band interference filter centred on 680 nm); $rg8$ and $rg9$ (broad-band glass filters, each at about 820 nm) and i (a 30 nm wide interference filter at 1020 nm). The ($r - rg9$) colour matched Kron's $(R - I)_K$ fairly closely, while ($r - i$) could be reliably converted to Johnson's $(R - I)_J$ through a linear transformation. Only 300 late-type stars were observed in this system.

In 1976 Alan Cousins introduced a VRI system based on the new RCA 31034A GaAs photomultiplier, which gave much higher quantum efficiency in the far red ($\lambda < 920$ nm) than provided by the S1 photocathode [140]. The Cousins system was developed on the Cape 18-inch reflector and employed an *R*-band interference filter and *I*-band Schott glass filter, with mean wavelengths of 670 and 810 nm. This system therefore resembles that of Kron, which it has now largely replaced, in part because of the excellent E-region standards established by Cousins in the southern hemisphere.

9.5.3   A comment on new photometric systems

The four years 1959–63 saw a bewildering variety of new photometric systems being developed. The systems of Strömgren, Crawford, Geneva, Walraven, Borgman and Vilnius, as well as the Johnson multicolour system, all first appeared during this brief interval. One reason for this was probably the simultaneous developments in the computation of the first line-blanketed model atmospheres for stars by Eugene Avrett (b. 1933) and Stephen Strom (b. 1942) at Harvard [174] and by Dmitri Mihalas (b. 1939) at Princeton [175]. Mihalas folded his Balmer-line blanketed A-type star fluxes with *UBV* filter functions to predict colour indices which agreed well with those observed [176]. Thus theoretical calibrations of photometric indices became possible. Moreover, the availability of high quality coudé spectra showing the absorption features in stellar spectra of different type, and the narrow-band observation of stellar energy distributions led astronomers to consider far more carefully the placement of their photometric passbands. Most of the new systems had intermediate bands carefully selected for special purposes. Until 1963 most new systems used the 1P21 photomultiplier, but the S20 cathodes available at this time also opened up new observational possibilities, as, for example, in the Vilnius system.

9.6   Photomultiplier photometry in the southern hemisphere

Although the electrical measurement of starlight was initiated in the northern hemisphere in the 1890s, none of this technology was practised south of the equator for over half a century. The earliest photoelectric photometry in the south was apparently that of Arthur Hogg (1903–66) in Australia using a gas-filled Osram diode photocell on the 30-inch Reynolds reflector at the Commonwealth Observatory on Mt Stromlo [177]. His photometer had no Fabry lens, no filters and a Lindemann electrometer.

When the 1P21 became available, Hogg was one of the early pioneers of southern hemisphere photomultiplier photometry. He used the new tube on the 9-inch Oddie refractor as well as on the Reynolds reflector from

1948 [178, 179]. This was the same year that Richard Stoy introduced the photomultiplier for photometry at the Cape, using a 931-A tube on the 7-inch refractor [180]. The following year George Eiby (1918–92) was using another 931-A photometer on a 9-inch refractor at the Carter Observatory in Wellington, New Zealand [181, 182].

9.6.1   Early photoelectric photometry in South Africa

These early and tentative experiments in photoelectric photometry were transformed, however, by a series of distinguished visitors to the observatories in South Africa as well as to the Commonwealth (Mt Stromlo) Observatory in Australia during the 1950s. The visitors brought with them the technical know-how of photomultipliers from the observatories of North America and Europe. The first of these travellers was Jan Schilt from Columbia University, who came to use a 931-A photometer on the 26-inch refractor of the Yale-Columbia Southern Station in Johannesburg. Observing began in October 1948 with the assistance of Cyril Jackson (1903–88), the Yale-Columbia observer, and the colours of over two thousand southern stars were obtained using blue and yellow filters [183, 184].

In 1950 Richard Stoy invited John Irwin (b. 1909) and Arthur Cox (b. 1927) from the Goethe Link Observatory of Indiana University to South Africa. After a short stay at the Radcliffe Observatory in Pretoria from June, they were at the Cape from September, where they installed their 1P21 'Kirkwood' photometer on the 24-inch Victoria refractor. This was a most opportune time for Stoy and his assistant Alan Cousins (b. 1903) to become familiar with new photoelectric techniques from North America. Cousins, who had joined the Cape staff in 1947, had made the early trials with Stoy the following year. He was to become one of the great practitioners of precise photoelectric photometry in the second half of the twentieth century. One of Cox's main concerns was the transfer of the NPS standards of the International System to the southern hemisphere, using stars in the Harvard E-regions at −45°, with C-region stars (at +15°) as an intermediate calibration [185, 186, 187]. This theme was taken up by Stoy and Cousins, with the aim of calibrating the Cape photographic S-system (see section 7.8.2), and indeed this goal became a major one for the Cape observers during most of the 1950s [188, 189].

In another paper, Cousins and Stoy stressed the essential properties of standard magnitude stars which are used to define a photometric system [190]. A wide range of spectral type, luminosity class and interstellar reddening was required, together with accessibility of the stars, a high

Fig. 9.12 Alan Cousins in 1952.

precision (better than one per cent) for the standard magnitudes and a specification of the response of the telescope-photometer system at each wavelength.

Another group of photometrists to visit South Africa in 1950 was from Harvard. Bart Bok (1906–83) came with his wife Priscilla Bok and Ivan King (b. 1927), as well as the Indonesian astronomer and Harvard graduate student Uco van Wijk (1924–66). The Boks and van Wijk used the Linnell-King 1P21 photometer on the 60-inch Rockefeller reflector of Harvard's Boyden Station to observe B stars in the southern Milky Way [191, 192]. Van Wijk also established the first photoelectric sequence in the Large Magellanic Cloud [193]. As with Irwin and Cox, they also visited the Union Observatory in Johannesburg and the Radcliffe Observatory in Pretoria, thereby ensuring that the expertise in photomultiplier techniques was widely disseminated at South African observatories. Like the Indiana and Cape observers, King also obtained standard magnitudes in the southern E-regions using two-colour (P, V) photometry, and in fact his doctoral thesis at Harvard was written on this subject – see [194].

Finally the close association between the Union and Leiden Observatories since 1923 resulted in a photoelectric programme by Leiden observers in South Africa, also from 1950. Pieter Oosterhoff (1904–78) visited the southern station in the winter of 1950 and he measured the colours of early-type stars in three filters (415, 500, 532 nm) using a 931-A photomultiplier [195] – see also [196]). Also in this year Theodore Walraven (b. 1916) became the southern station director. With A. Muller he installed a photoelectric photometer on the Radcliffe 74-inch reflector in 1951, and David Thackeray (1910–78) immediately commissioned another photometer for Radcliffe from Leiden at that time, which was delivered from Holland in 1952. These photometers were mounted at the newtonian focus, and the output was on a Brown strip-chart recorder [197, 198].

The Leiden 36-inch reflector was installed at Hartebeesport in 1957, which enabled Walraven to extend greatly his photometry in the south. Here he developed the $VLBUW$ Walraven photometer system from 1958 [130].

9.6.2   Early photoelectric photometry in Australia

Australia also benefited from visitors from North America bringing their photometric expertise with them. Gerry Kron and Olin Eggen from Lick both arrived at the Commonwealth Observatory at Mt Stromlo in January 1951 for an extended programme of photometry. Kron brought his Lick $(RI)_K$ photometer, using a Continental CE-25 gas-filled diode photocell, and established with Ben Gascoigne the first red and near infrared photoelectric magnitudes in the southern hemisphere [170, 199, 171]. For Eggen this was the first of several extended visits to Mt Stromlo prior to his becoming the observatory's director in 1966. These visits resulted in data for many bright southern stars in the $(P, V)_E$ and, later, the UBV systems [56].

Other observers also came to Mt Stromlo in the 1950s, no doubt because of the rapid expansion in the observatory initiated by Richard Woolley (1906–86), at about the time it became a part of the Australian National University in 1957. Thus when the Yale-Columbia 26-inch refractor was moved to Mt Stromlo from South Africa in 1952, Jan Schilt from Columbia supervised the new installation and also undertook photoelectric observations [200]. Another distinguished visitor was Frank Bradshaw Wood as a Fulbright Fellow from the University of Pennsylvania in 1957–58, to observe southern eclipsing binary stars on the Mt Stromlo reflectors [201], while Bart Bok with his wife was active in photoelectric photometry during his first year as Stromlo director from 1957 [202, 203].

Meanwhile Gascoigne, working on Cepheids in the Galaxy and Magel-

Fig. 9.13   Olin Eggen.

lanic Clouds, and Hogg, observing bright field stars and galactic clusters in *UBV*, continued to be active throughout this decade. William Tifft (b. 1932) from Caltech, at Mt Stromlo from August 1958, also studied Magellanic Cloud Cepheids photoelectrically [204]. Another significant influence on Australian photometry was the arrival of Uppsala observers from Sweden to use the new Uppsala Schmidt telescope on Mt Stromlo. Bengt Westerlund (b. 1921) was the Uppsala observer in Canberra from 1958, and he also undertook photoelectric photometry on the Stromlo reflectors [205].

9.6.3   Further developments in photoelectric work in South Africa

Meanwhile several interesting developments took place in South African photometry in the mid-1950s. These included a pulse-counting photoelectric polarimeter at the Cape, installed on the Victoria refractor by D. W. Beggs from Cambridge in 1953. Also Arthur Code (b. 1923) with Theodore Houck (b. 1926) came to Radcliffe and the Cape in 1953 and undertook tests on the ultraviolet transmission of the Victoria objective lens. The result was the introduction of the unique Cape system of $U_C BV$ photometry on the 24-inch refractor, and 13-inch astrograph – see section 9.3.3. Halton Arp (b. 1927) from Caltech was one observer using this system at the Cape during 1955–56 [206], and he showed that no simple transformation to the Johnson UBV system was possible, because of the different U passbands. When the Cape Observatory installed an 18-inch reflector in 1957, this became the preferred telescope of Alan Cousins, who used it for UBV photometry in the Johnson system, so as to be able to tie the Cape S system of photographic photometry to the UBV system widely adopted elsewhere [207]. The question of the multivalued relationship of the Cape and Johnson UBV systems was also considered by Olin Eggen during his visit to the Cape in 1958 [208]; like Cousins, he mainly used the new reflector for $(P, V)_E$ and UBV photometry.

Wilhelm Becker came to the Cape from Basel in 1958 to make photographic exposures of southern galactic clusters in his RGU system. Some photoelectric calibrations were taken for this work. One of the most interesting of the southern photometric programmes was that of Roderick Willstrop (b. 1934) from Cambridge, who installed a special 4-inch refracting telescope at the Cape in 1958 and undertook photometry in four 20-nm-wide bands at 541 (y), 460 (b_1), 439 (b_2) and 422 (b_3) nanometres using an EMI photomultiplier with interference filters to define the bands [209, 210]. The bands y and b_2 were close in wavelength to V and B of Johnson. Willstrop's observations of 221 southern stars were the first photomultiplier observations where the data were calibrated against a standard lamp in an artificial star, with the fluxes expressed in units of ergs cm^{-2} sec^{-1} $(100 \text{ Å})^{-1}$ outside the Earth's atmosphere.

Southern hemisphere photoelectric photometry both was born and quickly came of age in the 1950s. It was a decade of vigorous growth in photometric work in South Africa and Australia and a tradition was established, which is regarded as commonplace today, for observers based in the northern hemisphere to travel south explicitly to gather data on the less well observed southern stars. The photomultiplier tube was the unifying link in this story.

Fig. 9.14   Uncooled photoelectric photometer on the 40-inch Elizabeth reflector at the Cape, 1964. (r.: R. H. Stoy.)

For the first time astronomers had a photoelectric detector which was robust, relatively easy to use and readily transportable to distant telescope sites overseas.

9.7   Photoelectric spectrophotometry

The first experiments in the photoelectric recording of stellar spectra were made by Theodore Dunham (1897–1984) at the Mt Wilson 100-inch telescope and coudé spectrograph in 1933, using a potassium hydride photocell [211]. These were high resolving power observations from which Dunham recorded the profiles of solar absorption lines. Hermann Brück (b. 1905) in Cambridge continued this type of work a few years later, using a technique to record automatically the profiles on bromide paper mounted on a rotating drum, exposed by a light spot galvanometer [212].

For stellar spectral scans John Hall was the early pioneer, with his low resolving power objective grating scans from the blue to near infrared made at the Sproul Observatory in 1934–35 and recorded using an S1 photocell [213] – see section 5.5.1. However, the photomultiplier tubes available after the Second World War opened up a new dimension to narrow-band spectrophotometry. Albert Hiltner and Arthur Code (b. 1923) at Yerkes Observatory used a 1P21 on the coudé spectrograph at McDonald in 1949 and they devised a method of compensating for seeing fluctuations at the coudé slit by using a second monitor channel [214]. This was the first photomultiplier spectrophotometer. When Code moved to Mt Wilson in 1951 he installed a spectrophotometer with a 1P21 on the 60-inch coudé prism spectrograph and hence obtained blue spectral scans on a Brown recorder of some 25 bright stars [215]. The resolution was 5 to 10 Å. The remainder of this section will review this lower resolution spectrophotometry of stellar energy distributions.

Code's work at McDonald, and especially Mt Wilson, marked the beginning of successful photoelectric spectrophotometry in the United States from the 1950s. Three observatories dominated this new type of work: Mt Wilson, Michigan at Ann Arbor, and Warner and Swasey at Cleveland. Later Whitford and Code also developed a photoelectric scanner at Wisconsin [216]. In Europe, early photoelectric spectrophotometry was undertaken in France by Pierre Guérin [217] at Haute Provence and by N. A. Dimov in the Crimea [218].

The spectrophotometry of William Liller (b. 1927) and Lawrence Aller (b. 1913) at Michigan [219] and of Donald MacRae (b. 1916) [220], Jurgen Stock (b. 1923) [221] and Walter Bonsack (b. 1932) [222] at Cleveland was initially with the Schmidt telescopes at these institutions. The spectra were scanned simply by trailing the telescope in the dispersion direction. A photomultiplier was mounted behind a narrow slit so as to define a passband of a few tens of ångstrom units and continuous scans were output to a Brown recorder and, for the Cleveland data, reduced relative to unreddened O9–B0 stars at 23 wavelengths from 350 to 500 nm.

A major development was the work of Code to obtain an absolutely calibrated scan of α Lyrae, by comparison with a standard tungsten filament lamp, which was in turn calibrated against a black-body furnace in a laboratory. This enabled the relative fluxes (in ergs cm^{-2} sec^{-1} Å^{-1}) to be determined. Code's earliest calibration was published in 1960 [223] and used by Bev Oke (b. 1928) in a paper defining six standard stars for photoelectric spectrophotometry [224]. In the Code and Oke spectrophotometry, the data were presented at discrete wavelengths, where early-type stars were relatively free of lines, as provided by the data of William Melbourne at Caltech, who measured the line blanketing in A to G dwarfs from photographic coudé spectra [225]. This work allowed spectrophotometry in bands typically 50 Å wide to be corrected to the continuum values, which would in turn allow comparison with the fluxes predicted from the early non-grey model atmospheres.

Oke had soon extended this calibration to beyond 1 μm in the near infrared, using an RCA 7102 (S1) photomultiplier for the red part of the scan [226]. Moreover, he had built a compact Cassegrain spectrophotometer [224, 226] in which the scan was made by a slow rotation of the plane diffraction grating. Oke's instrument was used on the 60- and 100-inch telescopes at Mt Wilson for his studies of the energy distribution of Cepheids [227, 228] at different phases, and of RR Lyrae variables to obtain effective temperatures and surface gravities [229, 230]. It was also used by Alex Rodgers (b. 1932) for spectrophotometry of O stars [231], and by Code for subdwarfs [232].

In the mid-1950s a similar Cassegrain scanner was built at Michigan by Aller and Liller [233]. This instrument also operated into the infrared with a Farnsworth 16-stage S1 photomultiplier, or in the blue it used Lallemand or EMI tubes. This Michigan scanner, mounted, however, at the newtonian focus of the Curtis Schmidt telescope, was used by Robert Bless (b. 1927) to obtain blue spectrophotometric continuum scans of A stars [234]. Code's unpublished Vega calibration was used, and the results were an excellent illustration of how spectrophotometric fluxes could be compared with the computed predictions for non-grey model atmospheres.

The Michigan scanner was taken to Australia by Aller in 1960, where he observed the energy distributions of selected southern early-type stars at Mt Stromlo Observatory and the Mt Bingar field station with Don Faulkner [235, 236]. The Aller and Faulkner observations were the first with a narrow-band grating spectrometer in the southern hemisphere. But they were followed soon afterwards by the spectrophotometry of Roderick

Fig. 9.15   The Liller-Aller spectrophotometer at Michigan, 1957.

Willstrop, who took his photoelectric spectrum scanner from Cambridge to South Africa, where he used it on the newtonian focus of the Radcliffe reflector during 1962 [237]. Willstrop did not directly calibrate his data relative to α Lyrae, which is not well placed for southern observers, nor to Oke's secondary spectrophotometric standards. Instead he interpolated in his earlier Cape narrow-band filter photometry which had been compared with a calibrated standard lamp [209]. Some significant discrepancies were obtained in a comparison with the data of Code and Oke.

The problem of the absolute calibration of spectrophotometry was discussed by Code in 1960. He wrote:

> The apparent simplicity of a direct comparison of stellar radiation
> with that from a black body is illusory. It is not an undertaking to be
> approached casually. The operation of a true black-body radiator, at a
> well-defined temperature, is an exacting enough procedure in a
> laboratory, to say nothing of its use at a site convenient for telescopic
> observation. In addition many telescopes are not constructed so that it
> is convenient to focus on a nearby source or to point toward the
> horizon [223].

This fundamental problem of the absolute calibration was tackled by several observers during the 1960s, and experiments were published at intervals, including by Klaus Bahner (b. 1921) from Heidelberg, who made his observations on the 36-inch telescope at the McDonald Observatory [238], by A. V. Kharitonov in the Crimea [239], by Don Hayes (b. 1939) [240, 241] and by Oke and Rudy Schild (b. 1940) [242].

A review article by Oke in 1965 discussed the need for the absolute calibration of standard-star spectrophotometry, if the observations were to be compared with computed fluxes from model atmospheres [243]. The practical problems of comparing a standard lamp with a star were discussed. Oke noted: 'Until very recently the absolute calibration of α Lyrae by comparison with a standard lamp has yielded distressingly discordant results' [243] and he also commented that α Lyrae (A0 V) with its broad converging hydrogen lines in the Balmer series, was 'to some extent an unfortunate choice' as a primary standard.

By 1966 it was clear there were some problems with Oke's 1964 calibration of α Lyrae, if the temperatures of A and B stars derived from the Paschen continuum slope (that is, in the blue, visual and red spectral regions), and from the size of the Balmer discontinuity at 365 nm, were to be in mutual agreement – see e.g. [244]. Such problems, arising from the difficulty of calibrating a star with a lamp, were largely removed in the calibrations of Don Hayes in 1967 and of Oke and Rudy Schild in 1970. Hayes obtained his observations on the Crossley telescope using a new Lick Observatory scanner designed by Joseph Wampler (b. 1933) [245], while Oke and Schild used a new scanner built by Oke for the 200-inch Palomar telescope, but used here on α Lyrae by attaching it to a special 10-cm-aperture newtonian reflector to enable the observation of such a bright star [242]. One feature of Wampler's instrument is that it did not scan continuously, but the grating moved so as to record and integrate on selected discrete wavelength regions only, which increased the efficiency of telescope time and enabled fainter stars to be reached.

9.8   Ultraviolet photometry above the Earth's atmosphere

The high extinction of the terrestrial atmosphere at wavelengths below about 320 nm prevents ground-based photometry in this spectral region. This section records the early development of ultraviolet photometry from rockets and satellites prior to 1970. Altitudes of about 100 km above the earth's surface are required to obtain unobstructed measures of radiation in the 100–320 nm region.

9.8.1   Ultraviolet photometry from rockets

Rocket astronomy was first undertaken from 1946 by the US Naval Research Laboratory using the technology of V2 rockets captured from Germany. Richard Tousey (b. 1908) at NRL obtained the first ultraviolet solar spectrum from a V2 in 1946. Soon afterwards the American Aerobee rocket was developed and in the 1950s this launch vehicle was used for the first attempt at detecting ultraviolet radiation from stars. The Naval Research Laboratory conducted Aerobee launches from the White Sands site in New Mexico in 1955 and 1957 for ultraviolet stellar photometry, but it is probable that neither of these flights detected far ultraviolet stellar radiation [246, 247]. However, the second flight recorded the radiation from bright early-type stars in a single band at 270 nm. Albert Boggess (b. 1929) thus reported the first stellar photometry below the atmospheric cutoff [248].

Successful rocket photometry at shorter wavelengths followed in 1960–61, by which time three groups were undertaking this type of programme. Talbot Chubb (b. 1923) and Edward Byram from the US Naval Research Laboratory reported two flights in 1960 that detected over 50 stars in bands at 142.7 and 131.4 nm [249]. Ionization chamber detectors collecting radiation from small 10 and 15-cm parabolic mirrors were used. Also in 1960, Theodore Stecher and James Milligan at the Goddard Space Flight Center undertook successful narrow-band spectrophotometry of seven bright OB stars and of Canopus using a grating spectrometer with EMI photomultipliers on an Aerobee rocket [250]. Their wavelength interval was 160 to 400 nm. Finally, a British group from University College London launched a Skylark rocket from Woomera in Australia in May 1961 and detected about 15 early-type stars at 200 nm, also using EMI photomultipliers [251].

Rocket photometry was always difficult. The flights lasted only a few minutes, the rocket photometers had no pointing capability and their calibration was always a problem. The early data were reviewed by Douglas Heddle (b. 1928) [252] and by Albert Boggess [253].

9.8.2   Ultraviolet photometry from satellites

The first proposals to use satellites for ultraviolet astronomy came from astronomers such as Arthur Code and Lyman Spitzer (b. 1914) in the late 1950s. This idea was supported by the US National Aeronautics and Space Administration, and a series of Orbiting Astronomical Observatories was planned. Four satellites in this series were built and two were operated successfully in orbit. The first of these two was the OAO-2, launched in December 1968. This 2-tonne spacecraft was the heaviest unmanned vehicle that had then been put into orbit. It revolutionized our knowledge of the ultraviolet radiation from stars. The other was the Copernicus satellite for ultraviolet spectroscopy (launched in 1972).

The OAO-2 carried two experiments, from the University of Wisconsin and from the Smithsonian Astrophysical Observatory. The latter Celescope programme involved imaging photometry (see section 10.4.2); the former comprised five small telescopes for ultraviolet filter photometry with photomultipliers, and another two telescopes for grating spectrophotometry.

The instrumentation on this satellite was described in detail by Arthur Code and his Wisconsin colleagues [254]. The five photometric telescopes had sixteen intermediate bandwidth filters covering the wavelength range from 133 to 425 nm, with some deliberate redundancy. EMI and Ascop photomultipliers were the detectors used. The two grating spectrometers also covered the range from 105 to 380 nm, but in narrower bands.

Preliminary results from the OAO-2 Wisconsin experiment were reported by Code [255]. The effective temperatures of early-type stars and the wavelength dependence of interstellar extinction in the ultraviolet were the primary goals. The early results at once showed anomalously high extinction around 220 nm, which was discussed in more detail by Robert Bless (b. 1927) and Blair Savage (b. 1941) [256] and ascribed to graphite particles in the interstellar medium [257]. This phenomenon confirmed somewhat earlier rocket data obtained from spectrophotometry by Theodore Stecher (b. 1930) at Goddard [258, 259]. Stecher was the first explicitly to identify the peak seen with graphite† grains [260].

---

† The idea that graphite particles may be ejected from cool carbon stars and contribute to interstellar extinction has a longer history. This was first suggested by Evry Schatzman (b. 1920) and Roger Cayrel (b. 1925) in Paris [261] in 1954 and was discussed further by Fred Hoyle and Nalin Wickramasinghe (b. 1939) in 1962 [262].

OAO-2 was just the first of a series of ultraviolet astronomy satellites that opened up this new window on the universe. OAO-3, the Copernicus satellite (launched in 1972), TD-1A (1972), ANS (1974) and IUE (1978) all made substantial contributions to this new branch of astronomy in the 1970s decade, but lie beyond the time frame being considered here.

References

[1]   Hull, A.W., *Proc. Inst. Radio Engineers*, **6**, 5 (1918).
[2]   Iams, H. and Salzberg, B., *Proc. Inst. Radio Engineers*, **23**, 55 (1935).
[3]   Penning, F. and Kruithof, A., *Physica*, **2**, 793 (1935).
[4]   Weiss, G., *Zeitschr. Tech. Phys.*, **17**, 623 (1936).
[5]   Zworykin, V.K., Morton, G.A. and Malter, L., *Proc. Inst. Radio Engineers*, **24**, 351 (1936).
[6]   Whitford, A.E. and Kron, G.E., *Rev. Sci. Instruments*, **8**, 78 (1937).
[7]   Kron, G.E., *Oral History Interview with G.E. Kron by D.H. DeVorkin*, Amer. Inst. Phys., Niels Bohr Library, pp. 37 and 61 (1978).
[8]   Siedentopf, H., *Astron. Nachr.*, **269**, 269 (1939).
[9]   Görlich, P., *Zeitschr. für Phys.*, **101**, 335 (1936).
[10] Görlich, P. and Meyer, E. *Zeitschr. für Astrophys.* **16**, 343 (1938).
[11] Görlich, P., *J. Optical Soc. America*, **31**, 504 (1941).
[12] Glover, A.M. and Janes, R.B., *Electronics*, **13** (8), 26 (1940).
[13] Rajchman, J.A. and Snyder, R.L., *Electronics*, **13** (12), 20 (1940).
[14] Glover, A.M., *Proc. Inst. Radio Engineers*, **29**, 413 (1941).
[15] Janes, R.B. and Glover, A.M., *RCA Rev.*, **6**, 43 (1941).
[16] Zworykin, V.K. and Ramberg, E.G., *Photoelectricity and Its Application*, J. Wiley & Sons, N.Y. (1949). See p. 152.
[17] Engstrom, R.W., *J. Optical Soc. America*, **37**, 420 (1947).
[18] Kron, G.E., *Astrophys. J.*, **103**, 326 (1946).
[19] Whitford, A.E., *Ann. Rev. Astron. Astrophys.*, **24**, 1 (1986).
[20] Whitford, A.E., *Oral History Interview with A.E. Whitford by D.H. DeVorkin*, Amer. Inst. Phys., Niels Bohr Library, p. 35 (1977).
[21] Lallemand, A., *J. Phys. et le Radium*, **10** (8), 235 (1949).
[22] Lallemand, A., in *Astron. Techniques*, ed. W.A. Hiltner, *Stars and Stellar Systems*, vol. **2**, chap. 6, p. 126, Univ. Chicago Press (1962).
[23] Lenouvel, F., *Comptes Rendus de l'Acad. des Sci.*, **232**, 385 (1951).
[24] Lenouvel, F., in *Astron. Photoelectric Photometry*, ed. F.B. Wood, p. 89, Amer. Assoc. Adv. Sci., Philadelphia (1953).
[25] Oort, J.H. and Walraven, Th., *Bull. Astron. Inst. Netherlands*, **12**, 285 (1956).
[26] Bouigue, R. and Chapuis, J.-L., *Ann. Observ. Astron. Méteo. Toulouse*, **24**, 55 (1956).
[27] Cocito, G. and Masani, A., *Mem. Soc. Astron. Ital.* (new series), **31**, 135 (1960).
[28] Kron, G.E., Greeby, R.W. and Willson, J.R., *Publ. Astron. Soc. Pacific*, **68**, 544 (1956).
[29] Kron, G.E., *Publ. Astron. Soc. Pacific*, **70**, 285 (1958).
[30] Kron, G.E., *Publ. Astron. Soc. Pacific*, **70**, 561 (1958).
[31] Kron, G.E., *Harvard Coll. Observ. Circ.*, **451**, 37 (1948).

[32] Smith, S., *Astrophys. J.*, **76**, 286 (1932).
[33] Bay, Z., *Rev. Sci. Instr.*, **12**, 127 (1941).
[34] Allen, J.S., *Rev. Sci. Instr.*, **12**, 484 (1941).
[35] Strömgren, B., *Oral History Interview with B. Strömgren by L. Hoddeson and G. Baym*, Amer. Inst. Phys., Niels Bohr Library, p. 16 (1976).
[36] Blitzstein, W., in *Astron. Photoelectric Photometry*, ed. F. B. Wood, p. 64, Amer. Assoc. Adv. Sci., Washington, DC (1953).
[37] Yates, G.G., *Mon. Not. R. Astron. Soc.*, **108**, 476 (1948).
[38] Yates, G.G., *Observatory*, **69**, 3 (1949).
[39] Beer, A., Redman, R.O. and Yates, G.G., *Mem. R. Astron. Soc.*, **67**, 1 (1954). See also *ibid. Mon. Not. R. Astron. Soc.*, **114**, 271 (1954).
[40] Redman, R.O. and Yates, G.G., in *Astron. Photoelectric Photometry*, ed. F.B. Wood, p. 93, Amer. Assoc. Adv. Sci., Washington, DC (1953).
[41] Blitzstein, W., in *The Present and Future of Telescopes of Moderate Size*, p. 95, ed. F.B. Wood, Univ. Penn. Press (1958).
[42] Blitzstein, W., *Vistas in Astron.*, **32**, 181 (1988).
[43] Thackeray, A.D., *Mon. Not. R. Astron. Soc.*, **115**, 168 (1955).
[44] Baum, W.A., *Astron. J.*, **58**, 211 (1953).
[45] Baum, W.A., *Astron. J.*, **60**, 25 (1955).
[46] Baum, W.A., *Sky & Tel.*, **14**, 264, 330 (1955).
[47] Baum, W.A., *Astron. J.*, **59**, 422 (1954).
[48] Johnson, H.L., in *Stars & Stellar Systems*, vol. **2**, *Astron. Techniques*, p. 157, ed. W.A. Hiltner, Chicago Univ. Press (1962).
[49] Eggen, O.J., *Astrophys. J.*, **111**, 65 (1950).
[50] Stebbins, J. and Whitford, A.E., *Astrophys. J.*, **108**, 413 (1948).
[51] Johnson, H.L., in *Stars & Stellar Systems*, vol. **3**, *Basic Astron. Data*, p. 204, ed. K.Aa. Strand, Chicago Univ. Press (1963).
[52] Kron, G.E. and Smith, J. Lynn, *Astrophys. J.*, **113**, 324 (1951).
[53] Stebbins, J., Whitford, A.E. and Johnson, H.L., *Astrophys. J.*, **112**, 469 (1950).
[54] Johnson, H.L. and Morgan, W.W., *Astrophys. J.*, **114**, 522 (1951).
[55] Johnson, H.L., *Astrophys. J.*, **116**, 272 (1952).
[56] Eggen, O.J., *Astron. J.*, **60**, 65 (1955).
[57] Eggen, O.J., *Astron. J.*, **60**, 401 (1955).
[58] Kron, G.E., *Vistas in Astron.*, **3**, 171 (1960).
[59] Kron, G.E. and Mayall, N.U., *Astron. J.*, **65**, 581 (1960).
[60] Stoy, R.H. and Becker, W., *Trans. Int. Astron. Union*, **10**, 369 (1960).
[61] Johnson, H.L. and Morgan, W.W., *Astrophys. J.*, **117**, 313 (1953).
[62] Johnson, H.L. and Harris, D.L. III, *Astrophys. J.*, **120**, 196 (1954).
[63] Johnson, H.L., *Ann. d'Astrophys.*, **18**, 292 (1955).
[64] Morgan, W.W., *Oral History Interview with W.W. Morgan*, Amer. Inst. of Phys., Niels Bohr Library, p. 17 (1978).
[65] Greaves, W.M.H., *Trans. Int. Astron. Union*, **9**, 338 (1957).
[66] Stoy, R.H., *Mon. Not. R. Astron. Soc.*, **114**, 305 (1954).
[67] Cousins, A.W.J., Eggen, O.J. and Stoy, R.H., *R. Observ. Bull.*, **25** (1961).
[68] Cousins, A.W.J. and Stoy, R.H., *R. Observ. Bull.*, **64**, 103 (1963).
[69] Cousins, A.W.J., Lake, R. and Stoy, R.H., *R. Observ. Bull.*, **121** (1966).
[70] Johnson, H.L., Mitchell, R.I., Iriarte, B. and Wiśniewski, W.Z., *Comm. Lunar and Plan. Lab.* (No. 63), **4** (Part 3), 99 (1966).
[71] Blanco, V.M., Demers, S., Douglass, G.G. and Fitzgerald, M.P., *Publ. US Naval Observ.* (2nd series), **21**, US Gov. Printing Office, Washington, DC (1968).

[72]   Eggen, O.J., *R. Observ. Bull.*, **125** (1966).
[73]   Straižys, V., *Multicolor Stellar Photometry*, Pachart Publishing House (1992).
[74]   Ažusienis, A. and Straižys, V., *Astron. Zhurn.*, **46**, 402 (1969). English translation in *ibid. Sov. Astron.*, **13**, 316 (1969).
[75]   Johnson, H.L., *Astrophys. J.*, **135**, 975 (1962).
[76]   DeVorkin, D.H., *Proc. Inst. Electric. Electron. Engin.*, **73**, 1205 (1985).
[77]   Kron, G.E., Int. Astron. Union (Comm. 42) *Bull. of the Panel on Orbits of Eclipsing Binaries*, No. **4** (1946).
[78]   Kron, G.E., *Harvard Coll. Observ. Circ.*, **451**, 10 (1948).
[79]   Kron, G.E., *Sky & Tel.*, **6**, 7 (1946).
[80]   Whitford, A.E., *Handbuch der Physik*, **54**, 240 (1962).
[81]   Engstrom, R.W., *Rev. Sci. Inst.*, **18**, 587 (1947).
[82]   Kron, G.E., *Electronics*, **21** (8), 98 (1948).
[83]   Kron, G.E., *Publ. Astron. Soc. Pacific*, **59**, 173, 190 (1947).
[84]   Kron, G.E., *Publ. Astron. Soc. Pacific*, **60**, 253 (1948).
[85]   Öhman, Y., *Ark. Mat. Astron. Fys.*, **29B**, No. 12 (1943).
[86]   Öhman, Y., *Ark. Mat. Astron. Fys.*, **32B**, No. 1 (1945).
[87]   DeWitt, J.H. and Seyfert, C.K., *Publ. Astron. Soc. Pacific*, **62**, 241 (1950).
[88]   Carpenter, E.F. and Wood, F.B., *Astron. J.*, **54**, 182 (1949).
[89]   Cox, H.W., *J. Brit. Astron. Assoc.*, **58**, 101 (1948).
[90]   Sterling, H.T., *Harvard Coll. Observ. Circ.*, **451**, 30 (1948).
[91]   Baum, W.A., *Astron. J.*, **60**, 24 (1955).
[92]   Argue, A.N., *Proc. R. Irish Acad.*, **55A**, 117 (1953).
[93]   Engstrom, R.W., *RCA Rev.*, **21**, 184 (1960).
[94]   Sommer, A.H. and Turk, W.E., *J. Sci. Instr.*, **27**, 113 (1950).
[95]   Sommer, A.H., *Rev. Sci. Instr.*, **26**, 725 (1955).
[96]   Sandage, A. and Smith, L.L., *Astrophys. J.*, **137**, 1057 (1962).
[97]   Weitbrecht, R.H., *Rev. Sci. Instr.*, **28**, 883 (1959).
[98]   Gehrels, T., *Astrophys. J.*, **123**, 331 (1956).
[99]   Wilkes, M.V., *Nature*, **164**, 341 (1949).
[100] Wilkes, M.V., *Nature*, **164**, 557 (1949).
[101] Wilkes, M.V., *Nature*, **166**, 942 (1950).
[102] Porter, J.G., *J. Brit. Astron. Assoc.*, **61**, 185 (1951).
[103] Buscombe, W. and Gollnow, H., *Observatory*, **75**, 131 (1955).
[104] Gray, T.W., *Astron. J.*, **61**, 346 (1956).
[105] Arp, H.C., *Astrophys. J.*, **129**, 507 (1959).
[106] Johnson, H.L., *Lowell Observ. Bull.*, **4**, 123 (1959).
[107] Schulte, D.H., *Astron. J.*, **65**, 500 (1960).
[108] Schulte, D.H. and Crawford, D.L., *Kitt Peak Natl. Observ. Contrib.*, No. **10** (1961).
[109] Sharpless, S., in *Astron. Techniques*, ed. W.A. Hiltner, *Stars and Stellar Systems*, vol. **2**, chap. 9, p. 209, Univ. Chicago Press (1962).
[110] Tremko, J., *Mitt. Astron. Ges.*, **21**, 113 (1966).
[111] Arp, H.C., *Astron. J.*, **63**, 58 (1958).
[112] Smart, W., *Mon. Not. R. Astron. Soc.*, **94**, 115, 839 (1934).
[113] Hardie, R., in *Astron. Techniques*, ed. W.A. Hiltner, *Stars and Stellar Systems*, vol. **2**, chap. 8, p. 178, Univ. Chicago Press (1962).
[114] Hardie, R., *Astrophys. J.*, **130**, 663 (1959).
[115] Stoy, R.H., *Trans. Int. Astron. Union*, **11A**, 241 (1962).
[116] Stebbins, J., *Astron. J.*, **60**, 27 (1955).
[117] Seares, F.H. and Joyner, M.C., *Astrophys. J.*, **98**, 302 (1943).

[118] King, I., *Astron. J.*, **57**, 253 (1952).
[119] Forbes, J.D., *Phil. Trans. R. Soc.*, **132**, 225 (1842).
[120] Blanco, V., *Astrophys. J.*, **125**, 209 (1957).
[121] Wood, F.B. (ed.), *Astron. Photoelectric Photometry*, Amer. Assoc. Adv. Sci., Philadelphia (1953).
[122] Irwin, J.B. (ed.), *Proc. Natl. Sci. Foundation Astron. Photoelectric Conf.*, Univ. Indiana, Bloomington (1954). See also summaries in Irwin, J.B. (ed.), *Astron. J.* **60**, 17–32 (1955).
[123] Hall, J.S., in *Astron. Photoelectric Photometry*, ed. F.B. Wood, p. 41, Amer. Assoc. Adv. Sci., Philadelphia (1953).
[124] Whitford, A.E., in *Astron. Photoelectric Photometry*, ed. F.B. Wood, p. 126, Amer. Assoc. Adv. Sci., Philadelphia (1953).
[125] Whitford, A.E., *Astron. J.*, **60**, 22 (1955).
[126] Stebbins, J. and Whitford, A.E., *Astrophys. J.*, **98**, 20 (1943).
[127] Strömgren, B., *Astron. J.*, **57**, 196 (1952).
[128] Gyldenkerne, K., *Astrophys. J.*, **121**, 38 (1955).
[129] Crawford, D. L., *Astrophys. J.*, **128**, 185 (1958).
[130] Walraven, T. and Walraven, J.H., *Bull. Astron. Inst. Netherlands*, **15**, 67 (1960).
[131] Borgman, J., *Bull. Astron. Inst. Netherlands*, **15**, 255 (1960).
[132] Strömgren, B., *Quart. J. R. Astron. Soc.*, **4**, 8 (1963).
[133] Straižys, V., *Bull. Vilnius Observ.*, **6**, 1 (1963).
[134] Johnson, H.L. and Mitchell, R.I., *Comm. Lunar Plan. Lab.*, **1**, 73 (1962).
[135] Golay, M., *Publ. Observ. de Genève*, **64**, 419 (1963).
[136] Eggen, O.J., *Astrophys. J. Suppl.*, **14**, 307 (1967).
[137] Argue, A.N., *Mon. Not. R. Astron. Soc.*, **135**, 23 (1967).
[138] Johnson, H.L., Mitchell, R.I. and Latham, A.S., *Comm. Lunar & Plan. Lab.*, **6**, 85 (1967).
[139] Dickow, P., Gyldenkerne, K., Hansen, L. Jacobsen, P.-U., Johansen, K.T., Kjaergaard, P. and Olsen, E.H., *Astron. & Astrophys. Suppl.*, **2**, 1 (1970).
[140] Cousins, A.W.J., *Mem. R. Astron. Soc.*, **81**, 25 (1976).
[141] Strömgren, B., in *Stellar Populations*, p. 385, ed. D.J.K. O'Connell, S.J., Vatican Observ. (1958).
[142] Strömgren, B., *Astron. J.*, **56**, 142 (1952).
[143] Strömgren, B. and Gyldenkerne, K., *Astrophys. J.*, **121**, 43 (1955).
[144] Strömgren, B., in *Stars & Stellar Systems*, vol. **3**, *Basic Astron. Data*, p. 123, ed. K.Aa. Strand, Chicago Univ. Press (1963).
[145] Strömgren, B., *Ann. Rev. Astron. Astrophys.*, **4**, 433 (1966).
[146] Davis Philip, A.G. and Perry, C.L., *Vistas in Astron.*, **22**, 279 (1978).
[147] Lindemann, E. and Hauck, B., *Astron. & Astrophys. Suppl.*, **11**, 119 (1972).
[148] Borgman, J., *Bull. Astron. Inst. Netherlands*, **17**, 58 (1963).
[149] Borgman, J., *Astrophys. J.*, **129**, 362 (1959).
[150] Johnson, H.L. and Mitchell, R.I., *Rev. Mexicana Astron. y Astrofis.*, **1**, 299 (1975).
[151] Walraven, T. and Walraven, J.H., *Bull. Astron. Inst. Netherlands*, **15**, 67 (1960).
[152] Walraven, J.H., Tinbergen, J. and Walraven, T., *Bull. Astron. Inst. Netherlands*, **17**, 520 (1964).
[153] Oosterhoff, P.T. and Walraven, T., *Bull. Astron. Inst. Netherlands*, **18**, 387 (1966).

[154] Golay, M., *Vistas in Astron.*, **14**, 13 (1972).
[155] Golay, M., *Vistas in Astron.*, **24**, 141 (1980).
[156] Rufener, F., Hauck, B., Goy, G., Peytremann, E. and Maeder, M., *Publ. Observ. de Genève*, **66**, 1 (1964).
[157] Rufener, F., *Astron. Astrophys. Suppl.*, **3**, 181 (1971).
[158] Zdanavičius, K., Nikonov, V.B., Sūdžius, J., Straižys, V., Sviderskienė, Z., Kalytis, R., Jodinskienė, E., Meištas, E., Kavaliauskaitė, G., Jasevičius, V., Kakaras, G., Bartkevičius, A., Gurklytė, A., Bartkus, R., Ažusienis, A., Sperauskas, J., Kazlauskas, A. and Žitkevičius, V., *Bull. Vilnius Observ.*, **34**, 3 (1972).
[159] Stebbins, J. and Whitford, A.E., *Astrophys. J.*, **102**, 318 (1945).
[160] Stebbins, J. and Kron, G.E., *Astrophys. J.*, **123**, 440 (1956).
[161] Sears, R.L. and Whitford, A.E., *Astrophys. J.*, **155**, 899 (1969).
[162] Breckinridge, J.B. and Kron, G.E., *Trans. Int. Astron. Union*, **12A**, 471 (1964).
[163] Mianes, P., *Ann. d'Astrophys.*, **26**, 1 (1963).
[164] Brunet, J.P., Mianes, P., Perrin, M.-N., Prévot, L., and Rousseau, J., *Astron. & Astrophys.*, **15**, 320 (1971).
[165] Johnson, H.L., *Bol. Observ. Tonantzintla y Tacubaya*, **3**, 305 (1964).
[166] Johnson, H.L., *Ann. Rev. Astron. Astrophys.*, **4**, 193 (1966).
[167] Fernie, J.D., *Publ. Astron. Soc. Pacific*, **86**, 837 (1974).
[168] Spicer, W.E. and Bell, R.L., *Publ. Astron. Soc. Pacific*, **84**, 110 (1972).
[169] Weistrop, D., *Publ. Astron. Soc. Pacific*, **87**, 367 (1975).
[170] Kron, G.E., White, H.S. and Gascoigne, S.C.B., *Astrophys. J.*, **118**, 502 (1953).
[171] Kron, G.E., Gascoigne, S.C.B. and White, H.S., *Astron. J.*, **62**, 205 (1957).
[172] Eggen, O.J., *Astrophys. J. Suppl.*, **16**, 49 (1968).
[173] Eggen, O.J., *Astrophys. J.*, **163**, 313 (1971).
[174] Avrett, E.H. and Strom, S.E., *Ann. d'Astrophys.*, **27**, 781 (1964).
[175] Mihalas, D.M., *Astrophys. J.*, **141**, 564 (1965).
[176] Mihalas, D.M., *Astrophys. J. Suppl.*, **13**, 1 (1965).
[177] Hogg, A.R., *Mon. Not. R. Astron. Soc.*, **106**, 292 (1946).
[178] Hogg, A.R. and Bowe, P.W.A., *Mon. Not. R. Astron. Soc.*, **110**, 373 (1950).
[179] Hogg, A.R. and Hall, B., *Mon. Not. R. Astron. Soc.*, **111**, 325 (1951).
[180] Jackson, J., *Mon. Not. R. Astron. Soc.*, **109**, 158 (1949).
[181] Eiby, G.E., 'An astronomical photometer using a 931-A photomultiplier', M.Sc. thesis, Victoria Univ. Coll., Wellington (1949).
[182] Thomsen, I., *Mon. Not. R. Astron. Soc.*, **110**, 163 (1950).
[183] Schilt, J. and Jackson, C., *Astron. J.*, **55**, 9 (1949).
[184] Schilt, J. and Jackson, C., *Astron. J.*, **56**, 209 (1952).
[185] Cox, A.N., *Mon. Not. Astron. Soc. S. Africa*, **10**, 8 (1951).
[186] Cox, A.N., *Astron. J.*, **57**, 159 (1952).
[187] Cox, A.N., *Astrophys. J.*, **117**, 83 (1953).
[188] Cousins, A.W.J., *Mon. Not. Astron. Soc. S. Africa*, **10**, 11 (1951).
[189] Cousins, A.W.J. and Stoy, R.H., *R. Observ. Bull.*, **49**, 59 (1962). See also *ibid.*, *Cape Mimeogram*, **11** (1958) for preliminary results.
[190] Cousins, A.W.J. and Stoy, R.H., *Mon. Not. R. Astron. Soc.*, **114**, 349 (1954).
[191] Bok, B.J. and van Wijk, U., *Astron. J.*, **56**, 122 (1951).
[192] Bok, B.J. and van Wijk, U., *Astron. J.*, **57**, 213 (1952).

[193] van Wijk, U., *Astron. J.*, **57**, 27 (1952).
[194] King, I., *Astron. J.*, **60**, 391 (1955).
[195] Oosterhoff, P.T., *Bull. Astron. Inst. Netherlands*, **11**, 299 (1951).
[196] Oosterhoff, P.T., *Bull. Astron. Inst. Netherlands*, **12**, 271 (1955).
[197] Thackeray, A.D., *Mon. Not. R. Astron. Soc.*, **112**, 318 (1952).
[198] Thackeray, A.D., *Mon. Not. R. Astron. Soc.*, **113**, 342 (1953).
[199] Kron, G.E. and Gascoigne, S.C.B., *Astrophys. J.*, **118**, 511 (1953).
[200] Woolley, R. van der R., *Mon. Not. R. Astron. Soc.*, **113**, 349 (1953).
[201] Bok, B.J., *Mon. Not. R. Astron. Soc.*, **118**, 361 (1958).
[202] Bok, B.J. and Bok, P., *Astron. J.*, **63**, 303 (1958).
[203] Bok, B.J. and Bok, P., *Mon. Not. R. Astron. Soc.*, **121**, 531 (1960).
[204] Bok, B.J., *Mon. Not. R. Astron. Soc.*, **119**, 402 (1959).
[205] Westerlund, B., *Publ. Astron. Soc. Pacific*, **71**, 156 (1959).
[206] Arp, H.C., *Astron. J.*, **63**, 118 (1958).
[207] Cousins, A.W.J., *Mon. Not. Astron. Soc. S. Africa*, **18**, 46 (1959).
[208] Eggen, O.J., *Mon. Not. Astron. Soc. S. Africa*, **18**, 91 (1959).
[209] Willstrop, R.V., *Mon. Not. R. Astron. Soc.*, **121**, 17 (1960).
[210] Willstrop, R.V., *Mon. Not. Astron. Soc. S. Africa*, **17**, 40 (1958).
[211] Dunham, T., *Phys. Rev.*, **44**, 329 (1933).
[212] Brück, H., *Mon. Not. R. Astron. Soc.*, **99**, 607 (1939).
[213] Hall, J.S., *Astrophys. J.*, **84**, 369 (1936).
[214] Hiltner, W.A. and Code, A.D., *J. Optical Soc. America*, **40**, 149 (1950).
[215] Code, A.D., *Observatory*, **72**, 201 (1952).
[216] Code, A.D. and Liller, W.C., in *Astron. Techniques*, ed. W.A. Hiltner, *Stars and Stellar Systems*, vol. **2**, p. 281, Univ. Chicago Press (1962).
[217] Guérin, P., *Ann. d'Astrophys.*, **22**, 611 (1959).
[218] Dimov, N.A., *Astron. Zhur.*, **37**, 464 (1960).
[219] Liller, W. and Aller, L.H., *Astrophys. J.*, **120**, 48 (1954).
[220] MacRae, D.A., *Astron. J.*, **58**, 43 (1953).
[221] Stock, J., *Astrophys. J.*, **123**, 253 (1956).
[222] Bonsack, W. and Stock, J., *Astrophys. J.*, **126**, 99 (1957).
[223] Code, A.D., in *Stellar Atmospheres*, ed. J. L. Greenstein, *Stars and Stellar Systems*, vol. **6**, p. 50, Chicago Univ. Press (1960).
[224] Oke, J.B., *Astrophys. J.*, **131**, 358 (1960).
[225] Melbourne, W.G., *Astrophys. J.*, **132**, 101 (1960).
[226] Oke, J.B., *Astrophys. J.*, **140**, 689 (1964).
[227] Oke, J.B., *Astrophys. J.*, **134**, 214 (1961).
[228] Oke, J.B., *Astrophys. J.*, **133**, 90 (1961).
[229] Oke, J.B. and Bonsack, S.J., *Astrophys. J.*, **132**, 417 (1960).
[230] Oke, J. B., *Astron. J.*, **67**, 278 (1962).
[231] Rodgers, A.W., *Mon. Not. R. Astron. Soc.*, **122**, 413 (1961).
[232] Code, A.D., *Astrophys. J.*, **130**, 473 (1959).
[233] Liller, W., *Publ. Astron. Soc. Pacific*, **69**, 511 (1957).
[234] Bless, R.C., *Astrophys. J.*, **132**, 532 (1960).
[235] Aller, L.H., Faulkner, D.J. and Norton, R.H., *Astrophys. J.*, **140**, 1609 (1967).
[236] Aller, L.H., Faulkner, D.J. and Norton, R.H., *Astrophys. J.*, **143**, 1073 (1966).
[237] Willstrop, R.V., *Mem. R. Astron. Soc.*, **69**, 83 (1964).
[238] Bahner, K., *Astrophys. J.*, **138**, 1314 (1963).
[239] Kharitonov, A.V., *Astron. Zhur.*, **40**, 339 (1963). English translation in *ibid. Soviet Astron.*, **7**, 258 (1963).
[240] Hayes, D., Ph.D. Thesis, Univ. California, Los Angeles (1967).

[241] Wolff, S.C., Kuhi, L.V. and Hayes, D., *Astrophys. J.*, **152**, 871 (1968).

[242] Oke, J.B. and Schild, R.E., *Astrophys. J.*, **161**, 1015 (1970).

[243] Oke, J.B., *Ann. Rev. Astron. Astrophys.*, **3**, 23 (1965).

[244] Whiteoak, J.B., *Astrophys. J.*, **144**, 306 (1966).

[245] Wampler, E.J., *Astrophys. J.*, **144**, 921 (1966).

[246] Byram, E.T., Chubb, T.A., Friedman, H. and Kupperian, J.E., *Astron. J.*, **62**, 9 (1957).

[247] Kupperian, J.E., Boggess, A., Milligan, J.E., *Astrophys. J.*, **128**, 453 (1958).

[248] Boggess, A. and Dunkelman, L., *Astron. J.*, **63**, 303 (1958).

[249] Chubb, T.A. and Byram, E.T., *Astrophys. J.*, **138**, 617 (1963).

[250] Stecher, T.P. and Milligan, J.E., *Astrophys. J.*, **136**, 1 (1962).

[251] Alexander, J.D., Bowen, P.J., Gross, M.J. and Heddle, D.W.O., *Proc. R. Soc.*, **279A**, 510 (1964).

[252] Heddle, D.W.O., *Int. Astron. Union Symp.*, **23**, 167 (1964).

[253] Boggess, A., *Int. Astron. Union Symp.*, **23**, 173 (1964).

[254] Code, A.D., Houck, T.E., McNall, J.F., Bless, R.C. and Lillie, C.F., *Astrophys. J.*, **161**, 377 (1970).

[255] Code, A.D., *Publ. Astron. Soc. Pacific*, **81**, 475 (1969).

[256] Bless, R.C. and Savage, B.D., *Astrophys. J.*, **171**, 293 (1972).

[257] Wickramasinghe, N. and Gillaume, C., *Nature*, **207**, 366 (1965).

[258] Stecher, T.P., *Astrophys. J.*, **142**, 1683 (1965).

[259] Stecher, T.P., *Astrophys. J.*, **157**, L125 (1969).

[260] Stecher, T.P. and Donn, B., *Astrophys. J.*, **142**, 1681 (1965).

[261] Schatzman, E. and Cayrel, R. *Ann. d'Astrophys.*, **17**, 555 (1954).

[262] Hoyle, F. and Wickramasinghe, N.C., *Mon. Not. R. Astron. Soc.*, **124**, 417 (1962).

10 Photometry with area detectors

10.1 Introduction to area detectors

In 1930 the photographic emulsion was the only two-dimensional or area detector used in astronomy. Generally photography was considered to be the ultimate detector and it was widely used for many large programmes of stellar photometry, such as the *Mt Wilson Catalogue of Photographic Magnitudes* by Seares, Kapteyn and van Rhijn in 1930 and the *Cape Photographic Catalogue*, published from 1954 to 1968 by Jackson and Stoy. Each of these major works contained about 70 000 stars with a precision for the blue magnitudes of about $\pm 0^{m}.15$ and $\pm 0^{m}.04$ respectively – see sections 7.2 and 7.8.2.

The 1930s was also the era of the first image tubes, which were designed either to convert an image in the far red or near infrared to shorter wavelengths, or to intensify a faint image. These tubes were area detectors using the high quantum efficiency of the photoemissive photocathode or (for the S1 cathode) the long wavelength response, so as to produce an image that could be recorded on a photographic plate or transformed into an electrical signal.

The potential of image tubes for astronomy was recognized very early by André Lallemand in Strasbourg. He foresaw the advantages of an electronic area detector which might avoid the intrinsic problems of photography, namely low quantum efficiency, non-linearity of response and small dynamic range.

Other early image-tube pioneers were Jan Hendrik de Boer and his group in the Netherlands, who produced the first image converter tube in 1934 [1], and V. K. Zworykin and colleagues at RCA, who constructed image intensifiers from the mid-1930s, with focussing using either electrostatic or magnetic fields – see for example [2, 3]. An informative review is given in [4].

Image tubes and the related television tubes were intensively developed from the 1950s, and were used on an experimental basis by several observatories for photometry from that time. In the end they never seriously challenged photography for photometric observing, because of the small photocathode area and non-uniformity of response, even though their use became routine in astronomical spectroscopy. When the charge-coupled device (CCD) was developed in the 1970s, this solid-state area detector soon overtook photoemissive vacuum tube devices for most astronomical applications. Nevertheless, the development of image and television tubes as astronomical detectors, including those for photometry, was pursued intensively for several decades, and an interesting phase of astronomical history has left behind a considerable volume of technical literature. An indication of the astronomical interest in these devices was the holding of the joint discussion at the General Assembly of the IAU in Dublin in 1955 on image tubes and their astronomical applications [5], and the formation of an IAU sub-commission for image converters under the presidency of William Baum [6].

10.2   Electrographic image tubes

10.2.1   The Lallemand electronic camera

André Lallemand began his development of what he at first termed 'the electronic telescope' at the Strasbourg Observatory in 1934, having been influenced by his colleague Gilbert Rougier. His first articles in 1936 described a device for accelerating the electrons liberated by an optical image on a photocathode and for focussing these electrons by electrostatic fields onto a photographic plate [7]. He wrote:

> The photoelectric effect, even for very faint illumination, is practically instantaneous. The photoelectrons liberated can be accelerated in an electric field and hence acquire a very high energy, which can be used for making an impression on a photographic plate. One can thereby obtain an amplification of the available luminous energy and significantly increase the sensitivity of the photographic plate. This might have a considerable interest, especially in astrophysics. I have, as a result, obtained some excellent electronic images [7].

Unfortunately Lallemand's early work in Strasbourg was interrupted by the war. He resumed his development of the electronic camera with Maurice Duchesne in 1951 at the Paris Observatory, having obtained a position there from 1943. At this time, Lallemand's papers were referring to the concept of the ideal photon detector, which recorded the arrival position of every photon or photoelectron in a two-dimensional image [8].

Fig. 10.1 Early design of an electronic camera by Lallemand, in the period 1936–39.

With Duchesne he developed an operational version of the electronic camera [9, 10]. The tube comprised a CsSb photocathode of 20-mm diameter prepared in a separate glass capsule and installed in the tube after the focussing electrodes. An accelerating voltage of 25 to 40 kV was applied to the tube to accelerate the emitted electrons, which were focussed to produce an electron image on the electrographic plate. The plates were coated in nuclear track emulsion and cooled to liquid-air temperature to prevent water vapour outgassing and destroying the cathode. The plates were installed in a cassette, the tube evacuated to 10^{-6} torr and the photocathode capsule broken with a magnetic hammer. On releasing the vacuum to recover the plates after exposure, the cathode was destroyed.

Lallemand described his electronic device at the Dublin IAU General Assembly in 1955 [11], when he reported some of the impressive advantages of electrographic imaging, namely linearity of response to very high densities in electrographic exposures, a fine grain and hence high resolution, and the possibility of speed gains of several hundred times relative to conventional photography – see also [12].

In the mid-1950s the Lallemand electronic camera was being used in France at the Paris and Meudon Observatories and at Haute Provence Observatory, mainly for stellar spectroscopy. It was also used at Pic du Midi Observatory from 1960 for very short exposures for double star astrometry and for planetary imaging – see [13]. Undoubtedly the visit of Lallemand and Duchesne to the Lick Observatory in late 1959 was a significant event for the new detector. Here Merle Walker collaborated with the French

Fig. 10.2   Lallemand electronic camera at the Lick Observatory, 1959. (l. to r.:
M. Duchesne, G.E. Kron, A. Lallemand, M.F. Walker.)

visitors in using the electronic camera, mainly on the 120-inch telescope
[14, 15].

A detailed discussion of the first tests on the 36-inch refractor showed
stars in the globular cluster M15 down to $V = 17.5$ could be reached in 25
minutes [16]. This is one of the first successful direct electrographic images
with the Lallemand camera. It was analysed by Lallemand with Renée
Canavaggia and Françoise Amiot, using a Schilt photometer in Paris [17].
A linear relationship between the density in a stellar image and the flux
of starlight was demonstrated, quite dissimilar to the non-linear response
of photographic emulsions. Later work by Walker with this detector was
almost entirely spectroscopic, at times (from 1964) with an S1 photocathode
– see [18, 19].

Meanwhile in France, Gérard Wlérick (b. 1921) from Paris was obtaining deep Lallemand camera exposures of faint radio galaxies for optical
identification [20] using the 1.93-m telescope at Haute Provence. Some of

Fig. 10.3   Diagram of the Lallemand electronic camera, 1960.

these exposures used filters in the Johnson-Morgan *UBV* system. Limiting magnitudes as faint as $B = 24$ were obtained in an hour.

10.2.2   *Yerkes and Carnegie electrographic image tubes*

The Lallemand electronic camera was regarded by many to be an impractical device because of the destruction of the photocathode, normally after each night's observations. Several groups strove to overcome these problems by isolating the cathode in a separate vacuum chamber, either using a thin film through which the electrons could penetrate, or using a valve which was opened when required for use.

Thin-film technology was explored by Albert Hiltner at Yerkes. His first experiments were in 1954 [21]. With Jay Burns (b. 1924) he described a tube with a very thin protecting foil which could withstand differential pressures of no more than 10^{-3} torr [22].

At the same time the Carnegie Institution established an exploratory committee for the development of image tubes for astronomy in February 1954 under the chairmanship of Merle Tuve (1901–82). William Baum and

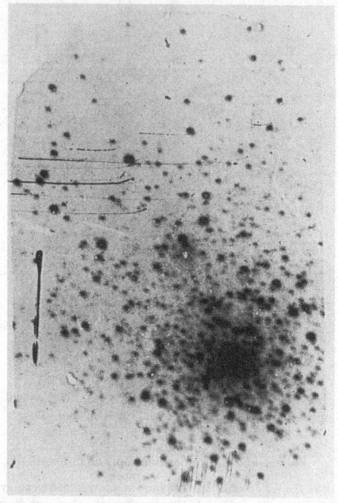

Fig. 10.4   M15 recorded with the Lallemand electronic camera at Lick, 1959.

John Hall were also on the committee [23, 24]. Thin-film electrographic tubes were part of the Carnegie programme, in collaboration with the Farnsworth Co. (later part of ITT). An electrographic tube of this type was tested in 1957 at the US Naval Observatory, Flagstaff Station, on the 40-inch reflector [25]. An aluminium foil, 70 nm thick, protected the photocathode. In 1958 at the Moscow IAU General Assembly, Baum reviewed progress on the Carnegie image-tube programme, including those tubes with phosphors and television tubes [26]. The results were still largely experimental at this time.

Strong field emission from the electrodes, loss of photocathode sensitivity, poor resolution and non-uniform response, even over a small photocathode, were the problems encountered in these early experiments. Such problems were described by the Yerkes team [27]. The field emission, which fogged the electrographic plates, was largely overcome at Yerkes by 1961, and cathode lifetimes were greatly extended [28]. In spite of significant progress, it would be fair to conclude that these tubes were never practical photometric area detectors.

10.2.3   The Kron and McGee electrographic image tubes

Ingenious solutions to the problem of the preservation of image-tube photocathodes, to allow ease of changing electrographic films or plates, were sought for and found, both by Gerry Kron at Lick and by James McGee at Imperial College, London.

Kron's solution was to devise a tube in which the chamber was in two parts separated by a gas-tight ball valve, which opened to allow the passage of the electron beams when in operation, but which closed so as to seal off the cathode chamber and preserve the high vacuum there when changing plates. Design and development work was already underway at the time of Lallemand's visit to Lick [29]. Kron was evidently well aware of the potential advantages of electrography before then. This knowledge came in part from Kron's 1950 visit to Australia, where he met the French astronomer, Gérard de Vaucouleurs (1918–95), who had a good understanding of Lallemand's work. As a result, Kron had corresponded with Lallemand and also visited his laboratory in Paris, before starting his own development in 1958. Although the idea of using a valve was Kron's own solution to this problem, the idea was independently proposed by Gerhard Lewin at Princeton [30].

A considerable amount of effort was expended on devising a suitable valve mechanism so as to maintaining a good vacuum, as well as on the cooling of the emulsion in liquid air so as to reduce outgassing, and hence protect the CsSb S9 photocathode [31]. Laboratory trials gave cathode lifetimes of several weeks. In 1960–61, Kron again visited Mt Stromlo Observatory in Australia. Albert Whitford, the new Lick director from 1958, had not supported the intensive laboratory work on the new detector, and hence the Mt Stromlo Observatory, with the encouragement of Bart Bok as director, continued this programme on the so-called Lick-Stromlo image tube [32]. A new coin-shaped valve was devised at this time [33].

The first observational tests were at Lick in 1964 and included direct

Fig. 10.5   The Kron electronic camera on the 61-inch US Naval Observatory
reflector at Flagstaff. (l. foreground: plate changing apparatus for the
camera; r. middle: 30-kV power supply.)

images of the globular clusters M13 and M15 on the 20-inch astrograph
[34]. A limiting magnitude of $m_{pg} = 21$ was reached in 100 minutes, about
half the exposure that would be required on baked Kodak IIaO plates.

In 1965 Kron resigned from Lick to take up a position at the US Naval
Observatory's Flagstaff Station. Here he brought his new detector and,
with Harold Ables (b. 1938), he made the first practical use of it at the
telescope [35]. On the 61-inch astrometric reflector an image of the cluster
M13 was recorded and measured on the Schilt photometer (using a fixed
aperture). Linearity over two magnitudes was demonstrated. In practice
at least a five-magnitude range was available, if the density profile of each
stellar image was measured on a microdensitometer [36]. A detailed paper
by Merle Walker and Gerry Kron followed, in which several blue and visual
M13 plates exposed in Flagstaff were analysed by microdensitometry. No
calibration stars were necessary for these electrographic plates, although a
few bright stars of known magnitude in the field were required, so as to

give the zero-point. Magnitudes to about $m = 21$ in blue and visual light were obtained with precisions of about $\pm 0^{m}09$. This can be regarded as the first reliable electrographic photometry reported in the literature.

Later work at Flagstaff showed there to be a measurable dynamic range of over six magnitudes for a single electrographic exposure. The precision for these faint stars was comparable to that from photoelectric photometry [37]. Magnitudes to $m = 23.6$ in one-hour exposures were possible [38, 39], and a promising future for electrographic image tubes was foreseen. A detailed description of the Kron camera was presented in 1968 at the fourth McGee symposium on photoelectronic image devices in London [40]. Photometry to $\pm 0^{m}035$ over six magnitudes was obtained in just 25 minutes of telescope time followed by two-dimensional microdensitometry.

The final electrographic image tube to be described is the famous Spectracon tube of James McGee (1903–87) at Imperial College, which was developed from about 1960. An early version was described in McGee's extensive image-tube review paper of 1961 [41], and early tests were presented at the second of McGee's symposia on photoelectronic image devices, held at Imperial College in 1961 [42].

The essential feature was a sealed image tube with a thin mica window at the end further from the S9 photocathode. Electrons accelerated through 40 kV were magnetically focussed onto the window, which they penetrated, and then were recorded on electrographic film in contact with the mica. Although thin-film tubes were not new, the window of McGee's tube was able to withstand atmospheric pressure and yet allow the passage of most of the electrons. This, and the magnetic focussing, were the main differences between the McGee tube and those tubes with thin foils used in the Yerkes and Carnegie experiments. The mica window was itself a development from light-emitting phosphor image tubes, in which the phosphor was deposited on the inner surface of the mica window [41].

By the time of the 1965 McGee symposium, the name Spectracon had been chosen for this type of tube [43]. The mica windows were now only 4 microns thick and 10 × 30 mm in area, allowing the passage of 75 per cent of 40-kV electrons [44]. The resolution was about 90 line pairs/mm for the finest grained emulsion (Ilford L4) – comparable to that of the Kron camera – and the densities recorded were proportional to exposure time. Field emission from the tube was practically eliminated by ensuring no caesium was deposited on the tube's electrodes during the preparation of the photocathode. Spectracons with larger windows, 5 cm in diameter, were also developed [45].

Being a permanently sealed tube, without the need for cryogenic cooling of the emulsions, nor for high-vacuum apparatus at the observatory, the

Fig. 10.6   The McGee Spectracon at the Cerro Tololo Interamerican
Observatory.

Spectracon was by far the easiest of the electrographic tubes to use. In
1967 several Spectracon tubes were acquired by Merle Walker at Lick [46]
and used initially for coudé spectroscopy on the 120-inch telescope. A
critical comparison of the Lallemand and McGee tubes was made as a
result. From this time Walker became one of the foremost observers with
the Spectracon for both spectroscopy and photometry. He was also the
most experienced astronomer in the world in obtaining useful astronomical
results from electrography, having worked with images acquired by the
Lallemand, Kron and McGee tubes.

In 1968–69 Walker took the Spectracon to the Interamerican Observatory
on Cerro Tololo in Chile, and here he recorded images of 14 Magellanic
Cloud blue globular clusters in the B and V passbands, with exposures of
up to three hours [47, 48, 49, 50], using the 60-inch telescope. Narrow-band
area photometry of southern planetary nebulae, to deduce their structures
in different spectral lines, was also part of his observing programme. The
data were all reduced on the US Naval Observatory's microdensitometer
in Flagstaff. The result of these observations was reliable electrographic
area photometry to unprecedentedly faint limits and high precision. For
example, a magnitude for a star at $B = 21$ had a precision of $\pm 0^{\text{m}}06$, and

Fig. 10.7   Images of the Small Magellanic Cloud cluster, Kron 3, recorded by
Merle Walker using the Spectracon. Also shown is a 1-hour
photograph of the same cluster (second from top).

at $B = 18$ of only $\pm 0^{m}.02$. The colour-magnitude diagram of the first cluster
analysed, Kron 3, was determined to about $V = 21.6$. However, the limiting
magnitude of a 3-hour exposure was about 22.5 on Walker's films [48].

It is interesting to quote Merle Walker's comments following these productive observations:

> Promising as these results are, their greatest significance is in
> demonstrating that we are on the threshold of a new era in
> astronomical photometry. Eventually, electronography should bring an
> advance in this field equal in importance to those that resulted from
> the introduction of the photographic plate and photomultiplier.
>
> Electronography combines the best features of both photographic
> and photoelectric photometry. In the first we can simultaneously record
> all stars and the sky background in a field, and in the second we have
> linearity and high quantum efficiency. Consequently electronographic
> photometry will permit using moderate-sized reflectors for problems
> heretofore restricted to the 200-inch telescope [47].

10.3   Photometry with phosphor image tubes

Image tubes which gave an optical output when electrons were focussed on a light-emitting phosphor were always at the forefront of image-tube development, no doubt because of their wide application in non-astronomical imaging. Phosphor image tubes have less good resolution than electrographic tubes, and their response can show large variations over the photocathode area. This non-uniformity was at once recognized as a difficulty for precise photometric work [51]. Since the output has to be photographed, all the usual problems of photographic photometry are compounded in phosphor-image-tube photography. Paul Hodge (b. 1934) in 1970 concluded that 'photometry with [phosphor] image tubes is not likely to be profitable at this stage' [52]. However, their use for astronomical spectroscopy was widespread at this time.

Nevertheless, some attempts were made to use these devices for photometric work. The advantage was a large speed gain, giving very short exposures, which was in any case necessary to avoid the sky brightness saturating the emulsion. At Kitt Peak Observatory, James de Veny attempted photometry in the M13 globular cluster using a Westinghouse image tube with a fibre-optic faceplate to couple the phosphor to the photographic emulsion [53]. The best precisions after iris photometry were $\pm 0^{\text{m}}14$ for stars of about 18th blue magnitude. The radial dependence of the image-tube response was allowed for in the reduction procedure.

At the University of California (UCLA), Donald Gudehus used an RCA image tube to undertake photometry in the open cluster M67, using the interesting technique of extrafocal images and subsequent microdensitometry [54]. The precision was slightly better ($\pm 0^{\text{m}}11$), possibly a result of more careful mapping of the tube's sensitivity over the photocathode, or because of the extrafocal technique and the brighter stars used ($V = 10$ to 15).

10.4   Television systems and photometry

10.4.1   The image orthicon

A television camera tube accepts a two-dimensional optical image as its input and converts this to an analogue electrical signal. The earliest tubes of this type, such as the iconoscope and the orthicon, were developed in the 1930s. They had a low sensitivity to light. After the war, the image orthicon was developed at the RCA Princeton Laboratories [55]. This had a higher sensitivity and became the most widely used television

Fig. 10.8 Schematic diagram of an image orthicon.

camera tube for commercial broadcast television in the 1950s and 1960s. In the image orthicon, electrons from a CsSb photocathode were accelerated and magnetically focussed onto an insulating target, so that secondary electrons left behind an image of positive charge. The target was scanned sequentially by an electron gun, and the current in the return beam was amplified in a dynode multiplier chain to give the output signal. According to Peter Fellgett, the detective quantum efficiency of the image orthicon was comparable to the human eye or the photographic plate [56].

Fellgett at Cambridge was one of the first astronomers to recognize the potential of the image orthicon as an astronomical detector. Using tubes from Pye in Cambridge, the first experiments at astronomical imaging were in November 1952 on the Cambridge spectrohelioscope and on the 24-inch Newall refractor [56, 57]. A demonstration of the Pye system was also made on the 12-inch Grubb refractor at the Dunsink Observatory, at the 1955 IAU meeting in Dublin. Fellgett wrote at that time:

> It was decided to use image-orthicon camera tubes for experiments at the telescope... We believe signal-generating tubes to have important advantages. They give rise directly to the wave-form which constitutes a measurement, whereas the output of image converters must be recorded and measured by a microphotometer in some manner. We also have found it a considerable advantage of television systems that the effects of adjustment are presented at once to the observer. The image orthicon has so far proved the most sensitive tube in practice... [58].

The interest in image tubes and television systems among the astronomical community in 1955 was such that subcommission 9a was established on photoelectric image tubes, including television systems. Baum from

Mt Wilson was the first president, while the members included Fellgett (Cambridge), McGee (Imperial College) and Morton (RCA), all of whom pioneered the astronomical application of television cameras.

In the 1950s the main centres producing commercial image orthicons were Pye, RCA and the Bendix-Friez Corporation (the Lumicon). In addition McGee at Imperial College was from the mid-1950s making specialized television tubes for astronomy, using targets able to integrate and store the charge for a relatively long time. The McGee tubes also employed a slower readout, with the charging and discharging processes being sequential rather than simultaneous, so as to improve the signal-to-noise ratio [59]. The operating principle of the image orthicon was described by V. K. Zworykin and E. G. Ramberg [60], while astronomical applications were discussed by George Morton [61] and Albert Whitford [51, see p. 283].

Several astronomical tests of image orthicons were made in the mid-1950s, in all cases on an experimental basis. In some instances these tests were for the purpose of recording images of Mars at its July 1954 opposition, in others they were as a detector for solar spectroscopy. The astronomical work up to 1958 is summarized in Baum's IAU report to subcommission 9a [26], and included observations made at the Lowell Observatory [62], at Cambridge [63], at Bloemfontein, at Michigan and at Sacramento Peak [64]. At Pulkovo Observatory, N. F. Kuprevich was also using experimental television techniques and recorded lunar images in May 1956 [65].

None of these experiments had attempted stellar photometry. However, improvements in image-orthicon performance made photometry a realizable goal from about 1958. The MgO target (developed by GEC in Schenectady) allowed much longer integration times in the image orthicon – see [66], while William Livingston (b. 1927) at Kitt Peak showed that refrigeration of the target using dry ice allowed exposures of over 20 minutes without the charge leaking away [67].

Between December 1958 and July 1959 Ewen Whitaker (b. 1922) and Robert Hardie tested a General Electric image orthicon at the Yerkes and McDonald Observatories on the 40-inch refractor and the 82-inch reflector. Images of star fields and nebulae were included in these trials – see [66]. These tests marked the start of experimental programmes which included stellar photometry as their goal, at at least four US observatories, as well as one in the Soviet Union. The active American observers were William Baum at the Mt Wilson and Palomar Observatories, William Livingston at Kitt Peak, John DeWitt at the Dyer Observatory and a team at the Dearborn Observatory comprising Richard Aikens, J. Allen Hynek (b. 1910), Justus Dunlap and William Powers. In the Soviet Union, A. N. Abramenko and

Fig. 10.9 Light curve of an eclipsing binary star in the cluster NGC 1893 recorded using an image orthicon by J. Allen Hynek *et al.*, 1966.

his colleagues undertook stellar photometry with a television system at the Crimean Astrophysical Observatory.

The Dearborn work originated with Aikens and Hynek in 1958 (then at the Smithsonian) with an image orthicon mounted on a 10-inch Baker-Nunn camera at Organ Mountain, New Mexico [68], with further tests being carried out at Mt Palomar in 1959 on the 20-inch telescope. Further work was undertaken at the Dearborn Observatory (Northwestern University, Illinois) on the 18.5-inch Clark refractor and on the 12-inch reflector at Organ Mountain in New Mexico [69, 70, 71, 72]. Magnitude 16 stars were recorded in a 15-s exposure, using an uncooled target. The apparatus was limited to such short exposures, and hence short-period variable star photometry was one application. The light curve of an eclipsing binary with a three-hour period in the open cluster NGC 1893 was obtained [71]. The method of extracting magnitudes was rather primitive, namely photographing the TV monitor and measuring the stellar image diameter with a travelling microscope. A photoelectric calibration was required to convert the diameter to a magnitude.

The programme of John DeWitt at the Dyer Observatory (Vanderbilt University) also attempted photometry with a GE image orthicon [73, 74]. He reported magnitude 11 stars being visible on the 24-inch telescope at the TV frame rate of $\frac{1}{30}$ s, or $m = 15$ in an 8-s exposure. In July 1961

DeWitt tested this tube on the 24-inch refractor at Lowell and recorded 19th magnitude stars in the globular cluster M13 in a 100-s exposure.

William Livingston at Kitt Peak used a GE image orthicon on the 36-in reflector, cooling the target in dry ice to −65°C to allow long integration times [75, 76, 77]. Livingston discussed techniques of image-orthicon photometry; this could be achieved by measuring the scanning beam current at the centre of a stellar image, by adjusting the target mesh voltage so as to achieve a given beam current, or simply by measuring the image diameter on the monitor, which was related linearly to stellar magnitude. Livingston applied the last of these techniques to obtain UBV magnitudes for 75 stars in the old open cluster M67 to a precision of about 0.1 magnitudes. This was a notable experiment in television-tube astronomical photometry.

The Russian work on television-tube photometry was at the Crimean Astrophysical Observatory from 1963 by E. S. Agapov, A. N. Abramenko and others [78, 79, 80, 81]. These observers used the image-diameter method, after photographing the television monitor. They demonstrated a linear diameter-magnitude relationship over a 7-magnitude range, and used this to measure magnitudes to a precision of $\pm 0^{\text{m}}.15$.

The image orthicon achieved a modest success in all these various photometric trials. But photometry was never a major application of television tubes in astronomy, nor was it ever a routine detector, preferred over the photomultiplier tube. Single-channel photomultiplier photometry in the 1960s was delivering random error bars for stellar magnitudes, which were ten or more times smaller than was achievable with the image orthicon.

10.4.2   The SEC vidicon

From 1964 at the Westinghouse Corporation a new type of television camera was developed by Gerhard Goetze (b. 1930) based on the phenomenon of secondary electron conduction in an insulating target, such as a thin deposited layer of potassium chloride [82, 83]. The SEC target was used in the SEC-vidicon camera tube manufactured from the mid-1960s at Westinghouse [84]. The target was scanned with an electron beam to read it out, with the signal current being collected by a conducting signal plate on which the target was deposited. This was then amplified externally to the tube.

The SEC vidicon largely displaced the image orthicon as the preferred television tube in astronomy from 1970. One of its principal advantages was the ability to hold an image on the target over long integration times without cooling. The first astronomical tests by Wallace Beardsley (1922–91) and Richard Hansen (b. 1928) were made on the Thaw 30-inch refractor at the Allegheny Observatory in October 1967 [85]. Integration times of up to 2 minutes were used on various star clusters. Other tests were made by Martin Green of Westinghouse, using his 10-inch newtonian reflector [86, 87].

In February 1968 Green and Hansen took the Westinghouse SEC vidicons to McDonald Observatory and undertook further tests on the 36-inch reflector [88]. In 19 minutes the night sky limit was reached, with stars of $V = 19.0$ being recorded. An intensified tube (with a one-stage electrostatic image tube in front of the SEC vidicon) was also tested, and shown to be about one hundred times faster in reaching the same limits.

An ultraviolet-sensitive variant of the SEC vidicon was developed at Westinghouse [89]. It was known as the Uvicon, and featured a lithium fluoride window and a caesium telluride or caesium iodide photocathode, the latter giving a good response down to 110 nm. Four Uvicon tubes were used for the Smithsonian Celescope experiment on the Orbiting Astronomical Observatory satellite, OAO-2 [90]. The OAO-2 was launched in December 1968 and the Celescope experiment gave photometric data in four broad ultraviolet passbands between 105 and 320 nm on about 50 000 stars to a precision of 0.2 magnitudes over 16 months of operation. The Celescope images were subjected to digital image processing, to extract the stellar fluxes, by integrating the stellar images above the surrounding background. This was therefore the start of a new phase in sophistication in two-dimensional area photometry, which has become commonplace in recent times.

The Celescope was the first attempt at ultraviolet stellar photometry using television techniques from space. Meanwhile, ground-based experiments continued. A major engineering development of the SEC vidicon took place at Princeton University Observatory by P. M. Zucchino and John Lowrance [91]. Phillipe Crane (b. 1943) from Princeton was one observer who used the Princeton camera tube for galaxy photometry at Kitt Peak [92].

In the late 1960s and 1970s, other types of vidicon target were devised, including the target consisting of an array of silicon diodes, and also the so-called electron-bombarded silicon target (EBS vidicon) and the silicon-intensified target (SIT) vidicon. Tubes with a silicon-diode target were first used for astronomy in 1971 by James Westphal (b. 1930) and Thomas McCord (b. 1939) [93, 94]; they will not be discussed further in this review. The state of the art of television detectors in astronomy as at the early 1970s was reviewed by Livingston in 1973 [95].

At one stage, the SEC vidicon was seriously considered as a detector for the wide-field and planetary camera on the Hubble Space Telescope. In the event it narrowly lost being selected in 1977, in favour of the charge-coupled device (CCD), in spite of the recent arrival of CCDs on the detector scene, and their relatively poor ultraviolet response – see the review article by Robert Smith and Joseph Tatarawicz [96].

10.5   The CCD – the fourth revolution in astronomical photometry

The history of astronomical photometry is largely the story of instrument and detector technology. Each major advance in detectors brought about a revolution in the practice of astronomical photometry. The revolutions of visual photometry, photographic photometry and photomultiplier photometry have been described in preceding pages. The charge-coupled device was the fourth revolution, which swept aside many other competing developments, such as those in image tubes and television camera tubes, that had at one stage (in the 1960s) seemed so promising for photometric work.

The first mention of the charge-coupled device (CCD) was in a technical Bell Laboratories report by Willard Boyle (b. 1924) and George Smith (b. 1930) in 1970 [97]. They described a semiconductor doped-silicon chip in which charge could be stored in potential wells and shifted from one well to another for readout. Various possible applications were cited, including optical imaging.

The earliest CCDs available commercially were 100×100 pixel arrays from Fairchild in 1973, followed by 100×160 and 400×400 Texas Instruments CCDs for the Jet Propulsion Laboratory. Astronomers first used these detectors in 1975, notably Roger Lynds (b. 1928) at Kitt Peak [98] and the Princeton observers, Edwin Loh (b. 1948) and David Wilkinson (b. 1935), on the 36-inch telescope [99, 100]. Soon afterwards, Bev Oke at Palomar was using the RCA-JPL CCD for spectroscopy on the 200-inch telescope at Palomar [101].

These developments mark the beginning of the fourth revolution in the measurement of starlight, which is now underway.

References

[1]   Holst, G., de Boer, J.H., Teves, M.C. and Veenemans, C.F., *Physica*, 1, 297 (1934).
[2]   Iams, H., Morton, G.A. and Zworykin, V.K., *Proc. Inst. Radio Eng.*, 27, 541 (1939).

[3]   Zworykin, V.K. and Morton, G.A., *J. Optical Soc. America*, **26**, 181 (1936).

[4]   Malatesta, S., *Rev. Gén. d'Electricité*, **38**, 455 (1939).

[5]   Baum, W.A., *Trans. Int. Astron. Union*, **9**, 673 (1957).

[6]   Baum, W.A., *Trans. Int. Astron. Union*, **9**, 67 (1957).

[7]   Lallemand, A., *Comptes Rendus de l'Acad. des Sci.*, **203**, 243 (1936).

[8]   Lallemand, A., *Bull. Astron.*, **16**, 197 (1952).

[9]   Lallemand, A. and Duchesne, M., *Comptes Rendus de l'Acad. des Sci.*, **235**, 503 (1952).

[10]   Lallemand, A. and Duchesne, M., *Comptes Rendus de l'Acad. des Sci.*, **238**, 335 (1954).

[11]   Lallemand, A., *Trans. Int. Astron. Union*, **9**, 673 (1957).

[12]   Lallemand, A. and Duchesne, M., *Comptes Rendus de l'Acad. des Sci.*, **241**, 360 (1955).

[13]   Rösch, J., Wlérick, G. and Boussuge, G., *Adv. Electron. & Electron Phys.*, **16**, 357 (1962).

[14]   Whitford, A.E., *Astron. J.*, **65**, 531 (1960).

[15]   Lallemand, A., Duchesne, M. and Walker, M.F., *Publ. Astron. Soc. Pacific*, **72**, 76 (1960).

[16]   Lallemand, A., Duchesne, M. and Walker, M.F., *Publ. Astron. Soc. Pacific*, **72**, 268 (1960).

[17]   Lallemand, A., Canavaggia, R. and Amiot, F., *Comptes Rendus de l'Acad. des Sci.*, **262B**, 838 (1966).

[18]   Lallemand, A., *Adv. Electron. & Electron Phys.*, **22A**, 1 (1966).

[19]   Walker, M.F., *Adv. Electron. & Electron Phys.*, **22B**, 761 (1966).

[20]   Wlérick, G., *Adv. Electron. & Electron Phys.*, **28B**, 787 (1969).

[21]   Hiltner, W.A., *Astron. J.*, **60**, 26 (1955).

[22]   Burns, J. and Hiltner, W.A., *Astrophys. J.*, **121**, 772 (1955).

[23]   Hall, J.S., *Trans. Int. Astron. Union*, **9**, 697 (1957).

[24]   Baum, W.A. and Hall, J.S., *Astron. J.*, **60**, 154 (1955).

[25]   Baum, W.A., Ford, W.K. and Hall, J.S., *Astron. J.*, **63**, 47 (1958).

[26]   Baum, W.A., *Trans. Int. Astron. Union*, **10**, 143 (1960).

[27]   Miller, R.H., Hall, J.S. and Burns, J., *Astrophys. J.*, **123**, 368 (1956).

[28]   Hiltner, W.A. anmd Niklas, W.F., *Astron. J.*, **66**, 286 (1961).

[29]   Kron, G.E., *Publ. Astron. Soc. Pacific*, **71**, 386 (1959).

[30]   Lewin, G., *Rev. Sci. Instruments*, **32**, 206 (1961).

[31]   Kron, G.E. and Papiashvili, I.I., *Publ. Astron. Soc. Pacific*, **72**, 353, 502 (1960).

[32]   Kron, G.E. and Papiashvili, I.I., *Publ. Astron. Soc. Pacific*, **74**, 404 (1962).

[33]   Kron, G.E., *Adv. Electron. & Electron Phys.*, **16**, 25 (1962).

[34]   Kron, G.E., Breckinridge, J.B. and Papiashvili, I.I., *Publ. Astron. Soc. Pacific*, **77**, 112 (1965).

[35]   Ables, H.D. and Kron, G.E., *Publ. Astron. Soc. Pacific*, **79**, 422 (1967).

[36]   Kron, G.E. and Walker, M.F., *Astron. J.*, **72**, 307 (1967).

[37]   Ables, H.D., Kron, G.E. and Hewitt, A.V., *Bull. Amer. Astron. Soc.*, **1**, 231 (1969).

[38]   Lewis, M. and Kron, G.E., *Bull. Amer. Astron. Soc.*, **1**, 352 (1969).

[39]   Guetter, H., *Astron. J.*, **73**, 515 (1968).

[40]   Kron, G.E., Ables, H.D. and Hewitt, A.V., *Adv. Electron. & Electron Phys.*, **28A**, 1 (1969).

[41]   McGee, J.D., *Rep. Progress in Phys.*, **24**, 167 (1961).

[42]   McGee, J.D. and Wheeler, B.W., *Adv. Electron. & Electron Phys.*, **16**, 47 (1962).

[43]   McGee, J.D., Khogali, A., Ganson, A. and Baum, W.A., *Adv. Electron. & Electron Phys.*, **22A**, 11 (1966).

[44]   McGee, J.D., Khogali, A. and Ganson, A., *Adv. Electron. & Electron Phys.*, **22A**, 31 (1966).

[45]   McGee, J.D., McMullan, D., Bacik, H. and Oliver, M., *Adv. Electron. & Electron Phys.*, **28A**, 61 (1969).

[46]   Walker, M.F., *Adv. Electron. & Electron Phys.*, **28B**, 773 (1969).

[47]   Walker, M.F., *Sky & Tel.*, **40**, 132 (1970).

[48]   Walker, M.F., *Astrophys. J.*, **161**, 835 (1970).

[49]   Walker, M.F., *Astrophys. J.*, **167**, 1 (1971).

[50]   Walker, M.F., *Mon. Not. R. Astron. Soc.*, **156**, 459 (1972).

[51]   Whitford, A.E., *Handbuch der Phys.*, **54**, 240 (1962).

[52]   Hodge, P.W., *Sky & Tel.*, **39**, 234 (1970).

[53]   de Veny, J., *Publ. Astron. Soc. Pacific*, **82**, 142 (1970).

[54]   Gudehus, D., *Publ. Astron. Soc. Pacific*, **82**, 1324 (1970).

[55]   Rose, A., Weimer, P.K. and Law, H.B., *Proc. Inst. Radio Eng.*, **34**, 424 (1946).

[56]   Fellgett, P.B., in *The Present and Future of Telescopes of Moderate Size*, ed. F.B. Wood, p. 51, Univ. Pennsylvania Press (1958).

[57]   Fellgett, P.B., *Vistas in Astron.*, **1**, 475 (1955).

[58]   Fellgett, P.B., *Trans. Int. Astron. Union*, **9**, 699 (1957).

[59]   McGee, J.D., *Trans. Int. Astron. Union*, **9**, 696 (1957).

[60]   Zworykin, V.K. and Ramberg, E.G., *Photoelectricity and Its Application*, J. Wiley & Sons, N.Y. (1949). See p. 393.

[61]   Morton, G.A., *Trans. Int. Astron. Union*, **9**, 676 (1957).

[62]   Morgan, R., Sturm, R. and Wilson, A., *Trans. Int. Astron. Union*, **9**, 690 (1957).

[63]   Somes-Charlton, B.V., *Brit. Commun. and Electron.*, **3**, 192 (1956).

[64]   Dennison, E.W., *Astron. J.*, **64**, 328 (1959).

[65]   Kuprevich, N.F., *Astron. Circ., (USSR)*, **171**, 12 (1956).

[66]   Baum, W.A., *Trans. Int. Astron. Union*, **11A**, 34 (1962).

[67]   Livingston, W.C., *Publ. Astron. Soc. Pacific*, **69**, 390 (1957).

[68]   Aikens, R., Barton, G., Hynek, J.A., Baum, W.A. and Kimmel, J., *Astron. J.*, **65**, 339 (1960).

[69]   Powers, W.T., *Astron. J.*, **67**, 584 (1962).

[70]   Powers, W.T. and Aikens, R.S., *Applied Optics*, **2**, 157 (1963).

[71]   Hynek, J.A. and Dunlap, J., *Sky & Tel.*, **28**, 126 (1964).

[72]   Hynek, J.A., Bakos, G., Dunlap, J. and Powers, W.T., *Adv. Electron. & Electron Phys.*, **22B**, 713 (1966).

[73]   DeWitt, J.H., *Astron. J.*, **65**, 343 (1960).

[74]   DeWitt, J.H., *Adv. Electron. & Electron Phys.*, **16**, 419 (1962).

[75]   Livingston, W.C., *Adv. Electron. & Electron Phys.*, **16**, 431 (1962).

[76]   Livingston, W.C., *Proc. Image Intensifier Symposium*, NASA SP-2, p. 167 (1961).

[77]   Livingston, W.C., *Publ. Astron. Soc. Pacific*, **73**, 331 (1961).

[78]   Agapov, E.S., Anissimov, V.F., Nikonov, V.B., Prokofieva, V.V. and Sinenok, S.M., *Izvestia Crimean Astrophys. Observ.*, **30**, 3 (1963).

[79]   Abramenko, A.N. and Prokofieva, V.V., *Izvestia Crimean Astrophys. Observ.*, **36**, 289 (1967).

[80]   Abramenko, A.N. and Prokofieva, V.V., *Izvestia Crimean Astrophys. Observ.*, **35**, 289 (1966).

[81] Abramenko, A.N., Istomin, L.F. and Prokofieva, V.V., *Izvestia Crimean Astrophys. Observ.*, **41–42**, 372 (1970).

[82] Goetze, G.W. and Boerio, A.H., *Proc. Inst. Elec. & Electron. Eng.*, **52**, 1007 (1964).

[83] Goetze, G.W., Boerio, A.H. and Green, M., *J. Appl. Phys.*, **35**, 482 (1964).

[84] Goetze, G.W., *Adv. Electron. & Electron Phys.*, **22A**, 219 (1966).

[85] Beardsley, W.R. and Hansen, J.R., *Astron. J.*, **73**, 54 (1968).

[86] Green, M., *Sky & Tel.*, **35**, 140 (1968).

[87] Green, M., *Astron. J.*, **73**, S14 (1968).

[88] Green, M. and Hansen, J.R., *Adv. Electron. & Electron Phys.*, **28B**, 807 (1969).

[89] Doughty, D.D., *Adv. Electron. & Electron Phys.*, **22A**, 261 (1966).

[90] Davis, R.J., Deutschman, W.A., Lundquist, C.A., Nozawa, Y. and Bass, S.D., *Scientific Results from the Orbiting Astronomical Observatory (OAO-2)*, NASA SP-310, p. 1 (1972).

[91] Zucchino, P.M. and Lowrance, J.L., *Adv. Electron. & Electron Phys.*, **33B**, 801 (1972).

[92] Crane, P., *Bull. Amer. Astron. Soc.*, **3**, 399 (1971).

[93] Westphal, J.A. and McCord, T.B., *Publ. Astron. Soc. Pacific*, **84**, 133 (1972).

[94] Westphal, J.A. and McCord, T.B., *Appl. Optics*, **11**, 522 (1972).

[95] Livingston, W.C., *Ann. Rev. Astron. Astrophys.*, **11**, 95 (1973).

[96] Smith, R.W. and Tatarawicz, J.N., *Proc. Inst. Elec. & Electron. Eng.*, **73**, 1221 (1985).

[97] Boyle, W.S. and Smith, G.E., *Bell Systems Tech. J.*, **49**, 587 (1970).

[98] Lynds, C.R., *Quart. Rep. Kitt Peak Nat. Observ.*, Apr.–Jun. 1975, p. 3 (1975).

[99] Loh, E.D. and Wilkinson, D.T., *Bull. Amer. Astron. Soc.*, **8**, 350 (1976).

[100] Loh, E.D., *Bull. Amer. Astron. Soc.*, **8**, 350 (1976).

[101] Babcock, H.W., *Ann. Rep. Dir. Hale Observ. 1975–76*, reprinted from *Carnegie Inst. Washington Yearbook*, **75**, 277 (1976). See p. 320.

Sources of illustrations

Note: The notation [200, Ch. 8] refers to an illustration that appeared originally in literature reference [200] cited in Chapter 8.

Abbreviations

IE	Photograph supplied by Dr. I. Elliott, Dublin.
MG	Photograph supplied by Prof. M. Golay, Geneva.
JSH	Photograph supplied by the late Dr J. S. Hall, Sedona, Arizona.
HCO	Courtesy of Harvard College Observatory archives.
GEK	Photograph supplied by Dr G. E. Kron, Honolulu.
ROE	The photographic work was undertaken by the photographic department of the Royal Observatory, Edinburgh, from material in the library of that institution.
photog. ROE	The photographic work was undertaken by the photographic department of the Royal Observatory, Edinburgh.
SAAO	Photographic work courtesy of the South African Astronomical Observatory, Cape Town, from material in the SAAO library.
RHS	Photograph supplied by the late Prof. R. H. Stoy, Edinburgh.
UoC	The photographic work was undertaken in the photographic section of the Audio-Visual Department of the University of Canterbury.

Fig.	Reference	Other sources and acknowledgements
1.1	[3, Ch. 1]	ROE
1.2	[20, Ch. 1]	ROE
1.3	[30, Ch. 1] – from 1661 edition	ROE
1.4		SAAO
2.1		
2.2		SAAO
2.3	[39, Ch. 2]	ROE
2.4	*Pop. Astron.*, **4**, 337 (1896)	ROE

Fig.	Reference	Other sources and acknowledgements
3.1	[7, Ch. 3]	photog. ROE
3.2	Herrmann, D., *Archenhold Sternwarte Vorträge und Schriften*, **52** (1976)	ROE
3.3	[7, Ch. 3]	photog. ROE
3.4		HCO
3.5	[40, Ch. 3]	ROE
3.6	Shearman, T.S.H., *Pop. Astron.*, **21**, 479 (1913)	ROE
3.7		SAAO
3.8	*Vierteljahrschr. Astron. Ges.*, **60**, 158 (1925)	ROE
3.9	*Vierteljahrschr. Astron. Ges.*, **55**, 144 (1920)	ROE
3.10	[43, Ch. 3]	ROE
3.11		MG
3.12	Nordmann, C., *Bull. Astron.*, **26**, 5 (1909)	ROE
4.1		HCO
4.2	Norman, D., *Osiris*, **5**, 560 (1938)	ROE
4.3	Norman, D., *Osiris*, **5**, 560 (1938)	ROE
4.4	[31, Ch. 4]	ROE
4.5	*Trans. Int. Union Solar Res.*, **2**, *frontispiece* (1908)	ROE
4.6	[46, Ch. 4]	ROE
4.7		SAAO
4.8		SAAO
4.9	*Bull. Astron.*, **9**, 281 (1892)	ROE
4.10	[53, Ch. 4]	ROE
4.11	[122, Ch. 4]	UoC
4.12	Eberhard, G., *Handbuch der Astrophys.*, **2**, 431 (1931)	ROE
4.13	[150, Ch. 4]	ROE
4.14	Barrett, S. B., *Pop. Astron.*, **33**, 281 (1925)	ROE
4.15	[157, Ch. 4]	ROE
4.16	[126, Ch. 4]	ROE
4.17	[123, Ch. 4]	
4.18	*Pop. Astron.*, **40**, 65 (1932)	ROE
4.19	[186, Ch. 4]	ROE
4.20	Jones, H. S., *Nature*, **107**, 173 (1921)	ROE
4.21	Joy, A. H., *Publ. Astron. Soc. Pacific*, **52**, 69 (1940)	ROE
4.22	[221, Ch. 4]	ROE
5.1		IE
5.2		IE; originally from Mary Lea Shane Archives, Lick Observatory

Fig.	Reference	Other sources and acknowledgements
5.3	[6, Ch. 5]	ROE
5.4	[15, Ch. 5]	ROE
5.5	[15, Ch. 5]	ROE
5.6	*Pop. Astron.*, **47**, 117 (1939)	ROE
5.7	*Annuario della Pontificia Academia della Scienze*, **1**, 397 (1937)	Volume supplied by Prof. H. A. Brück, Edinburgh; photog. ROE
5.8		Photograph courtesy of the late Prof. Z. Kopal, Manchester
5.9	[31, Ch. 5]	ROE
5.10	[31, Ch. 5]	ROE
5.11	[31, Ch. 5]	ROE
5.12	[27, Ch. 5]	ROE
5.13	[60, Ch. 5]	ROE
5.14	[60, Ch. 5]	ROE
5.15		GEK
5.16		Photograph courtesy of Dr A. E. Whitford
5.17	[62, Ch. 5]	ROE
5.18	[78, Ch. 5]	ROE
5.19	[70, Ch. 5]	ROE
5.20		GEK
5.21		GEK
5.22	[108, Ch. 5]	ROE
5.23		Photograph courtesy of Dr V. I. Burnashev, Crimean Astrophys. Observatory
5.24	[126, Ch. 5]	ROE
5.25	[126, Ch. 5]	ROE
5.26		GEK
5.27	[126, Ch. 5]	ROE
5.28		JSH
6.1		SAAO
6.2	Hale, G. E., *Astrophys. J.*, **1**, 162 (1895)	ROE
6.3	[91, Ch. 6]	
6.4	[77, Ch. 6]	ROE
6.5	[102, Ch. 6]	ROE
6.6	[97, Ch. 6]	UoC
6.7	Lovell, D. J. & Miczaika, G. R., in *The Present and Future of the Telescope of Moderate Size*, p. 111, ed. F. B. Wood, Univ. Pennsylvania Press (1958)	UoC. Reproduced courtesy F. B. Wood and Univ. Pennsylvania Press.

Fig.	Reference	Other sources and acknowledgements
6.8	Lovell, D. J. & Miczaika, G. R., in *The Present and Future of the Telescope of Moderate Size*, p. 111, ed. F. B. Wood, Univ. Pennsylvania Press (1958)	UoC. Reproduced courtesy F. B. Wood and Univ. Pennsylvania Press.
7.1	[31, Ch. 7]	UoC
7.2	[35, Ch. 7]	ROE
7.3	Eberhard, G., *Handbuch der Astrophys.*, **2**, 431 (1931)	ROE
7.4	[92, Ch. 7]	
7.5	[122, Ch. 7]	ROE
7.6	[123, Ch. 7]	
7.7	From Ph.D. thesis of A.W.J. Cousins (1953)	Thesis supplied by Dr R. V. Willstrop, Cambridge; photog. ROE
7.8		RHS
7.9		RHS
7.10	[162, Ch. 7]	UoC
7.11	*Observatory*, **72**, 66 (1952)	UoC
8.1	King, E.S., *Pop. Astron.*, **39**, 456 (1931)	ROE
8.2	Bailey, S.I., *Pop. Astron.*, **30**, 197 (1922)	ROE
8.3	[23, Ch. 8]	ROE
8.4	Forbes, G., *David Gill, Man and Astronomer*, J. Murray, London (1916), opp. p. 168	ROE
8.5		HCO
8.6	[86, Ch. 8]	ROE
8.7	[83, Ch. 8]	ROE
8.8	*Publ. Astron. Soc. Pacific*, **69**, 304 (1957)	UoC
8.9	[115, Ch. 8]	UoC
8.10	[119, Ch. 8]	UoC
8.11		Photograph courtesy Mrs R. Hiltner, Ann Arbor, Michigan
8.12	[155, Ch. 8]	
8.13	[160, Ch. 8]	UoC
8.14	[215, Ch. 8]	UoC
8.15	[268, Ch. 8]	
8.16	[269, Ch. 8]	
8.17	[285, Ch. 8]	
8.18	[286, Ch. 8]	
9.1		UoC
9.2	[78, Ch. 9]	UoC
9.3		UoC

Fig.	Reference	Other sources and acknowledgements
9.4		MG
9.5	[41, Ch. 9]	Photograph provided by courtesy of Prof. W. Blitzstein
9.6	*Sky & Tel.*, **60**, 270 (1980)	Photograph provided by *Sky & Telescope*
9.7	From Ph.D. thesis of A.W.J. Cousins (1953)	Thesis supplied by Dr R. V. Willstrop, Cambridge; photog. ROE
9.8		GEK
9.9	[49, Ch. 9]	UoC
9.10		Photograph courtesy of Dr A. G. Wright, Thorn-EMI, Ruislip, UK
9.11		MG
9.12		RHS
9.13	Courtesy Mt Stromlo Observ., Australian National Univ.	Photograph supplied by Dr M. S. Bessell, Canberra
9.14		RHS
9.15	[233, Ch. 9]	UoC; reproduced courtesy of Prof. W. Liller
10.1		MG
10.2		GEK
10.3	[16, Ch. 10]	
10.4	[16, Ch. 10]	
10.5		GEK
10.6	[47, Ch. 10]	Photograph reproduced courtesy of Dr M. F. Walker
10.7	[47, Ch. 10]	Photograph reproduced courtesy of Dr M. F. Walker
10.8	[61, Ch. 10]	
10.9	[72, Ch. 10]	
Cover		Photograph courtesy of Dr R. C. Bless, Univ. Wisconsin

Name index

Note: Dates are given on pages with numbers in **bold face**.

Star index

Subject index